MW00783095

Louisiana Law of Sale and Lease

Louisiana Law of Sale and Lease: Cases and Materials
Second Edition 2020

Nadia E. Nedzel and David Gruning

Published by:

 Vandeplas Publishing, LLC – August 2020

801 International Parkway, 5th Floor
Lake Mary, FL. 32746
USA

www.vandeplaspublishing.com

Copyright © 2020 by Nadia E. Nedzel and David Gruning
All rights reserved.

No part of this book may be reproduced, stored in a retrieval system, or transmitted by any means, electronic, mechanical, photocopying, recording, or otherwise, without written permission from the author.

ISBN 978-1-60042-515-8

LOUISIANA LAW OF SALE AND LEASE: CASES AND MATERIALS
Second Edition 2020

Nadia E. Nedzel and David Gruning

TABLE OF CONTENTS

To our students:

A book designed as a tool for teaching a defined area of law to students who are largely unfamiliar with it at the outset must, by necessity, be a work in progress. This one is no exception. We have taught the law of sale and lease for many years now, in several places, to many groups of students, and we have had experience with this area of the law outside the classroom as well, both in practice and as contributors or commentators on the process of legislation. Our hope is that we have been able to incorporate the right ingredients in the correct proportions so that it will work for us and for our students, as well as for other teachers and their students.

A book like this of necessity goes on in another way, into the past. This book connects us, in a small but definite way, with our own teachers and colleagues, too. We are tempted sometimes to think of law as a sort of vast book, in which all the chapters are connected, all striving for reason and balance. Certainly, this is true of the development of the civil law, in which we hope this effort will be judged worthy of participating. We hope, in particular, that our teachers, some of whom have left us, may look upon this effort with sympathy, and with at least a touch of pride.

We wish to thank the several publishers who kindly granted us the right to use and to excerpt material: To Thomson Reuters for material first published in the Southern Reporter, the Federal Reporter, and the Federal Supplement; to the Tulane Law Review for permission to use an excerpt from Wendell H. Holmes & Symeon C. Symeonides, Representation, Mandate, and Agency: A Kommentar on Louisiana's New Law, 73 Tul. L. Rev. 1087(1999), to the Louisiana Law Review for permission to use an excerpt from Tanya Ann Ibieta, Comment, The Transfer of Ownership of Movables, 47 La. L. Rev. 841 (1987), to the Loyola Law Review for permission to use an excerpt from Michael Palestina, Comment, Of Registry: Louisiana's Revised Public Records Doctrine, 53 Loy. L. Rev. 989 (2007), and to Basic Books for permission to publish an excerpt from Hernando de Soto, The Mystery of Capital: Why Capitalism Triumphs in the West and Fails Everywhere Else (2000).

How to Use the Second Edition

In this second edition, we have added three features that we hope will help in studying the subject. Admittedly, those features make the textbook longer, but content-wise, it remains quite similar to the original.

First, we've added a "Flowchart" to the beginning of each chapter to provide an introduction to the topic and its contents. You may also choose to use it as the beginning of your course outline but bear in mind that it is a summary and does not include all that we (or your professor) considers important about the topic.

Second, we've added "Review Notes" to the end of each chapter in order to provide a quick review of the chapter before class, and perhaps a greater understanding of the contents of the chapter. We are concerned that students might attempt to simply read the Review Notes and skip reading the chapters themselves – that would be a mistake as you would not be well prepared for a Socratic discussion of the individual cases in class. It is likely, however, to help you put the topic in context and prepare for any hypothets the professor may present in class. While more complete than the "Flowchart," it still does not necessarily include everything that your professor may consider important about the topic. You are still responsible for preparing your own course outline.

Third, we've added a hypothet at the end of each chapter. Some of them, especially at the beginning of the book are very simply, but others towards the end of the book become increasingly complicated in order to help in preparing for a final exam.

We hope you find this second edition study-friendly and helpful!

Nadia E. Nedzel

&

David Gruning

CHAPTER 1

BASICS OF THE CONTRACT OF SALE

Flowchart

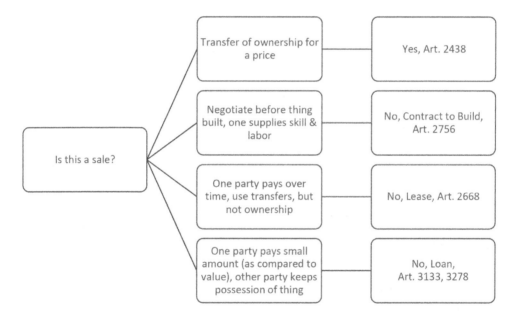

Flowchart 1.2

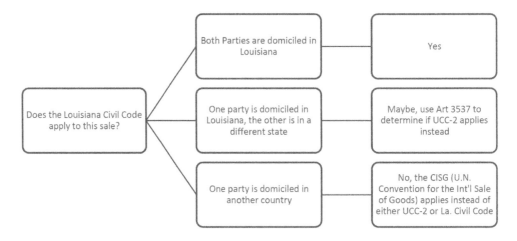

Section 1: Distinguishing Sales from Other Contracts

The Civil Code states: "Sale is a contract whereby a person transfers ownership of a thing to another for a price in money. The thing, the price, and the consent of the parties are requirements for the perfection of a sale." La. Civ. Code art. 2439. Thus, the key elements of a sale are: 1) the **thing** sold and bought, 2) the **price**, and 3) the **transfer** of the ownership of the thing by seller to buyer. Consent is also key simply because sale is a contract and therefore is formed or perfected by the agreement of the parties. La. Civ. Code art. 1906.

This first chapter will consider the definition of a sale, determining the difference between a sale and another kind of contract such as a contract to build (Articles 2756-76); a lease (Article 2668); a giving in payment (Article 2655) or an exchange (Article 2660); and a secured loan (Article 3133) or mortgage (Article 3278). It will then help you understand when the Civil Code applies to a sale, and when it does not under either conflict of law principles (Articles 3515-3518, 3537-3541) or the United Nations Convention on the International Sale of Goods. The chapter will finish by considering when a person may lack the capacity to enter into a sale.

a. Sale or Contract to Build?

Generally, it is easy to determine whether or not the contract at issue is a sale, but occasionally it's not so clear. The following cases provide guidance on distinguishing between a sale and a contract to build. Determining which is which is important because they have different effects: different remedies, different prescriptive periods, etc. For example, in a sale, if the seller does not deliver what the buyer expected or if it is defective, the buyer can demand that the seller either replace the item or return the money paid. In contrast, if a builder does a poor job, the extent of that failure to perform will be measured under the substantial performance factors. If the failure is complete, the contract will be dissolved, and the other party will pay only for any benefit received. If the builder substantially performed, then the othere party pays for the job minus any amount he can prove will be required to bring the object up to the quality promised.

While a sale requires an object, a price, and transfer of ownership, a contract to build is defined as a contract whereby one person undertakes to furnish his work and industry to build a thing for a stipulated price to be paid by the other person. Article 2757. The price and the specifications for the object are negotiated before construction. Determining the difference between a sale and a contract to build has been described as follows:

> "There are three major factors in determining whether a contract is a contract of sale or a contract to build or to work by the job. First, in a contract to build, the "purchaser" has some control over the specifications of the object. Second, the negotiations in a contract to build take place before the object is constructed. Lastly, and most importantly, a building contract contemplates not only that the builder will furnish the materials, but that he will also furnish his skill and labor in order to build the desired object. *Duhon v. Three Friends Homebuilders Corporation,* 396 So.2d 559 (La.App. 3 Cir.1981); *Airco Refrigeration Service, Inc. v. Fink,* 242 La. 73, 134 So.2d 880 (1961)."

Acadiana Health Club, Inc. v. Hebert, 469 So.2d 1186, 1189 (La. App. 3 Cir. (1985)).

Study Questions:

What does each of the following cases say about the test for distinguishing between a sale and a contract to build?

Why do you think the two cases show two different ways to distinguish between them?

HUNT V. SUARES (1836)
9 LA. 434

BULLARD, J., delivered the opinion of the court.

¶1   The plaintiffs sue to recover the price of various articles, as detailed in their account, which they allege were sold and delivered to the defendant, the principal articles consisting of marble mantle pieces and hearths.

¶2 The answer contains a general denial, and the defendant further avers, that he made a contract with the plaintiffs for the building and putting up of certain marble mantle and chimney pieces, the plaintiffs obligating themselves to furnish the materials and the work and labor; that before any of the mantle pieces had been put up, the house was destroyed by fire, and that if any of the materials were in the house at the time, they were at the risk of the plaintiffs.

¶3 The delivery of most of the articles charged, is proved; but there is no positive evidence of such a contract as is set up by the defendant. He seeks to bring the case under article 2729 of the Civil Code [now article 2758], which provides that:

> "When the undertaker furnishes the materials for the work, if the work be destroyed, in whatever manner it may happen, previous to its being delivered to the owner, the loss shall be sustained by the undertaker, unless the proprietor be in default for not receiving it, though duly notified to do so."

¶4 It appears to us from the evidence, that the principal contract was one of sale of the mantle pieces ready made, and that the agreement to put them up and furnish materials for that purpose, does not take the contract as to the mantle pieces out of the rule which governs that species of contract, and that as soon as they were delivered, they were at the risk of the purchaser, unless a special agreement to the contrary be shown. There is nothing in the record to show that the plaintiffs understood the contract at the time, as it is now interpreted by the defendant, and the cost of putting up is trifling, compared with the cost of the article. . . .

¶5 It is, therefore, ordered, adjudged and decreed, that the judgment of the District Court be reversed and annulled, and proceeding to render such judgment as in our opinion ought to have been given below, it is further considered, that the plaintiffs recover of the defendant the sum of five hundred and one dollars and seventy-five cents, with costs of the District Court; those of the appeal to be borne by the plaintiffs and appellees.

Comment:

Many years have passed since Hunt v. Suares was decided, and later decisions have set forth other criteria for the distinction between a sale and a contract to build. Still, to distinguish sales from contracts to build Louisiana courts continue to compare the cost or price of the materials used to the value or price of the labor or work done on those materials: the comparative value test. See, e.g., Price v. Huey Childs Builder, Inc., 426 So. 2d 398 (La. App. 2d Cir. 1983).

HENSON V. GONZALEZ (1976)
326 SO. 2D 396 (LA. APP. 1ST CIR.)

BARNETTE, Judge.

¶1 This is an appeal from a judgment rendered in the City Court of Baton Rouge for $600.00 plus legal interest and costs for the failure of the defendant-appellant to pay for three jewelry display cases. The defendant alleges that his refusal to pay is justified in that the showcases were poorly constructed and were unfit and unsafe for the installation of the glass front and top. In rendering judgment for the plaintiff, it was the trial court's finding that the plaintiff substantially complied with the contract to build the type of showcases requested.

¶2 The contract between the parties is completely oral. The record reflects that on November 7, 1973, defendant-appellant, Porfirio Gonzalez, a jeweler, approached the plaintiff-appellee, Samuel G. Henson, to build the three above-mentioned cases. Henson, a cabinet-maker by trade, had no prior experience with display cases. However, he saw no problem with construction and agreed to build the cases for the undisputed amount of $200 each.

¶3 During the initial negotiations, a sketch of a counter design taken from a magazine by Gonzalez was shown to Henson with verbal instructions that he wanted '. . . a showcase built like this.' It was also agreed initially that Gonzalez would arrange for the glass to be put on after the cases were delivered.

¶4 The magazine sketch is labeled as follows:

"Sit Down Type Showcase"

"Plastic laminate covered or wood veneer on closed base or on tubular steel legs with storage drawers under in back and display drawers inside case." To the left there is a profile view of the side that is cut away to show the general method of construction. This drawing is labeled with basic exterior width and height measurements in inches. Just to the right there is a three-dimensional drawing of the showcase as it would look when completed. It is clear from the drawing that the case is of typical rectangular construction with a small overhang extending about six inches to the front or customer side. There is a glass counter top and a vertical piece of glass full length across the front and extending down about six inches to cover the front face of the overhang.

¶5 One of plaintiff's allegations is that he '. . . built the jewelry cases in accordance with the plans submitted by the defendant . . .' and thus being, for this reason, in compliance with their contract. An examination of the sketch entered into evidence by the plaintiff will reveal that it is at most a guide to construction. By no stretch of the definition could it be considered a plan or blueprint. Only a few general external dimensions are given. There are no details of the construction shown, no methods of joining the various pieces where they come together, and no specifications for fasteners, such as nails, screws, dowels, clips, glue, etc. The cutaway profile view is only of one side, and it is vague and lacks detail. There is neither a requirement for the type of material to be used in construction nor is a thickness or grade of quality specified in the sketch. The construction of a showcase using the drawings and specifications in the exhibited sketch would require the craftsman to significantly enlarge upon the detail of design using his own skill and improvisation, and it is the opinion of this court that the sketch was meant for illustrative purposes only.

¶6 Since the trial court found that there was substantial compliance on the part of the plaintiff and rendered judgment accordingly, it must be assumed that it was the opinion of the trial court that this was a construction contract rather than a contract of sale. It is our opinion that the trial court was correct in this respect and that the contract between Gonzalez and Henson is a building contract within the meaning of Article 2756 of the Civil Code. That article is found under the section headed 'Of Constructing Buildings According to Plots, and Other Works by the Job, and of Furnishing Materials' reads as follows:

"Building by plot and work by job, definitions

"To build by a plot, or to work by the job, is to undertake a building or a work for a certain stipulated price."

¶7 The above section and article are in Title IX of the Code entitled 'Of Lease.' Building or Construction contracts involve primarily the furnishing of labor and the contractor's skill in the performance of the job, rather than the mere sale of materials (citations omitted).

¶8 In the instant case, the contract involved the hiring or 'letting out' of the labor and skill of the plaintiff, a craftsman, in the construction of a work for a certain stipulated price, rather than the sale of an existing thing. See also Hermeling v. Whitmore, 140 So.2d 257 (La. Ct. App. 1st Cir. 1961). In Hermeling, a contractor purchased a lot and using his own plans constructed a house as a speculation. It was completed and then put on the market. The court distinguished the facts from the earlier case of Matthews v. Rudy, 4 La. App. 226 (1926), that was factually similar except that there was an agreement made with the prospective purchaser for an agreed price prior to the construction of the house. The court in Hermeling declared that "under these facts we find that the building was not 'undertaken to make by the job' and that '. . . the builder is treated as a vendor . . . ." Thus, in Hermeling, although of necessity the house had to be constructed, it was a sale of a finished house as it sat on the lot. The house was already in existence at the time negotiations were entered into.

¶9 It is not the purpose of this opinion to determine the cut off point in the negotiation of a contract which distinguishes the contract for construction from one of sale, that is, whether the contract is negotiated before or during the construction process. It is clear from our jurisprudence and the pertinent articles of the Civil Code, supra, that where, as in this case, negotiations are completed prior to the commencement of construction, that the obligation is governed by the articles on building contracts rather than sales.

¶10 In building or construction contracts, substantial performance is the standard rule for determining if the contractor is entitled to recover the contract price. Airco Refrigeration Service, Inc. v. Fink, [134 So.2d 880 (1961), and citations listed therein; (citations omitted). Airco further stated that it is a question of fact whether or not there has been substantial performance so as to permit recovery on the contract. Since this is a question of fact, the court on appeal is bound by the directive of the manifest error rule.

¶11 The Supreme Court in Airco listed several factors to be considered in determining whether there has been substantial performance. "Among the factors to be considered are the extent of the defect or nonperformance, the degree to which the purpose of the contract is defeated, the ease of correction, and the use or benefit to the defendant of the work performed." 134 So.2d at 882. We cannot say that the trial court was manifestly wrong in its finding of substantial performance by the plaintiff contractor.

¶12 Once substantial performance has been proven by the plaintiff, he is entitled to recover the contract price less whatever damages the owner may prove attributable to the breach. Airco, supra, and citations listed therein, Cortiza v. Rosenblat, 291 So.2d 425 (La. Ct. App. 4th Cir. 1974). Subsequent cases have held that:

> "An owner seeking to recover from the contractor has the burden of proving both the existence and nature of the defects, that the defects are due to faulty materials or workmanship and the cost of repairing the defects." [citations omitted]

¶13 The defendant has alleged three defects in the jewelry cases as they were delivered: (1) that the cases are 'weak all over' and unsafe for the installation of glass, (2) that the cases were poorly made, and (3) that the cases were not constructed properly to facilitate the installation of glass without modification.

¶14 The defendant has failed to establish allegations numbers one and two above. One of the showcases was introduced into evidence and examined by the trial court judge. The court did not comment on its observation nor is the showcase or any other evidence in the record before us on appeal that would tend to establish that that the case were unsafe or that they were constructed in an unworkmanlike manner.

¶15 However, the record is replete with testimony and it is abundantly clear that the showcases as made would not accommodate the glass counter top or the glass front. There is no question that the agreement between Henson and Gonzalez required that Gonzalez was to arrange to have the glass put on. It is implicit from this, and also the illustrative drawing, that Henson knew that the showcases would eventually have glass fitted to them in some manner. When completed, however, the installation of the glass presented some problems which might have been avoided by some modification of the design.

¶16 The defendant under Airco and Cortiza, supra, upon proof could deduct this amount from the original contract price, upon proof of the cost of the modification or correction necessary to enable the glass to be installed properly. However, he has failed to allege or prove any dollar amount for the cost of such modification. The most desirable evidence would be a firm competitive bid for the necessary remedial work. [citation omitted] Lacking this, an estimate by an expert witness at trial based on firm computation of the work undertaken would suffice in establishing the cost.

¶17 There is testimony from a witness from each side qualified as an expert in glass installation. Of the two experts, the witness offered by Gonzalez speculated on a remedial cost figure. He testified that for an estimated $150 to $200 he could install a minimum of quarter inch glass in a professional manner. This is not a certain estimate, nor is it broken down to itemize the cost of remedial work, as distinguished from the cost of the glass and the glaziers labor, which had been contemplated as an expense to be borne by the defendant, Gonzalez. The defendant has failed to discharge this essential element of proof and no consideration can be given to a reduction in the contract price.

¶18 For the foregoing reasons, the judgment appealed is affirmed at the appellant's cost.

Affirmed.

b. Sale or Lease?

A sale requires a thing, a price, and a transfer of ownership. A lease is "a synallagmatic contract by which one party, the lessor, binds himself to give to the other party, the lessee, the use and enjoyment of a thing for a term in exchange for a rent that the lessee binds himself to pay." La. Civ. Code art. 2668. Both require that one person provide a thing and that another person agree to pay for access to that thing. In a sale, the first party alienates and transfers the ownership of the thing, but in a lease the first party only permits the second party to use and enjoy the thing but only for a limited time.

Study Question:

While the following case is admittedly old, it presents a principle of contractual interpretation that is still followed – regardless of what name the parties give to their contract, a court will look to the nature of the agreement between two parties to determine whether it has the character of that title or whether, in fact, the title is a mere simulation and the parties' true intent shows it to be a different kind of nominate contract. That being said, what did Cooper and Matney call their agreement, and what does the court conclude about its nature?

BYRD V. COOPER 1928
117 SO. 441 (LA.)

ST. PAUL, J.

[Plaintiff Byrd is suing to be declared the owner of thirteen mules that are in the court's possession. Defendant Cooper claims that he bought them from Matney, and that Matney had bought them from Byrd. Byrd claims that he had only leased, not sold, the mules to Matney. Matney is not a party to the suit.]

¶1 The facts are practically undisputed, but not the conclusions to be drawn therefrom. Matney says he bought the mules; plaintiff says he only leased them to Matney. And the circumstances were these, that plaintiff delivered the mules to Matney, and Matney gave plaintiff six notes aggregating $4,750, the full value of the mules, payable from month to month, one for $1,000 and five for $750 each. When Matney would have paid all the notes, he was to have the privilege of buying the mules for no other consideration than the amount of the notes so paid. Matney paid only the first four notes, aggregating $3,250, but did not pay the last two notes, aggregating $1,500. All notes bore interest at 8 percent from date.

¶2 Now it is clear that a so-called contract of lease by which the lessee binds himself at once and irrevocably for a rental equal to the full value of the thing leased, and is to become owner thereof when the so-called rental is paid in full, and without the payment of any further consideration, is nothing else than a conditional sale disguised under the form of a so-called lease; and the effect of such a contract is to vest title in the so-called lessee, i. e., purchaser. Grapico Bottling Works v. Liquid Carbonic Co., 113 So. 454 (La. 1927)

¶3 Plaintiff directs our attention to Doullut v. Rush, 77 So. 110 (La. 1917), wherein this court held:

> Where parties enter into a contract, by authentic act, which they call a lease, in which they call themselves lessor and lessee, . . . the fact that it also contains an option to the lessee to buy the property, upon specified conditions, and certain stipulations, predicated upon the . . . right so conferred, is . . . insufficient . . . for the defense, set up by the lessee, in an action of ejectment, for nonpayment of rent, that the contract is one of sale, where it is admitted that none of the conditions required to convert it into a contract of sale have been complied with.

¶4 That case is readily distinguishable from the case at bar. Thus the very same case, upon some other phase thereof, came before the Court of Appeal for the parish of Orleans, and that court held, quite in consonance with ruling of this court, as follows:

> 1. A contract by which a party binds himself to pay in installments a certain sum for the use of a thing, with the privilege of becoming the owner thereof upon paying a further sum, for which, however, he has not bound himself absolutely, is simply a lease with an option to purchase, and is not a sale. [But]

> 2. An alleged lease, in which at the end of the term the lessee is to become the owner of the thing leased, in consideration of the rent to be paid, is in fact a sale translative of the property from its very inception. Doullut v. Rush (No. 7270) Tessier's Digest, p. 98. [Cf. Grapico Bottling Works v. Liquid Carbonic Co., supra.]

¶5 In Doullut v. Rush, the lessees had bound themselves only for 22 months at $500 per month, with the privilege of buying the property at any time during said period for $25,000, less a credit for any rent paid; so that there was at least $14,000 of the stipulated price for which they had never bound themselves at all, and might never bind themselves. On the other hand, in this case, Matney had bound himself at once for the full amount of the stipulated price. So that the Doullut v. Rush case falls clearly within the first category above, and the present case clearly within the second.

***

The judgment appealed from is therefore affirmed.

c. Sale or Loan with an Interest in Collateral?

A sale involves the transfer of ownership in exchange for a price in money. Under a chattel mortgage or security right, one party loans money to another, in exchange for interest. Security is an accessory right, established by statute or contract, to secure the debtor's repayment of the loan. If the debtor does not repay, then the creditor may have the secured property seized and sold and obtain repayment out of the proceeds. (See La. Civ. Code art. 3136.)

Study question:

Using the same policy at issue in Byrd v. Cooper, why does the Louisiana Supreme Court in the following case hold that the contract between the two parties was NOT a sale, even though the contract at issue specifically said it was?

COLLINS V. PELLERIN 1850
5 LA. ANN. 99 (LA.)

Eustis, C. J.

¶1 The plaintiffs allege themselves to be the owners of two hydraulic presses, having purchased them from the defendant on or about the 1st of May, 1846. They pray that the presses may be delivered to them or, in default thereof, that they have judgment for $2250, the value of said presses, together with interest in the sum of $1400 from said 1st of May, 1846, and on the balance from judicial demand. The presses were sequestered and bonded by the defendant.

¶2 These presses were in the cotton press of the defendant, where they have remained. It appears that on the day stated, the defendant made a bill of sale for the presses for the nominal sum of $1500, on which two payments, amounting to $1400, were made at different times in the month of April following. But on the same day the plaintiffs gave the defendant a counter letter, by which it was stated that the bill of sale was given as a collateral security for the sum of $1500 loaned him for twelve months from date, which sum, if returned within said term, the bill of sale was to be void; otherwise to be absolute, and the presses to belong to the plaintiffs thereafter. The presses were to remain in the defendant's cotton press for said term of twelve months, and on the default of the defendant in returning the money the plaintiffs were to be the owners of them, and make such disposition of them as they thought proper.

¶3   Their petition presented a distinct demand for the presses or their value, based on an allegation of ownership. And the bill of sale and the counter letter in evidence, the district judge considered did not establish the ownership of the presses in the plaintiffs, but merely a pledge for the payment of a debt. He dismissed the plaintiffs' petition, as he considered they had no action for the presses or their value, and had mistaken their remedy. The plaintiffs have appealed.

¶4   It is clear to us that the contract between the parties was not a sale with power of redemption, but merely an hypothecary contract. The sum of fifteen hundred dollars, we think the evidence shows, was far less than the value of the objects, and the circumstance of the vendor's remaining in possession, we consider as a distinctive sign of the real nature of the contract. The want of delivery of the thing sold by the vendor, is held by civilians to be a badge of simulation, and as depriving the contract of the essential characteristics of a sale. Redeemable sales unaccompanied by delivery of the thing sold, of which the considerations are inadequate, courts are bound to consider, without sufficient evidence to the contrary, as contracts for which the thing nominally sold stands as security and nothing else. Merlin Rep. verbo Contrat Pignoratif. Troplong, de la Vente, § 695.

¶5   The contents of the counter letter, we think, authorized the district judge in his conclusions on this point.

¶6   The plaintiffs have their remedy for the recovery of their debt, on which no decision was rendered by the district judge. Evidence was received relating to a partnership between the plaintiffs and the defendant, which we do not pass upon; because the action of the district court, in confining its decision to the issue first presented by the plaintiffs' petition and defendant's answer, was regular and correct: the defective pleading of the defendant to the contrary notwithstanding.

¶7   The judgment of the district court is therefore affirmed, with costs.

Lagniappe question:

The court concludes that the purported sale between Collins and Pellerin was a "simulation," accompanied by a "counterletter" that expressed the parties' true intent. What is a simulation? What is a counterletter? Where are they defined in the Civil Code?

Why was the simulation itself not enforced here – were there any indicia of fraud? See Article 2025, et seq.

1. John gives Mary a pair of blue suede shoes, and she gives John $200

2. John gives Mary a pair of blue suede shoes, and Mary gives John a yellow sweater.

3. John gives Mary a pair of blue suede shoes, and though she was supposed to give him $200, he accepts a yellow sweater instead of the money.

Section 2: What Law Applies?

Article 2439 of the Louisiana Civil Code defines a sale as "the transfer of ownership of a thing to another for a price in money." But first we have to decide that Louisiana law, including the Civil Code, applies to the facts. When does Louisiana sales law apply, and when does some other body of law apply?

a. Civil Code or UCC-2?

What if the parties are in different states when they agree to the sale? Which state's law applies? (Remember, states other than Louisiana have all adopted a version of UCC-2). Article 3537 provides that in an issue involving a conventional obligation, one should use "the law of the state whose policies would be most seriously impaired if its law were not applied to that issue." Specifically, one should look to several sets of factors. The first set of factors can be described as factual contacts: "the pertinent contacts of each state to the parties and the transaction, including where the contract was negotiated, formed, performed, the location of the object, and the parties' domiciles or businesses."

The second set of factors are concerned with the contract itself: "the nature, type, and purpose of the contract." Finally, the third set of factors concerns public policy: each state's relationship to the parties, the needs of interstate commerce, the need to uphold the parties' justified expectations. A party to a contract is capable if he possesses capacity under the law of either the state he was domiciled in at the time the contract was made or the state whose law applies to the contract. Finally, the parties may choose to be governed by a body of law, unless it would contravene the public policy of the state whose law would otherwise apply. (Articles 3538-3540).

Study Question:

Why does the court in the following case over-ride the parties' choice of law clause and how does that comply with Article 3537?

PLUNK V. LKQ BIRMINGHAM, INC. (2013)

2013 WL 5913755, (W.D. LA.)

¶1 Before the Court are cross-motions for summary judgment in the above captioned matter with respect to whether Illinois or Louisiana law should apply to an asset purchase agreement involving a restrictive covenants provision.

BACKGROUND INFORMATION

¶2 In June 2010, Donald Plunk, Sr. and Donald Plunk, Jr. (the "Plunks") and LKQ executed an Asset Purchase Agreement (the "Agreement"), whereby the Plunks (and another business partner) sold several businesses and assets to LKQ for the approximate sum of $3.8 million. The Agreement, a document in excess of twenty pages, contained a clause that, upon closing, required LKQ to employ the Plunks on an at-will basis. The Agreement also contained a "Restrictive Covenants" provision whereby the Plunks essentially agreed not to compete against LKQ for a period of five years from the date of the sale. The Restrictive Covenants provision also included a blanket prohibition that prevented the Plunks from competing against LKQ *"anywhere within the United States ..."* for the five-year period. The parties determined that the Agreement would be "governed by and construed in accordance with the laws of the State of Illinois ..."

¶3 Following the sale, and as provided in the Agreement, LKQ retained the Plunks as at-will employees. On September 12, 2012, however, LKQ abruptly terminated the Plunks' employment. Two days later, the Plunks filed a Petition for Declaratory Judgment against LKQ in the 4th Judicial District Court for the Parish of Ouachita, State of Louisiana.

¶4 Applying Louisiana law to the Agreement, the Plunks contend that the Restrictive Covenants are unenforceable because, inter alia, they exceed the two-year legal maximum. Thus, the Plunks seek a judgment declaring the restrictive covenant set forth in paragraph 10.1.1 of the Agreement null and void. LKQ removed the case to federal court on the basis of diversity jurisdiction, [and] LKQ filed a motion for summary judgment.

1. Standard of Law

¶5 Summary judgment is proper when, after reviewing "the pleadings, the discovery and disclosure materials on file, and any affidavits," the court determines there is no genuine issue of material fact. Fed.R.Civ.P. 56(c). The party seeking summary judgment always bears the initial responsibility of informing the court of the basis for its motion and identifying those portions of the record that it believes demonstrate the absence of a genuine issue of material fact.

2. Which State Law Applies: Illinois or Louisiana?

¶6 [T]he threshold issue in this case is which state law applies: Illinois or Louisiana? Although the contract states that Illinois law should apply, this Court, exercising diversity jurisdiction and applying the conflicts of law principles of Louisiana, holds that Louisiana law applies.[1]

¶7 To determine which state law applies, the Court first looks to Louisiana Civil Code Article 3540, which provides:

> All other issues of conventional obligations are governed by the law expressly chosen or clearly relied upon by the parties, except to the extent that law contravenes the public policy of the state whose law would otherwise be applicable under Article 3537.

¶8 Louisiana Civil Code Article 3537 states, as a general rule, that an issue of conventional obligations is "governed by the law of the state whose policies would be most seriously impaired if its law were not applied to that issue." Article 3537 also states:

> That state is determined by evaluating the strength and pertinence of the relevant policies of the involved states in the light of: (1) the pertinent contacts of each state to the parties and the transaction, including the place of negotiation, formation, and performance of the contract, the location of the object of the contract, and the place of domicile, habitual residence, or business of the parties; (2) the nature, type, and purpose of the contract; and (3) the policies referred to in Article 3515, as well as the policies of facilitating the orderly planning of transactions, of promoting multistate commercial intercourse, and of protecting one party from undue imposition by the other.

¶9 Thus, the Court must first determine which state's law would apply in the absence of the choice of law provision in the agreement by considering the factors of Article 3537. In this case, the Article 3537 factors strongly support the Plunks' argument. The Plunks are both domiciled in Louisiana. The Plunks executed the Agreement in Louisiana. The subject of the Agreement was the acquisition of three businesses: two Louisiana entities and one Mississippi entity. Other than the fact that Illinois is the headquarters of LKQ, Illinois had marginal contact with the asset purchase and the subsequent employment dispute at issue in this case.

¶10 In addition, the Court finds that application of Illinois law would significantly impair the policies of Louisiana in protecting its employees from restrictions on the common right to work. Louisiana's statutory and jurisprudential law expresses a strong public policy against restrictions on the Plunks right to work in Louisiana. Although Illinois has an interest in promoting freedom of contracting which may be arguably impaired by the application of Louisiana law, this impairment is insignificant under the required analysis.

¶11 The strong public policy to protect employees from restrictive covenants on the employees' right to work is evidenced by Louisiana Revised Statute § 23:921. This statute precludes employers and employees from choosing the state law that will apply to employment agreements, providing:

> The provisions of every employment contract or agreement, or provisions thereof, by which any foreign or domestic employer or any other person or entity includes a choice of forum clause or choice of law clause in an employee's contract of employment or collective bargaining agreement, or attempts to enforce either a choice of forum clause or choice of law clause in any civil or administrative action involving an employee, shall be null and void except where the choice of forum clause or choice of law clause is expressly, knowingly, and voluntarily agreed to and ratified by the employee after the occurrence of the incident which is the subject of the civil or administrative action.

¶12 LKQ argues that Section 23:921 does not apply to the Agreement because "this matter does not implicate rights under an employment relationship." This argument fails on multiple levels, including under a common sense analysis. LKQ attempts to use the Agreement, a document in excess of twenty pages, as a clever veil to shroud the employment relationship clearly embedded within the lengthy contract.

¶13 To reiterate: the Agreement undoubtedly implicates rights under an employment relationship. Section 10.1 of the Restrictive Covenants specifically states that the parties "shall not, directly or indirectly, either for himself or itself or for any other person, for a period of five years ... engage in, represent, furnish consulting services to, *be employed by* or have any interest in ..." The restrictive covenants at issue in this case are incredibly broad and preclude the Plunks from working in any capacity in the industry for five years. LKQ concedes that "the covenant prohibits the Plunks from competing nationwide. As shown by the Plunks advertising, the geographical good will of Plunks extended nationwide and is being pushed into new areas every day." Furthermore, the Agreement required LKQ to hire the Plunks on an at-will basis following the closing. Section 10.7 is entitled "Employment" and set a yearly salary for Mr. Plunk, Sr. and Mr. Plunk, Jr. at $50,000 .00 and $100,000.00 plus bonuses, respectively. Ultimately, these facts acutely and unquestionably evince an employment relationship sufficient to trigger Section 23:921.

¶14 This Court next notes that covenants must be strictly construed against the party seeking its enforcement. The Fifth Circuit has recognized that Louisiana has a strong public policy restricting non-competition agreements and similar types of restrictive covenants and narrowly construes such agreements. *See Arthur J. Gallagher & Co. v. Babcock,* 339 F. App'x 384, 387 (5th Cir.2009). Likewise, Louisiana's approach to non-competition agreements "requires mechanical adherence to the requirements listed in the law (especially the geographical and time limitations)." *L & B Transp., LLC v. Beech,* 568 F.Supp.2d 689, 693 (M.D.La.2008). LKQ's argument simply fails under these critical standards.

¶15 Because of the strong public policy expressed by the Louisiana legislature, by the Louisiana Supreme Court, and by the other state and federal courts interpreting this law, the choice of law statement in the Agreement contravenes the public policy of Louisiana. *See Lobrano v. C.H. Robinson Worldwide Inc.,* 10–CV–1775, 2011 WL 52602 (W.D.La, Jan. 7, 2011). For these reasons, Louisiana law applies to the interpretation of this contract. Accordingly, there is no need to discuss whether the provision would survive under Illinois law.

3. Do the Restrictive Covenants Comply With Louisiana State Law?

¶16 Because Louisiana law applies, this Court must determine whether the five year period specified in the restrictive covenants provision complies with the strict requirements of Louisiana Revised Statute § 23:921(B), which provides as follows:

> Any person ... who sells the goodwill of a business may agree with the buyer that the seller or other interested party in the transaction, will refrain from carrying on or engaging in a business similar to the business being sold or from soliciting customers of the business being sold within a specified parish or parishes, or municipality or municipalities, or parts thereof, so long as the buyer, or any person deriving title to the goodwill from him, carries on a like business therein, *not to exceed a period of two years from the date of sale.* (Emphasis added).

¶17 In sum, the statute requires that restrictive covenants cannot extend beyond two years from the date of sale. The date of sale was June 1, 2010. As such, the Plunks were no longer bound by the restrictive covenant after June 1, 2012. Ultimately the restrictive covenants are no longer enforceable.

4. Can the Agreement Be Reformed To Comply With Louisiana Law?

¶18   The next issue before this Court is whether reformation is possible or the Agreement is null and void in its entirety. The Agreement contains a "Savings Clause" set forth in paragraph 10.1.2 which states that if any provision is held to be invalid or unenforceable, it "shall in no way affect any other provision or any other part of this Agreement ..." In some limited instances, Louisiana courts have applied severability clauses to enforce otherwise invalid non-competition agreements.

¶19   As noted earlier, the Agreement is incredibly broad both geographically and temporally. As such, this Court refuses to reform the Agreement here. This Court also notes that LKQ argues that reformation is feasible but makes no effort to explain how a modification is possible under existing law. [Doc. 29]. Ultimately, because the non-compete restrictive covenants do not comply with the strict requirements of Louisiana Revised Statute § 23:921, reformation of the contract is not possible.

b. International Law in Louisiana

In Louisiana, the Civil Code is not the sole body of law that may apply to a sale: The Convention on the International Sale of Goods ("CISG"), a multinational treaty, is United States law and therefore applies to sales within its scope. Seventy-four countries have ratified CISG, which means that as of this writing, 75% of all world trade in goods is subject to it. Article 1 stipulates that:

> (1) This Convention applies to contracts of sale of goods between parties whose places of business are in different States:
> (a) when the States are Contracting States; . . . .

To simplify, 1) if the sale is of a good, and 2) while one party's place of business is in Louisiana, the other party is in some other country that has itself ratified CISG (and most of them have), then the CISG applies, rather than the Civil Code. There are some significant differences between Louisiana's Civil Code and the CISG, and (interestingly) international jurisprudence (i.e. case law) applies in its interpretation. In their contract, however, the parties may choose that a law other than the CISG will apply, for example, the law of one of the United States. For more detail on the subject, go to www.uncitral.org or www.cisg.law.pace.edu.

CISG Hypothet:

In the following fact pattern, which law governs – the Louisiana Civil Code or CISG?

Taylor Petroleum in Louisiana agrees to buy gasoline from PetroVenezuela in Venezuela. The contract contains two key provisions. First it states: "Jurisdiction: Laws of Louisiana." Second, the gasoline must have a gum content of less than three milligrams per one hundred milliliters, to be determined at the port of departure.

Although the gum content tested below the maximum at the port of departure, it exceeded the maximum when it arrived in Louisiana. Taylor Petroleum refused to accept the gasoline.

What law applies to the resulting suit for breach?

(Hint: see BP Oil International, Ltd v. Empresa Estatal Petroleos de Ecuador, 332 F.3d 333 (5th Cir. 2003).

Comment:

Generally both federal and state courts enforce a choice of law term in a contract without any particular need for either party to the contract to 'opt out' in express terms from the application of the law that would otherwise apply.

If a country has ratified the CISG, however, it becomes the domestic law of that country for the international sales of goods the CISG describes. Therefore, parties must specifically opt out of the CISG if they do NOT want it to apply to their particular sale. However, this is not to imply that an attorney drafting a contract for an international sale of goods should want to apply local law, as opposed to CISG. There may be significant advantages to applying CISG as opposed to Louisiana or other local law.

For more information about CISG and choice of law concerns see e.g. Henry Mather, Choice of Law for International Sales: Issues Not Resolved by the CISG, 20 J.L. & COM. 155 (2001); Lisa Spagnolo, A Glimpse through the Kaleidoscope: Choices of Law and the CISG (Part I), 13 VINDOBONA J. INT'L COM. L. & ARB. 135 (2009).

Lagniappe Question:

While the CISG might apply where a contract involves the sale of a good and one party is in Louisiana while the other is in another country, what law applies if one party is in Louisiana while the other is in a different state?

Section 3: Review of Obligations and Limitations on Capacity

a. Quick Review of Obligations in General and Conventional Obligations

An entire review of a subject you studied is impossible in the space of an hour or two, but because the rules on Obligations in General and Conventional Obligations apply to both sales and lease, where not specifically displaced, a cursory review exercise is helpful.

Obligations in General

1. What is an obligation, how does one arise, what effects do obligations have, how are they terminated, and what kind of obligation is a sale or lease? (Arts. 1756-1758)

2. _____ _____"shall" govern the conduct of both the obligor and the obligee in whatever pertains to the obligation. (Art. 1759)

3. What is a natural obligation, what are its effects, and how can it be elevated to a civil obligation? (Arts. 1760 & ff).

4. What is a strictly personal obligation? (Art. 1766)

5. A sale in which the transfer of ownership is delayed until financing is approved is one subject to a _____ condition (Art. 1767)

6. A lease that ends on a specific date given in the contract is an obligation with an _____ __ _____. (Art 1777).

7. Where several obligors are liable for the same performance, their obligation is either _____ or _____. (Arts. 1815, 1818).

8. The substitution of one person to the rights of another is called _____. (Art. 1825).

9. The transfer of immovable property must be made by _____ or _____. Nevertheless, _____. (Art. 1839).

10. How does an act under private signature differ from an act under private signature duly acknowledged? (Arts. 1836-1837).

Conventional Obligations

1. What is the definition of a contract? (Art. 1906)

2. What four elements are required for a conventional obligation? (Arts. 1918-1926, 1927, 1966, 1971-1972).

3. What is the difference between a gratuitous contract and an onerous one? (Arts. 1909-1910).

4. An irrevocable offer is _____. Acceptance of an irrevocable offer is effective _____. (Arts. 1928, 1934).

5. Error vitiates consent when _____. (Arts. 1949-50).

6. Fraud vitiates consent if _____, unless _____. (Arts. 1954-55).

7. Cause is _____. (Art. 1967)

8. The object of a contract must be determined at least as to its _____, but _____ may be undetermined. (Art. 1973).

9. A contracting party may _____ a _____ for a third person, called the _____ _____. (Art. 1978).

10. The interpretation of a contract is the determination of the common _____ of the parties. (Art. 2045).

b. Limitations on Capacity

As you've remembered from the previous review, all conventional obligations (and that includes both sales and leases) require the presence of four elements in order to be enforceable: consent, capacity, cause, and a lawful determinable object. In case you have not look closely at "capacity" previously, review the pertinent articles now (Articles 1918-1926). All persons are presumed to have contractual capacity, and that includes the capacity to buy or sell, except for unemancipated minors, interdicts, and those deprived of reason at the time of contracting.

In addition to these basic rules, there are a few special circumstances where someone may lack the capacity to buy or sell something. For instance, officers of a court may not buy litigious rights subject to contestation in the jurisdiction where they perform their professional duties, as in article 2447, nor may a person buy a thing he already owns (Article 2443), or sell to a third party something that belongs to another (unless he is authorized to do so by the owner)(Article 2452). Furthermore, one spouse cannot sell or otherwise alienate immovable property owned by the community – the consent of both spouses is required, see arts. 2346-47, and there are limits on the sale of immovable property by parents to some of their children where that sale is in fact a simulation in violation of the rules of forced heirship. (Article 2444).

The following two cases illustrate two of these instances: one involves a sale to a person, since deceased whose family had filed (but not completed) an interdiction process. Thus, it interprets one or more of the capacity articles you should already be familiar with (Articles. 1918-1926). The other involves one of the specific sales-only limitations on capacity.

Study Question:

Exactly which Civil Code article is at issue in the Jumonville case?

Why was the family even allowed to argue that the Senator was deprived of reason at the time he bought jewelry from Mr. Cohen?

JULIUS COHEN JEWELER, INC. V. SUCCESSION OF JUMONVILLE 1987
506 SO. 2D 535 (LA. APP. 1ST CIR.)

WATKINS, Judge.

¶1 Plaintiff, a jeweler, brought this lawsuit to recover the balance due on a sale of jewelry to former Louisiana State Senator John E. Jumonville, Sr. The Senator's Succession defended on the ground that the senator was mentally incapable of contracting to buy the jewelry. The jeweler appeals from the trial court's judgment in favor of the Succession. We reverse.

FACTS

¶2 Although the central incident in this suit, the sale of over $190,000 worth of jewelry, took place in February of 1983, we will first describe the relevant incidents leading up to the sale.

The Prior Dealings

¶3 Julius Cohen, a New York jeweler, first met Senator John E. Jumonville, Sr. in March of 1981 while they were patients at the Pritikin Institute in California. On the day they met, the Senator bought a fifteen-carat diamond from Cohen for more than $30,000. Cohen's testimony indicates that the Senator was a free and generous spender. For example, one afternoon in Beverly Hills, California, Cohen was present when the Senator purchased an automobile for the Senator's mother for $75,000. The Senator made a number of other jewelry purchases from Cohen, totaling in excess of $200,000, through February of 1982. Many of the items were purchased as gifts for the Senator's family members.

The Interdiction Suit

¶4 In May of 1982, the Senator's mother, brothers and sister filed a petition to have the Senator interdicted, and sought to have provisional curators appointed during the pendency of the suit. Their petition alleged that the Senator was "mentally and physically infirm" and "completely incapable of taking care of his person and of administering his estate." Annexed to the petition was the affidavit of a physician, who gave his opinion that the Senator was "both mentally and physically incapable of caring for his person and his property, and that this condition is irreversible."

¶5 On May 10, 1982, the trial court, without a contradictory hearing, ordered that the Senator's two brothers be appointed as his provisional curators. The trial court subsequently denied two motions by the Senator to set aside the appointment of the provisional curators. Senator Jumonville died on May 4, 1983, and no judgment of interdiction was ever rendered against him.

The Jewelry Sale

¶6 On February 19, 1983, Julius Cohen and an assistant flew to New Orleans, at Senator Jumonville's request, to show the Senator various pieces of jewelry. During the evening, more than 300 pieces of jewelry were examined by the Senator; the Senator's sister, Sese Halstead; his girlfriend, Rosemary Norris; and his alleged illegitimate daughter, Debra Pylant. The Senator finally agreed to purchase a number of items valued at $194,840, most of which were selected as gifts for Rosemary Norris, for Rosemary's daughter, and for Debra Pylant's daughter.

¶7 The next day, after learning that the Senator's mother and sister were unhappy that the Senator had bought so much jewelry for people "out of the family," Mr. Cohen unsuccessfully attempted to dissuade the Senator from the sale. It was not until the following day, February 21, 1983, that Mr. Cohen first learned, after speaking with the Senator's son, of the pending interdiction suit. Cohen then attempted, again unsuccessfully, to convince the Senator to cancel the jewelry sale. Cohen was able, however, to regain most of the jewelry from Rosemary Norris, who he met by chance while preparing to return to New York. Ms. Norris gave Mr. Cohen all but two items of jewelry selected for her, and told him that she would try to retrieve two other items given to her daughter.

¶8   Cohen then returned to New York, and ultimately submitted a bill to the Senator for the unreturned jewelry, that is, for a diamond bracelet ($5,400) and diamond ring ($16,800) given to Rosemary; a garnet bracelet ($6,800) and emerald neck chain ($8,400) given to Rosemary's daughter; and a diamond ring ($2,800) and sapphire bracelet ($1,440) given to Debra Pylant's daughter, Melissa. Cohen made no further effort to get any of the jewelry from the recipients. As stated above, Senator Jumonville died on May 4, 1983.

The Present Suit

¶9   The jeweler filed the present suit in December 1983 against the Succession of John E. Jumonville, Sr. and its representatives ("the Succession") for the value of the unreturned jewelry bought by the senator, $41,640. Plaintiff contended that the Senator had entered into a binding contract and that the Succession was responsible for payment of the balance due. Plaintiff also sought attorney's fees under Louisiana Revised Statute 9:2781, and contended that the defendants were equitably estopped from asserting the defense of incapacity to contract. Defendants argued that the contract was null because the filing of the petition for interdiction and appointment of the provisional curators voided any attempt by the Senator to contract after that date. Defendants also contended that Cohen's retrieval of most of the jewelry from Rosemary Norris "vitiated" the contract, but that, in any event, Cohen's failure to retrieve all of it was a failure on his part to mitigate his damages.

¶10   After a trial in September 1985, the trial court rendered judgment in favor of defendants, and the jeweler appealed.

STATEMENT OF LAW

¶11   Plaintiff filed suit to enforce a contract for the sale of jewelry. A contract is an agreement, in which one person obligates himself to another, to give, to do or permit, or not to do something, expressed or implied by the agreement. La. Civil Code art. 1761 (Amended by Acts 1984, No. 331, § 1). See La. Civil Code art. 1906 (Acts 1984, effective Jan. 1, 1985).

¶12   There are four elements required for the confection of a valid contract: (1) the parties must have the capacity to contract; (2) the parties' mutual consent must be freely given; (3) there must be a certain object for the contract; and (4) the contract must have a lawful purpose. La.

Civil Code art 1779; First Nat'l Bank of Shreveport v. Williams, 346 So.2d 257, 260 (La. 3d Cir. Ct. App. 1977. See La. Civil Code arts. 1918, 1927, 1966, 1971 (effective January 1, 1985).

¶13 The testimony presented at trial established that the agreement between the jeweler and the Senator was the product of their mutual consent, that it had a certain object and a lawful purpose. The issue, then, is whether the Senator had the capacity to make a binding contract on February 19, 1983.

Capacity to Contract

¶14 The general rule is that all persons are presumed capable of contracting, except those who have been declared incapable by law. See Standard Life & Acc. Ins. Co. v. Pylant, 424 So.2d 377, 379 (La. 2nd Cir. Ct. App. 1982); La. Civil Code arts. 25, 1782, 2445. See also La. Civil Code art. 1918.

¶15 Attacks on contracts for lack of mental capacity are governed by Civil Code articles 400-403 and 1788-189. As a general proposition, the acts of a deceased person may not be attacked unless a petition for his interdiction was filed, or a judgment of interdiction was rendered, before his death. La. Civil Code arts. 403, 1788(4). See La. Civil Code art. 1926. The exceptions, which are not applicable here, are (1) when the contract is gratuitous, (2) when the contract itself contains evidence of insanity, and (3) when the contract was made within thirty days of the alleged incompetent's death. La. Civil Code arts. 403, 1788(5)-(8). See La. Civil Code art. 1926 Because a petition for the Senator's interdiction was filed before his death, his Succession may seek to invalidate the contract.

¶16 Under the Civil Code, where a judgment of interdiction is ultimately rendered, the judgment of interdiction is conclusive evidence of an incapacity to contract, retroactive to the date the petition for interdiction was filed. La. Civil Code arts. 400, 401, 1788(1), 1788(13). See La. Civil Code art 1918. It is undisputed that no judgment of interdiction was ever rendered against Senator Jumonville. The Succession contends, and the trial court found, that the appointment of provisional curators for Senator Jumonville, on May 10, 1982, prevented the Senator from contracting after that date and raised the conclusive presumption of incapacity.

¶17 Under La. Civil Code art 1788(1), the conclusive presumption of incapacity to contract arises only after a judgment of interdiction. A judgment of interdiction restricts the person interdicted from exercising his civil rights, such as the right to sue and be sued in his own name, La. C. C. P. arts 684, 733; the right to manage his own estate, La. Civil Code art. 31; and, of course, the right to enter into contracts, La. Civil Code arts. 31,1788(1). Because interdiction is such a harsh remedy, it may be declared only after a contradictory trial, at which the defendant is given the opportunity to cross examine the adverse witnesses. Stafford v. Stafford, 1 Mart. (n.s.) 551, 552-53 (1823; La. Civil Code art 393; La. C.C.P. art 4547. In the interdiction proceeding, the plaintiff has the burden of proving the defendant's incapacity to care for himself and his property, In re Ohanna, 88 So.2d 665, 666 (1956), Interdiction of White, 463 So.2d 53, 55 (La. 3d Cir. Ct. App. 1985), and the proof must be clear and conclusive, Interdiction of White, 463 So.2d at 55, In re Adams, 209 So.2d 363, 364 (La. 4th Cir. Ct. App. 1968). Such a contradictory trial was never held to determine the question of the Senator's incapacity. The ex parte appointment of provisional curators, pursuant to La. Civil Code art. 394 and La. C.C.P. art 4549, is insufficient to raise the legal presumption of incapacity afforded a judgment of interdiction after a full contradictory trial. See, e.g., La. Civil Code art 1919 comment (d). ("Under this Article, a contract made by an interdict after the date of successful application for interdiction is relatively null.") (Emphasis added.)

¶18 We believe the Succession's burden of proof in this case is analogous to the burden of one attacking an onerous contract made by a noninterdicted person before the filing of any petition for interdiction. In such a case, the party attacking the contract has the burden of proving

(1) that the alleged incompetent was deprived of reason at the time of contracting, and

(2) that the other party knew or should have known of his incapacity.

La. Civil Code arts. 402, 1788(2)-(3), 1789. See La. Civil Code art 1925.

¶19 The Succession failed to meet its burden of proving these elements. There was no admissible evidence presented that Senator Jumonville was deprived of reason on February 19, 1983. The only evidence of incapacity introduced, a physician's affidavit dated May 7, 1982 and attached to the petition for the Senator's interdiction, is inadmissible hearsay and is not entitled to any weight. See In re Aaron, 417 so.2d 105, 107 (La. 3d Cir. Ct. App. 1982); Board of Comm'rs v. La. Comm'n on Ethics, 416 So.2d 231, 238-39 (La. 1st Cir. Ct. App. 1982). Similarly, there was no evidence presented that Senator Jumonville was "notoriously" insane, or that Mr. Cohen knew or should have known that the Senator was incapable of contracting. To the contrary, it was undisputed at trial that Mr. Cohen was unaware of the interdiction proceedings against the Senator until he spoke with the Senator's son two days after the sale. The jeweler was summoned to New Orleans after a phone call by the Senator's sister, his hotel room was paid for by the Senator, and he was the Senator's guest, along with fourteen others, for dinner at a prominent New Orleans restaurant that evening. Considering the past dealings between them and the surrounding circumstances, Mr. Cohen had no reason to question the capacity of the Senator to enter into the contract before us.

Equitable Estoppel

¶20 Because of our finding that the Succession failed to meet its burden of proof to rescind the contract of sale, we find it unnecessary to address the jeweler's contention that defendants should be equitably estopped from asserting the defense of incapacity.

Mitigation of Damages

¶21 Defendants contend that even if the contract is valid, the jeweler failed to mitigate his damages and that his award should be reduced accordingly.

¶22 The doctrine of mitigation of damages applies to Louisiana contract law. Unverzagt v. Young Builders, Inc., 215 So.2d 823, 825 (1968).

¶23 The doctrine provides for a reduction in the amount of damages awarded to the victim of a contract breach if it is shown that all or part of the damages sustained should have been avoided. La. Civil Code art. 2323; Alex W. Rothchild & Co. v. Lynch, 129 So. 725, 727 (1930). The standard applied in determining which damages should have been avoided is that of "a reasonably prudent person acting under the facts and circumstances in which the nondefaulting party found himself...." Unverzagt, 215 So.2d at 826 (emphasis omitted). If a reasonably prudent person would have prevented or limited the extent of an injury, the defendant will not be cast in judgment for the full measure of the harm. Armistead v. Shreveport & RR. Val. Ry, 32 So. 456, 459 (1901).. The doctrine of mitigation of damages does not require a plaintiff to give up valuable legal rights and privileges. Langlois v. Allied Chem. Corp., 249 So.2d 133, 141 (1971). It may, however, require him to expend reasonable sums to avoid additional losses. See Comment, 30 Loy.L.Rev. 901, 918-19 (1984).

¶24 The question is, then, what would a reasonably prudent person in Mr. Cohen's position have done upon learning of the pendency of the interdiction suit against Senator Jumonville. Mr. Cohen twice tried, unsuccessfully, to encourage the Senator to rescind the sale. He was successful, however, in retrieving more than $153,000 worth of jewelry from Rosemary Norris, out of a $194,840 sale, before returning to New York. On the facts before us we do not find that Mr. Cohen breached any duty to mitigate his damages.

Attorney's Fees

¶25   Plaintiff seeks an award of attorney's fees pursuant to La. R. Stat. 9:2781, for suits on open accounts. At the relevant time, this statute provided, in part:

> A. When any person fails to pay an open account within thirty days after receipt of written demand thereof correctly setting forth the amount owed and a copy of the invoices in support thereof, that person shall be liable for reasonable attorney fees for the prosecution and collection of such claim when judgment on the claim is rendered in favor of the claimant.

(Emphasis added.)

¶26   After the sale, the plaintiff sent written demand letters with invoices, setting forth the correct amount owed, to Senator Jumonville, the Senator's son, the Senator's business, and to the Senator's wife after his death. The amounts owed were never paid. As such, we believe that plaintiff is entitled to an award of reasonable attorney's fees.

¶27   Among the factors to be considered in making an award of attorney's fees are: (1) the ultimate result obtained, (2) the responsibility incurred, (3) the importance of the litigation, (4) the amount involved, (5) the extent and character of the labor performed, (6) the legal knowledge, attainment and skill of the attorney, (7) the number of appearances made, (8) the intricacies of the facts and law involved, (9) the diligence and skill of counsel, (10) the court's own knowledge, and (11) the ability of the party liable to pay. Guillory v. Guillory, 339 So.2d 529, 531 (La. 4th Cir. Ct. App. 1976).

¶28   After an examination of the record and briefs, we find that plaintiff is entitled to an award of attorney's fees in the amount of 10% of the principal amount awarded.

CONCLUSION

¶29 For the foregoing reasons, the judgment of the trial court is reversed. Judgment is rendered in favor of plaintiff and against the Succession of John E. Jumonville, Sr. in the amount of $41,640.00, with the legal interest thereon from the date of judicial demand, and for attorney's fees in the amount of $4,164.00. All costs of this proceeding are assessed against the defendant Succession.

REVERSED AND RENDERED.

Study Questions:

Why did the plaintiff in the case below lose on appeal?

What does this case have to do with capacity?

What current Civil Code article would be at issue were the case to be decided today?

BANKS V. HYDE 1840

15 LA. 391

[Plaintiff's immovable was offered for sale at a public auction. It was adjudicated to the defendant for $19,000.00. When the defendant failed to comply with his bid, a second sale was made to yet a third person for $7,000.00. However, this third person was in fact acting at the plaintiff's request – the plaintiff had asked him to buy the property at the second auction, and after doing so, the third party reconvened the immovable back to the plaintiff as requested. Plaintiff then filed suit to recover the $12,000.00 difference between the two sales, relying on the authority of Civil Code art. 2611.]

MORPHY, J., delivered the opinion of the court.

¶1 The defendant appeals form a judgment condemning him to pay twelve thousand dollars, the difference between the price at which certain property was adjudicated to him, and that which it brought on a resale at public auction, on his refusal to carry into effect the first adjudication...

¶2 From the evidence, it appears, that when the property was put up for sale the second time, it was adjudicated apparently to Joseph E. Whitall, but, in reality, to the plaintiff himself. The name of the former was given in to the auctioneer, as being the purchaser, without his knowledge or consent, and shortly afterwards the property was reconveyed to the latter. No consideration was given or received by Whitall, in either sale. He declares, explicitly, that he always thought he was holding the property for Banks, whose agent he was. The plaintiff must then be considered as having himself become purchaser at this second sale, qui facit per alium, facit per se.

¶3 The first adjudication was for nineteen thousand dollars; the second for seven thousand dollars. We cannot consider the difference as a loss to plaintiff. If it was allowed him, he would be receiving his property back, and besides, a sum of twelve thousand dollars. A vendor must take his choice, either to regain possession of his property, or to insist on the payment of the price by bringing suit against the purchaser, or by resorting to the course authorized by article 2589 [2611] of the Louisiana Code. This article provides that the thing sold is to be again exposed for sale, as if the first adjudication had never been made. If, at this second exposure for sale, the vendor buys in the property, he must be considered as withdrawing it, or renouncing the right of reselling, for the account and risk of the first purchaser. He can claim of the latter, no deficiency of the price when there has been no resale. The plaintiff could no more buy at this second sale, than he could at the first. Louisiana [Civil] Code, art. 2418 [2443]; See the recently decided case of Municipality No. 2 vs. Hennen, 14 Louisiana Reports, 559.

¶4 It is, therefore, ordered, adjudged and decreed, that the judgment of the District Court be avoided and reversed, and that ours be for the defendant, with costs.

Lagniappe question:

You've seen a case involving interdiction, and one showing that a person is not capable of purchasing something he already owns. What are the Louisiana rules regarding the other two major exceptions to the presumption of capacity: the lack of contractual capacity of minors and those deprived of reason at the time of contracting? Concerning the latter, see Morris v. Malagarie, 607 So. 2d 1032 (La. App. 3d Cir. 1992).

Study Question:

What does the following case add to the Civil Code's rules regarding the contractual capacity of minors?

BOUDREAUX V. ST. FARM MUT. AUTOMOBILE INS. CO. 1980
385 SO. 2D 480 (LA. APP. 1ST CIR.)

PONDER, Judge.

¶1 These are two tort suits arising from a one vehicle accident. We intend no discourtesy by the use of given names; we find it necessary to distinguish the different Boudreaux's.

¶2 Michael Boudreaux (Michael), a minor, agreed to purchase a car from Jerry Aucoin for $450.00. After Michael paid $300.00 in installments, Aucoin's attorney drew up a bill of sale and a promissory note for $150.00. Michael signed the note and took possession of the vehicle. He kept the car at his sister's home for several days, but then drove the car home and to work that night.

¶3 The next day, Michael's father, Nathan Boudreaux (Nathan) objected to Michael's having the car and took the keys from him, saying he would not be responsible for his son's driving the car. There is some confusion concerning whether or not Nathan would have permitted Michael to keep the car if someone else had agreed to be responsible for it. Michael apparently tried unsuccessfully to convince his mother and his sisters to assume the responsibility.

¶4 Nathan spoke to Aucoin's parents and told them he would not be responsible for the car. He subsequently spoke to Aucoin and told him Michael was a minor and that he would not be responsible for the car. Aucoin agreed to come to some agreement to take the car back.

¶5 Nathan gave Michael the car keys with the understanding Michael was to meet Aucoin in Thibodaux and return the car. Instead, Michael met a friend, John Boudreaux (John), not related to him, and they decided to drive to California.

¶6 The boys picked up two hitchhikers in Texas. Michael asked one of them to drive so he could rest. Approximately 10 hours later, while still in Texas, the hitchhiker-driver veered close to a truck, pulled sharply on the steering wheel and pushed down on the accelerator. The car swerved off the road and rolled over several times. Michael, who was asleep in the front seat, was killed instantly. John suffered a broken back and other injuries. The hitchhikers were only slightly injured. Their whereabouts are now unknown.

¶7 Nathan sued State Farm Mutual Auto Insurance, his insurer on two other vehicles, for damages for the wrongful death of his son. John's parents sued Nathan and State Farm for their son's injuries.

¶8 The trial court found that the driver's gross negligence was the cause of the accident; that neither Michael nor John was neither negligent nor contributorily negligent, and neither had assumed the risk; that the driver was an uninsured motorist at the time of the accident; that the vehicle involved was a non-owned vehicle and had not been furnished for the regular use of Michael under the terms of the State Farm policies; that the two policies should be stacked to provide $55,000.00 uninsured motorist coverage per person and $110,000.00 per accident; that the sale entered into by Michael was null and void. The trial court permitted all parties to recover from State Farm. Michael's parents recovered $55,000.00 for the wrongful death of their son. John recovered $55,000.00 for his injuries.

¶9 The issues are: Was the hitchhiker-driver negligent? Was Michael negligent or contributorily negligent? Was John negligent or contributorily negligent? Was the sale to Michael an absolute nullity? If not, did Michael own the car or had the sale been nullified? Was the car an unowned vehicle under the terms of the policy? Was it furnished for the regular use of Michael? Did Michael have permission to drive the car? Did the hitchhiker-driver become a second permittee? Has the driver been proved to be an uninsured motorist? Is Nathan entitled to recover under the uninsured motorists provision of his policies? Is John entitled to recover under the uninsured motorist provision of Nathan's policies? Was an excessive award given to Michael's parents?

NEGLIGENCE

¶10 The trial court found that the hitchhiker-driver was negligent. This conclusion is not being seriously contested on appeal. We agree.

¶11 Michael was found to be not negligent. We agree. He was not operating the vehicle at the time of the accident; he was asleep. It is argued that he was negligent by allowing the hitchhiker to drive. John, the only witness to testify said he had found no cause to question the driver's competency until the accident occurred. We find insufficient proof of negligence in allowing him to drive.

¶12 There was no proof of John's negligence.

¶13 We therefore find no negligence, either primary or contributory, on the part of Michael or John. There being no negligence on the part of Michael, Nathan cannot be held liable therefor.

¶14   Contrary to this circuit's holding in Ellis Electric Co. v. Allstate Ins. Co., 153 So.2d 905 (La.App. 1st Cir. 1963) a contract entered into by a minor is not an absolute nullity but rather a relative nullity. La.C.C. Arts. 1785, 1791 and 3542. Harris v. Ward, 224 So.2d 517 (La.App. 2nd Cir. 1969), Scott v. Continental Ins. Co., 259 So.2d 391 (La.App. 2nd Cir. 1972).

¶15   The sale between Michael and Aucoin was valid but voidable. The question then becomes was the sale voided by Nathan's actions or was the car owned by Michael at the time of the accident.

¶16   Nathan informed Aucoin of Michael's minority and his refusal to take responsibility for the car. Nathan had the authority under C.C. 1794 to either confirm or annul the contract on behalf of his minor son. He left no doubt that his intent was to disaffirm the contract. In the case of a minor's contract, restitution need not be made before the contract can be declared null. D. H. Holmes Co. v. Rena, 34 So.2d 813 (La.App. Orleans, 1948). Therefore, we hold that the contract had been disaffirmed at the time of the accident.

¶17   Under the terms of the policies, a non-owned vehicle is an automobile not owned or furnished for the regular use of either the named insured or any relative. State Farm argues that the vehicle was for the regular use of Michael.

¶18   The facts of this case point to the opposite conclusion. Michael was forbidden to use the car. The keys were taken from him. Regular use must be more than casual or incidental use. Moreau v. Keller, 144 So.2d 281 (La.App. 4th Cir. 1962); Diagle v. Chastant, 271 So.2d 290 (La. App. 3rd Cir. 1972); cf. Romano v. Girlinghouse, No. 13,198, decided March 31, 1980. The facts indicate that the use of the vehicle was merely incidental to returning the car to Aucoin. There is a question of whether the deviation by Michael changed the use of the car from being merely incidental or casual to regular use. At the time of the accident, Michael had had the car under his control for approximately 24 hours. However, we hold the use was still incidental or casual. The fact that Michael intended to take the car to California and use it regularly in the future is irrelevant.

¶19   We therefore hold that the vehicle was a non-owned vehicle not furnished for the regular use of Michael.

PERMISSION TO DRIVE

¶20   Aucoin at least impliedly gave Michael permission to drive the vehicle with the intention that the car be returned to him. Though the permission was limited, deviations by the initial permittee, given expressly or impliedly, are immaterial for purposes of insurance coverage. Gathe v. Aetna Casualty & Sur. Co., 345 So.2d 117 (La.App. 1st Cir. 1977) writ refused, 346 So.2d 709.

¶21   However, we hold that the hitchhiker was not a second permittee driver. In Morgan v. Matlack, Inc., 342 So.2d 167 (La.1977) and Hughes v. Southeastern Fidelity Ins. Co., 340 So.2d 293 (La.1976), the Supreme Court found certain specific circumstances in which a permittee driver can give permission to a second permittee. It has even been argued that permission to use should always include the right to give permission to a second permittee. However, in this case, no discretion was given to Michael, certainly not to allow someone else to drive the car while en route to California. He was to drive the car for the purpose of returning it to Aucoin. He certainly did not have any discretion to allow a second permittee to drive it. It was not foreseeable that Michael would allow any one else to drive the car. Therefore, the hitchhiker was not a second permittee driver.

RECOVERY UNDER UNINSURED MOTORIST PROVISIONS

¶22   The above reasoning forces the conclusion that the car was not covered under the liability portions of Nathan's policy.

¶23   State Farm argues that the plaintiffs have not proved that the driver was uninsured. The statement from the Department of Public Safety does not comply with the literal terms of La.R.S. 22:1406d(6), which, however, is not the exclusive method of proving the non-existence of a liability insurance policy. See Campbell v. American Home Assurance Company, 260 La. 1047, 258 So.2d 81 (1972). We have held above that Nathan's policies did not afford coverage. There is creditable evidence that there was no other insurance covering the driver's operation. We agree with the trial court's conclusion.

¶24   The recovery is then limited to the uninsured motorist provisions of State Farm's policies.

¶25   A relevant provision of those policies is:

> "'Insured' means:
>> "(a) The named insured and any relative;
>> "(b) any other person while occupying an insured automobile; and

"(c) any person, with respect to damages he is entitled to recover because of bodily injury to which this Part applies sustained by an insured under (a) or (b) above."

¶26 Clearly, both Nathan and Michael were insureds and recovery for Michael's death was proper.

¶27 John's situation is quite different. He is not the named insured under Nathan's policy nor is he a relative of Nathan. The definition of insured automobile under the uninsured motorist coverage includes a non-owed automobile only while being operated by the named insured. John would not be entitled to recovery because of injury to another. We are therefore unable to find that he was an insured under Nathan's policies so as to be entitled to recovery thereunder.

DAMAGES

¶28 State Farm complains of the amounts awarded to Nathan, Michael's father, and Mary Armond, his mother.

¶29 Awards given in other cases are not binding on the court. Each set of facts determines what the appropriate award for that case will be. Michael was a troubled child. However, there is much evidence of a close relationship with his mother and father. The instances when he stayed away from home for a night or two were not to escape a bad home situation. He went to New Orleans and Lafayette on several occasions for fun. His father, in particular, aided Michael in every way he could to receive an education. His father also encouraged him when he decided to work.

¶30 The awards to Nathan, Michael's father, and to Mary Armond, Michael's mother, are high but not excessive. They are within the discretion of the trial court.

AFFIRMED.

Section 1: Distinguishing Sales from Other Contracts
Initial Definitions

Sale:

A contract by which seller transfers ownership of a thing to buyer for a price in money. Essential elements: thing, price, and consent. La. Civ. Code Art. 2439.

Sale: transfer of ownership – Thing, Price $, Consent

Contract to Build:

One party agrees to furnish either work or both work and materials; the other party for whom the work is done stipulates specifications; and the parties negotiate the job prior to the work being done. (Jurisprudential definition; La. Civ. Code art. 2757.)

K to Build: 1) skill/materials, one party, 2) specs, other party, 3) prior negotiation and agreement.

Lease:

Synallagmatic contract by which one party, the lessor, binds himself to give to the other party, the lessee, the use and enjoyment of a thing for a term in exchange for a rent that the lessee binds himself to pay. The consent of the parties as to the thing and the rent is essential but not necessarily sufficient. Art. 2668

Lease: Use of thing, Rent, Consent, (term)

Security right:

Right created by accessory contract to secure performance of another obligation (the principal obligation created by the principal contract). La. Civ. Code art. 1913. Security right may bind a person (personal security, e.g., suretyship) or may encumber a thing (either immovable, e.g. mortgage or movable, traditionally pawn but now the "security interest" governed by Article 9 of the Louisiana Uniform Commercial Code).

La. Civ. Code arts. 3133-3139, 3278; Rev Stat 10:9-101 et seq.

Section 1: Distinguishing a Sale from other kinds of contracts

Sale v. Contract to build

Contract to build: A contract whereby one party agrees to furnish his work and skill or his skill and materials, the other party provides specifications, and the parties negotiate the job prior to construction. Art 2557.

Tests to distinguish:

1. 3 factor test
2. Value test

Examples: mantel pieces, jewelry cases

Sale v. Lease

Lease: A synallagmatic contract by which one party, the lessor, binds himstlf to give to the other party, the lessee, the use and enjoyment of a thing for a term in exchange for a rent that the lessee agrees to pay. Elements: thing, rent, consent, term

Example: 13 mules –

Take-away: Although the parties called this a 'lease,' that was a relative simulation. They intended this to be a collateralized sale instead, as the buyer would own the mules once he finished making the payments. It was not in the proper form to be collateralized.

Security right: Arises from contract or operation of the law, whereby a thing or another person's promise is used to secure repayment of a loan. If a thing is used as collateral, then the promise is secured by a mortgage. If another person's promise to pay is used, then the debtor's promise is secured by a suretyship. A mortgage or chattel mortgage must be set up in accordance with statutory law, perhaps UCC-9 (Chattel mortgage) or Civil Code articles on mortgages if collateral is an immovable.

Sale v. Loan for Money

A loan for consumption is a contract by which a person, the lender, delivers consumable things to another, the borrower, who binds himself to return to the lender an equal amount of things of the same kind and quality. When the loan is of money, the borrower is bound to pay the same numerical amount in legal tender of the country whose money was lent regardless of fluctuation in the value of the currency. (arts 2904-2907).

Example: 2 hydraulic presses

Take-away: If the thing remains in the seller's possession and the 'price' paid was low, then the agreement is presumed to have been a loan, not a sale. (Again, it was not in the proper for to be a collateralized loan).

Giving in Payment: When an obligee accepts a thing instead of the money he is owed, Art. 2655

Exchange: When each party transfers to the other the ownership of a thing other than money, Art 2660.

One of the 3 elements of a sale is <u>price</u> (see art 2439 quoted above). Art 2464 provides that "the price must be fixed by the parties . . . There is no sale unless the parties intended that a price be paid." It further provides that

> The Price must not be out of all proportion with the value of the thing sold. Thus, the sale of a plantation for a dollar is not a sale, though it may be a donation in disguise.

Hint: review Simulation (art. 2025-2028).

Section 2: What Law Applies?

If both parties to a sale are from Louisiana (and the sale took place in Louisiana), then the Civil Code applies. However, if one party is in Louisiana and the other party is in another U.S. state or territory, then the law of the state whose policies would be most seriously impaired if its law were not applied dominates. Under Civil Code Article 3537, one considers 1. The pertinent contacts of each state to the parties of the transaction, 2. The nature, type, and purpose of the contract, and 3. The states' policies and the policy of promoting multistate commercial intercourse. In most cases, if Louisiana law does not apply, then the other state's UCC-2 articles would apply, but in the Tunica Tribe case, the tribe's sales law would have applied, had the contract not been a Louisiana contract.

If one party to the sale is in Louisiana and the other party is in a different country, then (unless the contract EXPRESSLY prohibited it), the United Nations Convention for the International Sale of Goods will displace the Civil Code. (In that case, the parol evidence rule is excluded, and if, as in many cases, the buyer is the U.S. party, then the buyer can use any and all evidence to prove that what the seller delivered did not conform to the contract, as in MCC Marble).

Section 3: Limitations on Capacity

The Civil Code provides a few special circumstances where someone may lack the capacity to buy or sell. For instance, officers of a court may not buy litigious rights subject to contestation in the jurisdiction where they perform their professional duties (article 2447), nor may a person buy a thing he already owns (Article 2443), or sell to a third party something that belongs to another (unless he is authorized to do so by the owner)(Article 2452). Furthermore, one spouse cannot sell or otherwise alienate immovable property owned by the community – the consent of both spouses is required, see arts. 2346-47, and there are limits on the sale of immovable property by parents to some of their children where that sale is in fact a simulation in violation of the rules of forced heirship. (Article 2444). All of these are more accurately regarded as legal prohibitions instead of a lack of capacity – the difference is that where there is a lack of capacity, the contract is relatively null, not absolutely null.

The Jumonville case is one of the few applications of Article 1926, which stipulates that the only time that one can argue that a sale made by a person since deceased is relatively null because he or she was deprived of reason at the time of the sale is if the sale was 1. Gratuitous, or 2. Shows a lack of understanding, or 3. Took place after interdiction had been filed, or 4. Took place within 30 days of death. The only reason the family was able to even argue that the Senator lacked capacity to buy the jewelry from Mr. Cohen was because they had filed an interdiction before the sale. Nevertheless, their argument failed because they were unable to prove that he was deprived of reason at the time he made the purchase and they were also unable to prove that Mr. Cohen knew or should have known that he was deprived of reason at the time.

Michael Boudreau, the minor who purchased a car and then tried to drive to California with his friends instead of returning it to the seller is included because it illustrates the fact that such a sale is a relative nullity, as well as the fact that the sale had been dissolved (by Michael's father) before Michael's actions.

Hypothetical

Boris, who owns a well-known shop selling blue suede shoes in New Orleans, was looking for a carpenter to build floor displays when he saw Natasha's beautiful work on the internet. He decided that her displays, done in black veneer, would be just the thing to show off his shoes to their best advantage.

He contacted her by email, and although she is headquartered in Florida, she agreed to work with him. They agreed that her standard black veneer pre-made floor display, in the standard size, would work perfectly. All that would need to be done is to secure them to the wall with a few screws when they arrived.

The display shelving arrived, Boris installed it and was very happy with it, but died two weeks later, before he had paid for them. His daughter, Anna, the executor of his estate, refuses to pay for them, arguing that the sale is relatively null because he was deprived of reasoning at the time – everyone knows that the blue shoes won't show up well against the black.

You are the first-year associate and have been assigned the task of evaluating Anna's claim. Answer the following question for your supervising attorney:

1. What law applies to this case, Louisiana or Florida?

2. Is this a sale or a contract to build?

What chance does Anna have of winning her argument that the sale was relatively null?

CHAPTER 2

PERFECTION OF SALE - PRICE

Flowchart

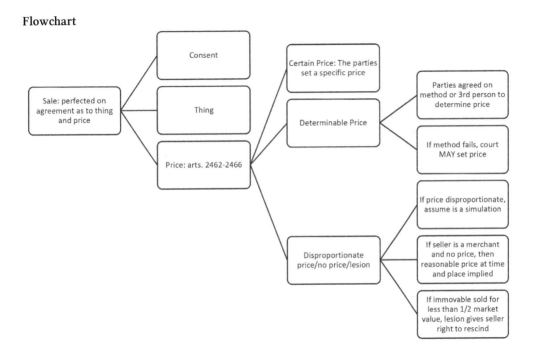

Introduction

Article 2439 of the Louisiana Civil Code defines a sale as "the transfer of ownership of a thing to another for a price in money. The thing, the price, and the consent of the parties are require-ments for the perfection of a sale." Article 2456 further provides that "[o]wnership is transferred between the parties as soon as there is agreement on the thing and the price is fixed, even though the thing sold is not yet delivered nor the price paid." Thus, as of the moment the parties agree on the thing and the price, the sale is perfected and the buyer is the proud new owner of the thing. Nevertheless, this rule that transfers ownership immediately upon agreement has limited practical significance. First, it is effective only between the parties to the sale. Additional requirements are imposed before third parties are bound. For example, creditors of the seller may be able to seize the thing until delivery occurs. La. Civ. Code art. 518. Second, risk of loss of the thing sold caused by a fortuitous event does not transfer to the buyer until the thing has been delivered to him. La. Civ. Code art. 2467. And third, in spite of the absolute language in article 2456, seller and buyer may agree that ownership will transfer only upon the occurrence of a condition or upon the arrival of a term.[1]

Hypothetical Question:

Olivia was finally getting married, and no one was prouder than her 55-year-old mother, Maggie, who had been saving up for Olivia's wedding for years. The two women went to Saks Fifth Avenue on Canal Street in New Orleans to find Olivia the perfect wedding dress. They spent several hours, looked at over fifty dresses, and Olivia tried on ten of them, but Olivia still could not say "Yes" to any dress. Kevin, the sales manager, told the women that Saks expected a new shipment in three days. Exhausted and famished, the women decided to head to the French Quarter for some well-deserved cocktails and from there to Galatoire's for dinner. Before they left, Maggie pulled Kevin aside and told him that she wanted the first Vera Wang dress in the expected shipment, giving Kevin her business card and her phone number. Kevin assured Maggie that he would take care of her.

When the new wedding dresses arrived in the store three days later, as promised, Kevin set aside the first Vera Wang dress in Olivia's size and called Maggie. The two women returned to the store the next day, Olivia tried on the dress and fell in love. Kevin put the dress in a garment bag and brought it to the cash register. As he was recording the sale, Maggie took out her American Express card, but when she saw that the dress was listed at $18,000, she fainted. She came to ten minutes later and stormed out of the store, pulling Olivia by the hand.

Is there a valid sale between Saks Fifth Avenue and Maggie?

While you should have concluded that there was no agreement as to price, and therefore no contract of sale, it isn't always so easy to tell if a sale is perfected. Must the price be in money? Must it be in proportion to the value of the thing? (Check the second paragraph of Article 2462.) And is it always true that ownership transfers on mere agreement? What if the blue suede shoes you agreed to buy from the seller in Mamou (you're in New Orleans) go up in flames before the seller even takes your size 20s off the shelf – do you still have to pay for the shoes you won't get? What if they leave his store safely, but they fall off the UPS truck and into the Atchafalaya Basin while en route – do you have to pay for them if that happens? What if they are packed up when the seller's creditor seizes them for nonpayment of a preexisting debt – can you get them

---

[1]   DIAN TOOLEY-KNOBLETT & DAVID GRUNING, *A. The Immediate-Transfer-of-Ownership Rule*, in 24 LOUISIANA CIVIL LAW TREATISE §3.3 (West 2012)

back as your property? Thus, as you can see, while articles 2439 and 2456 provide some necessary background rules, more is needed to determine whether a given sales agreement is perfected.

Section 1. How Price Distinguishes Sale from Other Contracts

Article 2456 states: "A price is an essential element in a contract of sale. If there is no price then the contract, if valid, is one of a different kind or description." In addition to Article 2456, familiarize yourself with Articles 2464-2466 and especially the comments to Article 2464.

Article 2464 provides first that "[t]he price must be fixed by the parties . . .. There is no sale unless the parties intended that a price be paid." The second paragraph provides that "[t]he price must not be out of all proportion with the value of the thing sold. Thus, the sale of a plantation for a dollar is not a sale, though it may be a donation in disguise." As indicated in Comments b-d, if the price is not in money or is nominal (i.e. "out of all proportion"), then the transaction at issue, though it may still be valid, is not a sale – it might be an exchange, a giving in payment, a donation inter vivos, or an innominate agreement. Thus, the "out of all proportion" language DOES NOT mean the transaction is invalid; it simply means that the transaction is likely to be something other than a sale. The price may be fixed in two ways: the parties may agree to a certain price, or they may fix it by agreeing on an objective method by which the price will be fixed. In the first instance, the price is "certain;" while in the latter case, the price is "determinable." Article 2464.

To return to the previous hypothet, if one party gives the other a pair of blue suede shoes in exchange for $250, then the agreement is a sale. However, if one party gives the other a pair of blue suede shoes in exchange for an electric guitar, then the agreement is an exchange, as defined in Articles 2660-2667. If the parties originally agreed on $250, but the buyer is short of cash and so the seller takes the electric guitar instead, then the contract as modified is a giving in payment (*dation en paiement*), Articles 2655-2659. If the parties agree that one party gets the blue suede shoes for $1.00 "and other consideration," then the price is out of all proportion to the value of the shoes, leading to the presumption that this is not a sale, but is instead a simulation (either relative or absolute, Articles 2025-2028) and may in fact be a donation inter vivos (Articles 1523-1526, 1541-1551). Finally, if the parties agree that one party gets the blue suede shoes in exchange for services to be rendered or an obligation of support, then the agreement is not a sale but may be either a remunerative donation or an innominate contract, as indicated in Article 2464 comment. (c).

Study Questions:

What kind of contract is at issue in the following cases? What rules apply?
Which price article discussed above is relevant?

MONROE, J.

¶1   Plaintiffs are grandchildren of Mrs. Evalina Gamper, who died in April, 1909, and they seek to annul an act of conveyance made by her to defendant on November 26, 1907, which reads, in part, as follows:

> 'Said Mrs. Evalina Gamper declared to me, notary, and witnesses, that the said Mrs. Edna S. Craig is her niece, and that during her continued and painful illness the said Edna S. Craig has devoted her entire time in nursing and caring for declarant, and for that purpose has abandoned a lucrative position, her only means of support, and she further declared that in consideration of the devoted services thus rendered to her by the said Mrs. Edna S. Craig, and in further consideration of the undertaking by Mrs. Craig, as hereinafter set out, she does hereby give to the said Mrs. Edna S. Craig, in part consideration for her devoted services, past, present and to be rendered, the following described property [describing a piece of real estate, No. 749 Dryades street, New orleans (sic), worth about $1,500]. And, in addition to the said property, she hereby pays to her the sum of $1,755.59, now on deposit with Mr. Harry H. Hall of this city, authorizing him hereby to transfer and deliver the said sum to the said Mrs. Edna S. Craig; and the said Mrs. Edna S. Craig, on her part, hereby declares that she obligates herself to devote her entire time and services to said Mrs. Evalina Gamper so long as she shall live, and to defray from said sum, or, if necessary, the above-described property, all the expenses of her illness and support, and to provide for such expense as may be rendered necessary by her death.'

¶2   The grounds of attack are: (1) That there is no estimation of the value of the services or real estate; . . .

***

¶3   The answer then recites the services alleged to have been rendered by respondent to the decedent and the sacrifice thereby entailed, alleges that the property and money conveyed by the contract in question would but moderately compensate the same, and prays that plaintiffs' demand be rejected.

***

¶4 Plaintiffs' allegations that the conveyance here attacked was not the voluntary act of the decedent, and that defendant rendered no services or that the services rendered were insignificant, have been, practically, abandoned, and the grounds of attack, set up in the petition, which are now relied on, are (1) that:

'There is no estimation of the value of the services, rendered, or to be rendered, and no estimation of the value of the real estate conveyed; and (2) that the act is a transfer of all the property possessed by the donor, or transferrer, leaving her without any means of support, and hence is absolutely null and void and violative of a prohibitory law.'

¶5 The provisions of the Civil Code which appear to bear upon the question at issue are as follows: [The court quoted the articles on onerous and remunerative donations inter vivos.]

¶6 Articles 2656, 2658, and 2659 provide that giving in payment differs from a sale only in two respects: (1) That a sale is perfect by the consent of the parties, whereas giving in payment is completed only by the delivery of the thing given; and (2) that an insolvent may lawfully sell for the price paid him, whereas the law forbids the giving in payment to one creditor to the prejudice to the others of anything save money.

¶7 From which it follows that in the giving in payment, as in the contract of sale, it is essential that the price or value of the thing given be fixed and agreed on.

¶8 There is, however, no such rule with regard to donations, though, in the case of a gratuitous donation, the value of the thing given may be inquired into for the purpose of ascertaining whether or not it exceeds the disposable portion, and, in cases of conveyances, purporting to be remunerative or onerous donations, such values may be inquired into in order to determine whether they are what they purport to be, or whether they are real, or gratuitous, donations, and subject to the rules applicable thereto. In Kleinpeter, Adm'r. v. Harrigon, 21 La. Ann. 196 (upon which plaintiffs seem to rely), it was held that a transfer of real estate is null as a sale, if the act does not show that a price has been fixed and agreed on; and that a fixed price is of the essence of the contract of dation en paiement. Referring to the contract there under consideration, however, the court said: "It is not pretended that it is an exchange or donativon inter vivos."

¶9 We therefore conclude that the validity of the conveyance here attacked, purporting, as it does, to be, at once, a remunerative, and an onerous, donation, is not affected by the failure of the parties to estimate, or fix, in exact terms, the value of the real estate conveyed or of the services rendered, or charges imposed, as the consideration of such conveyance.

¶10 It is ordered, adjudged, and decreed that the judgment appealed from be annulled, avoided, and reversed, and that there now be judgment rejecting the demands of the plaintiffs and dismissing this suit at their cost in both courts.

Hypothetical:

Plaintiff Orban Company sued defendant Lakco Supply on the unpaid purchase price for steel pipe allegedly sold to defendant. The parties entered into what each believed to be an agreement for the sale of pipe, agreeing that the price would be $400.00 per net ton based on the actual weight of the pipe. Lakco picked up a total of 103 segments of pipe, 73 segments of which remain in its possession, but the balance of pipe had been sold or otherwise disposed of. Upon reviewing the accounts, Lakco discovered that Orban was billing Lakco based upon the theoretical weight of the pipe rather than its actual weight. Consequently, Lakco was overcharged $730.88 on the first invoice. A third invoice similarly overcharged Lakco, though it contained a notation that the billing would be adjusted after all of the pipe was shipped. Lakco objected, stating that it had agreed to pay $400.00/ton based on the actual weight of the pipe, not the theoretical weight. Orban countered, claiming that it understood the agreement to be that Lakco would pay based on the theoretical weight of the pipe with a credit to be issued later.

a. Who should win and why? In answering, consider the Louisiana Civil Code provisions on formation and interpretation of contracts as well as the sales provisions on price.

b. If the contract was invalid, then Orban would have a cause of action for unjust enrichment (Lakco would have to either pay for the pipe or return it). But, assuming there was a contract in place, and the court decided to enforce it, who would have the responsibility for paying expenses incidental to the sale in the absence of a contrary agreement – buyer or seller (read article 2463). See D.B. Orban Co., v. Lakco Pipe & Supply, Inc., 496 So. 2d 1382 (La. App. 3d Cir. 1986).

Section 2. Price Provisions as Suppletive Law

The previous section focused on price as being necessary to a contract of sale. But, as you should know by now, many of the Civil Code provisions on conventional obligations (including Sales) are suppletive, meaning that they only apply if the parties' contract failed to otherwise provide for the issue in question. Sometimes parties forget to set an exact price, or for one reason or another delegate the setting of the exact price to a third person. Article 2466 provides that in a few such cases the sale may still be valid:

When the thing sold is a movable of the kind that the seller habitually sells and the parties said nothing about the price, or left it to be agreed later and they fail to agree, the price is a reasonable price at the time and place of delivery. If there is an exchange or market for such things, the quotations or price lists of the place of delivery or, in their absence, those of the nearest market, are a basis for the determination of a reasonable price.

Nevertheless, if the parties intend not to be bound unless a price be agreed on, there is no contract without such agreement.

As a second suppletive rule relating to price, unless the parties provided otherwise, the expenses of the act and other expenses incidental to the sale are borne by the buyer. La. Civ. Code art. 2463. Finally, the parties may leave the price "to the determination of a third person, and if the parties fail to agree on or to appoint such a person, or if the one appointed is unable or unwilling to make a determination," the court may (but is not required to) determine the price. La. Civ. Code art. 2465.

Study Question:

Read the following cases in light of the preceding three suppletive articles.
Why is Benglis Sash cited in the comment to Article 2466?

BENGLIS SASH & DOOR CO. V. A.P. LEONARDS 1980
387 SO. 2D 1171 (LA.)

Lemmon, J.

¶1 This suit to collect the reasonable retail value of bay windows ordered by defendant Leonards' architect (with admitted authority) presents the issue of whether a valid contract was struck although the parties at the time of contracting did not state a price certain in money.

¶2 Leonards had employed the architect in connection with the renovation of a building into apartments. While Leonards was out of the country, his wife selected certain bay windows for the building, and the architect contacted plaintiff, a building material wholesale dealer, to furnish the windows. Plaintiff had previously furnished other materials to defendant for this and other jobs. Since the desired windows were not stock items, it was necessary to order them specially from the manufacturer. Plaintiff estimated that delivery would take about eight to ten weeks, and the architect indicated satisfaction, without requesting a guaranteed delivery date or otherwise indicating a need for delivery within a certain period. The price of the windows was not discussed, and plaintiff did not require the usual deposit for a special order because of the previous dealings between the parties. Plaintiff placed the order on July 22, 1977 and received delivery on October 6, about 11 weeks later.

¶3 In the meantime Leonards had returned home and, being displeased with the progress of the renovation, fired his office manager. Leonards claimed he wrote a letter to plaintiff on September 24, cancelling the order because of failure to deliver within the time promised, but plaintiff denied receiving the letter. When the windows arrived, plaintiff contacted Leonards for delivery instruction, whereupon Leonards refused to accept the windows. This suit ensued, with Leonards' sole defense being that the windows were not delivered within the agreed time.[2]

¶4 After trial on the merits the trial court found that delivery was timely and rendered judgment awarding plaintiff the invoice price of the windows and interest, but denying attorney's fees and other items of damages. The court of appeal reversed and dismissed the suit, holding that there was never an enforceable contract, since the parties had never agreed upon a price as required by C.C. arts. 2439 and 2464. 378 So.2d 992. We granted certiorari. 380 So.2d 97.

¶5 The four requisites of a valid contract are capacity of the parties, their consent, a certain object and a lawful purpose. C.C. art. 1779. Particular types of contracts, such as a contract of sale, may have other requisites, and if the requisite is missing there is either no contract or a contract of another description. C.C. art. 1764.

¶6 C.C. art. 2439 defines the contract of sale and states the circumstances which must concur for the perfection of the contract.[3][FN2] Thus, the contract of sale is perfected when one party consents to give a certain thing for a price in money and the other consents to give the price in order to have that thing. Although there must be consent to give and to accept a price, it is not essential that the specific sum of the sales price be stated at the time of contracting. The parties can agree that the price may be ascertained by computation[4] [FN3] or that the price may be fixed by arbitration.[5][FN4] Or the parties can consent to buy and to sell a certain thing for a reasonable price, and when they do, the contract of sale has been perfected. The essential thing is that there be a meeting of the minds (as opposed to a disagreement) as to price.

---

2   FN1. At trial Leonards testified the price of the windows did not affect his decision not to accept them.

3   FN2. C.C. art. 2439 provides:

"The contract of sale is an agreement by which one gives a thing for a price in current money, and the other gives the price in order to have the thing itself.

"Three circumstances concur to the perfection of the contract, to wit: the thing sold, the price and the consent."

4   FN3. See General Fin. Corp. of N. O. v. Harrell, 188 So.2d 211 (La.App. 1st Cir. 1966).

5   FN4. Shell Oil Co. v. Texas Gas Transmission Corp., 210 So.2d 554 (La.App. 4th Cir. 1968).

¶7   The crucial question in this case is whether the parties expressly or impliedly agreed to buy and to sell these specific windows at a reasonable price, or stated otherwise, whether there was a meeting of the minds as to price. Since the parties did not discuss price at all at the time of contracting, there was no express agreement to buy and to sell at a reasonable price. However, C.C. art. 1811 provides that the proposition and the assent to a contract may be either express or implied, and there are factors indicating the parties consented to buy and to sell those windows at a reasonable price.

¶8   The parties had a history of dealings in which Leonards ordered materials and paid the price stated on the delivery invoice. In the present transaction, moreover, Leonards' authorized agent ordered a specific item which had to be specially ordered from the manufacturer. Although an exact price was not immediately ascertainable, Leonards did not object to the price which was eventually charged. Under these circumstances one could reasonably infer that Leonards and plaintiff intended to buy and sell these particular windows at a reasonable price. Thus, the case differs from those cases relied on by defendant such as Stupp Corp. v. ConPlex, Div. of U. S. Indus., 344 So.2d 394 (La.App. 1st Cir. 1977), in which the parties negotiated price but failed to agree, thereby creating circumstances under which one could not reasonably infer the parties' implied consent to a reasonable price.

¶9   We accordingly hold that consent of the parties to buy and sell the specific item at a reasonable price may be implied from the circumstances of this case and that the contract of sale was perfected before plaintiff ordered the windows from the manufacturer in reliance thereon. The contract was valid and may be enforced by plaintiff.

¶10   Since no specific time of delivery was sought or promised, the trial court correctly found that plaintiff did not breach the contract by failure to deliver timely. And since there is no dispute that the price charged was reasonable, we reinstate the award of the trial court in that amount.

¶11   Plaintiff also sought to recover (1) the loss of the profit it would have gained if it had been able to reinvest the sales proceeds into its business and (2) attorney's fees under R.S. 9:2781 for a suit on an open account.

¶12   The loss plaintiff characterizes as loss of profits is actually a loss occasioned by the delay in payment, and the only award of damages due for delay in performance of an obligation to pay money is interest. C.C. art. 1935. Since interest was elsewhere awarded, plaintiff's demand for damages for the socalled loss of profits was properly rejected. However, all debts bear interest from the date due, rather than from judicial demand, and interest should have been awarded from October 6, 1977.

¶13   As to attorney's fees, it is unnecessary to review the trial court's holding that this was not a suit on an open account, inasmuch as plaintiff did not comply with the statute's requirement for a written demand.

¶14   Accordingly, the judgment of the court of appeal is reversed, and the judgment of the trial court is reinstated, except that interest is awarded from October 6, 1977. All costs are assessed against defendant.

REVERSED AND RENDERED.

DENNIS, Justice, concurring.
I respectfully concur in the result reached by the majority, but I respectfully decline to join in the conclusion that the contract between the parties was that of a sale. There is ample codal, jurisprudential and doctrinal authority that a contract which cannot be considered a sale for the lack of certain price can, nevertheless, be construed as an enforceable innominate contract. La.C.C. arts. 1777, 1778; Thielman v. Gahlman, 119 La. 350, 44 So. 123 (1907); Helluin v. Minor, 12 La.Ann. 124 (1857); 1 S. Litvinoff, Obligations '' 113115 in 6 Louisiana Civil Law Treatise 19799 (1969); Hebert and Lazarus, Some Problems Regarding Price in the Louisiana Law of Sales, 7 La. Law Review, 378, 38487 (1942); Mashaw, A Sketch of the Consequences for Louisiana Law of Adoption of "Article 2: Sales" of the Uniform Commercial Code, 42 Tul.L.Rev. 740, 74647 (1968). See also H. T. Cottam & Co. v. Moises, 88 So. 916 (La. 1921).
    WATSON, J., recused.

MARCUS, Justice (dissenting).
I agree with the court of appeal that there was never an enforceable contract since the parties had never agreed upon a price as required by La. Civ. Code arts. 2439 and 2464. Section 2305 of the Uniform Commercial Code provides in pertinent part that the parties may conclude a contract for sale even though the price is not settled. In such a case, the price is a reasonable price at the time of delivery if nothing is said as to the price. However, the Louisiana legislature did not adopt this section of the Uniform Commercial Code. Accordingly, the articles in the Civil Code on sales should control.
    I respectfully dissent.

Comment and Lagniappe Question:

As mentioned previously, Benglis Sash, decided in 1980, is cited in the comment to Article 2466, which was new as of 1993. One of the aims of the 1993 revision was to harmonize the Louisiana Civil Code sales law with that of the Uniform Commercial Code Title 2 on sales, so as to facilitate cross-border sales of movables. It also made clear that the legislature was rejecting the line of argument presented in Justice Marcus's Dissent. The corresponding UCC article is 2-305 provides:

§ 2-305. Open Price Term.

(1) The parties if they so intend can conclude a contract for sale even though the price is not settled. In such a case the price is a reasonable price at the time for delivery if
    (a) nothing is said as to price; or
    (b) the price is left to be agreed by the parties and they fail to agree; or
    (c) the price is to be fixed in terms of some agreed market or other standard as set or recorded by a third person or agency and it is not so set or recorded.

(2) A price to be fixed by the seller or by the buyer means a price for him to fix in good faith.

(3) When a price left to be fixed otherwise than by agreement of the parties fails to be fixed through fault of one party the other may at his option treat the contract as cancelled or himself fix a reasonable price.

(4) Where, however, the parties intend not to be bound unless the price be fixed or agreed and it is not fixed or agreed there is no contract. In such a case the buyer must return any goods already received or if unable so to do must pay their reasonable value at the time of delivery and the seller must return any portion of the price paid on account.

Study Questions:

1) How is the UCC Open Price Term similar to Louisiana Civil Code Article 2466? How does it differ? Does your opinion change if you consider art. 2466 in concert with other Louisiana Civil Code articles?

2) Article 2465 did not exist when the following case was decided in 1904. (Like Article 2466, it was added in the revision of Title VII on Sale that became effective January 1, 1995.) If it had been in effect, would the court have reached a different result?

LOUIS WERNER SAWMILL CO. V. O'SHEE 1904

35 SO. 919 (LA. 1904)

PROVOSTY, J.

¶1 Plaintiff and defendant entered into the following contract:

'Alexandria, La., 1-28-'03.

'We, Jas. A. O'Shee and Louis Werner Sawmill Co., on this 28th day of January, 1903, mutually
agree as follows: O'Shee agrees to sell and L. W. S. M. Co. agrees to buy all the lands of said
O'Shee, lying in townships four and five north, and range one and two east, in Rapides Parish,
La., in all about 4000 acres. The consideration to be one dollar and fifty cents per M. for each
thousand feet of merchantable pine timber found on said lands. The quantity of timber, and
therefore the value of the lands and amount of money which L. W. S. M. Co. is to pay O'Shee for
said lands, is to be arrived at by two estimators, one to be chosen by each of the parties to this
agreement. This estimate is to be made at a time to suit the convenience of the parties hereto,
but to be commenced not later than March 1st next. It is understood that the term 'merchantable'
used herein is intended to mean sound timber not less than 14″ in diameter at the stump.'

¶2 In execution of this contract, the parties appointed each an estimator, and the estimators
proceeded to their work. Plaintiff's estimator proposed that the estimate be made by the acre;
defendant's proposed that it be made by 40's; and the latter mode was adopted. After four
40's had been estimated, the experts compared notes, and found themselves wide apart; and
defendant's estimator declared that to proceed further was of no use, as they evidently should
not agree. They, however, made the attempt at another 40, but, the estimates being widely
divergent, defendant's estimator refused to go on any further, and the attempt at estimating
was abandoned.

¶3 Defendant then notified plaintiff that he considered himself no longer bound by the contract, and that he would not execute the same, and plaintiff has brought this suit to compel him
to do so.

¶4 Plaintiff alleges the contract and the above-recited facts, and that 'the estimate of said
West [defendant's estimator] exceeded the estimate of said Marks [plaintiff's estimator] by an
amount so great as to indicate there was no intention on the part of said West and defendant to
make a true and correct estimate'; that plaintiff expected to make a profit of $10,000 from the
contract; and plaintiff prays that the defendant be ordered 'to appoint an estimator to complete

the estimate on his part,' and that in default of his doing so the court appoint one, and that 'the said contract be ordered completed, and defendant be ordered to make title to plaintiff.' Plaintiff also prays for an injunction restraining the defendant from cutting the timber on, or selling, the lands in question pending this suit.

¶5 Defendant interposed an exception of no cause of action, and, this exception having been sustained, plaintiff appeals.

¶6 The contention of defendant is that the contract is sought to be enforced as a promise of sale, and that as such it is fatally defective in not fixing a price.

¶7 Plaintiff, on the other hand, contends that the price is fixed, namely, $1.50 per thousand feet of timber on the land, and that the only thing not fixed is the quantity of the timber, and that this quantity is a matter ascertainable very much as in any sale by weight, tale, or measure; and plaintiff invokes the maxim, 'Id certum est quod certum reddi potest.'

¶8 Of these two contentions we readily adopt defendant's. Plaintiff cannot but admit that there is something left undetermined in this contract; something as to which the parties themselves were at the moment of the contract unable to come to any conclusion, and the fixing of which they found themselves compelled to leave to the future arbitrament of experts. Now, what was that thing?

¶9 To the completion of a contract of sale four things are essential: (1) Parties legally capable of contracting; (2) their consent legally given; (3) a thing; and (4) a price. [citing then C.C. arts. 1779, 2439] Now, there is no question in this case as to the parties, their capacity, or their consent, nor as to the thing sold, viz, 'all the lands of O'Shee,' etc. Plaintiff does not pretend to say there is any indeterminateness as to the parties, the consent, or the thing sold. Where, then, is the indeterminateness, if not in the price?

¶10 The contract in so many words says 'the value of the lands and amount of money which L. W. S. M. Co. is to pay to O'Shee for said lands, is to be arrived at by two estimators.' Therefore it was the price of the sale which was indeterminate, and the fixing of which was left to the arbitrament of experts.

* * *

¶11 The case being one, then, where the parties have agreed that the amount of the price should be determined and fixed by the agency of estimators or experts to be thereafter named by themselves, the question is whether such a contract is valid as a sale, for it is as a sale that plaintiff is seeking to enforce it.

¶12   With the exception of Duvergier (volume 1, No. 155) and one or two of the less authoritative writers, the French commentators on the Code Napoleon (article 1592, the exact counterpart of our article 2465) seem to agree that, if the price is left to be determined and fixed by experts to be named by the parties, the contract is null, since either of the parties has it in his power to nullify it by refusing to appoint the expert. See particularly Delvincourt, vol. 3, p. 65, note 7; Duranton, vol. 16, No. 114; Troplong, Comm. on art. 1592, No. 157; Marcadé, same article, No. 2; Aubry et Rau, vol. 3, p. 232, note 19; Laurent, vol. 24, No. 76; Baudry-Lacantinerie, vol. 3, No. 464.

¶13   And to the same effect are the decisions of the courts. See, particularly, the case of Grosjean c. Tissier, Journal du Palais, 1894, part. 2, p. 144, and the footnote, where it is said: 'It is now generally admitted that a sale made in consideration of a price to be determined by experts to be thereafter appointed has no binding character.' Citing Cassation, 31 Mars, 1862; Grenoble, 1 Juin, 1865; Rennes, 26 Jan. 1876; Bordeaux, 6 Fev. 1878; Dijon, 15 Dec. 1881. See, also, Limoges, 4 Apr. 1826; Toulouse, 5 Mars, 1827.

¶14   If, however, the parties do name the experts, and the latter do fix the price, this perfects the sale. Cass. 31 Mars, 1862; Aubry & Rau, vol. 4, p. 337, § 349, note 28; Laurent, vol. 24, No. 76.

¶15   But if the parties do not name the experts, the court is without authority to do so. Same decision of Grosjean c. Tissier, supra cit.; Dijon, 15 Fev. 1881; Aubry & Rau, vol. 4, p. 337; and the other commentators cited above.

¶16   'What is essential,' says Marcadé, Comm. on art. 1592, C. N., 'is that the parties should have bound themselves in such way that the price may be thereafter determined as a mere consequence of the consent given by them, without any new act of volition on their part. If, for example, after the parties had said that the sale was made for a price as to which they would agree thereafter, they added, or which, in case of disagreement, should be fixed by an expert to be appointed by the parties themselves or by the judge of the district, it is clear that there would be a sale, since it would no longer be within the power of the parties to prevent the fixing of the price. The result would be the same if, without expressing themselves thus explicitly, the parties had, however, manifested the idea of leaving matters to the courts, if need were, to name one or more experts; but, when nothing indicates such a consent, the fixing of the price will have to be by the expert or experts that the parties will have designated, and if one of them refuses, or dies, or is unable to make the estimation, there will be no sale, the condition upon which it depended not having materialized.'

¶17 'It will be said, perhaps,' says Troplong, Comm. on same article, 'that the default [of the party to the contract] to name the expert may be righted by the courts. But if nothing in the contract indicates that, in the event of refusal by one of the parties, the courts shall name the experts, it is not permissible to substitute the act of the court to that which should be the voluntary act of the contractants themselves, or of those to whom they have intrusted the fixing of the price. The contract, then, must not be added to, and the parties be compelled to submit to a fixing of price to which they have not dreamed of subjecting themselves.'

¶18 The exception of no cause of action was properly sustained.

***

¶19 Plaintiff asks that the right be reserved to sue in damages. The right, such as it is, is reserved. Interesting decisions in that connection are those of Bordeaux, 6 Fev. 1878; and Dijon, 15 Dec. 1881; and, by same court, Grosjean c. Tissier, supra cit.

¶20 Judgment affirmed.

Study Question:

Would the decision in the following case be any different under current Louisiana law?

LANDECHE BROS. CO. V. NEW ORLEANS COFFEE CO. 1931
173 LA. 701, 138 SO. 513

ODOM, J.

¶1 Plaintiff and defendant entered into a written contract which reads, in so far as it need be quoted, as follows:

'Sugar-Contract.

'New Orleans, La., June 4, 1920.

'The Landeche Bros. Co., Ltd., Killona, La., have sold and the New Orleans Coffee Co., Ltd., have bought.

'Quantity: Approximately Five Thousand (5000) barrels of Mary open pan syrup from the growing crop.

'Quality: Syrups to be good grade and to beaume 38 1/2 at 65/o Fahrenheit, and to be made from sound cane.

'Price per Gallon: If sugar sells at 15¢ to 20¢ per lb., 6 1/2 times the price of Prime Y. C. Sugar.

'If sugar sells at 20¢ to 25¢ per lb., 6 1/4 times the price of Prime Y. C. Sugar.

'If sugar sells at 25¢ to 30¢ per lb., 6 times the price of Prime Y. C. Sugar.

'Deliveries: To begin with grinding and to continue until quantity has been completed.'

¶2   When the date of delivery arrived, which was the beginning of the grinding season in 1920, defendant refused to accept any syrup from plaintiff. By the present suit, plaintiff seeks to recover of defendant $11,628.93, alleged to be the amount of damage sustained on account of the breach of the contract. Defendant excepted to the petition on the ground that it set out no cause and no right of action. The exception was sustained, and plaintiff appealed.

¶3   The exception is well founded and was properly sustained. The contract is in writing and speaks for itself. Plaintiff contends that the document evidences an unconditional obligation to sell and to buy. The defendant on the contrary contends that, under the express provisions of the document, there was to be no sale unless the market price of prime Y. C. sugar for the grinding season of 1920 ranged from 15 cents to 30 cents per pound; that it was not contemplated that either party should be bound if the price dropped below 15 cents or went above 30 cents, and that, inasmuch as plaintiff alleged that the highest market price of sugar for the season was 5.91 cents, it affirmatively appears that neither party is bound.

¶4   It will be noted that the price of the syrup was made to depend upon the market price of Prime Y. C. sugar. The contract stipulates that the price of the syrup per gallon was to be 6 1/2 times the price of Prime Y. C. sugar 'if sugar sells at 15¢ to 20¢ per lb.'; 6 1/4 times the price of sugar 'if sugar sells at 20¢ to 25¢ per lb.'; and 6 times the price of sugar if it sells for 25 cents to 30 cents. So that if sugar had sold, for instance, at 18 cents per lb., the price per gallon for the syrup would have been 6 1/2 times 18 cents, or $1.17, and, if it had sold for 26 cents per lb., the price of the syrup would have been 6 times 26 cents, or $1.56. The lowest price fixed for syrup was 6 1/2 times 15 cents, or $.97 1/2, and the highest was 6 times 30 cents, or $1.80.

¶5   It seems that on June 4, 1920, the date on which this contract was entered into, the market price of Prime Y. C. sugar was 22 cents per lb. It may be that the parties did not anticipate that during the grinding season of 1920, in which the syrup was to be delivered, the price of sugar would drop below 15 cents or go above 30 cents, and for that reason thought it unnecessary to provide for the fixing of a price for the syrup except as they did. Or it may be that both parties or one of them did not care to enter into such a contract unless sugar sold at prices ranging from 15 cents to 30 cents. But whatever they had in mind, the contract evidences the fact that the plaintiff did not bargain to sell nor the defendant to buy the syrup except on condition that the market price of sugar ranged from 15 cents to 30 cents per lb.

¶6   If they had intended, as plaintiff contends they did, to enter into an unconditional obligation to sell and to buy the quantity of syrup mentioned, regardless of the price of sugar which regulated the price of the syrup, it is reasonable to assume that they would have provided some method of fixing the price in case sugar dropped below 15 cents or went above 30 cents.

¶7   The fact that they failed to do so must be construed to mean that they did not intend to do so, and that they did not intend to bind themselves except under the conditions stipulated.

¶8   The contract literally construed means not merely that plaintiff was to sell and defendant to buy a certain quantity of syrup. It means more than that. It means that the syrup should be sold in case the price of sugar, which regulated the price of syrup, ranged between 15 cents and 30 cents, as stipulated.

¶9   The case of Held v. Goldsmith, 153 La. 598, 96 So. 272, 275, involved the interpretation of a contract under which one merchant agreed to ship rice to another on the steamer 'Sylvanian.' Justice St. Paul, the organ of the court, said in the opinion on rehearing:

'In the case before us one party agreed to sell, and other to buy, rice to be shipped by the steamer Sylvanian. The stipulation to ship by the Sylvanian was put into the contract for reasons best known to the parties who put it in. As merchants, they were not likely to have put it in unless they attached some value and importance to it; and they owed no explanation why they put it in, but are entitled to stand by the contract as deliberately expressed by them in writing.

'We are therefore of opinion that plaintiff bound itself to ship by the Sylvanian, and by no other ship, and that, when it became impossible for it to ship by the Sylvanian on account of the outbreak of the war between England and Germany, plaintiff was discharged from fulfilling same.'

¶10 When parties reduce their agreements to writing, and when such writing exihibits no uncertainty or ambiguity as to the nature, extent, or object of the agreement, it is presumed that the document expresses their true intent; and, in the absence of an allegation of fraud, error, or mistake, their intents and purposes cannot be sought outside the four corners of the instrument. [citations omitted]

¶11 Under our interpretation of the contract, the parties did not intend to bind themselves to sell and to buy except on condition that sugar sold at prices named in the contract, and, inasmuch as the market price at no time during that season reached the lowest price named, they were not bound.

¶12 Plaintiff's counsel in oral argument and in brief earnestly contend that the contract itself shows that this was an unconditional sale, and they lay stress upon the opening paragraph, which reads:

'The Landeche Bros. Co., Ltd., Killona, La., have sold and the New Orleans Coffee Co., Inc., have bought.'

¶13 But we must not look to this clause alone for the intent of the parties. Contracts must be construed as a whole.

'All clauses of agreements are interpreted the one by the other, giving to each the sense that results from the entire act.' Civil Code art. 1955.

¶14 In order to ascertain the intent and meaning of a contract, all its clauses must be construed together. Escoubas v. Louisiana Petroleum Co., 22 La. Ann. 280; Succession of Allen, 48 La. Ann. 1036, 20 So. 193, 55 Am. St. Rep. 295.

¶15 The above-quoted clause must be construed along with the one fixing the price. But if it be conceded that counsel's contention is correct, their client is in no better plight, for the reason that there was no agreement at to the price of the commodity if sugar sold for less than 15 cents, which it did. The three essential elements of a sale are the thing, the price, and the consent of the parties. Civil Code art. 2439. In the absence of any one of these essentials, there is no sale.

¶16 The learned district judge in closing his written opinion well said:

'Therefore, as there was never any time that prime yellow clarified sugar sold for fifteen cents a pound and over, there was never any fixing of a price for syrup and no obligation on the part of the seller to deliver and the buyer to receive and pay for it.'

¶17   The judgment appealed from is affirmed.

Lagniappe Question:

What articles in the Louisiana Civil Code are necessary to resolve the previous case, in addition to those articles on price?

Section 3. Lesionary Price and Rescission for Lesion Beyond Moiety

As you should have realized from the previous discussion above, caveat emptor generally applies in Louisiana so that in the absence of a vice of consent (error, fraud, or duress), a court will not dissolve a sale if a seller accepts a low price for the thing he sells or a buyer pays more than he should. The Civil Code statement that a price must be proportionate to the value of the thing does NOT mean that a sale for a disproportionately low price will be invalidated, it just means that the court will presume that the transaction is not a sale, but is in fact some other kind of contract.

There is, however, one instance where an 'unfair' price may be questioned, and that is where the seller alleges that the price he received for the sale of a corporeal immovable was lesionary and he wants the court to rescind the sale. A claim for rescission for lesion is extremely limited: it applies only to the sale of a corporeal immovable, only to the seller, only if the seller received less than ½ the value of the immovable, and only for one year after the date of the sale. La. C.C. art. 2589 & 2595. Article 2595 provides that the one-year limitation period is "peremptory," which means that it is strictly applied, as opposed to a prescriptive period, to which there are typically a number of exceptions. Furthermore, the right to lesion cannot be waived by the seller, as per Article 2589 which states: "Thee seller may invoke lesion even if he has renounced the right to claim it."

The effects of a claim of lesion beyond moiety are quite simple. When a sale is subject to rescission for lesion, the buyer has a choice of either returning the immovable (and getting a refund) or paying the seller the difference in value between the price paid and the fair market value of the immovable at the time of the sale. La. C.C. art. 2590 & 2591. If the buyer chooses to return the immovable, he must also return the value of any fruit accruing from the time the demand for rescission was made, and similarly, in addition to refunding the price, the seller must pay interest on the price from the same time. Art. 2592. If the buyer resold the immovable prior to the demand for rescission, a good-faith third-party purchaser is protected from any claim made by the seller, whose only recourse is to sue the original buyer for any profit realized from the resale. Art 2594.

Hypothetical Question:

Jim, a Louisiana law student, was taking Sale and Lease. He had already been called on twice but was unprepared because he had been unable to purchase the textbook as the bookstore was sold out, and other law students had already checked out the law library's copies. Finally, Jim decided to send out a request on Facebook, and two hours later, Paul, an upper classman at another Louisiana law school (and a book collector) responded, saying that he would willingly sell a copy of the textbook to Jim for $200. Although the book normally retailed for $95, Jim was too desperate to wait any longer, and agreed to meet Paul at the Starbucks in Tanger Mall.

Once at Starbucks, Jim slid $200 in cash to Paul, and Paul slid a copy of the textbook to Jim. The textbook was covered in clear heat-sealed plastic wrap, bigin the impression that it was brand-new. That evening, Jim ripped off the wrapping, and while inspecting the book, he noticed some notes in the margins. On the fronts-piece was even a signature by the book's original owner and author, Saul Litvinoff himself! Jim knew that Professor Litvinoff, the famous law professor, was deceased. So, he took the book to Professor Walker, a civil law historian.

Professor Walker told Jim that the signature was Professor Litvinoff's, and that the book was probably an original edition and therefore very valuable – at least $2,000! Two days later, Paul contacted Jim and told him that he wanted to exchange the textbook for another copy. Jim politely refused. Paul continued to call Jim, but Jim ignored each one of his calls.

Can Paul have the sale to Jim of the original edition rescinded under lesion? If not, can you think of another argument Paul could make under obligations rules?

Study Question:

Explain how the Civil Code provisions for lesion beyond moiety and Articles 2660-2664 on exchange operate in the following two cases. The section was updated in 2010 and changed somewhat. Read comment a to Article 2663 especially carefully. Were both cases properly decided, or are they inconsistent with each other?

JOINER V. ABERCROMBIE 2007
968 SO.2D 1184 (LA. APP. 2D CIR.)

BROWN, C.J.

¶1 On February 18, 2004, plaintiff, Luzon Joiner, an elderly World War II veteran, sold a 198-acre tract of land located on Highway 33 in Union Parish to defendants, Robert S. Abercrombie and Brenda Kay Hobson Abercrombie, for $110,000. Robert Abercrombie, a timber buyer and manager, had bought and cut timber on this tract from Joiner in the past. The deed was drafted and notarized by attorney Bruce Hampton. Within one month of the sale, on March 17, 2004, defendants transferred the property by an exchange deed to Pinoak Investments, LLC, which developed and sold the property as a residential area. Attorney Hampton, one of the owners of Pinoak, signed the exchange deed as the duly authorized manager of Pinoak. Exactly what Pinoak paid for the property is at issue in this action for damages. Plaintiff alleges lesion beyond moiety, contending that the sale price of his transfer to the Abercrombies was less than one-half of the value of the property. The trial court found that plaintiff did not prove lesion and dismissed his lawsuit. We reverse and render judgment in favor of plaintiff.

Discussion

¶2 Lesion beyond moiety is a sale of a corporeal immovable for which the buyer paid less than one-half of its fair market value. Lesion can be claimed only by the seller. La. C.C. art 2589. Fair market value is defined as the amount a willing and informed buyer would pay a willing and informed seller for a particular piece of property, with neither being under any compulsion to buy or sell. Cook v. Mixon, 29,491, 700 So.2d 1264 (La.App.2nd Cir. 1997), writ denied 705 So.2d 1101 (La. 1998); Mullins v. Page, 457 So.2d 538 (La. 1984). The immovable sold must be evaluated according to the state in which it was at the time of the sale. La. C.C. art. 2590.

¶3 When the sale price is lesionary, the buyer may elect to either return the immovable to the seller or keep the property and pay the seller a supplement equal to the difference between the price paid and the fair market value. La. C.C. art. 2591. However, when the buyer has sold the immovable, the seller may not bring an action in lesion against a third person. In such a case, the seller may recover whatever profit the buyer realized from the sale, not to exceed the supplement the seller would have received had the buyer kept the property. La. C.C. art 2594. The seller carries the burden of proving lesion. Mullins, supra; Caillouet v. Zwei Brudeland, 746 So.2d 752 (La. App. 3d Cir. 1999). The trial court's determination of fair market value is a finding of fact and is reviewed on appeal under the manifest error standard. Id.

***

The Purchase Price

¶4 This lesion case arises from the sale of 198 acres on Highway 33 between Farmerville and Ruston, by plaintiff, Luzon Joiner, to defendants, Robert and Brenda Abercrombie. Robert Abercrombie had bought and cut the timber on this tract and had the trust of Joiner. The Abercrombies, without obtaining an appraisal, purchased the land for $110,000 on February 18, 2004.

¶5 Approximately one month after purchasing the property from Joiner, the Abercrombies sold the land to Pinoak Investment, LLC. The purchase price paid by Pinoak is in conflict. The Abercrombies contend that they sold the property to Pinoak for $155,000 cash and the exchange of a 22-acre tract of property worth $55,000. Thus, the price was $210,000 and not lesionary.

¶6 This price, however, does not include the $90,000 timber management agreement that Robert Abercrombie entered into with Pinoak. The $90,000 was considered an advance, and it bound Robert Abercrombie to provide timber management services to Pinoak for either 35 years or until Pinoak ceased to own the subject property, whichever occurred first.

¶7 Three things cause this court to seriously question the propriety and actual purpose of the timber management agreement. First, Larry Culp testified that he offered the Abercrombies $300,000 for the entire tract, but that Robert Abercrombie informed him that he was selling it to Bruce Hampton for more. Second, Robert Abercrombie testified that he has been in the timber business for 12 years and, as far as he knows, he has never heard of or seen anyone getting paid in advance for timber management services. Finally, Pinoak immediately started developing and selling the subject property as residential, with all of the lots being sold before the case went to trial. Once all of the property was sold, Robert Abercrombie's agreement to manage the timber terminated. In fact, the "timber management" agreement terminated without Abercrombie ever going onto the property or performing any service after he sold it to Pinoak.

¶8 It is clear that the timber management agreement was a sham, designed to conceal the true purchase price received by the Abercrombies, which was $300,000. We again note that the trial court disallowed Joiner's attorney's attempts to question Bruce Hampton or the Abercrombies about their dealings on the Pinoak purchase. This was error.

Fair Market Value

¶9 At trial Robert Horton and William Maxwell testified as experts in the area of real estate appraisal and valuation, respectively. Horton valued the property at $237,500 as of February 2004, and Maxwell valued the property at $2,500 per acre. However, John Messina, an expert in real estate appraisal testifying by oral deposition for the defense, determined that the fair market value of the property was $134,000.

¶10 Testifying by oral deposition, Joel Kent Antley was tendered by plaintiff as an expert in real estate valuation. Defendants, however, objected to his being accepted as an expert and the trial court never ruled on the objection. Antley testified that he believed that the property was worth $300,000 because that was what he thought Pinoak, in which he and Bruce Hampton were partners, paid for the tract of land.

¶11 The Abercrombies contend that Joiner failed to prove the fair market value of the property through clear and convincing evidence. Moreover, the Abercrombies assert that Joiner's, as well as his experts', valuations of the property were speculative, as they were based on the property being classified as residential and not cutover timberland. To support this assertion, the Abercrombies cite Valley Land Corp. v. Fielder, 242 So.2d 358 (La. App. 2d Cir. 1971), in which this court found that in lesion cases, evaluations may not be based on conjecture, possibility or speculation.

¶12 In Valley Land Corp., supra, the plaintiff's experts concluded that the highest and best use of the property in question was for the development of a residential subdivision. While noting that the highest and best use of property may be considered, along with other evidence of value, to show the value of the property at the time of the sale, this court found that to evaluate that particular piece of property as a residential subdivision would be indulging in speculation. Id.

¶13 Based upon our finding in Valley Land Corp., supra, the Abercrombies argue that for this court to value the property based upon its highest and best use, i.e. residential, would require us to indulge in speculation. We, however, do not agree with this argument as the property currently at issue and the property at issue in Valley Land Corp. are different. In Valley Land Corp., this court found that the disputed land was "not suitable for a subdivision" and that "there were no residential areas within miles." The property in the instant action, however, is located in an area with rapid residential growth, is propitiously situated between Ruston and Farmerville, and has a large amount of road frontage. Furthermore, three out of four experts testified that the highest and best use of the property was residential.

¶14 In an attempt to invalidate the experts' conclusion that the highest and best use of the property was residential, the Abercrombies posit that at the time of the sale the property was cutover timberland and that Joiner had no intentions of using the property for residential purposes. Thus, the Abercrombies conclude, to value the property based on the possibility that it could be used as residential is speculative and does not show the value of the property in the condition it was in at the time of the sale.

¶15 After reviewing the jurisprudence, we find that there is no rule of law restricting the application of the highest and best use, when determining fair market value in a suit for lesion, to the actual use of the property at the time of the sale. This court previously stated in Mullins, 457 So.2d at 72:

> [T]he plaintiff in a lesion suit may present proof of the highest and best use of the property rather than solely the actual use of the property at the time of the sale. Such proof may be considered along with all the other evidence of property value provided that it tends to show the value of the property at the time of the sale.

> See also Nation v. Wilmore, 525 So. 2d 1269 (La. App. 3d Cir. 1988).

¶16 We find that the trial court's reliance solely on the appraisal of the one expert who evaluated the property as cutover timberland without considering the testimony of the three experts who concurred that, inasmuch as the property in question was ideally located and in an area with a burgeoning residential market, its highest and best use was residential was clear error. Further, within a month of the sale, the land was bought and developed as residential property.

¶17 Having found that the property should have been evaluated as residential, we must now determine the fair market value of the property at the time Joiner sold it to the Abercrombies. As we have found, within one month of the sale from petitioner to the Abercrombies the property was sold for $300,000 for residential development. Larry Culp testified that the Abercrombies were asking $300,000 before they purchased the property and that he offered $300,000 for the property. This price is supported by the valuations determined by the three experts who considered the property as residential rather than cutover timber.

¶18 Louisiana Civil Code art. 2594 states:

> When the buyer has sold the immovable, the seller may not bring an action for lesion against a third person who bought the immovable from the original buyer.

¶19 In such a case the seller may recover from the original buyer whatever profit the latter realized from the sale to the third person. That recovery may not exceed the supplement the seller would have recovered if the original buyer had chosen to keep the immovable.

¶20 Finding the fair market value to be $300,000 and that the profit realized by the Abercrombies was $190,000, we find that Joiner is entitled to damages in the amount of $190,000.

Conclusion

¶21 For the foregoing reasons, the judgment of the trial court dismissing Luzon Joiner's petition for lesion is hereby reversed and judgment is rendered in favor of plaintiff in the amount of $190,000, together with interest from the date of judicial demand. Costs are assessed to defendants, Robert and Brenda Abercrombie.

SAIZAN V. CENTURY 21 GOLD KEY REALTY 1984
447 SO. 2D 41 (LA. APP. 1ST CIR.)

SAVOIE, Judge.

¶1 Plaintiff appeals the trial court's finding that no right of action exists on his petition to rescind a contract for lesion beyond moiety.

¶2 Plaintiff entered into an agreement to sell certain property to Century 21 Gold Key Realty, Inc. (hereinafter referred to as Century 21). This agreement stated that Century 21 agreed to pay $120,000.00 for the subject property upon the following terms: "$90,000.00 Cash at act of sale thru-property exchanges with the balance ($30,000.00) to be financed for 12-Months $ ten (10%) interest." Thereafter, by document entitled "Act of Exchange Between Century 21 Gold Key Realty, Inc., Floyd S. Saizan," plaintiff transferred to Century 21 the property for and in consideration of (1) certain immovable property, (2) a $10,000.00 promissory note, (3) a $30,000.00 promissory note, and (4) $25,405.00 cash. The "Act of Exchange" stated that this exchange was being made mutually by the parties and that the properties exchanged were of equal value. Several months later, plaintiff brought this action to rescind the contract, alleging lesion beyond moiety. Defendant filed a Peremptory Exception of No Right of Action under L.S.A.-C.C. art. 2666, which exception was maintained by the trial court.

¶3 We note that the trial court failed to provide either written or oral reason for judgment. However, we assume his decision was based on the law advanced in the exception, that being, L.S.A.-C.C. art. 2666.

¶4 On appeal, plaintiff alleges two assignments of error. However, neither assignment has any bearing on the question posed to the trial court at the hearing on defendant's exception, that being, whether plaintiff is barred by L.S.A.-C.C. art. 2666 from bringing this action. Accordingly, we will not address the specific assignments raised by plaintiff on appeal but will address that issue which faced the trial court.

¶5 An exchange is a contract by which the parties to the contract give to one another one thing for another, whatever it be, except money, for in that case, it would be a sale. L.S.A. art. 2660.

¶6 It is clear from the facts that the contract in question was that of exchange. As consideration for the property plaintiff transferred, he received certain immovable property, three promissory notes, and some cash.

¶7 Contracts of exchange are subject to rescission on account of lesion except in two cases: (1) when one party gives immovable property to the other in exchange for movable property, and (2) if a balance has been paid in money or immovable [in movable] property, and if the balance paid exceeds by more than one-half the total value of the immovable property given in exchange by the person to whom the balance has been paid. L.S.A.-C.C. arts. 2664, 2665, and 2666, respectively.

¶8 Under the present factual circumstances, L.S.A.-C.C. art. 2665 is not applicable because the exchange was not immovable property for movable property. The exchange was immovable property for immovable property and movable property. Thus, L.S.A.-C.C. art. 2666 is controlling.

¶9 Using art. 2666 as our legal basis, we pretermit a factual finding of whether the balance paid exceeds by more than one-half the total value of the immovable property given in exchange by the person to whom the balance has been paid. We note that a factual determination thereon is not necessary because under art. 2666, it is only the person who has paid such balance who may demand rescission of the contract on account of lesion, and that person is not the plaintiff herein.

¶10   Since factual circumstances of plaintiff's exchange fail to invoke the application of either exception, plaintiff's contract of exchange cannot be rescinded on account of lesion.

¶11   Accordingly, the judgment of the trial court is affirmed. Plaintiff is to pay all costs.

AFFIRMED.

Study Question:

Title VIII on Exchange was amended effective August 15, 2010. Article 2663 now reads:

A party giving a corporeal immovable in exchange for property worth less than one half of the fair market value of the immovable given by him may claim rescission on grounds of lesion beyond moiety.

Revision Comment (a) begins, "This Article changes the law...." Does it change the result in *Saizan v. Century 21 Gold Realty*?

Treatise Note: The 2010 revision makes it clear that the party giving the corporeal immovable for any other property whose value is less than ½ the fair market value of the immovable may rescind for lesion, and the type of property given in exchange is no longer an issue, whether it is a mix of movable and immovable, corporeal or incorporeal.[6] The earlier version indicated that the party giving up the mixture of movables and immovables was the party that could rescind the sale if the immovable received was worth less than ½ the value of the mixture given. That was anomalous to the concept of lesion, which applies ONLY to immovables.

Lesion Hypothetical:[7]

Marge sold a mansion in New Orleans' garden district to Sue for $1,000,000. The actual fair market value of the property at the time of the sale was $2,100,000. The act of sale contained a waiver of any right to rescind the sale on the basis of lesion. This provision was mentioned at the sale, discussed in Marge's presence, the clause containing the waiver was initialed by Marge and Sue, and the act of sale was signed by Marge and Sue in authentic form in the presence of Sue's counsel and two witnesses. Six months following the sale, Marge brought an action to rescind the sale on the basis of lesion. On the date of the filing of the petition, the property was worth $4,000,000.

---

6   24 Civil Law Treatise §13:23, *Lesion and exchange*

7   Adapted from Louisiana Code III Bar Exam (July 2019)

Question: Can Marge prevail in his action against Sue, and what rights should Sue have if Marge prevails? Discuss.

REVIEW NOTES

Price & Lesion

Perfection of a sale: A sale is perfected on agreement as to the thing and the price and ownership is transferred even if the thing is not yet paid for nor the object yet delivered.

If there is no price (or the price is disproportionate), then the agreement is not a sale, though it may be something else.

Example: Hearsey v. Craig:

Aunt gave an immovable to her niece in exchange for nursing care, niece had given up her job. Other successors argued that the agreement was invalid as a sale and also invalid as a giving in payment because it lacked a price.

The court agreed – it was invalid as either a sale or as a giving in payment because it lacked a price. HOWEVER it was valid as an onerous or remunerative donation inter vivos where not price is needed. (NOTE: if the value of the services given in an onerous/remunerative donation is < 2/3 the value of the thing given, then the donation is presumed to be gratuitous and an authentic act is needed or else the donation is absolutely null. Review articles 1523-26, 1541-51 on donations inter vivos.

Open Price Term Art 2466

If the seller is a merchant and is selling things he normally sells and no price is stated (**or a method to determine the price was agreed on and it failed or the seller was to determine the price in good faith),** then the price is a reasonable price at the time and place of the sale.

Example: Benglish Sash:

Hubby and wife renovating apartment building ordered windows, Hubby objected when they came in, claiming late – and that no price had been given (parties had dealt with each other before). La. SCT held that the agreement implied a reasonable price, and was valid, and that objection was groundless. The case was used in drafting Article 2466, which coordinates with the UCC-2 open price term

Determinable price:

if the parties agree on an objective method to determine price, and that method fails, then the court MAY determine a reasonable price. Aft 2465

Examples:

1. Timber tract & land, price was to be determined by 2 experts (one appointed by each party), but 2 experts estimates were very far apart. Court held that it had no power to determine the price. Would probably be decided differently now.

2. Sugar: Parties set three different prices based on the market price range, but the market price was much lower than the range. The court held that the parties had intended to contract ONLY if the price was within that range. (But see current art 2466, this case might well be decided differently today – the entire issue would depend on the parties' intent, Prof. Nedzel is not convinced that the parties intended to be bound only if the price was within the range given in their contract, and one if not both parties were merchants).

Lesion Beyond Moiety Art 2589 & FF

1. If the price paid for an immovable is < ½ its market value at the time of the sale, then the seller (and only the seller) can bring an action under Lesion.

2. A successful action for lesion gives the buyer the choice of either supplementing the price or dissolving the sale (in which case, seller would return price + interest, and buyer would return thing + fruit).

3. 1 year peremptory period

4. No waiver possible

5. The value of the immovable is AT THE TIME OF THE SALE, not afterward – unless the buyer reduced the value of the thing by disposing of parts of it, in which case he or she will have to return the value received for those parts plus)

Example: Jim & Litvinoff casebook
Example: Joiner v Abercrombe:

Joiner sold his immovable to the Abercrombres, who exchanged it to Pinoak. The J-A sale was for $110K, the exchange was for $115K cash, $55K exchange for another immovable, and $90K timber management contract.

Abercrombe argued that Joiner had failed to prove the fair market value at the time of the sale was more than $115 K, however, court says that the "highest and best use value" was the appropriate measure, not the value of the immovable's actual use at the time of the sale.

Saizan: another exchange of immovables – court must determine value of each immovable to see if there was lesion beyond moiety. Article 2663 has changed since then.

Lesion Hypothetical:[8]

Marge sold a mansion in New Orleans' garden district to Sue for $1,000,000. The actual fair market value of the property at the time of the sale was $2,100,000. The act of sale contained a waiver of any right to rescind the sale on the basis of lesion. This provision was mentioned at the sale, discussed in Marge's presence, the clause containing the waiver was initialed by Marge and Sue, and the act of sale was signed by Marge and Sue in authentic form in the presence of Sue's counsel and two witnesses. Six months following the sale, Marge brought an action to rescind the sale on the basis of lesion. On the date of the filing of the petition, the property was worth $4,000,000.

Question

Can Marge prevail in his action against Sue, and what rights should Sue have if Marge prevails? Discuss.

HYPOTHETICAL

Anna, the owner of a New Orleans shop that sells blue suede shoes, placed an order with her favorite whole-sale seller of blue suede shoes, Singapore Slings' (who has a Monroe, Louisiana office). She ordered her customary refill order of loafers, high-heeled sandals, and sneakers. The order arrived timely, but nothing was said about how much it would cost. The delivery includes an invoice in the amount of $10,000. Anna thinks it is too much and does not want to pay.

---

8   Adapted from Louisiana Code III Bar Exam (July 2019)

In the interim, Anna sold the old fixtures to Ralphs' Refurbishing – she doesn't need them anymore, now that she has installed Natasha's new ones. She sold them last year, for approximately 1/50th of their value when she was desperately trying to stay afloat after Boris's death, and they have stayed in her warehouse since then. Ralph is now demanding possession.

Anna also sold the farm she inherited from Boris to Harold nine months ago. She sold it for $500,000, and just heard that Harold turned around and sold it for $750,000 and a "timber management" fee of $300,000 to a developer who plans on building a subdivision there. No one has ever heard of a 'timber management fee' in or out of the timber business. Anna thinks that Harold had set this all up beforehand to get her to sell the land to him cheaply. It is now worth $1,000,000.

1. What legal advice can you give Anna with regard to the Singapore Slings' invoice?
2. Ralph's demand?
3. The sale of the farm to Harold?

CHAPTER 3

PERFECTION OF SALE - THE THING SOLD

Flowchart

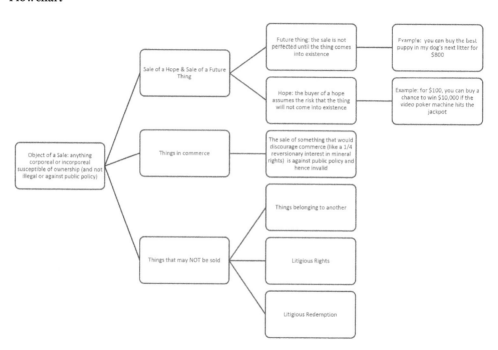

In addition to consent and price, a sale must include a lawful, possible, determined, or determinable thing as the object of the sale. Thus, anything – any thing – that a person may own may be sold and bought. As Article 2448 states: "All things corporeal or incorporeal, susceptible of ownership, may be the object of a contract of sale, unless the sale of a particular thing is prohibited by law." As that last phrase hints, the Civil Code does make some exceptions from the broad class of things that may be sold. In addition, the Code expressly permits the sale of certain things whose susceptibility to being sold might surprise us.

In preparation for this section, read Articles 2448 through 2453.

Section 1. Sale of a Hope versus Sale of a Future Thing

Study Question:

What does the following classic case teach us about the difference between the sale of a hope and the sale of a future thing?

LOSECCO V. GREGORY 1901
108 LA. 648, 32 SO. 985

[In this famous case of the sale in advance of two annual crops of oranges, followed by a very hard freeze, the trial court found for the plaintiff buyer, the appellate court reversed and found for the defendant seller, and in its first opinion (Jan 7, 1901), the Louisiana Supreme Court reversed the appellate decision and held for the buyer, ordering that the seller reimburse the buyer's $4000 initial payment. It then reverses itself twice in the two subsequent rehearings.

BLANCHARD, J.

¶1   Plaintiff is an orange merchant of New Orleans, in the habit of purchasing the produce of orange orchards in Louisiana in advance of the growth and maturity of the crops. Defendant was the owner of an orange orchard, and in November, 1898, he agreed to sell to plaintiff, and the latter to buy, the oranges which his orchard would produce in the years 1899 and 1900. The agreement was reduced to writing and is as follows:-'I have this day, in consideration of the terms hereinafter named, sold unto Vincent Losecco of the city of New Orleans, two crops of oranges on my place as follows, i. e.: 1st. All oranges that my trees may produce in the year eighteen hundred and ninety-nine (1899). 2nd. All oranges that my trees may produce in the year nineteen hundred (1900). For the sum of eight thousand dollars ($8,000). Four thousand dollars paid cash down and the balance four thousand dollars to be paid on the 1st day of December, 1900. Purchaser assumes all risks. Vendor to furnish teams and carts and drivers to move the two (2) crops.' This was signed by both parties. The plaintiff (Losecco) paid the $4,000 stipulated for. In February, 1899-on the 12th, 13th and 14th days thereof-less than three months from the execution of the contract aforesaid, there occurred an unprecedented freeze, the thermometer going down to 7° above zero in the city of New Orleans and eight degrees above in the parish of Plaquemines, below the city, where defendant's orange orchard was situated. This freeze, plaintiff alleges, killed and utterly destroyed the orange trees of defendant. The latter admits this in his answer, and the proof establishes it. Because of the utter destruction of the orchard and no possibility of the production of any crop thereon in the contract years, plaintiff demanded the return of the $4,000 he had paid. This was refused and the present suit followed. The allegation is made that a freeze such as that which destroyed the orchard was never considered nor contemplated by the parties in making the contract, since no orange groves in the section of country, where the one in question was located, had ever before been destroyed by cold. The destruction of defendant's grove is ascribed to a fortuitous event, an act of God, and by reason thereof the cause or consideration of the contract is averred to have wholly failed, entitling plaintiff to the relief sought. Resistance is made on the ground that the agreement between the parties evidences an aleatory contract. The contention is that Losecco purchased an uncertain hope, an expectancy, a chance — classifying ungrown crops as such— and must take the consequences of his bargain. It is claimed that all risks are included by the nature of an aleatory contract, and, besides, that Losecco expressly assumed all risks. Judgment below was in favor of plaintiff and defendant appeals.

¶2 Is this an aleatory contract? If it be, the defense is good against plaintiff's alleged right of recovery. 'A contract,' says Civ. Code, art. 1776, 'is aleatory or hazardous when the performance of that which is one of its objects depends on an uncertain event. It is certain when the thing to be done is supposed to depend on the will of the party, or when in the usual course of events it must happen in the manner stipulated.' Judged by this definition of the law, the contract under consideration is not an aleatory one, because the performance of that which was one of its objects-the growing of oranges-did not 'depend on an uncertain event,' within the meaning of the article of the Code. It is a 'certain' contract, in the sense of the article, because 'in the usual course of events it must happen.' The cold of February, 1899, which killed all the trees of the grove and prevented the happening of the event-the growing of the crops of oranges in 1899 and 1900-was unusual in the course of events, was phenomenal and extraordinary. The evidence establishes this. There had been cold weather-very cold weather for an orange-growing country-in certain years, attended with destruction of the orange crop of the years when occurring, and sometimes with partial destruction of the orange trees-the killing of the upper and outstanding twigs and branches, requiring trimming and pruning. There, too, was one year, 1895, when it is said by one witness that about half of the orange trees were destroyed. But the total destruction of entire groves of orange trees had not been known since, certainly, the year 1830, when, as we are vaguely informed by Martin's History of Louisiana (new edition, continuation by Condon), 'the severity of the winter * * * destroyed the orange trees.' The evidence discloses that for days following the great freeze of February, 1899, the remarkable spectacle was presented of ice floes in the Mississippi river passing the city of New Orleans, borne by the river's current to the Gulf of Mexico, and that some of the blocks of ice were from 20 to 30 feet in length by from 10 to 15 feet thick. It does not appear that the like was ever known before on the lower stretch of the river. It is shown that the temperature at the time of the freeze of 1899 was from 6° to 7° lower than ever before-the lowest point reached prior to that time of which any information is given having been in 1895 when the thermometer registered 14°>> above zero. The principal witness for the defense, who has lived in the parish of Plaquemines for 25 years, and who seems to have kept a record of the cold of the winters, admits that he had never known of a freeze in the parish which approached that of February either in intensity or duration.

¶3 We are justified, then, in holding that the contract between these parties litigant was 'certain,' as contradistinguished from 'aleatory,' in the meaning of the law, since in the usual course of events it must happen that the trees composing defendant's orange grove, or at least some of them, would have continued to exist during the contract years, and that their total destruction by the freeze in question must be considered as unusual in the course of events. Defendant sold by the contract 'two crops of oranges.' He did not sell the hope, or the chance of two crops. What he sold was oranges, and what he must be understood as warranting was that his trees would be there to do their part towards growing oranges. Lanata v. O'Brien, 13 La. Ann. 229. The contract certainly contemplated the continued existence of the trees, for the language is 'all oranges my trees may produce in the year 1899; all oranges my trees may produce in the year 1900.' The trees, however, disappeared, ceased to exist, were not there to produce oranges, or to make the effort of nature to produce oranges. But it is said 'the purchaser assumed all risks.' True, those words are in the contract, and are not to be read out of it. On the contrary, they meant something and effect must be given to them. We differ from defendant's counsel only in the scope of their meaning. They are to be considered as meaning all usual, known, or foreseen risks that may attend the inception, growth, development and maturity of the orange crop. This assumption of risk is held to apply to the thing sold, viz:-the orange crop of each year; not that which was to produce the crops-the trees themselves. Plaintiff took his chances on the crops, whether bountiful, or meager; whether of good quality or bad. His risk may have included all the vicissitudes of the season as to the effect of same on the orange crop proper. If the season were such that only an orange or two were produced in the grove, the same would have been 'the crop' of the year and that was what he bought and he would have no cause to complain. It may be that he took his chances as to whether there would be any oranges grown at all, the trees remaining. But his risk cannot be extended to an inclusion of the life of the trees themselves. The contract meant they were to remain in esse, to afford the orange crops which plaintiff purchased an opportunity to grow. Plaintiff did not purchase the trees; he purchased only what the trees were to produce. If the trees had remained and afforded the oranges nature's chance to grow, the fact that they were unable to grow because of unpropitious seasons, would not have availed plaintiff and he must abide his contract. But where the trees did not remain, were all destroyed and nothing was left to afford an orange a chance to grow, the case is different. Plaintiff took the risk only of the appearance on the trees, the growth, development and maturity of the oranges-not the risk that the orchard itself would continue to exist. See Walker v. Tucker, 70 Ill. 527. The contract may be likened unto a lease of the trees to gather the fruit they may produce in the years named. 'If,' says the law (Civ. Code, art. 2697), 'during the lease, the thing be totally destroyed by an unforeseen event * * * the lease is at an end.' If, then, the trees of defendant were destroyed by an uncontrollable event, par cas fortuit, or force majeure, it is a loss which must be held to fall on him. It would come under the head of an unforeseen accident. Plaintiff did not stipulate in the contract to run all chances of all foreseen and unforeseen accidents. Civ. Code, art. 2743. He stood to take all chances of foreseen accidents only. If, following the execution of the contract, war had been declared and an invading army had occupied the country, cutting down all the trees of this orange grove-would this be considered a risk which plaintiff assumed by the words:-'the purchaser assumes all risks'? We think not. If the great river which washed the front side of this orange grove had exerted its mighty force and engulfed the whole tract of land-not merely overflowing it, but appropriating it for its bed, causing the whole of it 'to cave into the river,' as the vernacular phrase is-would this come within the scope of the risks assumed by the purchaser? We cannot hold so. Yet these catastrophies would not have been more utterly destructive of the tree life of this orange orchard than was the freeze of February, 1899. The destruction of the orange trees was the destruction of the subject-matter on which the contract was to operate. The term vis major (superior force) is used in the civil law the same way that the words 'act of God' are used in the common law. These are not considered included in the assumption of risks such as that here disclosed. To be held so included it must clearly appear that such was the intention of the parties. Civ. Code, arts. 1933, 2743, 2219, 2120, 2697, 2754, 2939, 2970; Viterbo v. Friedlander, 120 U. S. 731, 7 Sup. Ct. 962, 30 L. Ed. 776. When the orange grove of defendant ceased to exist, the contract between him and the plaintiff became a contract 'without cause' in the meaning of Civ. Code, art. 1897, which says:-'The contract is also considered as being without cause when the consideration for making it was something which, in the contemplation of the parties, was thereafter expected to exist or take place, and which did not take place or exist.' Here the consideration for making the contract, on part of the plaintiff, was the orange grove from which he expected to derive a crop of oranges in each of the contract years. He and defendant certainly expected the grove 'thereafter to exist'-to continue to exist following the execution of the contract and for the two years of the life of the contract. But the grove did not continue to exist, and, thus, the consideration or cause of the contract failed. See Civ. Code, art. 1899; Mayor, etc., v. Caldwell, 14 La. 501; Hall v. School Dist., 24 Mo. App. 213. 'Where the consideration or cause of the contract,' says Civ. Code, art. 1898, 'really exists at the time of making it, but afterwards fails, it will not affect the contract if all that was intended by the parties be carried into effect at the time.' It surely cannot be claimed that all that was intended by the parties to this contract at the time of its execution has been carried into effect, nor that all that was intended was carried into effect at the time. 'When the certain and determinate substance,' says Civ. Code, art. 2219, 'which was the object of the obligation, is destroyed * * * so that it is absolutely not known to exist, the obligation is extinguished * * *.' Here, the 'certain and determinate substance' constituting the object of the contract was a grove of orange trees. Its destruction carried with it the destruction of the obligations growing out of the contract. Thus, if plaintiff were to sue defendant for the crop of oranges in the year 1899, had in contemplation in this contract, or were to sue him for damages because no crop of oranges was delivered that year, he could not, under the terms of this law, recover. See, also, Civ. Code, art. 1933, cl. 2. So, too, if Losecco had not paid in advance part of the purchase price and were, at the end of the contract period, sued for the whole of the $8,000 he stipulated to give for the two crops of oranges, no recovery against him could be had. The orange grove having been destroyed by a fortuitous event, a vis major, the purchaser of the crops of oranges which the grove was expected to grow in the contract years, had the right to recede from the contract. This being so, the seller is bound to make him restitution of that portion of the price received. Civ. Code, arts. 2497, 2301, 2302, 2304.

¶4   The judgment appealed from is found to be correct and is affirmed.

The CHIEF JUSTICE and MONROE, J., dissent.

PROVOSTY, J. On Application for Rehearing, March 31, 1302
¶1   Defendant owned an orange grove in the parish of Plaquemines, about 60 miles south of the city of New Orleans. Plaintiff was, and had been for 25 years, an orange-crop buyer. He had frequently bought orange crops in advance, some of which, as a result of cold weather, had failed entirely. Plaintiff had been known to buy crops as far in advance as three years. The parties entered into the following contract:

> "I have this day, in consideration of the terms hereinafter named, sold unto Vincent Losecco, of the city of New Orleans, two crops of oranges on my place, as follows, i.e.:

> "1st. All oranges that my trees may produce in the year (1899) eighteen hundred and ninety-nine.

> "2nd. All oranges that my trees may produce in the year (1900) nineteen hundred.

> "For the sum of eight thousand dollars ($8,000). Four thousand dollars paid cash down, and the balance, four thousand dollars, to be paid on the first day of December, 1900. Purchaser assumes all risks. Vendor to furnish teams and carts and drivers to move the 2 (two) crops."

¶2   Within three months after the execution of this contract, and therefore during the same winter, and before the trees had had a chance to even put out the blossoms of the crop of 1899, a freeze came that killed the trees, root and branch. Cold weather had been known to destroy the crops of the year, and even to kill the trees halfway down; but never, within the memory of the oldest inhabitant, had the trees been killed entirely, or even so injured as not to produce a crop the following year. In the several histories of Louisiana, mention is made of such a killing frost having occurred in 1748, 1768, and 1830, but whether the trees then killed were so far south as these of defendant's, does not appear; and nothing shows that the parties, when they entered into their contract, had any knowledge of these events of the distant past.

¶3 Plaintiff claims back the $4,000 paid under the contract, and defendant demands in reconvention the $4,000 payable on the 1st day of December, 1900. Plaintiff contends that the subject of the sale was the future crops, and that the contract was conditional upon these crops eventually coming into existence, and that the failure of this condition annuls the contract. He contends further that so long as crops continue to be attached to the realty they are part of the realty and belong to the owner of the soil, and if they perish by cas fortuit extraordinaire, or vis major, their loss falls upon such owner, and not upon the purchaser, unless the latter has specially assumed such risk; the presumption, otherwise, being that he has assumed only ordinary risks. Defendant contends that the subject of the sale was not the crops themselves, but only the hope of them, coupled with the right to take them in case they materialized, and that, even if the sale was of the crops themselves, plaintiff assumed the risk of their loss.

¶4 If the sale was of the hope, merely, then plaintiff got what he bargained for, and there is an end of the matter. If, on the other hand, the sale was of the crops themselves, then the loss must fall upon one or other of the parties according to the interpretation placed upon the risk clause. It cannot be, and is not, contended that the plaintiff could not validly assume the risk of the trees being destroyed by cold. The question must be, therefore, simply whether or not he made the assumption. It was possible, under our Code, for the parties to make either the crops themselves, or the hope of them, the subject of their contract. Civ. Code arts. 2450, 2451. Had they made the crops themselves the subject of their contract, the sale, in the absence of contrary stipulation, would have been conditional upon the crops eventually coming into existence, as contended by plaintiff. Duranton, Vente, Nos. 169, 171, 172; Troplong, Vente, No. 240; Delsol, Vente, art. 1, pp. 28, 29; Pothier, Vente, No. 132; Baudry-Lacantinerie, vol. 2, No. 842. Had they made the mere hope of the crops the subject of their contract, the sale would have been proof against all eventualities, as contended for by defendant. Same authorities; also Baudry-Lacantinerie, Vente, No. 97; Laurent, Vente, No. 99.

¶5 Plaintiff argues that, even if the sale was merely of a hope, there went along with it a certain warranty of the continued existence of the trees during the time required for the production of the crops; that even in the case of the sale of the cast of the fisherman's net, which is the example given by the Code as an illustration of the sale of a hope, there goes with the sale a warranty that the net shall continue in being until the time shall arrive for the casting of it. And in support of this plaintiff quotes as follows:

> 'Celui qui me vend un coup de filet garantit que le filet sera jeté, et que la totalité de son produit me sera remise; si donc le pêcheur refuse de jeter son filet ou de me remettre la totalité du poisson qui en provient, on déterminera l'étendue de cette garantie: savoir, au premier cas, en estimant l'espérance du coup de filet, et au second cas, en estimant le poisson que le pêcheur refuse de livrer. . . . Dictionnaire de Digeste, Thevenot-Dessaules, t. 1, vo. 'Eviction,' p. 266.

¶6   We do not think that anything further is meant here than that the fisherman warrants that he shall not refuse to cast the net or to give up the fish.

¶7   The seller of a hope has satisfied his obligations fully and completely when he has executed the act of sale. Delivery accompanies the act, and nothing further remains for him to do. The hope is a presently existing incorporeal thing, and since it is, of itself, and separately from the thing on which it bears, made merchantable by the Code, its sale cannot be differentiated from the sale of any other thing, corporeal or incorporeal. Of course, the seller warrants that the basis of the hope is not illusory; that is to say, he warrants that there is in reality an existing hope, and that he is the owner of it; but so does the seller of a horse warrant that there is a horse, and that he is the owner of it. The horse must be actually delivered, whereas the hope cannot be delivered, and hence delivery accompanies the act of sale; but beyond this there is no difference between the two sales. The vendor of the hope no more warrants the continued existence of the hope, or of the conditions serving as the basis of it, than the vendor of the horse warrants the continued existence of the horse.

¶8   The question of whether the crops, or the mere hope of them, was the subject of the sale, is to be determined by the terms of the contract, read in the light of the attending circumstances. Chief among these, according to the unanimous sentiment of the civil-law writers, is the comparison between the price agreed upon and the value of the thing; the inference being one way or the other accordingly as the disparity between price and value is wide or narrow. Unfortunately, in this case, the question of this value has been left by the evidence as much in doubt as the main question itself, by the contract. Both sides argue from this value in favor of their own theory; one placing the value low, and the other high. Plaintiff proved that the crop of 1898 was sold for $2,700; but at what stage of the growth of the crop this sale was made, and whether the purchaser assumed any risks, as in the present case, is not shown. Plaintiff proved, in addition, that the entire plantation of the defendant is assessed at $3,000; . . . The age of the trees seems to be conceded to have been eight years. As to what is the value of the average yield of an orange tree of that age, there is no evidence.

***

¶9 Therefore, not knowing with any degree of certainty what was the number of the trees, and knowing still less what was the value of the average crop of an orange tree eight years old, we are not in a position to establish a comparison between the value of the crops and the price of the sale.

¶10 Another circumstance on which defendant places reliance is the fact that plaintiff had made it part of his business to buy orange crops in advance, on a speculation, as he himself testifies. He was a speculator in orange crops, says defendant, assuming all risks, and securing thereby a material reduction in the price. But there is no proof as to how the prices of the crops thus bought in advance compared with the value of the crops after maturity; nor is there any proof that payment was exacted for the lost crops, nor of any local custom in that connection. Orange crops, like all other crops, vary in quantity and quality, affording a margin for speculation irrespective of the risk of total failure from extreme cold; and, besides, assumption of risk of loss of crop would not necessarily mean assumption of risk of loss of grove. Then, again, there is a broad and marked distinction between the purchase of a crop in advance, and the purchase of the hope of the same crop. As already stated, the one sale is valid only if the crop materializes, whereas the other is valid whatever befall. These previous purchases go to show that plaintiff must have been well up in the knowledge of what risks an orange crop was exposed to, but do not show that he consented to assume risks so extraordinary as to amount clearly to vis major or cas fortuit extraordinaire.

¶11 Coming to the contract, there is no denying that the wording of it is peculiar. After the statement that what is sold is two crops of oranges, there is added, as if by way of explanation, the videlicet, 'all the oranges that my trees may produce'; not what the trees will, but what they may; the use of the subjunctive from of the verb expressing uncertainty; implying that the trees might and might not produce any oranges, and that the plaintiff took his chances in that regard; and there is no denying that this peculiarity of language, when considered in connection with the sweeping assumption of risks, gives rise to an implication of considerable strength that the mere hope of the crops was the subject of the sale. Of course, if given the latitude of construction that its terms call for, this clause of assumption of all risks would show beyond a peradventure that nothing more than a mere hope was sold, for one who assumes literally all risks does not buy anything more than a mere chance, but when we come to consider later on, in another connection, the extent of the assumption of risks under this clause, we shall show, we think, that clauses couched in such general terms are not to be construed according to their very letter, but according to what, under all the circumstances of the matter, was most probably the intention of the parties, and that by this clause the purchaser did not intend to assume any other risks than such as the crops were at that time supposed to be liable to. So construing this clause, the theory of the sale's having been of nothing more than a mere hope finds neither in the surrounding circumstances, nor in the terms of the contract, any support, other than the implication arising, as stated, from the peculiarity of the wording of the contract. This implication stops short of legal certainty. It leaves the mind in doubt, and hesitation in the premises must forebode failure to the defendant's theory.

¶12 'The seller,' says the Code (article 2474), 'is bound to express himself clearly respecting the extent of his obligation; any obscure or ambiguous clause is construed against him.' We do not forget that the rule of interpretation by which uncertainty is construed against the vendor is to be applied only in last resort, when all other means of knowing the intention of the contracting parties have failed; but has not that extremity been reached in the present case? Have we not, both on the submission of the case and on this application for a rehearing, exhausted all known means of interpretation in the vain endeavor to reach a satisfactory conclusion on this question? We shall give heed to the conservative wisdom of our predecessors, who, after deciding against the vendor in a case of considerable analogy with the present one, added the following: 'But even were the case doubtful with us, we would come to the same conclusion. The price stipulated for plaintiff's pretensions was a large one, and, in a case of doubt, would incline in favor of a party striving to avoid a loss against one seeking to obtain a gain.' Therior v. Chandor, 17 La. 448. A consideration of this kind does not look strong from the standpoint of pure logic, but it addresses itself strongly to the conscience of the court.

¶13 Relinquishing as hopeless the attempt to determine, except by means of the presumption enforced above, the question of what, as between the crops themselves and the mere hope of them, formed, in reality, the subject of this sale, we address ourselves to the task of ascertaining what risks the parties intended that the purchaser should assume; in other words, what scope should be given to the clause 'purchaser assumes all risks.' Writings designed to express the conditions of an agreement are not to be read in the abstract, and to be construed by mere verbal criticism, but are to be read in connection with the facts of the case, and to be construed according to what, all things considered, was most probably the intention of the contracting parties. The clause now in question, for instance, taken in its literal meaning, would embrace such unforeseen risks as those pointed out in our original opinion, namely, the invasion of the country by a foreign foe, or the irruption of the mighty river flowing near by, and the consequent destruction of the grove; and yet it must be clear to any one that nothing could be more improbable than that the contractants should have given a single thought to any such contingencies as these, in connection with their contract. The clause, then, is not to be construed according to its literal meaning. 'However general may be the terms in which a contract is couched,' says article 1959 of the Civil, Code, 'it extends only to the things concerning which it appears the parties intended to contract.' 'The reason of this rule,' says Poth. Obl., No. 86, 'is evident. The contract being formed by the will of the contracting parties, it can have effect only in regard to what the contracting parties have intended, or have had in contemplation.'

¶14 Our question, then, is, what risks did the contracting parties have in contemplation? Or, more specifically, did they have in contemplation a freeze that, occurring before the end of the same winter, would cut off the crops bargained for? That question resolves itself into another: Had such a thing happened before? In so far as the cutting off of one crop is concerned, it had. According to plaintiff's witness Martin, and crop of 1881 failed as the result of a freeze that occurred on the 10th of January, 1881, and it failed entirely. The freeze that cut off the crop of 1899 came on the 12th-14th of February,-one month later than that of 1881. True, 17 years had gone by without a recurrence of this experience, but speculators in orange crops had nevertheless to keep note of it and govern themselves accordingly. It had to enter as one of the prime factors in their calculations. They had to know that what had happened might happen again, and that the crop ran the risk, and that the purchaser would assume it if he assumed the risks to which the crop was exposed. This fatal freeze of 1881 had happened within plaintiff's own experience, and therefore he had double reason to know of it, and to be guided accordingly; and, besides, there had been other years when the temperature had fallen low enough to kill the crops,-notably in 1886 and 1895. We hold that plaintiff assumed this risk, and that he must abide the consequences. But in his 25 years' experience, plaintiff had not known the trees to be killed, or even to be so injured as not to produce a crop the following year; nor had the oldest inhabitant known of such a thing. Some of the trees on the adjoining farm were 38 years old. Under the circumstances, we think it would be putting a most strained construction on the situation to hold that the parties, in making this contract, took into consideration the contingency of the trees being thus killed or injured. The most prudent and cautious speculator would hardly have done so. If he had thought of the matter at all, he would have assumed that nature would not deviate from her usual course. We hold, therefore, that the parties did not contemplate this risk, and that, as a consequence, plaintiff did not take it upon himself.

¶15 We have to assume that the degree of cold which proved fatal to the crop of 1881 proved equally fatal to that of 1899, and that therefore the crop of 1899 would have been cut off just the same if the temperature had not gone lower than in 1881. This being so, the loss of the crop is to be attributed to the fact that the temperature fell as low as in 1881, and not to the fact that it fell lower. The excess of cold beyond the degree of 1881 is therefore immaterial, in so far as the loss of the crop of 1899 is concerned. If the trees had not perished, the crop would have failed just the same as in 1881. At least, we are bound so to assume. The same is not true of the crop of 1900. For the freeze of February, 1899, to cut it off, a lower, and, for ought we know, a much lower, temperature was required than the degree attained in 1881. The freeze of 1881 did not prevent the crop of 1882. And we have to assume that if the freeze of 1899 had not been greater, and, for aught we know, very much greater, than that of 1881, or of any of the other frost years, the crop of 1900 would not have failed. If we had held the sale to have been of the hope of the crops, all risks of whatsoever nature would have fallen to the lot of the purchaser, under the maxim, 'Res perit domino;' but holding, as we have done, that the sale was of the crops themselves, the legal situation is that the vendor warranted the continued existence of the grove during the time required for the production of the crops, and that he is relieved of this warranty only to the extent that the purchaser assumed the risk of the loss of the crop. Between the lease of a grove and the sale of the future fruits of the same grove there is a close analogy. Both contracts purport to procure to the taker the fruits of the grove in consideration of a fixed sum of money. The destruction of the grove would annul the lease, and for the same reason a destruction of the grove ought to annul the sale. A lessee may assume the risk, but a clause by which he should have assumed 'all risks of whatsoever nature, including those of an extraordinary character,' would not be construed as an assumption of the risk of the destruction of the leased premises, in whole or in part. The intention to assume such a risk would have to be 'clearly manifested,' and the assumption would have to be 'restrictively construed.' Marcadé, Comm. on Art. 1773, Code Nap.

¶16   It is therefore ordered, adjudged, and decreed that the decree heretofore entered in this case be set aside in so far as it condemned the defendant to restore the $4,000 paid for the crop of 1899, and condemned defendant to pay the costs of suit, and that said decree be maintained in so far as it rejected the reconventional demand of the defendant. And it is further ordered, adjudged, and decreed that the plaintiff's suit be rejected, with costs in both courts. Rehearing refused.

NICHOLLS, C. J.,

is of the opinion that the contract in question was an aleatory contract of sale of a hope. He therefore concurs in the decree in so far as it relieves the defendant of returning to plaintiff the portion of the price received, but dissents from that portion of the decree which relieves the plaintiff from payment of the balance of the price. BLANCHARD, J., dissents in so far as the judgment appealed from is disturbed by this decree; adhering to the opinion and decree first handed down by this court.

BREAUX, J. (dissenting).

In this case, unquestionably, there is hardship. None the less, the loss cannot be divided on the ground that it seems hard that either party should sustain it entirely. The obligation is indivisable. Either the vendor owes a return of that portion of the price he has received, or the buyer the remainder unpaid. If the risk of the destruction of the fruit carries with it the implied assumption of the risk of the destruction of the trees by which it was expected that the fruit would be produced, then the buyer owes the whole price, and he should be held bound to pay the whole of the purchase money. If, on the other hand, the loss incurred did not fall within the terms of the contract, as a loss assumed by the buyer, then the seller should return that part of the purchase price already received. The pleadings and the arguments at bar did not suggest the possibility in any manner of dividing the obligation between the buyer and the vendor. I dissent.

PROVOSTY, J. On Application for Rehearing, Nov. 11, 1302
[After the March decision, the Louisiana Supreme Court decided to hear the case yet a third time, based on the plaintiff's complaint that he had not been accorded oral argument on the rehearing. The court again reversed itself, finding this time entirely for the defendant, and ordering the plaintiff to pay the remaining $4000 balance. The court based its reasoning on a number of French authorities' discussion of contractual interpretation, stating that the use of the future tense (e.g. 'all the oranges my trees shall bear') would have meant that the plaintiff's assumption of risk was limited to the loss of the crops only, not the trees, but that the odd and intentional use of the conditional tense in the contract "all the oranges my trees *may* bear" (emphasis added), along with the proviso that the vendor would provide transportation (thus, if there were no oranges, the buyer-plaintiff would not have had to pay for the trouble of providing potential transportation) meant that the plaintiff was assuming all risks, including that the trees themselves would perish. The Court then ordered that the plaintiff's suit be dismissed and that he pay the defendant the sum of $4,000 with legal interest from December 1, 1900, as well as the costs of the final appeal].

Comment on Losecco v. Gregory:

The procedural history of this case is remarkable. The trial court held for the plaintiff, the appellate for the defendant. The Supreme Court first held for the plaintiff buyer and returned the $4000 he had paid to him, then revised its opinion and split the difference, and finally after third hearing held entirely for the defendant seller and ordered the buyer to pay the balance of the price. The discussion of the sale of a hope versus the sale of a future thing given in the first rehearing is still helpful, as indicated in the Comments to Article 2451.

Given that the final decision relies almost completely on a parsing of one sentence of the contract, and that the final appeal was brought by the plaintiff after the Court had already issued two opinions on the matter, one could wonder whether the decision could have been influenced by the Court's irritation with the plaintiff, rather than the purported contractual interpretation basis.

Review articles 2045-2057 on contractual interpretation. See also, Karl Lewellyn, Theory of Appellate Decision and the Rules or Canons About How Statutes Are to Be Construed, 3 Vand. L. Rev. 401 (1950), with a famous argument that the parsing of contractual or statutory language based on such Canons of Interpretation can be manipulated to achieve a pre-determined result.

How would you have counseled plaintiff Losecco after the first rehearing? Would you have counseled him to proceed with a request for a second rehearing given that he had won twice (at trial and on the Supreme Court's first hearing? Or would you have counseled him to quit while he was ahead – that the decision split the loss between himself and defendant, but that a second rehearing could mean that he would lose entirely?

Study Question:

As decided, Losecco v. Gregory involved the sale of a hope. In contrast, read Article 2450. What does it say about a suspensive condition and how does it operate in the following case?

PLAQUEMINES EQUIPMENT & MACH. CO. V. FORD MOTOR CO. 1963
245 LA. 201, 157 SO. 2D 884 (LA.)

[Plaintiff buyer special-ordered a Ford pickup truck from dealer Pearce Ford, Inc. Pearce Ford was to buy the truck cab and chassis from Ford Motor Company and "to have installed on the chassis a special oil field body, a heavy winch, and other mechanical equipment." The buyer paid a deposit of $707.30 toward the total price of $6,029.18. Plaintiff was to pay the balance on delivery. Although Pearce Ford procured the truck cab and chassis from Ford Motor, Pearce Ford went into liquidation before the equipment was installed. Ford Motor seized the truck from Pearce Ford for nonpayment. Plaintiff then sued, claiming ownership of the truck. The District Court found that plaintiff did not have title to the truck, and the Court of Appeal affirmed. The Louisiana Supreme Court then granted a writ of certiorari.]

SANDERS, Justice.

1 It is clear that future things may be the object of a sales contract. Commercial transactions involving objects to be manufactured or fabricated are quite common. Such a contract is not aleatory, but certain, since the price is to be paid for a specific future object, the production of which depends upon the will of the seller.

2 In the absence of an expression of intent to the contrary, such a contract is not immediately translative of the ownership of any property. Title to the future thing cannot pass for it is not

yet in existence. Title to the component parts does not vest in the purchaser because they are not the object of the contract.

3 In the instant case, the object of the contract was a specially built truck to be produced. The agreement of the parties specified in detail the body type and other equipment to be installed on the cab and chassis. The body and other special equipment represented a major factor in the cost.

4 The dealer surrendered the cab and chassis to The Ford Motor Company without making the installation required to place the truck in deliverable form. It follows that the contract remained executory. It did not ripen into a sale. Title did not pass to the purchaser [citations omitted].

5 [Former] Articles 2439 and 2456 of the Louisiana Civil Code [of 1870], provide:

> Article 2439: The contract of sale is an agreement by which one gives a thing for a price in current money, and the other gives the price in order to have the thing itself.
>
> 'Three circumstances concur to the perfection of the contract, to wit: the thing sold, the price and the consent.'
>
> Article 2456: The sale is considered to be perfect between the parties, and the property is of right acquired to the purchaser with regard to the seller, as soon as there exists an agreement for the object and for the price thereof, although the object has not yet been delivered, nor the price paid.'

6 In express terms, Article 2439 requires the concurrence of the thing sold, the price and the consent for the perfection of the contract of sale. If the thing sold has not come into existence, as in the instant case, the concurrence is lacking.

7 Article 2456 provides for the vesting of title in the purchaser by operation of the law prior to actual delivery. For the transfer of title to be operative under the Article, the object of the contract must exist in a deliverable state. The law does not presume to pass title to anything other than the object of the contract.

***

8 We conclude, as did the Court of Appeal, that the plaintiff, Plaquemines Equipment & Machine Co., Inc., has no title to the property in controversy.

9 For the reasons assigned, the judgment of the Court of Appeal is affirmed.

Note:

Under the current law, the power of a creditor to seize goods that the creditor's debtor has sold depends on whether the debtor is still in possession of them. La. Civ. Code art. 518 ¶2. If that debtor has both sold and delivered them, then the buyer in possession of them can defeat the claim of a creditor of the seller.

Quite often, creditors such as Ford Motor, or Pearce Ford's bank lender, will take a security interest in both the cab and chassis and in the equipment to be installed under Chapter 9 of the Louisiana Uniform Commercial Code.

Section 2. Things in Commerce

Study Question:

The recognition that commerce – i.e. trade – increases the wealth of a nation led to a public policy encouraging sales and discouraging perpetual ownership, particularly of immovables, in both common law and civilian jurisdictions.

Explain how and why this public policy determined the decision in the following case.

HICKS V. CLARK 1954
225 LA. 133, 72 SO. 2D 322 (LA.)

[A landowner, Raines, sold his land in Bossier Parish but tried to reserve for himself the right of reversion over one-fourth of the mineral interest. Plaintiff Hicks and others, subsequent owners of the land then resold it to a third party, Red Chute Land Company, but specifically reserved the right of reversion of Raines' one-fourth mineral interest. The land was subsequently transferred to defendants. Plaintiffs sued defendant owners of the land for recognition of their mineral interest.]

HAWTHORNE, Justice.

¶1 The plaintiffs, S. B. Hicks, J. R. Querbes, and W. M. Phillips, instituted this suit against the defendants, Prentice O. Clark, Sam Brown, M. Daley Brown, and Odie Waites, to be recognized as owners of one-fourth of the oil, gas, and other minerals in 1142.88 acres of land owned by the defendants in Bossier Parish, Louisiana. Plaintiffs' suit was dismissed on exceptions of no cause or right of action, and they have appealed.

¶2   It is plaintiffs' contention that on December 9, 1951, the date the mineral servitude created by Raines by his reservation of one-fourth of the minerals in his deed to Brown was extinguished by liberative prescription, this one-fourth mineral interest reverted to them as transferees of Hicks Company, Ltd., Inc., under the reservation of the right of reversion in the deed from Hicks Company to Red Chute Land Company.

¶3   It is defendants' contention that, when the servitude in favor of Raines was extinguished by prescription, one-fourth of the minerals reverted to the land of which they are the fee owners.

¶4   The question of whether a landowner who has mineral servitudes outstanding against his estate can sell the land and reserve the reversionary rights, or as the owner sell to another the reversionary rights, . . . is squarely presented, . . . for the first time in this case.

¶5   Appellants in support of their contention rely on Articles 2448, 2449, 2450, and 251 of the Civil Code, which provide that any effects of commerce may be sold when there exists no particular law to prohibit the traffic thereof, that not only corporeal objects may be sold but also incorporeal things, such as a servitude or any other right; that a sale can be made of a thing to come, and that an uncertain hope may be sold, as the fisher sells a haul of his net before he throws it, and, although he should catch nothing, the sale still exists because it was the hope that was sold together with the right to have what might be caught. They argue from these articles that in the instant case the reservation of the reversionary right was nothing more than the reservation or sale of a hope and consequently was an object, thing, or right susceptible to sale.

***

¶6   Since we are here dealing with a future right to go on the land and explore for oil, gas, and other minerals, or a right which is to come into existence upon the extinguishment of the outstanding mineral servitude, we must look for a solution to the problem to the articles of our Code dealing with servitudes found in Book II, 'Of Things, and of the Different Modifications of Ownership', in addition to the articles on sales cited and relied on by appellants. Under the articles in this book dealing with conventional servitudes, the right of imposing a servitude permanently on an estate belongs to the owner alone, Civil Code art. 729; see Long-Bell Petroleum Co., Inc., v. Tritico, supra; U.S. v. Nebo Oil Co., 190 F.2d 1003 (5th Cir. 1951); and this servitude, once created, becomes a charge upon the estate or lands and not upon a person, C.C., Art. 709. If the right of servitude is not exercised within 10 years, the servitude is extinguished by liberative prescription, C.C. Arts. 783, 789, and the estate is no longer charged or burdened with this servitude.

¶7   Under the law relative to predial servitudes, therefore, such servitudes are extinguished by the liberative prescription of 10 years. If the reservation of the reversionary right is analogous to a sale of a hope as contended by appellants, liberative prescription would not extinguish this hope, as this kind of prescription is not applicable to a fully executed sale, even the sale of a hope. It is the servitude, the right to explore for oil, gas, and other minerals, which is extinguished for non-usage for 10 years. If the reservation of the reversionary right in the instant case was, strictly speaking, the reservation of a hope governed by the articles of our Code dealing with sales, that hope could never be lost by liberative prescription. Under appellants' contention that the sale of the reversionary right is the sale of a hope, the owner of an estate by conveying the oil, gas, and other minerals lying thereunder would create a servitude, and in the same act in which this servitude was created he could convey also unto his vendee the reversionary right, and thus the vendee would acquire the hope of the extinguishment of his own servitude. In effect, the person acquiring the servitude would have the right to go upon and explore the lands of the vendor for oil, gas, and other minerals for a period in excess of 10 years, because, when the existing servitude became extinguished for non-use at the end of 10 years, he could then exercise the right under his reversionary right. If appellants are correct in their contention that the sale of the reversionary right is the sale of a hope, the hope thus sold could be fulfilled at any time in the future, and the mineral servitude which would become effective would cause the land to be burdened with a mineral servitude for a longer period than 10 years without user, contrary to the public policy of this state that the right to explore for oil, gas, and other minerals in the absence of use reverts to the land in a period of 10 years. Palmer Corp. v. Moore, 171 La. 774, 132 So. 229, and authorities therein cited and authorities therein cited; see Daggett on Louisiana Mineral Rights (Rev.Ed.1949), p. 53.

¶8   We consider the reservation of the reversionary interest in this case as an effort to circumvent the public policy of this state, and we therefore refuse to recognize or give effect to it. . . .

¶9   For the reasons assigned, the judgment of the lower court dismissing plaintiffs' suit on exceptions of no cause or right of action is affirmed; plaintiffs-appellants to pay all costs.

Section 3: Things that may NOT be sold

As Article 2448 indicates, all things corporeal or incorporeal that are susceptible of ownership may be the object of a sale – unless the sale of a particular thing is prohibited by law, or as in the case of Hicks v. Clark, by a public policy aimed at keeping rights connected with immovables in commerce. Articles 2452, 2447, and 2652 prohibit the sale of three categories of things: things of another, litigious rights, and a related concept, litigious redemption. (You should also remember that the succession of a living person may not be the object of a contract, as stated in Article 1976.)

A. Things of Another (Art. 2452)

One exception to the general rule that all corporeal or incorporeal things may be the object of a sale is when the thing belongs to another – the sale of a thing belonging to another does not convey ownership (Article 2452), and a seller who purports to sell a thing he does not own is liable for damages (art. 2452 cmt. d). Nevertheless, such a sale may become valid if the seller acquires ownership from the true owner before the buyer brings an action for nullity. This is the after-acquired title doctrine, as delineated in comment e.

Notice that comment d indicates that the sale of a thing belonging to another results in the seller being liable for damages, not liable necessarily for the return of the object. Often the true owner of the object cannot demand return because the third-party purchaser is protected by the bona fide purchaser doctrine or the public records doctrine, which will be discussed in Chapter 4.

B. Litigious Rights

Article 2453 stipulates that "when the ownership of a thing is the subject of litigation, the sale of that thing during the pendency of the suit does not affect the claimant's rights." In contrast, however, Article 2447 says that "[o]fficers of a court, such as judges, attorneys, clerks, and law enforcement agents, cannot purchase litigious rights under contestation in the jurisdiction of that court." Consider why allowing something that is the subject of litigation can be sold pending the suit is in accord with public policy, while allowing officers of the court to purchase a right in a lawsuit is not. The latter means that the defendant now faces an officer of the court instead of the original plaintiff, which would raise potential issues of corruption of the entire judicial process. Rather than being absolutely null, however, so the debtor who is now being sued by a court officer, can resist the officer's claim by raising the issue of nullity, and it makes the purchaser liable for all costs, interest, and damages.[1] Thus, an attorney's contract with his client may not provide that payment of his fee will be a portion or percentage of the subject of the lawsuit. That brings us to Huey P. Long's participation in a case involving mineral rights.

---

1   24 Louisiana Civil Law Treatise §14:5 Incapacity of officers of the court

DAWKINS, J.

¶1   On April 9, 1919, Huey P. Long, a member of the Caddo bar, entered into the following contract with one W. M. McClung, to wit:

'Before me, the undersigned authority, personally came and appeared W. M. McClung, married, wife living, and Huey P. Long, Jr., married, wife living, who being sworn, depose, say and declare:

   'That, whereas the said McClung is the owner of one-half the minerals of the following described property, to wit:

   'N. 1/2 of S. W. 1/4 and S. W. 1/4 of S. W. 1/4 of Sec. 28, S. 1/2 of S. E. 1/4 and S. E. 1/4 of S. W. 1/4 and S. E. 1/4 of N. W. 1/4 of section 29, all lying in Tp. 21 N. R. 7 west. La. Mer.; and

   'Whereas the Atlas Oil Company or its vendee is claiming the ownership of the said mineral rights, and inasmuch as it is necessary that the said McClung secure judgment against the said Atlas Oil Company, or its vendee or any other claimants, decreeing him to own the said mineral rights, the said appearers have and do, by these presents, enter into the following agreement and the following transfer of rights is made hereby to wit:

   'In consideration of the professional services of the said Huey P. Long, Jr., in bringing whatever action or actions he may deem necessary, in order to secure judgment in favor of said McClung for the mineral rights as above set out, and in further consideration of the said Long paying whatever court costs decreed against said McClung in said suit or suits, the said McClung does by these presents, transfer, set over and deliver to the said Huey P. Long, Jr., one-half of his undivided one-half mineral rights of the property described above and in this instrument, excepting a 1/16 royalty on all property described herein.

'The appearers said McClung and Long, further stipulate that the said Huey P. Long shall have free and exclusive power to sue for the said property, to compromise such suit or suits in any court, and to represent the said McClung before any court and in any action he may see fit to institute, and it is agreed that rights herein conferred upon the said Long do not affect rights for rentals and royalties that may be due to the said McClung under any previous agreement, should the same be held by the court to be valid, but which said parties consider of no effect;

   'Thus done and signed in my presence and in the presence of the undersigned competent witnesses on this the 8th day of April, 1919.

'Sm. M. McClung.

'Huey P. Long.

'Attest:

'B. H. Moore.

'F. N. Moore.

'Leroy P. Fulmer, Notary Public'

- which contract was properly recorded in Claiborne parish.

¶2   On April 25th of the same year this suit was filed both in the name of McClung and Long [as owners of the mineral rights and naming Atlas and others as defendants for allegedly breaching a mineral lease of the property.]

* * *

¶3   May 17, 1919, answer was filed, in which defendants denied that Long had any interest in the property; admitted the execution by McClung of the leases to Wilder, the failure to drill during the first period, the subsequent extension, and the failure to pay any rental before March 27, 1918, but averred that none was due, for the reason that they had fully complied with the terms of the lease. They further denied that the payments under the last extension were not made timely, and averred that the transfers made by the Atlas Oil Company were in good faith. They also denied that Long had acquired any interest in the mineral rights in said property, and averred

> 'That the said W. M. McClung has ratified and confirmed said lease, and that he has revoked
> and set aside the rights of the attorney herein to prosecute or further carry on this suit, as will
> appear by an authentic act of ratification, made and signed by him, which is hereto attached and
> made part hereof; that, the said W. M. McClung being the owner of said property, having ratified
> and confirmed the lease made and held by your defendants, and having withdrawn from the said
> attorney of record the right to prosecute this suit, the same should be dismissed for that if for no
> other reason.'

¶4   The prayer was for the rejection of plaintiffs' demands.

¶5   The act of ratification referred to in the last paragraph of the answer just quoted and made part thereof is as follows:

> 'State of Louisiana, Parish of Claiborne.

'Before me, the undersigned authority, personally came and appeared W. M. McClung, married, wife living, who declared that, whereas he is the owner of the following described real property, to wit:

'S. W. 1/4 of S. W. 1/4, Sec. 28, S. 1/2 of S. E. 1/4, E. 1/4 of S. W. 1/4 and S. E. 1/4 of N. W. 1/4, Sec. 29, and N. 1/2 of N. E. 1/4, Sec. 33, all Twp. 21, Range 7 W. in Claiborne Parish, Louisiana; and

'Whereas, said land is held under mineral lease by various parties under lease heretofore given to A. E. Wilder, and whereas D. L. Davis, married, wife living, who holds under said lease, has heretofore begun the erection of a derrick for the purpose of exploring said land in search for oil and gas, which action I have at all times encouraged and acquiesced in, by reason of which fact said lease had become valid, as to the portion held by Atlas Oil Company and D. L. Davis:

'Now, therefore, in consideration of said D. L. Davis, continuing operations for the drilling of said well as agreed by him and the Atlas Oil Company, under whom he holds, I hereby declare said lease valid and binding in so far as it applies to and covers the above described land, and hereby revoke all powers of attorney heretofore given by me to any and all persons for the purpose of bringing suit thereon to cancel said lease.

'In testimony thereof, witness my hand at Homer, Louisiana, this the 24th day of April A. D. 1919:

[Signed] W. M. McClung.
'Attest:
'[Signed] W. A. McKenzie.
'G. T. Shaw.
'[Signed] J. Melton Oakes, Notary Public.'

¶6   May 21, 1919, defendants filed the following exception, to wit:

'In this case now comes the defendants, and show unto the court that the only plaintiff remaining in said cause is Huey P. Long, and that he is without right or authority to prosecute or maintain the suit in question.

'In any event, whatever rights he has, he acquired with the view to bring a suit thereon, and such rights were litigious rights, and being an attorney at law practicing in the courts of this state, he was absolutely prohibited from acquiring the same, and for that reason, if no other, said suit should be dismissed;'

¶7   This exception was tried and sustained, the suit as to the remaining plaintiff, Long, was dismissed, and he brings this appeal.

Opinion.

¶1   As we read the contract, it was not alone a transfer of an interest in the subject-matter of the contemplated lawsuit, but it was a present conveyance of a fixed undivided interest in such title as McClung then owned in the mineral rights of the property described. The consideration was a real one, i. e., the professional services to be rendered, and when the act was recorded in the conveyance records McClung could not thereafter have sold to any one else the rights in question so as to give them a claim superior to Long's any more than he could have done in any other conveyance of real property. If Long acquired a title in the property, then he undoubtedly had a standing in court to test the same with others making claim to the same thing. He has a real interest to assert. C. P. 15.

* * *

¶2   We are therefore of the opinion that the petition, which was brought, both in the name of Long and of McClung, but from which the latter has been dismissed at his own instance, does allege a cause of action; provided of course Long was not prohibited by law from acquiring the interest which his deed called for.

¶3   Leaving out of consideration for the present Act No. 124 of 1906, we will inquire whether or not the interest which Long acquired involved a litigious right within the meaning of the law. As was said by us in Sanders v. Ditch, 110 La. 899, 34 South. 860 (decided before the act of 1906 was passed), there is nothing wrong or immoral in the act itself of conveying a right which is either in the process of litigation or may become litigated, and its illegality arises when and to the extent only which the express law makes it such. In that case, we took occasion to review the codal provisions and jurisprudence on the subject up to that time, and to point out that the Code itself (article 2653) in unequivocal terms defines a litigious right as one about which a suit exists. **Until there is a lawsuit actually pending, no right is litigious, no matter how apparently necessary one may be to enforce i**t. And the term has the same meaning in article 2447, applying to attorneys and court officers, as under article 2652, applying to all other persons, the only difference being that in cases where the first article applies the attempted transfer is null, while under the latter the party against whom the litigious rights exists may relieve himself by paying to the purchaser 'the real price of the transfer, together with the interest from date.' In the present case, there was no suit pending when Long acquired his interest in the mineral rights; and, while it is true that the consideration which he agreed to give was his professional services in such actions as he might deem necessary to obtain judgment in favor of McClung therefor, yet, even this could not have the effect of supplying the condition which the Code requires, i. e., the pending of a suit. Sanders v. Ditch, supra; Succession of Landry, 116, La. 970, 41 South 226; Saint v. Martel, 122 La. 93, 47 South. 413.

* * *

¶4 For the reasons assigned, the judgment appealed from is annulled and reversed, and this cause is hereby remanded, to be proceeded with according to law and the views herein expressed. Appellee to pay costs of this appeal and other costs to await final judgment.

Study Question

As the McClung court stipulated, until a lawsuit is filed, no right is litigious. However, under the Rules of Professional Conduct, a lawyer must still be very careful in how she constructs her fee. What differences in fee structure meant that Huey Long was safe, while attorney Martin Sanders in the next case was found to have violated the rules?

LA. ST. BAR ASS'N V. SANDERS 1990
568 SO. 2D 1025 (LA.)

WATSON, Justice.

¶1 In this disciplinary proceeding against attorney Martin S. Sanders, Jr., the issue is the appropriate sanction for Sanders' violation of Disciplinary Rule 5-103(A)1 which prohibited a lawyer from acquiring a proprietary interest in his client's cause of action.

FACTS

¶2 Urzula Cloud Hatch was the record owner of a twenty-acre tract of property, part of a forty acre farm which had been owned by her parents, Noah and Lucy Cloud. Urzula was one of the Clouds' five children. She acquired the record title in a property settlement with her former husband, Bonnie M. Hatch. Sanders represented her husband in the divorce. Bonnie M. Hatch testified that he had purchased the property from Noah Cloud for $2,000. His former in-laws said title had been placed in Hatch's name to keep Noah Cloud, invalid and senile, from giving away the royalties. Urzula Hatch was deposed before trial, testified at trial and was deposed a second time after trial. Her testimony about ownership of the property was not consistent.

¶3 In 1964, when title to the twenty-acre tract was put in the name of B. M. Hatch, Mr. and Mrs. Cloud went to live with Mr. and Mrs. Hatch. Noah Cloud survived until December of 1966. Shortly after his death, his widow was interdicted. The interdict, Lucy Cloud, stayed with her daughter for a total of sixteen years and seven months. Bonnie Hatch said the care of Mr. and Mrs. Hatch was not a consideration for the deed.

¶4 Noah Cloud had leased the property's mineral rights in 1963. Placid Oil Company made royalty payments on the production to Noah Cloud from October of 1965 until January of 1968.

¶5 After Noah Cloud died, Urzula Hatch was named administratrix of his estate. . . .

¶6 Following her mother's death on March 11, 1980, Urzula Hatch consulted attorney Sanders about a dispute with her four siblings over ownership of the property. Sanders had no prior involvement with the succession proceedings. Urzula Hatch wanted a ten-acre portion, not eight, because she had cared for her parents. She was unable to pay Sanders, who told her she had title to the tract. On June 20, 1980, she transferred one-fourth of the tract's minerals to him in exchange for $10,000.00 in legal services.

¶7 On May 19, 1981, the four Cloud siblings filed a rule to show cause in the succession of Noah Cloud, alleging that the administratrix had been receiving royalty checks from Placid Oil Company; that the succession should be audited; and that Urzula Cloud Hatch should be removed as administratrix. On July 17, 1981, Sanders answered the rule on behalf of Urzula Hatch, alleging that the tract and its royalties belonged to her rather than the succession. On August 31, 1981 Urzula Hatch transferred an additional one-twelfth of the minerals to Sanders in exchange for $10,000.00 in legal services.

¶8 Between 1981 and 1985, Sanders was paid $108,945.51 by Placid. During the same period, Urzula Hatch was paid $249,809.95. According to Sanders, there was a dramatic increase in the royalties after he acquired his interests, creating an unanticipated windfall.

¶9 On May 7, 1984, the Cloud siblings attacked the transfers to Sanders. The trial court dismissed their suit. The court of appeal held that Sanders did not violate the Code of Professional Responsibility because the mineral interests he acquired were not litigious rights. A writ was granted to review the judgment of the court of appeal.

¶10 In Succession of Cloud, the transfers from Urzula Cloud Hatch to Martin S. Sanders, Jr. were declared a nullity because Sanders violated DR 5-103(A). Succession of Cloud pretermitted the question of whether Sanders' acquisition of the minerals constituted the purchase of a litigious right contrary to LSA-C.C. art. 2447.8. Sanders was adjudged guilty of violating the Code of Professional Responsibility, and the only remaining issue is the appropriate sanction.

¶11   After the decision was rendered in Succession of Cloud, the Committee on Professional Responsibility of the Louisiana State Bar Association advised Sanders that a formal investigatory hearing concerning his conduct would be held. After the hearing, the Committee agreed that Sanders was guilty of professional misconduct. A Commissioner was appointed, who concluded that Sanders had unintentionally violated the Code of Professional Responsibility, specifically DR 5-103(A), by acquiring a proprietary interest in the subject matter of his client's dispute. In addition, the minerals became the subject of litigation before the second transfer to Sanders on August 31, 1981. The Committee has suggested eighteen months' suspension as an appropriate sanction.

LAW

¶12   LSA-C.C. art. 2447 prohibits attorneys and other public officers connected with courts of justice from purchasing litigious rights. Although prohibited, such a purchase is not necessarily dishonest: it is not malem [sic] in se. Sanders v. Ditch, 110 La. 884, 34 So. 860 (1903). An exception in LSA-R.S. 37:218 allows attorneys to acquire an interest in the subject matter of a suit to secure their fees.

¶13   There are two exceptions to DR 5-103(A): a lien to secure a lawyer's fee and a contingent fee contract. Buck & Beauchamp v. Blair & Buck, 36 La. Ann. 16 (1884) discusses the contingent fee exception to the prohibited purchase of a litigious right. Compare Hope v. Madison, 192 La. 593, 188 So. 711 (1939) where the attorney's recovery was contingent on the favorable decision of a lawsuit and production from the property.

¶14   Gautreaux v. Harang, 190 La. 1060, 183 So. 349 (1938) held that Civil Code article 2447 did not prohibit an attorney from purchasing an interest in a client's disputed claim to immovable property when no suit was pending at the time of the purchase. Gautreaux is contrary to the French commentators, who interpreted the corresponding article of the French Code to prohibit not only the purchase of rights in litigation but rights requiring litigation.

¶15   Succession of Cloud did not overrule Gautreaux but held that the prohibition in DR 5-103(A) against an attorney acquiring a proprietary interest in the cause of action or subject matter of litigation being handled for a client is broader than the Gautreaux interpretation of Civil Code article 2447. DR 5-103(A) forbids an attorney from acquiring any right "which is genuinely disputed and likely to become the subject of litigation." The interpretation of DR

5-103(A) in Succession of Cloud was new and represented a change in the law.14 See Succession of Powers v. Howcott, 137 La. 818, 69 So. 198 (1915).

¶16 Transactions between a lawyer and client are closely scrutinized because of the advantage held by a lawyer in dealing with a lay person. See Phipps v. Willis, 53 Or. 190, 96 P. 866 (1908). When a lawyer is guilty of overreaching in dealing with a client, an appropriate punishment must be imposed. Determining the proper discipline involves weighing the attorney's conduct in light of any aggravating or mitigating factors.

AGGRAVATING FACTORS

¶17 Although the recited consideration for the transfers was $20,000, Sanders has received $108,945.51. All attorney's fees must be reasonable. The amount of Sanders' compensation casts doubt on his good faith; it is an aggravating circumstance.

¶18 Sanders testified that he disbursed many of the royalties he received: $19,000 to Urzula Hatch; $38,000 to one D. F. Miles; over $12,000 to First Federal; and other cash to the Hatch children. None of these payments are documented. Sanders admitted keeping approximately $18,000 in fees but no accounting was furnished to Urzula Hatch. Sanders' failure to account for the funds is an aggravating factor.

¶19 At the time of the second transfer, August 31, 1981, Ms. Hatch's right to the royalties from the tract had been challenged by a rule to show cause filed in the succession of Noah Cloud by her four siblings. Her answer to the rule, filed by Sanders on July 17, 1981, asserted that she, rather than the succession, owned the tract and its royalties. By July 17, 1981, at the latest, the mineral interests in the twenty acre tract had become a litigious right. This is a further aggravating factor.

MITIGATING FACTORS

¶20 Sanders' first acquisition was not a litigious right. Before the decision in Succession of Cloud, the prohibition in DR 5-103(A) only extended to a client's property which was the subject of litigation. Thus, the rule did not apply to Sanders' first acquisition at the time of transfer. This is a mitigating circumstance.

¶21 The Commissioner concluded that Sanders' transgression was unintentional. This is a mitigating factor.

¶22   The client, Urzula Hatch, was not financially harmed by the transaction. Placid paid her $249,809.95 in royalties between 1981 and 1985, substantially more than her one-fifth interest justified. This is a mitigating factor.

¶23   In view of Urzula Hatch's conflicting testimony, it is impossible to know what representations she made to Sanders in 1980. He could reasonably have believed that her former husband had purchased the twenty-acre tract from Noah Cloud. This factor weighs in Sanders' favor.

¶24   Ms. Hatch owned at least one-fifth of the twenty acre tract. Sanders could have guaranteed his fee either by taking a contingent interest in the remaining four-fifths or placing a lien on the undisputed one-fifth. As an attorney dealing with a client, Sanders had to structure his fee arrangement within the parameters of the law. However, the fact that he could have obtained a similar result without censure is a mitigating factor.

CONCLUSION

¶25   Considering all of the circumstances, nine months' suspension from the practice of law is an appropriate sanction.

ORDER

IT IS ORDERED, ADJUDGED AND DECREED that Martin S. Sanders, Jr. be suspended from the practice of law for a period of nine months. All costs are assessed to respondent.

DENNIS, J., concurs and will assign reasons.

Study Question

The Louisiana Rules of Professional Conduct impose a number of strictures on contingent fees. Contingent fees may not be used in domestic or criminal cases, the lawyer must thoroughly explain the basis for and calculation of the fee to the client even when it is allowed. Consider the following statutes and Rules of Professional Conduct and explain how Mr. Sanders went wrong and how he should have constructed his fee.

La. State Bar Rule of Professional Conduct 1.5

Rule 1.5 sets forth rules with regard to fees and provides in part:

(a) A lawyer shall not make an agreement for, charge, or collect an unreasonable fee or an unreasonable amount for expenses. The factors to be considered in determining the reasonableness of a fee include the following:

(1) the time and labor required, the novelty and difficulty of the questions involved, and the skill requisite to perform the legal service properly;

(2) the likelihood, if apparent to the client, that the acceptance of the particular employment will preclude other employment by the lawyer;

(3) the fee customarily charged in the locality for similar legal services;

(4) the amount involved and the results obtained;

(5) the time limitations imposed by the client or by the circumstances;

(6) the nature and length of the professional relationship with the client;

(7) the experience, reputation, and ability of the lawyer or lawyers performing the services; and

(8) whether the fee is fixed or contingent.

(b) The scope of the representation and the basis or rate of the fee and expenses for which the client will be responsible shall be communicated to the client, preferably in writing, before or within a reasonable time after commencing the representation, except when the lawyer will charge a regularly represented client on the same basis or rate. Any changes in the basis or rate of the fee or expenses shall also be communicated to the client.

(c) A fee may be contingent on the outcome of the matter for which the service is rendered, except in a matter in which a contingent fee is prohibited by Paragraph (d) or other law. A contingent fee agreement shall be in a writing signed by the client. A copy or duplicate original of the executed agreement shall be given to the client at the time of execution of the agreement. The contingency fee agreement shall state the method by which the fee is to be determined, including the percentage or percentages that shall accrue to the lawyer in the event of settlement, trial or appeal; the litigation and other expenses that are to be deducted from the recovery; and whether such expenses are to be deducted before or after the contingent fee is calculated. The agreement must clearly notify the client of any expenses for which the client will be liable whether or not the client is the prevailing party. Upon conclusion of a contingent fee matter, the lawyer shall provide the client with a written statement stating the outcome of the matter and, if there is a recovery, showing the remittance to the client and the method of its determination.

(d) A lawyer shall not enter into an arrangement for, charge, or collect:

(1) any fee in a domestic relations matter, the payment or amount of which is contingent upon the securing of a divorce or upon the amount of alimony or support, or property settlement in lieu thereof; or

(2) a contingent fee for representing a defendant in a criminal case.

La. R.S. 37:218: Contract for fee based on proportion of subject matter; stipulation concerning compromise, discontinuance, or settlement

A. By written contract signed by his client, an attorney at law may acquire as his fee an interest in the subject matter of a suit, proposed suit, or claim in the assertion, prosecution, or defense of which he is employed, whether the claim or suit be for money or for property. Such interest shall be a special privilege to take rank as a first privilege thereon, superior to all other privileges and security interests under Chapter 9 of the Louisiana Commercial laws. In such contract, it may be stipulated that neither the attorney nor the client may, without the written consent of the other, settle, compromise, release, discontinue, or otherwise dispose of the suit or claim. Either party to the contract may, at any time, file and record it with the clerk of court in the parish in which the suit is pending or is to be brought or with the clerk of court in the parish of the client's domicile. After such filing, any settlement, compromise, discontinuance, or other disposition made of the suit or claim by either the attorney or the client, without the written consent of the other, is null and void and the suit or claim shall be proceeded with as if no such settlement, compromise, discontinuance, or other disposition has been made.

B. The term "fee", as used in this Section, means the agreed upon fee, whether fixed or contingent, and any and all other amounts advanced by the attorney to or on behalf of the client, as permitted by the Rules of Professional Conduct of the Louisiana State Bar Association.

C. Litigious Redemption

A lawyer's lack of capacity to purchase a pre-existing litigious right and his professional responsibilities with regard to structuring his fees appropriately differ from Article 2652, which provides:

"When a litigious right is assigned, the debtor may extinguish his obligation by paying to the assignee the price the assignee paid for the assignment, with interest from the time of the assignment.

"A right is litigious, for that purpose, when it is contested in a suit already filed.

"Nevertheless, the debtor may not thus extinguish his obligation when the assignment has been made to a co-owner of the assigned right, or to a possessor of the thing subject to the litigious right."

Article 2652 can be more easily understood if one begins by substituting the word "defendant" for "debtor" and "co-plaintiff" for "co-owner," and if one begins by reading Articles 2642-2654 on Assignment of Rights. Remember that anything, corporeal or incorporeal, can be sold. A right is an incorporeal movable or an incorporeal immovable. Almost any right can be "assigned," meaning that any right can be transferred from one owner to another, unless it would be illegal to do so. One such illegal transfer is the transferring of a right in a lawsuit to a clerk of court, another is the transfer of interest in a succession of a living person. Otherwise, however, rights are assigned all the time. Consider the stock market, where shareholders buy and sell shares of stock, or patent licensing, or timeshares (where you might invest in a right to have a vacation somewhere) – the list is endless, and such rights are often more valuable than land.

Article 2652 is considering the issue of selling – assigning – an interest in a right in a lawsuit to someone who is neither an officer of the court nor a co-plaintiff. While it does not make such an assignment illegal, it provides the defendant for an easy way to settle the lawsuit by paying the new plaintiff (the "assignee") whatever he had paid, plus interest. If there were not such an article, then people could buy and sell their interests in lawsuits left and right – perhaps we could even have a stock market in lawsuits! Why do you think that might be undesirable? What affect would if have on a court if the plaintiff in interest was no longer part of the suit?

Litigious redemption requires that the suit must be filed and active, because the purpose is to end litigation, not to end potential litigation. As implied in the previous paragraph, one purpose of litigious redemption is to discourage speculators from buying lawsuits in which they had no true interest. Another purpose is to protect creditors from being coerced into selling out their claim for less than it was worth. A third purpose is to put an end to litigation and reduce the burden on scarce public resources.[2] In terms of case law, Article 2652 has led to some interesting litigation. Consider the following case.

---

2   24 Louisiana Civil Law Treatise §14:4, Litigious Rights

LUK-SHOP, L.L.C. V. RIVERWOOD LAPLACE ASSOCS. L.L.C. 2002

802 SO. 2D 1291 (LA.)

PER CURIAM.

¶1 This per curiam addresses whether plaintiff's claim against defendant is based upon plaintiff's purchase of a litigious right and whether defendant is entitled to terminate the litigation by paying to plaintiff what plaintiff paid to the assignor.

¶2 On March 27, 1996 CFSC Capital Corp., XXVII (CFSC) filed suit against Riverwood LaPlace Associates, L.L.C. (Riverwood). The suit sought a judgment against Riverwood for sums allegedly due on promissory notes, mortgage notes, and guaranty agreements, and in connection therewith sought a writ of sequestration to seize the revenues and rents from the Riverwood's shopping center operations. On April 3, 1996, the writ of sequestration was issued in the United States District Court for the Eastern District of Louisiana. On April 9, 1996, Riverwood filed a motion to dissolve the sequestration. Thereafter, Riverwood dismissed its motion to dissolve the writ, without prejudice, on April 30, 1996 (apparently coincident with ongoing settlement negotiations). On June 23, 1996 Riverwood answered the federal lawsuit denying liability on the promissory notes. In September 1996 Riverwood filed a petition in bankruptcy, which resulted in the imposition of an automatic stay of the Federal court suit. Thereafter, on July 8, 1999, CFSC assigned its claims against Riverwood to Luk-Shop L.L.C. (plaintiff in this state court proceeding).

¶3 On July 15, 1999, Riverwood emerged from bankruptcy. On October 25, 2000, Luk-Shop filed suit against Riverwood in the 40th Judicial District Court, Parish of St. John the Baptist. Luk-Shop's petition sought judgment on the promissory notes, mortgage notes and guarantee agreements that were assigned by CFSC as well as a writ of sequestration regarding revenues from Riverwood's shopping center. Riverwood responded, claiming entitlement to litigious redemption, seeking to terminate this litigation by paying to Luk-Shop what Luk-Shop paid to its assignor, CFSC.

¶4 The trial court found that CFSC'S assignment to Luk-Shop was not the sale of a litigious right because Riverwood had dismissed its motion to dissolve the writ of sequestration in the prior federal court litigation. The trial court held that the "effect of Riverwood's motion to withdraw the writ of sequestration is that the sequestration was no longer contested ... Accordingly, at the time that the assignment in question was confected, CFSC's suit against Riverwood was uncontested. Therefore, Luk-Shop was not the assignee of a litigious right." The court of appeal denied writs, and Riverwood has sought supervisory review by this court.

¶5   Upon consideration, we find error in the trial court's holding as the facts indicate that the assignment from CFSC to Luk-Shop was the sale of a litigious right pursuant to Louisiana Civil Code article 2652.2

¶6   While the writ of sequestration against Riverwood may not have been in contest in the Federal Court suit at the time of CFSC's assignment to Luk-Shop (it having been dismissed without prejudice), the underlying monetary obligation, i.e. Riverwood's liability on the promissory notes, mortgage notes and guarantee agreements was highly contested in the Federal proceeding. Riverwood did withdraw its motion in federal court to dissolve the writ of sequestration, but Riverwood never withdrew its answer in which it denied liability on the promissory notes. The underlying obligation, the debt, was a litigious right because it was "contested in a suit already filed." La. Civ. Code art. 2652. Thus Riverwood is entitled under La. Civ. Code art. 2652 to extinguish the obligation by paying to Luk-Shop what Luk-Shop paid to CFSC. Once that obligation is extinguished, the state court sequestration and claim on the debt fall. The sequestration is simply a procedural mechanism for enforcing the underlying obligation. Once the underlying obligation is extinguished, there is no remaining claim on the debt, and hence, no valid reason for the sequestration.

¶7   For the foregoing reasons, we find that defendant, Riverwood, is entitled to be apprised of the sum that Luk-Shop paid to CFSC for the assignment CFSC'S rights against Riverwood and is entitled to terminate the litigation by paying that amount to Luk-Shop. The district court judgment finding that the CFSC assignment of its claims against Riverwood to Luk-Shop not to be the sale of a litigious right was erroneous and is therefore reversed. The case is remanded to the trial court for further proceedings in this ongoing litigation.

MARTIN ENERGY CO. V. BOURNE 1992
598 SO. 2D 1160 (LA. APP. 1ST CIR.)

CARTER, Judge.

¶0   This is an appeal from a trial court judgment granting defendant litigious redemption.

BACKGROUND

[Ken G. Martin purchased a home through his company, Martin Energy Company (MEC) in 1986. That home was in the beautiful, exclusive subdivision of Beau Chene in Mandeville. His next-door neighbor was defendant Melville F. Borne, Jr. Later that year, Martin filed suit against

Borne, alleging that Borne had violated a number of Beau Chene Homeowners Association's rules, including its servitude rules, building restrictions, and that he had conducted other activities on his property that caused damage to Martin's MEC-owned home as well as causing Martin personal injuries.

[On his part, Borne filed a reconventional demand against MEC, claiming malicious prosecution, abuse of right, false imprisonment, false accusation, and defamation, all of which caused injury to Borne, his reputation, and his standing in the community.

[Sometime after the suit was filed, Martin started rearranging his business. He entered into several transactions involving the house in Beau Chene, all of which involved companies of which he was President: MEC sold the house to Hojew, Inc. on July 24, 1989. A few weeks later, on August 15, 1989, Hojew transferred the house to EJT, Inc. for the same price, then on November 3, 1989, EJT, Inc. transferred it to Martin Riverside Gas Company. All three transfers cited the exact same payment and commitments by the buyer:

> [TEN DOLLARS ($10.00) and other valuable services, in part payment and deduction whereof the purchaser(s) has (have) well and truly paid unto the vendor(s) the sum of TEN DOLLARS ($10.00) and other valuable services, receipt of which is hereby acknowledged and complete acquittance and discharge granted therefor. And for the balance of said purchase price the purchaser(s) does (do) hereby assume, jointly and solidarily with the vendor(s) herein, the following obligations, . . .]

¶1   On November 28, 1989, Martin Gas filed a motion to be substituted, in place of MEC, as one of the petitioners in the suit filed against Borne. Thereafter, on August 20, 1990, Borne filed a peremptory exception pleading the objection of litigious redemption. Contemporaneously with the filing of the exception, Borne deposited into the registry of the court the sum of $10.00, together with $0.92, which represented the legal interest on such amount at an annual rate of 11.5% from the date of the alleged transfer of the litigious rights on November 3, 1989, through the date of the filing of the exception. After a hearing, the trial judge determined that the real price for the transfer of the litigious rights was $10.00 plus interest. Accordingly, the trial judge maintained Borne's exception and allowed Borne to redeem the litigious right against him.

¶2   From this adverse judgment, Martin Gas appealed

REQUISITES OF A LITIGIOUS RIGHTS CLAIM

¶3   LSA-C.C. art 2653 makes it clear that, for the purposes of litigious redemption, there must exist a suit and contestation on the same. In Hawshorne v. Humble Oil & Refining Co., 210 So.2d 110, 112 (La. App. 1st Cir.), writ denied, 252 La. 832, 214 So.2d 160 (1968), the court noted that "a right transferred after suit is instituted and an answer filed thereto, and before the judgment therein is final, is a litigious right, since there is a suit and contestation thereon."

¶4 In the instant case, MEC and Martin filed the instant suit for damages against Borne on June 10, 1986. Borne answered petitioners' suit and filed a reconventional demand against Martin. Thereafter, on July 24, 1989, the rights to this pending litigation were transferred by MEC. Subsequently, the property was transferred twice more. Prior to the rendition of judgment, an exception pleading the objection of litigious redemption was filed by Borne. Thus, it is clear that the requirements set forth in LSA-C.C. art. 2653 have been met. See Calderera v. O'Carroll, 551 So.2d 824, 826-27 (La.App. 3d Cir. 1989), writ denied, 556 So.2d 60 (La. 1990).

¶5 LSA-C.C. art 2652 provides as follows:

> He against whom a litigious right has been transferred, may get himself released by paying to the transferee the real price of the transfer, together with the interest from its date.

¶6 As a general rule, transfer of a litigious right subject to the provisions of LSA-C.C. art 2652 must be made in consideration of a price. It follows, therefore, that only sales and onerous transfers in which a price can be determined are contemplated by the codal provisions governing litigious redemption. However, a plaintiff does not have an absolute right to be released. To be released, the plaintiff must pay to the transferee the "real price of the transfer," whatever that price may be. Charrier v. Bell, 380 So.2d 155, 156 (La.App. 1st Cir. 1979), writ denied, 382 So.2d 165 (La. 1980). In Charrier, the court noted that LSA-C.C. art. 2652 speaks of interest on the real price, which leads to the conclusion that redemption should only apply to transfers made in return for the payment of a certain or determinable amount of money.

¶7 Moreover, the law does not require that the "real price" paid for the litigious right be equal to the value of the right transferred. In Calderera v. O'Carroll, 551 So.2d at 825-26, the plaintiffs obtained a money judgment against the defendant, O'Carroll. When the judgment creditors attempted to seize his automobile in satisfaction of their judgment, O'Carroll filed suit for wrongful seizure. During the pendency of the proceedings, O'Carroll filed a voluntary bankruptcy petition. The district court rendered, but did not sign, a judgment in favor of O'Carroll on the wrongful seizure claim. Thereafter, the Bankruptcy Trustee sold to O'Carroll the rights to the litigation over the wrongful seizure for $250.00 and 10% of the monies recovered in the litigation. The court then permitted the judgment creditors to release themselves from the litigious right by paying to O'Carroll the "real price of the transfer," which the court determined was $250.00. The appellate court, in affirming the trial court judgment, quoted from the district court's reasons as follows:

"If his assignee [O'Carroll] made a recovery, he [Trustee] was to receive 10% of the recovery. If O'Carroll made no recovery, whatever the reason, the Trustee would receive nothing more than the $250.00." "The codal article [La. C.C. art. 2652] does not speak in terms of what the seller of a litigious right has expectations of receiving. It only speaks of reimbursement to the purchaser of the price."

Caldera v. O'Carroll, 551 So.2d at 827.

¶8   Additionally, a partial transfer of a litigious right may take place when a sole owner of the right transfers a portion thereof or when one of several co-owners transfers his entire partial interest in the thing in litigation. See Comment, The Transfer of Litigious Rights in Louisiana Civil Law, (pt. 2), 1 La. L. Rev. 818, 822 (1939). In such cases, the exercise of rights under LSA-C.C. art 2652 will not operate to end the litigation. Moreover, if a litigious right is transferred with a non-litigious right in a lump sum transaction, an apportionment of the price must be made in order to determine the amount of reimbursement due the transferee.

¶9   Although there is no time period set out in the codal provisions governing litigious redemption, a debtor should promptly exercise the redemption. As pointed out in Comment, The Transfer of Litigious Rights in Louisiana Civil Law, (pt. 2), 1 La. Law Rev. 818, 827 (1939), a person entitled to invoke litigious redemption "may not fight the case on its merits until it is apparent that the case is lost and, at the last moment, exercise redemption."

* * *

ANALYSIS

¶10   Applying the legal principles governing litigious redemption to the facts of the instant case, we must determine whether the trial court was manifestly erroneous or clearly wrong in granting Borne litigious redemption for the sum of $10.00.

¶11   At the hearing on the exception, the testimony of Ken Martin, who testified as general manager of MEC and as president of each of the other three Martin corporations, formed a majority of the evidence. Martin testified that the document, which was introduced into evidence as Borne 1, represented the transfer of the lot and improvements from MEC to Hojew. Martin also testified that the litigious rights of MEC were also specifically transferred in that document. However, Martin explained that, in item three of the recited consideration, he intended to transfer the litigious rights from MEC directly to Martin Resources, which was not a party to any of the agreements. . . . The consideration in each of these transactions was $10.00

cash, the other three items listed in the cash sales, and "other valuable services." . . . Martin testified that this mortgage was later cross-collateralized with two other debts to the same creditor prior to the transfers among the various Martin corporations. According to Martin, the difference between the total indebtedness (the original mortgage and the subsequent cross-collateralized amounts) of $418,000.00 and the $325,000.00 appraised value of the property represents the amount for which the litigious right was transferred, namely $90,000.00. However, Martin acknowledged that nothing in the documents reflects this $90,000.00 consideration. . . .

¶12   Martin testified that he intended to transfer the litigious right, but not for $10.00. Martin testified that he meant for the rights to be transferred for $90,000.00. Martin testified that Martin Resources had not paid anything for the right, but that he anticipated receiving about $90,000.00 from the suit against Borne.

¶13   In his oral reasons for judgment, the trial judge noted that there was no dispute as to the sale of the litigious right against Borne. A series of transfers was made among Martin's various corporations, and the consideration for each of these transactions was identical:

(1) ten dollars and other valuable services performed by the purchaser;
(2) assumption of the mortgage indebtedness relating to the property, which had a balance of $251,307.00;
(3) assumption of a mortgage indebtedness in the sum of $150,000.00, which indebtedness had never been funded and upon which nothing was owed; and
(4) obligation for the purchaser to pay to Martin Resources the proceeds recovered from the instant suit up to $1,000,000.00.

¶14   The trial judge determined that Martin Gas was unable to show that it performed any "valuable services" as consideration for the sale. The trial judge determined that the hand notes allegedly cross-collateralized were not executed in connection with either of the two loans referred to in the acts of cash sale, had not been reduced to writing, and were not referenced to the mortgage note in question. Moreover, the trial judge determined that the value of the East Ruelle property at the time of the transfers was $325,000.00. The trial judge concluded that the evidence established that the real price paid for the transfer of the litigious rights was $10.00. Accordingly, the trial judge determined that Borne could redeem the litigious rights sold for the real price paid for them by Martin Gas, namely $10.00, plus interest.

¶15   After carefully reviewing the entire record and based upon the law and the great deference accorded to trial court determinations as to credibility, we find that the trial judge was not manifestly erroneous in finding that the real price paid for the transfer of the litigious rights was $10.00. Accordingly, the trial court did not err in granting Borne litigious redemption.

¶16   Additionally, although the trial judge's reasons did not specifically address the issue of timeliness of Borne's plea of litigious redemption, inherent in the granting of litigious redemption is a finding that Borne timely asserted his right to this remedy. We have reviewed the record and find that the trial judge was not manifestly erroneous in finding that Borne had timely exercised this right. On November 28, 1989, Martin Gas filed a motion and order to substitute itself as party plaintiff in place of MEC, which the trial court granted on December 4, 1989. At the same time, petitioners amended their original petition. Shortly after the pre-trial conference, on August 20, 1990, Borne filed the exception pleading litigious redemption. Martin Gas does not allege, nor does the record show, that the litigation had advanced significantly during the interim

CONCLUSION

¶17   Accordingly, the judgment of the trial court is affirmed. Martin Gas is cast for all costs on appeal.

AFFIRMED.

REVIEW NOTES

The last chapter focused on price. This chapter focuses on the object of the sale: "All things corporeal or incorporeal, susceptible of ownership, may be the object of a contract of sale, unless the sale of a particular thing is prohibited by law." Art. 2448

Consistent with this, there are one or two things that you might not have thought about that susceptible of being sold, as well as a few things that you might not have realized are illegal to sell (such as the succession of a living person).

Section 1: Sale of a Hope v. Sale of a Future Thing

A thing that does not yet exist – a future thing – can be the object of a sale. Art 2449. So, for example, you can sell in advance the next foal that your mare produces, or your next crop of wine grapes. In that case, however, the sale is not complete – not perfected - until the object comes into existence. In other words, the sale is subject to the suspensive condition of the thing coming into existence. If the vines never produce grapes, or the horse never has a foal, then the sale is null.

On the other hand, the buyer can assume the risk that the thing will not come into existence. In this case, what the buyer bought was the "sale of a hope." Art 2451. It is, in essence, a gamble. So, every quarter you put into a one-armed-bandit is the sale of a hope: you hope to hit the jackpot when you pull the handle. In essence, what you bought for your quarter is a pull of the handle. The example given in the Civil Code is the next casting of a fisherman's net: you could end up with a million dollars in redfish, or you could end up with an old boot.

Losecco v. Gregory:

This famous case was heard three times by the Louisiana Supreme Court, and it gave a different opinion each time.

The facts are simple. Losecco was an orange merchant and speculator in New Orleans, and was in the habit of buying crops ahead of time at a low price, Gregory owned an orange orchard. Losecco agreed to buy two years' worth of orange crops from Gregory for $8,000: $4,000 in advance in 1899, and the balance to be paid when the second crop was harvested (December 1, 1900). The contract said that Losecco would buy "all the oranges that my trees may produce" and "buyer to assume all risks." In an unusually hard freeze, the trees were destroyed in 1899, and no oranges were produced. Losecco sued, demanding that his $4,000 be returned. The trial court found for Losecco, the appellate court reversed, finding for Gregory, and when Losecco appealed to the Louisiana Supreme Court, it reversed the appellate decision, reinstating the trial court's holding for Losecco.

In the first opinion, written by Justice Blanchard, the Supreme Court did not believe that the contract depended on an uncertain event because under normal conditions, the trees would have produced at least some oranges – if not one year, then the other. It was not anticipated that the trees themselves would die. The language "purchaser assumes all risks" is interpreted as being limited to the risks of which the parties would have been aware – a freeze that would cause one crop to fail, but not a freeze that would kill the trees themselves. Thus, this was not the sale of a hope, and so when force majeur killed the trees, the contract became impossible to perform, and had to be dissolved.

From this, Gregory appealed. On its first rehearing (written by Justice Provosty), the court discusses at length the difference between the sale of a hope and the sale of a future thing. It finds that, as it had been known that a hard freeze could ruin one year's crop, the first year (1899) was the sale of a hope – Losecco knowingly took the risk that the crop might fail for one year, but that he did not knowingly take the risk that it would fail for both years. Thus, the sale of the second crop (1900) was the sale of a future thing. When it did not come into existence, he did not have to pay for it. Thus, Gregory kept the first $4,000, but Losecco does not have to pay the second half. In a sense, the court 'split the baby' – the parties' shared the loss.

Apparently this was not good enough for Losecco, who appealed yet again to the Supreme Court. This time, Justice Provosty was not as compassionate. In a careful reading of the contract in connection with the Civil Code's articles on contractual interpretation, the court found that the words were not ambiguous, and that the contract should be interpreted as written. The language "all the trees that my trees MAY produce" implies that the trees may not produce any fruit, and that coupled with "purchaser to assume all risks" means exactly that – the purchaser (Losecco) was assuming ALL risks, including the risk that the trees themselves would be destroyed.

Remember, a court's last opinion invalidates all other contrary opinions before it. Consequently, it is this third hearing that is the only one that is actually law.

Plaquemines Equipment

Plaintiff special-ordered a Ford pickup truck from a Ford dealer, putting a $707 deposit down against the full price of $6,029. The truck was to be outfitted with special oil field equipment. After the cab and chassis had been delivered to the dealer, but before it had been outfitted, the dealership went into liquidation. Plaintiff sued for delivery of the truck. The court held that the sale was of a future thing, and that as the truck had not been outfitted, it had not 'come into existence,' and therefore plaintiff could not get title to the truck. In effect, the only thing the plaintiff could get was an unsecured claim against the defunct dealership in the amount of the deposit.

Section 2: Things in Commerce

An underlying public policy is that commerce creates value because it increases the wealth of the individuals who engage in it and therefore of the nation in which they reside. Therefore commerce should be encouraged, and hindrances to commerce should be discouraged. For example, a perpetual lease of a thing would hinder any other transaction in that thing. (The Civil Code limits the term of a lease of an immovable to ninety-nine years. La. Civ. Code art. 2679.)

Hicks v. Clark

Raines granted a mineral lease on his immovable. He then sold the immovable, reserving for himself and his heirs and assigns a right of reversion of a ¼ interest in the mineral rights that would return to Raines if the mineral lessee's rights ended for any reason, for example, by ten years nonuse. Raines's buyer subsequently resold the land to a third party who then sold it to a fourth party, the Defendant. Plaintiffs acquired Raines's reversionary interest; they filed suit for recognition of the ¼ reversionary interest in the mineral rights.

Plaintiffs argue that the ¼ reversionary interest in mineral rights is an incorporeal thing susceptible of ownership and a sale of the hope that eventually oil would be produced from the immovable and that they would obtain ¼ of the production.

The court held, however, that this has the nature of a servitude on the land, and that any predial servitude is extinguished by the liberative prescription of 10 years because otherwise the land would be burdened so as to take it out of commerce. Recognition of the 'reversionary interest' would circumvent the state's public policy of keeping things in commerce. Therefore its reservation was absolutely null.

Section 3: Things that may NOT be sold

In addition to things that might violate public policy, the Civil Code lists a few other things that may not be sold: the thing of another (Art 2452), litigious rights (Art 2447), and litigious redemption (Art 2652).

A. Thing belonging to another

The sale of a thing belonging to another does not convey ownership (Art 2452), and a seller who purports to sell such a thing is liable for damages when the real owner comes forth to challenge the buyer's ownership. Such a sale may become valid, however, if the seller acquires ownership before the buyer becomes aware of the problem. This is known as the after-acquired title doctrine. At times, the real owner may not be able to reclaim the thing because the third-party purchaser is protected by the bona fide purchaser doctrine or the public records doctrine. All of these complications, some of which are mentioned in the comments to Article 2452, are further discussed in later chapters.

B. Litigious Rights

A right it litigious when a lawsuit has already been filed. Article 2447 states that it is unlawful for officers of a court to purchase a litigious right that is being contested in a jurisdiction in which they practice their profession. It is thus unlawful for lawyers and other court officers to buy and sell an interest in a lawsuit. There are a number of professional responsibility rules that make it unlawful as well and likely to lead to sanctions.

McClung v. Atlas Oil

Huey P. Long, Jr., as a young lawyer long before he became governor of Louisiana, purchased ½ of the mineral rights in land that Mr. McClung owned, knowing that Atlas Oil was claiming ownership of those mineral rights. Nevertheless, the court lets the lawsuit go forward because Long purchased the interest before the lawsuit was filed: "Until there is a lawsuit actually pending, no right is litigious, no matter how apparently necessary one may be to enforce it."

While Huey Long got away with it, under the Rules of Professional Conduct 1.5 , a lawyer must be very careful in how he constructs his fee: A lawyer may not collect an unreasonable fee or make an agreement for an unreasonable fee, and any fee or method of collecting a fee must be made clear to the client at the onset of the representation, and must be within certain parameters. Reasonableness depends on the extent and difficulty of the representation, the attorney's experience, etc. An attorney can, however, by written contract signed by his client acquire a privilege in the subject matter of a suit to secure his fee. La. R.S. 37:218.

Louisiana v. Sanders

Attorney Sanders acquired as his fee an ¼ mineral interest in his client's immovable and later an additional 1/12 interest, as in McClung, he acquired the mineral interests before the lawsuit was filed and therefore they were not illegal litigious rights. He performed the services as required, but was eventually paid $108,945. However, he was found guilty of violating the Code of Professional Responsibility by acquiring a proprietary interest in the subject matter of his client's dispute. Furthermore, by the time of the second acquisition (the 1/12 interest), a lawsuit had been filed. As a result, his license to practice law was suspended for 9 months, and he had to pay back all amount above and beyond what the court calculated was a reasonable fee for the serviced performed.

C. Litigious Redemption

Litigious Redemption, Article 2652 applies when a plaintiff to a lawsuit transfers his interest in it to someone (not a lawyer) who is not otherwise involved in it. The article stipulates that when this happens, "the debtor (i.e. the defendant) may extinguish his obligation by paying to the assignee the price the assignee paid," plus interest. In other words, if the plaintiff sells his interest in a lawsuit, the defendant can go to the buyer, pay whatever it was the buyer paid, and thus get the case dropped. This makes sense in a couple of different ways. First, it discourages a market in lawsuits. Can you imagine what would happen if we allowed people to buy and sell their interest in a lawsuit? It would create havoc in the courts because the people pursuing the case would not be the ones who claimed that the defendant did something wrong. Furthermore, when a plaintiff sells out his interest, what he is in essence telling the world is that the price he receives is what he feels the case is worth – so then there is no need to pursue a larger amount.

Luk Shop v. Riverwood

CFSC sued Riverwood, claiming that the Riverwood shopping center owed it money. Riverwood answered, denying liability, and subsequently filed a petition in bankruptcy, which meant that the CFSC lawsuit was automatically stayed. While the bankruptcy suit was pending, CFSC assigned its claims against Riverwood to Luk-Shop. A week or so later, Riverwood emerged from bankruptcy, and Luk-Shopt filed suit seeking judgment on the CFSC debt. The Appellate court found that this was a non-illegal sale of a litigious right, because Luk-Shop purchased them after the lawsuit had been filed. Therefore, Riverwood could avail itself of litigious redemption to get the lawsuit dropped.

Martin Energy v. Bourne

Ken Martin was in the energy business and bought a home through his company (Martin Energy) in an exclusive subdivision in Mandeville. Shortly after purchasing that home, he filed suit against his neighbor, alleging that Bourne had violated a number of the HOA rules, conducted other activities that were damaging Martin's property, and causing Martin personal injuries. Bourne filed a reconventional demand, claiming malicious prosecution, abuse of right, false imprisonment, false accusation, and defamation.

Sometime after the suit was filed, Martin started to rearrange his business, and as part of that transferred ownership of the house through several corporations that he had created. Along with ownership of the house, he transferred the interest in the lawsuit for $10. When Bourne found out that he was not being sued by the "Martin Riverside Gas Company" instead of the Martin Energy Company," he claimed litigious redemption – and the court cancelled the lawsuit once Bourne paid "Martin Riverside Gas Company" the $10 it had paid.

HYPOTHET

Anna, the owner of a New Orleans shop that sells blue suede shoes met Guiseppe, a shoemaker who makes beautiful shoes. She agreed to buy his entire next-year's production of blue suede shoes for her spring collection, for $5,000, knowing that he usually makes $500 hand-made pairs/year. Unfortunately, he took sick and has been unable to make any shoes this year. Must she still pay him?

She also purchased a ½ reversionary interest in the mineral rights to her brother, Mikhail's Bossier City tract 15 years ago. He has since sold the tract, but she wonders if she can collect on the mineral royalties now that the tract is producing oil.

Finally, she and her sister Marsha, a doctor, had purchased the building in which she has her shoe store some time ago. Her next-door neighbor is a store, Markus Music that sells musical instruments. They often stack cardboard boxes against her back door, blocking it, they have raucous band rehearsals with no sound-proofing, and their customers hang out in front, blocking customers from getting to her door, and even making fun of those who try to come. All of this is against city code, so she and Marsha filed a lawsuit about six months ago. However, the lawsuit has become a nuisance, her attorney wants her to do this and that, read this, that and the other motion, and it's dragging on and becoming expensive. She's ready to get out of the lawsuit, but Marsha is not, so they agree that for $500, Marsha will take over the lawsuit, and Anna will get out of it. Does this benefit Markus in any way?

CHAPTER 4

THE FORM OF THE CONTRACT OF SALE

Flowchart

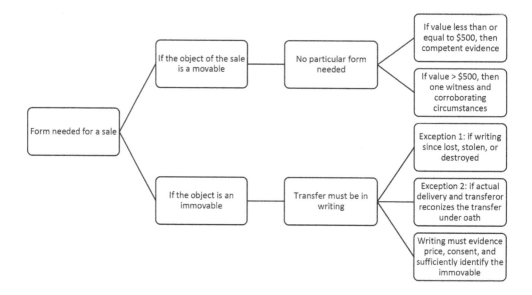

Section 1. Movables

As a general rule, the Civil Code requires no particular form for the sale or other voluntary transfer of ownership of movable property, although the Revised Statutes some special exceptions, such as the sale of agricultural commodities, as provided in Revised Statute §3:3414. Of course, parties may agree that they will not be bound until their contract has been reduced to writing, as per Article 1947. As indicated in article 2456 and discussed in the previous chapter, a contract of sale of movable property is perfected as between the parties on agreement as to the thing and the price, and ownership transfers at that time. However, it is only on delivery of the thing to the buyer that the contract is effective against third parties and risk of loss due to fortuitous events transfers.[1]

These principles are true even for movables subject to mandatory registration such as motor vehicles. Therefore, an oral sale of a registered movable is valid as between the buyer and the seller but does not bind third parties until it is registered. A seller who fails to register the sale faces criminal liability, but Louisiana courts have uniformly rejected the registration requirement as having any effect on the validity of the sale.[2]

Article 1846 provides that:

> When a writing is not required by law, a contract not reduced to writing, for a price, or, in the absence of a price, for a value not in excess of five hundred dollars may be proved by competent evidence.
>
> If the price or value is in excess of five hundred dollars, the contract must be proved by at least one witness and other corroborating circumstances.

Study Question:

How does Article 1846 apply in the following case? On what evidence and what witnesses did the court rely in reaching its decision?

JOYNER V. LIPRIE 2010
33 SO. 3D 242, (LA. APP. 2D CIR.)

PEATROSS, J.

¶1 A jury found that Defendant, Samuel F. Liprie, breached an oral agreement to form a joint venture with Plaintiff, Lee Roy Joyner, M.D., for the development and potential marketing of a device invented by Liprie to administer radiation treatment to the coronary artery. The jury awarded damages to Dr. Joyner in the amount of $4.3 million, plus attorney fees. Liprie now appeals. For the reasons stated herein, we affirm.

FACTS

¶2 [Liprie is a nuclear pharmacist and inventor who works primarily with radiation therapy. He developed a cutting-edge technology for directing "high doses" . . . of radiation therapy at

---

1   24 Louisiana Civil Law Treatise §6:3.

2   *Id.* at §4:3.

a specific part of the body.] This breakthrough technology treated the cancer from within the body. Liprie licensed this "high dose" technology to Omnitron, a company owned by Liprie.

¶3 In 1993, Liprie then began testing the technology to deliver "low doses" (below 4 curies) of radiation directly and, specifically, to the coronary artery. The procedure was to be used following angioplasty surgery to prevent re-clogging or "restenosis" of the arteries. Liprie shared the idea for this intracoronary radiation therapy ("ICRT") with Dr. Joyner and a radiation oncologist, Dr. Mark Harrison. The three men had discussions regarding a joint venture to move forward with the development and promotion of ICRT.

¶4 The record . . . reflects that discussions regarding the heart project began among Liprie and Drs. Joyner and Harrison around February 1994, culminating in a meeting of the three in Atlanta in May 1994. Orlando Gurdiel, a Venezuelan cardiologist, among other Latin American representatives, was also at this Atlanta meeting to discuss conducting human trials of the technology in Caracas, Venezuela. The ultimate goal of the venture was to have the abstract accepted by American College of Cardiologists ("ACC") for publication at the annual convention in New Orleans in March 1995.

¶5 According to the testimony of Dr. Joyner, it was at this Atlanta meeting, following the discussions with the Venezuelans, that the joint venture agreement was reached between Liprie, Dr. Harrison and himself. He testified that, otherwise, he would not have gone forward with the project.

¶6 Regarding the economics of the agreement, Dr. Joyner testified that the three agreed that he and Dr. Harrison would each pay one-half of the expenses of the joint venture and one half of a monthly salary to Liprie. For this, Drs. Joyner and Harrison received 25 percent ownership interest each in the joint venture. Liprie retained 50 percent ownership and would supply all of the materials and intellectual property rights to the low-dose ICRT applications for the exclusive use of the joint venture. Dr. Joyner described his contribution to the venture as follows:

Q: What was Lee Roy Joyner required to bring to the deal to be entitled to a percentage of the profits?

A: The ability to do a clinical study with a resume documenting this has been done many times in the past by Lee Roy Joyner and that this would subsequently then be published not in just peer review literature, but in prestigious peer review literature as directed specifically to the publication of what you're doing. And further that this new treatment or this new project turns out at least for a period of time changing the way that this disease is treated worldwide.

***

I had to pay half of Sam Liprie's salary at the same level of the salary that he was making of (sic) the time with Omnitron. A hundred and fifty thousand dollars a year. And I had to pay half of the expenses related to the completion of the study down to and including the ... acceptance of this study to be published in the cardiology literature.

¶7   At one point in his testimony, Dr. Joyner states that Liprie assured him at the meeting in Atlanta that he would not be required to provide any security. Later in his testimony, Dr. Joyner states that the first he knew of a requirement of security was by way of a letter dated July 15, 1994. There are, in fact, two versions of this July 15th letter in the record. Both letters bear the typed names of Lee Roy and Mark as authors. The copy relied on by Dr. Joyner ("the Joyner letter") outlines the agreement as described above, making no mention of a $2.5 million security requirement. The Joyner letter does reference efforts to "perfect the Bahamian security agreement," but Dr. Joyner urges that that is not a reference to any independent security arrangement (for $2.5 million) as suggested by Liprie. . . .

¶8   The second version of the July 15th letter ("the Liprie letter") is substantially the same as the first, with the addition of the following language:

> We fully intend to honor our commitment of 2.5 million even if the project fails. If the project is successful and revenues are forthcoming, we would like to extend to you the option of taking the first 3 million off the top, satisfying our obligation, prior to any distribution to us.

¶9   It is this letter that Liprie cites as the first time there was an agreement reached by the three men. Liprie denies that any agreement was reached at the meeting in Atlanta. Despite the discrepancy in the terms contained in the letters of intent, the three men continued to move forward with the project. Drs. Joyner and Harrison were paying the expenses and Liprie's salary and the plans were set for the trip to Caracas. Dr. Harrison and Liprie arrived in Caracas on July 21, 1994, and, due to passport issues, Dr. Joyner arrived the following day.

¶10   Dr. Joyner testified that it was within his expertise to determine how the human trials should be conducted in Caracas, including how many patients would be necessary to validate the procedure in order to obtain FDA approval. Dr. Joyner also testified that he was instrumental in overcoming the setback experienced in Caracas. For this reason, Dr. Joyner testified, while the Venezuelans were debating whether to allow the study to proceed, Liprie reassured him that, if the trials proceeded, no security would be necessary from Dr. Joyner.

***

¶11 Despite the fact that he did not participate in the second round of trials in Caracas, Dr. Joyner submits that he assisted in authoring the abstract of the heart project in September 1994. In fact, the abstract bears the names of Drs. Joyner, Harrison and Liprie, among others. The ACC accepted the abstract for publication in New Orleans the following March (1995).

¶12 The record reflects that, during the months surrounding the November 1994 deadline, there were many conversations among the players in this venture regarding the requirement of $2.5 million and/or the security therefor. Dr. Joyner testified that "the closer the venture got to the finish line, i.e., publishing a medical abstract, the higher the bar was raised by Liprie for Dr. Joyner to perform the oral agreement." Dr. Joyner testified that he ultimately acquiesced in Liprie's demand and approached businessman and friend David Harter, with whom he had had discussions about becoming involved in the heart project and others, about securing $1.25 million, or his share of the $2.5 million. Dr. Joyner provided information on the project to Mr. Harter, who, in turn, sought the counsel of European heiress and long-time friend of Mr. Harter, Jacqui Biwer.

¶13 Ms. Biwer and Mr. Harter testified by deposition that they were both excited about the prospect of being involved in the heart project. Ms. Biwer further testified that she sought the advice of several doctors and concluded that she "absolutely" desired to provide funding for the project on behalf of Dr. Joyner. The record contains an agreement dated November 19, 1994, executed by Dr. Joyner, Mr. Harter and Ms. Biwer reflecting, inter alia, that Dr. Joyner transfer 50 percent of his ownership in the project to Mr. Harter and Ms. Biwer in exchange for the availability of $1.25 million payable to Liprie on demand. Ms. Biwer testified that she spoke with Liprie by telephone and advised him that she would be providing the security for Dr. Joyner.

¶14 It is not disputed that Liprie did not "call" upon the money made available by Ms. Biwer and Mr. Harter. To the contrary, Liprie testified that there was no conversation in which he was told that security was being offered on behalf of Dr. Joyner.

¶15 In March 1995, Art Berner, another attorney hired by Liprie, advised Dr. Joyner by letter that Dr. Joyner would no longer own 25 percent of the joint venture and that the venture would be incorporated into a new entity, Angiorad, Inc. On behalf of Liprie, Mr. Berner offered Dr. Joyner 5 percent of Angiorad, Inc. for an additional $180,000. This offer was made to Drs. Joyner and Harrison, but only Dr. Harrison accepted. Subsequently, by letter dated March 14, 1995, Mr. Berner advised Dr. Joyner that the offer for Dr. Joyner to participate in the joint venture was withdrawn.

¶16   Dr. Joyner filed the current suit on February 8, 1996. Thereafter, on September 6, 1996, United States Surgical Corporation bought the rights to the ICRT from Angiorad, Inc. The only evidence of record reveals that Liprie collected profits totaling $17 million from the technology.

DISCUSSION

¶17   The case sub judice presents a complex and sometimes confusing scenario of the evolution of the so-called joint venture efforts of Liprie and Drs. Joyner and Harrison. This litigation turns on (1) the existence of an enforceable oral joint venture agreement among the three men, (2) the terms of such agreement, if confected, and (3) whether Dr. Joyner and/or Liprie satisfied the terms of such agreement or whether Liprie breached the same.

Oral Agreement

¶18   In his first three assignments of error, Liprie challenges the factual findings of the jury that the terms of the oral agreement between the doctors did not include the security provision, that Liprie defrauded Dr. Joyner and that he breached a fiduciary duty to Dr. Joyner as his partner.

***

¶19   Before determining the terms of the alleged oral agreement, we must first examine whether such agreement was confected. If the price or value of an oral contract is in excess of $500, the contract must be proved by at least one witness and other corroborating circumstances. La. C.C. art. 1846. The phrase "other corroborating circumstances" means general corroboration and does not require independent proof of every detail of the agreement. Smith v. Dishman & Bennett Speciality Co., Inc., 35,682 (La.App.2d Cir.1/23/02), 805 So.2d 1220. Whether there are corroborating circumstances sufficient to establish an oral contract is a question of fact. Treen Const. Co., Inc. v. Schott, 03-1232 (La.App. 5th Cir.1/27/04) 866 So.2d 950.

¶20   As stated, in the case sub judice, the parties state in brief that it is "undisputed" that Liprie and Drs. Joyner and Harrison entered into an oral joint venture agreement. Liprie and Dr. Joyner, however, also argue that they had differing ideas regarding the initial terms of the oral joint venture agreement. If that is the case, the question arises whether there was, in fact, a meeting of the minds resulting in an enforceable agreement. Dr. Joyner maintains, and the jury so found, that the initial agreement did not require contribution of $1.25 million in capital or security therefor. In support of his testimony that there was no security required under the initial oral agreement, Dr. Joyner provided the July 15, 1994 Liprie letter of intent and the subsequent draft of a written partnership agreement, as described hereinabove, both of which contained the security provision and both of which he refused to sign because of that additional term. Significantly, Dr. Joyner notes the actions of Liprie throughout the early phases of the venture, prior to the ACC acceptance of the medical abstract. Dr. Joyner emphasizes that Liprie proceeded eagerly with the venture, accepting the salary paid by Drs. Joyner and Harrison and allowing Dr. Joyner's participation in testing the technology in the first round of human trials in Caracas and co-authoring the medical abstract. Dr. Joyner further emphasizes that, on several occasions, Liprie assured him that he would not be required to provide security for $1.25 million. Most notably, while in Caracas awaiting a decision of the Venezuelan doctors as to whether the trial could continue, Dr. Joyner was instrumental in procuring a solution that allowed the project to proceed and was assured at that time that he would be included in the project to its end without having to "come up" with any additional security. According to Dr. Joyner, it was not until after the first round of successful trials in Caracas that Liprie became insistent on the furnishing of the $1.25 million or the security therefor. According to Dr. Joyner, it was at that point that Liprie knew that he had the potential to make millions, if not billions, on this technology.

¶21 After a complete review of the evidence in this case, we conclude that there exists a reasonable factual basis in this record on which the jury could have concluded that the three men reached an oral agreement, either in late May in Atlanta or in July surrounding the time of the two "letters of intent" exchanged among the three men. Liprie's actions in continuing the project and accepting the benefits of the bargain as described herein provide sufficient, albeit marginally sufficient, evidence of corroborating circumstances sufficient to support the jury's finding that an oral agreement existed and that security was not required as a term of the agreement.

***

Damages

¶22 A fact finder's determination of damages is also subject to the manifest error standard of review and is entitled to great deference on review. Mazel v. Gould, 4 So.3d 979 (La.App.2d Cir. 2/25/09), citing Williams v. Enriquez, 935 So.2d 269 (La.App.2d Cir. 6/28/06). The total profit from Liprie's radiation technology, according to his testimony, was $17 million. The jury chose to accept that figure and awarded Dr. Joyner 25 percent of that profit in accordance with his 25 percent ownership share in the joint venture [i.e. $4.3 million]. We find no abuse of discretion in this award.

Comment: Writings and the Parol Evidence Rule

As you just learned, contracts for large amounts of money will be enforced, even if not written, as long as the one alleging the contract proves its existence with at least one witness and corroborating evidence. Nevertheless, even if no particular form is required, if the parties choose to write out their agreement, then the parol evidence rule as set forth in Article 1848 comes into play. It reads:

> "Testimonial or other evidence may not be admitted to negate or vary the contents of an authen-
> tic act or an act under private signature. Nevertheless, in the interest of justice, that evidence
> may be admitted to prove such circumstances as a vice of consent, or a simulation, or to prove
> that the written act was modified by a subsequent and valid oral agreement."

Thus, the rule provides that if parties to a written instrument intend it to be the final manifestation of their mutual understanding, no evidence may be admitted contradict or modify.

The American common law addresses the same issue. As expressed in the Restatement (Second) of Contracts, if the instrument is a complete expression of the parties' understanding, the agreement is said to be integrated and the parol evidence rule attaches; but, if the writing produced is not complete, though a final instrument, the writing can be complemented, but not contradicted, by additional evidence. The instrument is then termed 'partially integrated.' To determine whether the instrument as executed by the parties is the final and complete expression of their will, courts sometimes use the 'four corners' rule: all information relating to the interpretation of the contract must be gleaned from the document itself and not from extrinsic sources, whether oral or written. Alternatively, the court may look to see if the contract itself provides that it is the final and complete agreement of the parties. The concept of 'total integration' is a major area of conflict concerning the scope and applicability of the rule, and has led to a number of exceptions to the rule.

Extrinsic writings not excluded

The Louisiana version of the parol evidence rule is less exclusive of extrinsic evidence than the Restatement's version. At common law, the parol evidence rule excludes both oral and written extrinsic evidence on the basis that the subsequent written evidence is as irrelevant to a fully integrated written contract as is oral evidence. In contrast, under Louisiana's civil law, the theory of exclusion is grounded upon a distrust of parol itself. Consequently, the Louisiana Supreme Court generally recognizes that the parol evidence rule excludes only oral testimony and does not extend to extrinsic writings.

Collateral evidence that does not contradict, add, or vary terms not excluded

Furthermore, Article 1848's prohibitions apply only when the evidence is offered to negate the terms of the act – to contradict, vary, or "prove the falsity of what is therein stated." Consequently, parol evidence may be introduced if it is intended to prove a fact collateral to the agreement.

Evidence that the writing not effective between the parties not excluded

The most important exception to Louisiana's parol evidence rule allows use of parol to establish that the writing in question was not effective, in whole or in part, between the parties due to a vice of consent, or that it is a simulation, or that the cause of the agreement was unlawful, or that the instrument does not accurately reflect the parties' intent. Art. 1848 comments. b, d.

Evidence used to interpret the writing is not excluded

The Louisiana Supreme Court allows use of parol evidence to aid in the interpretation of a written agreement, usually when an ambiguity in the writing requires resolution, because in these circumstances the evidence is "consistent with the agreement and not offered for the purpose of altering, contradicting, varying, enlarging, or restricting."

Study Questions:

In the following lawsuit between brothers, is the decision grounded in Article 1846 or Article 1848.? If it's based on Article 1846, then what evidence did the court use in reaching its decision concerning ownership of the movable?

JEANFREAU V. JEANFREAU 1935
182 LA. 332, 162 SO. 3 (LA.)

FOURNET, Justice.

¶1 Louis Jeanfreau filed suit against his brother Edward Jeanfreau for the ownership and possession of a motorboat, the Alice D, alleging that he purchased the boat at Biloxi, Miss., and 'had the title to same placed in the name of Edward Jeanfreau for convenience sake only,' and that the defendant 'agreed to return the said motorboat * * * whenever he so demanded.' In another paragraph of the petition, he alleged that since the purchase of the motorboat, all the expenses for the upkeep thereof were borne by him at the approximate cost of $2,500.

¶2 The defendant filed a plea of vagueness and, in pursuance to the order of the district judge, the plaintiff filed an amended petition, asserting that he purchased the boat from the Foster Packing Company of Biloxi, Miss.

¶3 Defendant then filed his answer denying the allegations of plaintiff's petition, and, further answering, averred that he had been the owner of the boat since January 1, 1927, and that plaintiff had always recognized and acknowledged his ownership; that the boat had been seized by the United States government, and though plaintiff was present at the trials in the United States District Court, he made no claim for the boat, and specially pleaded that to be an estoppel by conduct. Defendant later filed pleas of prescription of three and of five years, respectively, which were referred to the merits by the district judge, and after trial of the case, the pleas of prescription were dismissed and judgment was rendered in favor of the plaintiff as prayed for. The defendant has appealed.

¶4 There is no evidence in the record, except the deposition of C. A. Delacruz, of Biloxi, Miss., who stated, in answer to the interrogatories propounded to him, that he was connected with the C. B. Foster Packing Company and that the motorboat Alice D was sold by the C. B. Foster Packing Company to Louis Jeanfreau; that the purchase price thereof was paid by Louis Jeanfreau in the presence of Fred Jeanfreau, who took the boat from Biloxi to Violet, La.; that the boat was equipped with a 40-horse power engine, but that the same had been replaced with a 100-horse power engine at the request of Louis Jeanfreau, and at his expense.

***

¶5 The possession of the boat in defendant as owner is clearly negatived by the plaintiff's petition wherein he alleges that the boat 'was placed in the name of Edward Jeanfreau for convenience sake only.' The only evidence in the record, the depositions of Delacruz, corroborates plaintiff's allegations that he purchased the boat. Defendant's counsel, however, indicated by his exception of vagueness and in his brief that since the plaintiff had placed the title to the boat in defendant's name, he should have a counterletter to establish that fact. Evidently counsel has confused the law of evidence touching upon the transfer of immovables; i. e., the inadmissibility of parol evidence to establish title to immovables. This is not true as to movables, the ownership of which can be established by the corroborating testimony of one witness. [former] Civil Code art 2277.

***

¶6 For the reasons assigned, the judgment of the lower court is affirmed.

Section 2. Immovables

Quick Review of Articles 1833-1838:

What is an authentic act?

An act under private signature?

An act under private signature duly acknowledged?

As shown in the previous section the sale of a movable requires only the seller's and buyer's agreement on the thing and the price. The sale of an immovable – or other transfer of ownership of an immovable – under Louisiana law is subject as well to a writing requirement, though there are some exceptions, as stated in articles 2440, 1839, and 1832:

> Art. 2440: Sale of immovable, method of making
>
> A sale or promise of sale of an immovable must be made by authentic act or by act under private signature, except as provided in Article 1839.
>
> Art. 1839: Transfer of immovable property
>
> A transfer of immovable property must be made by authentic act or by act under private signature. Nevertheless, an oral transfer is valid between the parties when the property has been actually delivered and the transferor recognizes the transfer when interrogated on oath.
>
> An instrument involving immovable property shall have effect against third persons only from the time it is filed for registry in the parish where the property is located.
>
> Art. 1832: Written form required by law
>
> When the law requires a contract to be in written form, the contract may not be proved by testimony or by presumption, unless the written instrument has been destroyed, lost, or stolen.

Comment:

In contrast to any transfer (or sale) of a corporeal or incorporeal movable, the transfer (or sale) of an immovable must be in writing. La. Civ. Code arts. 2440 & 1839. Moreover, an accessory contract that relates to the transfer of an immovable must also be in writing. This includes the transfer of an interest in minerals, a contract of mandate that grants the mandatary the power to sell or transfer an immovable, or any other accessory contract relating to the transfer of an immovable.

Note that an authentic act is required for the donation inter vivos of an immovable, but an authentic act is NOT required for a valid sale of an immovable. Thus a sale of an immovable is effective as between the parties if it is in the form of an authentic act, of an act under private signature duly acknowledged, or merely of an act under private signature. Note that the simple act under private signature could be written on a paper napkin. As of the 2001 Louisiana Uniform Electronic Transactions Act, an e-commerce conveyance is also effective. Regardless of the form used, and though the writing need not designate the price, it must contain language documenting or promising the transfer of ownership and must be signed by the parties.[3] A photocopied signature page attached to the contract is insufficient.[4]

There are two exceptions to this writing requirement. First, parol testimony may be accepted if the written instrument was destroyed, lost, or stolen. Article 1832. Second, if there never was a written instrument, then the transfer is effective if there was actual delivery and the transferor acknowledges the transfer under oath. Article 1839.

Study Question:

What do the cases below add to your understanding of these articles?

PIERCE V. GRIFFIN 1957
95 SO. 2D 190 (LA. APP. 1ST CIR.)

TATE, Judge.

¶1 Plaintiffs, the widow and the daughter of the late L. J. Pierce, appeal from dismissal of their petitory action claiming ownership of Lot 4 of Square 12 of the Pierce Addition to the Town of Golden Meadow in Lafourche Parish. The action was filed in October of 1952.

¶2 The uncontradicted facts show: L. J. Pierce acquired a tract including the lot in question in 1925. Defendant Griffin went into possession of said Lot 4 in March of 1936, with the consent of Pierce. Immediately afterwards, Griffin built his home thereupon, in which he has resided since that date. L. J. Pierce died in 1940. No conveyance of the property in question from L. J. Pierce or his surviving spouse and heir to defendant Griffin has ever been recorded.

¶3 Plaintiffs-appellants rely upon Articles 2275 and 2240 of the LSA-Civil Code, which provide that every transfer of immovable property must be in writing, and that oral sales of such

---

3   24 Louisiana Civil Law Treatise §§6:8, 6:9.

4   Wheeler v. Carber, 2012 WL 3526786 (M.D. La. 2012) (unpublished).

property are null, even as between the parties concerned (unless the vendor confesses the sale when under oath after actual delivery of the property thus sold).

¶4 Defendant Griffin claims there was a sale of Lot 4 in writing, relying upon the following evidence:

> An admittedly authentic receipt signed by both L. J. Pierce and defendant Griffin, dated February 22, 1936, showing that Pierce owed Griffin $100 which was to be paid upon a lot subsequently to be sold by Pierce to defendant;

> his own testimony, corroborated by that of Gustave Guidry who was present, that subsequently an oral agreement was reached between Pierce and the defendant that Pierce would sell defendant the lot in question for the balance of $100 due; and

> his own testimony that immediately thereafter Pierce pointed out the corners of Lot 4 to him, immediately following which he commenced building his residence thereupon, during which time Pierce prepared four wooden stakes, writing in Pierce's own hand upon each of such stakes, the following:

> 'In 1936 this Lot 4 sold to Silas Griffin by L. J. Pierce.'

¶5 These stakes were placed at the four corners of the lot sold, which Griffin stated was 44 100 in dimensions, thus omitting a 5-foot strip along the canal to the south of Lot 4 as a passage for pedestrians. Malbrough, a carpenter working on the home at the time, corroborated Pierce's testimony. Malbrough had furnished the pencil and the stakes upon which Pierce wrote, and further testified that although he could not read or write, he remembered very plainly Pierce reading from such stakes to the effect that he, Pierce, was selling the property so staked to defendant Griffin.

¶6 Able counsel for plaintiffs-appellants does not cite us to any authority that the writing required for a valid sale of immovable property must be upon paper or parchment. As between the parties, there does not seem to be any substantial reason why it should be sacramental that the writing must be upon such material, providing that the writing is adequately proved. That the writing in question was adequate, if sufficiently proved, to convey title as explained by the corroborative evidence, seems to be well established by the jurisprudence. Guice v. Mason, 156 La. 201, 100 So. 397, Saunders v. Bolden, 155 La. 136, 98 So. 867; cf. also Lemoine v. Lacour, 213 La. 109, 34 So.2d 392, and Walker v. Ferchaud, 210 La 283, 26 Lo.2d 746.

¶7 The stakes themselves have been destroyed, to which we will advert below. While the weight of the parol evidence as to the writing of almost 20 years before raises a substantial question of credibility, we cannot say the District Court committed manifest error in accepting it, in view of the corroborative testimony of a disinterested person, and the strong corroborating circumstances of the delivery and possession, the construction of a home thereupon by the purchaser, and the unprotested possession thereof and residence thereon by the purchaser for the 18 years prior to the present suit.

* * *

¶8 Pierce's widow, the co-plaintiff herein, testified that the sale had not been completed because defendant Griffin had not paid the balance of the purchase price, apparently referring to a system of operations whereby the formal sale was not executed and recorded until after the entire purchase price had been paid. She testified that her husband had several times requested payment of the balance from Griffin, and she further testified that after her husband's death in 1940, she went to defendant, and

'A. I asked Mr. Griffin if he wants to pay what he owed. He say that I am not going to pay you and nobody can make me get out of here. Better you go out of here and he was very dirty.

'Q. You asked him to pay for the lot or the rent? A. What he owed Mr. Pierce. He owed on the lot and on the house.

'Q. You mean what he owed on the lot? A. On the lot and house. There was only $100.00 deposit on the lot.' (Tr. p. 12.)

¶9 This testimony can be construed to being an admission under oath by the vendor's successor that the verbal sale had indeed taken place as testified to by defendant, which is sufficient to convey title under Article 2275, LSA-C.C., although the defendant had never completed payment of the purchase price. (The pleadings simply requested recognition of plaintiffs' ownership of the property, and we are therefore not concerned herein with the validity at this date of any claim by plaintiffs for any alleged balance due.)

¶10 Plaintiffs further urge that, even accepting that the written instrument conveying title has been adequately proven, parol evidence is only admissible to enforce its contents when said writing 'has been lost or destroyed, by accident or force,' Article 2279.

¶11   Defendant Griffin testified that following construction of the house, he erected a fence along the lines shown by the stakes, in consequence thereof removing the stakes, which were subsequently burned along with the other debris remaining from the construction. Plaintiffs urge most ably that this intentional destruction is not such a destruction 'by accident' as would satisfy the requirements of the codal article.

¶12   The codal article's intent is to admit of proof of the contents of a writing conveying title when such writing has been unintentionally lost or destroyed. We do not think it means that the party relying thereupon is barred from proving the contents of such a writing thrown away or burned without realizing the effect of such action. The word 'accident' in the codal article is used, in our opinion, as contradistinguished from knowingly and intentionally destroying what one knows to be instrument in writing upon which one relies to prove one's rights. It should no more bar defendant's proof of the lost writing herein than that of a person seeking to prove the contents of a deed which fell by mistake into a trash barrel, and which the person intentionally burned without knowing he was burning an instrument of title.

* * *

¶13   For the above and foregoing reasons, the judgment of the District Court herein is affirmed.

Affirmed.

Comments:

Compare Pierce v. Griffin to the following more recent case.

HARTER V. HARTER 2013
127 SO. 3D 5 (LA. 2ND CT. APP.)

BROWN, Chief Judge.

Plaintiffs David Harter and his sister, Jan Harter Pipkin, sued their brother Mike Harter and his business, Harter Oil Company, for breach of contract. They claim that Harter Oil sold them each a 25% working interest in certain mineral leases for $250,000, and that Harter oil had agreed to finance the purchase price, to be paid out of proceeds. Plaintiffs claim that defendants unilaterally terminated their ownership interests.

Discussion

Facts

¶1   Marilee Davis Harter died on December 24, 2005. She was predeceased by her husband, Earl Michael Harter, Jr., with whom she had four children: Steven S. Harter ("Steve"), Earl Michael Harter, III ("Mike"), David Allen Harter ("David"), and Jan Harter Pipkin ("Jan"). Pursuant to their mother's last will and testament, Steve was named as the Independent Administrator of the estate. [The four children owned a one-fourth interest each in the estate. Steve, in his capacity as the Independent Administrator, sued Mike (who managed the family oil business), and they reached a settlement: Mike was to pay off three notes, purchase the interest of Harter Energy, LLC, in certain oil and gas leases, and transfer those leases to his own Harter Oil Company. In return, Mike forfeited his interest in the estate proportionally increasing the other heirs' shares.

¶2   However, this settlement did not solve the family dispute. David, Jan, and Mike all believed that Steve was mismanaging the estate. So, the three agreed that Harter Oil would sell a 25% interest in the mineral leases Mike had purchased to each David and Jan for a total price of $500,000, to be financed out of lease proceeds at 7% interest. In return, David and Jan agreed to institute legal action to remove Steve as the Independent Administrator of the succession and that any recovery, including real estate, cash, and oil and gas leases, would go to Mike. In addition, Mike agreed to loan the money to David and Jan (neither of whom worked) to finance the cost of the litigation against Steve.

¶3   At some point in the latter half of 2007, Mike instructed Harter Oil's corporate officer and secretary, Roslyn Hull, to make an entry in Harter Oil's internal records showing the transfer of a 25% interest each to Jan and David in the subject oil and gas leases. The production from these leases was to be attributed retroactively from July 1, 2007. Initially, all of David and Jan's working interest revenues from July 1, 2007, until December 31, 2007, were applied to the $500K loan. David and Jan received no cash payments during this period; however, they were issued 1099 forms by Harter Oil showing compensation to each in the sum of $148,187 and they paid the taxes due for 2007.

¶4   In late 2007, David, Jan, and Mike met with an attorney Billy Pesnell to discuss the legal action against Steve, and Mike issued a $10,000 personal check payable to Pesnell as a fee advancement. In anticipation of Steve's negative reaction to the lawsuit and fear that he might withhold David and Jan's monthly payments from the estate, the alleged agreement was modified (though it was never memorialized in writing). Mike agreed to make $6,000 monthly payments from their working interests to David and Jan commencing on January 1, 2008. The checks were issued by Harter Oil. When David requested an increase in those payments on April 1, 2008, the payments were modified such that David and Jan were paid all their working interest revenues minus $8000/month applied towards the loan. At that time checks for $17,342 were issued to both David and Jan.

¶5   Harter Oil's books and records listed David and Jan as working interest owners for each lease established. The accounts receivable ledger showed David and Jan's purchase price loans, the credits for their monthly loan payments, and the interest charges. The company's lease analysis reports showed David and Jan as owners. Harter Oil sent them regular monthly reports such as joint interest billing and lease operating expense reports. David and Jan were both sent 1099 forms from Harter Oil for 2008 showing compensation of $236,712 each for that year.

¶6   Mike testified under oath that, "I said (to Rosalyn Hull) put it on the books as working interest owners. Yes, I told her to treat it like a sale." At trial, when asked if he implemented the agreement, Mike replied, "[W]ell, if you mean by implementing by me putting it in my books of my company for accounting purposes, yes."

¶7   During this time period, David sent Mike three written requests asking that the parties finalize the purchase of the oil properties, which include a standard promissory note on which David had handwritten the terms. Despite these requests, no written agreement or promissory notes were executed. Furthermore, none of the drafts from David included the obligation of plaintiffs to file suit against Steve.

¶8   In 2008, Mike decided to sell two of Harter Oil's leases acquired from the estate, Urania G and Tensas Delta, to Voyager Energy for a purchase price of $2.5 million (he actually received $2,070,968) after he received a letter of interest from Voyager. When Voyager conducted its due diligence, it reviewed Harter Oil's records and discovered that in addition to Harter Oil there were four working interest owners: David and Jan's 50%, 7.5% was owned by two other individuals, and Harter Oil the remaining 35%. Only Harter Oil's original assignment was recorded in the public records.

¶9   The dispute that led to this lawsuit began shortly thereafter, when Mike instructed Roslyn to remove David and Jan from all of Harter Oil's records as of August 2008. The two other individuals were paid their 7.5% interest, but not David and Jan. On September 28, 2008, Mike sent a handwritten note to David and Jan notifying them of his dissatisfaction with the lack of progress made in their suit against Steve. The note also stated that Mike would compensate both David and Jan $12,000 per month for the remainder of the year, at which point they would re-evaluate their "deal." Harter Oil followed through, paying them $12,000/month each for September, October, and November 2008, and then ceasing payments entirely after that.

¶10 On October 26, 2008, David sent an email to Mike stating that he and Jan had paid attorney Pesnell an additional $10,000, and a draft of the lawsuit was to be distributed for approval no later than October 30, 2008. On December 17, 2008, David and Jan finally filed a petition against Steve to recover damages for the breach of fiduciary duty or mismanagement of the succession, and subsequently entered into settlement agreements with Steve on or before January 14, 2009. Under that agreement, Jan and David each received (what they actually already owned) a 1/3 share of the estate without any compensation for damages.

¶11 In May 2011, Mike sold the remaining leases acquired from the estate plus other leases owned by Harter Oil to RYCA Energy ("RYCA") for a total of $11.2 million. Mike testified that Harter Oil received $11,036,721, but, due to expenses, Harter Oil netted only about $10 million. David and Jan claim that their working interest shares in these sales should have been $798,078 from Voyager and $1,012,956 from RYCA.

* * *

¶12 Mike argues that because the mineral interests in question are classified as incorporeal immovables, they are insusceptible of delivery. As a result, he urges that the transfer failed to meet the delivery requirement of Article 1839.]

Requirements For Valid Transfer of Mineral Interest

¶13 A working interest in an oil and gas lease is a mineral right. La. R.S. 31:18 provides that a mineral right is an incorporeal immovable. It is alienable and heritable and subject to the laws of registry. Mineral interests are subject to the general rules regarding immovables set forth in the Louisiana Civil Code. La. R.S. 31:2. The Civil Code states that rights and actions that apply to immovable things are incorporeal immovables. Immovables of this kind include personal servitudes established on immovables, predial servitudes, mineral rights, and petitory or possessory actions. La. C.C. art. 470; *Trident Oil & Gas Corp. v. John O. Clay Exploration, Inc.,*622 So.2d 1191 (La.App. 2d Cir.1993). La. C.C. Art. 1839 provides:

> A transfer of immovable property must be made by authentic act or by act under private signature. Nevertheless, an oral transfer is valid between the parties when the property has been actually delivered and the transferor recognizes the transfer when interrogated on oath.

An instrument involving immovable property shall have effect against third persons only from the time it is filed for registry in the parish where the property is located.

¶14 Two requirements must be met for a valid oral transfer of immovable property, namely, actual delivery of the property and recognition by the transferor under oath. Delivery must be actual, that is, the physical possession of the property must be in the transferee who claims title thereto. That is so because, in the absence of a writing, the symbolic delivery that always accompanies an authentic act of transfer simply cannot have taken place. Delivery alone is not enough, however, as possession might have been given to the alleged transferee in performance of an obligation arising from a contract of lease, or for custodial purposes, rather than in performance of a contract that effects a transfer of ownership. For that reason, actual delivery of the property to the transferee must be followed by recognition of the transfer by the transferor when interrogated on oath. Saul Litvinoff, *5 La. Civ. L. Treatise, Law Of Obligations* § 12.40 (2d ed. 2001).

¶15 Once the two requirements are met, an oral transfer of immovable property is valid because, when taken together, those requirements perform the same evidentiary function as, and perhaps even in a stronger way than, a writing would perform. *Id.*

* * *

¶16 In order for property to be actually delivered, the immovable which is the object of the verbal sale must have been transferred or placed into the possession of the buyer. The determination of delivery must be ascertained by the circumstances of each case. *Martin v. Brister,* 37,011 (La.App.2d Cir.07/23/03), 850 So.2d 1106, *writ denied,* 03–2374 (La.11/21/03), 860 So.2d 550.

¶17 In the case *sub judice,* Mike Harter's actions constituted an actual delivery of the two 25% working interests. Harter Oil's internal records indicate a transfer of 25% working interests to both David Harter and Jan Pipkin and showed loans to each representing their purchase payments. Additionally, Harter Oil created documents indicating the transfer and labeled them "David Harter and Jan Pipkin's share of 'Energy Purchase'." Harter Oil's accounts receivable ledger reflected the total amount of the purchase price loans. David and Jan were added to the "ownership decks" as working interest owners. Initially, the money earned from their working interests was applied toward the loans. Harter Oil issued David Harter and Jan Pipkin monthly checks from January until November 2008, as well as 1099s for the years of 2007 and 2008. David and Jan were kept abreast of production through regular monthly joint interest billing reports and lease operating expense reports sent by Harter Oil. Based on the company's records, Mike Harter treated the two other working interest owners, Gaiennie and Burroughs, in the same manner as David and Jan. During his testimony, Mike admitted that an objective third person viewing Harter Oil's records would assume that David and Jan were working interest owners. In September 2008, Mike terminated David and Jan's interests and "changed back" the records. This court finds that based upon the facts presented above, Mike delivered the interests by placing David and Jan in possession of ownership.

¶18 Secondly, Mike contends that he unequivocally denied transferring the working interests to David and Jan every time he was interrogated under oath.

¶19 This court has held that only the admission under oath by the grantor or the transferor may be used against him in an effort to establish a verbal immovable property transfer. *Langevin, supra*. Jurisprudence establishes that article 1839 **requires the recognition of the transfer or delivery by the transferor under oath, not necessarily that the transferor judicially confess the ultimate conclusion.** *Langevin, supra; Pierce v. Griffin*, 95 So.2d 190 (La.App. 1st Cir.1957)[emphasis added].

¶20 This court held that the transfer of rights pertaining to an incorporeal immovable may be verbally created upon the transferor's judicial admission of delivery. In *Langevin, supra*, the defendant admitted at trial that he accepted a $200 check from his neighbor, the owner of the dominant estate, in exchange for permission to utilize the servient estate owner's driveway for two years. This court found that the defendant's admission of accepting the plaintiff's payment and allowing him use of the driveway constituted a verbal creation of a predial servitude.

¶21 Mike asserts that David and Jan failed to prove that he recognized the transfer of mineral interests under oath because he never judicially admitted transferring the working interests. We disagree and find that the art. 1839's [sic] requirement of "recognition under oath" is satisfied by Mike's admissions concerning the events surrounding the agreement during his trial testimony.

¶22 While under oath, Mike admitted several pertinent facts concerning the delivery of the working interests. He admitted issuing monthly payments to David and Jan from January 2008 until August 2008 which were derived from the leases' revenues. Mike admitted instructing Roslyn Hull to make entries in the company's internal records evidencing a transfer of 25% of the working interests to both David and Jan and to add them as working interest owners to the ownership decks. We find that Mike's admissions made during trial constitute an oral confession under oath. Since Mike's actions evidence an actual delivery of the interests and he subsequently recognized such delivery under oath, the requirements for a valid oral transfer found in Article 1839 have been met.

* * *

¶23 The courts have held that when parties substantially comply with an oral agreement, neither one can subsequently withdraw on the basis that they failed to execute a writing despite the fact that all parties had initially agreed to reduce their agreement to writing. *Southern Scrap Material Co. v. Commercial Scrap Materials Corp.,* 239 La. 958, 120 So.2d 491 (La.1960); *O'Glee v. Whitlow,* 32,955 (La.App.2d Cir.04/07/00), 756 So.2d 1288. In *O'Glee, supra,* the plaintiff entered into an agreement with the defendant to sell his café. The defendant drafted a document in his own handwriting entitled "promissory note" that contained the purchase price, interest rate, and an amortization schedule for repayment. Both parties testified that they had agreed that a subsequent "sale document" would be drafted containing the terms of the sale. Regardless, the plaintiff transferred possession of the café to the defendant who began operating it and making monthly payments in accordance with the amortization schedule. Within a year of making the oral agreement, the defendant ceased making payments, claiming that the sale was never perfected due to lack of a written sales agreement. This court ruled that the defendant's actions constituted substantial performance . . . .

¶24 In the case at hand, we find that the agreement to transfer the working interests in the leases was complete.

* * *

¶25 After a review of the evidence presented, we find that the trial court erred in concluding that the evidence was insufficient to prove an assignment of the working interests and in dismissing plaintiffs' action before defendants' presentation of evidence.

Conclusion

¶26 For the reasons set forth above, this court reverses the trial court's judgment granting defendants' request for involuntary dismissal of plaintiffs' action and remands the matter for the receipt of defendants' evidence and a decision on the entire record.

Study Question:

The next case involves a relative simulation and the parol evidence rule. Isabel Mitchell wanted to buy a house for herself, and eventually wanted her nephew to inherit it, but without the trouble of going through an inheritance procedure. What additional information does this case provide about Louisiana's parol evidence rule as it applies to the transfer of ownership of an immovable?

MITCHELL V. CLARK 1984
448 SO. 2D 681 (LA.)

DIXON, Chief Justice.

[Isabel Mitchell sued her nephew, Willie Clark as well as W. Orie Hunter, Jr., the Caddo Parish Clerk of Court, to change the conveyance records and show Mitchell to be the owner of an immovable property, rather than Clark. She alleged that she is the true owner of the property and has been since its purchase from Harriet Holmes in 1958. The trial court found that as Mitchell had paid the purchase price for the home as well as all taxes and other costs, that the property should be transferred into her name. The court of appeal reversed on the basis that parol evidence provided by Mitchell was not admissible to prove her title.]

¶1 Isabel Mitchell negotiated with Holmes (who lived in Kansas City) for the purchase of [the immovable] located at 1718 Rex Street, Shreveport, Louisiana. She presented the sum of $1200.00 cash to an agent of Holmes as the purchase price, and specifically stipulated that Willie Clark be named the vendee.

¶2 Holmes, acting on Mitchell's instructions, executed a deed in authentic form conveying the property to Willie Clark, a single man who lived in Atlanta, Georgia. Neither Clark nor Mitchell signed the authentic act. Clark did not even know of the transaction. The deed was recorded in the Caddo Parish Conveyance Records on July 9, 1958.

¶3 Since that sale, Mitchell has paid all expenses related to ownership of the home, has made improvements to the home and has lived in the same as her own. Clark did not learn that he was the beneficiary of this sale until sometime in 1981. It was then that he sought to occupy the home as owner, prompting this action by the plaintiff.

¶4 In response to Mitchell's petition to have the vendee's name changed from Clark's to hers, Clark filed an exception of no cause of action. He stated that Mitchell's petition failed to allege any fraud, error or counter letter which would permit parol evidence to be adduced at trial in attacking an authentic act. He argued that Mitchell was precluded from offering parol evidence to create title in one who never owned the land, and that she had no case without the parol. The exception was overruled.

¶5 The defendant did not appear at trial, but was represented by counsel. He objected to the admission of parol evidence, but the objection was overruled. The judge treated the defendant's absence at trial, and consequent failure to testify, as a confession under oath that the allegations of the plaintiff's petition were true. Because a verbal sale of an immovable is recognized when confessed under oath, provided actual delivery has been made (C.C. 2275), the trial judge recognized Mitchell as the true vendee and ordered Hunter to transfer the property into her name.

¶6 The court of appeal was convinced that parol evidence should not be admitted to prove title in one who never had title. It quoted Barbin v. Gaspard, 15 La.Ann. 539, 540 (1860): "... plaintiff claims title ... by virtue of a sale, but is without any evidence in writing, ... and relies on testimonial proof to establish her demand. Evidence of this kind is insufficient to establish title..."

¶7 Mitchell then sought review by this court.

¶8 The trial judge correctly denied Clark's exception of no cause of action, and correctly permitted Mitchell to produce whatever documents that might support her position. Mitchell was a party to the transaction that resulted in naming Clark the vendee of the Rex Street property, but Mitchell was not a party to the authentic act by which the property was actually transferred. Clark was a party neither to the transaction nor the act. Written evidence, therefore, was admissible.

¶9 But the trial judge should not have permitted the oral or testimonial proof of any facts relating to the land purchase because this litigation concerns the ownership of an immovable whose sale was effected by a written act. No mutual error in the description of lands is claimed. Nor is this an action by a vendor who alleges fraud or error, or by an heir or a creditor who argues that no sale has taken place and that the property remains in the vendor's estate.

¶10 By paying the purchase price, Mitchell had a right to demand that a deed translative of title be executed in her favor; she chose, instead, to have the property transferred to her nephew. The property was conveyed in accordance with the plaintiff's instructions. She brings this action not based on error but based on a change of mind.

* * *

¶11 In two separate articles the Civil Code requires a writing to transfer immovable property. "Every transfer of immovable property must be in writing ..." C.C 2275. "All sales of immovable property shall be made by authentic act or under private signature." C.C. 2240. The writing provides reliable evidence of the parties' consent. It provides certainty and diminishes the possibility of fraud. 35 La.L.Rev. 779 (1975).

¶12 However, in the absence of a writing, a verbal sale of an immovable is effective if the delivery has been made and if the sale is confessed by the contesting parties under oath. C.C. 2275; Barbin v. Gaspard, supra. The answers of a party when interrogated under oath supply the place of written proof. Wright-Blodgett Co. v. Elms, 106 La. 150, 30 So. 311 (1901).

¶13 Louisiana courts have admitted parol evidence to show error in the description of lands when, because of accident or negligence, the instrument does not express the meaning and intention of the contracting parties. Agurs v. Holt, 232 La. 1026, 95 So.2d 644 (1957); Palangue v. Guesnon, 15 La. 311 (1840). "The reception of parol evidence to establish a clerical error, ... is no infringement of the rule which demands that title to real estate be evidenced in writing only." Levy v. Ward, 33 La.Ann. 1033, 1035 (1881).

¶14 That action, sometimes called an action for reformation of a deed, seeks to correct the mutual error or mistake that occurred in the preparation of the instrument. The property description is changed to describe the property which the vendor intended to sell and which the vendee intended to purchase. Brulatour v. Teche Sugar Co., 209 La. 717, 25 So.2d 444 (1946); Waller v. Colvin, 151 La. 765, 92 So. 328 (1922).

¶15 Parol evidence is admissible to invalidate a sale when the vendor was induced to sell by fraud or error. Baker v. Baker, 209 La. 1041, 26 So.2d 132 (1946); LeBleu v. Savoie, 109 La. 680, 33 So. 729 (1903). It is also admissible to show that a sale did not take place, and that the property continues to belong to the pretended vendor. Hodge v. Hodge, 151 La. 612, 92 So. 134 (1922).

¶16 Parol evidence can be used by a creditor to bring back into the estate of the debtor property which the debtor has fraudulently transferred, as in a revocatory action. C.C. 1970. It may be used by forced heirs to annul simulated contracts of those from whom they inherit. C.C. 2239.

¶17 However, parol "... is insufficient to create a title in one who never owned the property or to show that the vendee was in reality some other person than the person named in the act of sale." Scurto v. LeBlanc, 191 La. 136, 184 So. 567 (1938); Ceromi v. Harris, 187 La. 701, 706, 175 So. 462, 464 (1937). This rule applies whether the party proffering the parol is an heir of the alleged vendee, Eberle v. Eberle, 161 La. 313, 317, 108 So. 549, 551 (1926), or a creditor of the alleged vendee, Hoffmann v. Ackermann, 110 La. 1070, 1076, 35 So. 293, 295 (1903).

¶18 It is the policy of this state that acts appearing to transfer immovable property be read and interpreted from the face of the instrument. "... there would be no security whatsoever for purchasers of real estate, if they were not entitled to rely upon the title deeds to such property, as being exactly what they purport to be." Beard v. Nunn, 172 La. 155, 159, 133 So. 429, 430 (1931).

***

¶19 The admissible evidence in this case establishes that Mitchell paid Holmes for the lot, and that Holmes followed Mitchell's instructions and executed a deed to Clark. The inadmissible evidence establishes that Mitchell's intention — to make a gift of immovables to take effect upon Mitchell's death — could not be accomplished in the way attempted.

¶20 We cannot give relief to the plaintiff without abrogating the consistent rule of property that excludes parol evidence to prove that one not named in the deed is the real vendee.

¶21 The judgment of the court of appeal is amended and, as amended, affirmed, and there is now judgment in favor of defendants, Willie Clark, Jr. and W. Orie Hunter, Jr., dismissing plaintiff's suit at her cost.

LEMMON, J., dissents.

Comment:

The salient language of Mitchell is that while parol evidence rule that varies or negates a written instrument is admissible to show a vice of consent or even a simulation, it is not sufficient to "create a title in one who never owned the property." As Isabel was never listed as owner, she is out of luck:

> Because of the requirement that all transfers of immovable property be shown by a writing,
> parol evidence cannot be admitted to create a title in one who never owned the property or to
> show that the vendee was in reality some other person than the person named in the act of sale.[5]

The following case involves a written agreement to purchase an immovable, but this time the issue is whether an agreement to cancel the forthcoming agreement must itself be in writing or whether parol evidence may be admitted to show an oral cancellation.

---

5 Peter S. Title, 1 La. Prac. Real Estate §729 (2ⁿᵈ ed.).

FRANK V. MOTWANI 1987

513 SO. 2D 1170 (LA.)

MARCUS, Justice.

¶1 This lawsuit involves an agreement to purchase or sell real estate. On May 9, 1983, Verhomal Motwani (purchaser) offered to purchase a piece of property located at 620 South Peters Street in the City of New Orleans for the sum of $690,000. The owners, C.W. Frank, Jr., P.L. Frank, Sr., Muriel S. Hochstein, Ann Hochstein and Lynn Hochstein (sellers), accepted the offer by signing the agreement. The agreement provided that upon acceptance of the offer, purchaser was obligated to deposit with sellers' agent ten percent of the purchase price amounting to $69,000. The deposit of $69,000 was to be made as follows:

> 1) C.D. in a Metropolitan Area Bank (FDIC insured) in the amount of $50,000.00, said certificate to be in the joint names of purchaser and C.W. Frank Jr. (representing the sellers). All interest earned to belong to purchaser.

> 2) $19,000.00 to be represented by non-negotiable demand note due at act of sale executed by purchaser to the order of C.W. Frank, Jr.

¶2 The agreement further provided that:

> [F]ailure to do so shall not void this agreement but shall be considered as a breach thereof and seller shall have the right, at his option, to demand liquidated damages equal to the amount of the deposit or specific performance, and purchaser shall, in either event, be liable for agent's commission, attorney's fees and costs.

¶3 The demand note was executed May 9, 1983 (the date the agreement was signed) and delivered to sellers' agent. [On May 11, 1983, defendant buyer issued a check in the amount of $50,000 . . . so that a certificate of deposit could be purchased pursuant to the agreement to purchase or sell.] The events that occurred on the following day, May 12, 1983, are in dispute. Purchaser alleges that the agreement . . . was verbally (sic) cancelled by agreement of all the parties. Sellers allege that there was no such verbal cancellation but that purchaser placed a stop payment order on the $50,000 check and that the remainder of the deposit was never made. Sellers wrote purchaser on May 12, 1983, placing him in default.

¶4 In June 1983, sellers filed suit against purchaser alleging breach of the agreement and demanding liquidated damages in an amount equal to the deposit, plus attorney fees and costs.

After limited discovery, sellers filed a motion for summary judgment contending that there was no genuine issue of material fact because an agreement that has to be in writing to be valid cannot be cancelled verbally. After a hearing, the trial judge held that a verbal cancellation was not a viable defense as a matter of law and rendered summary judgment in favor of sellers and against purchaser in the amount of $69,000 plus attorney fees, interest and costs. The court of appeal affirmed, stating that evidence of "defendant's claim of an oral agreement to cancel the written purchase agreement is not admissible." On purchaser's application, we granted certiorari to review the correctness of that decision.

***

¶5   It is well-settled law that a transfer of immovable property must be in writing. Louisiana Civil Code Article 1839 states: "A transfer of immovable property must be made by authentic act or by act under private signature." It is also well settled that a promise or an agreement to sell immovable property may not be enforced unless it is in writing. La. Civ. Code art. 2462; Kaplan v. University Lake Corp., 381 So.2d 385 (La.1979); Quarles v. Lewis, 219 La. 194, 52 So.2d 713 (1951); Conklin v. Caffall, 189 La. 301, 179 So. 434 (1938).

¶6   La. Civ. Code art. 1848 provides:

> Testimonial or other evidence may not be admitted to negate or vary the contents of an authentic act or an act under private signature. Nevertheless, in the interest of justice, that evidence may be admitted to prove such circumstances as a vice of consent, or a simulation, or to prove that the written act was modified by a subsequent and valid oral agreement.

> [Emphasis added.]

¶7   This article deals with the situation where a party to a written contract is trying to prove that the contract exists but differently from the way it is written. In other words, it addresses the question of whether parol evidence may be used to prove a verbal modification of a contract. It does not address the question of whether parol evidence may be used to prove a verbal cancellation of a contract. Therefore, art. 1848 does not apply here because this case only involves an alleged verbal cancellation, not a modification.

¶8   Written contracts may be revoked or cancelled by the mutual consent of the parties. La. Civ. Code art. 1901 (1870) provides:

> Agreements legally entered into have the effect of laws on those who have formed them.

They cannot be revoked, unless by mutual consent of the parties, or for causes acknowledged by law.

They must be performed with good faith.

¶9 Article 1901 does not indicate how the parties' mutual consent is to be effected.

* * *

¶10 There is no reason why a party to a contract that has to be in writing should not be able to offer evidence that the parties verbally agreed to cancel the contract. Clearly, the burden of proof will be on the party asserting that it was cancelled. La. Civ. Code art. 1831. Although this may very well be a difficult burden to meet in the face of a signed written contract, the party claiming cancellation should be allowed to present evidence to prove that the contract was verbally cancelled.

¶11 Accordingly, we conclude that a writing is not required to cancel a contract which has to be in writing to be valid. Therefore, the court of appeal erred in affirming the summary judgment. There is a genuine issue as to whether or not there was a verbal cancellation of the agreement to purchase or sell.

DECREE

¶12 For the reasons assigned, the judgment of the court of appeal affirming the summary judgment granted by the district court is reversed. The motion for summary judgment . . . is denied. The case is remanded to the district court for further proceedings in accordance with law.

LEMMON, Justice, concurring.

¶1 A contract to sell immovable property must be in writing to be enforceable. La.C.C. art. 2462. The question here is whether a contract to extinguish or modify a previous contract to sell immovable property must also be in writing to be enforceable.

¶2 In the case of a modification which changes the terms of the original contract, the answer depends on whether the modification (modifying the previous contract to sell immovable property) would be required to be in writing if it were the original contract. For example, when a contract calls for the sale of two lots of ground, a modification to call for the sale of three lots must be in writing to be enforceable because an original contract calling for the sale of the third lot would not have been enforceable unless in writing. The modification constitutes a contract to sell immovable property.

¶3 However, in the case of a later contract which extinguishes a previous contract to sell immovable property, the later contract (extinguishing the obligation) need not be in writing because it does not constitute an agreement to sell immovable property. There is no codal or statutory requirement that a contract extinguishing an obligation to sell immovable property be in writing. Article 2462's oblique incorporation of a parol evidence rule only requires a contract to sell (not a contract to extinguish a contract to sell) to be in writing to be enforceable.

Study Question:

The previous cases discuss when the parol evidence rule excludes oral testimony concerning the purported sale of an immovable, and provide two instances when it does not: 1. If the oral testimony establishes the previous existence of a writing, 2. If the oral testimony is being used to establish that a contract to sell was extinguished (i.e. "the written act was modified by a subsequent and valid oral agreement, Art. 1848). What does the following case illustrate about another of the exceptions to the parol evidence rule listed in Article 1848: "may be admitted to prove such circumstances as a vice of consent, or a simulation . . . ."

MATHEWS V. MATHEWS 2008
1 SO. 3D 738, (LA. APP. 2D CIR.)

CARAWAY, J.

¶1 This action concerns a family dispute between two brothers over their mother's tract of land. In 1996, the mother executed an act of sale to one son, now a defendant. The defendant admits that no price was paid for the property and no sale occurred, but he defends the action claiming that a disguised donation was intended by his mother. In 1999, the mother made a second transfer of the property to the other son, the plaintiff, which she executed in the form of a donation. The plaintiff now claims that the 1996 sale to his brother was an absolute nullity and that a subsequent donation of a portion of the land by his brother to their cousin, [Charles "Rusty" Gilbert], also a defendant, should likewise be annulled. The trial court determined that the 1996 sale transaction was a disguised donation and ruled in favor of the defendants. Finding manifest error in the ruling, we reverse.

Facts and Procedural History

¶2 The land in question consists of 51 acres (hereinafter the "Farm") and was acquired by Lavada Gilbert Mathews, wife of Alfred Mathews, Sr., in 1971. This parcel, and the Mathews' house in the Town of Hodge, were described as community property in Mr. Mathews' succession in 1980. The judgment of possession recognized his widow, Lavada, as the surviving spouse in community, the owner of her undivided one-half interest in the community and usufructuary. Their two children, Alfred and Emmett [plaintiff and defendant, respectively], were recognized as the sole heirs and naked owners of the property, subject to their mother's usufruct.

***

¶3 The disputed Sale of the Farm occurred on January 22, 1996 and was executed on a cash sale deed by both Mrs. Mathews and Emmett as an authentic act. The price was recited in the instrument as $2,000 "and other good and valuable consideration." Acting as the notary for the Sale was Bobby L. Culpepper, an attorney who testified as a witness in the trial of this case. Emmett has now stipulated that the price was not paid to his mother and the Sale was simulated. However, he asserts that the transaction was in actuality a relative simulation or disguised sale in which his mother intended to donate the Farm to him.

¶4 Following the Sale, and Emmett's donation to Rusty on June 15, 1998, Emmett and Rusty partitioned the Farm into two tracts. Rusty testified that he grew up in the house on the Farm and also lived at his Aunt Lavada's house with his grandmother (Mrs. Mathews' mother) after his father died at a young age. The northerly portion consisting of 26.5 acres was acquired by Emmett, and the southerly portion with a dilapidated farmhouse containing 24.5 acres, went to Rusty.

¶5 One month prior to this partition between Emmett and Rusty, a Ruston attorney representing Mrs. Mathews wrote a letter to Emmett under the caption, "Suit to set aside deed." Threatening legal action by Mrs. Mathews, the May 19, 1998, letter states:

> Mr. Mathews, there are actually two separate matters with which we are dealing, the invalid
> deed by your mother and the interest your brother has in the inherited property. Further, there
> are complications that have arisen with your purported donation and lease. If suit is filed, there
> will be other parties who will have to be brought into the proceedings, all of which will lead to
> great cost, financial and otherwise, on the part of many, including yourself.

¶6 At the latest visit you had with your mother, you indicated that you were "going to clear things up shortly;" however, nothing has happened.

¶7 This letter, which was copied to Lavada and Alfred, was filed into evidence at trial.

¶8 On December 8, 1999, Mrs. Mathews executed an Act of Donation purportedly donating a full ownership interest in the Farm to Alfred by an authentic act of donation passed before Culpepper. Alfred had appeared before a Delaware notary public and two witnesses and signed the instrument accepting the donation six days earlier, on December 2, 1999. The donation was filed in Jackson Parish on December 13, 1999, the same day Alfred brought this action against Emmett and Rusty to nullify the 1996 Sale, the 1997 donation to Rusty and the 1998 partition of the Farm.

¶9 On May 26, 2000, Mrs. Mathews executed a revocation of her donation of the Farm to Alfred. Emmett testified that he accompanied his mother to Culpepper's office, where Culpepper notarized the revocation of the donation to Alfred on the following grounds:

> Donor made said donation to Donee at Donee's insistence and for the consideration that Donee would not file litigation against his brother, Emmett A. Mathews. When in fact, Donee did the opposite after the donation was secured by Donee as per suit filed in the records of Jackson Parish, Louisiana, styled "Alfred L. Mathews v. Emmett A. Mathews, et al, No. 27,575 " records of Jackson Parish, Louisiana all of which constitutes cruel treatment as per Louisiana Civil Code Article 1560.

¶10 In spite of Mrs. Mathews's inter vivos donation to Alfred, his petition prayed that ownership of the Farm be recognized in his mother upon nullification of the Sale to Emmett.

¶11 In June 2000, Mrs. Mathews, then age 91, gave her deposition in this case at Pine Hill Nursing Home. She testified as follows concerning the 1996 deed:

Q. Did you know that you sold the farm to Emmett?

A. No, I didn't sell it.

Q. In [the deed]?

A. I didn't sell it.

Q. At the top it says cash sale deed. It says this sale is made for the consideration of two thousand dollars cash in hand paid.

A. Well, it wasn't paid.

***

Q. Mrs. Mathews if you will refer to [the deed], which is this document here. By signing [the deed], did you intend, what did you intend?

A. All I know, I want them to have their parts, their equal part, I wasn't trying to beat them out of nothing.

Q. When you say their equal part, you're referring to Emmett, Al & Rusty?

A. Yes.

* * *

¶12 Mrs. Lavada Mathews died on February 18, 2001.

¶13 [After her death, at the trial, the remaining parties testified, including attorney Culpepper.], Culpepper stated that he "knew Lavada well." He prepared the 1996 Sale pursuant to her instructions and acted as the notary for that instrument and other later transactions which affected the property. Culpepper testified as follows:

Q. Okay. Uh-at whose request did you prepare that deed?

A. Well the parties came in the office, Mrs. Mathews and Emmett Mathews came into my office.

Q. Okay. And what did Mrs. Mathews ask you to do?

A. There was some problem going on somewhere I don't remember what it was, but she said she wanted to give this property to Mr. Mathews, to her son, I believe.

Q. Okay, that was Emmett?

A. Emmett, whoever Emmett is.

Q. Okay. And did you counsel with her as to how she should do that?

A. She wanted it done in the form of a cash sale deed although there was no money was changed hands. She was donating it to him but then she had in her idea that she wanted it done like this and I explained to her that this would actually be a donation in disguise. But I did it the way she wanted it prepared.

¶14   In his testimony, Emmett stated as follows:

[I]n '96 I assumed possession of it [the Farm] and in order to relieve her of any cost insurance wise and maintenance wise to help her financially and to attempt to more or less keep the farm in the name of Gilbert and Mathews and in a complete packet of 51 acres to be descended down to future relatives.

¶15   According to his testimony, Emmett thought he was to pay his mother $2,000 when the 1996 deed was executed, but she refused it. Thereafter, he paid the taxes and "made sure somebody was living on the farm." The evidence indicates that in 1996, Emmett was not living in Louisiana. Emmett testified he leased the farmhouse to his cousin, Lonnie Ray Clark, who was already living there previously.

¶16   The trial court [found] that Emmett A. Mathews owned the 26.5-acre tract and Rusty and his wife owned the 24.5 acre tract previously partitioned, together comprising the Farm. The trial court [also found that] "the testimony of Bobby Culpepper was crucial showing donative intent of Lavada Gilbert Mathews," and found that defendants established that the 1996 deed was thus valid as a disguised donation. The trial court discounted Mrs. Mathews' deposition testimony, stating:

In examining Mrs. Lavada Gilbert Mathews' deposition, it becomes obvious that she didn't want to be there. In fact a letter from her Doctor is attached to the deposition indicating it would be detrimental to her health to participate. Alfred Mathews, Jr. and Rusty Gilbert were present at the deposition which may have made her uncomfortable about her testimony in her deposition. Her age, agitation for being involved, presence of parties plaintiff and defendant, and the fact that the transaction in question occurred more than four years ago, indicates to the Court that her deposition testimony as to her intent in the Act of Sale is of little value.

¶17   The trial court judgment declaring defendants the respective owners of the two tracts was signed on March 6, 2008. Alfred appeals the judgment.

Discussion

¶18 The Civil Code defines a simulation as follows:

> A contract is a simulation when, by mutual agreement, it does not express the true intent of the parties.

¶19 If the true intent of the parties is expressed in a separate writing, that writing is a counterletter.

> La. C.C. art. 2025.

¶20 The simulation can be a feigned or pretended sale clothed in the formalities of a valid sale. Russell v. Culpepper, 344 So.2d 1372, 1377 (La.1977).

¶21 The Civil Code defines two types of simulations. Article 2026 provides:

> A simulation is absolute when the parties intend that their contract shall produce no effects between them. That simulation, therefore, can have no effects between the parties.

¶22 This contrasts with a relative simulation, where the parties intend that their contract produce effects between them which are different from those recited in their contract. La. C.C. art. 2027.

¶23 The Civil Code's writing requirement for the sale or transfer of immovable property states that "an authentic act" or "act under private signature" must be executed by the parties. La. C.C. arts. 1839 and 2440. Article 1839 places that requirement in the chapter on "Proof of Obligations" and is followed in that same chapter by Louisiana's parol evidence rule, Article 1848, which provides:

> Testimonial or other evidence may not be admitted to negate or vary the contents of an authentic act or an act under private signature. Nevertheless, in the interest of justice, that evidence may be admitted to prove such circumstances as a vice of consent, or a simulation, or to prove that the written act was modified by a subsequent and valid oral agreement.

¶24 As recognized in the jurisprudence before the addition of the new exception for simulations in Article 1848, another basis for the allowance of parol/extrinsic evidence to resolve a dispute between the parties to a relative simulation is the Civil Code's provision concerning an untrue expression of cause. Article 1970 states the principle as follows:

When the expression of a cause in a contractual obligation is untrue, the obligation is still effective if a valid cause can be shown.

¶25   The jurisprudence allowed that "the motive or real consideration can always be established by parol evidence," and that "the cause of a contract is always open to proof explanatory of its nature, as between the parties." Love v. Dedon, 239 La. 109, 118 So.2d 122 (1960).

¶26   The jurisprudence has allowed the consideration of extrinsic evidence for the determination of a disguised donation made in the form of a written sale of an immovable where no price was paid. See, Moore v. Wilson, 34,135 (La.App. 2d Cir.11/3/00), 772 So.2d 373 (deed stating nominal consideration in authentic form was invalid as disguised donation because evidence failed to establish grantor's donative intent); Nofsinger v. Hinchee, 199 So. 597 (La.App.1941) (deed conveying interest in family farm for a stated price of $1,000 was upheld as a valid donation when executed as an authentic act and with extrinsic evidence showing intent); Wood v. Martin, 2 So.2d 665 (La.App.1941) (authentic act of sale reciting nominal consideration invalid as donation because donee failed to accept donation and did not possess the property); Reinerth v. Rhody, 52 La. Ann.2029, 28 So. 277 (1900) (deed transferring immovable for $1.00, valid as a donation).

***

¶27   The Civil Code addresses in general the required consent for a contract in Article 1927, providing that a contract is formed by the consent of the parties established through offer and acceptance. Consent may be vitiated by error. La. C.C. art. 1948. For a valid contract, the court must find that there was a meeting of the minds of the parties to constitute consent. Hanger One MLU, Inc. v. Unopened Succession of Rogers, 43,120 (La.App. 2d Cir.4/16/08), 981 So.2d 175. The existence or nonexistence of a contract is a question of fact which will not be disturbed by the appellate court unless clearly wrong. Id.

¶28   In this case, Emmett conceded that the disputed written transaction was never completed as a sale and that no price was ever paid. He therefore had the burden to prove the parties' mutual intent to give the written act of sale some other legal effect resulting in a valid transfer of the ownership of the Farm. Emmett's reconventional demand asserted that the transaction was a disguised donation. Such transaction would be a relative simulation, which by definition would require a showing of the "mutual agreement" between his mother and himself. La. C.C. art. 2025. The fact that both immovable property and an inter vivos donation are involved implicates the important formalities required by our law for the transfer of immovables and the manifestation of donative intent and the donee's acceptance. La. C.C. arts. 1536 and 1839.

Nevertheless, Civil Code Article 1848 allows that a court "may" admit for consideration "in the interest of justice," testimonial and other evidence to negate the written act of sale and establish it instead as a simulation.

¶29 The trial court's ruling ultimately rested on the testimony of the attorney who notarized the authentic act of sale. We believe that the starting point for consideration of the parties' "mutual agreement" for the alleged disguised donation must be with the parties themselves. With this perspective, the trial court's written ruling significantly did not consider Emmett's testimony concerning his understanding of the transaction.

¶30 In his testimony, Emmett was shown the 1996 Sale and questioned by his counsel, as follows:

Q. All right. Now so you have admitted that you didn't pay your mother for the property?

A. Right.

Q. Is that correct?

A. Yes.

Q. Did she ask for payment?

A. No.

Q. Did you-uh-at the time of that document did you understand that you were not to pay her?

A. No, I did not. I understood I was to pay her. But she refused it. She said there would be no money paid.

¶31 Later, on cross examination, Emmett was asked if he understood what his mother wanted. He indicated that he understood that she wanted the property to be kept intact, and that the three, Rusty, Charles, and himself, would divide the benefits. He testified that he tried to do that, and when asked how, responded:

A. I attempted to bring my brother, Alfred, into the use of the land by either cutting the timber or farming it or whatever, research to be utilized and we'd spread the profits or pay the cost or whatever. We'd set it up as an agreement between he and I with Rusty being the beneficiary in the event that down the road we deceased and he would get the property in total. Rusty would - Charles R. Gilbert would get the property in total.

* * *

¶32 This last, somewhat puzzling comment concerning Emmett's attempt to "spread the profits" with Alfred was not further elaborated upon by either Emmett or Alfred. Nevertheless, in his testimony, Emmett depicts his role as one who "assumed possession" of the Farm "to attempt to more or less keep the farm" as a caretaker for his mother and to foster some ultimate sharing of the ownership between the Mathews and Gilbert families.

¶33 This evidence reveals that at the time of the Sale in 1996, Emmett did not understand that his mother was donating the complete and irrevocable ownership of the Farm to him. He did not know his mother's motive for not selling the property to him and choosing the language in the written act which ultimately proved untrue when she declined payment. He did not know that he was a donee of the Farm since he expected to pay a price.

¶34 This lack of a mutual understanding by the parties at the time of the execution of the Sale is also consequential for determining Emmett's acceptance of the donation in 1996 or thereafter as a donee before his mother's death. Though his signature is on the cash sale deed form, the Sale obviously does not express language of his acceptance of the property as a donee. From his testimony, he said he "understood I was to pay her." **The contract of donation, even a disguised donation, is formed by the donee's acceptance "in precise terms."** La. C.C. art. 1540 (emphasis added). Additionally, we find in the record no clear evidence of Emmett's corporeal possession by his physical acts on the property after 1996 which shows the tacit acceptance of the alleged donation permitted under Civil Code Article 1541. See, La. C.C. art. 3425.

¶35 Turning to consideration of Mrs. Mathews' expressions of her intentions for the Sale, there is significant evidence apart from her deposition testimony and before the litigation began. That evidence indicates that she did not intend a complete and irrevocable transfer of the Farm to Emmett which, under the definition of a donation inter vivos, is the essence of a gratuitous conveyance. La. C.C. art. 1468. In 1998, her attorney threatened suit against Emmett over "the invalid deed." In 1999, she executed an instrument purporting to donate the entirety of the ownership of the Farm to Alfred. These acts clearly imply that the prior Sale was not intended to transfer the ownership of the Farm irrevocably to Emmett, and since all agree that her written act of sale was not in fact a sale, she demonstrated by these actions that she likewise had no donative intent to transfer the Farm to Emmett.

¶36 With those adverse actions on her part already established by the evidence, her deposition testimony following the filing of this suit confirms that no sale was intended between her and her son, and that she had a motive for something other than a donation of complete and irrevocable ownership to Emmett as her donee. In fact, when she was directly asked whether she donated the Farm to Emmett, she denied a donation.

* * *

¶37 Mrs. Mathews's ambivalence and Emmett's intentions for a purchase do not demonstrate to us that at the time of the execution of the written act of sale in 1996, the parties shared a mutual intent and agreement for a donation of the Farm's ownership to Emmett. Their transaction, which our law requires in writing to transfer the immovable and, more importantly, as an authentic act to insure the proper written expression of the donative intent, should not be recognized as a donation of this immovable under these extrinsic circumstances which do not show mutuality of the parties' intentions.

* * *

¶38 Accordingly, finding manifest error in the trial court's ruling, we do not find that Emmett sustained his burden of proving that he and his mother intended a relative simulation or disguised donation by the 1996 Sale. We find that there was no showing of a meeting of the minds of the parties to constitute their mutual consent for a donation. Therefore, the 1996 Sale is an absolute nullity. Furthermore, according to our initial ruling in Mathews I, supra, defendant, Charles R. Gilbert, was not a protected third party and is therefore also subject to the determination of absolute nullity of the Sale. The subsequent acts between Emmett and Rusty affecting the property are likewise annulled.

Conclusion

¶39 For the above reasons, the judgment of the trial court is reversed. The 1996 Sale and the subsequent acts affecting the property executed between the defendants are annulled. Costs of the appeal are assessed to appellees.

Lagniappe Question:

The Second Circuit reversed the trial court's decision for Alfred. Who now owns the Farm? Do you think this decision is in keeping with the wishes of Lavada Mathews, Alfred and Emmett's mother?

Comment:

Shortly before Mathews v. Mathews was issued (in fact, only two weeks before), the Second Circuit said the following about the 1984 Revision to Article 1848 in Sonnier v. Conner, 998 So.2d 344, 353 (La. App. 2 Cir. 12/3/08), a similar family dispute over a purported simulated transfer of an immovable:

> "Although a simulation in many instances is intended to operate as a fraud on one's creditors or to impair the rights of forced heirs, that need not be the case. As Planiol observed, "a person can have honest reasons for concealing from third persons the veritable nature of his transactions and the state of his affairs, but this is rare." 2 M. Planiol, Traité élémentaire de droit civil, no. 1190 (11th ed. La. State L. Inst. transl.1959). However, regardless of the motive concerning one's creditors or forced heirs, or any other fraudulent motive giving rise to the simulation, disputes sometime arise thereafter between the parties to a simulation when the one receiving the simulated transfer refuses to later acknowledge the simulation.

> ***

> "Prior to 1984, jurisprudential exceptions to the parol evidence rule had developed, even with regard to transactions involving immovables. In 1984, as a new codal addition to the parol evidence rule, express exceptions to the general rule prohibiting parol evidence were set forth. The legislature added these exceptions in the second sentence and included the allowance for proof of a simulation. Revision Comment (c) indicates that "simulation" as used in Article 1848 refers to either the absolute or relative simulation.

> "The exception regarding simulations under Article 1848 contains no limitation that the parol/extrinsic evidence may only be offered by an heir or creditor of the vendor to attack the simulated sale or transfer of property. Thus, it indicates that either party to a simulation may prove the true intent of the parties to the transaction by oral/extrinsic evidence. The exception regarding simulations likewise does not expressly turn on the important fact of the continued possession of the transferor which in the case of immovables, might be considered a prerequisite before any written act transferring an immovable can be challenged. As reviewed below, continued corporeal possession by a seller is the predicate fact for the presumption of simulation addressed in Article 2480.

> "This exception for simulations under Article 1848 indicates that for proof of the true intent of the parties that is not reflected on the sham written act, "testimonial or other evidence" may now be admitted as between the parties to "negate" the simulated act. In the context of an absolute

simulation of a sale of an immovable, the purported transferor/seller would not be offering such evidence to prove an oral transfer of the property back to him. He would be offering the evidence to show that the prior written act of sale did not reflect the parties' true intent to their "mutual agreement" for the simulation. La. C.C. art. 2025. As such, the exception for simulations now allowed in the second sentence of Article 1848 is analogous to another exception also listed in the article, the exception for vices of consent."

Study Question:

Article 1540 (on acceptance of a donation inter vivos) was replaced in 2008 with Article 1544:

A donation inter vivos is without effect util it is accepted by the done. The acceptance shall be made during the lifetime of the donor.

The acceptance of a donation may be made in the act of donation or subsequently in writing.

When the donee is put into corporeal possession of a movable by the donor, possession by the done also constitutes acceptance of the donation."

Would Mathews v. Mathews be decided the same way under current law?

Section 3. Sufficiency of Description

While the Civil Code states that the sale of an immovable must be in writing, it does not state what that writing must contain. Consequently, some requirements have developed through the jurisprudence.

To prove a sale, the writing should indicate the thing, the price, and the consent of the parties. Thus, it should address each element of the contract of sale. Consent is generally demonstrated by the parties' signatures. Nevertheless, as indicated in Comment (b) to Article 1838, the writing may be valid even though it is signed by only one party, if the party who signed it asserts the validity of the contract contained in the writing against a party who did not sign it, but whose conduct reveals that he availed himself of it. Consequently, a transfer of immovable property in return for the transferee's assumption of a mortgage was held enforceable against a transferee who had not signed the act of transfer, but who had later granted a mineral lease on the property transferred. Succession of Jenkins v. Dykes, 91 So. 2d 416 (La. App. 2d Cir. 1956). In addition to one or both signatures indicating consent, the writing must indicate a price and describe the immovable.

Whether or not a description is sufficient has been the issue in a number of cases. Because the property description is "an integral part of a sale," it must be contained in the writing. "A description of immovable property in an act of sale is sufficient if it enables a person to locate and identify the property." Thus, as long as the description identifies the property, it will be considered sufficient even if it is incomplete and needs to be supplemented by additional evidence, whether parol or written, to locate it precisely.[6]

Study Questions:

How, exactly, does the writing at issue in the following classic case describe the property? Was the description sufficient? (Consider both the parol evidence rule and the question of sufficiency of description.)

LEMOINE V. LACOUR 1948
213 LA. 109, 34 SO. 2D 392 (LA.)

HAMITER, Justice.

¶1 The main demand of plaintiff herein is for specific performance to compel the defendants to make formal conveyance of a one-acre parcel of land, with improvements thereon, located in Rapides Parish.

¶2 He alleges that defendants agreed verbally, during the first part of July, 1944, to sell the property to him for the sum of $350, payable in ten monthly installments of $35 each; that he made nine of the monthly payments, as is fully shown by the receipts therefor attached to the petition, and that the tenth payment, which was tendered to defendants but by them declined, has been deposited in the registry of the court; and that defendants have refused to give him a deed to the property, notwithstanding he has fully complied with the agreement.

¶3 Plaintiff prays that defendants be ordered and commanded to execute an appropriate deed. Alternatively, he asks judgment for all sums expended by him in connection with the property.

¶4 Defendants excepted to the petition as stating no cause of action. The exception was sustained by the district court, and the suit dismissed, as to the demand for specific performance; it was overruled as to the alternative or money demand. On appeal to the Court of Appeal the

---

6   24 Louisiana Civil Law Treatise §6:10

judgment was affirmed. The case is presently before us on a writ of certiorari or review granted on plaintiff's application.

¶5 The Court of Appeal, as well as the district court, correctly concluded that the petition in its present form states no cause of action. Plaintiff expressly alleges that the agreement of sale, under which he seeks specific performance was verbal. Civil Code Article 2440, states:

'All sales of immovable property shall be made by authentic act or under private signature.

'Except as provided in Article 2275, every verbal sale of immovables shall be null, as well for third persons as for the contracting parties themselves, and the testimonial proof of it shall not be admitted.'

¶6 And there is nothing in the petition to bring the case within the provisions of the referred to Civil Code Article 2275 reading:

'Every transfer of immovable property must be in writing; but if a verbal sale, or other disposition of such property, be made, it shall be good against the vendor, as well as against the vendee, who confesses it when interrogated on oath, provided actual delivery has been made of the immovable property thus sold.'

¶7 There are nine receipts, of course, attached to and made a part of the petition, which the to be considered in passing upon the exception of no cause of action. All of them are identical, except for their respective dates, and recite:

'Received from Mr. Clifton Lemoine $35.00 for payment on place.
'W. L. Lacour
'C. P. Lemoine.'

¶8 Plaintiff's counsel contends that these receipts constitute written evidence of his contract of sale with the defendants and are sufficient to permit the introduction of parol testimony to identify the property. And in support of the contention he cites Saunders v. Bolden, 155 La. 136, 98 So. 867, Guice et al. v. Mason et al., 156 La. 201, 100 So. 397, 398, and Walker v. Ferchaud et al., 210 La. 283, 26 So.2d 746, 747. The cited cases are not appropriate here. In each of them the writing relied on contained a substantial description of the affected property. Thus in the Saunders case the property was described as the 'Judie Lewis place.' In Guice v. Mason the description was 'a certain 80-acre tract of land laying broadside with the 160-acre tract that he [vendee] now lives on' (brackets ours). And in Walker v. Ferchaud the contract of sale made reference to $124 Stella Street, on grounds measuring about 60 x 150, as per title.' In the instant case, however, each of the receipts merely evidences a 'payment on place;' it contains no description whatever of any property.

¶9   There is applicable here, we think, the doctrine of Kernan v. Baham, 45 La.Ann. 799, 13 So. 155, which was followed in Jackson v. Harris et al., Second Circuit, 18 La.App. 484, 136 So. 166, viz.:

> 'The writings which defendants present as establishing their title are not only insufficient per se for that purpose, but they are so defective as not to serve as a basis upon which a title could be built up or eked out by parol. The declaration that the promissory note was given as 'the price of certain lands in the parish of St. Tammany' is entirely too general to justify the admission of parol evidence to establish possession of particular property by the party named in the instrument as the vendee, and from such possession to assume or infer it to be that referred to in the writing. Parol evidence to establish identity is allowable, as is likewise parol evidence of possession, in aid of a defective or ambiguous description; but this is only in cases where there is a sufficient body in the description to leave the title substantially resting on writing, and not essentially on parol, as it would have to rest, if at all, in the case at bar. [45 La.Ann. 799, 13 So. 159.]'

¶10   But it is our opinion that the Court of Appeal, as well as the district court, after concluding that the petition stated no cause of action, should have granted to plaintiff (as he requested in the alternative) permission to supplement his pleadings and to interrogate defendants on oath regarding the verbal sale, pursuant to the provisions of Civil Code Article 2275. Plaintiff has already alleged that immediately after entering into the contract of sale he moved on to the property and that he has lived there continuously since that time. If he can show also that the defendants, in their answers to interrogatories on facts and articles, have confessed the existence of the asserted agreement, clearly his petition will state a cause of action.

***

¶11   For the reasons assigned the judgments of the Court of Appeal and of the district court, which dismissed plaintiff's suit as to his demand for specific performance, are amended to the extent of reserving to plaintiff the right to supplement his pleadings in the manner above indicated so as to state a cause of action; and the case is remanded to the district court for further proceedings according to law and not inconsistent with the views herein expressed.

Comment:

Generally, if a writing identifies the particular property intended to be conveyed, it will be held sufficient even though the description is incomplete. A writing is insufficient if parol evidence is required to identify the property, even though an intent to transfer is clearly indicated.

The following descriptions have been held to be sufficient to identify the immovable sold:

'Prudhomme Place; 'a certain 80-acre tract of land laying broadside with the 160-acre tract that he now lives on,'

'124 Stella Street, on grounds measuring about 60x150 as per title,' and

'all my land in Lafourche Parish.'

The supreme court has stated several times that the description of a residence or plantation by name and locality is sufficient, though additional evidence is necessary to complete the description.

In contrast, the following have been held insufficient to identify the immovable allegedly being sold:

'Received from Mr. Clifton Lemoine $35,000 for payment on place,'

a declaration on a note that it was given as 'the price of certain lands in the Parish of St. Tammany,' and

'Received from Archie Jackson in full payment of land ($600) Six Hundred Dollars.'

Also insufficient were

"100 feet off of the west end,"

"Property #137 — Gilliam, Louisiana — Vacant Land 21 acres — call for directions.," and

a purchase agreement that did not identify the specific condominiums that were to be sold.[7]

Furthermore, a perfect description of the wrong property cannot be cured.[8]

---

7   Wheeler v. Carber, 2012 WL 3526786 (M.D. La. 2012)(unpublished).

8   24 Louisiana Civil Code Treatise §6:10.

While an omnibus description like the ones listed in the previous paragraph is not sufficient to give third parties notice of the transfer of an immovable, as between the parties, however, such a description will transfer the intended property as effectively as if it had been specifically described. For example, in Noel v. Noel, 312 So.2d 134 (La. App. 1st Cir. 1975), the court held that because the co-owners of an immovable had conveyed their interest to the defendant, they were not third parties and therefore could not assert that the sale was invalid on the basis of an insufficient description. In contrast, however, a similar description in a lease was not binding on a third party because it was insufficient. United Gas Pub. Sev. Co. v. Mitchell, 188 La. 651, 177 So. 2d 697 (1947).

Section 4. Mandate and other Ancillary Contracts

Not only must the sale of an immovable be in writing, so must any ancillary contract that relates to the sale of an immovable, such as a contract to sell in Article 2623, an option in Article 2620, a right of first refusal in Article 2625 (or the sale of mineral rights)

In several places in the Civil Code, the writing requirement is referenced, but not perhaps as directly as one might expect. Article 2993 provides one such example:

"The contract of mandate is not required to be in any particular form.

"Nevertheless, when the law prescribes a certain form for an act, a mandate authorizing the act must be in that form."

HOLMES & SYMEONIDES, REPRESENTATION, MANDATE, AND AGENCY:

A KOMMENTAR ON LOUISIANA'S NEW LAW

73 TUL. L. REV. 1087, 1122-26 (1999).

a. Form and "Equal Dignity"

The comments to article 2993 aver that it "reproduces the substance of Article 2992 of the Louisiana Civil Code of 1870." This is true of the first sentence of the new article, which indeed is essentially the equivalent of former article 2992. The second sentence of the new article, however, enunciates a substantive rule which has no counterpart in the former code articles, although it is firmly grounded in the jurisprudence. According to this jurisprudence, whenever the extrinsic law demands that an act be in a certain form, the authority of a mandatary to consummate that act for his principal must be in the same form. That rule in turn is similar, but not identical, to an early common-law agency doctrine, the "equal dignity rule," which required an agent's authority to execute an instrument to be in writing, if the instrument itself was required to be in writing.

While the general principle espoused by the second sentence has been recognized in a long line of opinions, the Louisiana Supreme Court most recently addressed it in Tedesco v. Gentry Development, Inc., 540 So. 2d 960 (La. 1989). In Tedesco, the plaintiffs entered into a written contract to purchase immovable property from the defendant corporation, signed by the corporation's president. The court held that the contract was unenforceable because the president had no written authority to sell the property. In so doing, the court refused to distinguish between actual and apparent authority; in the court's words, "[j]ust as testimonial proof cannot be used to prove the sale of immovable property (or the agreement to sell such property), testimonial proof cannot be used to prove the agent's authority to execute the contract, whether that authority was actual or apparent."

***

In that regard, it is also important to note that the rule of article 2993 is contrary to that of the modern common law. Under the early common law, it was clear that, for instruments required to be under seal, sealed authority of an agent was generally likewise required. The significance of the seal, however, has generally been abolished. Thus, in common law states, unless there is a specific statute requiring written authorization of certain transactions, written authority is not necessary for the execution of a writing. Simply put, the "equal dignity rule" no longer generally obtains under modern common law doctrine. In this respect, then, the revision does not move Louisiana law towards the national commercial mainstream. Instead it arguably creates a minefield, especially for out-of-state lawyers.

b. Application of the Rule

The comments to article 2993 offer two examples of the application of the rule as to form. First, because donations must be by authentic act, a mandate authorizing a mandatary to make a donation must also be by authentic act. Second, because an act of compromise must be written, a mandate authorizing a mandatary to execute a compromise must likewise be in writing.

As the foregoing discussion illustrates, however, the choice of these examples may have the unfortunate effect of obscuring the area in which the rule of form has been clearly the most important, which are transactions in immovable property.

Study Question:

In addition to article 2993 on mandate, how do Articles 2299-2305 on Payment of a Thing Not Owed apply to the following case?

TRIANGLE FARMS, INC. V. HARVEY 1934
178 LA. 559, 152 SO. 124 (LA.)

BRUNOT, Justice.

¶1   This is a petitory action coupled with an injunction. The defendant, in his answer, alleges that he is in possession of the property described in the petition without title thereto, but that he is holding under a written contract executed in his favor by the Sherburne Industries, Inc., with full written authority of the plaintiff, to sell to defendant the said land for $9,482.50, one-half of said price to be paid in ninety days from the date of the contract, and one-half thereof to be paid in five equal annual installments with 6 per cent. per annum interest thereon, to be represented by notes identified with the deed and mortgage reserved to secure their payment; that in compliance with his contractual obligations he paid the Sherburne Industries, Inc., $4,741.25 timely, but no deed to the property has been tendered him, and that the bringing of this suit is an active breach, and a judicial repudiation, of said contract.

¶2   The defendant expressly consents that the contract be rescinded, but, as plaintiff in reconvention, he prays for judgment against the plaintiff for $4,741, the one-half of the purchase price of the property paid by him to Sherburne Industries, Inc., with legal interest thereon from March 14, 1930, and for costs.

¶3   It is not necessary to state the incidental pleadings and rulings, for the reason that the only question presented for decision by this court is whether or not, under the established facts, the plaintiff in reconvention can recover from the Triangle Farms, Inc., the $4,741 he paid to the Sherburne Industries, Inc.

¶4   We have read the record carefully and concur in the finding of the trial judge that the Sherburne Industries, Inc., had no written contract of agency from the plaintiff to sell the land involved in this suit. Some parol testimony was introduced to show a verbal authorization to do so, but parol testimony cannot be received to establish an agency to sell land. R. C. C. art. 2992; Mumford v. McKinney, 21 La. Ann. 547. This testimony was doubtless admitted to prove that the plaintiff consented to, participated in, ratified or profited by, the contract, but the trial judge held, and our appreciation of the testimony leads us to the same conclusion, that the evidence fails to establish, with reasonable certainty, a single fact upon which a judgment against the plaintiff can be based.

¶5 This is a regrettable case. The defendant, like numberless victims of misplaced confidence, was led to the shambles and sheared by courteous and affable promoters, who thought little and cared less for the consequences which might follow in the wake of their activities.

¶6 The learned trial judge has written a carefully prepared opinion in which he has correctly resolved the facts and rendered judgment thereon in favor of the plaintiff as prayed for in its petition, and rejecting the demand of the defendant, as plaintiff in reconvention, all at defendant's cost.

¶7 The judgment is correct, and it is therefore affirmed at appellant's cost.

O'NIELL, C. J., and ROGERS and ODOM, JJ.,
are of the opinion that the defendant's reconventional demand should be dismissed as in case of nonsuit.

On Rehearing.

LAND, Justice.

¶1 In our original opinion the court said:

'We have read the record carefully and concur in the finding of the trial judge that the Sherburne Industries, Inc., had no written contract of agency from the plaintiff to sell the land involved in this suit. Some parol testimony was introduced to show a verbal authorization to do so, but parol testimony cannot be received to establish an agency to sell land. R. C. C. art. 2992; Mumford v. McKinney, 21 La. Ann. 547. This testimony was doubtless admitted to prove that the plaintiff consented to, participated in, ratified or profited by, the contract, but the trial judge held, and our appreciation of the testimony leads us to the same conclusion, that the evidence fails to establish, with reasonable certainty, a single fact upon which a judgment against the plaintiff can be based.'

***

¶2 It is well settled that parol testimony is inadmissible to establish an agency to sell land, and that defendant cannot establish title to the property in dispute by such proof. At the same time, parol testimony is, without doubt, admissible to show that plaintiff received the purchase price, or part of same, paid by defendant under a verbal agreement to sell, since defendant would have the clear right, under such state of facts, to recover the amount so paid.

¶3   Our former decree in this case rejected the demand of defendant, as plaintiff in reconvention, at his costs.

¶4   For the reasons assigned, it is ordered that our original decree be amended so as to dismiss the demand of defendant, as plaintiff in reconvention, as of nonsuit, at his costs; and, as thus amended, our original decree is reinstated and affirmed.

REVIEW NOTES

Section 1: Movables

No particular form is needed for the sale of corporeal movables, and because it has not adopted UCC-2 and is not a common law state, Louisiana does not have a writing requirement for a sale over $500 or even for one over $5000. The sale of incorporeal movables such as stocks, bonds, negotiable instruments is governed by law specific to each type, and is beyond the scope of this textbook.

Article 1846 stipulates that a contract not reduced to writing for a value less than or equal to $500 must be proven by competent evidence, and one over $500 must be proven by at least one witness and other corroborating circumstances.

Joyner v. Liprie

Dr. Joyner sued for breach of an oral agreement to form a joint venture to develop, market, and sell a device designed to clear coronary arteries by means of radiation. To prove the existence of the agreement, Joiner recounted how defendant Liprie approached him along with doctor Harrison in 1994. They, along with a Venezuelan cardiologist, met in Atlanta and an agreement was reached shortly thereafter. Liprie wanted him to lead a human trial of the procedure in Venezuela, and eventually to present a paper at the 1995 Annual Cardiologist's convention in New Orleans.

Joyner testified that the three men agreed that he and Dr. Harrison would each pay ½ of the expenses of the joint venture and ½ of a monthly salary to Liprie, and that Joyner would develop and publish the all-important article. In exchange, Joyner and Harrison would each receive 25% ownership in the venture. Liprie would retain 50% ownership and would supply all of the materials and intellectual property rights. Joyner went to Venezuela, conducted the trial, and wrote the paper.

Joyner also presented a subsequent letter discussing some sort of security Liprie subsequently said he wanted, and a later letter on the same topic. Joyner testified that Liprie's demands kept increasing the closer they got to the 'finish line' – the presentation and publication of the paper. In connection with these demands, Joyner sought funding from two possible sources, both of whom testified: Mr. Harter and Ms. Biwer, and Joyner presented a third letter sent by Liprie's attorney advising Joyner that he would no longer own 25% of the joint venture, and that the venture would be incorporated into a new entity, and offering him 5% of the new entity for an addition sum of $180,000.

The jury found for Dr. Joyner in the amount of $4.3 million in damages. The second circuit affirmed the award.

Parol Evidence Rule

Article 1848 states Louisiana's parol evidence rule: "Testimonial or other evidence may not be admitted to negate or vary the contents of an authentic act or an act under private signature. Nevertheless, in the interest of justice, that evidence may be admitted to prove such circumstances as a vice of consent or a simulation, or to prove that the written act was modified by a subsequent and valid oral agreement."

Louisiana's version generally does not exclude extrinsic writing. The equivalent common law rule does, but Louisiana distrusts only 'parol,' i.e. oral evidence. Additionally, it does not exclude evidence intended to prove a fact collateral to the agreement, or needed to interpret the writing itself – in addition to the exceptions listed in the article itself.

Jenfreau v. Jenfreau

Brothers Louis and Edward Jeanfreau bought a motor boat, Louis sued for recognition that he was, in fact, the owner of the boat even though the title was in Edward's name. (The boat cost approximately $2,500). Edward claimed that he owned the boat and that plaintiff had always acknowledged his ownership, and that the boat had since been seized by the U.S. government, and plaintiff made no claim against the seizure.

Plaintiff presented the deposition of Delacruz, who represented the seller of the boat, and stated that Louis paid the money, that the boat was then moved from Biloxi (where the sale took place) to Violatee, La. Where the boat's engine was replaced with a much stronger one at Louis's request and expense. Louis also alleged that the boat was put in Edward's name for convenience sake only.

The court found in favor of Louis, and that finding was affirmed by the Louisiana Supreme Court.

[Question: why do you think the U.S. government might have seized the boat sometime between 1930 and 1935, when the decision was made?]

Section 2: Immovables

After a review of the Civil Code articles on proof of obligations and the differences between an authentic act, an act under private signature duly acknowledged, and an act under private signature (Articles 1833-1838), this section reminds you that a transfer of an immovable, corporeal or incorporeal, must be made in writing, whether by an act under private signature or by authentic act. Art. 2440, 1839.

There are two exceptions: if the written instrument of transfer was lost, stolen, or destroyed, then parol testimony may be accepted to prove the transfer. Art. 1832. Additionally, if there never was a written instrument, then a transfer is still effective if there was actual delivery of the immovable and the transferor (in some way) acknowledges the transfer under oath. Art.1839.

Pierce v. Griffin

In this classic case, a widow and her daughter (Pierce) are suing defendant who built a home on property that the plaintiffs claim is theirs. Defendant claims that the deceased sold him the immovable some 20 years previously, and that the sale was originally written on four wooden stakes, which had been pounded into the boundary of the property "In 1936, this Lot 4 sold to Silas Griffin by L.J. Pierce." In the intervening time, however, Griffin built his home and burned the stakes.

The widow claims that the sale had not been completed because defendant had not paid the balance of $100 – testifying that her husband had several times requested that Griffin pay the balance, and that after his death, she asked him to pay what he owed.

The court held for the defendant, that he had in fact purchased the lot from Pierce. Whether it had been paid for or not was not discussed in the opinion – apparently plaintiff had not presented evidence that it had not been paid.

Which of the two exceptions applies? Or do they both apply?

Harter v. Harter

This modern family fight is over ownership of incorporeal immovables, i.e. a 25% working interest in a mineral lease. Parents Harter had four children, one of whom, "Steve" was named as independent Administrator of the estate in their mother's will. The four children (Mike, Steve, Jan, and David) were each left a ¼ interest in their parent's estate, which included Harter Energy. Two of the children did not work but received monthly payments of $6,000 from their mother's estate; nevertheless, they felt that Steve was mishandling the estate's money. After some discussion, the four agreed that Harter Oil would sell a 25% interest in the family oil company, the purchase price of $250 K for each would be financed at 7% through the company, and taken out of proceeds, and production from the leases was to be attributed retroactively from July 1, 2007. Internal entries from the oil company showed payments made to the siblings from the proceeds, however no written agreement was executed.

A year later, Mike, instructed the Oil Company to remove David and Jan from the records, saying that Mike would compensate them at $12K/month for the remaining months of the year, and then re-evaluate their 'deal." David and Jan then sued Steve, claiming breach of fiduciary duty. Two years later, Mike sold the remaining leases form the estate and the family oil company for a lump sum of $11.2 million. The issue is whether the mineral leases, as incorporeal movables, were ever actually delivered to Jan and David and whether Mike breached the agreement that they owned a 25% interest each.

The court held that the oil company's records demonstrated the transfer, and that the transfer had been recognized – though Mike claimed he never judicially admitted transferring the interests, he admitted several pertinent facts while under oath concerning the delivery of the working interests: monthly payments derived from the leases' revenues for several months to his siblings, instructing his bookkeeper to make entries in the company's internal records evidencing a transfer of 25% of the working interest.

Mitchell v. Clark

In both Pierce and Harter, plaintiffs were able to prove their ownership of an immovable even though the transfer (for one reason or another) was not recorded in writing. Mitchell has the opposite result.

Plaintiff Mitchell wanted to purchase an immovable and leave it to her nephew, the defendant but without the formalities of a will. So, when she purchased it, she instructed the seller to put the title in her nephew's name. When her nephew learned of it, he demanded immediate possession.

Thee trial court held that a verbal sale was recognized under oath coupled with actual transfer, and that Mitchell was the true vendee. However, the court of appeal was convinced that parol evidence should not be admitted to prove title in one who never had a title.

The Louisiana Supreme court affirmed the appellate court's holding, reasoning that acts appearing to transfer immovable property must be interpreted from the face of the instrument because otherwise purchasers of real estate could not be entitled to rely on title deeds. Mitchell paid for the lot, and the seller followed her instructions and put the title in Clark's name – consequently, she cannot now object and claim ownership of the property.

Frank v. Motwani

While the previous cases dealt with when the sale of an immovable is valid or invalid because of the lack of a writing, this case deals with whether the cancellation of the sale of an immovable must be in writing.

Defendant Motwani offered to purchase plaintiff Frank's immovable in New Orleans. The sellers accepted the offer by signing the agreement. Purchase was obligated to deposit 10% of the purchase price, and had agreed to do so with a certificate of deposit for $50K in one bank, and a non-negotiable demand note for $19K. The agreement further provided that "failure to do so shall not void this agreement but shall be considered a breach, and seller shall have the right to demand liquidated damages equal to the amount of the deposit or specific performance AND shall be liable for agent's commission, attorney's fees, and costs."

Purchaser submitted a $50K check to purchase the CD, but then put a stop payment order on it, and never made the remainder of the deposit, seller brought suit, and defendant purchaser Motwani claims that the sale was cancelled orally by agreement of all the parties.

Article 1901 of the Code of 1870 provided that agreements have effect of law, and cannot be revoked unless by the parties' mutual consent. It does not stipulate any particular form needed for the cancellation of a contract, and there is no reason why a party to a contract that has to be in writing should not be able to offer evidence that the parties verbally agreed to cancel it.

In his concurrence, Justice Lemmon says that while a contract to transfer an immovable must be in writing, the cancellation of such a contract need not be in writing because it does not constitute an agreement to sell immovable property.

Mathews v. Mathews

In this family fight, Mom simply wanted her two sons to share the land and not fight. She began by 'selling' the property to one son, Emmett by authentic act. Emmett later admits that he did not pay the $2,000 recited in the Act, and that it was a simulation. Following the 'sale' to Emmett, Emmett partitioned the farm into two tracts, and Emmett prepared to give the southern portion with the farmhouse he had grown up in to Rusty, their cousin. A month before the partition, Mom's attorney wrote a letter to Emmett saying that she was invalidating the donation in disguise. She then executed a different Act of Donation giving ownership to Emmett's brother Alfred., After which she revoked that donation (apparently she was angry that Alfred had filed a suit against Emmett) – she was 91 years old, and in her deposition stated that 1. She did not sell the farm to Emmett, that she wanted them to have equal parts. She said that each of her sons were supposed to get equal parts and Rusty was supposed to get the house so he could keep it up, that it was to be shared among the three of them.

The court held that the "sale" was never completed as a sale and that no price was ever paid. Emmett never manifested to accept the land as a donation. Emmett admitted that he understood she wanted the property to be kept intact, and claims he tried to bring Alfred into it by having him cut timber or farm, or research how to use it, and that he had assumed possession of it as a caretaker. He did not understand that his mother was donating the complete and irrevocable ownership of the Farm to him, because he expected to pay a price. The court then held that Emmett did not prove that he and his mother intended a relative simulation or disguised donation, there was no meeting of the minds, and therefore the sale to Emmett was an absolute nullity.

Section 3: Sufficiency of Description

To prove a sale of an immovable the writing should indicate the thing, the price, and the parties' consent. Under Comment b to Article 1838, it may be valid even if only one party signed it – if the party who signed it can show that the one who did not sign it's conduct revealed that he availed himself of it or if it is the one who did not sign it who proves its existence by the signature of the other party.

Additionally, the writing must indicate a price and identify the immovable. There is a body of caselaw that demonstrates what kind of description of the property sufficiently identifies it to the sale, and what does not. Even if the description is incomplete, but it is supplemented by additional evidence that can locate and identify the property, the writing may be sufficient.

Lemoine v. Lacour

Cancelled receipts stating "received from Clifton Lemoine $35 for payment on place" was not enough to establish the sale because it did not identify the property being sold.

Section 4: Mandate and other Ancillary Contracts

Under the equal dignity rule, a contract that is ancillary to another contract that is required to be in writing must itself be in writing. Thus, an agency or 'mandate' to sell an immovable must itself be in writing, as must a right of first refusal or option to buy an immovable, and ohther similar contracts.

Triangle Farms, Inc. v. Harvey

Defendant claims that he possesses an immovable and purchased it from a third party, Sherburne Industries, for $9,482. He made the first payment of $4,741 to Sherburne, but did not receive title, and that plaintiff is unjustly breaching that sale. Plaintiff claims the immovable belongs to it, and is suing for possession. Sherburn did not have a written contract of agency from the plaintiff to land, and while there might have been a verbal authorization to do so, that is insufficient to establish the agency. Consequently, the court says it is regrettable that the defendant was cheated, but nevertheless, plaintiff owns the immovable and does not need to reimburse defendant for the funds lost.

HYPOTHET

Guiseppe recovered from his illness, and he and Anna agreed in writing that he would make her 10 pairs of women's high-heeled blue suede sandals in assorted sizes plus 10 pair of men's blue suede loafers in various sizes for $2,000, to be delivered in January. Now he claims that they subsequently agreed orally that he need only make half the number of pairs for the same amount of money because his material costs have risen precipitously. Anna does not remember any such conversation. If the dispute goes to court, can he introduce his claim?

Anna's mother, Lubov, bought a condominium in New Orleans from Sterling twenty years ago and has been living in it since. The condo originally cost $40,000, she paid $35,000 down, and the last $5,000 six months later. The thing is, the parties never wrote out any actual agreement, and Sterling recently died and his widow claims the condo is hers. Lubov has a note from Sterling, from when she made the final payment saying: Received $5000 in full payment on condo in New Orleans, (signed) Sterling. Is this enough to prove her ownership?

CHAPTER 5

AGREEMENTS PREPARATORY TO THE SALE

Flowchart

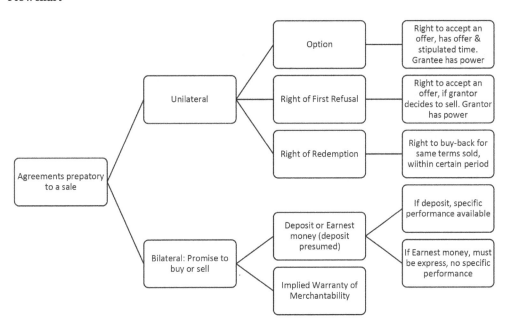

While Article 2456 provides that ownership is transferred as soon as there is agreement on the thing and the price is fixed, there may be a number of reasons why the parties to a sale may execute a preliminary agreement or may agree to delay the transfer of ownership until the occurrence of some suspensive condition. Thus, they may agree that the transfer of ownership will take place at some future time, such as at the moment of delivery, or at the moment the price is paid, or (especially with immovables) at the moment a formal writing or a notarial act is executed. These kinds of agreements are termed a contract to sell by the Civil Code, and while the obligee (buyer) is not yet the owner, he still has certain obligations. In other circumstances, a potential seller may grant the buyer the right to purchase the thing, if the buyer chooses to do so, for a specified period of time, or she may grant the potential buyer the right to purchase the thing ahead of any other potential buyer should the seller ever decide to sell the thing. The first agreement is an option; while the second is a right of first refusal. Begin by reading Articles 2620-2030 of the Louisiana Civil Code, where the rules governing such agreements preparatory to a sale are collected.

Section 1: Unilateral Promises to Sell

Options and rights of first refusal bind only one party and hence are unilateral promises. As such, they will be discussed first, prior to bilateral promises.

A. The Option

Article 2620 provides that an option to buy, or an option to sell, "is a contract whereby a party gives to another the right to accept an offer to sell, or to buy, a thing within a stipulated time. An option must set forth the thing and the price and meet the formal requirements of the sale it contemplates." Thus, if it relates to the sale of an immovable, it must be in writing.

Study Questions:

What are the required elements of an option as indicated in the next case?

Have they changed under the articles as currently formulated? What do you think happened on remand?

BECKER & ASSOC., INC. V. LOU-ARK EQPT. RENTALS CO., INC. 1976
331 SO. 2D 474 (LA.)

DENNIS, Justice.

¶1 These consolidated cases present a suit by a lessee of heavy equipment against its lessor for the specific performance of an option to purchase the equipment and a suit by the lessor to recover the movable property and accrued rental from the lessee

¶2 Lou-Ark Equipment Rentals Co., Inc., applicant herein, by a written agreement dated July 13, 1971, leased to respondent, Becker and Associates, Inc., a 45 ton crawler crane at a rental of $2,000.00 per 30 calendar days plus sales tax, for a minimum lease period of 30 days. On the same date the parties executed and made part of the lease a written agreement granting Becker the option to purchase the equipment, which provided that 99% of the rental paid for the crane would apply toward the purchase price and that the value of the equipment would be determined 'by an independent appraiser or by mutual agreement.'

¶3 Becker paid Lou-Ark rental in accordance with the terms of the lease from July, 1971 through February, 1973, totaling $41,200.00 including taxes. In January and February, 1973, Becker informed Lou-Ark of its desire to exercise the option. At the request of Becker the value of the crane was estimated by two different appraisers, both of whom determined it was worth $40,000.00. It is disputed whether Lou-Ark agreed to the designation of either appraiser as an 'independent appraiser' for purposes of determining the value of the property under the option. When Becker called upon Lou-Ark to sell the crane for the price of $40,000.00, Lou-Ark refused.

¶4 Becker filed suit against Lou-Ark for a declaratory judgment of ownership and alternatively for specific performance. It deposited $412 including taxes into the registry of the court as the balance between the appraisal value of the equipment and 99% of the amount it had paid Lou-Ark as rent. Lou-Ark brought suit against Becker seeking to be declared owner of the crane, for its return and for $12,000.00 accrued rent, as well as future rent, interest and attorney's fees.

¶5 The two suits were consolidated for trial; the district court rendered judgment for Lou-Ark, and Becker appealed. The court of appeal reversed, set aside the lower court decrees and rendered judgment for Becker ordering specific performance of the option to purchase. 314 So.2d 553 (La.App.4th Cir. 1975). Upon application of Lou-Ark, we granted writs. 318 So.2d 55 (La.1975).

¶6 Lou-Ark contends that the option agreement was null and void because it was without a fixed or definite term as required by Article 2462 of the La. Civil Code, which, in pertinent part, provides:

> 'One may purchase the right, or option to accept or reject, within a stipulated time, an offer or promise to sell, after the purchase of such option, for any consideration therein stipulated, such offer, or promise can not be withdrawn before the time agreed upon; and should it be accepted within the time stipulated, the contract or agreement to sell, evidenced by such promise and acceptance, may be specifically enforced by either party.'

¶7 In enforcing this provision we have held that perpetual options which would take property out of commerce are prohibited because they violate the doctrine of ownership established by the La. Civil Code. Bristo v. Christine Oil and Gas Co., 139 La. 312, 71 So. 521 (1916); See also

Delcambre v. Dubois, 263 So.2d 96 (La.App.3rd Cir. 1972); Clark v. Dixon, 254 So.2d 482 (La. App.3rd Cir. 1971).

¶8 The option agreement itself sets forth no time limit within which the offer to sell the property must be accepted. Nevertheless, the court of appeal held that the option stated a time within which it was to be exercised, because, being part of the same agreement as the lease, Becker could elect to exercise its right of option to purchase the leased property at any time during a thirty-day rental period for which the rent had been paid.

¶9 Had the lease contract provided a definite term we would agree with the decision below, because the failure to expressly state a termination date in an option agreement made part of a lease having a definite term does not render the option invalid if the time for its acceptance is necessarily limited by the term of the lease. Kinberger v. Drouet, 149 La. 986, 90 So. 367 (1922); Smith Enterprises Inc. v. Borne, 245 So.2d 9 (La.App.1st Cir. 1971). However, upon careful inspection, we find that the lease between Becker and Lou-Ark was not for a definite term but was dependent upon the will of the parties for its duration.

¶10 The lease instrument provided for a 'rental rate' of $2,000.00 plus tax 'per 30 calendar days.' The 'rental period' was described as beginning on July 13, 1971, and ending when the equipment 'is received by the Owner at their warehouse . . . or . . . on the date Bill of Lading is issued covering the return of the Equipment to the Owner. Additionally, a 'termination of agreement' clause provided that the lessor shall have the right to take possession of the equipment five days after the lessee's default on any payment. Therefore, the parties agreed to methods by which the lease could be terminated, but they did not agree upon a definite term for the lease.

¶11 Because no time for the duration of the lease was agreed on by the parties, it was subject to termination in accordance with La. C.C. art. 2686, which provides:

> 'The parties must abide by the agreement as fixed at the time of the lease. If no time for its duration has been agreed on, the party desiring to put an end to it must give notice in writing to the other, at least ten days before the expiration of the month, which has begun to run.'

¶12 Thus, in addition to the methods provided by the lease contract, the lease could be terminated by either party by the giving of notice in writing to the other, at least ten days before the expiration of the month.

¶13 The court of appeal apparently concluded that by operation of law a new 30-day lease was confected each month. Thus, the court reasoned that the option to purchase terminated upon the expiration of each 30-day rental period and was effectively limited thereby. We find, however, that the premise of the court of appeal decision was erroneous and at variance with the jurisprudence concerning month to month leases.

¶14 Under La.C.C. art. 2686, the presumed continuance of a lease by operation of law from month to month, resulting from holding over without notice, is called a 'tacit reconduction.' The effect of such a continuance is not to constitute a new lease each month or even to renew the old one, but rather to continue the original lease. Weaks Supply Co. v. Werdin, 147 So. 838 (La. App.2d Cir. 1933). Cf. Governor Claiborne Apartments, Inc. v. Attaldo, 256 La. 218, 235 So.2d 574 (1970). Accordingly, the month to month lease in the instant case did not terminate each month but endured continuously until put to an end in the manner provided by La.C.C. art. 2686 or by the lease contract.

¶15 Since there were no provisions in either the lease or the option itself limiting its duration, the option was null and void for failure to stipulate a time period for the acceptance of the promise to sell. La.C.C. art. 2462.

¶16 Accordingly, the judgment of the court of appeal must be set aside. However, we cannot fully reinstate the trial court's judgment because its conclusion that Lou-Ark is entitled to enforcement of the lease contract, including award of attorney's fees, was also erroneous. It is well settled under our Civil Code and the jurisprudence interpreting it that when one of the parties errs in perceiving the very nature of the contract into which he enters, the contract cannot be enforced against him. La.C.C. art. 1841 states:

'Error as to the nature of the contract will render it void.

'The nature of the contract is that which characterizes the obligation which it creates. Thus, if the party receives property, and from error or ambiguity in the words accompanying the delivery, believes that he has purchased, while he who delivers intends only to pledge, there is not (no) contract.'

¶17 See also Baker v. Baker, 209 La. 1041, 26 So.2d 132 (1946); Green v. McDade, 17 So.2d 637 (La.App.2nd Cir. 1944). In both cases, the courts refused to enforce a purported contract of sale against an owner of property who intended only to offer it as security.

***

¶18   In the instant case, Becker's officers mistakenly believed that it was entering into a rental agreement with a option to purchase. In fact, the option was null for lack of a specified time within which to accept the offer of sale. We are convinced from the evidence that Becker would not have entered the transaction if its officers had been aware that the contract consisted of a mere lease of the equipment. Thus, Becker erred as to the nature of the contract, and the lease agreement should not be enforced against it.

¶19   However, the principle of unjust enrichment, embodied in our Civil Code art. 1965 requires that Lou-Ark be compensated in the amount of the fair rental value of the equipment for the period it was in Becker's possession. Accordingly, it is necessary that we remand the case to the trial court to determine precisely this value.

¶20   The court of appeal judgment is set aside and the case is remanded to the trial court for further proceedings consistent with the views expressed herein.

¶21   Reversed and remanded.

Lagniappe:

Read the comments to Article 2620 and compare an option to an irrevocable offer as defined in Article 1928:

An offer that specifies a period of time for acceptance is irrevocable during that time.

When the offeror manifests an intent to give the offeree a delay within which to accept, without specifying a time, the offer is irrevocable for a reasonable time.

The definition of an option was clarified in the 1995 revision, and since that time, consideration is NOT a required element, though a specified period of time as well as a valid offer are required. Furthermore, because an option is a contract, it requires agreement by both parties, even though only one of them is bound.[9] In contrast, no agreement is required for an irrevocable offer because it is merely a policitation. An option is heritable and transferable, while an irrevocable offer is not, it can be enforced by specific performance, whereas the remedy for an offeror's failure to keep faith with an irrevocable offer can be, at most, detrimental reliance. Consequently, the only way to tell the difference between an option and an irrevocable offer with a specified term is to verify that both parties agreed to the option – that the option itself was offered by one party and accepted by thee other.

---

9   24 La. Civil Law Treatise §5:14.

Is the following an irrevocable offer or an option? "I'll let you buy my blue suede, diamond-encrusted Jimmy Choo shoes for $1500– and you can think about it for three days." Hint – you can't tell if this is an option or an irrevocable offer without further information, but why? And what would be the legal effects of one as opposed to the other?

Study Question:

What does the following case teach about what happens when a seller breaches an option to sell?

BADEAU V. SAVOIE 2007

970 SO. 2D 1126, (LA. APP. 5TH CIR.)

CLARENCE E. McMANUS, Judge.

¶1   Plaintiff, Barry Badeaux, filed a petition for damages and breach of contract, alleging that he and defendant, Warren Savoie, entered into a lease agreement with an option to purchase, and that defendant breached the agreement by selling the property to someone else. After trial on the merits, the court rendered judgment in favor of plaintiff, awarding damages of $19,200.00 plus interest and costs. All other relief was denied. Both parties have appealed from that judgment.

¶2   On August 11, 1993, Badeaux and Savoie entered into an agreement for the lease of property. The agreement, provided by Savoie, was a typewritten rental agreement which provided for monthly rental payments of $575.00 with a reduction of $25.00 for timely payments. Savoie also included handwritten terms at the bottom of the first page that provided:

House will be removed from the sales market during term of this lease.

Lessee may purchase at any time. All rent applied to purchase. (10/06 + $4,000.00 Approx.)

¶3   The original term of the lease was from July 17, 1993 to August 1, 1994. The lease also provided for "Automatic renewal on a month to month basis at the expiration of this contract allowing then either the Lessor or Lessee to void with a 30 day written notice."

¶4   Badeaux and Main took occupancy of the residence. After the expiration of the original term, no new agreement was made. They continued to make timely monthly payments to

Savoie until March of 2005. On the bottom of each payment, it was noted that the payment was for "house note." On March 16th, Badeaux received a letter notifying him to make his payments to a third party, Wilton and Courtnie Comardelle. On April 25, 2005, Badeaux sent Savoie a letter stating that he wanted to purchase the property in accordance with their lease agreement.

¶5 During that time, Badeaux discovered that Savoie had sold the property to the Comardelles. He testified that he was not given notice, nor was he provided the opportunity to exercise the option to purchase prior to the sale. At the time of the sale, Badeaux had paid in excess of $70,000.00 to Savoie. Badeaux received a notice to vacate the premises from the Comardelles in April of 2005, and was served with a Petition of Eviction on May 5, 2005.

¶6 Rachael Main testified that she cohabitated with plaintiff, and had done so for the previous 14 years. She resided with the plaintiff at the subject property. She stated that Savoie offered them the option of "rent to own," and that he provided the contract that they entered into. She further testified that she and plaintiff requested that he include the addendum that the payments would finish in October of 2006, with the payment of an additional $4,000.00, and Savoie made the handwritten notation on the bottom of the contract. Thereafter, they occupied the premises and made the required monthly payments. She further testified that they stayed in the house past the 1994 term, and there was never a new agreement executed between them.

¶7 Ms. Main testified that from August of 1991 until September of 1995, they made timely monthly payments of $550.00. In September of 1995, the taxes on the property increased, and they began to pay an additional $25.00 per month for the tax. She also testified that she and Mr. Badeaux made some repairs to the property, and that Mr. Savoie also made repairs, including replacing the air conditioner and the roof. She further said that at one point, she and Badeaux changed the locks on the property. Mr. Savoie was not given a key to the new locks.

¶8 Barry Badeaux testified that he and Savoie discussed the possibility of a lease purchase (rent to own) and that Savoie prepared the contract of their agreement. Savoie indicated that Badeaux would take over the house payment, which would be concluded in October of 2006. Thereafter, and after making an additional payment of $4,000.00, Badeaux would own the property. Savoie wrote the notation on the first page, representing their agreement. The agreement was orally modified twice, at the request of Savoie, first to include an extra $25.00 payment toward property tax, and second to request that payment be made on the 25th of the month instead of the following 1st, so that Savoie could make his payments timely. Badeaux testified that he did not receive any written notice from Savoie prior to the sale to the Comardelles.

¶9   Badeaux also testified that at the time he initially entered into the agreement with Savoie, comparable properties rented for approximately $350.00, but he paid more in exchange for what he believed was an ownership option.

¶10   Mr. Savoie testified that he originally purchased the property for $54,000.00 in 1981. In 1991, he placed an ad in the paper to sell or lease the property. He stated that he requested rent of $525.00, although he admitted that other properties were renting for $300.00. He stated that Badeaux paid $550.00 monthly because he was consistently late in his payments.

¶11   He further testified that he offered to sell the property several times, but was told that Badeaux could not come up with the balance. He sold the property to the Comardelles for $26,000.00. He further testified that the rent increase of $25.00 in 1995 was not to pay taxes, but was a penalty because Badeaux's rent payments were late "a couple of times." Other than that increase, he never raised the rent in the twelve years that Badeaux occupied the property.

¶12   Savoie testified that his monthly mortgage note on the property at the time he rented it was $511.00. He further stated that the lease agreement between he and Badeaux provided for an option to buy for the first year only, and after it was strictly a lease. He agreed that this one year limitation was not present on the document, but stated that he had discussed those terms with Badeaux. He admitted that he had several discussions with Badeaux concerning the purchase of the property. He further admitted that he had seen the notation "house note" on the payments, but considered that was a notation for rent. His intention on the written language was that it was a notation that his mortgage on the property would be paid in October of 2006, and that should Badeaux want to purchase the property at that time, it would cost no more than $4,000.00. Savoie testified that he notified Badeaux that he was going to sell the property via telephone, and that Badeaux indicated that he did not like the idea because they had an agreement to rent, and that Badeaux never stated that he thought he was purchasing the property. However, in his deposition of April 5, 2006, Savoie stated that "... he wasn't pleased that I was going to sell the property and he assumed that we had an agreement for him to purchase it the whole time."

¶13   In this appeal, Savoie contends that the trial court erred in finding that the agreement was a lease with an option to purchase. Badeaux argues that the trial court correctly found that the agreement contained an option to buy, but argues that the award of damages was erroneous.

¶14   Initially we note, as did the trial judge, that it is undisputed that Savoie provided all of the language in the agreement. Accordingly, any ambiguous language is to be interpreted against him, and in favor of the other party, Badeaux.

¶15   LSA-C.C. art. 2620 sets forth the requirements for such an agreement:

> An option to buy, or an option to sell, is a contract whereby a party gives to another the right to accept an offer to sell, or to buy, a thing within a stipulated time.
>
> An option must set forth the thing and the price, and meet the formal requirements of the sale it contemplates.

¶16   The trial judge evaluated the evidence presented and first found that the "thing" contemplated in the agreement was the mobile home and lot located at 124 Julia Street. He further found that Savoie gave Badeaux until October, 2006 to exercise his option to purchase.

¶17   The court also found that the parties reached an agreement as to the price for purchase, that being monthly payments of $575.00 (with a monthly discount of $25.00 for timely payments) from August 1, 1993 to October 2006, and an additional payment of $4000.00 in October, 2006. If the option had reached its term, applying the $25.00 on time discount to each payment and discounting the $25.00 increase for property taxes, the total amount paid would have been $81,950.00. After adding the $4000.00 lump sum due in October of 2006, the total purchase price was $85,950.00.

¶18   Finally, the court found that the agreement met a formality requirement for a sale of immovable property, namely an act under private signature.

¶19   After review of the record, we cannot say that the trial court erred in its findings, and thus we find that the trial court did not err in finding that the lessee agreement between the parties contained an option to purchase, and that Mr. Savoie breached that contract by selling the property to the Comardelles.

¶20   Badeaux's appeal challenges the award of damages given by the trial court. It is his contention that the trial court erred in giving credit for the fair rental value of the property and also in giving credit for the improvements made by Savoie, which were improvements incurred in connection with the maintenance of the property by the property owner. Badeaux did not become the property owner, and therefore should not be assessed with the cost of the improvements as a "penalty."

¶21   We find no error in the trial court's ruling awarding Savoie a credit for the fair rental value of the property.

¶22 We do find that the trial court erred in granting credit for the cost of replacing the roof and air conditioning system. We agree with Mr. Badeaux's assertion that these are expenses associated with the ownership of the property, and he never acquired that ownership. Furthermore, the lease agreement states that "If the residence is damaged beyond normal wear and tear or due to direct action or neglect on the part of the Lessee, Lessee shall be responsible for the costs of the repair." There was no evidence offered to show that the roof and air conditioner were replaced because of damage beyond normal wear and tear, or that Badeaux and/or Main either caused the damage or allowed it to happen due to neglect. Accordingly, we find that the trial court erred in granting to Mr. Savoie a credit of $9,000.00 ($6,000.00 for roof replacement and $3,000.00 for air conditioner replacement).

¶23 For the above discussed reasons, the judgment of the trial court is amended to increase the award to plaintiff, Barry Badeaux, from $19,200.00 to $28,200.00. In all other respects, the judgment of the trial court is affirmed. All costs are assessed against defendant/appellant.

AMENDED AND AFFIRMED.

Lagniappe Question:

Why do you think the court did not (or could not) award Badeaux specific performance?

Study Questions:

The following questions test your understanding of Articles 2620, 2621, and 2622 on Options.

1. When is an acceptance or rejection of an offer contained in an option effective? On dispatch or on receipt? Does rejection of the offer contained in an option terminate the option?

2. Jean gave Mary an option to buy her shoes (blue suede, naturally) for $600, good for three days, in exchange for $1. Mary called her up 24 hours later and said, "I'll pay $450, not a penny more." Does this statement terminate the option?

Comment:

The offeree's acceptance of the offer contained in the option is often described as 'exercising' the option. The offeree must do so in accord with any form or method requirements stipulated in the option contract, so if the option requires acceptance through certified mail, it must be accepted in that form, and if it requires acceptance 45 days before the end of a lease to which it is attached, then acceptance must be received prior to that date, as acceptance of an option is effective on receipt.[10] In addition to an option terminating if it is not accepted as per its terms, Article 2621 stipulates that [r]ejection of the offer contained in an option terminates the option but a counteroffer does not." Nevertheless, under Louisiana Supreme Court jurisprudence, an acceptance must be unqualified and give "full recognition to . . . thee terms and conditions of the proposal."[11]

B. The Right of First Refusal

An option is a contract. As such, it can be assigned or inherited, or enforced by specific performance. Because it is a contract as well, a right of first refusal is similarly binding. Article 2625 defines a right of first refusal as follows:

> "A party may agree that he will not sell a certain thing without first offering it to a certain person. The right given to the latter in such a case is a right of first refusal that may be enforced by specific performance."

As with an option, "an agreement for a right of first refusal may be attached to another contract, such as a sale or lease." Id., comment (b). Notice that the grantor is conditionally bound only if he needs to offer the thing for sale to the promisee: if he (the promisor) decides to sell it. Furthermore, because an offer to sell pursuant to a right of first refusal need not be irrevocable, the offeror (grantee of the right) can revoke that offer before its acceptance by the holder of the right of first refusal. In that case, the grantor remains bound. Id. comment (d).

In contrast with an option to buy or sell, which must set forth the thing, the price, and meet the formal requirements of the sale contemplated, a right of first refusal must indicate the thing and satisfy the requirements of form, but it need not state the price. The reason for this is that the owner of a thing who grants a right of first refusal is not promising to sell that thing at all. Instead, the grantor is promising to *offer* to sell it to the grantee first before the owner sells it to a third person. Thus, article 2626 declares that "the grantor of a right of first refusal may not sell to another person unless he has offered to sell the thing to the holder of the right on the same terms, or on those specified when the right was granted if the parties have so agreed."

Once the grantor has decided to sell the thing and has made an offer to the holder of the right of first refusal, Article 2627 provides a limited time for the grantee to accept: after all, presumably the grantor has another potential buyer waiting in the wings, and would lose that buyer if the grantee doesn't respond in a timely manner. Consequently, if the thing is a movable, the holder of the right of first refusal has ten days – thirty days if the thing is an immovable – from

---

10   24 La. Civil Code Treatise § 5:20.

11   Louisiana State Bd. Of Ed. V. Lindsay, 79 So. 2d 897, 885 (1954).

the time he receives the offer within which to accept it. If he rejects the offer or does not accept it within that period and the grantor does not sell to a third person within six months, then the right of first refusal subsists in the grantee. Notice that an option must have a specified period of time, but a right of first refusal need not – though both may remain effective for a maximum of 10 years if the thing is an immovable. La. Civ. Code art. 2628. This is discussed in more depth in the next section.

Study Question:

Which Civil Code articles are at issue in the following cases and how do they apply?

JONES V. HOSPITAL CORP. OF AMERICA 1987
516 SO. 2D 1175 (LA. APP. 2D CIR.)

SEXTON, Judge.

¶1   This suit against Hospital Corporation of America (HCA) was brought by Dr. Henry Jones seeking a declaratory judgment and injunctive relief based on theories of estoppel, unjust enrichment, negligent misrepresentation and detrimental reliance. The trial court sustained a motion for summary judgment filed by the defendant with respect to the "claims based on the existence of a contract of sale, the existence of a contract to sell, the estoppel of defendant from denying the existence of a contract of sale or a contract to sell and an injunction...." The summary judgment was denied as to the suit's "other claims." The plaintiff appeals asserting only that because there is a material issue of fact pertaining to the issue of estoppel, the trial court erred in dismissing the demands for injunctive relief.

¶2   The appellant, a Monroe, Louisiana, physician, purchased Lot 2 of Block B, Unit 1, Monroe Medical Park in Ouachita Parish from Hospital Corporation of America in June of 1983. HCA owned adjacent Lot 1.

¶3   Dr. Jones' petition alleged that at the time of the sale of Lot 2, the defendant orally agreed to give him the right of "first refusal" on Lot 1. He further alleged that he later entered into an oral agreement with the defendant to purchase the property at an agreed upon price and took certain actions in furtherance thereof, including obtaining plans for a new building and ordering a survey of the lot. He contended that the defendant refused to acknowledge the agreement and to complete the formalities of the sale. He thus sought a declaratory judgment that a valid contract of sale was entered into or, in the alternative, that a valid contract to sell existed. In the further alternative, he sought an injunction based on estoppel.

¶4   The act of sale contained no written restrictions on the use of Lot 1, nor was there any written agreement containing a right of preemption or first refusal on the part of Dr. Henry Jones.

¶5   HCA moved for a summary judgment contending that since there was no written contract, Dr. Jones could claim no interest in Lot 1 of any kind. The district judge granted summary judgment in favor of HCA on all claims whereby Dr. Jones claimed an interest in the land or sought to restrict its alienation. His claim for damages, however, remains for trial. The dismissed claims include a claim that a sale had occurred, that there was a contract to sell, that there was a right of first refusal, that HCA was estopped from alienating the land, and that the plaintiff was entitled to an injunction.

¶6   Dr. Jones' appeal assigns as error only the granting of the summary judgment as it pertains to the issues of estoppel and injunction. In so doing, the plaintiff concedes in brief that the lack of a written instrument is fatal to his claims with respect to a contract to sell or a contract of sale.

¶7   Appellant asserts that the defendant, HCA, should be estopped from denying the existence of the written contract to sell, even though he admits these agreements were not put in writing. He alleges that HCA represented at the time of the original negotiations that the property would not be sold to a competitor and that Dr. Jones would have a right of preemption or right of first refusal. Dr. Jones claims that as a result of these representations by HCA he agreed to buy the property upon which he built his clinic. He asserts, and the record supports, that HCA has offered to sell the property to two competitors. Dr. Jones alleges, however, that HCA discussed the possibility of a sale with him in January of 1986 and that HCA did in fact offer to sell the property to him for a dollar per square foot. He claims that he accepted the offer and agreed to purchase the adjoining property and has conducted acts of corporeal possession upon the property since that time. He contends that he is ready and willing to complete the necessary formalities of the sale pursuant to the alleged agreement between the parties but that the defendant refuses. Based upon these allegations, he asserts that HCA is estopped from denying the contract of sale or contract to sell and should be enjoined from selling the property to the competitors.

¶8   Equitable estoppel is defined as the effect of the voluntary conduct of a party by which he is barred from asserting rights or defenses against another party justifiably relying on such conduct and causing him to change his position to his detriment as a result of such reliance.

The three elements of estoppel are: (1) a representation by action or word, (2) justifiable reliance on the representation, and (3) a change in position to one's detriment because of the reliance. John Bailey Contractor, Inc. v. State, Department of Transportation and Development, 439 So.2d 1055 (La.1983); Wilkinson v. Wilkinson, 323 So.2d 120 (La.1975); First Federal Savings & Loan of Natchitoches v. American Bank and Trust Company, Coushatta, 461 So.2d 341 (La.App. 2d Cir.1984).

¶9 Defendant concedes that the summary judgment as it related to the existence of a contract of sale or a contract to sell was correct because these types of agreements must be written. Indeed, it is clear that any transfer of immovable property must be in writing. LSA-C.C. 1832, 1839 and 2440. Additionally, a contract to sell immovable property must be in writing. Harrell v. Stumberg, 220 La. 811, 57 So.2d 692 (1952); Reaux v. Iberia Parish Police Jury, 454 So.2d 227 (La. App. 3d Cir.1984), writ denied 458 So.2d 120 (La.1984); Gross v. Brooks, 130 So.2d 674 (La.App. 3d Cir.1961). As plaintiff acknowledges these points and was apparently aware of the law with respect to immovables, we cannot find that he justifiably relied on any unwritten representation made by the defendants. Moreover, the jurisprudence specifically holds that an unwritten contract to sell or contract of sale of realty cannot be proven by estoppel. Harrell v. Stumberg, supra.

¶10 The instant case specifically concerns the right of first refusal, about which there is very little Louisiana jurisprudence. The first recognition of the concept we found is in Price v. Town of Ruston, 171 La. 985, 132 So. 653 (1931). Price dealt with the validity of the right of first refusal under a forced sale and is therefore of no assistance in resolving the instant case. The only case discussing the definition and nature of the right is Keene v. Williams, 423 So.2d 1065 (La.1982) (footnote omitted).

¶11 In Keene v. Williams, the court specifically approved Professor Litvinoff's discussion of the right of first refusal in his obligations treatise. 7 S. Litvinoff, Louisiana Civil Law Treatise § 104, § 108 (1975). The court described the right of first refusal as "the option and preferred right to buy property at the price offered by a third party in the event the owner desires to sell it."

¶12 Professor Litvinoff's discussion of the right of first refusal is in the context of the classic civil law. He does not specifically refer to it later in the treatise in his section on the law of Louisiana. In discussing the right of first refusal, which he refers to as the pacte de préférence, he states that it is "certainly not a sale because even if an offer is made, the beneficiary of the pact is not bound to buy." He further points out that:It is not a simple promise of sale either, because the prospective vendor is always free not to sell the thing. It is rather a conditional promise of sale. The condition, although on the side of the obligor, is not truly potestative but it is simply potestataive and, consequently, it does not make the obligation null. The enforceability of a pacte de préférence is unquestionable. In regard to contractual requirements, transfer of ownership, risk and damages for nonperformance, a pacte de préférence is governed by the same rules as unilateral promises of sale. (footnotes omitted)

¶13 Thus, Professor Litvinoff indicates that the civil law treats the pact as a unilateral promise to sell and points out that it is not a pure option, though it has some of the features thereof. In light of the Supreme Court's approval of Professor Litvinoff's discussion on the subject, we adopt his cogent definition and classification.

¶14 Thus, a pacte de préférence is a type of contract to sell. As we have previously noted, such a contract must be in writing to be enforceable, therefore, estoppel will obviously not lie to prove the pacte de préférence or right of first refusal-a type of contract to sell. Plaintiff's contention that he should have the opportunity to pursue this claim by way of estoppel is thus in error.

¶15 This leaves for consideration appellant's request for an injunction. This demand is based on the theory of estoppel. Since estoppel will not lie to prove any contract to sell-in this case the right of first refusal-the remedy of an injunction based on estoppel is likewise not available.

¶16 However, we do need to note that the appellant suggests that if estoppel is inapplicable, the facts nevertheless may support the existence of a predial servitude or a building restriction, the existence of either of which appellant contends would entitle him to an injunction. However, predial servitudes must be in writing. LSA-C.C. Art. 2440; Langevin v. Howard, 363 So.2d 1209 (La.App. 2d Cir.1978), writ denied 366 So.2d 560 (La.1979). Likewise, building restrictions, which are classified as servitudes, must be in writing. LSA-C.C. Arts. 770, 776 and 777; McGuffy v. Weil, 240 La. 758, 125 So.2d 154 (1960). Again, the lack of a written instrument is fatal to the plaintiff's position.

¶17 The final issue is appellee's request made in brief for damages for frivolous appeal. However, a request for damages for frivolous appeal made in brief cannot be entertained. LSA-C.C.P. Art. 2133; Guidroz v. State Farm Fire & Casualty Co., 334 So.2d 535 (La.App. 1st Cir.1976).

¶18 The judgment of the trial court is affirmed at appellant's cost.

¶19 AFFIRMED.

CANNELLA, Judge.

¶1   Plaintiff, Pelican Publishing Company (Pelican), appeals from the district court judgment in favor of defendants, Justin Wilson and Justin Wilson and Associates, Inc. (Wilson), granting defendants' exception of no cause of action and dismissing plaintiff's lawsuit. For the reasons which follow, we affirm.

¶2   On May 14, 1986, Pelican and Wilson entered into a book publishing contract, which is the subject of this litigation. The contract, similar to the six prior contracts that the parties had entered, was for the publication of a book entitled Justin Wilson's Louisiana Outdoor Cookin. The contract included many of the customary trade clauses, including an option clause on the "next work" and a non-competition clause.

¶3   On March 30, 1990, Pelican filed suit against Wilson alleging that Wilson had violated the terms of the contract. After an exception of no cause of action was sustained, Pelican amended its petition, alleging that in May 1988 Wilson acknowledged that his "next work" was a book called Justin Wilson's Homegrown Louisiana Cookin (Homegrown Cookin) and acknowledging that Pelican had an option or "right of first refusal" on that "next work" under the option clause of their contract. Despite this, Wilson had already, in March 1988, allegedly entered into a publishing contract with another publisher in violation of the option clause and the non-competition clause contained in the contract and further in violation of the implied covenant of good faith and fair dealings found in all Louisiana contracts.

¶4   Wilson again filed an exception of no cause of action arguing that the two clauses in the contract upon which Pelican relies are invalid and, accordingly, that Pelican has no cause of action. The matter was heard on June 29, 1992. The trial court again granted the exception of no cause of action and dismissed Pelican's case by judgment rendered on September 23, 1992. It is from this judgment that Pelican appeals.

***

¶5   The two clauses in the contract upon which Pelican relies in support of its case provide as follows:

[The author] will grant to the Publisher an option on his next work. If the Publisher declines in writing to execute a publishing agreement within ninety (90) days of the receipt of the completed manuscript, the Author is under no further obligation.

***

[The Author] will not, without the consent of the Publisher, furnish to any other publisher any work on the same subject of such extent and character as to conflict with the sale of said work.

¶6   Wilson argues, in its memorandum in support of the exception of no cause of action, that both of the above clauses are invalid. The first clause, the option clause, is invalid because it is uncertain as to the price and the terms. Wilson argues that the second clause, the non-competition clause, is invalid because it is vague and unenforceable for failure of consideration, failure to specify a time period for the non-competition and failure to limit its application to a restricted area.

¶7   Pelican argues that the lower court erred in granting Wilson's exception of no cause of action based on the invalidity of the contract clauses. Pelican argues that the first clause establishes a right of first refusal, rather than an option, and as such is valid. Pelican further argues that consideration for the non-competition clause is not properly before the court on an exception of no cause of action. And finally, Pelican argues that specificity as to time and location may be inferred under the circumstances.

¶8   After reviewing the contract it is clear that the two clauses in question lack the specificity necessary for their enforcement. An option is an elective right that, when exercised, ripens into a binding contract. It therefore must be specific as to the thing, the price and the terms, as provided in La.C.C. art. 2462. Where any of these elements are lacking there is no contract between the parties. McMikle v. O'Neal, 207 So.2d 922 (La.App. 2nd Cir.1968). In this case, the option clause is clearly void of any mention of price or even a means from which to derive the price. And, while Pelican is correct that clauses establishing a right of first refusal are exceptions to this requirement, Pelican's argument that this is a right of first refusal lacks merit. There is nothing here to indicate that a right of first refusal was created. The clause only grants Pelican an option to attempt to come to an agreement with Wilson. It does not address Pelican's right to accept or reject terms that Wilson has negotiated with another publisher. Furthermore, the clause requires Wilson to submit his work to Pelican and it requires Pelican to decline in writing. Thus, Pelican may indefinitely tie Wilson to the option by not declining ... "in writing to execute a publishing agreement ..." Pelican may unilaterally keep Wilson from negotiating with another publisher. Thus, we find this clause lacks the specificity for its enforcement.

¶9 Similarly, the second clause, relied on by Pelican in support of its cause of action, the non-competition clause, lacks the essential elements necessary for its enforcement. Non-competition clauses are not favored in the law and are strictly construed against the person attempting to limit the completion. Desselle v. Petrossi, 207 So.2d 190 (La.App. 4th Cir.1968), writs denied, 209 So.2d 39 (La.1968). Also, three requirements are necessary, serious consideration, a specified time period and a restricted area. In this case the clause is too vague and broad to be enforceable. There is no specified time period and no restricted area. Other clauses in the contract do not indicate what is intended and the nature of the contract does not sufficiently define what would be improper competition. As such, it is unenforceable. Desselle, supra.

***

¶10 Accordingly, we affirm the trial court judgment, granting Wilson's exception of no cause of action and dismissing Pelican's petition. Cost of appeal is assessed to Pelican.

AFFIRMED.

Comment:

Contrary to both *Wilson* and *Jones*, the most common controversies relating to rights of first refusal are neither a poor statement of the right nor a lack of form, but instead a lack of clarity on the part of the grantor – the grantor must clearly and unambiguously offer the property to the grantee before selling it to a third person. If the right of first refusal does not specifiy the price at which it should be offered to the grantee, then the grantor needs to clearly designate the price as well as all other terms on which he is willing to sell. For example, in one instance, a grantor forwarded a copy of an offer received from a third party to purchase the property at issue as well as the following: "I have made no determination to dispose of this property, however, in view of the offer received, . . [you have ten days to respond]. When the grantor did not receive a response thirteen days later, she sold the property to the third party. The court held that because her letter to the grantee did not contain an offer, her subsequent sale was a violation of the grantee's rights.[12]

---

12 Robichaux v. Boutte, 492 So. 2d 521, 523 (La. Ct. App. 3d Cir. 1986).

C. The Right of Redemption

PEACOCK V. PEACOCK (1996)
674 SO. 2D 1030 (LA.)

¶1 In 1990, Roger Peacock needed money for a business venture. He proposed to convey to Jon his one-half interest in forty acres of immovable property they owned in indivision in Ouachita Parish. Roger proposed to sell his interest to Jon for $8,000, with the right to redeem his interest in the property upon return of the $8,000, together with 5% interest per year. Jon sent Roger a check for $8,000, dated January 13, 1990. Roger drafted a "quitclaim deed" dated January 5, 1990, selling his interest in the 40 acres to Jon for $8,000. In the deed, [Roger stated the following:]

> James Roger Peacock reserves the right to repurchase his equal ownership in the above
> described property from Jon Franklin Peacock for the amount of $8,000 (Eight thousand dollars)
> plus 5% (Five percent) interest per anum [sic] within five years from the date of this document if
> he still owns the property at the time.

* * *

¶2 Roger testified that he met with Jon over the Easter weekend in 1994. Roger told Jon at that time that he intended to send him a check for $8,000 and that he intended to exercise his right to redeem his interest in the property. On April 18, 1994, Roger sent a registered letter to Jon with a check for $8,000. The intent was to exercise the right of redemption. For whatever reason, Jon did not pick up the registered letter until April 28, 1994, although testimony indicated that the ordinary mailing time between the two addresses was much shorter. As previously noted, the original "quitclaim deed" was not recorded in Ouachita Parish until April 20, 1994. On April 25, 1994, Jon executed another "quitclaim deed" purporting to transfer all of his interest in the property to his wife, Sharon, for one dollar and other valuable consideration. Subsequently, Roger wrote Jon a letter dated April 30, 1994, indicating that Roger had received the return notice showing that Jon had received Roger's letter of April 18. In the letter, Roger stated that he would pay the 5% interest when Jon executed a deed returning Roger's interest in the property. On May 2, 1994, Jon sent a letter to Roger, returning the check and informing Roger that the property had been sold. Jon did not tell Roger that the "buyer" was Jon's wife.

¶3 Roger filed suit against Jon and Sharon Peacock on May 27, 1994, seeking to enjoin the defendants from alienating the property, seeking recognition of Roger's right of redemption, and seeking an order that the defendants convey to him his interest in the property upon payment of the agreed price.

* * *

¶4   The court then turned its attention to the purported sale from Jon to his wife, Sharon. The court concluded that Jon's attempt to explain the "other valuable consideration" at trial simply could not be accepted. According to the defendants, the property was sold to Sharon so that she could terminate her current employment and manage the couple's property. Sharon allegedly would give Jon her 125 shares of Federal Express stock as payment for the property. She claimed to be seeking a "quieter style of life," and testified that she had a medical problem that would be helped by less stressful work. The trial court . . . concluded that the purported transfer from Jon to Sharon was "a sham and a veiled attempt to avoid Roger's attempts to redeem or regain his interest in the subject property."

* * *

¶5   The court concluded that upon payment of the $8,000, plus all accrued interest, Roger was entitled to redeem his one-half interest to the property.

* * *

¶6   The defendants appealed the trial court judgment, arguing that the trial court erred in finding that Roger had a valid right of redemption and that the trial court erred in finding invalid the sale between Jon and Sharon Peacock.

RIGHT OF REDEMPTION

¶7   The defendants argue that the trial court erred in finding that the plaintiff had a valid right of redemption to the property. . . . This argument is without merit.

¶8   Under the provisions of LSA–C.C. art. 2567, the parties to a contract of sale may agree that the seller shall have the right of redemption which is the right to take back the thing from the buyer. Clearly, the quitclaim deed drafted by Roger and filed by Jon contains a right of redemption. Even in the face of numerous attempts by Jon to get Roger to execute a new deed without the right, Roger maintained that this right was an essential element of the agreement to convey his one-half interest to Jon.

* * *

VALIDITY OF SALE BETWEEN THE DEFENDANTS

¶9   Under the provisions of LSA–C.C. arts. 2025 and 2026, a contract is a simulation when, by mutual agreement, it does not express the true intent of the parties, and is an absolute simulation when the parties intend that the contract shall produce no effects between them.

¶10   A simulation is a transfer of property which is not what it seems. In a pure simulation, sometimes called a nontransfer, the parties only pretend to transfer the property from one to another, but in fact both transferor and transferee intend that the transferor retains ownership of the property. When this type of simulation is successfully attacked, the true intent of the parties is revealed; that is, that no transfer had in fact taken place. *Kennedy v. Bearden,* 471 So.2d 871 (La.App. 2d Cir.1985).

¶11   Two legal presumptions, one codal and one jurisprudential, apply in situations where a party seeks to prove a simulation. *Kennedy v. Bearden, supra.* The codal presumption is expressed in La.C.C. art. 2480 and is applicable where the vendor retains corporeal possession. The jurisprudential presumption of simulation applies where the evidence establishes the existence of facts and circumstances which create a highly reasonable doubt as to the reality of the putative sale. *Kennedy v. Bearden, supra.* When *1034 either the codal or jurisprudential presumption exist, the burden of proof shifts to the other party to the sale who may rebut the presumption by establishing a good faith transaction, resulting in a true alienation of ownership for consideration. *Kennedy v. Bearden, supra.* A transaction will not be set aside as a simulation if any consideration supports the transaction, because the reality of the transference is thus established. *Russell v. Culpepper,* 344 So.2d 1372 (La.1977).

¶12   In this case, by referring to the alleged sale by Roger to Sharon as a sham, the trial court indicated its conclusion that the transaction was an absolute or pure simulation. As such, it had no effect between the parties, and was subject to attack by Roger as being made in derogation of his right of redemption. The record supports the trial court finding. First, there was no showing that possession of the property passed from Jon to Sharon. Further, the record shows that facts and circumstances create a highly reasonable doubt as to the reality of a sale between Jon and Sharon. Roger testified that on Easter weekend, 1994, he told Jon that he intended to mail him a check for $8,000 to regain his interest in the property within the next few days. This was followed by a "flurry of activity" by Jon in recording the original deed from Roger, purportedly selling the property to Sharon and not accepting delivery of the registered letter and check from Roger until after the purported sale to Sharon. Further, the record shows that Jon had learned that Roger's interest in the property was worth much more than the $8,000 Jon paid Roger. The timber on the property alone was worth as much as $70,000.

¶13   Also, the trial court found that the defendants failed to show that any consideration was given for the purported sale between Jon and Sharon. Jon and Sharon had the burden of proving that the sale was an actual transfer of ownership and not a simulation. *Kennedy v. Bearden, supra.* Regarding the "other valuable consideration" Sharon testified that she *intended* to convey shares of stock to Jon and to leave her job in order to manage the couple's property. However, she had not taken either action at the time of the purported sale to her.

¶14   An appellate court may not set aside a trial court's finding of fact in the absence of manifest error; where there is conflict in testimony, reasonable evaluations of credibility and reasonable inferences of fact should not be disturbed upon review, even though the appellate court may feel that its own evaluations and inferences are as reasonable. *Rosell v. ESCO,* 549 So.2d 840 (La.1989). When findings are based on determinations regarding the credibility of witnesses, the manifest error standard demands great deference to the trier of fact's findings, for only the fact finder can be aware of the variations in demeanor and tone of voice that bear so heavily on the listener's understanding and belief in what is said. *Gardner v. McDonald,* 27,303 (La.App. 2d Cir. 8/25/95), 660 So.2d 107, writ denied 95–2349 (La. 12/15/95), 664 So.2d 453.

¶15   We find no manifest error in the trial court's decision that the sale of the 40–acre tract for one dollar and "other valuable consideration" was a sham and an absolute simulation, having no effect between the parties. Accordingly, that portion of the trial court judgment, finding that there was no sale from Jon to Sharon Peacock is affirmed.[1]

AMENDED, AND AS AMENDED, AFFIRMED.

Study Question:

Article 2567 defines a right of redemption as the "right to take back the thing from the buyer." Read Articles 2567-2572. How does this differ from the right of first refusal, as explained in the following case?

TRAVIS V. HEIRS OF FELKER 1985
482 SO. 2D 5 (LA. APP. 1ST CIR.)

EDWARDS, Judge.

¶1 In 1959, plaintiff sold some property to her sister for the stated price of "One Hundred Dollars and other considerations." The act of sale also contained the following clause: "It is understood and agreed that the Vendor (Mrs. Bernice Martin Travis) has the right to buy her interest back if ever sold; for the full sum and amount not to exceed $4,000.00."

¶2 Plaintiff brought this action in 1979 to enforce that clause, alleging that one of her sister's heirs had sold part of the property and that the succession administrator had made application to sell another part of the property. The trial court concluded that the 1959 transaction was a sale with the right of redemption and that since that right can only be reserved for ten years, LSA-CC. art. 2568, her right of redemption had prescribed. Accordingly the trial court dismissed her action. On appeal we reversed and remanded, holding that the transaction was not a sale with the right of redemption. Travis v. Felker, 434 So.2d 1222 (La.App. 1st Cir.1983). We reasoned that since the right of redemption gives the vendor the right to "tak[e] back the thing sold by returning the price paid for it," LSA-CC. art. 2567, the transaction could not have been a sale with a right of redemption because the stated redemption price of $4,000 was much more than the price paid in the sale. Id. at 1225.

¶3 On remand the trial court took more evidence on the issue of the characterization of the sale. Upon defendant's questioning, plaintiff admitted at trial that the agreed upon sale price was actually $4,000 although only $100 was paid. Based on that the court again found that the transaction was a sale with a right of redemption, and again granted the exception of prescription. Once again plaintiff appeals, asserting res judicata, i.e., the trial court should not have allowed evidence tending to prove that the sale was one with the right of redemption after this court had already held that the transaction was not a sale with the right of redemption. We find it unnecessary to deal with the question of res judicata because we conclude on other grounds that the court erred in sustaining the exception of prescription.

¶4 We must distinguish between redemption and the situation in which the vendee voluntarily resells the property to the vendor. "The right of redemption is an agreement ... by which the vendor reserves to himself the power of taking back the thing sold by returning the price paid for it." LSA-C.C. art. 2567. The defeasible condition rests solely with the vendor, Patterson v. Bonner, 14 La. 214, 234 (1839); the vendee has no choice in the matter. The right of the vendor to demand the return of the thing he sold simply by returning to the vendee the price paid for it is a sine qua non of a sale with the right of redemption. Redemption is a resolutory condition which operates to dissolve the original sale. 2 M. Planiol, Treatise on the Civil Law pt. 1, no. 1574 (11th ed. La.St.L.Inst. trans. 1959). Thus although the vendee is the actual owner of the thing until it is redeemed, his ownership is uncertain because of the existence of the redemption condition. Once the ten-year delay has run, however, without the seller having exercised his right to redeem the thing, the resolutory condition vanishes, and the buyer is then the irrevocable owner. LSA-C.C. art. 2568; Planiol, supra, no. 1581.

***

¶5 The agreement at issue in this case does not give the vendor the unqualified right to demand the return of her property. Rather she has the right to buy back her interest "if ever sold." Because the plaintiff does not have this right to demand the return of her property, the sale was not one with the right of redemption regardless of whether the original sale price and the resale price were the same. This agreement simply gives plaintiff the right to buy back the property in the event that it is sold, that is, the right of first refusal.

¶6 Although we draw our conclusion from the language of the agreement itself, our conclusion is strengthened by the fact that the purpose of the sale in the instant case was inconsistent with the function of the sale with the right of redemption. The sale with the right of redemption is a means by which a person who needs cash can procure it by selling his property and yet retain the hope of getting his property back in the future. Indeed this system of credit was used for centuries before the establishment of the mortgage system. Planiol, supra, no. 1573. In the instant case, however, plaintiff sold the property to her sister in an effort to help her sister get enough collateral for a loan. Thus it was the buyer, not the seller, who needed money. And the agreement simply provided that if the property were ever sold, plaintiff had the right to buy it for $4,000.

¶7 The right of first refusal, or pacte de préférence, is the option and preferred right to buy property from another if he ever decides to sell. Keene v. Williams, 423 So.2d 1065, 1069 (La.1982) (citing 2 S. Litvinoff, Obligations §§ 104, 108, at 187, 198, in 7 Louisiana Civil Law Treatise (1975)). The Supreme Court has held the right of first refusal enforceable as an option under article 2462 of the Civil Code despite arguments that it states no specified time and that it is contrary to public policy because it is a perpetual option. See Keene v. Williams, 423 So.2d at 1069, n. 2; Crawford v. Deshotels, 359 So.2d 118, 122 (La.1978); Price v. Town of Ruston, 171 La. 985, 132 So. 653, 656 (1931).

¶8 Accordingly the judgment of the trial court sustaining the exception of prescription is reversed and the case is remanded for further proceedings consistent with this opinion. Appellees are cast for all costs of this appeal.

REVERSED AND REMANDED.

D. Special Prescriptive Periods for Options, Rights of First Refusal, and Rights of Redemption

Article 2628 provides that an option or a right of first refusal concerning an immovable may not be granted for a term longer than ten years, and if a longer time was stipulated in a contract, that time "shall" be reduced to ten years. A similar prescriptive period is provided for a Right of Redemption in Article 2568—and it also limits a Right of Redemption for a movable to a maximum of five years. Article 2628 on Option and Right of First Refusal, however, goes on to provide:

> Nevertheless, if the option or right of first refusal is granted in connection with a contract that gives rise to obligations of continuous or periodic performance, an option or right of first refusal may be granted for as long a period as required for the performance of those obligations.

The question of what circumstances establish this exception to the peremptory period has been the subject of litigation.

Study Question:

What is the underlying basis for the rule that an option, a right of first refusal, and a right of redemption can be in effect for only a limited amount of time, especially with regard to immovables?

Article 2628 contains an exception to the time limit: "Nevertheless, if the option or right of first refusal is granted in connection with a contract that gives rise to obligations of continuous or periodic performance, an option or a right of first refusal may be granted for as long a period as required for the performance of those options." Read comment c to the article and then explain how and why the exception provided in Article 2628 does or does not apply to the two cases below.

Hint: Read the phrase "obligations of continuous or periodic performance" and be careful to distinguish it from a right of continuous or periodic performance.

YOUNGBLOOD V. ROSEDALE DEV. CO., L.L.C. 2005
911 SO. 2D 418, (LA. APP. 2D CIR.)

BROWN, C.J.

¶1 Plaintiffs, Ray Oden Youngblood, James Dee Youngblood, III, and Mary Anne Youngblood Shemwell, filed this lawsuit for a declaratory judgment. Rosedale Development Company, LLC ("Rosedale"), was named as defendant. Defendant's predecessors purchased 15 acres out of an undeveloped 363-acre tract from plaintiffs. An option to purchase the remaining acreage provided a three-year term and that "a partial exercise (of at least 12 acres) or any subsequent partial exercise shall have the effect of extending this option for an additional (3) year period." Plaintiffs claimed that this provision created an endless stream of three-year extensions that is prohibited by law. A stipulation of facts was agreed to by both sides. The trial court ruled in favor of defendant and plaintiffs have appealed. We reverse and render judgment reducing the term of the option to ten years.

Facts and Procedural History

¶2 Plaintiffs owned 363 undeveloped acres north of Bossier City off Airline Drive. On June 26, 1996, a group of developers purchased 15 acres for $12,000 per acre with the intent to build a residential subdivision. If successful, they contemplated buying more land from plaintiffs and eventually hoped to develop all of plaintiffs' land in stages. In furtherance of this plan, the developers obtained from plaintiffs an option to purchase the remaining 348 acres at the same price per acre adjusted by a change in the Consumer Price Index. The term of the option was three years; however, it provided for a partial exercise of the option as follows:

> It is understood and agreed that Purchaser may exercise its option on a portion of the Optioned Property, provided however that no such partial exercise shall be for less than twelve (12) acres. Such a partial exercise or any subsequent partial exercise shall have the effect of extending this option for an additional three (3) year period from the closing date of the property upon which the option has last been exercised.

¶3 In December 1996, the developers assigned and transferred all their rights under the agreement to defendant, Rosedale. Over the next six years and within each three-year period provided for, defendant partially exercised the option four times, purchasing approximately 56 acres. The last purchase was on March 8, 2002. On April 21, 2004, defendant gave plaintiffs notice of its intent to again exercise the option and purchase an additional 16.23 acres of land. Plaintiffs refused to sell the land. On June 24, 2004, plaintiffs filed this petition to declare the option null. Defendant filed an answer and the parties submitted the case on a joint stipulation of facts.

¶4   In a written opinion, the trial court held that the right to extend the stipulated time period three years from each purchase of twelve acres or more was not in violation of Louisiana Civil Code article 2628, which limits any option contract for immovable property to a maximum term of ten years. The court noted that this article allows an exception for a contract that gives rise to obligations of continuous or periodic performance. Plaintiffs have appealed from this judgment.

Discussion

¶5   Because options to buy immovable property restrict the free flow of commerce, the legislature imposed as a contractual limitation a maximum term of ten years. Therefore, Louisiana Civil Code article 2628 provides:

> An option ... that concerns an immovable thing may not be granted for a term longer than
> ten years. If a longer time for an option ... has been stipulated in a contract, that time shall be
> reduced to ten years. Nevertheless, if the option ... is granted in connection with a contract that
> gives rise to obligations of continuous or periodic performance, an option ... may be granted for
> as long a period as required for the performance of those obligations.

¶6   In this case, the exception is inapplicable. Never did the original purchasers of the first 15 acres of land, nor the defendant when it purchased land by means of the option to buy, obligate themselves to the development of the whole or any part of the 363 acres of land. There is no agreement or contract to the ultimate development by increments, nor any requirement of the defendant to purchase any additional acreage. Since the contract to buy was not granted "in connection with a contract that gives rise to obligations of continuous or periodic performance," then it cannot fall into the exception stipulated in Louisiana Civil Code article 2628.

¶7   According to the clear language of the option at issue, unhampered by the ten year limitation mandated by Louisiana Civil Code article 2628, defendant could purchase 12 acres every three years until achieving complete ownership of the estate, thus leaving the last 12-acre plot out of the stream of commerce for approximately 73 years. Plaintiffs argue that this is beyond their life span, and it was not their intention when they made the contract to tie up the property beyond their natural lives. Plaintiffs cite the 1993 Revision Comments to Article 2620, which provides:

Under this Article, an option for a perpetual or indefinite term is null. See Crawford v. Deshotels et al., 359 So.2d 118 (La.1978); Becker and Assoc., Inc. v. Lou-Ark Equipment Rentals, Inc., 331 So.2d 474 (La.1976); Bristo v. Christine Oil & Gas Co., 139 La. 312, 71 So. 521 (1916).

¶8 The language and intention of the Louisiana Civil Code is clear and unambiguous on the issue of term limits for options to buy immovable property. In this case, the term provided in the contract was for three years, which could be extended every three years, well beyond the ten-year limitation. Louisiana Civil Code article 2628 states that if the term for a option to buy exceeds ten years, it shall be reduced to ten years. Plaintiffs, however, ask that the option be declared null and void. This would be a drastic measure that would not give any effect to the intent of the parties. We find that the trial court was in error when it failed to reduce the term of the option to buy to ten years, or June 26, 2006 (footnote omitted).

Conclusion

¶9 For reasons set forth above, the judgment of the trial court is reversed.

¶10 IT IS HEREBY ORDERED, ADJUDGED and DECREED that judgment be rendered declaring the option to purchase in favor of defendant, Rosedale Development Company, L.L.C., is valid for a term of ten years to expire on June 26, 2006. Costs are assessed one-half to plaintiffs and one-half to defendant.

REVERSED and RENDERED.

BULLER V. CLARK 2009
7 SO. 3D 167 (LA. APP. 3D CIR.)

¶1 The plaintiff-appellant, Joyce Buller, seeks to enforce a right of first refusal against the defendant-appellee, Peggy Clark, over ten years after the agreement granting the right was entered into by the parties. The trial court granted Clark's exception of no cause of action. For the reasons set forth below, we affirm.

I. ISSUES

¶2 We must decide whether the trial court erred in applying La.Civ.Code art. 2628 and in granting the defendant›s exception of no cause of action.

II. FACTS AND PROCEDURAL HISTORY

¶3 [In 1996, Buller and Clark purchased a commercial building in Alexandria. They recorded a Joint Ownership Agreement in which they gave each other a right of first refusal should either party desire to sell her undivided one-half interest in the property, and they agreed to share equally in all costs on the property. Buller opened a beauty salon in one portion, and Clark operated a florist shop in the other portion of the building. The problems began when in 2008, Clark sold her undivided interest in the property to Larry Clark without first offering it to Buller. Buller claimed that Clark violated the Right of First Refusal, Clark argued that the right had expired because it was more than ten years, and Buller countered that the costs and expenses meant that the ten-year prescriptive period was tolled under the exception in Article 2628. The trial court found for Clark.]

III. LAW AND DISCUSSION

* * *

¶4 Louisiana Civil Code Article 2628 provides as follows: . . .

> An option or a right of first refusal that concerns an immovable thing may not be granted for a term longer than ten years. If a longer time for an option or a right of first refusal has been stipu-lated in a contract, that time shall be reduced to ten years. Nevertheless, if the option or right of first refusal is granted in connection with a contract that gives rise to obligations of continuous or periodic performance, an option or a right of first refusal may be granted for as long a period as required for the performance of those obligations.

¶5 Clearly, the first sentence of the article limits both an option and a right of first refusal con-cerning immovable property to a term of ten years. With regard to the third sentence of Article 2628, providing an exception for contracts giving rise to "obligations of continuous or periodic performance," we find that an agreement to share expenses is not the kind of obligation con-templated in the language of the exception. . . . The published comments to Article 2628 indicate that a lease would be such an obligation.

¶6 In any event, it is very clear that the right of first refusal cannot be indefinite and that any continuing obligation that would extend the right would itself have to have a definite term or ending date. More specifically, published comments (a) through (c) to Article 2628 provide as follows (emphasis added):

(a) This Article *changes the law* by providing a maximum term for options to buy and rights of first refusal that concern immovable things.

(b) A right of first refusal or an option to buy for a perpetual or indefinite term is null. . . .

(c) The failure to expressly state a termination date in an option or a right of first refusal made part of a lease *having a definite term* does not render the option or right of first refusal invalid *if the time for its acceptance* is necessarily *limited by the term* of the lease *Becker and Assoc. Inc. v. Lou–Ark Equipment Rentals, Inc.,* 331 So.2d 474 (La.1976); *Smith Enterprises, Inc. v. Borne,* 245 So.2d 9 (La.App. 1st Cir.1971); *Kinberger v. Drouet,* 149 La. 986, 90 So. 367 (1922).

* * *

¶7 The Second Circuit Court of Appeal specifically addressed the exception in Article 2628, finding it inapplicable in *Youngblood v.Rosedale Development Co., L.L.C.,* 39,939 (La.App. 2 Cir. 9/21/05). There, a developer purchased fifteen acres out of plaintiffs' 384 acre tract with an option to buy more acreage, as long as future purchases were for a minimum of twelve acres. The option was renewable for three additional years with each purchase. The developer transferred its rights within six months, and its successors exercised the option four times over the next six years, purchasing a total of only 56 acres. The plaintiffs refused the next attempt by the developers to exercise the option, arguing that they never intended to extend the option past their lifetimes. Such could occur where, applying the math, the developers could take 73 years to exercise their option on the last twelve acres.

¶8 The developers in *Youngblood* argued the exception to Article 2628. However, the court found that the developers never obligated themselves to develop all of the land by increments or to purchase any more acreage after the first 15 acres. Therefore, the option to buy was not granted "in connection with a contract that gives rise to obligations of continuous or periodic performance," and it could not fall into the [Article 2628] exception. . . *Youngblood,* 911 So.2d at 420. While the Second Circuit in *Youngblood* would not declare the option null and void, it did reverse the trial court and reduce the term of the option to ten years, . . .

¶9 In the present case, we find that an agreement to share expenses for maintenance, insurance, and taxes is not an obligation with a definite term, as contemplated by the language in Article 2628 providing an exception to the ten-year limit on a right of first refusal.

* * *

Section 2: Bilateral Promise to Sell

A contract to sell something or buy at a future time is different from a contract of sale. With a contract of sale, "[o]wnership is transferred between the parties as soon as there is agreement on the thing and the price is fixed, even though the thing sold is not yet delivered nor the price paid." La. Civ. Code art. 2456. In other words, once you have agreed on the thing and the price, the sale is perfected (i.e. immediately effective) and the buyer is the proud new owner of the thing. In contrast, a contract to sell, or a contract to buy, is not the sale itself. It is a preliminary agreement:

> An agreement whereby one party promises to sell and the other promises to buy a thing at a later time, or upon the happening of a condition, or upon performance of some obligation by either party, is a bilateral promise of sale or contract to sell. Such an agreement gives either party the right to demand specific performance.

> A contract to sell must set forth the thing and the price, and meet the formal requirements of the sale it contemplates.

La. Civ. Code art. 2623.

When a promise is unilateral, as with a right of first refusal or an option, the final contract is enforceable as soon as the promisee makes his choice. In contrast, with a generic bilateral promise, the existence of the final contract depends on some condition – which means that a bilateral promise to sell may or may not itself be enforceable. For example, the parties might intend that the enforceability of the final contract will depend on execution of some formal act, in which case, their bilateral promise itself may be unenforceable until such time as that act takes place (as with a promise to donate an incorporeal movable or an immovable). On the other hand, if the purpose of the formality is to protect the interest of third parties, then the bilateral promise to make a formal contract may itself be binding, as when a debtor borrows money in order to pay a debt and intends to subrogate the lender to the rights of his original creditor.

When the bilateral promise is one that promises a future sale, assuming that the agreement sets forth the thing and the price and is in the form required for the future sale, then the Civil Code provides that either party will have the right to demand specific performance should the other party fail to perform; however, the agreement must still be distinguished from the sale itself because the effects are different. To begin with, while a party may demand specific performance as a remedy for breach if the contract is for a movable, Louisiana courts generally prefer to award damages over specific performance. Furthermore, even in the case of an immovable, if the property has since been sold to a third party, the public records doctrine will usually bar specific performance, as explained in Chapter Nine.

Rules particular to bilateral promises to sell include 1) instances where the buyer puts up money to secure the promise (earnest money or deposit), 2) where the thing is destroyed before the actual sale, and 3) the seller's implied warranty of merchantability. The following subsections will discuss first the general rules that apply to a bilateral promise to buy or sell, then will cover each of the particular rules in turn.

A. Bilateral Promise to Sell – in general

Study Question:

What do the following cases teach about bilateral promises to sell?

PECK V. BEMISS 1855

10 LA. ANN. 160 (LA.)

Slidell, C. J.

¶1 [Bemiss's alleged agent, Sims, agreed in an authentic act to sell an immovable to Peck on September 23, 1847. When the sale had not gone through by the following year, Peck sued, alleging that he was the owner of the tract of land.] He admits that the defendant is in possession, and prays that he be adjudged the lawful owner, placed in possession, and quieted in his title. The defendant answers that she is the lawful owner of the tract, alleges an open and undisputed possession since October, 1846, and recites her titles as owner.

***

¶2 We shall overlook the grave questions which concern the authority of Sims to make this contract, the authority of another agent, Wilson, to approve it, or its tacit approval by Overton. Assuming the authority for the purposes of the only discussion which we deem material, we limit ourselves to the consideration of the meaning and legal effect of this instrument.

¶3 It remains to inquire what is the legal effect of such a contract with respect to the transmission of ownership. The contract, to this day, has never been executed, although a suit has been brought by Peck against Overton, to enforce a specific performance; and the question is, what rights passed by the instrument itself, assuming the authority of Sims to sign it.

***

¶4   This reciprocal promise of sale did not make Peck the owner of the land. It gave him only the right of becoming so at a future time. It created in his favor an obligation binding upon Overton, and by which, if he refused voluntarily to comply, he could be judicially constrained to a specific performance or subjected, if he had put it out of his own power to comply, to an action for damages. Until a voluntary or forced execution of the promise, the ownership did not pass to Peck.

***

¶5   The law would be censurable for a strange violation of the principles of reason and justice, and for a shortsighted view of expediency, if it deprived individuals of the right of making prospective agreements for a sale, or told them that if they make each other a reciprocal promise to buy and sell a thing a year hence, for example, that they should be absolutely considered as having made a present sale, with all the incidents of a shifting of the risk, revenues, accretion, &c., which pertain to a contract of sale.

***

¶6   Being of opinion that the plaintiff has not shown a right to maintain a petitory action, his suit against Mrs. Bemiss must fail.

Lagniappe Question:

Plaintiff Moss as buyer sues, praying for specific performance of a promise to sell an immovable.

In support he produces an unsigned typewritten promise to sell, a check for $100 (not negotiated), and a handwritten, signed paper at the top of which the purported seller/defendant Gifford wrote "Received of Moss, $100 toward purchase of 2427 Rose Street."

Below Gifford's signature was written (in Moss's handwriting):

Buy/Sell Agreement Purchase price $15,000, deposit of $100 by buyer, seller must provide up-to-date abstract, buyer to check same. (signed Moss).

Should the court grant Moss specific performance? See Moss v. Gifford, 974 So. 2d 104, (La. App. 3d Cir. 2007).

EDWARDS, Judge.

¶1   In this suit for the return of a deposit made pursuant to a purchase agreement, the defendant appealed the judgment ordering him to return the $1,000.00 deposit to the plaintiffs and to pay $2,958.35 in attorney's fees. The plaintiffs answered the appeal and asked that the attorney's fees be increased to $5,940.32.

¶2   The issues are whether an error existed as to the principal cause of the purchase agreement and whether the award of attorney's fees was proper. We affirm in part and reverse in part.

FACTS

¶3   The plaintiffs, Lyndle and Margaret Thomas, signed an agreement to purchase the residence owned by the defendant, Charles R. Pace, III. Shortly after the execution of this purchase contract, Mr. Thomas went to examine the property following a heavy rain and found it inundated. The Thomases sought to invalidate the contract alleging an error in the principal cause of the purchase agreement. They contended that the real estate agent had been informed about their desire for property which was not susceptible to flooding and that Mr. Pace had assured the agent that the property did not flood. At trial, the Thomases attempted to prove that Mr. Pace was aware that the property had flooded on three previous occasions. The trial court ruled that the plaintiffs met their burden of proving that the flooding of the property constituted an error which vitiated their consent and therefore invalidated the contract.

THE PURCHASE AGREEMENT

¶4   In order to invalidate a contract due to error, the error must relate to the principal cause for making the contract and the other party must either know or be presumed to know of this principal cause. LSA-C.C. art. 1823 (current version at LSA-C.C. art. 1949); Stack v. Irwin, 246 La. 777, 167 So.2d 363 (1964); Talley v. Blake, 322 So.2d 877 (La.App. 1st Cir.1975). The Thomases contend that their primary objective in searching for a home was to locate property with no flooding or water problems. The record reflects that they did inform the realtor of their concern and were assured that Mr. Pace's property was not susceptible to flooding. Since a reviewing court must accord great weight to the findings of the trier of fact, the factual conclusions made by the trial judge should not be disturbed unless the record reflects that the findings are manifestly erroneous. Hanagriff's Machine Shop v. Slaw Construction Co., 380 So.2d 146, 148 (La.App. 1st Cir.1979).

After a careful review of the record, we cannot conclude that the trial court erred in finding that the inundation of the property after the signing of the purchase agreement constituted an error as to the principal cause of this contract. Therefore, the part of the judgment ordering Mr. Pace to return the $1,000.00 deposit to the Thomases is affirmed.

***

AFFIRMED IN PART, REVERSED IN PART.

Lagniappe Question:

What principles or rules of the law of obligations and contracts did the previous case involve? Review the vices of consent. La. Civ. Code arts. 1948-1964.

NEWMAN V. CARY 1985
466 SO. 2D 774 (LA. APP. 4TH CIR.)

WARD, Judge.

¶1 Robert J. Newman appeals a judgment dismissing his suit for breach of contract. He alleges that defendants, Shawn Stevens Carey and her husband, R.F. Carey, agreed to sell a 1978 Ferrari 308 GTS to him for $32,500.00 on March 9, 1981 and that they refused to deliver the vehicle, instead selling it to someone else. Newman's suit sought specific performance of the contract, or alternatively, damages.

¶2 Only Newman and Shawn Carey testified at the trial. Newman submitted into evidence a memorandum, handwritten by Shawn Carey, which he alleges contains the terms of the parties' agreement. The Trial Judge dismissed Newman's suit without written reasons.

¶3 The parties substantially agree on the facts leading up to the disputed contract: Newman, a collector of Ferrari automobiles, was looking for a model like the one the Careys had for sale. A mutual acquaintance told R.F. Carey of Newman's interest, and Carey telephoned Newman. Either Friday afternoon or Saturday, Carey drove the Ferrari to Newman's home, where, after viewing and driving the car, Newman expressed interest in buying it. The Careys were advertising the car for $38,000.00; Newman and R.F. Carey agreed upon a cash sale for $30,500.00. Carey then told Newman that he could not complete the sale because the car was registered in his wife's name. The men drove to the Careys' home where it was discovered that the car was registered under the couple's names jointly, although Shawn Carey had purchased it during their marriage with money given her by a relative. In spite of the agreement between R.F. Carey and Newman, Shawn Carey insisted that Newman raise his offer, and an agreement was reached at the price of $32,500.00. Because the transfer of title required a release of a bank mortgage on the vehicle and because it was after banking hours, the parties agreed to complete the sale at the bank on Monday morning. Accordingly, Mrs. Carey wrote out the following statement:

"I, Shawn Stevens Carey, hereby agree to sell one said Ferrarri 308 GTS, for 32,500 dollars to Mr. Robert J. Newman to be transacted on Monday March 9 at 9 a.m. I guarantee to deliver free and clear title."

¶4   She and Newman signed the statement.

¶5   At this point, the parties differ on the facts. Shawn Carey insists that the memorandum of the agreement does not represent the true understanding among the parties. She contends the actual agreement was to sell the car to Newman for $32,500.00 on March 9, only if the Careys did not get a better offer from another buyer over the weekend. (In fact, they did sell the car to someone else on Sunday, March 8, for $38,000.00.) Shawn Carey testified that she wrote out the agreement for Newman only because he insisted that he needed it to show to his wife and because she trusted him since he claimed to be a friend of her deceased grandfather.

¶6   The Careys did not appear at the bank where Newman went to meet them on Monday morning, March 9. His efforts to contact the Careys were unsuccessful. He filed the present suit on March 23, 1981.

¶7   After examining the evidentiary record including the agreement signed by Mrs. Carey and Mr. Newman, we conclude that the parties had a binding contract which was breached by Mr. and Mrs. Carey.

¶8   A sale in Louisiana requires consent of the parties with agreement as to the price and the thing to be sold. La.C.C. art. 2439. Although a contract to sell movable property need not be written, the parties' written agreement in this case is persuasive evidence that there was consent of all parties, and agreement as to price and object.

¶9   Nonetheless, Shawn Carey testified, without objection from Newman's counsel, that the written agreement did not reflect that the parties agreed to the sale only if a better offer was not received over the weekend. This testimony violates Louisiana's parol evidence rule:

Neither shall parol evidence be admitted against or beyond what is contained in the acts, nor on what may have been said before, or at the time of making them, or since.

La.C.C. art. 2276.

¶10 Clearly, Shawn Carey's testimony was evidence "against or beyond" the terms of the written agreement.

¶11 The Careys argue that Newman should not be allowed to object to the parol testimony on appeal since he did not make timely objection to its admission at trial. We believe Wade v. Joffrion, 387 So.2d 1265 (La.App. 1st Cir.1980), is correct. Louisiana's parol evidence rule is not substantive law, but a rule of evidence. Therefore, inadmissible parol evidence admitted without objection may be considered by the Trial Court (and the Court of Appeal) in reaching a decision. However, simply because we consider Shawn Carey's testimony, does not mean that we find it persuasive.

¶12 Rather, considering the circumstances of the transaction, Shawn Carey's testimony is incredible, and we believe the Trial Judge erred in giving credence to it. We conclude his findings of fact are manifestly erroneous and we reverse.

¶13 Since we hold that the parties had a binding contract which the Careys breached, we now consider Newman's remedy. He sought specific performance of the sale as provided by Civil Code Article 2462. However, specific performance is impossible since the car is no longer in the Careys' possession. But Newman is entitled to damages.

¶14 Civil Code Article 1995 provides that "damages are measured by the loss sustained by the obligee and the profit of which he has been deprived." In general, the measure of the buyer's loss for the seller's refusal to perform a contract of sale is the difference between the contract price and the market value at the time and place of delivery. Mutual Rice Co. v. Star Bottling Works, 163 La. 159, 111 So. 661 (1927).

¶15 The contract price for the 1978 Ferrari 308 GTS was $32,500.00. Shawn Carey testified that on the day following the execution of the contract, she accepted an offer to sell the car for $38,000.00. On this evidence, we find the market value of the Ferrari to be $38,000.00. The difference between this value and the contract price is $5,500.00.

¶16 Accordingly, we render judgment in favor of Robert J. Newman for the sum of $5,500.00 with all costs of this appeal to be paid by Shawn Stevens Carey and R.F. Carey.

REVERSED AND RENDERED.

B. Earnest Money v. Deposit

If a person who has agreed to purchase a thing at some future date gives the future seller money in connection with a contract to buy, that payment has legal consequences. The current presumption is that the money is a deposit on account of the price – unless the parties agree explicitly that the sum is earnest money. Article 2624 provides:

> "A sum given by the buyer to the seller in connection with a contract to sell is regarded to be a deposit on account of the price, unless the parties have expressly provided otherwise. If the parties stipulate that a sum given by the buyer to the seller is earnest money, either party may recede from the contract, but the buyer who chooses to recede must forfeit the earnest money, and the seller who chooses must return the earnest money plus an equal amount.

> "When earnest money has been given and a party fails to perform for reasons other than a fortuitous event, that party will be regarded as receding from the contract."

The presumption that the sum is a deposit changes the rule of the Civil Code of 1870, whose Article 2463 provided that such sums were earnest. Thus be aware that old cases apply that rule, not the current Code Article.

Under the current article, money given with a promise to buy is presumed to be a deposit towards the price. Thus, it will be deducted from the amount owed at closing and if either party breaches the contract, the other can sue for specific performance. If, however, the parties instead agree that the sum will be earnest money, then they have agreed that the sum is the cost of canceling the contract to sell: i.e., if either party fails to go through with the sale, he loses that sum of money but the contract is otherwise regarded as unenforceable and neither can sue for specific performance. As with a deposit, however, assuming the sale goes through as planned, the earnest money is treated as a down payment towards the full price. The last paragraph provides that regardless of whether the sum is a deposit or earnest money, the contract will be dissolved in the case of force majeure.

WORLEY V. CHANDLER 2009
7 SO.3D 38 (LA. APP. 2ND CIR.)

STEWART, J.

¶1 Defendant-Appellant, Loren F. Chandler, et al., ("Chandlers"), is appealing a written judgment rendered in favor of Plaintiff-Appellee, Arnold Victor Worley, et al., ("Worleys"), awarding them damages totaling $71,705.48, in connection with a contract to buy and sell immovable property. Finding that the Chandlers' claims bear no merit, we affirm the trial court's judgment.

FACTS

¶2 The Worleys filed suit against the Chandlers, seeking damages for the Chandlers' failure to purchase the Worleys' home at 209 Canyon Road, West Monroe, Louisiana. The negotiations related to the sale of this home were reduced to writing in a Residential Agreement to Purchase and Sell.

¶3 On February 7, 2006, the Chandlers made the first offer on the home in the amount of $490,000.00 and deposited $5,000.00 in connection with the offer. The Residential Agreement to Purchase and Sell provided that the deposit would not be considered as earnest money and the parties opted for specific performance:

> This deposit shall not be considered as earnest money and this contract shall be considered a Specific Performance Contract.

¶4 On February 7, 2006, the Worleys made a counter offer to sell for $530,000.00 and added a handwritten provision that occupancy would be granted seven days after the closing, or sooner if possible.

¶5 On February 10, 2006, the Chandlers made a counter offer for $528,000.00 and included the following handwritten language related to the deposit and obligations in the event the sale failed:

> The deposit shall be non-refundable after all inspections by purchaser and approval for a loan, appraisal completed. If the sale falls through after March 6, 2006, the deposit shall be given to sellers.

¶6 The Chandlers' realtor, Mr. Dwaine Sutton of Coldwell Banker, testified that he wrote this language contained in the counter offer.

¶7 In April of 2006, Mr. Chandler terminated his recently acquired employment as the Chief Financial Officer at the Glenwood Regional Medical Center. He then notified the Worleys that he would not be purchasing the home. The Worleys subsequently filed this suit seeking specific performance. The Chandlers filed a counterclaim seeking the return of their deposit.

¶8 On July 3, 2008, the trial court rendered a judgment in favor of the Worleys, awarding them $71,705.48 in damages. The trial court determined that the handwritten language did not "do away with" what is written before it, and that the $5,000.00 at issue was not earnest money. The Chandlers are now appealing this judgment.

LAW AND DISCUSSION

Assignments of Error One and Two: Validity and Modification of the Contract

¶9 The Chandlers assert three assignments of error in their appeal. In their first assignment of error, the Chandlers assert that the trial court erred in finding that the parties had a meeting of the minds and entered into a binding contract. In the second assignment of error, the Chandlers allege that the trial court erred in finding that the handwritten language in the buy/sell agreement did not modify the printed provisions relating to the deposit and obligations between the parties because the sale was not consummated.

¶10 Because the intent of the Chandlers was completely different from that of the Worleys, the Chandlers argue that there was no "meeting of the minds" as it relates to the handwritten language in the Residential Agreement to Purchase and Sell. Therefore, the Chandlers assert that the parties failed to enter into an enforceable contract. Since assignments of error one and two are interrelated, we will discuss these issues together.

¶11 On appeal, the reviewing court may not set aside a trial court's findings in the absence of manifest error or unless they are clearly wrong. Where two permissible views of the evidence exist, the fact finder's choice between them cannot be manifestly erroneous or clearly wrong. Even though an appellate court may feel its own evaluations and inference are more reasonable than those made by the trial court, reasonable evaluations of credibility and reasonable inferences of fact are not disturbed on appeal where conflicting testimony exists. To reverse a trial court's factual determinations, the appellate court must find that a reasonable factual basis does not exist for the finding of the trial court and that the record establishes that the finding is clearly wrong. When findings are based on determinations regarding the credibility of a witness, the manifest error-clearly wrong standard demands great deference to the trier of fact's findings. Hanger One MLU, Inc. v. Unopened Succession of James C. Rogers, et al., 43,120 (La. App. 2 Cir. 4/16/08), 981 So.2d 175; Green v. Nunley, 42,343 (La.App. 2 Cir. 8/15/07), 963 So.2d 486.

¶12 A contract is an agreement by two or more parties whereby obligations are created, modified, or extinguished. La. C.C. art.1906. A contract is formed by the consent of the parties established through offer and acceptance. La. C.C. art 1927. The four elements of a valid contract are: (1) the parties must possess the capacity to contract; (2) the parties' mutual consent must be freely given; (3) there must be a certain object for the contract; and (4) the contract must have a lawful purpose. Provenza v. Central & Southwest Services, Inc., 34,162 (La.App. 2 Cir. 12/15/00), 775 So.2d 84. The court must find that there was a meeting of the minds of the parties to constitute consent. Hanger One MLU, Inc., supra. Consent may be vitiated by error, fraud, or duress. La. C.C. art.1948. Error vitiates consent only when it concerns a cause without which the obligation would not have been incurred and that cause was known or should have been known to the other party. La. C.C. art 1949. The existence or nonexistence of a contract is a question of fact not to be disturbed unless clearly wrong. Chapman v. Ebeling, 41,710 (La.App. 2 Cir. 12/13/06), 945 So.2d 222; Crowe v. Homeplus Manufactured Housing, 38,382 (La.App. 2 Cir. 6/21/04), 877 So.2d 156. The words of a contract must be given their generally prevailing meaning. Words of art and technical terms must be given their technical meaning when the contract involves a technical manner. La. C.C. art.2047.

¶13 A sum given by the buyer to the seller in connection with a contract to sell is regarded to be a deposit on account of the price, unless the parties have expressly provided otherwise. La. C.C. art. 2624. Under La. C.C. art 2624, when the parties' intention is that a sum of money be given as earnest, they must clearly express that intention. Edco Properties v. Landry, 371 So.2d 1367 (La.App. 3d Cir.1979).

¶14 Both Mr. Sutton, the Worleys' realtor, and Mrs. Inabnett, the Chandlers' realtor, testified that the handwritten language in the agreement prevails over the typed language. Additionally, the Residential Agreement to Purchase and Sell states:

> "If any of the pre-printed portions of this agreement vary or are in conflict with any handwritten, typed (not pre-printed), or other conditions of the sale, the handwritten, typed (not pre-printed), or other conditions of the sale provisions will control."

¶15 Mr. Worley and Mr. Sutton testified that the Worleys accepted the counter offer containing the handwritten language with the understanding that if the sale fell through the Chandlers would forfeit their deposit and the Worleys would retain the right to sue for specific performance. To support the assertion that they had a right to sue for specific performance, the Worleys pointed out the portion of the Residential Agreement to Purchase and Sell that states:

> In the event of default by either party, the non-defaulting party shall have all rights to demand specific performance or damages, at their option.

¶16   Sutton also testified that if the deposit was meant to be regarded as earnest money, then he would have addressed the money as earnest money, and not as a deposit.

¶17   Alternatively, Mr. Chandler and Mrs. Inabnett testified that the handwritten language altered the agreement to allow the Chandlers to forgo purchasing the property by forfeiting their deposit. The Chandlers argue that their intent in agreeing to the handwritten language was if the sale failed for any reason they would lose their deposit and nothing more. Additionally, Mr. Chandler testified that after the handwritten language was added, it became an earnest money contract.

¶18   The Residential Agreement to Purchase and Sell was a standard buy/sell agreement utilized by the Northeast Louisiana Realtors Association. The trial court found it to be clear and unambiguous. After reviewing the record, we must agree with the trial court that there was a "meeting of the minds" when the Chandlers entered into this binding contract to buy the property in question. Therefore, the first assignment of error is without merit.

¶19   As stated above, jurisprudence has established that when the parties' intention is that a sum of money be given as earnest, they must clearly express that intention. Unfortunately in the instant case, there is no clear indication that the $5,000.00 was to be given as earnest money. The additional handwritten language, which would prevail over the preprinted portions of the Residential Agreement to Purchase and Sell, failed to indicate that the $5,000.00 was to be given as earnest money. Rather, the Residential Agreement to Purchase and Sell clearly states that the deposit shall not be considered as earnest money and this contract shall be considered a specific performance contract.

¶20   Based on the facts and evidence presented, we find that the trial court did not err in determining that the Worleys are entitled to enforce the specific remedies provided in the Purchase Agreement. Doing so in no way conflicts with the requirement that the Chandlers also lose their deposit. The second assignment of error is also without merit.

C. Destruction of the Thing

Suppose the thing that is the subject of a contract to sell is destroyed or partially destroyed by a fortuitous event pending the actual sale. To determine what might happen, you'll need to look to general obligations articles 1876 and 1877, though article 2624 has some reference concerning what happens to a deposit or earnest money in that case.

Study Question:

What does the following case indicate about the interaction of Articles 1876, 1877, and 2624?

PAYNE V. HURWITZ 2008
978 SO. 2D 1000, (LA. APP. 1ST CIR.)

GAIDRY, J.

¶1 The prospective purchasers of a home under a purchase agreement sued the prospective seller, alleging the seller's noncompliance with the agreement and refusal to consummate the sale. The trial court rendered judgment in favor of the prospective purchasers for the return of their deposit, a contractual penalty, and attorney fees, expenses, and costs. The seller appeals and the prospective purchasers have answered his appeal, asserting error by the trial in failing to grant them specific performance. For the following reasons, we amend the judgment to grant the prospective purchasers specific performance, vacate the awards for the deposit return and contractual penalty, affirm the judgment in all other respects, and remand the case for further proceedings.

FACTS AND PROCEDURAL BACKGROUND

¶2 The plaintiffs, Wesley Payne and Gwendolyn Payne (the Paynes), decided to purchase a smaller home, and in July 2005 began searching for one. Using the Internet, they eventually located a home for sale at 4018 Willow Lane in Madisonville, Louisiana. The owner was Keefe Hurwitz. After viewing the home, the Paynes made an offer that was acceptable to Mr. Hurwitz, and a purchase agreement for the price of $241,500.00 was signed on August 22, 2005. On the same date, the Paynes wrote a check in the amount of $1,000.00, representing the required deposit, made payable to Houlemarde Realty, the real estate agency representing Mr. Hurwitz. The purchase agreement provided for a closing date for execution of the act of sale of September

26, 2005, or sooner if mutually agreed. However, it also provided for an automatic extension of the closing date for up to sixty days in the event repairs were necessary.

¶3 On August 29, 2005, Hurricane Katrina made landfall, causing extensive damage to property in southeast Louisiana, including Madisonville. Mr. Hurwitz's home sustained substantial roof damage from the hurricane winds and a fallen tree, as well as water damage to the sheetrock, windows, and other interior fixtures of the left side of the home. The costs of repair were estimated by Mr. Hurwitz, a self-employed contractor with experience as an insurance adjuster, at approximately $60,000.00.

¶4 Due to disruption of electronic communications systems and mail service following the hurricane, the Paynes, who had evacuated to Kansas City, Missouri, experienced considerable difficulty in contacting Mr. Hurwitz regarding the status of the sale of the home. On September 9, 2005, they hand-delivered a letter containing their contact information to Michelle Poliski, Mr. Hurwitz's wife, and attempted to contact Mr. Hurwitz by e-mail directed to Angela Houlemarde, Mr. Hurwitz's agent. The Paynes also contacted their loan officer, who suggested that they ask the lender's title attorney to attempt to contact Mr. Hurwitz regarding the status of the closing date and a proposed extension of that date, as authorized by the agreement.

¶5 On September 20, 2005, Mr. Hurwitz e-mailed the lender's title attorney, acknowledging a conversation of that date and stating:

> Per our conversation today I was blunt that the house was in need of major repair due to storm damage. It will take months to get this work completed. I will not be interested in selling for the same amount when and if I decide to sell my house. Naturally the house goes up in value each day. Your client states on the contract a sale for cash. That means no bank loan or approval is needed. I understand that Katrina was an inconvenance [sic] to every one[.] I'm sorry at this time I cannot afford to sell my house under the previous terms and conditions or the present status of my house and my life at this time. I thank you for your understanding. KH

¶6 On October 3, 2005, the Paynes filed a petition seeking specific performance and damages, alleging that Mr. Hurwitz breached the terms of the purchase agreement. On October 28, 2005, Mr. Hurwitz answered the petition, alleging that the agreement was unenforceable due to Hurricane Katrina and that his performance was impossible due to force majeure. He also alleged that the property could not be repaired within the automatic sixty-day extension for closing, or by November 24, 2005.

¶7   The matter was tried on May 8, 2006. At the conclusion of the trial, the trial court took the matter under advisement after ordering the submission of posttrial memoranda. On September 11, 2006, the trial court issued its judgment, incorporating its written reasons (footnote omitted). The court ruled in favor of the Paynes, awarding them the return of their $1,000.00 deposit and an equal amount representing a contractual penalty, as well as costs, fees, expenses and reasonable attorney fees, as provided in the agreement.

¶8   The Paynes answered the appeal, seeking amendment of the trial court's judgment to grant them the alternative remedy of specific performance in lieu of the return of their deposit and the contractual penalty.

ASSIGNMENTS OF ERROR

¶9   Mr. Hurwitz designates four assignments of error on the part of the trial court:

(1) The trial court erred in determining that he breached the terms and conditions of the purchase agreement;

(2) The trial court erred in determining that the home could have been repaired in time to accomplish the closing;

(3) The trial court erred in determining that the obligation was not rendered null and void due to force majeure or an "Act of God"; and

(4) The trial court erred in determining that he was in bad faith under the terms and conditions of the purchase agreement.
    In their answer to the appeal, the Paynes assign the following error on the part of the trial court:

(5) The trial court erred in holding that the Paynes were required to set a closing or to "put the seller in default," in order to be entitled to the remedy of specific performance authorized by the terms of the purchase agreement.

DISCUSSION

¶10   The purchase agreement at issue was signed by the Paynes on August 19, 2005 and presented in the form of an offer, and was accepted and signed by Mr. Hurwitz on August 22, 2005. It consisted of a two-page form agreement entitled "Agreement to Purchase or Sell," and bore language stating that it was produced through the use of a computer software program. The first page, bearing the parties' signatures, confirmed that the Paynes' offer was submitted to Angela Houlemarde, Mr. Hurwitz's designated real estate agent. The purchase agreement contained the following provision relating to the effect of necessary title work or repairs upon the date of the act of sale:

CURATIVE WORK/REPAIRS

In the event curative work in connection with the title is required, and/or if repairs are a requirement for obtaining the loan(s) upon which this agreement is conditioned, the parties agree
to and do extend the date for passing the Act of Sale to a date not more than fifteen (15) days
following completion of curative work/repairs; but in no event shall extension exceed sixty (60)
days without the written consent of all parties (footnote omitted).

¶11 The purchase agreement also included the following pertinent provisions:

BREACH OF AGREEMENT BY SELLER

In the event SELLER fails to comply with this agreement, for any reason other than inability
to deliver a merchantable title, within the time specified, PURCHASER shall have the right to
demand specific performance; or, at PURCHASER'S option, PURCHASER shall have the right to
demand the return of his deposit in full, plus an equal amount to be paid as penalty by SELLER.
In either event, PURCHASER shall have the right to recover any costs and/or fees, including
expenses and reasonable attorney's fees, incurred as a result of this agreement or breach thereof.

***

DEADLINES

Time is of the essence and all deadlines are final except where modifications, changes, or extensions are made in writing and signed by all parties.

¶12 Mr. Hurwitz testified at trial that no repairs had been made by the original scheduled closing date of September 26, 2005. According to Mr. Hurwitz, the roof repair began on October 21,
2005, and was completed on October 28, 2005. He received the final supplemental check from
his insurer for the estimated cost of repairs on November 15, 2005. He also testified that additional needed repairs were still incomplete at the time of trial.

¶13 Louisiana Civil Code article 2623 sets forth the requisite elements of a contract to sell, or purchase agreement:

> An agreement whereby one party promises to sell and the other promises to buy a thing at a later time, or upon the happening of a condition, or upon performance of some obligation by either party, is a bilateral promise of sale or contract to sell. Such an agreement gives either party the right to demand specific performance.

> A contract to sell must set forth the thing and the price, and meet the formal requirements of the sale it contemplates.

¶14 Delivery of an immovable is deemed to take place upon execution of the writing that transfers its ownership. La. C.C. art. 2477. Louisiana Civil Code article 2489 expresses the obligation of the seller as to the condition of the thing sold at time of delivery:

> The seller must deliver the thing sold in the condition that, at the time of the sale, the parties expected, or should have expected, the thing to be in at the time of delivery, according to its nature.

¶15 Under article 2489, the seller must care for and preserve the thing sold as a reasonably prudent administrator, in accordance with the overriding obligation of good faith. La. C.C. art. 2489. Revision Comments-1993, (b). Thus, Mr. Hurwitz as seller bore the risk of any damage to the home pending the sale, and had the legal duty to restore it to its expected condition prior to delivery to the buyers. As the obligor in that respect, the extensions provided for in the "Curative Work/Repairs" provision of the purchase agreement were primarily for his benefit as seller, to assist him in fulfilling that obligation.

¶16 Our Civil Code provides that "[a]n obligor is not liable for his failure to perform when it is caused by a fortuitous event that makes performance impossible." La. C.C. art. 1873. A fortuitous event is one that, at the time the contract was made, could not have been reasonably foreseen. La. C.C. art. 1875. Our jurisprudence uses the terms "fortuitous event" and force majeure (irresistible force) interchangeably. La. C.C. art. 1873, Revisions Comments-1984, (c). Force majeure is defined as "an event or effect that can be neither anticipated nor controlled." Black's Law Dictionary 673-74 8th ed.2004). It includes such acts of nature as floods and hurricanes. Id. It is essentially synonymous with the common law concept of "act of God," and the latter term has also found its way into our jurisprudence. See Saden v. Kirby, 94-0854, p. (La.9/5/95), 660 So.2d 423, 428; Bass v. Aetna Ins. Co., 370 So.2d 511, 513 n. 1 (La.1979); and A. Brousseau & Co. v. Ship Hudson, 11 La.Ann. 427 (La.1856). The parties concede, as we do, that Hurricane Katrina undoubtedly was a force majeure. But this is only part of the contractual defense of impossibility of performance.

¶17 To relieve an obligor of liability, a fortuitous event must make the performance truly impossible. La. C.C. art. 1873, Revision Comments-1984, (d). The nonperformance of a contract is not excused by a fortuitous event where it may be carried into effect, although not in the manner contemplated by the obligor at the time the contract was entered into. Dallas Cooperage & Woodenware Co. v. Creston Hoop Co., 161 La. 1077, 1078-79, 109 So. 844 (La.1926). In other words, if the fortuitous event prevents the obligor from performing his obligation in the manner contemplated at the time of contracting, he must pursue reasonable alternatives to render performance in a different manner before he can take advantage of the defense of impossibility. West v. Cent La. Limousine Serv., Inc., 03-373, p. 2 (La.App. 3rd Cir.10/1/03), 856 So.2d 203, 205. An obligor is not released from his duty to perform under a contract by the mere fact that such performance has been made more difficult or more burdensome by a fortuitous event. Schenck v. Capri Constr. Co., 194 So.2d 378, 380 (La.App. 4th Cir.1967). The fortuitous event must pose an insurmountable obstacle in order to excuse the obligor's nonperformance. 5 Saúl Litvinoff, Louisiana Civil Law Treatise: The Law of Obligations, § 16.17, at 476 (2nd ed.2001).

¶18 The leading commentator cited above has also made the following observations relevant to the situation of this case:

> A question arises when a fortuitous event prevents the timely performance of an obligation without making that performance impossible in an absolute sense. That is the case of a fortuitous event of limited duration that temporarily prevents the use of but does not destroy the means on which the obligor was counting in order to perform the obligation....

¶19 If the obligation is [such] that a delayed performance is still useful to the obligee, then the obligor remains bound to perform once the impediment ceases and owes no damages for the delay caused by the fortuitous event. Id., § 16.62.

¶20 Louisiana Civil Code article 1759 provides that good faith governs the conduct of both the obligor and the obligee in whatever pertains to the obligation. Similarly, La. C.C. art. 1983 provides that contracts, or conventional obligations, must be performed in good faith. Thus, a party to a contract has an implied obligation to put forth a good faith effort to fulfill the conditions of the contract. Bond v. Allemand, 632 So.2d 326, 328 (La.App. 1st Cir.1993), writ denied, 94-0718 (La.4/29/04), 637 So.2d 468.

¶21 The recent case of Associated Acquisitions, L.L.C. v. CarboneProperties of Audubon, L.L.C., 07-0120 (La.App. 4th Cir.7/11/07), 962 So.2d 1102, also arose in the aftermath of Hurricane Katrina. The defendant in that case also urged the defense of force majeure in an effort to excuse its nonperformance. The court there rejected the defense, observing that under settled Louisiana jurisprudence, "a party is obliged to perform a contract entered into by him if performance be possible at all, and regardless of any difficulty he might experience in performing it." Id., 07-0120 at p. 9, 962 So.2d at 1107, citing Picard Const. Co. v. Bd. of Comm'rs of Caddo Levee Dist., 161 La. 1002, 1007, 109 So. 816, 818 (La.1926). The court concluded: "The unexpected and unforeseen damage of Hurricane Katrina does not change the agreement between these parties; therefore, this is an agreement which can still be performed." Id. 07-0120 at p. 9, 962 So.2d at 1107-08.

¶22 Here, the only possible obstacle to Mr. Hurwitz's performance under the purchase agreement was a temporal one: the completion of the necessary repairs and the closing within the automatic sixty-day deadline or any additional extension agreeable to the parties. The Paynes, as obligees, unequivocally expressed their willingness to agree to the latter extension, but Mr. Hurwitz did not, and preemptively rejected the consummation of the agreement as impossible of performance even before the expiration of the automatic sixty-day extension. Mr. Hurwitz could certainly have rendered performance in a different manner, that is, at a later time based upon a mutual written extension of the closing deadline. We agree with the trial court's conclusion that the real basis of Mr. Hurwitz's failure to perform was volitional in nature, rather than the type of insurmountable obstacle necessary to invoke the defense of force majeure. The determination of whether performance was truly impossible was a factual one, and the trial court expressly concluded in its reasons that Mr. Hurwitz was disingenuous in his explanation regarding the availability of materials and delay in repairs (footnote omitted). Being based upon a reasonable credibility assessment, the trial court's conclusion cannot be manifestly erroneous.

¶23 In summary, we conclude that none of Mr. Hurwitz's assignments of error have merit. As to the Paynes' assignment of error, however, we conclude that there is merit. Louisiana Civil Code article 1986 provides:

> Upon an obligor's failure to perform an obligation to deliver a thing, or not to do an act, or to execute an instrument, the court shall grant specific performance plus damages for delay if the obligee so demands. If specific performance is impracticable, the court may allow damages to the obligee.

> Upon a failure to perform an obligation that has another object, such as an obligation to do, the granting of specific performance is at the discretion of the court.

¶24   The factual situation before us clearly falls within the mandatory relief provided in the first paragraph of the article, rather than the discretionary relief authorized by the second paragraph. Additionally, both La. C.C. art. 2623 (relating to purchase agreements) and the express terms of the purchase agreement at issue grant the Paynes the right to seek specific performance. The record does not support a finding that specific performance is impracticable as a remedy under the circumstances of this case.

¶25   The trial court based its finding that the Paynes were not entitled to specific performance because they "failed to demand specific performance as provided for in the [c]ontract by setting a closing date or otherwise … putting [Mr. Hurwitz] in default." We agree with the Paynes that the trial court erred in that regard as a matter of law. Putting the obligor in default is not a prerequisite to filing suit for specific performance because in such a case the judicial demand itself amounts to a putting in default. La. C.C. art.1989, Revision Comments-1984, (d). And even if a putting in default might somehow be considered a prerequisite to obtaining specific performance, our jurisprudence holds that "there is no need for a putting in default of a seller who has advised the buyer that he, the seller, will not appear to execute the final act of sale at the time fixed for that purpose." 6 Saúl Litvinoff, Louisiana Civil Law Treatise: The Law of Obligations, Part II: Putting in Default and Damages, § 1.18 (1999). Similarly, if the seller simply refuses to agree to the fixing of a mutually acceptable date for the closing, and affirmatively repudiates his obligation to sell under a purchase agreement, it is quite clear that there is no requirement for a putting in default as a prerequisite to seeking specific performance. See id., § 1.19 at 23. Such is the situation here. We conclude that the Paynes are entitled to specific performance under the facts before us, and will amend the judgment in their favor to grant them that relief.

DECREE

¶26   The judgment of the trial court is amended to vacate the award of $2,000.00, representing the return of the deposit of $1,000.00 and the penalty of $1,000.00, and in lieu thereof to grant the plaintiffs-appellees, Wesley Payne and Gwendolyn Payne, specific performance of the Agreement to Purchase and Sell, and to order the defendant, Keefe Hurwitz, to sell the immovable property to the plaintiffs-appellees for the sum of TWO HUNDRED FORTY-ONE THOUSAND FIVE HUNDRED AND NO/100 DOLLARS ($241,500), in default of which the trial court shall render a judgment that shall stand for the act, pursuant to Louisiana Civil Code article 1988. In all other respects, the judgment is affirmed. This matter is further remanded to the trial court for the entry of an order setting a convenient date and time for the execution of the act of sale, or the entry of a judgment that shall stand for the act. All costs of this appeal are assessed to the defendant-appellant, Keefe Hurwitz.

ANSWER TO APPEAL MAINTAINED; JUDGMENT AMENDED AND, AS AMENDED, AFFIRMED; CASE REMANDED.

D. Implied Warranty of Merchantability

Louisiana jurisprudence has long recognized that a prospective buyer who has contracted to buy an immovable may refuse to complete the purchase if doing so will embroil him in legal difficulties. For example, there might be significant doubt about the seller's clear ownership of the thing. Or there may be encroachments on the thing by a neighbor's property, or vice versa. In such cases, the buyer faces the strong possibility of having to resolve the problems through litigation, which is not his goal. After all, his primary purpose in purchasing the property is to obtain clear ownership of it, and if he cannot, then his principal cause of the contract to buy has failed. Thus, the seller is warranting (guaranteeing) that the property is merchantable.

Not all defects, of course, render a title unmerchantable. There must be outstanding rights in third persons (not parties to the sale) who might thereafter make claims of a substantial nature against the property. It has been said that the buyer is obligated to buy a property, but is not obligated to buy a lawsuit or even a potential lawsuit. If, after the sale occurs, the buyer discovers that there is a cloud on the title, then he has a different remedy under the seller's warranty against eviction, Articles 2500 and following, which will be studied in a later Chapter.

The standard for an effective defense based on the seller's inability to warrant the property's merchantability is that "third persons, not parties to the actions and unaffected by the judgments to be rendered, could thereafter make claims of a substantial nature against the titles and further subject the defendant [purchasers] to serious litigation." Schaub v. O'Quin, 214 La. 424, 38 So. 2d 63 (1948).

Study Question:

What do the following cases indicate about the Implied Warranty of Merchantability?

YOUNG V. STEVENS 1967
252 LA. 69, 209 SO. 2D 25

(On second rehearing)
[Defendant Stevens contracted to sell, in writing, a residential property on Arabella Street in New Orleans. Before the act of sale, a survey disclosed that the adjoining property owner's concrete drive strip and fence encroached on Stevens' property about one foot and one foot three

inches, and that the adjoining owner, Mrs. Gresham had refused to remove them. Furthermore, Stevens' own fences encroached on two other adjoining lots about ten and six inches, respectively. The contract to sell provided that "The seller shall deliver to purchaser a merchantable title, and his inability to deliver such title within the time stipulated herein shall render this contract null and void, reserving unto purchaser the right to demand the return of the deposit from the holder thereof." Nevertheless, the defendant refused to cancel the agreement and return the plaintiff's deposit. The plaintiff sued. The appellate court subsequently reversed the district court's dismissal of plaintiff's suit, and the Supreme Court granted certiorari on defendant's application.]

SUMMERS, Justice.

* * *

¶1   Property has a merchantable title when it can be readily sold or mortgaged in the ordinary course of business by reasonable persons familiar with the facts and questions involved. Roberts v. Medlock, 148 So. 474 (La.App.1933). '(O)ne should not be made to accept a title tendered as good, valid and binding unless it is entirely legal from every point of view.' Bodcaw Lumber v. White, 121 La. 715, 721, 46 So. 782, 784 (1908). The promisee in a contract to sell is not called upon to accept a title which may reasonably suggest litigation. Marsh v. Lorimer, 164 La. 175, 113 So. 808 (1927). And while the amount involved may be small, 'it cannot be said that because of this fact the danger of litigation is not serious. No one can be forced to buy a lawsuit * * *' Rodriguez v. Shroder, 77 So.2d 216, 224 (La.App.1955). See Patton on Titles s 46 et seq. (2d ed. 1957); 92 C.J.S. Vendor and Purchaser §§ 209, 211 (1955); 55 Am.Jur. Vendor and Purchaser §§ 252, 253, 254 (1946).

¶2   The encroachments upon the property in this case undoubtedly suggest litigation; for the purchaser could not take peaceful possession of the entire property if part of it is occupied by Mrs. Gresham, who, the record shows, refuses to surrender the controverted strips. No circumstance more clearly suggests litigation than this fact. Truly, Young would be buying a lawsuit, or he would have to take less footage than the agreement calls for, either condition being a violation of the requirement that he be furnished a merchantable title. In like a person buying property whose improvements encroach upon his neighbor is likely to sustain a law suit to defend his right to possession of the property sold to him beyond his title. Kay v. Carter, 243 La. 1095, 150 So.2d 27 (1963); DeSalvo v. Doll, 209 La. 1063, 26 So.2d 140 (1946); Jacobs v. Freyhan, 156 La. 585, 100 So. 726 (1924); Schroeder v. Krushevski, 186 So.2d 640 (La.App.1966); Clesi, Inc. v. Quaglino, 137 So.2d 500 (La.App.1962); Papalia v. Hartson, 52 So.2d 775 (La.App.1951).

¶3 The same result obtains, therefore, whether the adjoining property owner's improvements encroach upon the property to be sold or whether the property to be sold encroaches onto the adjoining property. What makes the title unmerchantable in either instance (and both occur here) is not necessarily the extent of the encroachment, but the fact that it suggests litigation. The law will not require Young to assume Mrs. Stevens' controversy with her neighbor.

¶4 Indeed, the prospect of litigation is the very circumstance which would destroy the principal cause of a contract to purchase a home. A person buying a home wants, above all, peaceful occupancy among peaceful neighbors. Selling him property which will probably bring on a lawsuit is contrary to that motive and furnishes a basis for nullifying the contract. La. Civil Code art. 1823 (1870).

¶5 It will not do in such a case to contend, as Mrs. Stevens does here, that the encroachments are De minimis. To begin with the encroachments consume about 1/40th of the lot area. This is significant. But what is more noteworthy is the fact that, until this time, no one has been able to remove the objectionable encroachments without a lawsuit, not even the vendor Mrs. Stevens who advances the contention that they are insignificant.

¶6 . . . We conclude that the title in question is not merchantable.

¶7 The pertinent part of the 'Agreement to Purchase or Sell', quoted in the beginning of this opinion, entitles the purchaser to a return of his deposit when the seller is unable to convey a merchantable title.

***

¶8 For the reasons assigned the judgment of the Court of Appeal is affirmed.

Review Notes

This chapter covers agreements preparatory to a sale: options, rights of first refusal, the right of redemption, and a contract to sell. The difference between the first three and the last one is that the first two are unilateral (i.e. only one party is bound), and the latter obligates both parties.

Section 1: Unilateral Promises to Sell or to Buy

A. The Option

An option is a contract whereby a party gives to another the right to accept an offer to sell or to buy a thing within a stipulated time. Art. 2620. It must set forth the thing and the price and meet the formal requirements of the sale it contemplates, thus, under the equal dignities rule, if it is an option to buy an immovable, it must be in writing. An option to buy differs significantly from a mere irrevocable offer in that the option is a contract. If the grantor of the option breaches it or sells the thing to someone else before the option-holder's time expires, then the option-holder can sue for specific performance or expectation damages. In contrast, an irrevocable offer is a mere "pollicitation," (Art. 2620 cmt. d), meaning that as it is NOT a contract, if the offeror does not wait the required period of time before selling to a third person, the offeree's only remedy is in detrimental reliance – and it is usually hard to prove that you relied to your detriment on an irrevocable offer.

The offeree's acceptance or rejection of the offer contained in an option is effective when the grantor receives it. Art. 2621. Rejection of the offer contained in an option terminates the option, but a counteroffer does not. An option may be assigned to a third party, in which case the assignor of an option to buy warrants the existence of the option, but does not warrant that the person who granted it can be required to make the sale. If the grantor of the option, in such a case, fails to make the final sale, then the assignee can demand from the assignor whatever he paid for the option. (Article 2622, in referring to 'buyer without warranty, the article is referring to eviction rules, which provide that if a buyer waives the warranty of title, he can still demand the price back from the seller, but cannot demand the other kinds of damages).

An option that concerns an immovable thing may not be granted for a term longer than ten years. If a longer time has been stipulated by the grantor, that time is reduced by law to ten years. Art. 2628. However, if the option is granted in connection with a contract that "**gives rise to obligations of continuous or periodic performance**," than an option may be granted for as long a period as required for the performance of those obligations.

Becker v. Lou-Ark

Defendant Lou-Ark agreed to lease a 45-ton crawler crane to Plaintiff Becker for $2,000/month plus sales tax. The lease included an option to purchase the crane such that 99% of thee rental paid would apply toward the purchase price, and the value of the crane would be determined "by an independent appraiser or by mutual agreement. Becker leased the crane for two years, paying $41,200 including taxes, and decided that it wanted to exercise the option. Two different appraisers determined that the crane was worth $40,000. When Becker demanded that

Lou-Ark sell the crane for that price, Lou-Ark refused and Becker filed suit, depositing $412 into the court's registry as the balance between the appraised value of the equipment and 99% of the amount it had paid in rent.

The Louisiana Supreme Court held that the "option" clause was invalid because it did not have a term, nor could one be derived from the terms of the lease. As the clause was absolutely null, that also means that one or both of the parties erred in its understanding of the very nature of the contract. Error is a vice of consent that renders a contract relatively null. If the error is unilateral, the party who made the error can dissolve the contract if it can prove that the error was to a cause of the contract and the other party knew or should have known of that cause.

Becker's officers thought it was entering into a rental agreement with an option to purchase. The option was absolutely null for lack of a specified time within which to accept the offer of sale, it was a mere lease of the equipment. The Court was convinced that Becker would not have entered into the transaction if its officers had been aware of that fact – therefore the error related to a cause of the contract. Furthermore, Lou-Ark knew or should have known that Becker was entering into the agreement with the understanding and expectation that it contained an option to buy.

Consequently, the Supreme Court held that the entire agreement was null, and that Lou-Ark can be compensated only in the amount of the fair rental value of the crane for the period it was in Becker's possession under the principle of Unjust Enrichment. So, to the extent that the $2,000/month was higher than it would have otherwise been had it been a mere lease, Lou-Ark may have to reimburse Becker for the difference – and the Court remanded the case back to the trial court for determination of that amount.

Badeau v. Savoie

Savoie and Badeau agreed that Savoie would lease an immovable to Badeau. According to Badeau, that agreement included an option to buy, which Savoie breached by selling the home to a third party. The agreement provided a monthly rental of $575, reduced by $25 if paid timely, as well as a handwritten provision stating "House will be removed from the sales market during term of this lease. Lessee may purchase at any time. All rent applied to purchase" and "Payments to finish in October 2006, with payment of an additional $4,000").

The original term of the lease was for one year, and it provided an automatic month-to-month renewal unless either party gives a 30-day notice. Badeau and his partner Main occupied the residence and stayed after the initial one-year term, continuing to make monthly payments, each of which included a notation saying it was for the 'house note.' Then, 12 years later, received a letter informing him that he should henceforth make the payments to a third party. At that point, Badeau sent Savoie a letter stating that he wanted to purchase the property in accordance with their agreement.

Main testified that she had been there from the inception of the agreement, and that Savoie offered "rent to own" and he provided the contract that they signed. She and Badeau requested the hand-written addendum. She further testified that they made timely monthly payments of $550/month until September 1995, when the taxes increased, and they began to pay an additional $25/month. Both Badeau and Savoie had made repairs to the property, and Badeau had even changed the locks.

Badeau testified that he and Savoie discussed the possibility of a rent to own, Savoie prepared the contract, and Savoie wrote in by hand the addendum.

The trial court held that the agreement was a lease with an option to purchase, and to the extent that the language in the addendum was ambiguous, as Savoie supplied it, it was to be interpreted against him. The court further found that the parties had agreed as to the price, and the term, and that Savoie breached the agreement by selling the home to a third party.

As Savoie cannot specifically perform (because he no longer owns the property), the court awarded Badeau damages in the form of a credit for the fair rental value of the property, giving a credit for the improvements he paid for.

Why do you think Badeau was not awarded expectation damages instead or in addition to the fair rental value – i.e. the difference in value between what he had paid and what the home sold for?

B. The Right of First Refusal

A right of first refusal (or 'pacte de preference'), like an option, is contractually binding. They can both be assigned or inherited or enforced by specific performance. A right of first refusal exists when a party agrees that he will not sell a certain thing without first offering it to the other party. Art. 2625. In a right of first refusal, the only thing the grantor is promising is that if he decides to sell the thing, he will offer it to the grantee first

As with an option, a right of first refusal may be an accessory to another contract, such as a sale or lease. One difference between the two is in who has the power to exercise the right. With an option, the power is in the hands of the grantee, who decides whether or not he wants to exercise the option. In contrast, a right of first refusal arises ONLY when the grantor decides that he actually wants to sell the thing. Another difference is that all of the offer's terms must be stated in an option, while a right of first refusal may or may not include a price – the price may be dictated by a third party's offer to the grantor, or it may otherwise be determined or stipulated. A third difference is that an option must have a term – a stipulated time period – while a right of first refusal does not. One similarity, however, is the 10-year maximum that both rights have when they involve an immovable (and the exception where they are in connection with an obligation of periodic performance).

The grantor of a right of first refusal may not sell to another person unless he has offered to sell the thing to the grantee on the same terms, or on those specified when the right was granted (if the parties so stipulated). Art. 2626. Unless otherwise agreed, the holder of a right of first refusal must accept the grantor's offer to sell within 10 days from receipt if the thing is movable, and within 30 days if the thing is immovable. Art 2627. If the grantee does not exercise his right when offered, and the grantor does not conclude a sale to a third person within 6 months, then the right of first refusal subsists in the grantee. Art 2627.

The most litigated issue with regard to the right of first refusal is where the grantor does not clearly and unambiguously offer the property to the grantee before selling to a third person. He must clearly designate the price as well as all the other terms on which he is willing to sell, and if he does not do so, he may be found to have violated the grantee's rights if he subsequently sells the property to a third person.

Jones v. Hospital Corp.

Dr. Jones claims that defendant gave him an oral right of first refusal on an immovable, and that promissory estoppel should be applied to block the hospital's denial of its existence. The hospital denied the existence of any right of first refusal. The court held for the defendant hospital because an oral right of first refusal for the purchase of an immovable is absolutely null, and as such promissory estoppel cannot be used to prove its existence.

Pelican Pub. V. Wilson

Celebrity Chef Justin Wilson and plaintiff Pelican Publishing entered into a book publishing contract, and Pelican published Wilson's book on "Louisiana Outdoor Cookin." That contract included two problematic clauses, the subject of the dispute:

> [The author] will grant to the Publisher an option on his next work. If the Publisher declines
> in writing to execute a publishing agreement within ninety (90) days of the receipt of the com-
> pleted manuscript, the Author is under no further obligation.

And

> [The Author] will not, without the consent of the Publisher, furnish to any other publisher any
> work on the same subject of such extent and character as to conflict with the sale of said work.

Pelican filed suit against Wilson alleging that Wilson had violated the terms of the contract in publishing a new work with a different publisher entitled "Homegrown Louisiana Cookin." Wilson argues in defense that the clauses are invalid.

The court held for Wilson. The first clause is not an option because it does not have an underlying offer nor a term, and the power is in the Publisher's hands, not Wilson's to accept. Thus, it looks more like a right of first refusal – the Wilson must offer the work to the Publisher first, before publishing elsewhere. The clause only grants Pelican an option to come to an agreement with Wilson, as with the option, it lacks essential specificity: it does not address any possible right on Pelican's part to accept or reject terms Wilson negotiated with another publisher. Furthermore, the "if the Publisher declines in writing" term means that Wilson will never know if he is free to publish elsewhere, unless the Publisher decides to say so within 90 days.

The second clause is absolutely null because it is in restraint of trade. Justin Wilson is a celebrity chef, known for his Cajun cooking (and fake Cajun accent and bad jokes). In order not to violate this clause, he would have to switch perhaps to a career in Zydeco music or start writing cookbooks on Italian or Chinese cooking. Consequently, the court affirmed the trial court's holding for Wilson.

C. The Right of Redemption

The right of redemption is the right to take back the thing from the buyer – in other words, it is the seller's right to buy back the thing, usually for the same price the buyer paid. Like an option and a right of first refusal, it is a unilateral and contractual right. Art. 2567. Unlike the other two, however, it is used primarily in a situation involving a family relation and is loan-like in nature. In fact, it is regarded as a simulation when the surrounding circumstances show that the parties' intent was to make a contract of security (for example, if the seller maintains possession of the thing). Art. 2569. If that is the case, any money, fruit, or other benefit received by the buyer as rent or otherwise may be regarded as interest. Pending redemption, any fruits produced by the thing belong to the buyer.

As with an option or right of first refusal, a right of redemption involving an immovable may not be reserved for more than ten years. Art. 2568. Unlike the other two, however, a time limit is also imposed on a right of redemption involving a movable: 5 years. Any provision for a longer period will be reduced. If the seller does not exercise his right within the time allowed or provided, then the buyer becomes the unconditional owner of the thing told. This period is preemptive and runs against all persons, including minors. Art 2571.

If the buyer makes improvements on the thing during the period subject to redemption, he is entitled to them if they can be removed once the seller exercises his right. If they cannot be removed, the buyer is entitled to enhanced value of the thing, just as he would be entitled to enhanced value resulting from un-gathered fruits and unharvested crops. Art 2577. On the other hand, if the thing naturally increases by accession, alluvion, or accretion during the time it is in the buyer's possession, the increase belongs to the seller. During the time allowed for redemption, the buyer is obligated to administer the thing with the degree of care of a prudent administrator. Art. 2578. Where that is the case, the redeeming seller must reimburse the buyer for all expenses necessary for the preservation of the thing. Art. 2587. If, instead of increasing the thing's value, the buyer violates this obligation and the value of the thing deteriorates as a result, then the buyer is liable to the seller for the difference in value.

Peacock v. Peacock

Jon Peacock wanted to raise money for a business, so he proposed to sell his immovable to his brother Roger. The sale was in the form of a quitclaim deed for $8000, and provided that Jon could buy back the immovable within 5 years for $8,000 + 5% interest/annum. Less than five years later, Jon told Roger he wanted to redeem the property, and followed up with a certified letter to that effect along with a check for $8,000, stating that he would pay the interest once Roger transferred the deed. Roger tried to duck the certified letter, and 'sold' the property to his wife. Jon eventually sued.

The court held that the sale contained a valid right of redemption, that Jon had properly exercised it, that the sale to his wife was an absolute simulation, and that Roger must return the property to Jon. The appellate court affirmed.

Travis v. Heirs of Felker

Travis sold an immovable to her sister in 1959 for $100 with the written condition that she had the right to buy it back if ever sold for the full sum of no more than $4,000. In 1979, she sued to enforce that clause because her sister's hers were in the process of selling of parts of the property. The issue was whether this was a right of redemption or a right of first refusal. The 1st Circuit found that it was not a right of redemption because she did not have the right to demand the return of her property. Instead, she had the right to buy it back in the event it was sold, i.e. a right of first refusal. Under the law at the time, a right of redemption prescribed after 10 years, at the time, a right of first refusal did not (see comments to Art 2628). Under current law, it would have prescribed in either case.

D. Special Prescriptive Periods

As mentioned previously, an option, a right of first refusal, and a right of redemption on an immovable all have a peremptory period of 10 years. A right of redemption for a movable is valid for a maximum of five years. Arts. 2628, 2568. Article 2628 concludes with the following:

> Nevertheless, if the option or right of first refusal is granted in connection with a contract that gives rise to obligations of continuous or periodic performance, an option or right of first refusal may be granted for as long a period as required for the performance of those obligations.

The important language is that pertaining to *obligations of continuous or periodic performance*. This means that the grantee of the option or right of first refusal has some continuous or periodic obligation, such as paying rent, that acts to extend the validity of the right. It does NOT mean that the grantee has some additional or periodic right, which is what is argued by the defendant in Youngblood v. Rosedale Development.

Youngblood v. Rosedale Development

Plaintiffs own 363 undeveloped acres in Bossier City, and agreed to sell 15 acres of it to the defendant at $12,000/acre. The defendant intended to develop the land as a residential subdivision. The agreement included an option for the defendant to purchase the remaining 348 acres at the same price per acre adjusted for inflation. The contract stipulated, to be precise, that:

> It is understood and agreed that Purchaser may exercise its option on a portion of the Optioned Property, provided however that no such partial exercise shall be for less than twelve (12) acres. Such a partial exercise or any subsequent partial exercise shall have the effect of extending this option for an additional three period from the closing date of the property upon which the option has last been exercised.

Over the next six years, defendant exercised the option four times, purchasing approximately 56 acres. When defendant notified plaintiffs that it intended to again exercise the option for an additional 16 acres of land, plaintiffs refused to sell and filed a petition to have the option declared null because if fully exercised, it would take approximately 75 years before the entire parcel would be sold, and is therefore unlawful because it extends beyond the 10 year limit. Defendants argued the last paragraph of 2628, that the option was valid because it was in connection with a periodic and continuous performance.

The court held in plaintiff's favor, finding the option invalid as extending beyond 10 years. The 2628 language does not apply because the option was not given in connection with an

OBLIGATION of periodic and continuous performance. Instead, it was given in connection with a right of continuous and periodic performance. A lease with an option to buy is "given in connection with an obligation of periodic and continuous performance" because the grantee of the option has the obligation to pay rent continuously. This clause, however, imposes no such obligation on the grantee. Instead, it imposes an obligation on the grantor – not to sell the land to anyone else for 75 years.

Buller v. Clark

Buller, a beautician, and Clark, a florist, bought a commercial building in Alexandria in 1996. They agreed that they would share the expenses of maintaining the property, and that each would have a right of first refusal should the other desire to sell her undivided one-half interest in the immovable. In 2008, Clark sold her interest to a third party without first offering it to Buller, who sued. Clark argued that the right had expired, as it was over 10-years old. Buller countered, claiming that the costs and expenses of maintaining the property that the parties shared amounted to an obligation of continuing and periodic performance under Article 2628.

The court disagreed, finding for Clark, because the costs and expenses of maintaining the property were not an obligation with a definite term, as contemplated by the language of Article 2628.

Thus, not only does 2628 require that the grantee of an option or right of first refusal maintain an obligation (not a right) of continuous performance, but also that the right have some term (it cannot be eternal). All leases have a term, either stipulated by the parties or supplied by law, so if a lease with an option to buy extends to (for example) 20 years, that option can extend to the end of the 20 year lease.

Section 2: Bilateral Promise to sell (or buy)

A. The nature of the bilateral promise to sell

A bilateral promise to sell, art 2623-24, differs from a contract of sale because it promises to sell (or buy) something at some future date. Generally, the sale of an immovable involves a contract to sell, followed approximately a month later by a contract of sale and the actual transfer of title and possession. Generally, the promise to sell contains clauses that suspend the transfer based on some uncertain event – for example, the sale is contingent on the buyer being approved for financing, or the immovable passing a termite inspection.

Rules specific to a contract to sell include 1. Instances where the buyer secures his promise with some money (either a deposit or earnest money); 2. Instances where the thing is destroyed before the actual sale, and 3. the seller's implied warranty of merchantability.

Peck v. Bemiss

Peck sued to be given title and put in possession of an immovable using a short form of action based on a document in which defendant's (alleged) agent promised to sell the property for a certain price. The court says, even assuming that the agent had the appropriate authority, the instrument is a contract to sell. It is 1. Inappropriate to pursue a petitory action; and 2. While he can sue for specific performance, he cannot sue for title as he was not the owner of the land – the instrument gave him the right to become the owner at a later time, it did not make him the owner.

Lagniappe:

Moss, an alleged buyer of an immovable, sued for specific performance based on a promise to sell. As evidence, he provided a check for $100 (not negotiated) and a receipt from the defendant Gifford saying "Received of Moss, $100 toward purchase of 2427 Rose Street." Below that, Moss wrote: Buy/Sell agreement purchase price $15,000, deposit of $100 by buyer, seller must provide up-to-date abstract, buyer to check same.

Issue: Should the court grant Moss specific performance?

Held: NO, while the thing and the price are apparent from the documents, there is no showing that Gifford consented to the sale – his signature would have needed to have been below Moss's notation of the agreement.

Thomas v. Pace

Plaintiffs Thomas wanted to purchase a home, and informed their real estate agent that they wanted a property that was not susceptible to flooding. The defendant-owner assured the agent that the property they agreed to buy did not flood, but before going to act of sale, they learned that the property had flooded on three previous occasions. Consequently, they sued to have the agreement to buy dissolved based on unilateral error and to get the return of the $1,000 they had deposited. The court held that there was an error as to the principal cause of the contract (and the seller knew or should have known of that cause), and dissolved the agreement.

Newman v. Cary

On a Saturday, defendants Cary agreed in a signed writing to sell their 1978 Ferrari 308 GTS to plaintiff for $32,500.000 the following Monday and subsequently refused to deliver it, selling it instead to a third party. Plaintiff sued for specific performance or damages.

Defendants claimed that the actual agreement was to sell the car only if they did not get a better offer from another buyer before the delivery date. The court held for the plaintiff, finding that 1. While defendant's claim of an oral condition was in violation of the parol evidence rule, as plaintiff did not object, neither will the court; however, 2. Neither the trial court nor the appellate court found it credible, and therefore found in favor of the plaintiffs, awarding Newman the difference between the price the car was actually sold for ($38,000), and the price they had contracted for ($32,500) – i.e. $5,500.00.

B. Earnest money v. Deposit

Article 2624 provides that any money given by a buyer in connection with a contract to buy is assumed to be a deposit. That means that the money will go towards the sale price at the act of sale. If the buyer breaches the contract, the seller can sue for specific performance. If, however, the parties stipulate that the money given is 'earnest money,' then the buyer can withdraw from the sale for any reason but will simply forfeit the earnest money. If the seller withdraws, then he must repay the earnest money to the buyer plus an equivalent amount. In other words, whichever party withdraws forfeits that amount of money to the other party, and neither party can sue for specific performance. Whether the money given is either earnest money or a deposit, in the event of a fortuitous event, the contract will be dissolved and the money returned to the buyer. (Originally the provision was reversed – money given was presumed to be earnest money, but as that does not match most parties' expectations, it was changed in 1995.)

Worley v. Chandler

Defendant Chandler appealed from a judgment in Worley's favor, awarding them $71,705 in connection with a contract to sell immovable property. Chandler had agreed to buy the Worleys' home. The original offer made by the Chandlers stipulated that the $5,000 deposit given towards the $490,000 offer would "not be considered as earnest money and this contract shall be considered a Specific Performance contract. The Worleys countered with an offer to sell for $530,000, and the Chandlers countered the Worleys' offer with one for $528,000, with hand-written languages stating that the "deposit shall be non-refundable after all inspections by purchaser and approval for a loan, appraisal completed. If the sale falls through after March 6, 2006, the deposit shall be given to sellers."

In April, 2006, Mr. Chandler terminated his employment at the local hospital and notified the Worleys that he would not purchasing the home. The Worleys subsequently filed suit seeking specific performance, and the Chandlers' reconvened seeking return of their deposit.

The Chandlers were under the impression that the handwritten language was 1. Newer than the "not earnest money" clause" in the original offer and changed the 'deposit' into Earnest money; 2. Was part of the offer that was actually accepted; and 3. Being hand-written would trump anything contradictory in the original offer.

The court held for the Worleys because the handwritten language does not expressly stipulate that the money would be considered earnest money and that specific performance would be unavailable to either party. In other words, they did not overcome the presumption that the money given was a deposit, not earnest money.

C. Destruction of the Thing: Fortuitous event

Articles 1876, 1877, and 2624 provide that when the entire performance owed by one party has become impossible because of a fortuitous event, the contract is dissolved and the other party may recover any performance he has already rendered. Art. 1876. If performance has been rendered impossible only in part because of a fortuitous event, then the other party's counter-performance may be reduced proportionally or (depending on circumstances) the contract may be dissolved. Article 2624 provides, consistent with this, that when earnest money has been given and the contract because impossible because of a fortuitous event, again the contract will be dissolved. However, if a party fails to perform for any other reason, that party will be regarded as receding from the contract and therefore forfeiting the earnest money.

Payne v. Hurwitz

Plaintiffs Paynes agreed to buy a home in Madisonville, Louisiana from Hurwitz. The agreement provided a price of $241,500, a deposit of $1,000, and a closing date of September 26, 2001, with an automatic extension for up to 60 days if repairs were necessary.

On August 29, 2001, Hurricane Katrina hit, and the wind caused substantial damage to the roof when a tree fell on the home, while water damaged sheetrock, windows, and other interior fixtures on one side. Repair costs estimated by the seller Hurwitz, a self-employed contractor and insurance adjuster, were $60,000. The Paynes tried to contact Hurwitz and proposed an extension of the closing, but on his side, Hurwitz said that it might take months to complete the work and he would not be interested in selling for the agreed-upon amount, but would demand more money. So, he was withdrawing from the sale. The Paynes sued for specific performance. Hurwitz's defense was that the agreement was unenforceable due to Hurricane Katrina and that the property could not be repaired within the 60-day window provided in the contract.

The court found for the Paynes because while Katrina was a fortuitous event, performance was not impossible. "An obligor is not released from his duty to perform under a contract by the mere fact that such performance has been made more difficult" and (of course) that good faith must govern the conduct of both parties to an obligation. Here, the only obstacle to Hurwitz's performance was the completion of the necessary repairs, and the Paynes unequivocally expressed their willingness to agree to a further extension. Hurwitz's excuse was disingenuous because he was primarily looking to profit from the damage by seeking a higher price. The court concluded that the Paynes were entitled to specific performance, and that Hurwitz was required to sell the home to them for the agreed-upon price.

D. Implied Warranty of Merchantability

One of the seller's obligations is an implied warranty against eviction, which is the buyer's loss or danger of losing the whole or part of the thing sold because of a third person's right that existed at the time of the sale. Art. 2500. If the warranty is breached, the buyer can dissolve the sale and recover the price he paid, any fruit he lost, and other damages. However, that warranty is available only after the sale is perfected. A different, jurisprudential remedy is available where the buyer under a contract to buy learns of a potential title problem. The saying is that one cannot be forced to buy a lawsuit, and the jurisprudential remedy is termed "the implied warranty of merchantability." If a third person, not party to the contract to buy, could thereafter make claims of a substantial nature against the title and potentially subject the purchaser to serious litigation.

Young v. Stevens

Stevens, defendant, agreed to sell a home to buyer-plaintiff Young. Before the act of sale, Young commissioned a survey which disclosed that there were boundary problems on all three sides: one adjoining property owner's driveway and fence encroached on the subject property approximately 1', and that owner refused to move either. Additionally, the subject property's offence encroached on two other lots approximately 10' and 6', respectively. Plaintiff sued to dissolve the agreement and get his deposit returned.

The court held for the plaintiff, that what makes title unmerchantable is not necessarily the extent of the encroachment, but the fact that it suggests litigation. Young was not obligated to assume Stevens' controversy with her neighbors.

Furthermore, the court stated that the prospect of litigation is the very circumstance which would destroy the principal cause of a contract to purchase a home: a buyer wants, above all, peaceful occupancy.

1. Anna's shoe store was so successful that she decided to open a second store and so entered into a 25-year lease that contained the following language: "Lessee to pay rent of $1,000/month plus 10% of any gross income over $10,000. Lessee also has an option to purchase the premises anytime before the end of the lease for $100,000."

Lessor now contends that this clause is invalid because it extends beyond 10 years. Is it?

2. In order to raise money quickly to buy more shoes from Guiseppe, Anna asked her sister, Nina, if Nina would be willing to buy her beloved antique Jaguar E-type (sports car) for $20,000, on condition that Anna could buy it back anytime within the next six years. Five and ½ years later, Anna finally has the money together and contacts Nina, demanding to buy back the car. Nina refuses.

Can Anna seek specific performance of her right to buy the car back?

3. Anna's businesses are taking off to such an extent that she agrees to buy a warehouse to hold all the blue suede shoes. Her contract for the warehouse stipulates that, assuming she can get the financing, she will pay $500,000, with $5,000 down as earnest money. If she doesn't go through with the sale, the seller can either keep the earnest money or sue for specific performance. In researching the property, Anna learns that the seller, Sue, has a long-standing argument with her next-door neighbor over ownership of the parking lot the two properties share. Can Anna get out of the contract and avoid the headaches?

CHAPTER 6

TRANSFER OF TITLE AND RISK

Flowchart

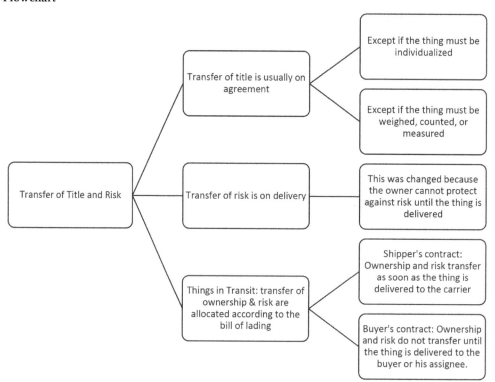

Section 1: Title and Risk in General

A sale is perfected once three things have been identified and consented to: the price, the thing being sold, and the transfer of ownership. La. Civ. Code art. 2456. Previous chapters have discussed the issue of price, what kinds of things can be sold, the form of a contract of sale, and agreements preparatory to a sale. This chapter will discuss when and how ownership and risk are transferred. While the general rule is that ownership is transferred on agreement, there are exceptions to that rule. Furthermore, special rules govern when the risk transfers, as opposed to ownership.

When you own a thing, you have the power to use it, keep any fruit it produces, and sell it or otherwise dispose of it. La. Civ. Code art. 477. Normally, you also own any risk that the thing may be destroyed (unless you secure adequate insurance, in which case an insurance company has assumed that risk in exchange for your payment of premiums). But what about when you just bought a thing, but don't yet have possession of it? Article 2456 provides that "ownership is transferred between the parties as soon as there is agreement on the thing . . . " This seems to suggest that risk has transferred at the same time, and originally this principle of *res perit domino* (risk follows ownership) was the case under both common law and Louisiana's civil code, as you will see in some of the older cases.

However, this was changed in the 1995 Revision as it is unfair to impose the risk of loss on the buyer when he neither controls the thing nor can prevent such loss—i.e., it's unfair to impose on you, the buyer, the risk that the blue suede shoes will burn up in the warehouse before you've ever seen them, and before you can put them in a fire-proof box to protect them. Consequently, the law was changed so that while ownership may transfer on agreement (there are exceptions to that as well), risk does not transfer until delivery. Article 2467 provides (in part): "The risk of loss of the thing sold owing to a fortuitous event is transferred from the seller to the buyer at the time of delivery."

As indicated in Article 2456, ownership is normally transferred on agreement, while risk transfers only on delivery. However, there are times when ownership cannot or does not transfer on agreement. Sometimes, the parties intend that ownership will not transfer until some suspensive condition is fulfilled. For example, very often a sales agreement stipulates that ownership of your new car or new house will not transfer until your financing is approved by the lender. The suspensive condition in this case is the lender's agreement to lend you the price. Once the condition is fulfilled, the effects of the contract of sale are retroactive to its inception. At times, the buyer may want to specify that ownership will not transfer until he has seen or tested the thing, and this sale "on view or trial" (Article 2460) is another sort of suspensive condition that delays the transfer of ownership.

Additionally, for a transfer of ownership to take place (and a sale to thereby be perfected), the object of the sale must be certain, meaning that the parties have agreed to exactly which thing has been sold, and it has been set aside, weighed, counted, or measured-off, as indicated in Civil Code article 2457 and 2458. Furthermore, there are special rules for movables in transit, where a third party (the shipper) is interposed between the buyer and the seller. These latter rules are influenced by both national and international shipping conventions, as recognized in Louisiana Civil Code articles 2613, 2616, and 2617 and the comments thereto. Read the articles mentioned previously on perfection of a sale in the Civil Code itself as preparation for the following.

Section 2. Appropriation or Individualization

Article 2457 provides:

> When the object of a sale is a thing that must be individualized from a mass of things of the same kind, ownership is transferred when the thing is thus individualized according to the intention of the parties.

This could apply in the blue suede shoes hypothet: now you should understand that you, as buyer, do not incur the risk of the blue suede shoes being lost in a fire until they are actually delivered to you, as per article 2467, nor do you have any other aspect of ownership until the shoes are taken off the seller's shelf and set aside for you (assuming he has other pairs of blue suede shoes he is selling).

Study Question:

Individualization normally takes place in accordance with the parties' intent. If they have clearly expressed their agreement on the time, place, and manner in which individualization will occur, than that agreement governs the process.[1] But, if the parties have not so expressed themselves, then individualization is inferred under Article 2457 and its jurisprudence. Normally, individualization of goods to be transported by a carrier does not occur until the seller delivers the goods to a carrier, as in *Collins v. Louisiana State Lottery* below. However, the result in *Edgwood v. Falkenhagen differs.* Why? How does Article 2457 apply?

COLLINS V. LOUISIANA ST. LOTTERY CO. 1891
43 LA. ANN. 9, 9 SO. 27 (LA.)

FENNER, J.

[Plaintiff claims that he owns 1/20th of a prize-winning lottery ticket; the defendant denies that ownership. Apparently, four days before the drawing, the plaintiff sent an order for 20 1/20 tickets, along with the requisite payment of $20.] His order was written on defendant's order form, which included the following disclaimer: 'It is of the utmost importance that correspondents send in their orders early. Many complaints arise from the fact that they wait for the last moment, thus causing a large accumulation of orders, and rendering it impossible to give them the careful attention we desire;' and also this: 'Remittances sent too late can only be attended

---

1   24 La. Civil Law Treatise 3:8.

to for the ensuing drawing.' The package was received by defendant at about 1 o'clock P. M. of January 13th, the day before the drawing. The defendant conducts its large and complicated business according to certain rules and forms of proceeding applicable to all orders. Letters are opened by one clerk, who hands the orders to another clerk, who fills them by selecting the tickets called for. He puts these tickets in the letter containing the order, and sends it, with others of like character, to the correspondence department, where a distributing clerk arranges the orders alphabetically, and sends them to an entry clerk, who enters the date, name, address, number, and size of tickets on sheets which are afterwards bound in a book. The letter and tickets are then passed to a clerk called the 'writer,' who puts the tickets in a letter and forwards them to the purchaser. The rules further require that all letters containing as much as $20 in tickets shall be sent by registered mail, and that no registerd (sic) letter shall be sent after the day before the drawing. In compliance with these rules, the filling of plaintiff's order was begun, but never completed. The letter containing the order was opened. The tickets to fill it were selected, including No. 12,122. The entries thereof were made on sheets. They were handed to the writer, to be forwarded according to instructions, or, in absence of instructions, according to the rules of the company. The order in this case contained no instructions, and reached the writer after the closing of the registry department of the post-office, rendering it impossible to comply with the rules. He therefore returned the order and tickets to the entry clerk, who canceled the entry which had been made, and handed the order and tickets to another clerk, whose duty it is to receive such orders as are too late to be filled, and are passed over to be filled with tickets for a subsequent drawing. He returned the tickets to the clerk who selected them, who, in fulfillment of his duty under the rules, canceled these, with all other unsold tickets, before the drawing on the following day. There is no dispute about the facts, and not the slighest (sic) hint of any fraud or unfair practice.

¶1 The plaintiff claims that the sale was complete from the moment the defendant selected and set apart the tickets to be sent to him, and he relies upon the elementary principles announced in the Code that the contract of sale is perfect when three things concur,-the thing sold, the price, and the consent, (Civil Code art. 2439;) that consent may be expressed in words or implied from actions, (articles 1811, 1819;) and that 'the sale is perfect between the parties, and the property is of right acquired to the purchaser with regard to the seller, as soon as there exists an agreement for the object and for the price thereof, although the object has not yet been delivered nor the price paid.' Article 2456. The real question is whether there did exist an 'agreement' as to the object. There was no express agreement on the part of defendant. Can his assent to such agreement be implied from his acts as above set forth? [former A]rticle 1816 says: 'Actions, without words, either written or spoken, are presumptive evidence of a contract, when they are done under circumstances that naturally imply a consent to such contract.' The article proceeds to mention certain classes of acts from which consent is implied, as, for instance, 'to receive goods from a merchant without any express promise, and to use them implies a contract to pay the value.' etc. Article 1818 provides:

> Where the law does not create a legal presumption of consent from certain facts, then, as in the case of other simple presumptions, it must be left to the discretion of the judge, whether assent is to be implied from them or not.

¶2 This is the article which defines our duty in this case. We are to determine whether, from the acts of defendant, we can imply its consent to a final and binding appropriation of the tickets selected to the order of plaintiff, as the object of the sale. We think we cannot. The selection of tickets made by defendant was simply a step in the process of filling an order which the defendant had adopted under its rules. The selection was merely a conditional appropriation of the tickets to the order which did not and was not intended to, become final or binding until the process had been completed, resulting in the actual filling of the order. When it became manifest that the filling of the order according to its rules could not be completed, defendant had the clear right to cancel the prior inchoate steps which had been taken for that purpose, and to treat the order as not filled. Of this plaintiff had no right to complain. He had notice of the importance of sending his order early, and of the danger that, if sent late, the accumulation of orders might render it impossible to give them attention; and he was further advised that, if received too late, his remittance would be applied to the ensuing drawing. This was exactly what occurred. His order came too late to be filled in accordance with the rules of the company. An attempt was made ot (sic) fill it, which was ineffectual. The company therefore did not fill his order. It was never filled, and the appropriation thereto of the tickets selected never became final and binding. Had the tickets drawn no prize, and had the company, having acted as it did, claimed the right to retain the price, such a pretension would have been absurd. In this case the company had a perfect excuse for not filling the order, because it was impossible to do so in accordance with its rules; but, even if it had no such excuse, and had had time to complete it, yet if it did not choose to do so, and saw fit to cancel the selection of tickets before completing the filling of the order by mailing them, it would have had the right to do so if its action were free from taint of fraud or malpractice. Says Mr. Benjamin, in his work on Sales:

> 'A very common mode of doing business is for one merchant to give an order to another to send him a certain quantity of merchandise, as so many tons of oil, so many hogsheads of sugar. Here it becomes the duty of the vendor to appropriate the goods to the contract. The difficulty is to determine what constitutes the appropriation; to find out at what precise point the vendor is no longer at liberty to change his intention. It is plain that the vendor's act in simply selecting such goods as he intends to send cannot change the property in them. He may lay them aside in his warehouse, and change his mind afterwards; or he may sell them to another purchaser without

committing a wrong, because they do not yet belong to the first purchaser, and the vendor may set aside other goods for him. It is a question of law whether the selection made for the vendor in any case is a mere manifestation of his intention, which may be changed at his pleasure, or a determination of his right, conclusive on him, and no longer revocable.' Benj. Sales, § 358.

¶3 This is objected to as a common-law authority, but it is also common sense, and in harmony with all principles of our own law. The rules adopted by the company were reasonable and conservative, and necessary for the safety of its correspondents, and for the preservation of its own good faith from suspicion or attack. If it should appropriate tickets to orders without dispatching them, or if it should dispatch them only on the day of the drawing, such proceedings would necessarily arouse suspicion as to their honesty and fairness, from the very nature of defendant's business. So the rule requiring tickets to be forwarded by registered mail is manifestly useful and proper. The acts of defendant relied on by plaintiff only exhibit an intention to appropriate specific tickets to the filling of plaintiff's order, conditioned on the order being actually and finally filled in accordance with its rules; and, when that condition failed, it had the perfect right to abandon the intention, and to cancel the inchoate appropriation, which had not become irrevocable.

¶4 Judgment affirmed.

EDGWOOD CO. V. FALKENHAGEN 1922
151 LA. 1072, 92 SO. 703 (LA.)

ST. PAUL, J.

¶1 Plaintiff sues for the price of 20 barrels of whisky sold to defendant in December, 1918, which defendant refused to accept. The question is whether the contract remained executory, leaving plaintiff only an action for damages, or did it ripen into an executed contract, so that the whisky became the property of defendant, entitling plaintiff to sue for the price.

¶2 The agreement was originally for 30 barrels, of which 10 were to be, and were, delivered at once, 10 to be delivered on January 10th, and 10 on January 25, 1919. On January 7th defendant wired plaintiff:

'Hold ten barrels to be shipped January 10th and 25th, and ship February 1st and 15th; am crowded for room.'

¶3 On January 13th plaintiff drew from its stock 20 barrels of whisky, had them regauged by the government, marked them with defendant's name and address, and put them aside in its warehouse to await the time of shipment, and thereupon sent defendant the official gauger's certificate showing the serial numbers and contents of the barrels. On January 20th defendant wrote plaintiff:

> 'Inasmuch as I am overstocked and the transportation of liquor into Texas is prohibited, you can cancel balance of my order.'

¶4 Plaintiff, however, refused to accept the cancellation, and this suit followed. At the time it was tried below (June, 1919) the whisky was still in plaintiff's warehouse and intact.

¶5 We think the sale became executed when the 20 barrels of whisky were segregated from the balance of plaintiff's stock and put aside as the property of defendant. This was an 'appropriation,' and completed the sale absolutely, whereby defendant became the owner of the 20 barrels of whisky thus appropriated, and plaintiff became entitled to the price. Thus:

> 'Any act indicating a definite intention to appropriate the goods to the contract is sufficient, such as setting apart and marking the goods for the buyer. * * * An appropriation by the seller alone will not pass title unless assented to by the buyer. This assent may, however, be either express or implied, and may be given by one party either before or after the act of appropriation by the other.' 16 Cyc. 296, 297.

¶6 As the buyer was here in Louisiana, and the goods were to be taken out of stock and shipped by plaintiffs from its warehouse in Cincinnati, it is clear that defendant assented in advance that the appropriation should be made by plaintiff. And by this appropriation the sale was completed, as there is no claim that the goods were not right.

¶7 In State v. Shields, 110 La. 547, 34 South. 673, Kessler v. Manhein, 114 La. 619, 38 South 473, and Witt Shoe Co. v. Seegars, 122 La. 145, 47 South. 444, the question involved was simply whether an executory agreement to sell and buy indeterminate objects was a completed contract of sale. The court held that such a contract was not a sale until there had been an appropriation of the specific objects which were to become the property of the buyer, and that no such appropriation had been made at the time of such agreement. What was said about delivery to a carrier or warehouseman was undoubtedly germane to the subject, since a delivery is necessarily an appropriation. But the two are not the same, the one being essential to the completion of the sale, the other not so; and the court was not specially concerned in those cases, as it is in this, with the precise issue whether there can be an appropriation without a delivery. Hence those cases cannot be taken as holding the negative thereof.

¶8   Defendant says in his brief:

'The plaintiff has lost nothing, for its suit is merely speculative, as it has the whisky or the proceeds thereof; and it is now trying to force the defendant to pay for something which plaintiff itself has in its possession, or has sold for a largely increased consideration.'

¶9   We deem it hardly necessary to say that, since defendant was the lawful owner of the 20 barrels of whisky from the time they were set aside as his, it follows that plaintiff was thereafter merely bailee thereof for his account (though with an interest), and that plaintiff is entitled to the possession thereof if still on hand, or to an accounting therefor if sold. Hence, if sold 'for a largely increased consideration,' defendant finds himself in an even more fortunate position than had his offer to cancel the sale been accepted. But the petition shows that the whisky was on hand when the suit was filed, and was then again tendered defendant, which was all defendant need do in the premises; so that, if the whisky be still on hand, any complications which may have arisen since, or may arise hereafter, cannot be laid to the charge of plaintiffs.

Decree.
The judgment appealed from is therefore affirmed.

Comment:

Article 2457 states that transfer of ownership is delayed until the thing has been individualized or properly appropriated, such as when the blue suede shoes are taken off the shelves, boxed, and addressed to you. Article 2458 similarly indicates that if the sale requires that the thing be weighed, countered, or measured, there is no transfer of ownership until that is accomplished, unless the thing is sold for a lump sum:

When things are sold by weight, tale, or measure, ownership is transferred between the parties when the seller, with the buyer's consent, weighs, counts, or measures the things.

When things, such as goods or produce, are sold in a lump, ownership is transferred between the parties upon their consent, even though the things are not yet weighed, counted, or measured. Articles 2457 and 2458 cover different kinds of sales. For example, if the thing sold must be segregated from a larger inventory, for example if the thing sold is 20,000 tons of processed, recycled concrete as in *Callou Corp. v. 3600 Alvar, LL.C.*, 2013 WL 5439152 (E.D. La. 2013), ownership does not transfer until the 20,000 tons is irrevocably separated from the rest of the seller's concrete. However, if the price depends on the quantity sold, then Article 2458 governs. For example, if the buyer wants 20,000 tons of concrete at $1,000/ton, that is a sale by weight. An agreement for 8,000 bushels of corn at $.65/bushel is a sale by measure. And if he wants 100 pairs of blue suede shoes at $150/pair, that is a sale by 'tale' (i.e. talley or counting).

Study Question:

Explain how Article 2458 applies in the following two cases. In addition, explain why in one case the court concludes that the buyer did not own the delivered merchandise (even though it had been weighed), and in the other case, that the buyer did own the delivered merchandise (even though it had not been counted).

PETERKIN V. MARTIN 1878
30 LA. ANN 894 (LA.)

SPENCER, J.

¶1 [The plaintiff alleges that he had agreed to pay the market price of good, sound corn, and was entitled to such an article, but that the defendant had delivered corn that had been subjected to heat and was damaged at the time it was weighed and delivered to plaintiff's vessel and mixed with both the plaintiff's corn and the corn belonging to the plaintiff in a related case, Oglesby v. Martin. Therefore the plaintiff demands appropriate damages or rescission of the sale. (Oglesby lost because he was unable to prove that the corn was damaged at the time of delivery.)]

¶2 The evidence shows that the plaintiff at time of contract agreed to pay the market price of good, sound corn, and he was entitled to such an article, unless there are circumstances in this case which vary the rule that a sound price entitles the purchaser to a sound article.

¶3 This the defendant contends is the case. He says that on the tenth April he sold the plaintiff all the mixed corn he had in the elevator, being six, seven, or eight thousand bushels, at sixty-five cents per bushel, to be taken away in a few days, and he contends that at that date it is not shown that the corn was unsound. That it was a sale of a determined lot, and that it put the thing at the risk of the purchaser from that date; that the sale was complete and perfect, there-fore, on the tenth April. We do not think so. Article 2458, Civil Code, provides: "When goods, produce, or other objects, are not sold in a lump, but by weight, by tale, or by measure, the sale is not perfect, inasmuch as the things sold are at the risk of the seller until they be weighed, counted, or measured, etc." Civil Code Article 2456 declares the sale "to be perfect between the parties, and the property of right acquired to the purchaser with regard to the seller, as soon as there exists an agreement for the object and for the price thereof, although the object has not yet been delivered, or the price paid."

¶4 We apprehend that in a case like this (admitting, for the sake of the argument, it was a purchase of all the mixed corn of Martin in the elevator, though Peterkin seems to deny this), where the quantity was stated to be between six and eight thousand bushels, at sixty-five cents per bushel, the price was not agreed upon and ascertained in the sense of article 2456. Had the elevator taken fire, and the corn been consumed before it was weighed, defendant could not have sued for any specific sum as the ascertained price of the corn. We think the rule of article 2458 governs this case. That by the very terms of that article a sale "by weight, tale, or measure," is not a sale "in lump." We agree with plaintiff's counsel that there can be no sale in lump, except for a lumping price. These views are, we think, in harmony with the jurisprudence of this State. See Goodwyn v. Pritchard, 10 A. 250, where the precise point is decided. Also, Larue v. Blair, 10 A. 242; 21 A. 235 and 414. Nothing short of an express agreement, in a case like this, will put the thing before it is weighed at the risk of the buyer. The argument of defendant's counsel as to the inexpediency or improbability of selling such articles as corn, eggs, butter, etc., subject to the call of the purchaser, can not (sic) vary a rule of law, or supply the place of proof that there was an agreement to vary it. It may be that a seller would do a very foolish thing in so doing, but if he does do it, he has no one to blame but himself.

¶5 We hold, therefore, that the sale was not perfect until the weighing and delivery (which are contemporary acts at the elevator) on the third and fourth of May.

***

¶6 It is therefore ordered, adjudged, and decreed that the judgment appealed from be avoided and reversed, and it is now ordered and decreed that plaintiff, William S. Peterkin, do recover of the defendant, George Martin, $1310 35, with legal interest from seventh day of June, 1871, till paid, and costs of both courts.

[Jacob Shuff, the plaintiff-buyer alleges that the boat, with the hoop-poles, had been delivered to him (but admittedly not counted or 'tallied') when they were wrongfully seized by the seller's creditor, the defendants.]

The defendants answer, that the property at the time it was attached, was not the property of Shuff, but of Mathews [the seller], and was, therefore, legally attached; . . .

MARTIN, J.

¶1 The defendants in this case contend that the hoop-poles were properly attached for the vendor's debt, because they had not yet begun to be the vendee's property, notwithstanding they were sold and delivered to him, and he had partly paid for them; having been sold by tale, and not having been all counted before the seizure, if any part of them was; for our statute provides that such a sale is not perfect, inasmuch as the things sold are at the risk of the seller till they be counted. Civ. Code, 346, art. 6. And it is hence held, that, according to the general principle, res perit domino suo, as the risk was for the vendor, he was the owner of the poles.

¶2 The principle is a general but not a universal one. It is of the nature, not of the essence of the contract of sale. As soon as the sale is perfected by the assent of the parties, the vendee becomes as to the vendor the owner of the thing; the latter cannot sell or abuse, may neglect to have a certain degree of care of it, without becoming liable to the former. If he be discharged of the obligation of delivering it by its destruction, without his fault, it is because an obligation to give a thing is dissolved by the destruction of it. As to third persons, the property of the thing sold does not pass to the vendee till after delivery.

¶3 Nothing prevents the parties to agree that the thing sold shall remain at the vendor's risk till, or even some time after the delivery. And this convention has not any other effect on the contract of sale, than to charge the vendor with the risk; it does not impair the vendee's right, it is merely for his advantage.

¶4 If it be agreed that the thing sold be at the vendor's risk till delivery, the vendee is not less the owner of the thing, as to the vendor, who can no more sell or abuse the thing, without being liable to damages.

¶5 The liability of the vendor, in the case just put, is introduced by the agreement of the parties. It is so, by the law, in cases of sales by tale. . .

¶6 The principle res perit domino suo applies between the owner and possessor; the object of it is that the former, not the latter, bear the loss of the destruction of the thing perishing without the fault of the latter.

¶7 I conclude, that the hoop-poles were, in the present case, the property of the plaintiff, the vendee, when they were attached.

¶8 If the property (sic) of A be seized, on a writ commanding the seizure of that of B, there cannot be any doubt of the right of A instantly to sue the officer at once, with the party authorizing the seizure as trespassers. He is not bound to interfere in the suit in which the seizure is made.

¶9 I think the judgment of this court ought to be, that the judgment of the parish court be annulled, avoided and reversed, and that the plaintiff do recover from the defendant the sum of $625, with costs in both courts.

***

¶10 It is therefore ordered, adjudged and decreed, that the judgment of the parish court be annulled, avoided and reversed; and this court, proceeding to give such judgment as in their opinion ought to have been given in the parish court, it is ordered, adjudged and decreed, that the plaintiff recover from the defendants the sum of six hundred and twenty-five dollars, with costs in both courts.

Comment

The previous discussion covered only the first paragraph of Article 2458, that relating to sales where the price is calculated as a price per unit, in which case, the transfer of ownership is suspended until the units are irrevocably separated from the mass of things and the price calculated, even where the sale is of a lump thing, though at a unit price, such as "all the mixed corn . . . in [plaintiff's] elevator" for $.65/bushel because what governs is the unit price. The second paragraph of Article 2458 refers to sales where the thing is "sold in a lump," in which case, ownership transfers on consent, even if the thing is not yet weighed, counted, or measured. So, for example, if the parties agreed that the buyer was buying a flatboat with all the hoop-poles it contained for $600, that is a lump sale for a lump price, as is the same sale where the seller promises that there are at least 20,000 hoop-poles on the flatboat, and they are being sold together with the flatboat for a 'lump price' of $600.

Section 3: Transfer of Risk

As mentioned previously, the law was changed in 1993, and Article 2467 now provides (in part): "The risk of loss of the thing sold owing to a fortuitous event is transferred from the seller to the buyer at the time of delivery."

Hypothetical Question:

Plaintiff Goodwyn, a New Orleans merchant, agreed with defendant Pritchard, a farmer who processed his sugar into molasses, to purchase Pritchard's crop at the rate of one dollar per gallon (Goodwyn would supply the barrels). The molasses was to be delivered to Goodwyn in barrels at the defendant's plantation, and the number of gallons as to be determined by weight, at twelve pounds to the gallon. The parties further agreed that Goodwyn would pay $1600 in advance, on account. Goodwyn made the advance payment and the molasses was put in barrels and weighed. But before Goodwyn picked it up, Pritchard's sugarhouse burned down and the molasses was destroyed. Goodwyn now wants his advance returned, claiming he did not receive anything. Pritchard argues that as the molasses had been weighed, Goodwyn owned it at the time it was destroyed, so not only should Pritchard get to keep the down payment, but Goodwyn should pay the remaining balance for the burnt sugar.

a. Under current law, who wins?

b. Would the result have been different under previous law?

c. In the original case, the molasses had not yet been weighed at the time of the fire. Explain why the court concluded that the risk of loss remained with seller Pritchard. See Goodwyn v. Pritchard, 10 La. Ann. 249 (La. 1855).

Study Questions:

Consider the interaction between ownership and risk in the following case. The case was decided under prior law, but would the decision be any different under current law? Even if the decision would not differ, would there be any difference in the court's reasoning?

BILLIOT V. LOVELL 1993

633 SO. 2D 280 (LA. APP. 1ST CIR.)

CARTER, Judge.

¶1 This appeal arises out of a trial court judgment granting a motion for summary judgment.

BACKGROUND

¶2 On or about August 28, 1991, Lynn Hubert Lovell, Jr. ("Lovell"), his mother, Cynthia Dyas, and Ray Gross Motors, Inc. engaged in discussions concerning Lovell's possible purchase of a used Pontiac LeMans from Ray Gross Motors. After paying the required down payment of one thousand dollars ($1,000.00) for the LeMans, Lovell was allowed to use and drive the automobile during the evening of August 28, 1991[, even though financing for the LeMans had not yet been approved.]

¶3 On the following afternoon, August 29, 1991, Lovell was informed by a representative of Ray Gross Motors that General Motors Acceptance Corporation (GMAC) would not provide financing for the LeMans, but that GMAC would finance a 1991 Dodge Colt. After test driving a 1991 Colt, Mrs. Dyas and Lovell entered into an agreement with Ray Gross Motors for its purchase.

¶4 Mrs. Dyas and Lovell then met with Ethel Sutfin, finance manager at Ray Gross Motors, who informed them that the down payment for the Colt was $500.00 more than the down payment which had been applied toward the LeMans. Mrs. Dyas and Lovell then presented Ms. Sutfin with two checks, each made payable for one hundred dollars ($100.00), and agreed to return on August 30, 1991, with three additional checks, each made payable for one hundred dollars ($100.00). It was agreed that Ray Gross Motors would deposit one check per week for the next five weeks. Mrs. Dyas and Lovell then signed various documents, which included the following: a retail installment contract, a buyer's order, a description of vehicle/disclaimer of warranties statement, an odometer statement, a bill of sale, a notice to cosigner, an application for title and registration, a customer statement, and an agreement with GMAC to keep the vehicle fully insured during the period of financing.

¶5 After Mrs. Dyas and Lovell had signed the documents, it was after 6:30 p.m., and Mrs. Dyas' insurance agency had already closed for the day. Ms. Sutfin allegedly assured Mrs. Dyas and Lovell that the newly acquired automobile would be insured for the evening under Ray Gross Motors' insurance policy. Lovell then drove the automobile home.

FACTS

¶6 In the early morning hours of August 30, 1991, at approximately 1:40 a.m., Lee Adam Billiot, Jr. was a guest passenger in Lovell's 1991 Colt. The automobile suddenly left the travelled portion of the roadway, struck a ditch embankment, and overturned. As a result of the collision, Lee Adam Billiot, Jr. was ejected from the vehicle and suffered fatal injuries.

¶7 On October 30, 1991, plaintiffs, Lee Adam Billiot, Sr. and Debra Businelle Billiot, parents of Lee Adam Billiot, Jr., filed this wrongful death and survival action under the provisions of La. Civil Code arts. 2315.1 and 2315.2, alleging that the sole cause of the accident was the negligence of Lovell. Named as defendants in the action were Lovell; Prudential Property and Casualty Insurance Company, Lovell's automobile liability insurer; Ray Gross Motors, Inc.; Chrysler Insurance Company, Ray Gross Motors' liability insurer; and the State of Louisiana, through the Department of Transportation (footnotes omitted).

¶8 On May 27, 1992, Ray Gross Motors filed an exception pleading the objection of no right of action, contending that plaintiffs had no right to assert a claim against them for failure to supply liability insurance coverage to Lovell. On August 12, 1992, the trial court signed a judgment maintaining the exception and dismissing all demands against Ray Gross Motors.

¶9 On May 27, 1992, Chrysler Insurance Company filed a motion for summary judgment, contending that, because the sale of the 1991 Colt occurred on August 29, 1991, the automobile was no longer owned by Ray Gross Motors at the time of the accident. Chrysler reasoned that, as a result, there was no coverage under the liability policy covering the dealership. Alternatively, Chrysler alleged that, even if the dealership owned the automobile at the time of the accident, language in its policy excluded coverage for Lovell because he had other insurance coverage available to him at the time of the accident.

¶10 On October 15, 1992, the trial court granted Chrysler's motion for summary judgment. Plaintiffs appealed, (footnote omitted) assigning the following specifications of error:

> 1. The trial court erred in granting defendant-appellee's motion for summary judgment when there exists a genuine issue as to material fact whether or not a sale of the automobile involved in the accident herein had occurred prior to the accident.
>
> 2. The trial court erred in granting defendant-appellee's motion for summary judgment on the alternative grounds that even if a sale of the automobile involved in the accident had not

occurred prior to the accident, there was no coverage for the accident under the policy issued by defendant-appellee due to certain exclusionary language contained in that policy.

***

SALE OF THE AUTOMOBILE

¶11 Plaintiffs contend that the trial court erred in finding that the sale of the 1991 Colt was complete on August 29, 1991.

¶12 It is clear that if the sale of the automobile was complete on August 29, 1991, then Chrysler's policy does not provide liability coverage in the instant case. Thus, the issue for our review is whether the trial court erred in finding that the sale of the 1991 Colt from the dealership to Lovell was complete on August 29, 1991. A sale is an agreement by which one gives a thing for a price in current money, and the other gives the price in order to have the thing itself. Three circumstances concur to the perfection of the contract: the thing sold, the price, and the consent. LSA-C.C. art. 2439; Evans v. Graves Pontiac-Buick-GMC Truck, Inc., 576 So.2d 1025, 1028 (La.App. 1st Cir.), writ denied, 581 So.2d 687 (La. 1991); DB Orban Co. v. Lakco Pipe & Supply, Inc., 496 So.2d 1382, 1384 (La.App. 3d Cir. 1986). A sale is considered to be perfect between the parties, and the property is of right acquired by the purchaser with regard to the seller, as soon as there exists an agreement for the object and for the price thereof, although the object has not yet been delivered, nor the price paid. LSA-C.C. art. 2456.

¶13 In the instant case, Mrs. Dyas testified in her deposition that, at the time of her son's accident, he was driving the 1991 Colt, which had just been purchased from Ray Gross Motors. She acknowledged that the sale of the vehicle was complete after she and her son signed all of the documents on August 29, 1991:

> Q. As far as you knew then, when you and your son left the dealership on August 29th, the only additional thing that needed to be done was that Ethel Sutfin [finance manager for Ray Gross Motors] needed to be called about the specifics of the insurance.
>
> A. Right.
>
> Q. But there were no other papers to sign, and as far as you knew at that moment in time?
>
> A. No.

Q. And the sale of the vehicle had been all completed.

A. Yes.

Q. Whereas, on the night before, you hadn't completed the sale, but were waiting for the credit to be approved or disapproved on the Lemans?

A. Yes.

¶14 An entry in Mrs. Dyas' notebook also noted that the vehicle's "date of purchase" was "8/29/91."

¶15 The deposition testimony of Tommy Chauvin, sales manager at Ray Gross Motors, reveals that he did not participate in the negotiations which led to the sale of the vehicle involved in this case. He explained that the dealership uses third-party closings, whereby the sales manager "pencils-in" a price for the salesman to negotiate to the buyer. Chauvin indicated that his approval is required before a salesman can negotiate a price. Chauvin stated that he must have approved the price of the red 1991 Colt because he recalled meeting Mrs. Dyas and Lovell on August 29, 1991, shaking their hands, and thanking them for their business.

¶16 Robert Tarleton, salesman at Ray Gross Motors, stated in his deposition that on August 29, 1991, Mrs. Dyas and Lovell test drove a blue 1991 Colt, but decided to purchase a red Colt. Tarleton testified that he reached an agreement with them as to the price of the red 1991 Colt. Mrs. Dyas and Lovell then met with Ethel Sutfin, the dealership's finance manager, to make financing arrangements.

¶17 Susan Gross, general manager at Ray Gross Motors, stated in her deposition that she was out of the office on August 29, 1991, when the sale took place, but that she signed the documents, on behalf of Ray Gross Motors, the following morning. Ms. Gross indicated that as soon as a customer signs all of the documents, the car becomes the property of the customer.

¶18 However, plaintiffs contend that the dealership's failure to have a representative sign the purchase documents on August 29, 1991, evidences that the sale was not complete at that time. More specifically, plaintiffs note that the Buyer's Order, containing the language "THIS ORDER IS NOT VALID UNLESS SIGNED AS ACCEPTED," was not signed by a representative of Ray Gross Motors on August 29, 1991.

¶19 In Van-Trow Olds-Cad-Toyota, Inc. v. Wiggins, 516 So.2d 1261, 1262 (La.App. 2nd Cir. 1987), the court considered a similar provision in the dealership's "deal sheet," which stated that "THIS ORDER SHALL NOT BECOME BINDING UNTIL ACCEPTED BY DEALER OR HIS AUTHORIZED REPRESENTATIVE." Even though the deal sheet was not signed by a representative of the dealership, the court ruled that there was a valid sale because the parties had verbally agreed on the object and price, and "[f]rom that point both parties acted as if they had a completed sale. Van-Trow delivered the car to Ms. Wiggins and she issued a check in partial payment of the price." Van-Trow Olds-Cad-Toyota, Inc. v. Wiggins, 516 So.2d at 1263.

¶20 Similarly, in the instant case, the deposition testimony shows that the parties reached an agreement as to the thing and the price on August 29, 1991. From that point forward, both parties to the sale acted as if the sale was complete. Mrs. Dyas and Lovell met with the dealership's finance manager and executed all of the required documents. A cash down payment was then accepted, and a temporary license was issued. Lovell then drove the vehicle away from the dealership.

¶21 Plaintiffs also argue that because Mrs. Dyas was called in to the dealership several days after the accident to sign an additional document regarding the purchase of the vehicle, the sale was not complete on August 29, 1991. However, Tommy Chauvin explained that GMAC merely returned a document for Mrs. Dyas to sign her name above that of her husband.

¶22 After reviewing the testimony and the documents in the record, we conclude that the sale of the 1991 Colt was complete on August 29, 1991. On that date, the parties reached an agreement as to the object sold (the red 1991 Dodge Colt) and the price $9,964.18 (including taxes). See LSA-C.C. art 2439; Evans v. Graves Pontiac-Buick-GMC Truck, Inc., 576 So.2d at 1028.

¶23 Therefore, it is clear that, at the time of the accident, the automobile was no longer owned by the dealership and that there was no coverage under Chrysler's insurance policy. Accordingly, no genuine issues of material fact were in dispute, and the trial court did not err in granting Chrysler's motion for summary judgment.

¶24 Given our resolution of assignment of error number one, we find it unnecessary to address plaintiffs' second assignment of error.

CONCLUSION

¶25 For the reasons set forth above, the judgment of the trial court, granting Chrysler's motion for summary judgment, is affirmed. Plaintiffs are cast for the costs of the appeal.

AFFIRMED.

Section 4: Things in Transit

In the transactions we've studied so far, the buyer and seller dealt directly with each other, face-to-face. But given today's global marketplace,

But today very often the parties are at some distance from one another. Indeed, they may have never dealt with each other before. That raises concerns on each side. On the buyer's side, the buyer cannot examine the item in person before deciding to buy it. So she wants to make sure that the movable she is purchasing is timely shipped to her, is exactly what she wants, and she doesn't want to pay for it otherwise.

Furthermore, sometimes the buyer (perhaps a wholesaler) is purchasing the things with the understanding that he will be reselling them, or perhaps he is purchasing them for a third party, and so he wants to be able to resell them even while they are en route.

On the seller's side, the seller wants to make sure that he gets paid and does not want to risk shipping his product otherwise.

In addition to protecting their ownership from the interests of third parties, seller and buyer want to know who will bear the loss if the goods are damaged en route.

Thus, the parties to sales where seller and buyer are remote from each other want to be able to allocate both ownership and risk while the things are in transit so that both buyer's and seller's interests are protected.

Ownership of Things in Transit & the Bill of Lading

Generally, under the Civil Code, ownership transfers on consent, unless one of the exceptions (weight, tale, measure, individualization) applies. Most goods shipped to the buyer through a carrier would require individualization, however, the contract between the carrier and the seller, called the bill of lading, can vary this, and those rules are set forth in Articles 2613, 2614, and 2615. A bill of lading serves several purposes. In addition to setting forth the terms of transport, it allocates risk and often serves as a document of title.

As a contract of transport, it shows what the carrier agreed to transport, from where to where, and the cost of that transportation. Should the goods be damaged or lost during shipment, for historical and policy reasons, a carrier's liability is strictly limited by legislation and treaty such as the Carriage of Goods by Sea Act (COGSA), 46 U.S.C. §§ 30710 & ff. (2006).). Nevertheless, carriers are very careful in accepting goods for shipment, and while they will not open the goods to verify condition before shipping, the bill of lading generally describes the condition the goods were on receipt by the carrier, the goods themselves are often described in an attached invoice. If the goods seem to be in good condition when inspected by the carrier, the bill of lading is described as "clean." If the carrier questions the condition, it may refuse to ship them, or may note the condition of the outside of the goods. **Examine the Bill of Lading in Figure 6-3 and see if it is 'clean' or not.**

In terms of serving as a document of title, a bill of lading can be either negotiable or non-negotiable. A non-negotiable bill of lading or "straight" bill of lading need not be given to the carrier in order for the recipient of the goods to obtain possession. In contrast, a negotiable bill of lading provides that whoever presents the bill to the carrier at the ultimate destination has title to and can obtain possession of the goods. Thus, the party who originally ordered the goods can sell them to a third party while they are still in the carrier's possession, and if the bill of lading is negotiable, that third party can obtain them by presenting the now negotiated bill to the carrier when the goods arrive at their final destination. **Examine Figure 6-3 and see if it is "straight" or negotiable.**

Usually, if the seller had the bill of lading issued to the buyer's order, that means that the seller has irrevocably allocated the goods to the buyer, just as with individualization. If, on the other hand, the seller is concerned about payment, he or she may instead have the bill of lading issued to himself or his own order, and thus can refuse to allow them to be retrieved from the carrier until the buyer proves that they have been paid for – this is another way of varying the underlying rule that ownership transfers on agreement.

Risk of Loss of Things in Transit

Since the 1993 revision of the Sales articles, as per Article 2467, the risk of loss of a thing sold due to a fortuitous event transfers from seller to buyer on delivery. However, before 1993, the default rule was that risk of loss transferred on agreement, along with consent, this was known as the principle of *res perit domino*. That general rule was changed in 1993 because until delivery, the buyer has no control over the goods and no way to minimize risk – for example, consider *Goodwin v. Pritchard*, discussed earlier where Goodwin bought molasses from Pritchard, but before it was delivered, it was lost in a fire. Under the default rule, Goodwin would still have to pay for the molasses. The only reason he did not was because the molasses had not yet been weighed, so neither ownership nor risk had transferred. Under current 2467, even if the molasses had been weighed, risk of loss due to a fortuitous event would not transfer to Goodwin until the molasses had been delivered.

Article 2616 considers allocation of the risk of loss when the thing is in transit, just as Article 2613 considers the transfer of ownership of things in transit. As it does with ownership, the bill of lading also allocates risk. The default rule is that the seller's responsibility ends when he places the goods in the carrier's possession. This is known as a *shipment contract* or *seller's contract*, and that means that the buyer bears the risk of the goods being damaged or destroyed in transit.

If the buyer does not want that risk, he can negotiate a *destination or buyer's contract* instead, in which case the risk of loss remains with the seller until the goods are actually delivered into the buyer's possession. Because it is a variation of the normal rule, a destination contract requires the seller to deliver the things at a particular destination.

An easy way to remember the difference between a seller's contract and a buyer's contract is to think of a seller's contract as being in the seller's favor – like a hot potato, he has gotten rid of the risk that the goods will be destroyed in shipment. The buyer's contract is similarly in the buyer's favor, meaning that the buyer has no worries until the seller actually delivers the goods.

The best way to determine the allocation of risk of loss is the use of well-established commercial symbols whose meaning is determined by a national or international organization, such as the International Chamber of Commerce's Incoterms (International Commercial Terms), as discussed in the comments to Article 2616. So, for example, the most common shipper's contract is probably "F.O.B.," which means "Free on Board" – the shipper's duties end when the goods have been loaded on the ship, plane, train, or truck. In contrast, assume the seller is shipping the goods from Alexandria to New Orleans, if one adds a destination after the symbol F.O.B. in the bill of lading, such as "F.O.B. New Orleans," that now indicates a buyer's contract. Thus, the seller is responsible for the goods until they reach the buyer in New Orleans. To sum up, it is generally assumed that a bill of lading is a shipment or sellers contract: no destination after the symbol indicates a shipment contract, destination after the symbol means buyer's contract. Other frequently used commercial symbols include F.A.S. ("Free Alongside"), meaning that the seller's risk ends when he delivers the things to the dock (alongside the vessel); C.I.F. (" Cost, Insurance, Freight"), another kind of shipper's contract under which the seller's duty and risk ends when he has paid any costs, the freight, and insurance. Often a buyer will negotiate which term will be used prior to the sale – in other words, he'll ask the seller to provide two or three prices – one for F.O.B. (the lowest) and another for C.I.F. He'll then choose whichever method he prefers.

Study Question

Examine Figures 6-2 (the invoice) and 6-3 in the Appendix. Determine whether the bill of lading is a shipper's or a buyer's contract. Determine what commercial symbol is at issue. (Hint: you will not find the symbol on the bill of lading, but it appears on the invoice).

The financial mechanism that has developed internationally for such sales generally involves five different entities: (1) the buyer; (2) the buyer's bank; (3) the seller; (4) the seller's bank; and (5) the carrier who transports the thing sold. Articles 2613 (Things in transit, ownership), 2616 (Things in transit, risk of loss), and 2617 (Payment against documents) are consistent with some of the law and business practices that have developed both nationally and internationally to deal with these concerns. However, it is difficult to make sense of these three articles without some additional background.

Documentary Sale: The Basics

In a documentary sale, banks handle the money part of the transaction and transmit it from buyer to seller, while the carrier (nowadays often a multi-modal transport system) handles getting the goods from seller to buyer. It is called a documentary sale because the performance of the contract is handled primarily through writings, documents or instruments, that evidence title to the goods, provide how payment occurs, and determine who bears the risk of accidental loss. See Figure 6-1, in the Appendix.

The Buyer's Basic Obligations: Pay Against Documents and Provide an
Irrevocable Letter of Credit

First, buyer and seller agree on the thing, the price, the method of payment, and shipping terms. This is usually in the form of a purchase order. Then, the buyer goes to his bank and requests that it issue a letter of credit, by which the bank irrevocably commits to pay a certain sum of money after the buyer's bank receives documents that prove that the seller has shipped the goods. The buyer's bank is called the 'issuing bank,' and it will issue the letter of credit on behalf of its customer, the buyer. The buyer either has deposited funds in the bank to cover the letter of credit or the issuing bank lends the buyer the price. The letter of credit is issued in favor of the seller, who is the letter of credit's "beneficiary."

The issuing bank then transmits the letter of credit to the seller's bank, known as the confirming or advising bank. The confirming bank then contacts the seller and informs him that it has a letter of credit drawn in his favor and will pay him if he produces the documents listed in that letter as required. The seller now has not one but two banks (his and the buyer's) assuring him that he will be paid once he proves that he has shipped the goods by providing the listed documents. If for some reason the buyer does not pay, the issuing bank is still required to honor the letter of credit, but its remedy is against its customer, the buyer. The seller's bank, the confirming bank, can refuse to 'confirm' the letter of credit if it believes the issuing bank is untrustworthy. This further protects the seller from having to risk shipping the goods before he has real assurance that he'll get paid once he does so. If you have dealt with Paypal, the process is similar: Paypal virtually holds the money in escrow for the seller pending proof that she has shipped the goods to the buyer.

Concerning letters of credit, the banks never want to receive any goods, nor will they be responsible for them. Their only responsibility is to deal properly with the documents and verify that the documents the seller delivers in order to obtain his money strictly comply with the requirements of the letter of credit (hence the expression payment against documents.) This principle of strict compliance and other banking practices dealing with letters of credit (i.e. documentary credits) are set forth internationally by rules such as the Uniform Customs and

Practices for Documentary Credit for the International Chamber of Commerce (the 'UCP500') and nationally by Title 5 of the UCC, both of which apply in Louisiana (but which are not the subject of this course).

Article 2617 sets forth this principle of payment against documents:

> In all cases where the parties have agreed that the seller will obtain a document showing that the things have been delivered to a carrier or a depositary the buyer must make payment against tender of that document and others as required. The seller may not tender, nor may the buyer demand, delivery of the things in lieu of the documents.

The Seller's Duty: Strict Compliance With the Letter of Credit

In terms of what documents are required by a letter of credit, generally, the documents often simply include the bill of lading and an invoice listing the goods shipped, but additional documents may be required as well: a certificate of insurance, a certificate of inspection, and any customs or required export documents. Whatever the letter of credit lists as required, the bank will not release funds to the seller until it has received all of the required documents, inspected them, and verified that they are in strict compliance with commercial standards. The bank, however, does not care at all about the goods themselves.

a. The Invoice

A standard invoice is a document prepared by the seller that gives information about the goods, identifies the buyer and the seller, and indicates the goods' country of origin. The seller must normally deliver the invoice to his bank as one of the requirements of the letter of credit.

b. The Bill of Lading

As described earlier, the bill of lading serves three important purposes: 1) it is the contract between the owner of the goods and the carrier and indicates the terms of shipping, and 2) it serves as evidence of ownership of the goods themselves and 3) it allocates risk to one or the other. The seller must normally deliver the bill of lading to his bank as one of the requirements of the letter of credit.

c. The Certificate of Insurance

As mentioned previously, the parties to a documentary transaction will need to consider how to allocate risk. Regardless of which party has the risk, they may decide to insure the shipment because by federal and international law, carrier's liability is extremely limited. For instance, COGSA (the Carriage of Goods by Sea Act) provides for $500/package if something is lost or damaged at sea; the Montreal Convention for the Unification of Rules for Carriage by Air, which the U.S. ratified, limits liability to 19 SDRs ("Special Drawing Rights) per kilogram (as of 2010, that equaled $29.53) ; and the Carmack Amendment allows U.S. carriers to limit liability by contract. For example, if Fed Ex loses or damages the blue suede shoes, their contract limits damages to the cost of shipping (read the twenty-seven some-odd pages of small print in their on-line contract). The historical reason for this limitation of liability is that governments recognized the importance of carriers to commerce – if a carrier's liability for loss or damage was not limited, then they might be discouraged from doing business or might raise rates so high that doing business at a distance becomes unfeasible. Consequently, insurance for valuable cargo is often a must.

Furthermore, often it is easier for the seller to research insurance options, as the goods will be shipped from her location. Consequently, as with C.I.F. shipments, the letter of credit may require the seller not just to provide the bill of lading itself, but also proof of insurance.

d. Certificate of Inspection and Other Documents

Given the built-in assurances of the international banking system and devices such as the letter of credit, a seller can be pretty confident that he will be paid once he provides the necessary documents. The buyer's concern that she receive the goods in a timely fashion is also relatively secure – the seller won't get paid until he provides proof that he has sent the goods. However, the buyer's concern that she get exactly what she paid for can still be problematic, and the assurances provided by international commercial practices are not as reliable for the buyer as they are for the seller. For instance, in bidding on Ebay (for the blue suede shoes), you may consider the ranking given by other purchasers concerning the seller's reliability and choose to bid on one item over another based purely on this ranking. In the commercial sector, especially with goods where the exact quality is important, a buyer may require that the seller provide a certificate of inspection as further assurance. This means that the seller must allow an independent professional testing agency to inspect the goods and certify that they are exactly what the buyer demanded. In the BP v. PetroEquador case, even this mechanism failed the buyer. In addition to a certificate of inspection, the parties may also specify import-export duties, so the letter of credit may also require proof that the seller has obtained the necessary customs documents in order to allow the goods to both leave his country and enter the buyer's.

Study Questions:

Consider how the court interpreted the language on the bill of lading in the following classic Louisiana case. Would the case be decided differently under current articles 2613 and 2616? Why or why not? (Hint: if you conclude that the result would be the same today, then you should read Comment (a) to Article 2616).

CALIFORNIA FRUIT EXCHANGE V. JOHN MEYER, INC. 1928
166 LA. 9, 116 SO. 575 (LA.)

ROGERS, J.

¶1 This is a suit to recover the difference between the invoice price of a carload of peaches, which plaintiff alleges it sold to defendant, and the amount realized from their sale at auction, after defendant had refused to accept them.

¶2 The defendant is a wholesale dealer in fruits in the city of New Orleans. In the early part of the month of August, 1920, it entered into an oral agreement with the district manager of the plaintiff for the sale and purchase of a carload of peaches. The peaches, which were shipped from California consigned to plaintiff on a straight bill of lading drawn in its name, reached New Orleans in the latter part of the month. Upon the arrival of the shipment, plaintiff's local manager notified defendant and offered to surrender the documents necessary to obtain its delivery from the carrier on payment by defendant of the invoice price. Defendant inspected the peaches and finding them to be in a damaged condition refused to accept delivery. Thereupon, plaintiff caused them to be sold at public auction, resulting in a loss equal to the amount herein sued for.

¶3 Plaintiff contends that the sale was made with acceptance at the shipping point in California and that the risk of loss in transit was assumed by defendant. Per contra, defendant contends that the sale was made subject to its right of inspection and rejection at New Orleans. The district court found that, on the facts, the peaches remained the property of the plaintiff until accepted by the defendant in New Orleans. The Court of Appeal, on the other hand, resolved the disputed question of fact in favor of plaintiff, holding that the contract was for "California acceptance." However, it affirmed the judgment on the ground that the delivery by the plaintiff of the peaches to the carrier in California consigned to itself in New Orleans on a bill of lading in its name was not an appropriation of the peaches to the contract calling for California acceptance so as to place the risk of transportation upon the defendant.

¶4 The finding of fact by the Court of Appeal necessitated its consideration and discussion of certain provisions of the Uniform Bills of Lading Act, which has been adopted in this state (Act 94 of 1912), invoked by the plaintiff. On this phase of the case, the court reached the conclusion, and so ruled, that, notwithstanding the qualifying clause in subsection (b) of section 40 of the statute, the law of this state did not recognize divided incidents of ownership subsisting in the seller and buyer of personal property. It is because of this ruling that the case was ordered up for review.

¶5 Plaintiff argues that whatever might have been the law of the state prior to the adoption of Act 94 of 1912, the general rule since that time has been that, upon a sale with acceptance at point of shipment, title passes from the vendor to the vendee at the moment of delivery to the carrier, and the goods sold are thereafter at the vendee's risk. Conceding the soundness of the argument, the operation of the rule is nevertheless subordinate to the intention of the contracting parties. In the case at bar, if the agreement was for California acceptance, as plaintiff contends, the rule applies. If, on the other hand, the agreement was for New Orleans acceptance after inspection, as defendant claims, the rule does not apply. The application vel non of the rule therefore depends upon the facts of the case. We have carefully examined these facts, and our conclusion is, contrary to that of the Court of Appeal but in consonance with that of the district court, that the plaintiff has not brought its claim within the statutory rule which it invokes.

¶6 Plaintiff's manager testified that he did not recollect who gave him the order for the peaches, whether it was Mr. Meyer, the president of the defendant company, or a Mr. Chalona, an independent operator, who was, as he thought interested in the deal. He declared, however, his recollection was clear on the subject-matter of the agreement; that a written confirmation of the order was sent by him to Mr. Meyer, and that the invoice bearing the notations. "Sold f. o. b. California," and "sold subject to California acceptance," was sent by him to the Fruit Auction Company for account of the defendant. It is clear from the testimony of Mr. Chalona that, even if he was interested in the shipment, which is not certain, he was not an actual party to the contract, which was entered into between Mr. Meyer, the president of the defendant company, and Mr. Johnson, the plaintiff's local manager. Mr. Meyer testified:

> That he had no recollection of receiving a written confirmation of the order calling for a sale f. o. b. subject to California acceptance. That if he had received such a letter he would have promptly returned it for the reason that he had no recollection and no record of any such purchase. The uncontradicted testimony in the record is that the universal custom among the wholesale dealers in fruits in New Orleans is to buy only upon arrival and after inspection of the fruit. This custom had always been observed between the New Orleans merchants and the plaintiff before Mr. Johnson became plaintiff's district manager at this point.

¶7   Mr. Meyer, in the course of his testimony, stated also:

> That he had had other transactions before and since with the plaintiff's local manager, all of
> which were entered into with the reservation of right of inspection and acceptance at New
> Orleans.

> That in all of his business experience, covering 30 years, except in two or three instances, he
> never had bought fruit from any one without the right of inspection and rejection on arrival, and
> that in the instances where he had departed from this rule special contracts had been drawn and
> signed.

¶8   Mr. Johnson, plaintiff's agent, testified that the carload of peaches was the first one he
had sold in New Orleans for California acceptance. It also appears, according to the record, to
have been the only one sold in that manner. The bill of lading shows that the shipment was
consigned to the shipper, care of its district manager, at the point of destination, and it bears
the notation, evidently placed thereon by plaintiff, viz.:

> "Note on Waybill.

> "Permit inspection before unloading without bill of lading. Deliver without bill of lading on writ-
> ten order of California Fruit Exchange."

¶9   Why is it, if the agreement was that the title to the peaches was to pass from the seller to
the buyer at the moment of delivery to the carrier, the bill of lading was not drawn to the consignee or its order? Plaintiff's explanation that it was not done because of its desire to secure
the payment of the purchase price is not convincing. The same object could have been attained
by attaching to a draft the bill of lading running to the consignee, deliverable only upon payment of the draft. This would have been the simple and usual method followed in such cases.
Again, by whom was the inspection to be permitted under the authorization marked upon the
waybill before the car was unloaded? If by defendant, then its contention that it had reserved
the privilege of inspecting and rejecting is corroborated; if by the plaintiff, then its contention
that the peaches became defendant's property at the point of shipment loses its force. If the title
to the peaches after they were placed in the car was in defendant, plaintiff was without interest
to inspect them. On the other hand, the right of inspection might have proved valuable, in the
event plaintiff had desired to divert the shipment en route as it would have had a right to do as
the consignee named in the bill of lading.

¶10 Our conclusion is that the plaintiff has not established by a preponderance of the evidence the contract for the alleged breach of which it seeks recovery in this suit.

¶11 For the reasons assigned, the rule nisi herein issued is recalled and the judgment of the Court of Appeal is affirmed at the cost of the relator.

Study Questions:

Read BP Oil Int'l, Ltd v. Empresa Estatal Petroleos de Ecuador, 332 F.3d 333 (5th Cir. 2003), the basis of the hypothetical at the beginning of Chapter 1.

1. What commercial term was involved?

2. Was BP paid? What makes you think it was (or wasn't)? A letter of guarantee is not the same as a letter of credit. Look up standby letter of credit and contrast it with letter of credit – what happened is that BP had guaranteed that the fuel would have the proper quality through means of a standby letter, so when PetroEquador believed the fuel was of lesser quality, it cashed out the standby letter. In the lawsuit, BP alleges "wrongful draw of a letter of guarantee."

3. Did the agreement include some sort of inspection or testing of the oil by an independent professional testing company? If so, what happened with that testing?

Figure 6-1: Documentary Sale

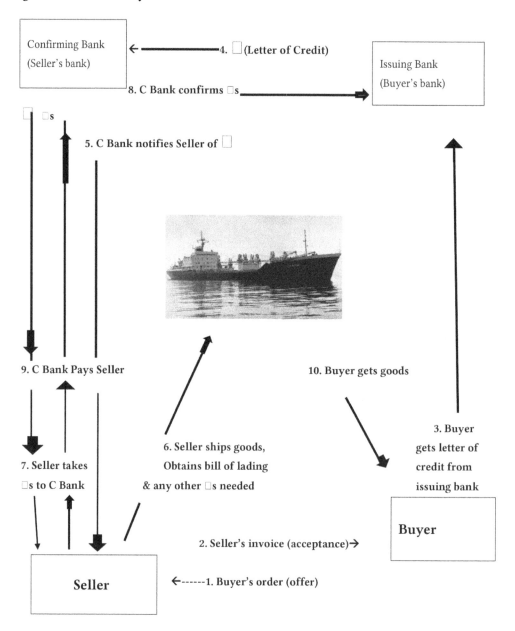

Confirming Bank (Seller's bank)

◄——————4. ☐ (Letter of Credit)

Issuing Bank (Buyer's bank)

8. C Bank confirms ☐s ——————►

☐ ☐s

5. C Bank notifies Seller of ☐

9. C Bank Pays Seller

10. Buyer gets goods

3. Buyer gets letter of credit from issuing bank

7. Seller takes ☐s to C Bank

6. Seller ships goods, Obtains bill of lading & any other ☐s needed

Buyer

2. Seller's invoice (acceptance)→

Seller

◄------1. Buyer's order (offer)

Figure 6-2

Singapore Slings: from 👠 to 👟
5432 Shoehorn Place, Singapore 8901234

Invoice

Order #	4321-2020
Order date	05/05/2020
Purchaser	Don't Mess with Mamou Shoes
Phone	01.863.123.4567
Shipping Company	N&N Shipping

Customer/Shipping Address

Don't Mess with Mamou Shoes
674 Cajun Way
Mamou, Louisiana.
70452
U.S.A.

Manufacturer	Model #	Quantity	Description	Unit price	Total Price
Jimmy Choo		10 pr	Blue Suede Sling-Back, Cork Platform	$750	$7,500
C. Louboutin	CL00357	10 pr	Blue Suede Pumps, 70mm heel	$1,500	$15,000
Puma	PM00978	10 pr	Blue Suede Sneaker, white	$100	$1,000
Sketchers	SK00567	10 pr	Blue Suede mule	$250	$2,500
Mia	M100564	10 pr	Blue Suede gladiator sandal	$300	$3,000
Fit Flops	FF00543	10 pr	Blue simulated Suede/black	$80	$800
Birkenstock	BK00999	10 pr	Blue Suede one-strap sandal	$80	$800

Shipping/Freight/ & Handling Charges:

F.O.B. Singapore: $1500

Inspection Certificate:

Payment Terms:
Currency: USD$

Figure 6-3

N&N SHIPPING

Bill of Lading

Shipper/Exporter Name:	Consignee Name:	Party to Notify:
Singapore Slings	**Don't Mess with Mamou Shoes**	**Bobbie Boudreaux**
Shipper/Exporter Address:	Consignee Address:	Party to Notify address/phone:

Initial mode of Carriage: VESSEL M/V Guppy,		Flag: Malaysia

Shipper's Memoranda

Booking #	BOL #	Point & Country of Origin: Singapore	Loading Pier :	Release of Original(s):
459-2020	123-2020		A-11	
Export References:	Freight Forwarder: Acme-Gets-There	Type of Move: Multi-modal	Routing & Instructions: M/V to port of New Orleans, truck to Mamou, La.	Final Destination: Mamou, Louisiana, USA

Shipping Details

MKS	#Packages	Description of Packages & goods	Gross Weight (kilograms)	Measurement (cu. meters)	Condition	Freight Charges
JC00123	1	Gemmy Chew shoes	100	1		125
CL00357	1	C. Louboutin shoes	100	1	+pkg water-damaged	125
PM00978	1	Puma sneakers	75	1		100
SK00567	1	Sketchers shoes	100	1		125
M100564	1	Sandals	50	1		100

INCOTERM: F.O.B. Singapore

DATE: 05-05-2020

AT SINGAPORE PIER A-11   By: _____

Figure 6-4

FIRST MAMOU BANK AND TRUST OF LOUISIANA

123 Main Street

Mamou, LA. 76543 U.S.A

Swift Address: FMBTL78; Telex Number ITT 455660 FJIOLYI

TRT123456 FBMEKTL.Ca; Email: FMB&TLa@gmail.com

IRREVOCABLE NON-NEGOTIABLE CREDIT

ADVISING BANK:

First Bank of Singapore

Date: 10/05/2020

ALL DRAFTS DRAWN MUST BE MARKED

WITH FMBTL

REFERENCE NUMBER _____

ADVISING BANK REFERENCE NUMBER

_____

GENTLEMEN:

By the order of Paul Boudreau, we hereby issue through you in favor of Singapore Slings, Inc,.
Our irrevocable credit for the account #123456 for an amount not to exceed, in the aggregate,
U.S.D. $50,800, available by your drafts at First Bank of Singapore on First Mamou Bank and
Trust of Louisiana, Mamou, La. U.S.A., when accompanied by the documents indicated below,
effective May 10, 2020 and expiring on May 30, 2020.

This Credit is Subject to the Following:

Ship From: Singapore

Ship To: Mamou, Louisiana, U.S.A.

Documents Required:

1. Invoice

2. Clean Bill of Lading that matches Invoice

3. Customs invoice

Covering Shipment of: Shoes

Shipping Terms: F.O.B. Mamou

Advising Bank must airmail or e-deliver one original commercial invoice, customs invoice, and bill of lading to business address above for our account and a certificate to this effect must be submitted with the remaining documents.

We hereby engage with the drawers' and with the advising bank and bankers that each draft drawn under and in compliance with the terms of this credit will be duly honored if presented for negotiation on or before the expiry date.

The amount of each draft must be endorsed on the reverse of this credit by the advising bank

This credit is subject to the uniform customs and practice for documentary credits (2000 Revision), International Chamber of Commerce Publication 400.

Very Truly Yours,
First Mamou Bank and Trust

Advising Bank's Notification:
Authorized Signature:

_____

Place, Date, Name & Signature   Authorized Signature:

REVIEW NOTES

Section 1. Title and Risk in General

A sale is perfected and ownership is transferred as soon as the parties have agreed on the thing and the price, even if the thing is not yet delivered or the money yet paid. Art 2456. Risk, however, does not transfer until delivery. Art 2467.

Prior to 1995, that was not the case (risk transferred on agreement too). However, that led to some anomalous results when the thing was destroyed while still in the seller's possession – there was no way the buyer could have protected his possession or prevented the destruction, yet he was still bearing the risk. Consequently, that was changed, but you may still find some old cases holding the opposite way.

While a sale is generally perfected on agreement, there are instances where that is not the case, and some sort of suspensive condition applies. For example, if the thing has to be individualized from a mass of identical things, or if it has to be weighed, tallied, or measured, then ownership does not transfer until the thing has been irrevocably set aside for the buyer or weighed-out.

Section 2: Appropriation or Individualization

Article 2457 provides that when the object of a sale is a thing that must be individualized from a mass of identical things, then ownership is not transferred until the thing is individualized according to the parties' intent, for example, when the seller delivers it to a carrier.

Collins v. Louisiana Lottery

Collins ordered a lottery ticket that turned out to be prize-winning, and is suing to collect. However, he ordered it at the last minute and while it had been set-aside for him, the lottery personnel did not have time to mail it out. Consequently, they did as they habitually do in that instance and roll it over to the next day's lottery. Thus, because it had not been irrevocably set aside for Collins, it had not been individualized, and ownership had not yet transferred. The court held for defendant.

Edgwood v. Falkenhagen

Defendant ordered 20 barrels of whisky from plaintiff, of which 10 were to be shipped in January, and the remainder in early February. In mid-January, plaintiff Edgwood withdrew 20 barrels, had them regauged, marked them with defendant's name and address, and set them aside in its warehouse to await shipping, sending the defendant the official certificate showing the serial numbers and contents of the barrels. A week later, the defendant wrote again, saying that as he was overstocked and importing liquor into Texas had just been declared illegal, he was cancelling his order. Plaintiff sued. The court held for the plaintiff, as the whisky had been appropriated. So, the whisky belonged to the defendant from the time it was set aside. What he could have done was simply sold it at a higher price to a third party, rather than breaching the contract.

Peterkin v. Martin

Plaintiff agreed to buy corn from defendant, but by the time it was weighted and delivered to his ship, it had been heat-damaged and mixed with bad corn. He wants the sale rescinded.

The plaintiff agreed to buy 'all the corn he had in the elevator' at $.65/bushel on the 10th of April. After that agreement, but before it was weighed, it was subjected to heat and damaged. Consequently, it did not belong to the plaintiff when it was damaged, and he need not pay for it.

Shuff v. Morgan

Plaintiff is suing for possession of a boat loaded with "at least" 20,000 hoop-poles (for $600) that had been delivered to him when it was seized by defendant-seller's creditors. The issue is who owned the boat and hoop-poles (wood for making barrels) at the time, because the hoop-poles had not yet been counted. Here, as they had actually been delivered, they were the buyer-plaintiff's property when seized. Furthermore, they were being sold for a lump price, not a price/hoop-pole. There is no suspension of the transfer of ownership when something is sold at a lump price. Only when it has to be individualized or has to weighed, counted, or measured.

Section 3: Transfer of Risk

As mentioned previously, under Article 2467, while ownership transfers on agreement, risk does not transfer until delivery.

This was not always the case. For example, in Goodwyn v. Pritchard, Goodwin agreed to buy molasses from Pritdhard. Goodwyn paid in advance. Before Goodwyn could pick up his molasses, Pritchard's sugarhouse burned down and the molasses was destroyed. Goodwyn wanted his advance payment returned, but under the law at the time, risk and ownership both transferred on agreement, so he lost. The result would be different today under the new code article, Goodwyn would have gotten his money back.

Billiott v. Lovell

Lovell and his mother were interested in buying a used car from third-party defendant dealer. They did not qualify for the first car they chose, but the dealer then showed them a different car, a Dodge Colt. The down payment was $500 more than the down payment on the original car, so Lovell gave them five post-dated checks for $100. After signing all the documents, it was after 6:30 pm. And the defendants' insurance agency had closed for the day, but the dealer assured Lovell that the dealer's insurance policy would cover the car for that night.

At approximately 1:30 am that night, Lovell and his friend Billiott went joy-riding in the car, Lovell lost control, the car flipped, and Billiott was killed. The issue is who is liable for Billiott's wrongful death: Lovell or the dealer. The court held that as the parties had acted as if the sale was complete by delivering the car, that the sale was, in fact, complete and both ownership and risk had transferred to Lovell, and so the dealer's insurance company did not cover the car at that time.

Section 4: Things in Transit

It can be relatively simple to buy something when you can go to the seller, pick it out, pay for it, and walk out of the store with it. It gets more complicated, however, when the parties are at some distance from each other. The buyer cannot simply pick up the thing but must trust to a shipping company to deliver it. The seller usually does not know the buyer, may not even use the same currency as the buyer, and wants to be assured that he is going to be paid promptly before he risks delivering the thing to a shipping company. Then there are the issues about the allocation of ownership and risk while the thing is in transit. In the days before credit cards and Paypal, payment problems were (and often still are) handled by a mechanism termed a documentary transaction, while shipping documents handled the allocation of ownership and transfer of risk through the use of certain standardized symbols. These mechanisms have allowed the immense growth of global trade.

Articles 2613 and 2616 discuss things in transit and focus on the bill of lading. The bill of lading is not just the contract between the shipper (the seller) and the carrier (the shipping company), it allocates risk, and it can serve as a document of title. If it is 'negotiable,' that means that the buyer can sell it to a third party while it is in transit. The third party then presents the negotiated copy of the bill of lading to the carrier, who will then give the thing to him.

Article 2613 discusses the ownership of things in transit, stating that the form of the bill of lading determines that ownership, as does Article 2616 discussing risk. Usually this is handled by standardized symbols: FOB, FAS, CIF. Most bills of lading are 'shipper's contracts' meaning that the thing is considered delivered to the buyer, and is now the buyer's problem: FOB means "free on board" – the thing belongs to the buyer and the risk is the buyer's once the thing is put over the ship's rail. FAS – "Free Along Side" – the thing belongs to the buyer and the risk is the buyer's once the thing is delivered alongside the ship. CIF: "Cost, Insurance, Freight" the thing belongs to the buyer and the risk is the buyer's once the shipper pays costs, freight, and insurance. The full range of shipping symbols can be seen in the chart found on the INCOTERMS (International Chamber of Commerce Terms) website.

Occasionally, however, the parties may instead choose to have a 'buyer's contract,' meaning that the shipper maintains the risk and the ownership until the thing is delivered to the buyer's address. This way, the shipper can also stop delivery while in transit if he learns that the buyer will not perform.

The reason that most contracts are in the shipper's favor (i.e. shipper's contracts) is because it has proven to be easier to assure that the shipper will be paid than that the buyer will get the goods, between credit cards, PayPal, and the system that was developed first, the documentary transaction. Before credit cards and PayPal, paying for international transactions was conducted by the system of trusted banks around the world. The banks would handle the paperwork between buyer and seller, and not pay the seller until the seller provided certain documents proving that he had complied with his side of the transaction. Because banks do not care about the actual content of the sale, and care only about whether the documents are in order, these kinds of transactions are called "Documentary transactions," and are facilitated by a letter of credit, a bank's written assurance that if certain documents are produced, it will pay a certain amount of money.

In general, the buyer, once he has been sent an invoice from the seller, takes the invoice to his bank and draws out a letter of credit specifying which documents the seller must produce in order to be paid: the bill of lading, the invoice, a certificate of insurance, a certificate of inspection, customs receipts, . . .That bank is called the 'issuing bank.' The bank sends the promise to pay along with the list of required documents to the seller's bank, called the 'confirming bank.' Once the seller brings the required documents to the confirming bank, he gets paid.

California Fruit Exchange

Defendant Meyer is a wholesale fruit dealer in New Orleans who purchased a train carload of peaches to be shipped to New Orleans in 1928. The bill of lading stipulated that the peaches were shipped on a 'straight bill of lading' (a shipper's contract) that stipulated that it was to permit inspection before unloading. When they arrived, Meyer found they were damaged, refused to accept them and plaintiff had them sold at auction, and is suing for the difference in price.

The court found that buyer had not breached the contract, so seller was unable to recoup his loss. This case was decided before the Civil Code incorporated Articles 2616, and is counter to current law.

Hypothet

Carefully compare the invoice, figure 6-2, to the BOL, figure 6-3 and the Letter of Credit, figure 6-4. You should find three issues that could cause serious problems for Singapore Slings, N&N Shipping, Or "Don't Mess with Mamou." What are they and what problems do you think might result?

CHAPTER 7

SALES SUBJECT TO CONDITIONS

Flowchart

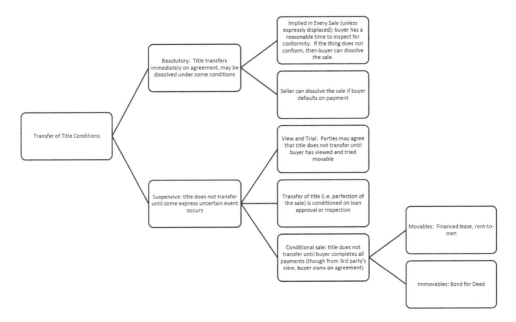

Section 1: Conditions in General

Chapter 6 answered one of the 'blue suede shoes' questions posed at the beginning of Chapter 2 – whether seller or buyer bore the risk if fire destroyed the shoes before the seller removed them from the shelf. Because the shoes were neither delivered nor individualized, the sale was not yet perfected, so the risk still belonged to the seller. We also considered what happened if they fell off the UPS truck and into the Atchafalaya Basin while *en route*. In that case, who bears the loss depends on the bill of lading or shipping terms given in the contract. For example, if they were shipped F.O.B., then the buyer bears the risk; if shipped C.I.F., then the insurance company does. In this chapter, we'll consider, among other things, what remedies the buyer has if the shoes the seller sends are the wrong size, or (Heaven forbid) some color other than blue.

Normally, ownership transfers on agreement, and risk transfers on delivery. There are situations, however, where the transfer of ownership depends on some condition. Article 1767 defines a conditional obligation as one dependent on an uncertain event. If the obligation may not be enforced until the uncertain event occurs, the condition is suspensive. If the obligation may be immediately enforced but will come to an end when the uncertain event occurs, the condition is resolutory. So, if a sale is not perfected (i.e. if ownership does not transfer) until some uncertain event, then the sale is subject to a suspensive condition. You have already seen some sales that were subject to a suspensive condition – the sale of a future thing is one such example because the sale is not perfected until the object of the sale comes into existence. Another example, especially common in immovable and vehicle sales, is where the parties agree that the sale will not be perfected (i.e. ownership will not transfer) until the buyer is approved for a loan with which to pay for the object. Sales can also be subject to resolutory conditions. One such resolutory condition is the buyer's right of inspection: if, on delivery, the buyer discovers that the thing delivered does not conform to what he had ordered, then he may reject it, and if the seller does not cure the problem, the buyer can dissolve the sale pursuant to Articles 2603-2610. In other words, all sales are subject to the resolutory condition that the seller delivers a conforming thing.

Lagniappe quiz:

Before getting started, review the rules pertaining to Obligations subject to conditions, Articles 1767-1776, and answer the following questions:

1. A suspensive condition occurs when the obligation _____.

2. A resolutory condition occurs when the obligation _____.

3. Must conditions be express?

4. If the suspensive condition is unlawful or impossible, then the obligation is _____.

5. A suspensive condition that depends solely on the whim of the obligor makes the obligation __ _____.

6. A resolutory condition that depends solely on the will of the obligor must _____.

7. If a condition is not fulfilled because of the fault of a party with an interest contrary to the fulfillment, then _____.

8. If the condition is that an event shall occur within a fixed time and that time elapses without the occurrence of that event, then the condition is considered _____.

9. If no time has been fixed for the occurrence of the event, then the condition may be fulfilled within a _____ time.

10. If the condition is that an event shall NOT occur within a fixed time, it is considered as _____ _____ once that time has elapsed without the event having occurred.

11. Fulfillment of a condition has effects that are _____ to the inception of the obligation. Nevertheless, that fulfillment does not impair the validity of acts of administration duly performed by a party, nor does it affect the ownership of fruits produced while the condition was pending.

Study Question:

What suspensive condition is at issue in the following case and how does it affect the sale?

CANAL MOTORS, INC. V. CAMPBELL 1970
241 SO.2D 5 (LA. APP. 4TH CIR.)

BARNETTE, Judge.

¶1 The plaintiff, Canal Motors, Inc., was awarded judgment of $3,137.50 against the defendant, Gerard C. Campbell, after a hearing of rule for judgment on the pleadings, pursuant to LSA-C.C.P. art. 965. The defendant Campbell has appealed devolutively.

¶2 A motion for judgment on the pleadings differs from a motion for summary judgment in that on the latter there may be submitted supporting affidavits and counter affidavits and depositions. LSA-C .C.P. art. 966. A motion for judgment on the pleadings is submitted on the pleadings which may include attached exhibits made a part of the pleadings. In either case the judgment may be granted as a matter of legal right if there does not appear to be a genuine issue of material fact. Our jurisprudential guidelines favor giving a party his day in court, hence summary judgments and judgments on the pleadings are granted only when the legal right is clearly established. Brown v. B & G Crane Service, Inc., 172 So.2d 708 (La.App.4th Cir. 1965), and cases cited therein at page 710. The issue on this appeal is whether that right has been clearly established on the pleadings, which for this purpose must be accepted as true.

¶3 The following pleaded facts are not in dispute. On May 28, 1969, the defendant Campbell selected a used automobile for purchase from plaintiff, an automobile dealer. The price was agreed upon, being $3,162.50. Campbell made a down payment or deposit of $25. The plaintiff in Article III of its petition alleged the $25 was '* * * a deposit to hold the said automobile until his loan with his Federal Credit Union had been approved * * *.' In his answer Campbell denied the allegations of Article III except the fact that defendant paid the sum of $25 as a deposit on the 1968 Chevrolet station wagon, which he admitted. Therefore for the purpose of the motion under consideration, we must accept as true that the $25 was a 'deposit' pending a loan approval. On that date the vehicle was delivered to Campbell and held in his possession and use until June 22, 1969, when it was seriously damaged in an accident. No further payment on the purchase price was made. Attached to plaintiff's petition and made a part thereof by reference are two exhibits showing Campbell as 'purchaser' of the described automobile, the price, the 'down payment' and 'net balance due.' One of these is signed by Campbell.

¶4 The disputed pleadings are plaintiff's allegation that it was assured by Sealco that Campbell's loan application was approved and in reliance upon that information it delivered possession of the automobile to Campbell on May 28, and that Sealco refused to make the loan to Campbell after the automobile was damaged. Campbell denied this allegation for lack of information sufficient to justify a belief. He reconvened seeking return of the $25 'cash deposit' and alleged: 'The balance of $3,137.50 due on the purchase price has not been paid, for reasons beyond the control of defendant; and no terms of credit were extended defendant for the balance of the purchase price.'

¶5 The foregoing summary of the pertinent pleadings shows a genuine issue of a material fact. If the $25 payment was a 'deposit' as alleged to 'hold the automobile' until the purchaser's loan application was approved, there was at that time (May 28, 1969) no completed sale, but at most a conditional obligation dependent upon an uncertain event. The condition of loan approval was a suspensive condition. LSA-C.C. arts. 2021 and 2471; Jackson Motors, Inc. v. Calvert Fire Insurance Co., 239 La. 921, 120 So.2d 478 (1960); Kershaw v. Deshotel, 179 So.2d 528 (La.App.3d Cir. 1965).

¶6 The plaintiff alleged that it delivered possession of the automobile to Campbell after assurance from Sealco that the loan application had been approved. This is denied by Campbell. Whether or not the suspensive condition was satisfied is therefore an issue of fact material to a determination if there was a completed sale of the automobile to Campbell when possession was delivered to him.

¶7 Having concluded that there is a genuine issue of material fact, the motion for judgment on the pleadings cannot be maintained. This conclusion makes unnecessary our consideration of the remaining questions argued and briefed at length by counsel.

¶8 For these reasons the judgment maintaining plaintiff's motion for judgment on the pleadings and granting judgment in favor plaintiff, Canal Motors, Inc., and against the defendant, Gerard C. Campbell, in the principal sum of $3,137.50 is annulled and the motion for judgment on the pleadings is denied.

¶9 The case is remanded for further proceedings according to law.

Judgment annulled; case remanded.

Section 2: Inspection by the Buyer v. View and Trial

As seen in Canal Motors, often sales are subject to an express or implied suspensive condition that the buyer will obtain a loan needed to pay for the object. This means that the transfer of title is suspended until such time as the buyer gets loan approval. Unless otherwise stipulated, however, all sales are subject to an implied resolutory condition that the buyer has a right to inspect the thing sold within a reasonable amount of time after delivery and if the thing delivered does not conform to the contract, and the seller cannot or will not cure the noncomformity, then the buyer may dissolve the sale. Read Louisiana Civil Code articles 2604-2610. Consider the following hypothet

Practice Hypothet:

Mr. and Mrs. Alexander wanted a new RV, and went to the dealer from whom they had purchased their two previous RVs, Kite Brothers. They bought a brand-new 2014 Torque RV on October 15, 2013, and traded in their 2006 Fleetwood Gearbox "toy-hauler." Even though the Kite Brothers inspected the Gearbox and complimented Mrs. Alexander on how well she had maintained the interior, they did not actually go into the Gearbox, but only inspected the outside, noticing storm damage to an awning, which the Alexanders promised to handle through their insurer. Kite Brothers gave the Alexanders $25,495 credit for the trade in. The sale and trade-in were finalized and the Alexanders moved their personal effects into the new RV.

In November, 2013, the Kite Brothers contacted the Alexanders to advise them that the Gearbox's roof had been damaged, and showed them an area that had been peeled back and a hole in the roof. The Alexanders assumed that the damage was done prior to the sale to Kite Brothers but were not sure. Because Gearbox had since gone bankrupt, it took several months for the Kite Brothers to obtain the awning, and so they left the RV out on their lot in the interim. When the parts arrived, in February 2014, they moved the Gearbox into the garage and discovered that the hole in the roof had led to deterioration of the interior. They now want the Alexanders to pay for those repairs, claiming that they had breached the contract as the trade-in value was based on the Gearbox having no leaks, no rotten wood or water damage.

Question

Based on your knowledge of Articles 2604-2610, are the Alexanders liable because the Gearbox did not conform to the buyer's expectation? (Adapted from Kite Bros. LLC v. Alexander, _____ So.3d _____, 2019 WL 6887259 (La. 3d Cir. Ct. App. 2019).

In contrast to the normal right of inspection (and the attendant possible resolutory condition), parties may expressly agree that title does not transfer until the buyer has viewed and tried the object of the sale. In such a case, the sale is subject to a suspensive condition – i.e., the sale is not complete until the buyer approves the thing. Read Article 2460. Thus, a sale subject to view and trial is subject to a suspensive condition just like the sale of something that must be weighed, counted, or measured. Remember, the general rule is that ownership transfers on agreement, but the buyer has a right to inspect the thing and dissolve the sale should the thing not conform to the contract of sale. As an exception to this rule, the parties can agree that the buyer must view or try the thing and approve it before title transfers. Distinguishing between an ordinary sale and a sale on view and trial depends on determining the parties' intent.

Study Questions:

Is the sale in the following case one on view and trial, or is it just a normal sale where the buyer has a right to inspect?

When and where did the sale take place, and what reasoning did the court use?

John V. PARKER, District Judge.

Stipulation of Facts

[On motion for summary judgment, the parties stipulated that the plaintiff Tunica-Biloxi Tribe of Louisiana is a federally-recognized Indian tribe enjoying a government-to-government relationship with the United States, and that it acts under a Constitution recognized by the federal government which became effective on January 1, 1999.

[Defendant Bridges was the secretary of the Louisiana Department of Revenue and he is charged with the collection of state taxes. Raymond Bertalotto was the Tribe's Transportation Manager of its wholly-owned enterprise the Paragon Casino and Resort, in Marksville, Louisiana, on the Tribe's Reservation. Sometime in October 2004, Bertalotto sent (from his office on the Reservation) a written solicitation for bids by fax to several Louisiana car dealerships on a van the Tribe wished to buy. He received three bids. After reviewing the bids and investigating a similar van sold to another casino, Bertalotto called Bolton Ford from his office and agreed to pay $32,064 and ordered the van, contingent on inspection. Anticipating imminent delivery of the van to the Tribe's reservation, Bolton Ford prepared a bill of sale, signed by an agent of the dealership. The Tribe took delivery of the van on its reservation on December 28, 2004, and Bertalotto hand-delivered a check for the purchase price to an agent of the dealership on the reservation when the van was delivered.

[The price paid to Bolton Ford included $2,876.14 in sales tax on the van, including $1,603.20 to the State and $1,272.94 to [Avoyelles] Parish. The Office of Motor Vehicles Vehicle Application lists the date of vehicle acquisition as December 22, 2004. The Tribe, through Paragon, paid a license fee for the van and obtained Louisiana license plates for the van.

[The Tribe then objected to the payment of sales tax, arguing that the sale of the van was completed on the reservation and therefore was not subject to Louisiana sales tax on motor vehicles, which led to the instant suit. The Tribe sought a refund of the sales tax paid on the van, and declaratory and injunctive relief.]

Conclusions of Law: Site of the Sale

¶1 The critical question at this stage of the litigation is whether the sale of the van occurred on the Tribe's reservation or whether it took place at Bolton Ford in Lake Charles. For tax purposes, a "sale" is defined as "any transfer of title or possession, or both, exchange, barter, conditional or otherwise, in any manner or by any means whatsoever, of tangible personal property, for a consideration ...." La.R.S. 47:301(12). The court has previously concluded that "[t]he word 'title,' as used in this context, is best understood as being synonymous with 'ownership.' " Tunica-Biloxi Tribe of Indians v. Bridges, 365 F.Supp.2d 782, 786 (M.D.La.2005). Therefore, a tax "sale" is perfected upon the earliest of the transfer of ownership or the transfer of possession. Since "[t]he jurisprudence of Louisiana is quite clear that the sale of a motor vehicle is governed by the articles in the Louisiana Civil Code relating to the sale of movables," Biggs v. Prewitt, 669 So.2d 441, 443 (La.App. 1 Cir.1995), writ denied, 674 So.2d 264 (La.1996), the court notes that a transfer of ownership occurs "as soon as the price is fixed, even though the thing sold is not yet delivered nor the price paid." La. Civ. Code art. 2456.

¶2   Mr. Bertalotto sent out a written solicitation for bids by fax to at least two Louisiana car dealerships, including Bolton Ford in Lake Charles. The Tribe concedes that the solicitation of bids was not an offer, but rather, an invitation for dealerships to make offers to the Tribe. Bolton Ford responded in kind and "offered"-by fax-to sell a van to the Tribe. Bertalotto called Bolton Ford in Lake Charles from his office on the reservation and agreed to pay $32,064 for the van.

¶3   The court cannot but comment upon how unhelpful the reply brief on behalf of defendant was to the court. In that brief, the State abandons all prior positions and advances the notion that the sale of a motor vehicle is not complete "until the [S]tate of Louisiana actually issues a paper title" (doc. 117, p. 3). In addition to a radical change in legal position by the State, that assertion contradicts established Louisiana law:

> The jurisprudence of this state does not require that the certificate of title to a vehicle be trans-
> ferred in order for the sale to be a valid one. Wright v. Barnes, 541 So.2d 977 (La.App. 2d Cir.1989);
> Shanks v. Callahan, 232 So.2d 306, 308 (La.App. 1st Cir.1969). Furthermore, sale of a vehicle is
> not affected by non-compliance with the Vehicle Certificate of Title Law, LSA-R.S. 32:701-738.
> Wright, 541 So.2d 977; Sherman, 413 So.2d at 646. Neither does the law require that an agreement
> to sell a motor vehicle be notarized or even reduced to writing. See Maloney v. State Farm Ins.
> Co., 583 So.2d 12 (La.App. 4th Cir.), writs denied, 586 So.2d 544, 589 So.2d 1058 (1991).

> "The law in Louisiana is clear that absent contrary intent by the parties, a contract is considered
> executed at the place where the offer is accepted or where the last act necessary to a meeting of
> the minds or to completing the contract is performed." Aetna Ins. Co. v. Naquin, 478 So.2d 1352,
> 1354 (La.App. 5 Cir.1985).

¶4   Bertalotto accepted Bolton Ford's offer from the reservation (and ultimately accepted delivery on the reservation), but the "last act necessary" was for Bolton Ford itself to receive the acceptance of its offer. An acceptance means nothing unless it is properly communicated to the offeror. A "meeting of the minds" cannot occur unless both minds are "on the same wavelength" and communication between them is required to accomplish this. Once the acceptance was received by the seller in Lake Charles, the thing, price, and consent all converged and the sale was perfected. The sale having taken place in Lake Charles, the tax on the van was proper but for the Tribe's new argument regarding inspection by the buyer.

Inspection by the Buyer

¶5　It is undisputed that Bertalotto ordered the van "contingent on inspection." Therefore, the Tribe argues the applicability of La. Civ. Code art. 2460, which reads as follows: "When the buyer has reserved the view or trial of the thing, ownership is not transferred from the seller to the buyer until the latter gives his approval of the thing." The comments to Article 2460 advise that the situation contemplated by the article "must be distinguished from the buyer's right to inspect things delivered by the seller in performance of a contract of sale. The [view or trial] is incidental to a special kind of sale where the transfer of ownership depends on approval by the buyer. The [usual sale] is the buyer's right to check whether the seller has complied with the contract."

¶6　Pertinent to this issue are La. Civ. Code arts. 2604 and 2605. Article 2604 provides that "[t]he buyer has a right to have a reasonable opportunity to inspect the things, even after delivery, for the purpose of ascertaining whether they conform to the contract." Article 2605 adds, in part, that "[a] buyer may reject nonconforming things within a reasonable time. The buyer must give reasonable notice to the seller to make the rejection effective."

¶7　Thus, under general sales law, the Tribe had the right to inspect the van even after it was delivered to the reservation and to reject it if it did not meet the Tribe's specifications. The Tribe, as buyer, had that right even without specifically noting that the sale would be "contingent on inspection." The exercise of that right does not bear upon the transfer of ownership of the thing under Article 2456 because at the time of delivery of the van, there already was "agreement on the thing and the price [was] fixed ...." The court therefore concludes that this was not a "special kind of sale." Rather, Bertalotto's "inspection" is more appropriately classified as an exercise of any buyer's right of inspection following any sale under Article 2604.

¶8　Ownership was transferred at the moment the Tribe and Bolton Ford agreed upon the thing and the price. That moment occurred in Lake Charles, not on the reservation. Therefore, the sales tax was lawfully imposed on the transaction.

¶9 For the foregoing reasons, there shall be judgment herein in favor of defendants and against plaintiff, dismissing this action.

Study Question:

Contrast Tunica-Biloxi Tribe with the following classic case.

HAMILTON CO V. MEDICAL ARTS BLDG. CO. 1931
17 LA. APP. 508, 135 SO. 94

TALIAFERRO, J.

¶1 Intervener and third opponent, United Iron Works, Inc., of Kansas City, Mo., in the month of November, 1928, sold, delivered to, and installed for, defendant, Medical Arts Building, Inc., of Shreveport, La., certain machinery and equipment for the production and application of refrigeration, for the price of $2,175 on which there was a balance due of $629.69 when this litigation began. The purchaser gave to intervener its promissory notes for the deferred part of said price, with 6 per cent. interest and 10 per cent. attorney's fees in event of suit thereon, but took no mortgage to secure the notes. Nothing was recorded to give notice that the machinery and equipment were unpaid for. This machinery and equipment was shipped from Kansas City, or other points in Missouri, and was installed in defendant's building at intersection of Travis and Louisiana streets, during the month of January, 1929.

¶2 On July 26, 1929, defendant gave a special mortgage on its lots of ground and office building, aforesaid, to the Hamilton Company, plaintiff herein, and to C. L. Shaw Company, for $30,000, evidenced by its several notes, described in the mortgage. This act of mortgage was duly recorded in the official records of Caddo parish the day of its execution, and subsequently plaintiff acquired the notes of Shaw & Co. Defendant defaulted on its said notes, and on January 11, 1930, foreclosure proceedings were instituted thereon by plaintiff, and in due course the mortgaged property, including said refrigeration plant, was seized by the sheriff and advertised for sale.

¶3 In the meantime the United Iron Works, Inc., was placed in the hands of a receiver at Kansas City by the federal court, and through said receiver this intervention and third opposition was filed on February, 26, 1930.

¶4 Intervener alleges that the machinery and equipment sold by it to defendant was installed in the basement of defendant's said office building very soon after sale and delivery thereof; that the notes evidencing the unpaid part of the purchase price were secured by a vendor's lien and privilege on said machinery, refrigeration plant, and equipment; that same has been seized with said office building and the land whereon same is located, by the sheriff of Caddo parish, in the foreclosure suit of plaintiff, and is being advertised for sale. The prayer is that said machinery, refrigeration plant, and equipment be separately appraised and separately sold by the sheriff, and that he be ordered to hold the proceeds of such sale until the further orders of the court; that intervener have judgment against defendant for $629.69, the balance due on the price of said machinery and equipment, with interest and attorneys' fees, and judgment against plaintiff and defendant recognizing its vendor's lien and privilege on said property as outranking and superior to any claim of plaintiff, and ordering the judgment rendered in its favor paid out of said proceeds by preference and priority over plaintiff and others. Order of court issued as prayed for requiring separate appraisement and separate sale of the property described on which defendant asserted a vendor's lien and privilege. This litigation now is over the proceeds of sale of said property held by the sheriff.

¶5 Plaintiff answered the intervention, but defendant did not. A judgment by default was entered against it.

¶6 The answer is a general denial of the allegations of intervener's petition, except as to those relating to the foreclosure by plaintiff and seizure of defendant's property, including that against which the vendor's lien and privilege is asserted, and the impending sale thereof by the sheriff. It is further averred that, if any machinery or equipment or refrigeration plant was installed in the Medical Arts Building, the same became a part of said realty and incorporated therein, and became subject to plaintiff's mortgage; that the refrigeration plant in said building rests upon, and is securely fastened to, concrete foundations, and that same is an immovable by destination.

¶7 Under the issues tendered by these pleadings, the case was tried, resulting in a judgment rejecting intervener's demand and dismissing its suit with costs. Intervener appealed.

¶8 The first negotiations looking to the purchase by defendant of the machinery and equipment for a refrigeration plant from intervener took place in Dallas, Tex., between their respective representatives. This was very soon followed by a written proposal of intervener, dated at Shreveport, November 10, 1928, on printed form for the purpose, wherein it proposed "to furnish certain machinery and equipment for the production and application of refrigeration as described in specifications hereto attached." Production of refrigeration at rate of six tons per day of 24 hours, under stipulated conditions, was guaranteed. On November 15, 1928, defendant signed written acceptance of the above-mentioned proposal at Shreveport, and same was either forwarded to intervener at Kansas City or to its agent at Dallas. The proposal with defendant's acceptance thereon was finally approved by the vice president of the seller at Kansas City, November 28, 1928.

¶9   Two propositions of law arise in this case. The first is, Was the contract between intervener and defendant a Louisiana contract? If so, as a consequence the unpaid purchase price was secured by a vendor's privilege. The second is, Has such vendor's privilege been lost as a result of the installation of the machinery and equipment in defendant's building, for the purpose purchased, and being attached thereto for its use and benefit, no chattel mortgage securing the unpaid part of the purchase price having been registered?

¶10   Logically, the first question to be determined is whether we are dealing with a Louisiana contract. If the contractual relation between intervener and defendant is not governed and controlled by the laws of the state of Louisiana, a finding by this court to that effect will make it unnecessary to consider the second question, for intervener will be without remedy or right to pursue the goods sold by it to defendant.

¶11   The original proposal of intervener, referred to supra, contains the following stipulation, holding in suspense, in so far as concerned intervener, the terms and conditions of the proposal already accepted by defendant, to wit: "This agreement is executed and signed in duplicate, but it is understood that it shall become binding upon the seller only when approved by an executive officer of the seller at its home office in Kansas City, Mo., U. S. A., and if not approved the payment accompanying this proposition shall be returned promptly to the seller."

¶12   The proposal and acceptance were forwarded to intervener's office in Kansas City, and on November 26, 1928, was approved by its vice president, thus completing all the requirements necessary to render the contract binding on both sides.

¶13   The following pertinent stipulations are contained in the contract under discussion:

"The seller shall furnish an engineer to supervise and assist in making installation of said equipment and machinery."

"The seller shall furnish all labor for ammonia work. Buyer to furnish labor for putting up water lines and cooling tower."

"It is agreed and understood that a test run of three days must be made on the plant, for the purpose of making adjustments, if any, that may be required."

"And it is hereby understood and agreed that a failure on the part of the buyer to reject the plant by notifying the seller in writing within three days from completion of installation above mentioned, shall constitute an acceptance on the part of the buyer."

¶14 The record does not disclose the date the plant was finally installed, but on January 30, 1929, defendant wrote a letter of acceptance to intervener, on form used for that purpose, to wit:

"The undersigned this day accepts as completed according to contract and specifications, dated 10 day of Nov., 1928, the #30 machine 4 x 4 and Drinking Water Cooling Equipment.

"This acceptance is subject to the provisions of said contract, if any, in respect of replacing defective materials."

¶15 Plaintiff argues that, when the contract under consideration, was accepted by the vice president of intervener company in Kansas City, pursuant to the suspensive stipulation therein, it became a Missouri contract, and therefore no vendor's lien arose to protect the seller as to the unpaid portion of the purchase price, and that, when the goods were loaded on cars in Missouri, consigned to defendant on open bill of lading, the title there passed, and thereafter the goods became the property of the purchaser. This argument overlooks other conditions of the contract, suspensive in their nature, which were to be eventually executed, and could only be executed, in the state of Louisiana, where the goods were destined for installation and use, and which, until complied with, caused the contract to be executory and incomplete in respect to its fulfillment.

¶16 A contract of sale is perfected by three concurring circumstances, viz. The object or thing, the price and the consent. Civ. Code, art. 2439. But the perfection of the contract so as to fix responsibility of the parties to it, in the event of its final execution or nonexecution, is one thing, while the actual passing of the title of the thing, the object of the contract, under conditions suspensive in their nature, is another.

¶17 It is contended by intervener that the ultimate consummation of the contract between it and defendant was suspended until all of the stipulations of the proposal, quoted supra, had been fulfilled as written, citing article 2460 of the Civil Code: "Things, of which the buyer reserves to himself the view and trial, although the price be agreed on, are not sold, until the buyer be satisfied with the trial, which is a kind of suspensive condition of the sale."

¶18   The case of De La Vergne Co. v. N. O. & Western R. R. Co., 51 La. Ann. 1733, 26 So. 455, in our opinion, is decisive of the issue before us as to whether the contract between defendant and intervener is a Louisiana contract, and whether the unpaid part of the purchase price is secured by a vendor's lien and privilege.

¶19   On these questions the syllabus of that case reads: "A contract made in New York, to be executed and consummated in Louisiana,-the acceptance of the thing forming the object of the contract being dependent upon a suspensive condition, to wit, that after completion a stipulated test is to be applied, which test is to be made, and can only be made, in Louisiana,-is a Louisiana contract, and the thing sold subject to the vendor's privilege accorded by the Louisiana law."

¶20   The contract under consideration by the court in the above-named case was signed in the state of New York, the domicile of both parties thereto. It was to be executed in Louisiana. It provided for the construction, erection, and delivery by the Delta Construction Company (assignor of defendant) of two cotton compresses in Louisiana within a certain time and for a stipulated amount. The finished compresses, it was stipulated, were to respond favorably to certain tests set out in the contract.

¶21   In the course of this opinion, Justice Blanchard, as the organ of the court, said:

> "The contract for the presses, while made in New York, was to be executed and consummated
> in Louisiana. The presses were to be erected and completed here, and there was a suspensive
> condition in the contract, viz. that after completion a test stipulated for in the contract was
> to be applied here, and the acceptance of the presses by defendant was dependent on their
> performance measuring up to the requirements of the test. The presses and their appurtenances
> remained the property of the plaintiff and at their risk until thus tested and accepted. Hence the
> delivery of the presses was to be accomplished here.

> "The contract therefore must be held to be a Louisiana contract, and the presses subject to the
> lien accorded by our law to a vendor"-citing McIlvaine v. Legare et al., 36 La. Ann. 362; McLane
> v. Creditors, 47 La. Ann. 135-141, 16 So. 764; Overend v. Robinson, 10 La. Ann. 728; Duncan v.
> Helm, 22 La. Ann. 418; Maillard v. Nihoul, 21 La. Ann. 412; Carlin v. Gordy, 32 La. Ann. 1288;
> Scannell v. Beauvais, 38 La. Ann. 218; and Shakspeare v. Ware, 38 La. Ann. 574; Benjamin on Sales
> §§ 308, 319, 651.

* * *

¶22 The syllabus in Overend, Gurney & Co. v. Robinson & Olroyd et al., 10 La. Ann. 728, so far as pertinent, is: "Where the sale between the parties was, in New York, executory merely, with the intention that it should be consummated in New Orleans, and it was so consummated, the contract must be considered as completed in New Orleans, and the vendor's privilege may be exercised according to the laws of Louisiana."

¶23 With regard to contract of sale where the goods are shipped from the seller in one state to the buyer in another, the contract being executory in its nature, and containing stipulations or suspensive conditions which may not be finally discharged until after the delivery of goods to the purchaser, the laws of the state where the conditions are fulfilled, the last act in consummation of the intention of the parties, will govern.

¶24 In the case at bar, the seller contracted with full knowledge that the purchased goods were destined for use in Louisiana; part of the purchase price was not to be paid until after the goods were delivered and installed; the notes representing the deferred part of the price were executed in Louisiana. It was a part of the seller's obligation to furnish an engineer to supervise in the installation of the goods sold and also furnish all labor for the ammonia work. After installation of goods, a test of three days "must" be made, and within this testing period the purchaser had the right to reject the plant. We do not think he had the right to arbitrarily reject the plant, but it is certain that, if the plant did not function as guaranteed, he would have had the right to reject it, and thereafter it would have been the property of the seller.

¶25 We are informed in brief by counsel for intervener that the judge of the lower court held the contract under consideration to be a Louisiana contract. We agree with that holding.

¶26 Having reached the conclusion that the contract between intervener and plaintiff was a Louisiana contract, and that a vendor's lien and privilege secured the unpaid part of the purchase price of the goods sold, the next question for determination is whether such lien and privilege has been lost to the seller as a consequence of the goods having been installed and constituted into the refrigeration plant in the basement of defendant's building, and attached thereto. [The portion of the opinion discussing the vendor's privilege is omitted.]

Section 3: Other Implicit Resolutory Conditions

As the previous section showed you, because ownership transfers on agreement, if the buyer later inspects the goods and finds that they don't conform to the contract, then he can dissolve the sale. Courts sometimes treat the buyer's discovery upon inspection that the thing doesn't conform as a resolutory condition. Yet there's a problem. A condition is an uncertain event, something outside the control of buyer and seller or either of them. Verifying that seller has done as he promised doesn't sound like an uncertain event at all. It's rather something that will normally occur. In addition, to say failing such an inspection for conformity is an uncertain event means that if the condition is satisfied (and the thing does not conform), then the contract is viewed as being unwound because of the condition, not dissolved because the seller breached. But if the seller does not deliver what he promised to deliver, he breaches. That's why the seller similarly has the power to dissolve the sale if the buyer breaches. Article 2561 provides in part: "If the buyer fails to pay the price, the seller may sue for dissolution of the sale. . . ." It would be odd to say that the seller exercises rights arising out of the occurrence of an implied resolutory condition if the buyer instead of paying with dollar bills issued by the Federal Reserve gave the seller dollars printed by Parker Brothers as part of the game of Monopoly.

Study Questions:

Read the rest of Article 2561 and consider the following case in light of that article – does it apply or does some other principle or article apply? (See La. Civil Code arts. 2013-2024).

Alternatively, consider the case in light of the previous comment. The court says that seller's refusal to accept the buyer's irregular payments was a "dissolving condition."

Would it make more sense to reason that seller breached the contract and therefore the buyer has the power to file suit to have it dissolved?

BERRY V. GINSBURG 1957

98 SO.2D 548 (LA. APP. 2ND CIR.)

GLADNEY, Judge.

¶1 The plaintiff brought this suit against the defendant to rescind a contract and obtain the return of that portion of the purchase price which had been paid, together with attorney's fees occasioned by this action. The defendant has answered by denying a breach of the agreement and has instituted a reconventional demand for the unpaid balance due on the contract. Principally on these issues the case was tried and resulted in a judgment in favor of plaintiff against defendant in the amount prayed for, namely $704. The demand for attorney's fees was rejected as was the reconventional demand. The defendant appealed and plaintiff has answered the appeal to preserve her right to collect attorney's fees.

¶2 The petition of Pearl Berry alleges that on May 7, 1949, she purchased from the defendant, Abraham Ginsburg, who owns and operates a business in Shreveport, Louisiana, known as

Caddo Jewelry & Loan Company, a diamond ring for $1,830, inclusive of tax; that the ring was sold under an agreement whereby it was retained by the seller until paid for through weekly payments. The subject agreement reads as follows:

> "I Pearl Berry, the undersigned, do agree and promise to pay each week from this date, the 7th day of May, 1949, on the purchase of ring No. 099 until the total sum of Eighteen Hundred and Thirty Dollars ($1,830.00) has been paid.

> "It is understood that no certain sum of money is specified to be paid weekly, but that if no payment be made within a period of thirty (30) consecutive days, all previous payments to this, The Caddo Jewelry and Loan Company, become forfeit and I hold no claim against this Company."

¶3 It is further alleged after she made payments as prescribed in the contract, that on November 29, 1956, the defendant declined to accept further payments from plaintiff and told her he desired to recede from the contract; and that as a consequence of such action, plaintiff demanded the return of the money which she had paid under the contract. Plaintiff also alleges Ginsburg has offered to allow her to purchase other articles from the store to the value of her credit, but refuses to return the money she has paid.

¶4 The defendant has filed an exception of no right or cause of action, and a plea of prescription predicated on the provisions of LSA-C.C. art. 2498. By way of answer he denied refusing to accept any payment by plaintiff, admitted that he received the sum of $704 in various payments from plaintiff, and declared that he was willing to complete the contract. The defendant then as plaintiff in reconvention alleged a demand for the balance due on the sale price of the ring in the sum of $1,124, and pleading further in the alternative, seeks enforcement of the forfeiture provisions of the contract, and alternatively, he again assumes the position of plaintiff in reconvention and demands the payment of $333.26, which he alleges was paid in taxes while holding the possession of the ring.

¶5 The judge a quo in a written opinion concluded that Ginsburg did refuse to accept a payment on the ring on November 29, 1956, and that as a result thereof the defendant defaulted on the contract and plaintiff was entitled to recover. He rejected the exception of no cause or right of action, the plea of prescription, and the reconventional demands asserted by defendant.

¶6 Plaintiff's cause of action is founded on certain articles of the LSA-Civil Code, which we set forth herewith:

Art. 2045:

'The dissolving condition is that which, when accomplished, operates the revocation of the obligation, placing matters in the same state as though the obligation had not existed.

'It does not suspend the execution of the obligation; it only obliges the creditor to restore what he has received, in case the event provided for in the condition takes place.'

Art. 2046:

'A resolutory condition is implied in all commutative contracts, to take effect, in case either of the parties do not comply with his engagements; in this case the contract is not dissolved of right; the party complaining of a breach of the contract may either sue for its dissolution with damages, or, if the circumstances of the case permit, demand a specific performance.'

Art. 2047:

'In all cases the dissolution of a contract may be demanded by suit or by exception; and when the resolutory condition is an event, not depending on the will of either party, the contract is dissolved of right; but, in other cases, it must be sued for, and the party in default may, according to circumstances, have a further time allowed for the performance of the condition.'

¶7 Thus, a dissolution of a contract, if desired by one of the parties, may be claimed only by suit. Mossy Motors v. McRedmond, La.App.1943, 12 So.2d 719. It is plaintiff's position, therefore, that when the defendant refused to accept further payments on the contract and refused to return to her the money she had paid, she was forced to institute this action, thereby incurring attorney's fees which she seeks to recover.

¶8 Upon the trial of the case plaintiff and her attorney both testified that Ginsburg on November 29, 1956, refused to return the money which was demanded. Ginsburg denied that he had done so, although he admitted that he had offered to permit plaintiff to receive merchandise to the amount which she has paid in. The defendant was corroborated to some extent by an employee, Mrs. Juliette Arnold, but the latter conceded that she was not present during the entire conversation between defendant and Pearl Berry on November 29th, and, of course, she did not testify that she was present at the conversation between the defendant and plaintiff's attorney, in which conversation the latter testified Ginsburg did decline to permit plaintiff to continue with her payments. The trial court resolved the issue in favor of plaintiff upon determining defendant had breached the contract.

¶9 The defendant testified the payments made by plaintiff were at first substantial, but gradually were so reduced that it appeared that she would take an unreasonable period of time to complete the contract, and accordingly, he took the position it would be unfair to request that the parties sustain the contract with such small payments. As to this point, we observe that the written contract, which undoubtedly the defendant himself wrote, expressly provided no certain sum of money to be paid weekly. He, therefore, cannot claim the equities to be in his favor, especially in view of testimony by him that the ring which he sold to plaintiff for $1,830 was purchased by him for $700. We find no error in the finding of the judge a quo upon the merits of the case.

¶10 The appellant does not urge before this court his exception of no cause or right of action and we consider it as abandoned.

***

¶11 Through a reconventional demand accompanying respondent's answer, the recovery of Federal excise taxes and property taxes was sought. We find no merit in this claim. Title to the ring passed to the plaintiff at the time the agreement was effectuated and this is true even though possession of the ring was retained by the defendant vendor. It, therefore, seems to us that any property taxes paid on account of the ring by the defendant were paid in error and plaintiff cannot be held responsible therefor. We observe that plaintiff alleges she purchased the ring at the price of $1,830, inclusive of all taxes, and the contract itself fixes the amount to be paid by plaintiff as the sum of $1,830.

***

¶12 It is our conclusion plaintiff is entitled to recover the amount paid by her on the purchase price of the ring and was justified in instituting this action for a rescission of the contract due to defendant's refusal to accept further payments pursuant to the provisions of the contract. We further hold under the authorities hereinabove cited, attorney's fees of $250 which were sufficiently proven before the trial court should be awarded.

¶13 For the foregoing reasons, the judgment from which appealed is amended by awarding to plaintiff attorney's fees in the sum of $250, and as so amended, the judgment is affirmed at appellant's cost.

Section 4: Common Law "Conditional Sales"

Like Louisiana law, Article 2 of the Uniform Commercial Code provides the buyer with an implied right to inspect the goods, as well as remedies should the goods fail to conform to the contract. UCC § 2-513 provides:

> (1) Unless otherwise agreed and subject to subsection (3), where goods are tendered or delivered or identified to the contract for sale, the buyer has a right before payment or acceptance to inspect them at any reasonable place and time and in any reasonable manner. When the seller is required or authorized to send the goods to the buyer, the inspection may be after their arrival.

> (2) Expenses of inspection must be borne by the buyer but may be recovered from the seller if the goods do not conform and are rejected.

> (3) Unless otherwise agreed and subject to the provisions of this Article on C.I.F. contracts (subsection (3) of Section 2-321), the buyer is not entitled to inspect the goods before payment of the price when the contract provides
>   (a) for delivery "C.O.D." or on other like terms; or
>   (b) for payment against documents of title, except where such payment is due only after the goods are to become available for inspection.

> (4) A place or method of inspection fixed by the parties is presumed to be exclusive but unless otherwise expressly agreed it does not postpone identification or shift the place for delivery or for passing the risk of loss. If compliance becomes impossible, inspection shall be as provided in this section unless the place or method fixed was clearly intended as an indispensable condition failure of which avoids the contract.

Study question:

Does UCC § 2-513 differ significantly from Louisiana law?

Comment:

"A fundamental principle of Louisiana sales law is that ownership of the thing sold is immediately transferred to the buyer on agreement as to the thing as the price, even if the thing has not yet been delivered nor the price paid. Art 2456. The immediate transfer of ownership takes place automatically – unless the parties intended otherwise. Normally the parties' performances are due simultaneously, as with any bilateral contract. A credit sale is one exception to this in that while ownership transfers immediately, the buyer is given time in which to pay all or some of the price.[1] Another alternative is a conditional sale where the parties to the sale have agreed that ownership does not transfer until the buyer has paid the entire price, in other words, the sale is subject to the suspensive condition of the buyer having fully paid for the thing.

There are a number of ways the parties to a conditional sale can structure this. One is to designate the sale as subject to the suspensive condition of the buyer's payment of the price. Alternatively, they could call it a contract to sell, a lease with an option to buy, a lease-purchase agreement, a financed lease, or a rent-to-own contract. The latter two types can be found in the Revised Statutes: The Lease of Movables Act is set forth in R.S. §§ 9:3301-3342, and the Rental Purchase Agreement Act is presented in R.S. §§ 9:3352-3361."Louisiana also adopted Article 9 of the Uniform Commercial Code, so such an agreement could be structured as a chattel mortgage. Under the La. UCC-9 variant, the movable is subject to a security interest which is enforceable against the debtor, meaning that the movable is collateral in case the debtor fails to pay. This requires that a financing statement be filed (i.e. 'perfected'), and in the event of a default, the secured party may take possession of the collateral only by means of judicial process (unless the defaulting debtor otherwise consented). Once the security interest is perfected, that creditor's interest takes priority over other of the buyer's secured creditors and over all unsecured creditors.

As you saw in Chapter 1 with the cases dealing with the 'lease' of 13 mules and the 'sale' of the two hydraulic presses, sellers have long looked for ways to secure payment of a price without going through the full formalities of a chattel mortgage, and Louisiana courts were traditionally hostile towards adoption of any direct or indirect form of the common law conditional sale contract where the buyer would forfeit all payments made in case of his defaulting payment of one installment, or where the seller was given a right to avail himself of self-help to repossess the thing. Self-help is still frowned-upon by Louisiana's courts, but the seller can accelerate payments or alternatively cancel the lease and recover possession in a financed lease if the buyer defaults (La. R.S. § 9:3318). Under a Rental-Purchase Agreement, the seller's only option if a buyer defaults is to recover possession and demand back rent, but the defaulting buyer can reinstate the Agreement under certain conditions. (La. R.S. § 9:3357). One important principle to be aware of, however, in studying conditional sales, dates from the time when Louisiana courts were hostile towards them: While the parties to the agreement have stipulated that the transfer of ownership is suspended; nevertheless, from the perspective of a third party, ownership has already transferred.

Study Question:

How do Louisiana Revised Statutes 9:3301-3342 apply to the following cases?

---

[1]   24 La. Civil Law Treatise §4:16.

KLIEBERT, Judge.

¶1 Plaintiff, Vernon A. Blackledge, was the owner of a 1984 Fleetwood mobile home which was subject to a chattel mortgage held by Louisiana National Bank (Bank). This suit arises out of an agreement to purchase in which plaintiff agreed to lease the mobile home to Fred and Rene Vinet, defendants, pending the passage of the act of sale. When defendants failed to pay the monthly rents and voluntarily agreed to return the mobile home, plaintiff again took possession of the mobile home and turned it over to the Bank for credit under the chattel mortgage indebtedness. Additionally, plaintiffs sued for a bad faith breach of contract. Defendants answered with a general denial.

¶2 Based on stipulated facts the trial judge rendered judgment in favor of plaintiff and against defendants for $4,800.76 plus legal interest and costs. Defendants appeal devolutively contending the damage award was improper and could only be fixed as an early termination or a default in the manner provided by the Louisiana Lease of Movables Act, LSA-R.S. 9:3301 et seq. Plaintiff contends defendants' argument is an affirmative defense and since it was not pleaded in the answer was not properly before the trial court or before this court. For the reasons hereinafter assigned we change the amount of the award from $4,800.76 to $350.00, and as revised, affirm.

¶3 The stipulation of the parties admitted into evidence the Agreement to Purchase and Sell entered into by the parties on February 9, 1986 and attached hereto as Appendix "I". The stipulation entered into in lieu of a trial acknowledged: (1) the existence of Louisiana National Bank's chattel mortgage, (2) the Bank was not a party to the February 9th agreement, and (3) the plaintiff had paid, pursuant to the chattel mortgage agreement, the following amounts to the Bank: (a) Downpayment $1,150.00, (b) Insurance on mobile home $1,078.00, (c) Monthly installment notes of $6,329.16. Additional facts stipulated to were as follows:

"(1) Defendant was late in his monthly payments for five months between May and October, 1986. The late fee was $20.00 per month.

"(2) Defendant notified plaintiff in the third week of November, 1986 that he could not pay for the trailer and to pick it up.

"(3) Defendant mailed plaintiff a letter that trailer was on defendant's property and plaintiff would be charged lot rent of $110.00 per month if it was not removed. This letter was mailed December 28, 1986 and was received by the plaintiff.

"(4) The defendant did not pay rent in November 1986, December 1986, January 1987, February 1987, March 1987 and April 1987.

"(5) Plaintiff paid the defendant $350.00 for lot rent when the trailer was returned. Plaintiff spent $15.00 for a certified check and mail.

"(6) The plaintiff advertised the trailer in November, 1986 at a cost of $52.00.

"(7) The plaintiff kept the deposit on the trailer."

¶4 In arriving at the total award of $4,800.76, the trial court totaled the following amounts: (a) down payment $1,150.00, (b) insurance $1,078.00, (c) note payments $1,846.01, (d) butane tank $89.00, (e) late fees $220.00, (f) ad in Times-Picayune $52.00, (g) lot rental $350.00, (h) service charges for $350.00 certified check to pay the $350.00 land rental, and (i) postage $10.75.

¶5 Plaintiff contends defendants' arguments constituted an affirmative defense which was not properly before the trial court or this court is grounded in the provisions of La.C.C.P. Article 1005.1 An affirmative defense raises a new matter which, assuming the allegations of the petition to be true, constitute a defense to the action and will have the effect of defeating plaintiff's demand on its merits. La.C.C.P. Article 1003, 1005. Webster v. Rushing, 316 So.2d 111 (La.1975). If he fails to especially plead an affirmative defense, a defendant will not be allowed to introduce evidence of his defense. City of Kenner v. Dwyer, 464 So.2d 824 (5th Cir.1985).

¶6 Defendants' reliance on LSA-R.S. 9:3301 et seq., the Louisiana Lease of Movables Act, is not barred by his failure to plead the provisions of the act. The defense is based on the provisions of or lack of provisions in the contract which was stipulated into evidence. Additionally, applying the provisions of LSA-R.S. 9:3301 et seq., does not defeat plaintiff's claim on the merits, hence, it is not an affirmative defense. Webster, supra.

¶7 The "Agreement to Purchase or Sell" (Appendix "I") is a conditional sales agreement whereby title is maintained in vendor (plaintiff) while vendees (defendants) enjoy the use of the object through the terms of the agreement. At the term's expiration, the lease payments made by defendants would equal the stated purchase price for the mobile home and title would transfer. Although previously prohibited in Louisiana, this type agreement is now valid and enforceable under the Louisiana Lease of Movables Act. LSA-R.S. 9:3301 et seq., enacted by Act No. 592 of 1985, effective July 13, 1985.

¶8   Although the lease in question here is primarily for a personal, family, or household purpose, since the total compensation under the lease exceeds twenty-five thousand dollars, it is considered a commercial lease. LSA-R.S. 9:3306(9), (16). Under the provisions of the act, the parties to a financial commercial lease agreement may contractually agree to pay late charges in any amount or at any rate on any delinquent rental payment which is not paid in full on the scheduled or deferred due date. Other charges, including deferral charges (Sec. 3315), early termination charges (Sec. 3316), and end of lease charges (Sec. 3317) may be contractually provided for in the lease.

¶9   The only evidence in the record entitling plaintiff to recover for any of the charges enumerated in the preceding paragraph is the contractual late charges of $20.00 per month and the stipulation between the parties that five monthly payments were late. Therefore, plaintiff has proven and is entitled to recover $100.00 in late charges.

¶10   After default of the lessee, under LSA-R.S. 9:3318, lessor has two options: (1) sue for accelerated payments or (2) he may cancel the lease, recovering possession of the property and such additional amounts and liquidated damages as may be contractually provided under the lease agreement. Here, plaintiff took the property back and disposed of it. He therefore cannot sue for accelerated payments as he has already made his choice. In any event, he could not fulfill the requirements of LSA-R.S. 9:3319(C) as the mobile home is gone. Campbell v. Pipe Technology, Inc., 499 So.2d 111 (1st Cir.1986) writ denied 502 So.2d 117 (La.1987).

¶11   Liquidated damages provided for in the lease agreement are allowed under LSA-R.S. 9:3325 and shall be awarded to the lessor if the amount is found to be reasonable. When the parties, by their contract, have determined the sum that shall be paid as damages for its breach, the creditor must recover that sum, but is not entitled to more. Mason v. Coen, 449 So.2d 1195 (2nd Cir.1984). Here, the contract called for a deposit of $250.00 "to be held as security on the above mentioned trailer in the event of damage or default." Defendants' default entitles plaintiff to recover $250.00 in liquidated damages.

¶12   Any damages besides the amounts awarded above as liquidated damages and late charges were improperly assessed. The parties contracted for no other damages. Plaintiff maintained ownership of the mobile home and was himself responsible for the down payment, insurance and notes. There is no stipulation regarding the butane tank and the award of $89.00. The

Times-Picayune ad for $52.00 also does not concern defendants and should not have been awarded.

¶13   Defendants notified plaintiff by letter, mailed December 28, 1986, that $110.00 per month would be charged for lot rent if the mobile home was not removed. The stipulations do not state when the mobile home was returned but it does provide that $350.00 was paid as lot rent upon the mobile home's return. This period may have been as long as four months. We find defendants properly charged plaintiff rent. The law provides remedies to require a lessee to surrender possession, if he refuses to return the object. See LSA-R.S. 9:3321 and 9:3322. Since plaintiff left the mobile home on defendants' property, he is liable for rent. The service charge and mail fee are both related to the rent charges and improperly awarded as damages.

¶14   For the foregoing reasons, the judgment of the trial court is amended to provide that the award to plaintiff is $350.00 in lieu of $4,800.76 and as thus amended, is affirmed. Each party is to bear his own cost of the appeal.

AMENDED AND, AS AMENDED, AFFIRMED.

IN RE APPEAL OF CHASE MANHATTAN LEASING CORP. 1994
626 SO.2D 433 (LA. APP. 4TH CIR.)

KLEES, Judge.

¶1   Defendant appeals the Civil District Court decision granting summary judgment to plaintiff. After reviewing the record and applicable law, we affirm.

¶2   The Louisiana Stadium and Exposition District (LSED), a political subdivision of the State and owner of the Superdome, and Facility Management of Louisiana (FML), a private company hired by the State to manage the daily operations of the Superdome, needed to replace the Superdome's old scoreboard and signage system before the 1986 Superbowl. Having neither the time nor the money to effect an outright purchase of the new system, LSED and FML granted the contractor, American Sign and Indicator Corporation (ASI), the right to lease advertising space on the system. In return, ASI agreed to make annual payments to FML and to grant FML an option to purchase the system at the expiration of their agreement. FML assigned its purchase option to LSED. ASI was notified of LSED's intention to exercise that option.

¶3 Chase was interposed in the transaction to advance funds to ASI and the other manufacturer, Diamond Vision, for the purchase of the system. Pursuant to the financing agreement, Chase took title to the system to secure its interest. Chase then leased the system to BRAE Media, a corporation formed solely for such purpose.

¶4 The Louisiana Tax Commission denied plaintiff, Chase Manhattan Leasing Corporation, a refund of $153,542.72 in ad valorem taxes Chase claimed it had erroneously paid on the system. On appeal, the Civil District Court granted summary judgment in favor of Chase. The defendant, City of New Orleans, appeals to this court requesting reversal of the summary judgment.

¶5 In Louisiana, the substance of a transaction generally prevails over the form, and designing a sale to appear in form as a lease does not alter the true nature of the transaction. Louisiana Power & Light Co. v. Parish School Board of St. Charles, 597 So.2d 578, 588 (La.App. 5th Cir.), writ denied, 604 So.2d 1316 (1992). In the instant case, the transaction is actually a financed sale designed to allow LSED to acquire the system by circumventing the bond process. The transaction will be a sale in form when LSED exercises the purchase option it now holds.

¶6 Public property used for a public purpose is exempt from ad valorem taxation. La. Const. art. 7, § 21 (1974). Since LSED has effectively acquired the system through a financing arrangement, the system is public property. In addition, the Superdome scoreboard and signage system is constantly used for public purposes. Given the above, ad valorem taxes do not apply.

¶7 Chase also prevails under La. Civ. Code art. 493.1. The article states that component parts of an immovable belong to the owner of the immovable. Under Equibank v. U.S.I.R.S., a thing is a component part if either of the paragraphs of La. Civ. Code art. 466 are satisfied. 749 F.2d 1176 (5th Cir.1985). In the instant case, the requirements of both paragraphs are met.

¶8 La. Civ. Code art. 466 provides:

> Things permanently attached to a building or other construction, such as plumbing, heating, cooling, electrical or other installations, are its component parts.

> Things are considered permanently attached if they cannot be removed without substantial damage to themselves or to the immovable to which they are attached.

¶9 Following the Equibank rationale, the first paragraph of the article is satisfied because the system qualifies as an "electrical or other installation" which is permanently attached to the Superdome. id at 1179. The system accesses the Superdome's electrical energy source through the interior wiring of the building. Furthermore, the system is connected to the Superdome structure by welds, concrete, and steel attachments.

¶10 The second paragraph of La. Civ. Code art. 466 is also satisfied. Removing the scoreboard and signage system would probably cause substantial damage to both the system and the Superdome. Attachments would have to be dislodged from concrete and from the building itself. Therefore, the system is a component part of the Superdome and is public property exempt from ad valorem taxation.

¶11 For the foregoing reasons, no genuine issue of material fact exists, and the judgment of November 18, 1992, granting Chase summary judgment is affirmed.

AFFIRMED.

Study Question:
How is a financed lease, as evidenced in the two previous cases, the same as a conditional sale?

Section 5: The Bond for Deed Contract

Just as a financed lease provides a way for parties to subject their sale of a movable to a suspensive condition of full payment by the buyer, the bond for deed contract, set forth in La. R.S. 9:2941 sets forth a similar format for the sale of an immovable.

R.S. 9:2941 provides:

A bond for deed is a contract to sell real property, in which the purchase price is to be paid by the buyer to the seller in installments and in which the seller after payment of a stipulated sum agrees to deliver title to the buyer.

Study Question:

Based on the following case, how does a Bond for Deed Contract (La R.R. §§ 9:2941-2948) compare to a Financed Lease?

KREHER V. BERTUCCI 2002

814 SO.2D 614 (LA. APP. 4TH CIR.)

GORBATY, Judge.

¶1 In this appeal, defendant/ appellant, Continental Casualty Company ("Continental"), contends that the trial court erred in apportioning forty percent of the fault for plaintiff's accident to defendant Jack Worley, its insured. For the reasons set forth below, we reverse and remand.

FACTS AND PROCEDURAL HISTORY

¶2 This lawsuit arises from an accident that occurred on June 12, 1992. Plaintiff Charles W. Kreher, IV alleges that he was severely injured when he slipped and fell on water on the kitchen floor of the property he was renting at 6642 Bellaire Drive ("the Bellaire property"). Plaintiff, who had lived in the Bellaire property for three years, asserts that the gutters above the frame of the sliding glass door were worn, causing rainwater to leak inside the premises onto the kitchen floor. Plaintiff initially filed suit against June Bertucci as the owner of the Bellaire property at the time of the accident and against her insurer, Allstate Insurance Company. Plaintiff later amended his petition to add Dr. Jack Worley as an additional defendant, as well as his insurer, Continental.

¶3 Dr. Worley sold the Bellaire property "as is" to Bertucci on May 8, 1992, pursuant to a bond for deed contract. As a result of the sale, the Bellaire property was removed from his homeowner's insurance policy issued by Valley Forge Insurance Company, and Dr. Worley was refunded the applicable portion of the premium. Worley was also insured under a personal umbrella excess insurance policy issued by Continental, which arguably only covered his primary residence.

¶4 Prior to the sale, HMA Home Inspection Service conducted an inspection of the Bellaire property on behalf of Bertucci. The inspection report revealed various deficiencies. Specifically, it disclosed defects in the gutters and significant interior water damage resulting from water leaking into the apartment through the sliding glass door. The report stated, "[T]he gutters are leaking at the left side, gutters are deteriorating at left side. Replace gutters at right side." The report also noted that the "wall covering is damaged at right side of sliding door....Evidence of prior leakage noted on ceiling at 6642 dinning [sic] area in kitchen. Monitor status." Stain marks were apparent down the side of the building to the top of the sliding glass door. Worley or his agent, D & L Properties, had placed a piece of wood above the sliding glass door in an apparent attempt to deflect the water from entering the premises through the sliding glass door.

¶5 Worley and Bertucci received and reviewed copies of the inspection report. Rather than make the repairs to the property himself, Worley agreed to accept a reduced purchase price for the property.

¶6 After a judge trial on the issues of liability and coverage only, the court found that Worley was liable to plaintiff under negligence and strict liability theories. The court apportioned forty percent of the fault to Worley, thirty-five percent of the fault to Bertucci, and twenty-five percent of the fault to plaintiff. Initially, the court rendered judgment against Valley Forge Insurance Company and Continental, as insurers of Worley. Later, it issued an amended judgment removing Valley Forge from the judgment and holding Continental solely liable for the fault attributed to Worley. Continental subsequently filed this appeal.

DISCUSSION

¶7 Continental asserts that the trial judge erred in finding that Worley was strictly liable for plaintiff's accident.

¶8 Worley sold the property to Bertucci pursuant to a bond for deed contract one month before this incident. La. R.S. 9:2941 defines bond for deed as a "contract to sell real property, in which the purchase price is to be paid by the buyer to the seller in installments and in which the seller after payment of a stipulated sum agrees to deliver title to the buyer."

¶9 Louisiana Civil Code Article 2317 provides:

> We are responsible, not only for the damage occasioned by our own act, but for that which is caused by the act of persons for whom we are answerable, or of things which we have in our custody. This, however, is to be understood with the following modifications.

¶10 At the time this accident occurred, Louisiana Civil Code Article 2322 provided:

> The owner of a building is answerable for the damage occasioned by its ruin, when this is caused by neglect to repair it, or when it is the result of a vice in its original construction.

¶11 In the instant case, Worley sold the property to Bertucci pursuant to a bond for deed contract more than one month prior to the accident that is the subject of this dispute. Under the bond for deed sale, Worley retained the title of the property until repayment, but relinquished possession, care, custody, and control of the property as of the time of the sale. Worley had no legal right to even enter the Bellaire property after the sale was completed. The requisite care, custody, and control of the property were transferred to Bertucci at that time. Worley's position can be analogized to that of a bank that holds a mortgage on a piece of property until a loan is completely repaid. As such, we find that Worley is not the "owner" of the property, as contemplated by the strict liability articles. Certainly, the Bellaire property was not in his "custody," as described in article 2317. Accordingly, Worley cannot be held strictly liable for plaintiff's injuries, and nor can Continental, as his insurer.

¶12 Continental next contends that the trial court erred in attributing fault to Worley under a theory of negligence, and finding that he owed a duty to plaintiff.

¶13 Louisiana Civil Code Article 2315 provides that "every act whatsoever of man that causes damage to another obliges him by whose fault it happened to repair it." The standard analysis of whether to impose liability for negligence under article 2315 is the duty/ risk analysis. As discussed earlier, Bertucci bought the property "as is," and was well aware of the many defects in the property, including the one that allegedly caused plaintiff's injury, before she purchased it. No evidence was presented at trial, nor was it argued, that Worley concealed the defect in any way. Consequently, any duty owed to plaintiff was specifically assumed by Bertucci as the putative owner when she purchased the property. Worley relinquished any duty owed to the plaintiff when he sold the Bellaire property.

¶14 Since we find that Worley is not liable to the plaintiff under any theory, we pretermit discussion of Continental's other assignments of error.

CONCLUSION

¶15 Accordingly, for the foregoing reasons, the judgment of the trial court is reversed, and this matter is remanded to the trial court for proceedings consistent with the law and this opinion.

REVERSED AND REMANDED.

PARRO, J.

¶1   Tayaneka S. Brooks appeals a judgment of eviction, ordering her to vacate the property she is occupying, which is owned by David and Misty Solet. For the following reasons, we reverse the judgment.

FACTUAL AND PROCEDURAL BACKGROUND

¶2   After being displaced by Hurricane Katrina in 2005, Ms. Brooks and her three children lived several years in Kansas City, Missouri, before she decided to return to Louisiana. Working through a real estate agent, on July 17, 2008, she entered into a "Lease to Purchase Option Agreement" (the Agreement) concerning a house owned by the Solets in Denham Springs. The Agreement granted Ms. Brooks "an exclusive option to purchase" the property, called for her to pay an initial "non-refundable fee" of $35,500 "toward the purchase of the property," noted that she was required to make monthly payments in the amount of $1650 during the "option to purchase period," and required her to pay property taxes and insure the property for $239,000. The Agreement further stated that at the expiration of the option period, the purchase price for the property was $239,000, but if the "Buyer/Tenant" exercised the option and was "not in default of the Lease Agreement," the purchase price would be the "actual mortgage(s) payoff amount." The Agreement did not include a legal description of the property, and the Solets did not record the Agreement in the conveyance or mortgage records of the parish.

¶3   Ms. Brooks paid the $35,500 "non-refundable fee" and the August and September payments to the Solets' real estate agent. The following month, the agent told her to make the October payment directly to the holders of the first and second mortgages. Because the monthly payments had included a $100 monthly property management fee for the agent, Ms. Solet told Ms. Brooks the remaining payments would be only $1550 per month. This reduction in the amount of monthly payments was not put in writing.

¶4   Both mortgage holders told Ms. Brooks that unless they had something in writing from the Solets, they could not discuss the mortgage accounts directly with her. During a three-way telephone conversation among Ms. Brooks, Ms. Solet, and Countrywide Mortgage Company (Countrywide) concerning the first mortgage, Countrywide informed them that the amount paid on the mortgage by the agent was only $34,800 and that the August payment had not been paid to Countrywide. Despite these difficulties, Ms. Brooks paid the October payment to the two mortgage holders. She also tried to purchase insurance on the house, but was told that she could not insure it, because she was not the owner and there was no recorded document showing her interest in the property. She could only obtain renter's insurance on the contents of the house. Ms. Solet then renewed the insurance, and she and Ms. Brooks verbally agreed that the insurance premium would be paid as part of the monthly payment for an additional $40 per month. This agreement was also not put in writing. Ms. Brooks went to the courthouse in Livingston Parish to get the information needed to pay the property taxes and was told something would be mailed to her. However, because the property was not in her name, she never received that information; apparently it was sent to the Solets' forwarding address.

¶5 Hurricane Gustav had passed through the area, causing fallen trees, branches, and other damage to the property, which ultimately cost Ms. Brooks $1200. Because of this and other financial difficulties, she did not pay the November and December payments, and on December 29, 2008, the Solets sent her a letter and a ten-day notice to vacate. Ms. Brooks did not move out, and on January 20, 2009, Ms. Solet filed a petition for eviction in the City Court of Denham Springs. Neither party was represented by counsel at the January 28, 2009 hearing. Ms. Solet and Ms. Brooks testified, and Mr. Solet interjected unsworn commentary. Although Ms. Brooks offered to bring all the payments current and make the remaining payments by automatic withdrawals from her account, Mr. Solet insisted on a judgment of eviction, because he was tired of dealing with her. Finding the monthly payments had not been made as agreed, the court rendered a judgment of eviction, ordering Ms. Brooks to vacate the premises by February 12, 2009. The judgment was signed January 28, 2009, and Ms. Brooks filed a motion for appeal on February 9, 2009.

¶6 In this appeal, Ms. Brooks assigns as error the court's conclusion that the Solets were legally entitled to evict her under the Agreement. She further contends the court erred in granting the judgment of eviction in the absence of the statutory notice required by LSA-R.S. 9:2945, and in allowing the Solets to proceed via summary proceeding.

DISCUSSION

¶7 The Agreement that is the source of this conflict has many irregularities. First, the "Seller/Landlord" of the property is shown as Dave Solet. However, the Agreement is signed only by Misty Solet as the Seller/Landlord, and at the hearing, the Solets claimed they both owned the property. Second, the Agreement states that the "Seller/Landlord and Buyer/Tenant have together executed a prior lease agreement, the subject of which is the aforementioned Property (the 'Lease Agreement')." The separate "Lease Agreement" is also referenced in paragraphs 4, 9, and 15 of the Agreement. However, no such "Lease Agreement" is in evidence, and from both parties' testimony, it appears there was no such document. Third, the Agreement states that the "Seller/Landlord will allow Buyer/Tenant the option to record this Option to Purchase Agreement in Public Records." However, Ms. Brooks stated she was not given an original of the Agreement, so she could not record it. Fourth, the Agreement states that no modifications or amendments will be effective unless in writing, but both parties testified that the payment amount and the insurance requirement were verbally modified.

¶8   Despite these problems and many other typographical errors, word omissions, and other deficiencies in the Agreement, the parties testified that they intended this contract to reflect their mutual obligations concerning the property at issue. Therefore, in order to resolve the issues raised on appeal, we must determine the nature and effect of the Agreement, if any. The proper interpretation of a contract is a question of law subject to de novo review on appeal. Montz v. Theard, 01-0768 (La.App. 1st Cir.2/27/02), 818 So.2d 181, 185. When considering legal issues, the reviewing court accords no special weight to the trial court, but conducts a de novo review of questions of law and renders judgment on the record. Id.

¶9   Ms. Brooks argues that the court erred in failing to recognize that the contract at issue is actually a bond for deed contract, rather than a lease with an option to purchase. A bond for deed is a contract to sell real property, in which the purchase price is to be paid by the buyer to the seller in installments and in which the seller agrees to deliver title to the buyer after payment of a stipulated sum. See LSA-R.S. 9:2941; Seals v. Sumrall, 03-0873 (La.App. 1st Cir.9/17/04), 887 So.2d 91, 94. An option to sell or buy is a contract whereby a party gives to another the right to accept an offer to sell or buy a thing within a stipulated time. An option must set forth the thing and the price, and must meet the formal requirements of the sale it contemplates. LSA-C.C. art. 2620.

¶10   We conclude that the Agreement is not a bond for deed contract. Had it provided that after all of the installments were received, an act of sale conveying title to Ms. Brooks would be passed, the Agreement could be characterized as a bond for deed contract. See LSA-R.S. 9:2941; H.J. Bergeron, Inc. v. Parker, 06-1855 (La.App. 1st Cir.6/8/07), 964 So.2d 1075, 1076. In a true bond for deed contract, upon payment of the stipulated sum, Ms. Brooks would become the owner of the property. See Tabor v. Wolinski, 99-1732 (La.App. 1st Cir.9/22/00), 767 So.2d 972, 974. The Agreement does not meet this definition, and thus, is not a bond for deed contract.

¶11   Because we conclude that the contract at issue is not a bond for deed contract, the statutory provisions concerning bond for deed contracts do not apply to the Agreement. Therefore, the forty-five day notice required by LSA-R.S. 9:2945 was not required, and Ms. Brooks' second assignment of error is without merit.

¶12 Additionally, because the document was not executed properly under Louisiana law, any provisions concerning an option to purchase this immovable property are null. According to LSA-C.C. art. 2347, the concurrence of both spouses is required for the alienation, encumbrance, or lease of community immovable property. The alienation, encumbrance, or lease of community property by a spouse is relatively null unless the other spouse has renounced the right to concur. LSA-C.C. art. 2353. Furthermore, a transfer of immovable property or an option to purchase or sell immovable property must be made by authentic act or by act under private signature. See LSA-C.C. arts. 1839 and 2620. In this case, the Agreement shows Dave Solet as the "Seller/Landlord," but he did not sign the Agreement. It was signed only by Misty Solet. At the eviction hearing, Misty Solet stated that the house was owned by her and her husband. Since it was community property, both spouses had to sign the Agreement. Additionally, because the Agreement was not executed before a notary public in the presence of two witnesses, it does not constitute an authentic act. See LSA-C.C. art. 1833. And, although it could be considered an act under private signature that was duly acknowledged before the court by Misty Solet as her signature, it could not operate as a transfer or option to transfer immovable community property without Dave Solet's signature. Therefore, the Agreement is not a valid option to purchase or sell the immovable property at issue, and all of the option to purchase provisions, including the $35,500 "non-refundable fee," are unenforceable.

¶13 Having concluded that the Agreement is not a valid bond for deed contract or a valid option to purchase contract, we are left with considering whether there is a valid lease between the parties. There is no mention of a lease in the eviction petition. Also, although the Agreement expressly states that the parties "have together executed a prior lease agreement," there is no separate "Lease Agreement" in evidence and, based on the testimony of the parties, none was actually executed. In her testimony, Ms. Solet referred to the Agreement as "the lease," and made no mention of a separate written lease document. However, by its own terms, the Agreement is not the lease between the parties.

¶14 As previously noted, LSA-C.C. art. 2347 requires the concurrence of both spouses to lease community property. But a lease agreement is not required to be in writing, and both Mr. and Ms. Solet indicated in open court that they had leased the property to Ms. Brooks. At the hearing, both Ms. Solet and Ms. Brooks testified that the initial rental payment was $1650 per month and that it was verbally modified in October to $1550 per month. They also told the court about their verbal agreement that property insurance payments of $40 per month would be added to the monthly rent. Their testimony did not establish a term for the lease. Therefore, we conclude that although the Agreement was not a written lease, the parties did have a valid verbal residential lease agreement with an indefinite term. See LSA-C.C. arts. 2668, 2671, and 2678.

* * *

[The court goes on to examine the terms of the oral lease as established by the Solets' testimony, and finds that because Ms. Brooks missed paying two months' rent, she breached those terms, and the Solets were entitled to evict her. But because they failed to give her proper notice to vacate, a summary proceeding was improper, which rendered invalid the eviction granted by the city court below.]

CONCLUSION

¶15   Based on the foregoing, we reverse the January 28, 2009 eviction judgment ordering Ms. Brooks to deliver the leased property to the Solets. All costs of this appeal are assessed to the Solets.

REVERSED.

Study Question:

What are the most important provisions of both a Bond for Deed contract and a Financed Lease?

Review Notes

Section 1: Conditions in General

A conditional obligation is one dependent on an uncertain event. If the obligation is immediately enforceable but comes to an end when the uncertain event occurs, then the obligation is subject to a resolutory condition. If the obligation is not enforceable until the uncertain event occurs, then it is subject to a suspensive condition. (Article 1767-1776). Be sure to review those rules. This chapter explores further some of the instances where a sale is subject to an implied or express condition.

Sales can be subject to conditions in a number of different ways. Normally with a sale, ownership transfers on agreement and risk transfers on delivery. That transfer of ownership of a movable is subject to an implied resolutory condition that the thing delivered conforms to what was promised when the sale was made, and if it does not, then the buyer may demand that the seller either replace the thing or dissolve the sale. Art. 2603-2610. Additionally, as explained in

Chapter 6, the transfer of ownership may be impliedly suspended where the thing must be individualized, weighed-counted-or-measured, or if it was subject to shipping terms.

Canal Motors v. Campbell

Defendant Campbell agreed to buy a used car (a 1968 Chevrolet station wagon) from plaintiff Canal Motors for $3,162. He deposited $25, allegedly pending loan approval. He then drove off in the car and used it until a little less than a month later, when it was seriously damaged in an accident. Campbell made no further payments on the car. Canal Motors claims that Campbell's loan application was approved before they delivered it to Campbell, and that the finance company subsequently refused to follow through with the loan when the car was damaged, but that in any case, the car belongs to Campbell and he must pay for it. Campbell denies this, claims that ownership was never transferred, and wants his deposit returned.

The court finds that as there was a genuine issue of material fact concerning whether the loan was ever approved, the case cannot be decided via summary judgment.

The reasoning not stated by the court in its opinion is that if the sale was subject to loan approval, then title was not transferred until the loan was approved – if Sealco (the loan company) approved the loan before the car was delivered to Campbell, then the suspensive condition was fulfilled and the car belonged to Campbell when it was damaged. If the loan was not approved, then the car still belonged to Canal Motors at the time of the accident. The case illustrates the fact that very often in a sale of a high-priced item, the sale is subject to the express suspensive condition that the buyer obtain financing. If the buyer cannot, after a reasonable good-faith effort obtain that financing, then the pending sale is never perfected.

Section 2: Inspection by the Buyer v. View & Trial

As explained previously, most sales of movables are subject to an implied resolutory condition that the thing conform to the buyer's reasonable expectations. However, that can be changed if the buyer expressly demands that the sale be subject to 'view and trial' as stated in Article 2460, in which case, the sale is subject to the suspensive condition that the buyer view or try the thing an approve it before the sale is perfected. As the following cases demonstrate, merely stipulating that the buyer has a right to inspect the thing is not enough to engage Article 2460, because all buyers have an implied right to inspect the thing and then dissolve a non-conforming sale. If a buyer wants to suspend the transfer of ownership pending his inspection, then he must stipulate that in a clear and unambiguous way.

Practice Hypothet

Sellers/defendants Alexander traded in their older 'toy-hauler' to the plaintiff dealer for a new RV. The dealer left the traded-in vehicle on his lot for several months before noticing that it had a leak in the roof and the interior was severely damaged, and he now wants the sellers to pay for the repairs. The court should (and did) hold that the sale was subject to the normal resolutory condition of inspection by the buyer, and as the buyer did not inspect within a reasonable amount of time, he cannot now complain.

Tunica Biloxi Tribe v. Bridges

Tribe agreed over the phone to purchase a van from plaintiff Bridges, a dealer. The sale stipulated that it was subject to inspection. The tribe objects to the fact that it paid sales tax to Louisiana, claiming that as the sale took place on tribal lands, it was exempt. The court held that the contract was seemingly concluded over the phone in Louisiana, and that under conflict of law principles, Louisiana law applied. The next issue was whether this was a normal sale subject to an implied resolutory condition, or whether it was subject to Article 2460's suspensive condition – in which case, the sale was NOT concluded in Louisiana, but instead on tribal land once the tribe inspected and approved it. However, as the 'inspection' clause was ambiguous and did not stipulate any suspensive condition, the normal rules applied, and so the sale was perfected in Louisiana, and sales tax was due.

Hamilton v. Medical Arts

The Medical Arts Building in Shreveport purchased some refrigeration equipment from United Iron Works, a Missouri company, in 1931 (probably an early air conditioning unit), and never finished paying for it. Plaintiff Hamilton company had a pre-existing mortgage on the building. The Medical Arts Building company became insolvent, and United Iron Works (though itself in bankruptcy) is intervening, claiming that its vendor's privilege over the refrigeration equipment in the building's basement trumps Hamilton Company's mortgage foreclosure. Hamilton claims that the equipment is an immovable by destination, and is therefore subject to the mortgage. If the sale was concluded in Louisiana, then the unpaid price was secured by a vendor's privilege, and the next issue is whether it was lost as a result of the installation. So, the first concern is which law applies under conflict of law principles: Louisiana or Missouri? The defendant accepted in Shreveport, but the contract was finally approved in Missouri. However, the contract stipulated that "Seller SHALL furnish an engineer to supervise and assist in making installation," that "a test run of three days must be made on the plant," and "a failure on the part of the buyer to reject the plant by notifying the seller in writing within 3 days from . . installation . . . shall constitute an acceptance on the part of the buyer."

Based on that Article 2460 language, the court concluded that the sale was completed in Louisiana once the buyer viewed and tried the equipment, that the vendor's privilege did apply [the rest of the opinion discussing the vendor's privilege & immovable by destination is omitted]

Section 3: Other Implicit Resolutory Conditions

Just as the buyer can dissolve a sale if the thing delivered does not conform to the contract, so too can the seller dissolve the sale if the buyer fails to pay, as provided in Article 2561. This means that the buyer's failure to pay is another implied resolutory condition.

Berry v. Ginsburg

Plaintiff buyer is suing jeweler Ginsburg for return of the money she paid towards the purchase of a diamond ring. Berry had agreed to pay a total of $1,830 for the ring by means of weekly installments. The contract provided that she did not have to pay any certain amount each week, but had to make some payment. While she did, in fact, make some sort of payment each week, the payments became less and less, until finally, when the remaining balance was approximately $1100, defendant declined to accept further payments, saying he wanted to recede from the contract. She demanded the return of the money she had paid, and he refused.

The issue is which of them had failed to perform. In this case, it was the defendant jeweler, because she had kept to the terms of the contract. Had he wanted to specify a minimum payment per week, he could have done so. She never failed to make a weekly payment. That being the case – that he was the one who breached the contract – she has the right to dissolve the contract and demand her money back.

The point of the case is that a failure to perform or refusal to perform by either party is an implied resolutory condition. When a contract is dissolved, the parties are to be returned to the financial condition they were in before the contract. Article 2018.

Section 4: Common law Conditional Sales

Under the Uniform Commercial Code, buyers in common law states have a comparable right of inspection to determine if a good conforms to the sale. Section 2-513 provides that the buyer has a right before payment or acceptance to inspect the goods, those expenses must be borne by the buyer (unless the goods do not conform and are rejected). However, the buyer is not intitled to inspect the goods before payment if the contract provides for C.O.D. delivery or in a documentary sale.

A credit sale is where the title to the goods does not transfer – though the goods are delivered – until the buyer finishes paying. This can be called a conditional sale, a lease with an option to buy, a lease-purchase agreement, a contract to sell, a financed lease, or a rent to own contract. Provisions for these kinds of sale are set forth in Article 9 of the Uniform Commercial Code, which (unlike Article 2) has been adopted in Louisiana, and also in Revised Statutes R.S. §9:3318 (financed lease) and R.S. §9:3357 (Rental-Purchase Agreement). Under a financed lease, the seller can accelerate payments or alternatively cancel the lease and recover possession if the buyer defaults. Under a Rent-purchase agreement, the seller can recover possession and demand back rent – thought the defaulting buyer may be able to reinstate the agreement.

Blackledge v. Vinet

Plaintiff Blackledge owned a mobile home. He leased it to the Vinets under a financed lease arrangement. However, the Vinets' could not make the payments and voluntarily agreed to return the mobile home, so Blackledge took it back (eventually letting it be taken by the Bank that had a chattel mortgage on it.). He then sued the Vinets for the outstanding $4,800 le1ft on the lease/purchase, plus costs and attorney's fees. The issue is, however, that while one can accelerate the fees if a buyer defaults as part of a lease-purchase, one cannot also seize the item that is the subject to the lease – the seller/lessor either gets the money or the thing, not both. The Vinets are liable only for the rental that they did not pay during the period they had possession of the mobile home. Had the contract provided for a penalty, they would have had to pay it, but it did not. The only thing they owe was back rent.

In Re Chase Manhattan Leasing (i.e. the Superdome scoreboard)

The superdome needed a new scoreboard, so it purchased one under an agreement whereby Chase Manhattan held the title until the Louisiana State government entity that owned the superdome could pay it off – in other words, under a financed lease. When the state charged Chase Manhatten for ad velorem tax, Chase argued that it did not actually own the scoreboard, that the state did, and therefore it should not have had to pay taxes. The court agreed: in fact, with a lease-purchase agreement, while the title does not transfer until all payments are made, from the view of a third party, the purchaser/lessee is, in fact, the owner. Here, the purchaser/lessee was the State.

Section 5: The Bond for Deed Contract

A financed lease or rent-to-own arrangement applies to movables. The Bond for Deed contract is a similar arrangement for the sale of an immovable, as provided by La. Rev. Stat. 9:2941 &

following – in other words, title transfers when the buyer finishes paying the price. Sometimes the buyer's doing so is considered a suspensive condition.

Kreher v. Bertucci

Ms. Bertucci was in the process of buying an immovable from Dr Worley, using a bond-for-deed arrangement: i.e. title would transfer once she completed all of the payments. In the interim, she rented the property to Mr. Kreher for three years. When he slipped and fell on rain-water that had leaked inside, he sued both Ms. Bertucci and Dr. Worley. Dr. Worley claimed that he was not liable, but the trial court found comparative liability: 40% to Worley, 35% to Bertucci, and 25% to Kreher. Worley's insurance company appealed. The court found for Worley because, as Kreher is not party to the contract between Bertucci and Worley. Just as in the Scoreboard case, from the point of view of a third party like Kreher, Bertucci is the owner of the property. Worley had no legal right to enter the property, no control over it, and was therefore not the 'owner' of the property for purposes of Louisiana's strict liability or negligence standards.

Solet v. Brooks

Defendant Brooks entered into a 'Lease to Purchase Option Agreement" for a home owned by the Solets in Denham Springs. Under this agreement, Ms. Brooks paid a 'non-refundable fee' of $35,500 toward purchase of the property, was required to make monthly payments of $1650 during the "option" to purchase period, and also required to pay property taxes and insurance. At the end of the 'option' period, the purchase price was $239, and Brooks would be allowed to pay off the mortgage and obtain title to the property. The agreement was not recorded. Ms. Brooks paid the $35,500 fee, and made the August and September payments, and then was told to pay the holders of two mortgages directly. The mortgage holders told her that unless they received something in writing from the Solets, they could not discuss the mortgage accounts with her. She was able to work out payment with one company, but then had difficulty obtaining insurance on the property because she was not the owner, and the agreement was not recorded.

Facing financial difficulties in November and December, Ms. Brooks failed to make the payments for those months and the Solets sent her a notice to vacate, which was eventually granted in early February 2009.

Held: the agreement was an improper Bond-for-Deed contract because it did not make all payments directly payable to the mortgage companies, nor did it provide that all the installments were received, an act of sale conveying title would be passed, nor was it signed by both Solet spouses. Consequently, the provision concerning an option to purchase was null, and this was an oral lease without a term. Furthermore, Brooks breached the lease by failing to pay the two months' rent, and so the Solet's were entitled to evict her, but not by summary proceeding.

[Omitted from the case – as the sale was null, the $35,500 fee was unjust enrichment and would have to be returned.]

The purpose of the case is to point out that a bond-for-deed is more like a sale than a lease, and that if there is a pre-existing mortgage, all periodic payment must be put into escrow and the mortgage holder must be aware and accept such payments –otherwise, sellers can pocket the payments, not pay the mortgage, and the buyer is then stuck without either money or title to the property.

HYPOTHETS

1. Anna received a shipment of shoes from "Don't Mess with Mamou," but when she opened the boxes, 3 months later, she discovered that some of them were green suede instead of blue suede. Usually she checks everything right away, but this time she was off on a buying trip when they were delivered. Is there anything she can do? Why or why not? Now she no longer trusts "DMWM", but they are one of the few wholesale companies who sell a broad range of suede shoes. Is there another way to set up future purchases to avoid such mistakes?

2. Anna wants to expand her shoe stores and saw the perfect property in Metairie. However, for a number of reasons, she does not want another mortgage with another bank on her hands, but would like to pay over time. The seller is willing but has a pre-existing mortgage. Is there some way the parties can structure such an agreement without bringing in a new bank?

CHAPTER 8

THE EFFECT OF SALE ON THIRD PARTIES

Flow Chart

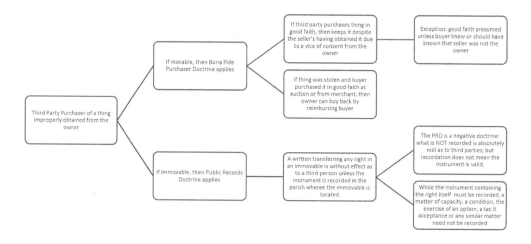

Section 1. Movables and the Bona Fide Purchaser Doctrine

What if you sell shoes, and you sold a pair of blue suede shoes to Max on credit. Before he even paid for them, however, Max turned around and resold them to Elvis and then refused to pay you. You know that you could sue to get the shoes back from Max, but can you do the same against Elvis? Or, perhaps Max forced you to sell them to him by threatening to hurt your Aunt Sara, and then immediately resold them to Elvis. Could you get the shoes back from Elvis at that point? The answer, generally, is no (though there is an exception). Although one cannot sell something that one doesn't own, and both sales were invalid, the law here protects a third party (i.e. Elvis) who purchases the thing in good faith. In doing so, the Civil Code has balanced two competing interests: the security of ownership and the security of transaction. While society must protect property rights, it must also protect commerce, and commerce wins out in instances such as these. Under common law, the third party is protected by the bona fide purchaser doctrine. Louisiana's Civil Code Article 522 similarly provides that: "A transferee of a corporeal movable in good faith and for fair value retains the ownership of the thing even though the title of the transferor is annulled on account of a vice of consent."

A. General Concepts

Though they apply generally to transfer of movables rather than just the sale of movables, read Civil Code Articles 518-525.

COMMENT, THE TRANSFER OF OWNERSHIP OF MOVABLES,
BY TANYA ANN IBIETA
47 LA. L. REV. 841, 841-45 (1987)

The rules of law governing the transfer of ownership of movables arise out of a conflict between two competing interests: the security of ownership and the security of transaction. This conflict is created by two opposing legal principles. The first is the rule codified in article 2279 of the French Civil Code which states that 'la possession vaut titre' (with respect to movables possession is considered equivalent to title). This rule promotes the security of transaction by protecting those who acquire possession of a movable in good faith from one they believe had the ability to transfer its ownership. The opposing principle is the common law rule 'nemo dat quod non habet' (no one can transfer a greater right than he himself has). Louisiana Civil Code article 2452 expresses this principle by providing that the sale of a thing belonging to another is null. This rule affords protection to the security of ownership by recognizing the rights of the dispossessed owner in the movable.

The conflict between these two legal principles arises in situations whereby, for one of several reasons, be it loss, theft, a vice of consent or misplaced confidence, the owner of a movable, X, is dispossessed of it by a second person, Y, who purports to transfer its ownership to a third person, Z. Both X and Z claim ownership of the movable and seek protection from Y's misconduct. X seeks security of ownership; Z seeks security of transaction.

Louisiana Law Prior to the Revision
Legislation

Prior to the revision of the Civil Code in 1979, Louisiana law did not contain a strong statement of the principle 'la possession vaut titre.' Article 2279 of the French Civil Code was not incorporated into the Louisiana Civil Code. On the other hand, article 2452 clearly stated the opposing principle of 'nemo dat quod non habet.'

Other strong legislative indications favoring the security of ownership prior to the revision were the articles on acquisitive prescription of movables. Article 3506 provided that a possessor of a movable for three years in good faith and by just title would acquire ownership by prescription, unless the thing had been stolen or lost. This article thus protected the dispossessed owner of a thing for three years. If the thing were lost or stolen, article 3509 would apply, which provided for ten-year acquisitive prescription if the possessor lacked the requirements of good faith or just title. The Code gave some protection to the good faith possessor in article 3507; if the possessor of a stolen or lost thing bought it at a public auction or from a person who usually sold such things, the true owner would be required to reimburse the purchase price before reclaiming the thing. These articles pointed to the conclusion that the legislature intended to protect the security of ownership of movables, but only for specific periods of time following dispossession.

Jurisprudence

In the absence of clear legislative direction, the Louisiana courts sought to balance the conflict between security of ownership and security of transaction. Recognizing that strict adherence to the principle that no one can transfer a greater right than he has would impede commerce and result in harsh consequences for good faith purchasers, the courts developed certain exceptions to the rule, similar to the common law bona fide purchaser doctrine. The requirements for the application of these exceptions were that the purchaser have acquired the thing in good faith, without notice that the seller was not the true owner, and for valuable consideration.

A study of the jurisprudence reveals two lines of reasoning used by the courts to avoid application of the rule in article 2452 that the sale of a thing belonging to another is absolutely null. Under one approach, the courts utilized the theory under which certain contracts are deemed to be burdened with a relative nullity. This generally involved cases in which title to the movable had passed from the original owner to the intermediate seller, but such title was deemed to be relatively null. Examples include cases in which there existed a vice of consent, such as fraudulent impersonation, and cases involving dishonored checks. The courts determined that, since title had passed, article 2452 did not apply, because the movable did not belong to another. The action to assert a relative nullity could only be brought by the original owner, who could assert it only against his vendee. Therefore, the person who acquired the movable from the original owner could validly pass title to the third party bona fide purchaser, who was protected from the claims of the original owner.

Under the second line of cases, the exception of equitable estoppel was applied in instances where title had not passed, but the owner had turned over possession to another along with some other indicia of ownership. This doctrine is based on the theory 'that where one by his words or conduct willfully causes another to believe the existence of a certain state of things, and induces him to act on that belief so as to alter his own previous position, the former is precluded from averring against the latter a different state of things as existing at the same time.' The owner must have surrendered not only possession to the seller, but must have clothed him with some indicia of ownership or authority to sell the thing, which induced the purchaser's reliance. These cases typically involved a breach of confidence by an agent or fiduciary. The owners were held to have contributed to their own loss by negligence in their dealings, and could not be heard to complain against an innocent purchaser.

Thus, as of 1979, the general rule was that the sale of a thing belonging to another was null, subject to certain jurisprudentially developed exceptions.

1979 Revision of Title II—Ownership and 1982 Revision of Title XXIV—Prescription

Upon recommendation from the Law Institute, the legislature added two new chapters to the Civil Code. Chapter 3, entitled Transfer of Ownership by Agreement, contains articles 517-525, and Chapter 4, entitled Protection of Ownership, includes articles 526-532. The drafters noted that the rule that possession is equivalent to title with respect to movables had been adopted by all modern civil codes and the Uniform Commercial Code (UCC), and was better suited to Louisiana's contemporary commercial economy. The Expose des Motifs to the chapter on transfer of ownership explained that 'Articles 518 through 525 . . . establish a significant change in the law in an effort to re-align Louisiana law with modern civil law and the Uniform Commercial Code.'

B. Lost or Stolen Things

As Article 522 indicates, if a third-party purchaser is in good faith, then his ownership of the movable is protected, even though the one who sold the thing to him obtained it through error, fraud, or duress. Article 523 goes on to define a good faith acquirer as follows: "An acquirer of a corporeal movable is in good faith for purposes of this Chapter unless he knows, or should have known, that the transferor was not the owner." Thus, in the hypothetical given above, even if you sold the blue suede shoes to Max under duress, Elvis's ownership of the shoes is protected, as long as he bought them in good faith – i.e. he neither knew nor did he have reason to know that Max had obtained them from you by a vice of consent, whether error, fraud, or duress.

When it comes to things that are lost or stolen, Article 522 does not apply. Instead, Article 521 provides:

> One who has possession of a lost or stolen thing may not transfer its ownership to another. For purposes of this Chapter, a thing is stolen when one has taken possession of it without the consent of its owner. A thing is not stolen when the owner delivers it or transfers its ownership to another as a result of fraud.

So, if the thing was stolen, the rightful owner can recover it from the thief, but can the rightful owner recover it from the third party who purchased it from the thief? Perhaps surprisingly, under the Civil Code, that right is limited. If the third party bought the stolen thing from a merchant or at a public auction, then the true owner can get it back from the third party, but only if he reimburses the third party the price he paid to buy it. And the same is true if the true owner lost the thing. Consequently, even when the thing was lost or stolen, security of transaction is preferred over security of ownership. Article 524 provides:

> The owner of a lost or stolen movable may recover it from a possessor who bought it in good faith at a public auction or from a merchant customarily selling similar things on reimbursing the purchase price.

> The former owner of a lost, stolen, or abandoned movable that has been sold by authority of law may not recover it from the purchaser.

Study Question:

Analyze how Articles 521 and 524 apply in the following cases.

BROWN & ROOT, INC. V. SOUTHEAST EQUIP. CO. 1985
470 SO.2D 516 (LA. APP. 1 CIR.)

GROVER L. COVINGTON, Chief Judge.

¶1 The plaintiff, Brown and Root, Inc. (Brown), appeals a judgment requiring it to reimburse the defendant, Southeast Equipment Company, Inc. (Southeast), the purchase price paid for a stolen Caterpillar wheeled loader, under LSA-C.C. art. 524, before recovering possession of it.

¶2 The facts surrounding this matter are undisputed. Brown is the owner of a wheeled loader, and it was stolen in Houston in April, 1982. Southeast purchased the loader from a Houston equipment dealer in May of 1982 for $23,000.00 and had it delivered to Louisiana. As the result of a police investigation of the equipment dealer by the Houston police department, the Louisiana State Police tracked the loader to a construction site in Convent, Louisiana, obtained a search warrant and seized the machine. Suit was brought by Brown seeking recognition of its ownership and seeking possession of the loader without being required to pay the defendant, Southeast, its purchase price. After a hearing on a rule filed by plaintiff, a stipulated partial judgment was signed recognizing Brown as owner and allowing it to obtain possession of the loader by posting a $23,000.00 bond.

¶3 The evidence left no doubt that the loader was stolen and that Southeast's vendor was a seller customarily engaged in the used equipment business. Accordingly, the only issue to be decided is whether Southeast is entitled to the proceeds of the bond as reimbursement of the purchase price as a good faith purchaser.

¶4 Articles 523 and 524 of the Civil Code are dispositive of cases involving the recovery of stolen movable property.

Art. 523:

An acquirer of a corporeal movable is in good faith for purposes of this Chapter unless he knows, or should have known, that the transferor was not the owner.

Art. 524:

The owner of a lost or stolen movable may recover it from a possessor who bought it in good faith at a public auction or from a merchant customarily selling similar things on reimbursing the purchase price.

The former owner of a lost, stolen, or abandoned movable that has been sold by authority of law may not recover it from the purchaser.

¶5 These articles reflect a change in public policy, as enunciated by the legislature, to the effect that the good faith purchaser of a stolen movable is to be protected at the expense of the true owner. Southeast Equipment Co., Inc. v. Office of State Police, 437 So.2d 1184 (La.App. 4th Cir.1983).1

¶6 In this case the only question is the good faith of Southeast. LSA-C.C. art. 523 defines good faith in terms of the knowledge of the purchaser. If the purchaser knows that the object is stolen prior to purchasing it, there is no good faith and these articles do not apply. But, where actual knowledge is absent, the article imputes knowledge if the purchaser has access to facts which would lead a prudent man to question the ownership of his vendor.

¶7 Since good faith is presumed, the true owner must establish sufficient facts to show the purchaser was put on notice his seller's ownership was questionable. In this case Brown attempted to show that Southeast had access to sufficient facts prior to purchasing the loader to indicate the movable might be stolen. The serial number plate on the front of the vehicle was glued on and the manufacturer's secret serial number under the identification number plate had been gouged out of the metal frame. Plaintiff also tried to show that the price Southeast paid was so low as to have put it on notice of the questionable ownership of the transferor. However, other testimony showed that Brown was selling similar loaders from its stock at prices even lower than what defendant paid for the loader in question. After a thorough review of the evidence in this case, we cannot say that the trial court erred in its decision that the plaintiff failed to carry its burden of proof that Southeast was in bad faith when it purchased the loader from the dealer. Arceneaux v. Domingue, 365 So.2d 1330 (La.1978).

¶8   For the reasons assigned the judgment of the district court is affirmed at appellant's costs.

AFFIRMED.

LIVESTOCK PRODUCERS, IN. V. LITTLETON 1999
748 SO. 2D 537 (LA. 2D CIR.)

GASKINS, J.

¶1   This case involves the sale of stolen cattle. The trial court allowed recovery to those who were damaged by the wrongful conduct of the cattle seller, but also applied the principles of comparative fault to reduce their recovery. Most of the parties have appealed the trial court judgment or have answered the appeal. For the following reasons, we reverse in part and affirm in part the trial court judgment.

FACTS

¶2   [Danny Smith and Charles Glasscock, Sr. had a partnership engaged in raising cattle in Bossier Parish: McDade Cattle Company. When Charles died in 1992, his three children, R.E., Charles Jr. and Dorothy Ann were substituted as partners. R.E., who lived in Houston, was the one who managed McDade with Smith. R.E. and Smith were involved in a second cattle operation at Shady Grove Farm in Bossier Parish. Smith leased the Shady Grove property from the Glasscock family for $12,000 and R.E. paid him to manage this second cattle company. R.E. provided all the money and land for a cow/calf operation and Smith supplied the labor. The two parties divided the Shady Grove profits.]

¶3   In 1994, Danny Smith told B.L. Littleton, an out-of-state rancher, that he and R.E. were selling 250 head of Brangus cattle from Shady Grove. Actually, Glasscock was the sole owner of the cattle which were not connected with the McDade Cattle Company. Littleton provided bull semen to artificially inseminate the cows, and then purchased the 200 cows that were pregnant. This sale occurred on August 1, 1994. [Littleton paid $150,000 for the cows and rebranded them with his "BL" brand, registered in Texas, and put sequentially numbered ear tags on them. Smith apparently gave the entire proceeds to R.E. When the cows began calving earlier than expected (in November 1994), Littleton and Smith agreed that the cattle would stay at the Shady Grove farm until February 28, 1995. In exchange for pasturing the cattle, Littleton paid Smith $11,000.]

¶4 [At about this time, Smith developed a gambling problem and started having financial difficulties as a result. Without Littleton's knowledge or approval, Smith began selling Littleton's cows at Livestock Producers, Inc., (LPI) an auction house run by Ronnie Stratton in Texas. Over time, he sold a total of 126 cows, some with their calves, this way in several separate sales, beginning in September 1994, even before Littleton agreed to let them stay at Shady Grove. In January 1995, Smith contacted Stratton, anxious to quickly dispose of the remaining 74 cows, so Stratton personally purchased the cows and immediately resold them to Don Sonnier, who took them to his farm.

¶5 On February 16, 1995, Littleton received an anonymous phone call at his office in Hot Springs, Arkansas, that the cows were gone and that Danny Smith had disappeared. Danny Smith was arrested and charged with theft. The Bossier Parish Sheriff's Office determined that the 74 cows should remain on the Sonnier farm until the matter was settled. When the ownership of the cows was called into question, LPI refunded Sonnier's purchase price. Then, the two civil suits at issue here were instituted.

¶6 LPI and Ronnie Stratton filed a petition for a temporary restraining order, injunction, declaratory judgment, or in the alternative, money damages. LPI claimed to be the owner of the 74 cows in Sonnier's possession.]

* * *

¶7 [B.L. Littleton sued LPI, Ronnie Stratton, Danny Smith, McDade Cattle Company and R.E. Glasscock, individually. Littleton alleged that LPI and Ronnie Stratton sold the cows without checking their ownership, even though the cows had a new and unfamiliar brand and even though Danny Smith was not a regular customer of the auction. He further alleged that Smith and Glasscock were partners in McDade Cattle Company and that they wrongfully received the proceeds from the sale of the cattle and should return the money to him.

¶8 On May 8, 1997, Donald E. Sonnier intervened, seeking to recover expenses for the 74 cows left in his care.] . . .

Trial Court Judgment

¶9 [The trial court consolidated the two cases and authorized the release of the 74 remaining cows to Littleton. It noticed that R.E. and Smith had a cattle operation separate from McDade Cattle Company, and that R.E. had received the entire $150,000 Littleton had paid for the 200 cows. The court found that both Stratton and LPI believed that Smith was acting in his capacity as partner of one or the other Glasscock ventures when he sold the 124 cattle at auction, and that Sonnier's purchase price for the 74 cattle had been refunded.

¶10 The court noted that during the time Sonnier kept the 74 cows, some calves were born, were sold and $39,000 was invested in a certificate of deposit. The court awarded Sonnier this money and any interest that had accumulated in satisfaction of his claim for caring for the cattle until they were released to Littleton.

¶11 Regarding the other claims in this case, the court found that, because these were suits requesting monetary damages, the principles of comparative fault applied.

* * *

¶12 The court found that Stratton was entitled to recover his purchase price for the cows, but that he was 40% at fault, therefore he was entitled to recover only $32,190 of his original purchase price of $53,650. The court found that Smith and Glasscock were solidarily liable to Stratton for $32,190. The court then found that Stratton was entitled to a judgment of $53,650 from Smith.

* * *

¶13 The parties were confused by the opinion and could not agree on the judgment. [The court then held a supplemental hearing and reallocated fault .]

THE APPEAL

¶14 B.L. Littleton appealed the trial court judgment arguing numerous assignments of error.

***

¶15 LPI and Stratton argue that the trial court erred in applying the theory of comparative fault, an affirmative defense, not pled or argued by any of the parties. LPI and Stratton also argue that the trial court erred in assessing any percentage of fault to them. R.E. Glasscock argues the trial court erred in finding any degree of fault attributable to him. Don Sonnier argues that the trial court erred in making an excessively low keeper's fee to him for caring for the 74 remaining cattle for an extended period of time.

***

AUCTIONEER'S LIABILITY

***

¶16 [Using principles of the Restatement of Agency and cases from other jurisdictions, the court finds that]

¶17 Under the facts of this case, we do not find that LPI and Stratton, acting for LPI, were guilty of any intentional wrong or complicity with Smith in the sale of the stolen cattle. The relationship between the livestock dealer, the seller and the bidder (purchaser) is in the nature of a dual agency. Tyler v. Elston, 236 So.2d 658 (La.App. 2d Cir.1970). LPI was an agent acting for Smith, a dishonest principal. Smith was not a regular customer of the business, the cattle had fresh brands not associated with Smith, and LPI and Stratton made no inquiry into the ownership of the cattle. Under these circumstances, we find that LPI is liable to Littleton for the price of the 126 cows sold at auction, $94,500. The trial court was manifestly erroneous or clearly wrong in holding otherwise.

LITTLETON'S LIABILITY

* * *

¶18 In the present case, we find that the trial court was clearly wrong and manifestly erroneous in finding that Littleton was liable in any way for the theft of his own property. The trial court based this determination on a finding that Littleton left the cows in Bossier Parish for an extended period of time without adequately securing them. The record fails to support that this action by Littleton was negligent or unreasonable in any way.

***

GOOD FAITH PURCHASER

¶19   Following the sale at auction of 126 cows, Stratton, in his personal capacity, purchased the remaining 74 cows and was reimbursed by LPI. Littleton argues that Stratton and/or LPI were not good faith purchasers and the trial court erred in ordering that Littleton reimburse LPI and/or Stratton the purchase price of the 74 cows, $53,650.

¶20   LPI argues that not only was it entitled to reimbursement for this amount, but the trial court should have ordered that Littleton make reimbursement for this amount before the remaining cows in Sonnier's care were returned to Littleton. According to LPI, it was a good faith purchaser when the 74 cows were purchased from Smith in January 1995 and, under La. C.C. art. 524, it is entitled to recover the purchase price.

¶21   La. C.C. art. 524 provides in pertinent part: "The owner of a lost or stolen movable may recover it from a possessor who bought it in good faith at a public auction or from a merchant customarily selling similar things on reimbursing the purchase price."

¶22   La. C.C. art 523 provides that an acquirer of a corporeal movable is in good faith unless he knows, or should have known, that the transferor was not the owner. If the purchaser knows that the object is stolen prior to purchasing it, there is no good faith. But, where actual knowledge is absent, the article imputes knowledge if the purchaser has access to facts which would lead a prudent man to question the ownership of his vendor. Brown and Root, Inc., v. Southeast Equipment Company, Inc., 470 So.2d 516 (La.App. 1st Cir.1985). In Brown and Root, Inc., the purchaser of equipment from a dealer was found to be in good faith even though the serial number on the piece of equipment had been tampered with and the price was low. The facts showed that the tampering was concealed, the purchase was made from an equipment dealer and other equipment was for sale at the establishment at similar or lower prices.

¶23   We find that the facts of the present case are distinguishable from those in Brown and Root, Inc. Regarding the purchase of the 74 cows, Stratton and/or LPI were not in good faith, as that term is construed under the provisions discussed above. Stratton had sufficient notice that something was amiss when Smith sought to quickly consummate a private sale of cattle that had a new brand that was not attributable to Smith or any of the concerns with which he was associated. According to Littleton, his "BL" brand was registered in Texas. Stratton testified that the brand on the cattle was referenced in a Louisiana brand book and determined to belong to a farmer in Coushatta with no connection to Smith, Glasscock or the McDade operation. Even though the brand actually belonged to Littleton and was registered in Texas, not only did Stratton fail to check the brand registry in neighboring states, but when the brand did not seem to fit with Smith, he made no further inquiry. Given the freshness of the brand, Stratton should have at least questioned the ownership of the cattle. Smith was pressing for a quick, private sale of the last of the cows from the herd. Stratton moved forward to purchase the cows and immediately resell them for a quick profit. Therefore, we find that, limited to the facts presented herein, and as construed under La. C.C. art. 523 et seq., Stratton and/ or LPI were not in good faith in purchasing the 74 cows, and are not entitled to reimbursement from Littleton for the purchase price of those cows. However, LPI may recover the amount paid from Smith, who knowingly sold property that he did not own.

¶24 [The court's reasoning is omitted as it relates to tort and agency law.]

CONCLUSION

¶25 We find that all of the losses in this case stem from the actions of Danny Smith. Although he is solidarily liable with some parties in this case, Smith is solely liable for those losses to all parties aggrieved in this case.

* * *

¶26 We find that principles of comparative fault are not applicable to this case. The trial court judgment to the contrary is reversed.

REVERSED IN PART; AFFIRMED IN PART; RENDERED.

C. Louisiana's Jurisprudential Improvisation

As discussed at the beginning of this chapter, the 1979 revision brought Louisiana's Civil Code more in line with the common law Bona Fide Purchaser doctrine. The revision put another article into place in the Civil Code, article 520, which was repealed in 1980, one year after its passage. That article dealt provided protection for a good faith purchaser – without it, protection is provided to a good faith acquirer, but not specifically for a good faith purchaser. In contrast, there is protection for security of ownership in articles dealing with both wrongful sales and other wrongful transfers. Article 2452 provides that "[t]he sale of a thing belonging to another does not convey ownership." Article 518 provides in part: "The ownership of a movable is voluntarily transferred by a contract between the owner and the transferee that purports to transfer the ownership of the movable."

Thus, together they provide security of ownership. Article 520 was intended to create a broad exception to the principle that an owner can transfer ownership via a contract, but that one who does not own the thing cannot convey ownership by selling it. It provided: "A transferee in good faith for fair value acquires the ownership of a corporeal movable, if the transferor, though not owner, has possession with the consent of the owner, as pledgee, lessee, depositary or other person of similar standing."

COMMENT, THE TRANSFER OF OWNERSHIP OF MOVABLES,
BY TANYA ANN IBIETA
47 LA. L. REV. 841, 849-50 (1987):

The repeal of Article 520 was in response to the confusion and apprehension generated by the article among Louisiana retailers and equipment leasing companies. Concerned with the ability of lessees to transfer ownership of leased equipment to third parties, representatives of these groups lobbied for the repeal of article 520. In enacting that repeal, the legislature intended to eliminate potential abuse by lessees and others who hold movables for owners; unfortunately, what appeared to be a simple remedy could potentially produce unintended consequences.

Article 520 codified a rule similar to but broader than the jurisprudential doctrine of equitable estoppel. Unlike equitable estoppel, which is based on the express or implied representation by the owner that the seller has the authority to sell the thing, article 520 was to be applied regardless of the nature of the original owner's actions in relinquishing possession of the thing. Its repeal may be seen as a rejection of the entire estoppel exception, or more probably, a return to the case by case approach to determining the effect of an owner's negligence on the validity of the sale of his property by another. In addition, it is reasonable to conclude that the repeal of article 520 indicates a legislative intention that a person who acquired possession of a movable from a transferor who had possession of such movable with the owner's consent should not acquire ownership. However, the force of such a conclusion is weakened by the failure of the legislature to repeal or amend the other articles of the revision that supported article 520.

In testimony before the Senate Judiciary A Committee, Professor Yiannopoulos characterized the repeal of article 520 as a "half-hearted' repeal of the law." Professor Litvinoff, at that same hearing, testified that "the repeal of article 520 would not extend those persons retailers and lessors as much protection as they feel it would." He added that the elimination of article 520 would only deprive Louisiana courts of the guidance it provides.

The problem to which these statements refer is that article 520 was originally passed not as an isolated provision, but as a part of an entire scheme of law; it was meant to be read in pari materia with the articles enacted in conjunction with it. The repeal of that single article ignored the rest of that scheme. Article 521 was enacted as an exception to 520. The other articles in the revision and in other parts of the code modified and qualified article 520.

Study Question:

Consequently, in light of the gap created by the repeal of Article 520, the solutions reached jurisprudentially prior to the revision of Articles 518 through 525 may remain relevant. Does the following case remain relevant, even though it was decided prior to the revision?

WILLIAM FRANTZ & CO., V. FINK 1909
125 LA. 1013, 52 SO.131

On Rehearing.

PROVOSTY, J.

¶1 Moss, one of the defendants, was a maker and repairer of jewelry. He had an office on the second floor of a building on one of the principal streets of this city, and also a workshop on the third floor of the same building. What this office consisted of, or what he kept in it, the record does not show. In a small way be bought and sold diamonds. The defendant Fink, in answer to the question, 'Q. He didn't have any store?' answered, 'He used to carry around a little paper of loose goods all the time; yes, sir.' From this, and from the evidence generally in the case, we understand that Moss was more of an artisan-a maker and repairer of jewelry and diamond setter- than merchant; and that he traded only in a small way in jewelry. That he did this, how-ever, was well known among the trade.

¶2 The plaintiff firm has a large jewelry establishment in this city. It had had some dealings with Moss in a small way, had sold him 'some small things,' for which he had duly paid, when the transactions which have given rise to the present controversy took place.

¶3 On March 16, 1906, he came into the store of the plaintiff firm, and said he had a customer for a pair of diamond earrings, and asked plaintiff to let him have the goods to show to his customer; and again, on April 4, 1906, he came with another similar request for another pair of diamond earrings; and both times plaintiff complied with his request.

¶4 A material point in the case is as to what were the terms and conditions on which the two pairs of earrings were thus put in the possession of Moss. The only witness on that point is the senior member of the plaintiff firm, and his testimony is accepted as true. He says that he fixed a price on the earrings, and let Moss have them on the condition that he should either return them or pay the price; that he did not sell them to him, but fixed the price low enough for him to make a profit in selling them to some one else. On both occasions the witness put this price on a piece of paper, and handed it to Moss, and made a memorandum for himself of what goods he had thus intrusted, and of the price set on them. This price was $502 on the first pair, and $975 on the second.

¶5   No time seems to have been fixed within which Moss should return the goods or pay for them, and the evidence does not show what was contemplated in that regard. It does show, however, that plaintiffs made inquiries of Moss, and were told that his customers were still deliberating.

¶6   As a matter of fact, he had taken the first pair of earrings on the day after he got them to the pawnbroker's shop of the defendant Fink and sold them to him for $300. This was $202 less than the low price set upon them by plaintiff.

¶7   The second pair of earrings he pledged at the pawnbroker's shop of one Koritzky for $465. The date of this pledge is not shown.

¶8   In the early part of February the defendant Fink had bought some small loose diamonds of Moss, and had left in his hands 171 small diamonds to be set in a pin or brooch. While the work was in progress, Fink kept an eye on his 171 diamonds. In one place he says that he went to Moss' shop every day; at another place he says that he went once or twice a week. After the pin had been apparently completed, Moss would not give it up, saying there was still something to be done to it. He had already been paid the price agreed on for doing the work, $110. The pin was worth $1,500. Fink had called at Moss' shop on several consecutive days to demand the pin and not found him in, when, determined to have the pin, he sought him out at his house; and Moss then acknowledged that he had pledged the pin at the shop of one Keil for $500. He at the same time said that he owned a pair of diamond earrings worth $975, which he had pledged to Koritzky for $465, and that Fink could have them if he would redeem them and pay the $500 to Keil in redemption of the pin. This Fink agreed to do, and on the same day did do.

¶9   On the evening of that day, April 28th, a Saturday, Moss came to plaintiff with a story that two armed men had come to his shop and robbed him of the diamonds. Plaintiff did not believe him and had him arrested, and at once instituted, with the aid of detectives, a search among the pawnbrokers' shops of the city. On the first visit to the shop of the defendant Fink he denied that he had had any dealings with Moss. When Moss saw that his tale of robbery would not hold, he confessed; and Fink also, on the second visit to his shop, acknowledge his transactions with Moss, and offered to restore the goods on being reimbursed the several sums which he had paid out, namely, the $300 to Moss, the $465 to Koritzky, and the $500 to Keil.

¶10   Plaintiff then brought this suit against Fink and Moss, demanding in the alternative a return of the goods or payment of the price set upon them.

¶11   Moss made no defense. Fink contends that the transactions between Moss and the plaintiff were sales; that Moss became owner of the goods, and could convey a valid title to them; that, at all events, the plaintiff firm is estopped in the premises, because it clothed Moss with the indicia of ownership, thereby enabling him to commit the fraud; and that, whenever one of two innocent persons must suffer by the acts of a third, he who enables such person to occasion the loss must sustain it.

¶12   The question of whether Moss became the owner of the goods or not depends upon what was the agreement of the parties. The parties had a perfect right to make any agreement they chose in that regard. The rights conferred upon Moss by that agreement were: (1) To become owner of the goods on paying the price set upon them; (2) to sell the goods to some one else at a cash price of not less than that set upon them. The right was not conferred upon him to buy the goods on a credit; or, in other words, to become debtor to plaintiff for the price of the goods. Whatever money he received from the person he sold the goods to was to be plaintiff's money; and, if he failed to account for it, he would be criminally responsible. The goods were not sold to him, and the only way in which he could become the owner of them was by paying cash for them. By the terms of the arrangement Moss could not sell the goods on a credit. Either the goods or the money would have to be in his hands, to be delivered to plaintiff.

¶13   The goods not having been sold to Moss, he could transfer no title to them. Nemo plus in alium transferre potest quam ipse habet. 5 Cyc. 207; 24 A. & E. E. 1163.

¶14   The learned counsel for the defendant Fink contend that the transaction was of the kind known at common law as 'sale and return,' and the Court of Appeal took that view. We repeat, the nature of a transaction is what the parties agree that it should be; and the distinct agreement in this case was that the goods were not sold, or agreed to be sold, on a credit to Moss, but that the only way he could become the owner of them was by paying cash for them. For the distinction between such an agreement and what is commonly known as 'sale and return,' see Sturm v. Boker, 150 U. S. 323, 14 Sup. Ct. 99, 37 L. Ed. 1099, and note; Sturtevant v. Dugan, 106 Md. 587, 68 Atl. 351, 14 Am. & Eng. Ann. Cas. 679.

¶15   Before passing to the consideration of how far plaintiff may be estopped, we will note that the law of agency can play no part in this case. Moss had no mandate to sell the goods at less than the price set upon them, and still less had he any mandate to give them in payment of his debts. And Fink did not deal with him as the agent of the plaintiff firm, but as the owner of the goods.

¶16 Coming to a consideration to the estoppel, it is a plain proposition that the mere possession of movable property is not such indicium of ownership as will enable the possessor to convey a good title as against the true owner. If it did, the borrower or hirer of a horse could validly sell it. The owner must have done something more than merely confide the possession of his property to the possessor before the latter can sell it or create a lien upon it. He must have to some extent accredited the title of the possessor-clothed him with more pronounced indicium of ownership than mere possession.

¶17 This may be done in various ways, and one way would be what the plaintiff firm did in this case, namely, consent that a vender of jewelry exhibit the jewels as part of his stock of goods, or as belonging to him.

¶18 'If a wine merchant be left in possession of wine, the fair inference is that it is his own, and a person may be justified in advancing money upon the security of it.' Per Bramwell, L. J., in Meggy v. Imperial, 3 Q. B. D., 717.

¶19 The decision in Conner v. Hill, 6 La. Ann. 7, is founded upon estoppel, agency, and ratification. From the facts as stated, the grounds of estoppel do not appear; but the writer of the present opinion knows that the flatboats coming down the Mississippi river before the War loaded with western produce were for sale, and that usually, if not always, those in charge of them had authority to sell; so that Anderson, who was in charge of the flatboat in that case, had more than mere possession. He had a possession which, according to custom, was accompanied by the power to sell. True, the owner had not consented to his being thus clothed with apparent authority to sell, but his son and agent had done so for him. It was upon this the court must have founded the estoppel, in so far as the decision is based on estoppel.

¶20 True, Moss was more of an artisan than merchant; but it was in his character of merchant that both plaintiff and Fink dealt with him. Plaintiff consented that he should exhibit the earrings to his customers as belonging to him, and that he should do so in his quality of a trader in jewelry. Fink, knowing him to be a trader in jewels, was justified in buying from him. It follows from this that Fink acquired a good title to the first pair of earrings. Although, we must say, that the great disparity in price gives some room for suspicion even as to that pair of earrings.

¶21 With respect to the second pair, Fink is not in a position to invoke equitable estoppel. For him to be in a position to do so, it would be necessary that he should 'not only have been destitute of knowledge of the real facts, but should also have been without convenient or ready means of acquiring such knowledge.' 16 Cyc. 739. And he must have been led to change his position for the worse. 16 Cyc. 722.

¶22 'Notice is to be distinguished from knowledge, and, if the buyer has notice of facts which would put a reasonably prudent man upon inquiry which would have resulted in the ascertainment of the adverse interest sought to be enforced against him, he will be deemed to have taken with notice, and cannot assert the rights of a bona fide purchaser.' 26 A. & E. E. 1175.

¶23 In so far as the earrings were taken in reimbursement of the $500 which Fink had to pay to Keil for redeeming his pin, his position was not changed for the worse, since that amount would have had to be paid to Keil even if Moss had never had possession of the earrings, and since it is not pretended that he was deprived of any recourse which he would otherwise have had against Moss. As to the circumstances under which one who has received property in payment of an antecedent debt may be considered to have parted with value, see 26 A. & E. E. 1171, 1173.

¶24 By the time Fink came to deal with Moss for this second pair of earrings, Moss had become utterly discredited. He was a confessed embezzler. He was no longer a merchant or trader having valuable goods for sale, but was a diamond setter who had pledged the goods of his employer and stood under the necessity of confessing his crime because of his inability to redeem the pledge. He was not a merchant offering to sell goods out of his stock, but at best an ex-merchant who was proposing to the person whose property he had embezzled that the latter should rescue from the pawnbroker's shop a certain piece of property and pay himself out of the margin between value of the thing and the amount for which it stood pledged. Fink testifies that he had lost confidence in Moss and would not trust him out of his sight with the $465 for redeeming the earrings from Koritzky. The fact itself, well known to Fink, that Moss was a diamond setter, to whom valuable jewelry was likely to be intrusted by third persons, was in itself sufficient to put Fink upon inquiry. We cannot help thinking that Fink was a willing victim, and that, if it had not been for the chance of getting back his $500, he would have dealt with Moss with a good deal less of confidence.

¶25 As to this $465, we put our decision distinctly on the fact that the earrings were not acquired from a merchant having them for sale to the public generally, but were redeemed from a pawnbroker's shop at the request of an embezzler as a means of settlement for the embezzlement.

¶26 It is therefore ordered, adjudged, and decreed that our former decree be reinstated and made the judgment of this court.

D. Registered Movables

Study Questions:

What do the following authorities indicate about how the Bona Fide Purchaser doctrine applies to a registered movable such as a car?

What is the seller's remedy in such a case?

TRUMBELL CHEVROLET SALES CO. V. MAXWELL 1962
142 SO.2D 805 (LA. APP. 2D CIR.)

HARDY, Judge.

¶1 Plaintiff brought this suit, praying for judgment recognizing it as the owner of a certain described 1960 Chevrolet automobile free and clear of all liens and encumbrances. Named as defendants were F. S. Naxwell, purchaser of the vehicle from Reed Motor Company of Monroe, Louisiana, and Maxwell's chattel mortgage holder, United Credit Plan, Inc. of Baton Rouge. To plaintiff's petition both defendants filed exceptions of no cause of action and pleas of estoppel, which, after hearing, were sustained and judgment rendered in favor of defendants. From this judgment plaintiff has appealed.

¶2 The petition of plaintiff, Trumbull Chevrolet Sales Company, Inc. of Michigan, alleged that the vehicle involved in this action was one of a group of eight cars it delivered to the O.K. Motor Company of Dresden, Tennessee, in or about the month of April, 1960; that delivery papers, invoices, titles and statements of origin on the said group of cars were not delivered; that plaintiff received from its vendee a check in the amount of $18,482.13 in payment for the said vehicles, payment on said check being dishonored; that despite the fact that plaintiff retained the original statement of origin, a false or forged statement on this particular vehicle was the basis for the transfer of title from the O.K. Motor Company of Dresden, Tennessee, to the Reed Motor Company of Monroe, which subsequently sold and delivered the vehicle to defendant, Maxwell, who executed a chattel mortgage thereon in favor of defendant, United Credit Plan, Inc.

¶3 Counsel for both appellant and appellee primarily rely upon the authority of Flatte v. Nichols, 233 La. 171, 177, 96 So.2d 477, in support of their opposed contentions. It is urged on behalf of plaintiff-appellant that the Flatte case is distinguishable by reason of the fact that, in addition to the delivery of possession of the vehicle, there was a delivery of license papers issued by another State and an invoice bill of sale. We think this asserted distinction is purely technical and cannot detract from the inescapable conclusion, on the basis of plaintiff's own pleading, that the transaction with the O.K. Motor Company constituted a valid sale despite the withholding of the statement of origin and other evidence of title. This point was covered in the opinion of the Supreme Court in Jeffrey Motor Company v. Higgins, 230 La. 857, 89 So.2d 369, which was cited in the opinion of the Supreme Court in the Flatte case.

¶4   In the Jeffrey case, upon the basis of LSA-C.C. Art. 2456, the court held that the original sale was complete when the seller accepted a draft which constituted an agreement as to the object and the price thereof. Upon this basis the court concluded that the original vendor could not recover the automobile from a subsequent bona fide purchaser. To the same effect is the holding in the very recent case of James v. Judice La.App. (3rd Circuit, 1962), 140 So.2d 169.

¶5   There is no allegation in plaintiff's petition in the instant case which so much as implies any fraud insofar as either of defendants or the Reed Motor Company is concerned, and it is therefore obvious that both Maxwell, as the purchaser from Reed Motor Company, and United Credit Plan, as Maxwell's mortgagee, are innocent parties.

¶6   It is too well established to necessitate citation that where one of two innocent parties must suffer loss through the fraud of another the burden of such loss is imposed upon the one who most contributes thereto (cf. James v. Judice, supra). The effect of plaintiff's allegations inescapably supports the conclusion that by its delivery of the vehicle in question and the acceptance of a check in payment therefor, it completed the necessary formalities of a sale, and, therefore, was solely responsible for laying the basis for the subsequent allegedly fraudulent transactions.

¶7   We observe no reason nor authority, either in law or equity, for penalizing the defendants in this suit for a fault exclusively chargeable to the actions of plaintiff.

¶8   The judgment appealed from is affirmed at appellant's cost.

La. Rev. Stat. 32:706

A. On and after December 15, 1950, except as provided in R.S. 32:705 and 32:712, no person buying a vehicle from the owner thereof, whether such owner be a dealer or otherwise, hereafter shall acquire a marketable title in or to the vehicle until the purchaser shall have obtained a certificate of title to the vehicle; however, neither the foregoing nor any other provisions of this Vehicle Certificate of Title Law shall be construed to have the effect of delaying, suspending or preventing the negotiation of a note secured by a chattel mortgage or security interest on a vehicle from being complete until the purchaser shall have obtained a certificate of title to the vehicle, . . .

La. Rev. Stat. 32:706.1

§ 706.1. Disclosure by persons who transfer ownership of vehicles with salvage or reconstructed titles, assembled title, or certificate of destruction; penalties [Section heading effective July 1, 2010]

A. Each person who sells, exchanges, donates, or otherwise transfers any interest in any vehicle for which a salvage title, certificate of destruction, assembled title, or a reconstructed title has been issued shall disclose the existence of that title to the prospective purchaser, recipient in exchange, recipient by donation, or recipient by other act of transfer. The disclosure shall be made by a conspicuous written document and shall be made prior to the completion of the sale, exchange, donation, or other act of transfer.

B. If any person sells, exchanges, donates, or otherwise transfers any interest in any vehicle for which a salvage title, certificate of destruction, assembled title, or a reconstructed title has been issued and does not make the disclosures required by this Section, the person to whom the interest in that vehicle was transferred may demand the rescission of the sale, exchange, donation, or other act of transfer and, in that event, shall be entitled to recover the price or other consideration for the transaction and any fees or taxes paid to any governmental agency in connection with that transaction.

C. Whoever knowingly violates the provisions of this Section shall be guilty of a misdemeanor and, upon conviction, shall be punished by imprisonment of not more than six months or by a fine not less than five hundred dollars nor more than five thousand dollars, or both. In addition, the violator shall be sentenced to not less than eighty hours of community service.

Section 2. Immovables: The Public Records Doctrine (PRD)

A. Basic Principles

Read Articles 517, 1839, 2442, 2629, 3338-3347

The Public Records Doctrine ("PRD") serves the same purpose for immovables that the Bona Fide Purchaser Doctrine serves for movables: it balances the security of transaction against the security of ownership. Article 2442 provides:

> The parties to an act of sale or promise of sale of immovable property are bound from the time the act is made, but such an act is not effective against third parties until it is filed for registry according to the laws of registry.

Articles 517 and 1839 are more general versions of the same principle, stating that although a transfer of ownership is effective immediately between the two parties to it, it is not effective against third parties until filed for registry in the conveyance records of the parish where the immovable is located. Article 2629 provides that options, rights of first refusal, and contracts to sell involving immovable property are likewise effective against third parties only from the time the instruments containing them are filed for registry.

The PRD is essentially a negative doctrine, in the following sense: a person may rely on the absence of something in the public record, but that doesn't mean that what is recorded is accurate. To rephrase, registration does not establish positive rights, but instead sets out negatives for both the parties to a recorded instrument and potential third party purchasers. For example, once an instrument is recorded, Article 3342 provides that parties to it may not contradict its terms or the statements of fact it contains to the prejudice of a third person who acquires an interest in the property after that recordation. Recordation itself is designed to put third parties on notice of what is contained in the recorded instrument, but as provided in Article 3341, recordation does not create a presumption that what is recorded is itself valid or genuine, nor does it create a presumption as to the capacity or status of the parties, and it is effective only with respect to immovables located in the parish where the instrument is recorded.

Prior to 2006, the PRD was contained in various Revised Statutes, referred to in the Civil Code, and elaborated upon in the jurisprudence. The 2005 Revision added "Of Registry" to the Civil Code itself in an attempt to put the PRD in one, easily accessible place. Thus, Articles 3338 through 3347 now set out the rules of the PRD.

Study Questions:

What do the following cases indicate about the PRD? Note that McDuffie v. Walker is still good law and still cited.

Would their reasoning and result change if the current Civil Code articles were in effect?

MONROE, J.

¶1 In 1907 plaintiff purchased a small tract of land at a sale made by order of court in the succession of Emma McClelland, and, finding that defendant was occupying a parcel (consisting of about an acre and a half) included in the tract so purchased, brought this petitory action for its recovery. Defendant answers, alleging that he bought the parcel in question by notarial act from Emma McClelland on September 23, 1899, and has been in open possession as owner, and has paid the taxes, since that time; that 'for some reason' the act was not recorded, but that he has recently (May 30, 1908) had it recorded; that there was, however, on record a plat of the tract owned by Emma McClelland, on which the parcel in question is shown as belonging to 'Sam Wallace,' which should be 'Sam Walker' (defendant herein); that said plat, with defendant's possession, was sufficient notice of his title; that plaintiff purchased with full knowledge of the fact that respondent was in possession as owner; that the sale by which plaintiff pretends to have acquired is void for want of proper notice; that no sale was necessary, because the succession of Emma McClelland owed no debts; that the property was appraised at less than its value; and that there was no intention to sell the parcel in question, which was excluded from the inventory and advertisement. There was judgment in the district court in favor of defendant, which was affirmed by the Court of Appeal, and to writ of review has issued from this court at the instance of plaintiff. In the opinion of the Court of Appeal, it is conceded that defendant's title was not recorded when plaintiff purchased the land, . . .

Opinion.

***

¶2 It is proved and admitted that the sale by Emma McClelland to defendant, though made in 1899, was not recorded until May 30, 1908, and we take it to be proved and admitted that the sale to plaintiff was made and recorded in 1907.

¶3 It can hardly be said that the Court of Appeal finds that plaintiff had actual knowledge of the defendant's title at the time that he made his purchase. The judgment of that court is predicated upon the presumption that plaintiff knew that which (it holds) he might have known, or ought to have known.

***

¶4 There were, however, differences between the provisions of the Code itself upon the subject of the registry of notarial acts and of acts under private signature, . . .

***

¶5 In 1855, therefore, the General Assembly took the matters up, and passed the Acts Nos. 259 (page 320), 274 (page 335), and 285 (page 345), which (save certain provisions concerning slaves) were subsequently incorporated in the Revised Civil Code of 1870 under the title, 'Of Registry,' as articles 2251 to 2266. Act No. 259 was entitled 'An act relative to notaries in the city of New Orleans.' Act No. 285 was entitled 'an act creating a register of conveyances for the parish of Orleans.' Act No. 274 was entitled 'An act relative to registry,' and was of general application throughout the state. It has been incorporated in the revised Civil Code as articles 2264, 2265, and 2266, with an addition (to the latter article) which will be noted. Section 1 of the act (now Civ. Code, 2264) provides:

'That no notarial act concerning immovable property shall have any effect against third persons until the same shall have been deposited in the office of the parish recorder [an officer created by Act of 1846, p. 71, No. 104] or register of conveyances of the parish where such immovable property is situated.'

Section 2 of the act (now Civ. Code, 2265, 2266) provides that all sales, marriage contracts, etc., and final judgments affecting immovable property, 'shall be recorded in the parish where the immovable property is situated,' and that 'all sales, contracts and judgments, affecting immovable property, which shall not be so recorded, shall be utterly null and void except between the parties thereto. The recording may be made at 'any time but shall only affect third persons from time of the recording.' In the revision of the Civil Code in 1870 there appears to have been added to the act of 1855 the following, which constitutes the last paragraph of article 2266, to wit:

'The recording shall have effect from the time when the act is deposited in the proper office, and indorsed by the proper officer.'

***

¶6 In Baker v. Atkins & Wideman, 107 La. 490, 32 South. 69, it was held (quoting from the syllabus) that:

'Where A., who is the owner of real estate by undisputed title, sells the same to B., and B. fails to record his title, the judgment creditors of A. can acquire judicial mortgages on such property by recording their judgments after the date of such sale and before its registry. And in such case the judicial mortgages recorded against A. prior to the registry of the sale prime all such mortgages recorded against B., whether the latter were recorded before or after the sale.'

¶7　It is evident that whether a person acquires an interest in real estate to the extent of its value or part of its value as a mortgagee or as a vendee the principle involved in the application of the law of registry is the same; and hence if it be true that one may acquire a valid first mortgage, though he know at the time that as between the mortgagor and another there already exists an unrecorded mortgage upon the same property, it must also be true that one may acquire a valid title to such property, though he know that as between his vendor and another an unrecorded title has already been passed. The law makes no distinction between mortgages and sales or between creditors and vendees or mortgagees; nor does it discriminate between those who acquire property with knowledge of unrecorded contracts and those who acquire without such knowledge.

¶8　Its purpose is to establish and enforce as a matter of public policy upon the subject of the most important property right with which it deals the rule that unrecorded contracts affecting immovable property 'shall be utterly null and void, except between the parties thereto.' No language could be plainer or more emphatic, and the courts have no more power to read into the rule established by it an exception, not contained in it, than they would have to read such an exception into the rule that a verbal sale of immovable property shall not affect third persons. It is true that 'fraud cuts down everything,' and, if it were alleged and proved in a given case that a mortgagee had been induced by fraudulent representation or device to leave his mortgage unrecorded or to abstain from reinscribing it, or that a vendee had been so induced to leave his title unrecorded and that loss had thereby resulted, such mortgagee or vendee would no doubt be granted relief as against the perpetrator of the fraud. But it cannot be said that one perpetrates a fraud who merely treats as utterly null and void a contract which the law in terms declares 'shall be utterly null and void.' To hold such doctrine is necessarily to hold that one who knows a particular contract to be denounced by the law as utterly void is bound in spite of the law to respect it as valid and binding, a paradox to which a court of justice would be unwilling to commit itself as an interpretation of law.

***

¶9　For the reasons thus given, we are of opinion that plaintiff should have judgment as prayed for . . . .

Study Question:

Why does the Public Records Doctrine NOT prevent the Maboules family from claiming fraud in the following Supreme Court case?

CIMAREX ENERGY CO. V. MAUBOULES 2010
40 SO.3D 931 (LA.)

JOHNSON, Justice.

¶1 This case arises out of a dispute involving royalty payments due under a mineral lease held by applicants, Cimarex Energy Co., Ceniarth, Ltd., Palace Exploration Co., and RZ, Inc. (hereinafter "Cimarex"). Alleging that there were competing claims to the royalty payments, Cimarex invoked a concursus proceeding and deposited the funds into the registry of the court. We granted this writ application primarily to review the lower courts' rulings that Cimarex had no reasonable basis to invoke a concursus proceeding in this case, and thereby unreasonably withheld royalty payments due to respondents, Orange River Royalties, L.L.P., Mission Royalty Quest, LLC, Fort Worth Operating Company, L.L.C., Richard Martter, and Coyote Ventures, Ltd. (hereinafter "Orange River").

* * *

¶2 For the following reasons, we therefore reverse the decision of the court of appeal.

FACTS AND PROCEDURAL HISTORY

¶3 The royalties at issue arise from a mineral lease between defendants, Katherine D. Mauboules, et al. ("Mauboules Family") and Cimarex. Various members of the Mauboules family own a tract of land in Vermillion Parish, Louisiana. In October of 1997, the Mauboules sold certain royalty interests in their land to Ereunao Oil & Gas, Inc. ("Ereunao") via five royalty deeds, all dated October 16, 1997. Ereunao subsequently assigned portions of its mineral interest to numerous entities.

¶4 The deeds executed between the Mauboules and Ereunao provided for a three-year prescriptive period for non-use. However, the deeds also included a prescription interruption clause which allowed off-premise production to maintain the entire royalty. The clause expressly provided:

It is expressly understood and agreed that an interruption of prescription resulting from unit production shall extend to the entirety of the aforedescribed tract or tracts of land regardless of the location of the well or of whether all or only part of the aforedescribed tract or tracts of land in included in a unit or units.

¶5 On November 14, 2001, the Mauboules' attorney, Kenneth Privat, sent a letter to Ereunao noting that the deeds had a three-year prescriptive period and thus had prescribed on October 16, 2000. Privat asked for a recordable instrument evidencing the extinction of the deeds. On November 20, 2001, Charles M. Fife, Jr., President of Ereunao, responded to Privat's letter, noting that although the deeds had a three-year prescriptive period, the deeds also included the prescription interruption clause relative to off-site production. Fife further stated in his letter: "Frankly, I did not realize the above clause was in these royalty deeds until recently. A member of my staff who prepares our royalty deeds advised me that he had inserted the clause as our information about the Key Production drilling program for this prospect was somewhat uncertain respecting its time frame for completion. Usually our royalty deeds have a three-year term and do not include the above clause."

¶6 In 2002, Key Production Company, predecessor to Cimarex, became interested in drilling on the Mauboules property, and contacted Privat to discuss and negotiate a lease. On May 29, 2002, an agent for Key Production sent a letter to Privat, extending an initial offer. Negotiations were difficult and continued over a two-year period, primarily due to Privat's assertions that the prescription interruption clause had been wrongfully inserted into the royalty deeds, possibly as a result of fraud, and that the royalty interests of Ereunao and the interests of its successors had therefore prescribed, and the royalty rights had reverted back to the Mauboules family.

¶7 On December 26, 2002, Cimarex continued the negotiations for the lease by making a revised offer to the Mauboules through Privat. In addition to stating the lease terms and price per acre, the offer included additional consideration: if the Mauboules pursued a cause of action against Ereunao, Cimarex would agree to pay up to $7,500 of legal expenses associated with that action incurred during the next twelve month period; and if that cause of action was pursued, but failed, Cimarex would agree to pay a cash bonus of $75,000 to the Mauboules upon 150% payout of the well.

¶8 The lease between Cimarex and the Mauboules Family was eventually executed on February 10, 2003.3 The lease contained the following miscellaneous provisions, summarized below:

In the event that the well is successful to the extent that the well reaches 150.00% payout, then the Mauboules shall be entitled to a one-time payment of $75,000.00, provided that the following has occurred:

1. At the time of payout, the Mauboules' royalty interest, which was conveyed unto Ereunao, remains outstanding;

2. That the well reaches 150.00% payout;

¶9   The Lease Purchase Report between the Mauboules and Cimarex, dated April 10, 2003, included the following note:

In the event that our well is successful, Lessor's attorney, Kenny Privat, will file suit against a royalty purchaser known as Ereunao Oil & Gas, Inc., et al.

Kenny Privat contends that representatives of this company altered Royalty Deeds after being approved by him; and further, misled the Royalty Owners as to what portion of the tract that they were actually selling.

The purpose of this suit will be to reduce the extent of the royalty deeds to cover only that portion of the leased premises situated within the confines of the Bourque unit, in lieu of the entirety of the tract.

* * *

¶10   Cimarex drilled a successful well and began production in January of 2004. On March 26, 2004, Privat sent a letter to Cimarex stating that the Mauboules were asserting that the royalty interests deeded to Ereunao had prescribed based on the three-year prescriptive period, and asking Cimarex to place the disputed royalties in suspense until a determination on this issue could be obtained from the courts. Cimarex forwarded the letter to its attorney, James Williams, who then contacted Privat. During a phone call with Privat, Williams learned that Privat was asserting that the off-tract production clause was ineffective because it had been inserted into the royalty deeds either fraudulently or under circumstances tantamount to fraud. Privat stated that he would have the clause declared invalid on the basis of fraud and that the royalty interests at issue had therefore reverted to the members of the Mauboules family.

* * *

¶11   Beginning in April of 2004, the Orange River Group ("Orange River"), a group of individuals and businesses who purchase mineral royalty interests for the purpose of investment and re-sale in the producing mineral royalties market, purchased shares of outstanding mineral royalties in the Mauboules' land from assignees of Ereunao.

¶12   On June 9, 2004, Cimarex advised Orange River of the Mauboules' adverse claim to the royalty interests, and further advised that Cimarex would be suspending the royalty payments. In August of 2004, Williams advised Cimarex that it would be necessary to file a concursus proceeding, and he received the authorization to do so. However, according to Williams, Orange River's attorney, Kerry Kilburn, asked him to delay the filing.

¶13   On November 16, 2004, Kilburn made written demand for payment on behalf of Orange River to Cimarex pursuant to La. R.S. 31:212.21.8 In his letter, Kilburn noted that Orange River was a "good faith purchase[r] relying on the public record for the validity of [its] title and there can be no reasonable claim against [Orange River] by the Mauboules Family members."

***

¶14   On December 20, 2004, Cimarex filed the concursus proceeding which forms the underlying basis of this writ application. Orange River was named as a defendant in the concursus, along with the Mauboules, Ereunao, and Ereunao's assigns. The Mauboules answered the concursus, admitted to the existence of a controversy concerning entitlement to the disputed funds, and sought to be recognized as the owners of the mineral royalty interests. The Mauboules did not specifically assert fraud in their answers. Orange River reconvened, seeking unpaid oil and gas royalties and penalties pursuant to La. R.S. 31:212.21, et seq.

¶15   Orange River subsequently filed a Motion for Summary Judgment, asking the Court to recognize their ownership of the mineral royalty interest at issue, and to award them all unpaid royalties allocable to such interest. In its opposition to the summary judgment, the Mauboules asserted that "the royalty deeds contain error that concerns the Mauboules principal cause of said contracts, and the error may have been induced by fraud." The Mauboules further stated that they had not yet had the opportunity to conduct discovery or depose Ereunao, and thus they could not yet prove that the error was induced by fraud.

¶16   On August 22, 2005, the Court granted summary judgment in favor of Orange River, recognizing Orange River as the owners of a certain undivided mineral royalty interest in the land at issue, and ordered the Clerk of Court to release the funds representing owed royalties.

¶17 Following a bench trial on Orange River's reconventional demand, the trial court found that Cimarex's reliance on the oral assertion of fraud by Privat was an unreasonable basis to suspend royalty payments, and thus Orange River was entitled to statutory penalties.

* * *

¶18 The court of appeal affirmed the trial court's finding that Cimarex's actions were unreasonable. The court found that Cimarex had no legitimate basis for initiating the concursus, and that it was merely orchestrated as a condition to the Mauboules granting the lease to Cimarex. The court also suggested that, given the history of the Mauboules' claim, the agreement Cimarex made with the Mauboules to obtain the lease violated the "clean hands doctrine." The court further found that Cimarex did not show how the Mauboules' assertions could present a claim that would challenge, much less defeat, Orange River's royalty interest and the public records doctrine. The court reasoned that to file a valid concursus, Cimarex needed to show that the Mauboules had a competing claim against Orange River. But, the Orange River claim was fully supported by the public records and public records doctrine. Thus, while the Mauboules may have a claim against Ereunao for fraud, the Mauboules had no claim to the funds due Orange River. Finally, because the concursus was improperly invoked, the court held that Cimarex was not entitled to immunity for depositing the funds into the registry of the court, and the action of depositing the funds did not constitute payment of the royalties due under the mineral code.

* * *

¶19 Cimarex (along with Ceniarth, Palace and Zeneco) applied for supervisory writs in this Court, which were granted.

DISCUSSION

¶20 Our decision addresses whether Cimarex properly invoked the concursus proceeding. Specifically, we examine whether the Mauboules' assertions relative to the Ereunao deeds constituted a competing claim, and whether Cimarex, as a stakeholder, was required to determine the merits of the competing claim prior to invoking the concursus.

¶21 Prior to its codification, concursus developed through jurisprudence as an equitable remedy. In 1922, the legislature officially enacted Act 123, providing for the concursus proceeding. This Act authorized one who held money, claimed by two or more persons, or upon which two or more persons claimed a lien or privilege, to deposit the money in the registry of the court, and to cite all claimants to litigate over the fund. La. Acts 1922, No. 123; American Surety

Co. of New York v. Brim, 175 La. 959, 144 So. 727 (La.1932). The Act further provided that the depositor was relieved of any liability to the persons cited, and provided the manner in which the deposit should be made and the manner for citing the persons who had an interest in the money. La. Acts 1922, No. 123. The Act was passed in order to avoid a multiplicity of suits and actions, and contemplated a proceeding leading to one judgment, which finally adjudicated all the issues between all the parties. Amerada Petroleum Corp. v. State Mineral Board, 203 La. 473, 485, 14 So.2d 61, 65 (La.1943); Hennington v. Petroleum Heat & Power Co. of Louisiana, 194 La. 188, 196-197, 193 So. 583, 586 (La.1940).

¶22 The Act was incorporated into La. R.S. 13:4811 et seq. La. R.S. 13:4811 was amended and reenacted by La. Acts 1954, No. 523 . . .

* * *

¶23 Given the background and purpose of concursus and interpleader, we find that the concursus proceeding was properly invoked in this case.

Contentions of Applicants and Respondents

* * *

Orange River

¶24 Orange River argues that the unique facts and circumstances of this case do not require this Court to pronounce a new rule regarding whether concursus is always a reasonable response by a royalty payor to competing claims. Orange River asserts that there was never a true "adverse claim" to justify the suspension of royalties, and that the suspension of royalty payments was prefabricated. The "adverse claim" was only pretext for doing what Cimarex was required to do under its deal with the Mauboules. There was never a bona fide dispute as to Orange River's ownership of the royalty interests and right to payment.

¶25 Orange River argues that it was entitled to rely on the prescription interruption clause in the Ereunao deeds to keep its interests alive, even if it was fraudulently inserted, because the deeds were recorded in the public records. The Mauboules took no action to pursue Ereunao, and there was no claim by the Mauboules of record. Further, the Mauboules have never asserted a claim for fraud, or made any claim that could be construed as competing or conflicting to the interests acquired by Orange River.

Analysis

¶26 First, we reject Orange River's assertion that there was no true competing claim made by the Mauboules. The language of Article 4652 allows persons "having competing or conflicting claims" to be impleaded into a concursus proceeding. There is no requirement in the article that claims must be made in a specific format, or with any formality. The Mauboules' written assertions that the Ereunao deeds had prescribed, and the verbal allegations of fraud against Ereunao were sufficient to constitute a competing claim to the royalty proceeds at issue. We find that Cimarex was reasonable in relying on the assertions by the Mauboules that they were entitled to the royalty proceeds. The assertions made by the Mauboules involved more than a mere possibility that a competing claim may be asserted. There was a positive assertion by the Mauboules that they were entitled to the royalty proceeds, whether or not a written assertion of fraud was ever made. Moreover, once the concursus was filed, the Mauboules did not disclaim any interest in the royalty proceeds. The Mauboules answered the petitions, claiming ownership of the disputed royalties, and additionally opposed Orange River's motion for summary judgment, specifically laying out the basis for their claim, and stating that fraud was certainly a possibility, pending further discovery.

***

¶27 The court of appeal based its decision on the merits of the Mauboules' claim, reasoning that it could not defeat the protections of the public records doctrine. The Louisiana Public Records doctrine generally expresses a public policy that interest in real estate must be recorded in order to affect third persons. Simply put, an instrument in writing affecting immovable property which is not recorded is null and void except between the parties. See Peter S. Title, Louisiana Real Estate Transactions, § 8.1 (2009). The public records doctrine is founded upon our public policy and social purpose of assuring stability of land titles. Camel v. Waller, 526 So.2d 1086, 1089 (La.1988). At the time the Cimarex lease was recorded, the public records doctrine was generally set forth in La. C.C. art. 1839,17 La. R.S. 9:272118 and 9:2756.19 Louisiana law relative to registry was restated and revised by the legislature in 2005 by Act 169. La. R.S. 9:2721 and 9:2756, which provided for the lack of effect of unrecorded instruments as against third parties, was repealed.

¶28 The public records doctrine is now generally set forth in La. C.C. art. 3338, which provides:

> The rights and obligations established or created by the following written instruments are without effect as to a third person unless the instrument is registered by recording it in the appropriate mortgage or conveyance records pursuant to the provisions of this Title:

(1) An instrument that transfers an immovable or establishes a real right in or over an immovable.

(2) The lease of an immovable.

(3) An option or right of first refusal, or a contract to buy, sell, or lease an immovable or to establish a real right in or over an immovable.

(5) An instrument that modifies, terminates, or transfers the rights created or evidenced by the instruments described in Subparagraphs (1) through (3) of this Article.

¶29 The public records doctrine has been described as a negative doctrine because it does not create rights, but, rather, denies the effect of certain rights unless they are recorded. Title, supra at § 8.16; Camel, 526 So.2d at 1089-1090; Phillips v. Parker, 483 So.2d 972, 975 (La.1986). In explaining the negative nature of the doctrine, this Court has stated that third persons are not allowed to rely on what is contained in the public records, but can rely on the absence from the public records of those interests that are required to be recorded. Camel, 526 So.2d at 1090 [citing Redmann, The Louisiana Law of Recordation: Some Principles and Some Problems, 39 Tul. L.Rev. 491 (1965)]. The primary focus of the public records doctrine is the protection of third persons against unrecorded interests. Camel, 526 So.2d at 1090; Phillips, 483 So.2d at 976.

¶30 Because recordation is not the source of legal rights, Orange River can not simply rely on, and only look to, the public records doctrine to support its position that the Mauboules' claim was not a competing claim for purposes of concursus. While a third party is entitled to rely on the absence from the public record of those interests that are required to be recorded, the public records doctrine does not provide that a third party may rely implicitly on what is shown in a recorded instrument, nor does it provide that a third party who relies on a recorded instrument can acquire good title from a vendor who does not have good title. Redmann, supra at 500 [citing Succession of Rosinski, 158 So.2d 467, 469 (La.App. 3 Cir.1963)]. Regardless of the final resolution of Orange River's ownership of the royalty interests and its right to the royalty payments, the question of whether the Mauboules' claims might affect Orange River's title certainly presented a legitimate basis for Cimarex to fear that Orange River's position possibly might not be protected by the public records doctrine. Simply put, "the rule that what is not recorded is not effective does not mean that what is recorded is effective at all events, despite forgery or any other defect." Redmann, supra, at 501. Even though the general protections of the public records doctrine indicated that the Mauboules had little chance of success, we decline to put the burden on Cimarex to make that final legal determination. Such a determination is properly placed in the hands of the courts.

¶31 Moreover, Orange River's ownership rights could not be determined simply by looking at the documents filed in the public records. Orange River's interests are dependent on the off-tract production clause in the Ereunao deeds. If such production occurred, prescription would be interrupted. However, if there was no such production, then, even under the documents recorded, the interests purchased by Orange River would be nonexistent. Thus, Orange River's rights are dependent on facts and documents that were not contained in the public records, necessitating a factual inquiry.

¶32 Furthermore, by focusing on the merits of the Mauboules' claim, the court of appeal focused only on the "multiple liability" purpose of concursus, and ignored the "vexatious litigation" purpose. Even assuming that the Mauboules' claim is tenuous at best, requiring Cimarex to choose which claimant to pay still exposes Cimarex to the costs and risks of defending multiple suits. We find that Cimarex was justified in its fear that it might be later faced with a suit brought by the Mauboules, and its use of concursus to avoid such multiple litigation was proper.

B. The Collision between the Public Records Doctrine and Other Protected Interests

Traditionally in certain contexts the PRD sometimes gives way when another public policy, such as protecting the rights of spouses in community or the rights of forced heirs, takes precedence as illustrated in the following cases.

1. The Public Records Doctrine and Rights of Spouses in Community

Study Question:

Historically, jurisprudence concerning the tug-of-war between the PRD and community property rights is mixed, with some cases finding for the community property interest, and others in which the PRD trumps. Consider the reasoning in the following two cases and analyze the equitable or policy-related reasons why one side or the other wins.

MONROE, C. J.

¶1 Defendant (a colored woman) was married in Alexandria on January 3, 1891, to William Johnson, and 2 1/2 years later, they came to New Orleans, where they established a domicile, which they maintained until the death of the wife, which took place, probably, in January, 1915. Johnson's trade, or occupation, was that of fireman upon ocean-going steamships, and his absences from home were of four or five months' duration, while the intervals between them did not usually extend beyond that many days. His wife engaged in the business of renting rooms, and for the purposes of that business retained her maiden name (Mary E. James). She also bought real estate in that name, imposed mortgages upon it to secure money borrowed in that name, and on December 3, 1914, made a will which she signed 'Miss Mary E. James,' and, in which she declares that she had never been married, that she wished her mother, Ada Texhada, to 'receive what is due her by law'; that she bequeaths certain furniture and $100 to Sarah Johnson; that she owes 'Mr. William W. Wren' $5,000, which she desires should be paid to him; that she gives the residue of her estate to her grandmother, Eliza Hines; appoints William W. Wren her executor, and Mr. Anthony J. Rossi, attorney of her estate, to have charge of all legal matters at her death. The transcript before us was prepared merely for the purposes of the particular issues brought up by the appeal, and leaves a good deal to be assumed. It, however, contains a copy of the will, as filed, and of an inventory, taken by order of court and filed on February 25, 1915, which shows real estate valued at $12,525, movable property valued at $1,614, cash in bank, $1, and a certain draft for $133. It also contains the various acts of purchase by which the real estate so inventoried was acquired, and whereby certain pieces, and perhaps the whole, was mortgaged; the acquisitions, and mortgages alike, having taken place and been imposed during the existence of the marriage with Johnson, but without his participation, and, as to the mortgages, without his knowledge or consent. It is to be assumed that the will was filed and ordered to be executed and the appointment of the executor confirmed, and it is shown by the transcript that in June, 1919, Paul Chretien took two rules on the executor, the civil sheriff, and William Johnson, alleging that in April, 1916, he had caused executory process to issue, in enforcement of mortgages so executed by decedent, as a result of which, and of a similar proceeding by another creditor, certain described real estate, inventoried in the succession, had been seized and sold, in satisfaction of debts due by the decedent and represented by her notes, secured by said mortgages, and that the proceeds had gone into the hands of the sheriff, who had made partial payments on mover's claims, leaving still due a balance of $3,316, and leaving in the hands of the sheriff two sums of $2,936.86 and $553, aggregating $3,490, which the sheriff refused to pay over 'because one William Johnson claims the whole of said balance,' and further alleging 'that all of the properties above described were, respectively, purchased and mortgaged, as aforesaid, by the late Mary E. James as a feme sole, and that the whole amount 'represented by the said mortgage notes was paid to her, as such, at the time that the said mortgages were given by her; and that the said notes were acquired in good faith, before maturity.'

¶2   Mover prayed that said sheriff, executor, and William Johnson be ordered to show cause why said balance should not be paid over to him. The sheriff made a pro forma defense, the executor made none, and Wm. Johnson excepted, on the ground that the rule disclosed no cause of action, and answered, setting up his marriage to decedent, and alleging:

> That the property mortgaged belonged to the community of acquêts which existed between his wife and himself;
>   that the mortgages, if executed by his wife, were unauthorized by, and without consideration as to him;
>   that the foreclosure proceedings were instituted during his absence from the state, but that he returned before the property was sold, and
>   that 'because of those conditions the purchasers of said property declined to take the titles to same;
>   but, by agreement made between the said purchasers and mover in rule, and the executor . . . and by defendant, the proceeds were deposited with the sheriff . . . subject to the further orders of court, and with full reservations of right of defendant on same, and the portion received by mover was the half belonging to his [defendant's] deceased wife;
>   that all the balance thereof belongs to defendant, William Johnson, and same should be paid to him.'

¶3   The agreement referred to bears date August 6, 1917, is signed by the attorneys representing plaintiff and defendants in rule (except the sheriff, who was without interest) and the purchasers of the property, and is to the following effect, to wit:

> The purchasers are authorized to pay, and the sheriff to receive, the amounts bid for the property, and the sheriff is authorized to make deeds thereto; the rights of the parties with respect thereto being referred to the proceeds.

> The sheriff is authorized to pay from the proceeds, the taxes due on the property, with interest, and his own costs and commission, and to pay one-half of the balance to Paul Chretien, plaintiff in rule to be applied on his claim, provided the claim equals or exceeds that amount.

The right of Chretien is reserved to make additional claim as an ordinary creditor against the interest of Mary E. James in the property, real, personal, or mixed, that she may have left, for any balance that may be due him.

That the agreement is made-

'without prejudice to the rights of William Johnson, claiming to be the surviving husband of Mary E. James, to assert such rights as he may have in, or to, or against, the property, but, on the contrary, the said Johnson reserves the right, which is hereby asserted, to assert his rights against the said fund, to the same extent that they could have [been] asserted against the property if it had not been sold, it being understood and agreed, however, that the said property shall pass to the respective purchasers thereof free from any claim by said Johnson in, or against, the same. It is further . . . agreed that the said fund shall remain in the hands of the sheriff until the . . . termination of the litigation in which the right to the same shall be involved, and . . . shall thereupon be paid to such person, or persons, as the court may decide entitled to the same.'

¶4   On the trial of the rule, a man who lived across the street from the decedent, and who was called as a witness by plaintiff in rule, testified that he had known decedent for a number of years, and that she never told him that she was married; that he supposed she was unmarried, and called her 'Miss Francis' without being corrected; but, as no one pretends that her name was Francis, the testimony only goes to show that it was a matter of indifference to her by what name the witness addressed her, or, perhaps, that she never observed it. Another witness, called by plaintiff in rule, was a boy, who testified that decedent was his godmother, and that he lived with her for 7 years; that when he gave his testimony he was 14 years old; at one time, that he had left decedent's house and gone to live with his mother about two months before decedent died; at another time, 'during the time I [he] was staying with her, I was 6 or 7 years old.' He also testified that Violet Texada and Cooper Haynes lived at decedent's when he was there, but that he never saw Johnson.

¶5   Violet Texada, decedent's grown sister, and Cooper Haynes (or 'Hynes,' or 'Hines'), the husband of her grandmother, testified that they lived at decedent's house, and corroborated Johnson's story of the marriage and the maintenance of the marriage relation. The marriage is, however, established by unchallenged documentary evidence. Neither the mother nor the grandmother of decedent, nor Sarah Johnson, her daughter, all mentioned in her will, were called as witnesses, nor was the executor; and, although the attorney named in the will testified that he and certain clients of his were the owners of the notes, sued on in the name of Paul Chretien, and that Chretien had no interest in them, he did not testify that he was ignorant of the fact that decedent was a married woman, and his clients were not called as witnesses.

There was judgment in the trial court in favor of plaintiff in rule, and defendant, Johnson, has appealed.

Opinion.

¶6 The purchasers of the property, having been warned of the condition of the title, held up the price until by the agreement between the parties they were able to pay it in safety, which having done, and having received a good title, they have no reason to complain, and are making no complaint. The appellees, who loaned this money upon the security of a mortgage imposed by a married woman, without the knowledge or consent of her husband, upon property which belonged to the community, having been awarded, by the judgment appealed from, as in payment pro tanto of the loans so made by them, not only the one half of the proceeds of the mortgaged property inuring to the succession of their debtor, the deceased wife and partner in community, but also the other half which belongs to the surviving husband, who owes them nothing, now seek to have that judgment affirmed; and they array against the law which denies the wife the power to sell or mortgage the property of the community during the life of the husband the law which declares that no sale or incumbrance of immovable property shall affect third persons unless recorded in the proper office. Whilst, however, the difficulty presented by the apparent conflict thus mentioned may be thought to require a remedy, the doctrine that the one rule is to be taken as an exception to the other is too well settled in our jurisprudence to justify the courts in attempting to supply such remedy. The husband, being head and master of the community, the title to property acquired for it is ordinarily acquired in his name, and yet when the wife dies and the community is thereby dissolved, though the title still stands recorded upon the public records as vested in the husband, and though the death of the wife is not so recorded, a purchaser, guided by the public records, cannot acquire the interest of the deceased wife by a conveyance from the husband, as the apparent holder of the title to the whole. And the same is true where, as in this case, the title stands in the name of the wife and the husband dies; the jurisprudence being as unvarying in the one case as in the other, and being in both cases founded upon provisions which are equally as explicit as those which declare that, as to third persons, the title to real estate is affected by nothing which is not recorded.

***

¶7 As to the alleged laches of the appellant, he appears to be an ignorant seafaring man, who probably could not have read a title if one had been shown him, and who, being told in the short intervals between his voyages that his wife had bought property, made no further inquiry upon the subject. On the other hand, the appellees were represented by an intelligent attorney, who seems to have made it somewhat of a business to lend money for himself and his clients, who knew that a married woman could not legally mortgage community property, and yet who, though on the stand as a witness, has altogether failed to state that he loaned the money here in question to the decedent upon any assurance by her, or any belief of his own, that she was an unmarried woman when the property mortgaged to secure the loans was acquired. The fact that decedent declared in her will that she had never been married appears peculiar, not to say, silly, since she left behind her a sister, mother, grandmother, stepgrandfather, and grown daughter, all of whom knew, or understood, that she had been married, and up to the moment of her death continued to be married, not to mention the record of the marriage in Alexandria, and the surviving husband on the high seas, perhaps homeward bound; but the peculiarity of the statement does not appear to us to affect the rights of the appellees, though it may have been so intended.

¶8 It is therefore ordered and decreed that the judgment appealed from be annulled; that the demands of Paul Chretien, plaintiff in rule, be rejected and his rule dismissed, and that there now be judgment in favor of William Johnson, defendant in rule, and against said Chretien, as also against William W. Wren, executor, and Louis Knop, civil sheriff, decreeing him (Johnson) to be the owner of and directing said sheriff to pay over to him the balance now in his hands of proceeds of sales of immovable property of this succession, amounting to $3,490.74.

¶9 It is further ordered that said Paul Chretien, plaintiff, pay all costs beginning with the rule first filed by him in this matter.

CAMEL V. WALLER 1988
526 SO.2D 1086 (LA.)

CALOGERO, Justice.

¶1 This is a suit for partition by licitation brought by a divorced wife against parties whose chain of title derives from her former husband. She claims to be an owner in indivision of two pieces of immovable property. The properties were purchased by her ex-husband during the marriage and during the existence of a community of acquets and gains. They were sold by him after the community was terminated by judgment of separation from bed and board. In both acquisitions and in the subsequent acts of sale of the two properties the husband declared that he was judicially separated from plaintiff. In fact he and plaintiff were not judicially separated at the time the property was acquired, although they were judicially separated by the time the property was sold.

¶2   The immediate parties to the suit (the plaintiff-wife and the current record owners of the property) agreed by stipulation on the issue to be decided in this case:

> Does the original plaintiff, Elizabeth Langley Camel, have any ownership interest in either unit number 1 or unit number 4 of the French Quarter Court Condominiums and-if so-in what percentage for each unit?

¶3   We granted this writ to decide whether the courts below were correct in dismissing plaintiff's suit for partition by licitation of these two pieces of property.

¶4   Elizabeth Langley Camel and Patrick Camel were married in East Baton Rouge Parish on June 16, 1962. The couple voluntarily separated on August 16, 1975. On December 29, 1975, Patrick Camel purchased Condominium Unit Number 4 in French Quarter Court located in the City of Baton Rouge from JDA Investment Properties, Inc. for the sum of $25,000.00. In the act of sale he declared that he had been "married but once and then to Elizabeth Langley Camel, born Langley, from whom he is judicially separated", when in truth the couple were still married at the time. On that same day, Patrick Camel and one Ellen H. Waller purchased Condominium Unit Number 1 of French Quarter Court Condominiums for the sum of $26,000.00. In that act of sale, Patrick Camel similarly declared that he had been "married but once and then to Elizabeth Langley Camel, born Langley, from whom he is judicially separated."

¶5   On January 12, 1977, a little over a year after the purchases, Elizabeth Camel filed a petition for separation from bed and board on the grounds of living separate and apart. She asked that a temporary restraining order be granted prohibiting Patrick Camel from alienating, encumbering or disposing of any and all community property. The temporary restraining order was granted on January 25, 1977. A preliminary injunction to the same effect was issued on February 3, 1977. On August 22, 1977, the judgment of separation was granted by default. Neither the temporary restraining order, the preliminary injunction, nor the judgment of separation were ever recorded.

¶6   On March 20, 1978, some eight months after the judgment of separation had been granted, Patrick Camel and Ellen Waller sold Unit # 1 to William Walker Squyres for $43,000.00. In the act of sale, Patrick Camel accurately declared that he was then judicially separated from Elizabeth Camel.

¶7   On March 23, 1978, just three days after the sale of Unit # 1 to Squyres, Patrick Camel sold Unit # 4 to Ellen Waller for $33,088.82. In this act of sale, Patrick Camel again accurately declared that he was judicially separated from Elizabeth Camel. Ellen Waller remains as owner of Unit # 4.

¶8   On December 15, 1978 Elizabeth Camel was granted a judgment of divorce. That judgment was recorded on that same date in the Parish of East Baton Rouge.

¶9   Some eight months after the judgment of divorce was rendered, William Squyres sold Unit # 1 to Karen Jayne Barber and Vaughn Barber on August 23, 1979 for the sum of $56,000.

¶10   To date no judicial partition of the community which existed between Patrick and Elizabeth Camel has been effected, nor do the parties contend that there has been a voluntary partition which has settled the couple's rights in these two condominium units.

¶11   On December 7, 1983, Elizabeth Camel filed in East Baton Rouge Parish the lawsuit which is the subject of the district court judgment below and this review, a petition for partition by licitation. She alleged that she was the owner of an undivided one fourth interest in Unit # 1, in common with the record owners, Karen and Vaughn Barber. She also alleged that she was an undivided one half owner of Unit # 4, in common with the record owner, Ellen Waller.

¶12   Plaintiff filed a second amended and supplemental petition in which she alleged the bad faith of defendant Ellen Waller in that "she knew or should have known his (Patrick Camel's) interest in the property was formerly community property ..." and that plaintiff "owned an undivided interest in the units." These allegations of bad faith were later withdrawn by plaintiff in an additional stipulation of facts.

¶13   In the course of this proceeding Ellen Waller moved for summary judgment, as did Karen and Vaughn Barber. Both motions for summary judgment were denied by the trial judge.

¶14   The trial judge rendered judgment in response to the stipulated issue, finding that Elizabeth Camel "has no interest whatsoever in either Unit No. 1 or Unit No. 4 of the French Quarter Court Condominiums." Plaintiff's suit was dismissed with prejudice. On appeal the First Circuit Court of Appeal affirmed the trial court's judgment. 515 So.2d 611.

¶15   A married person's rights in property purchased by the other spouse during the existence of a community vest in that person by operation of law at the time of the acquisition of the property. Thigpen v. Thigpen, 231 La. 206, 91 So.2d 12 (1956); Phillips v. Phillips, 160 La. 813, 107 So. 584 (1926). Thus, plaintiff, although not a named vendee in her husband's acquisition, acquired an interest in the two condominiums not apparent on the public records at or after the time her husband purchased them.

¶16 On the other hand, defendants purchased property on the strength of a public record which was silent regarding plaintiff's interest. The record showed that at the time of the acquisition of the two units Patrick Camel was the vendee and he was judicially separated from Elizabeth Langley Camel. When Patrick Camel and Ellen Waller sold Unit # 1 to William Squyres (who later sold it to defendants Karen and Vaughn Barber) and when Patrick Camel sold Unit # 4 to defendant Ellen Waller, the record reflected the same state of affairs existing then.

¶17 Thus, this case pits a plaintiff relying on longstanding legal principles favoring rights in community property against defendants relying on the public records doctrine. The competition between these conflicting legal principles has been noted in various law review articles and cases. Shapiro v. Bryan, 132 So.2d 97 (La.App. 4th Cir.1961); Comment, Registration of Title to Immovables in Louisiana, 32 Tul.L.Rev. 677, 683-85 (1958); Note, Sales-Community Property-Recordation of Divorce-Articles 2266, 2402, 2406, Louisiana Civil Code of 1870, 24 Tul.L.Rev. 375, 377 (1950); Comment, Recordation Problems in Louisiana Mineral Matters, 23 Tul.L.Rev. 259, 264-65 (1948). See also, Jackson v. D'Aubin, 338 So.2d 575 (La.1976); Speights v. Nance, 142 So.2d 418 (La.App. 2d Cir.1962); Redmann, The Louisiana Law of Recordation: Some Principles and Some Problems, 39 Tul.L.Rev. 491 (1965); The Work of the Louisiana Appellate Courts For the 1962-63 Term: Conventional Obligations, 24 La.L.Rev. 192, 196 (1964); Comment, "Tradition" In the Civil Law, 22 La.L.Rev. 418, 433-34 (1962); Note, Sales-Scope of the Public Records Doctrine-Succession Judgments, 12 La.L.Rev. 51 (1952).

¶18 The outset legal question posed by the parties is whether defendant purchasers may rely, to defeat plaintiff's community property rights and relative to the public records doctrine, upon the marital description given by Patrick Camel in the acts by which he acquired the property in dispute. As noted, he had stated that he was judicially separated.

¶19 The answer, of course, is that such purchaser cannot rely on that declaration of marital status so as to validate the purchaser's acquisition in preference to the interest of the ex-wife. Succession of James, 147 La. 944, 86 So. 403 (1920); Redmann, 39 Tul.L.Rev. at 500. See also, Gulf Union Mortgage Corp. v. Michael & Barber Construction Co., 251 So.2d 459 (La.App. 1st Cir.1971) ("The fact that an instrument is recorded does not have the effect of making all recitals contained therein true." Id. at 462).

¶20 The present statutes establishing the public records doctrine are Civil Code article 1839 and La.Rev.Stat. §§ 9:2721 and 2756.

¶21 Art. 1839, entitled Transfer of immovable property provides:

A transfer of immovable property must be made by authentic act or act under private signature ...

An instrument involving immovable property shall have effect against third persons only from the time it is filed for registry in the parish where the property is located.

La. Civ. Code art. 1839 (1987).

¶22 La.R.S. 9:2721 provides:

No sale, contract, counter letter, lien, mortgage, judgment, surface lease, oil, gas or mineral lease or other instrument of writing relating to or affecting immovable property shall be binding on or affect third persons or third parties unless and until filed for registry in the office of the parish recorder of the parish where the land or immovable is situated; and neither secret claims or equities nor other matters outside the public records shall be binding on or affect such third parties.

La.Rev.Stat. 9:2721 (West 1965).

¶23 La.R.S. 9:2756 provides:

All sales, contracts and judgments affecting immovable property, which shall not be so recorded, shall be utterly null and void, except between the parties thereto. The recording may be made at any time, but shall only affect third persons from the time of the recording.

The recording shall have effect from the time when the act is deposited in the proper office, and indorsed by the proper officer.

La.Rev.Stat.Ann. § 9:2756 (West Supp.1988).

¶24 These three statutes, operating in tandem comprise the public records doctrine as it applies here. See also, La.Rev.Stat.Ann. §§ 9:2721-2733, 2741-2759 (on Registry) (West 1965 & Supp.1988).

¶25 The public records doctrine is "founded upon our public policy and social purpose of assuring stability of land titles...." Blevins v. Manufacturers Record Publishing Co., 235 La. 708, 772, 105 So.2d 392, 414 (1958) (Tate, J. on rehearing). But as Justice Lemmon notes, that doctrine does not "create rights in a positive sense, but rather has the negative effect of denying the effectiveness of certain rights unless they are recorded." Phillips v. Parker, 483 So.2d 972 (La.1986) (Lemmon, J.) Also, as Judge Redmann has so aptly pointed out, it is an essentially negative doctrine. Third persons are not allowed to rely on what is contained in the public records but can instead "rely ... on the absence from the public record of those interests that are required to be recorded." Redmann, The Louisiana Law of Recordation: Some Principles and Some Problems, 39 Tul.L.Rev. 491 (1965). Thus, a third party is not protected by reliance on a recitation of marital status in the public records, Succession of James, supra 147 La. at 944, 86 So. at 403, but can rely on the absence of a claim from the records. State ex rel. Hebert v. Recorder of Mortgages, 175 La. 94, 143 So. 15 (1932); Westwego Canal & Terminal Co. v. Pizanie, 174 La. 1068, 142 So. 691 (1932). "[T]he primary concern of the public records doctrine is the protection of third persons against unrecorded interests." Phillips, 483 So.2d at 976. "[N]o right of any nature in immovable property can have any effect against third parties unless it is registered in the conveyance records or recorded in the mortgage records for the parish in which the property is situated...." Sarpy, Form in Louisiana Contracts Involving Rights in Property, 14 Tul.L.Rev. 16, 25 (1939).

¶26 Thus, the public records doctrine in its operative effect in a case of this sort, does not protect a third party purchaser by permitting him to rely upon a prior purchaser's misstated marital status in the latter's acquisition. But as will be recited in the reasons stated hereinafter, that doctrine does serve to protect these third party purchasers in a case like the one under consideration here.

¶27 The landmark decision of McDuffie v. Walker established the principle that a third person can acquire valid title from the owner of record even where the record owner is not the true owner since an act of sale of immovable property not recorded is null as to third parties. McDuffie v. Walker, 125 La. 152, 51 So. 100 (1909). See also, Bolding v. Eason Oil Co., 248 La. 269, 178 So.2d 246 (1965); Blevins v. Manufacturers Record Publishing Co., 235 La. 708, 105 So.2d 392 (1958); State ex rel. Hebert, 175 La. at 94, 143 So. at 15; Westwego, 174 La. at 1068, 142 So. at 691; Comment, Recordation Problems in Louisiana Mineral Matters, 23 Tul.L.Rev. 259, 259-60 (1948); Note, Sales-Recordation-Contract to Sell-Specific Performance-Article 1517, Louisiana Civil Code of 1870, 22 Tul.L.Rev. 208, 209 (1947). Thus third persons can take any rights to immovables that are free from unrecorded claims. Comment, "Traditio" in the Civil Law, 22 La.L.Rev. 418, 433 (1962).

¶28 This system of registry, designed to protect the security of title to real estate, stands in stark contrast to La. Civ. Code art. 2452's declaration that "the sale of a thing belonging to another is null". La. Civ. Code Ann. art. 2452 (West 1952).

¶29 The right to ownership of property is embedded in our law. La. Const. of 1974, art. 1, § 4; La. Const. of 1921, art. 1, § 2. Yet the public records doctrine has been given effect to the prejudice of the acquiring party where there is an absence of recordation. One type of acquiring party who has drawn special attention in the jurisprudence is the spouse in community. Courts favoring the acquiring spouse who does not appear in a recorded deed have often alluded to the long statutory and jurisprudential legal history that has evolved to ensure the protection of the community property system, e.g., Succession of James, 147 La. 944, 86 So. 403 (1920), a system designed to promote the stabilization and economic protection of the family. T.L. James & Co., Inc. v. Montgomery, 332 So.2d 834, 842 (La.1975); Daggett, Policy Questions on Marital Property Law in Louisiana, 14 La.L.Rev. 528 (1954).

¶30   Also of significant note for the purpose of this opinion is the fact that until the 1979 revision of Book III, Title VI of the Louisiana Civil Code (Matrimonial Regimes) accomplished by 1979 La.Acts, No. 709 (effective Jan. 1, 1980), the marital property law of this state characterized the husband as "head and master" of the community of acquets and gains. Under this scheme, the husband had sole authority to administer community effects and could alienate immovable property belonging to the community without his wife's participation or consent. La. Civ. Code Ann. art. 2404, repealed by 1979 La.Acts, No. 709, § 1 (effective Jan. 1, 1980); Pitre v. Pitre, 247 La. 594, 172 So.2d 693 (1965); Humphreys v. Royal, 215 La. 567, 41 So.2d 220 (1949).

¶31   In spite of her husband's false declaration in the act of acquisition that he was judicially separated at the time of the purchase (in effect, claiming that the property was his separate property), the property here in dispute is presumed to be community property since it was acquired during the existence of the community and since the act did not contain the required double declaration that he purchased the property with his separate funds and for his separate estate. Smith v. Smith, 230 La. 509, 89 So.2d 55 (1956); Slaton v. King, 214 La. 89, 36 So.2d 648 (1948); Succession of Bell, 194 La. 274, 193 So. 645 (1940). But even where the presumption of community applies, as here, the husband as head and master of the community was at liberty to sell community property standing in his name alone without his wife's consent. Azar v. Azar, 239 La. 941, 120 So.2d 485 (1960); Provost v. Harrison, 205 La. 21, 16 So.2d 892 (1944); Demarets v. Demarets, 144 La. 173, 80 So. 240 (1918); Op.Att'y Gen. 1942-44, p. 472.

¶32   It was inevitable that the tenets concerning the matrimonial regime of community property and the public records doctrine, both deeply embedded in this state's legal history, would collide. And of course they did. In Succession of James, 147 La. at 944, 86 So. at 403, this court rejected the argument that the public records doctrine protects the third party mortgagee from the undisclosed interest of a spouse in community, a husband in that case, where the acquiring, and later mortgaging spouse (a wife) declared in both instruments that she was single.

¶33   In the interim between the decision in James and the later decision of this Court in Humphreys v. Royal, the James case was cited as authority only rarely and then never in the context of a contest between community property law and the public records doctrine. Johnson v. Johnson, 213 La. 1092, 36 So.2d 396 (1948); Mathews v. D'Asaro, 14 La.App. 328, 126 So. 246 (1930); Bench and Bar: Trends in Louisiana Law of the Family, 9 La.L.Rev. 89, 100 (1934). However, other decisions reflected the continuing struggle between the two concepts in cases where a claimant's interest in land arose by operation of law on the termination of the community either by dissolution or by the death of one spouse. See, for example, Thompson v. Thompson, 211 La. 468, 30 So.2d 321 (1947); Stone v. Jefferson, 196 La. 1057, 200 So. 461 (1941); Bell v. Canal Bank & Trust Co., 193 La. 142, 190 So. 359 (1939); Chachere v. Superior Oil Co., 192 La. 193, 187 So. 321 (1939); Porterfield v. Parker, 189 La. 720, 180 So. 498 (1938); Long v. Chailan, 187 La. 507, 175 So. 42 (1937), after remand, 196 La. 380, 199 So. 222 (1940); Beard v. Nunn, 172 La. 155, 133 So. 429 (1931); Otis v. Texas Co., 153 La. 384, 96 So. 1 (1922) (reversed on rehearing).

¶34   Then came this court's decision in Humphreys v. Royal, 215 La. 567, 41 So. 2d 220 (1949). The relevant facts were different from those in James. There a husband acquired property during a marriage, declaring in the act of purchase that he was a single man. He then sold, following an unrecorded divorce. But the equities were also different. In Humphreys, it was not the divorced wife who was championing the cause of a wife's rights in community property, but a land speculator who had purchased his interest in the property from the wife.

¶35   The majority in Humphreys did not denigrate the wife's legally operative acquisition, but rather distinguished the James decision by stating that a judgment affecting immovable property had not been rendered in James (the James' community terminated upon the death of the vendee-mortgagor, Mrs. James) while a judgment of divorce had been rendered in Humphreys. The Humphreys majority held, without fuller explanation, that an "unrecorded divorce judgment affecting the immovable property in controversy is utterly null and void as to the defendant here, a third party". Id. at 573, 41 So.2d 222.

¶36   That opinion drew a dissent which complained that the settled law until then had resolved the conflict "in favor of the community owner rather than in favor of the one relying on the registry", and that the majority had permitted "the husband in this case, by his false and untrue statements made in the deeds that he was a single man, to take away from the wife her vested interest in the property." The dissenter, alluding also to James, opined that "it is the duty of a person who deals with a purchaser of immovable property to find out whether he or she was married or single at the date of such purchase." Id. at 575-77, 41 So.2d at 223 (Hawthorne, J., dissenting).

¶37 Humphreys and its legal analysis did not meet with consistent acclaim among the law review writers who discussed the case. See 39 Tul.L.Rev. at 502-04; 32 Tul.L.Rev. at 677; 24 Tul.L.Rev. at 375; Note, Sales-Effect of Recordation on Community Rights, 11 La.L.Rev. 389 (1951). But cf., 22 La.L.Rev. at 433-34; 12 La.L.Rev. at 513. But Humphreys was not wrong in its result, as will be seen hereinafter.

¶38 The debate on the interplay of community property rights and the public records doctrine continued following the Humphreys pronouncement. Head v. Bradley & Braud, Inc., 368 So.2d 723 (La.1979) (Tate, J., dissenting from denial of writs); Hodgeson v. McDaniel, 233 La. 180, 96 So.2d 481 (1957); Bishop v. Copeland, 222 La. 284, 62 So.2d 486 (1952); Gregory v. Womack, 300 So.2d 213 (La.App. 2d Cir.), writ denied, 302 So.2d 622 (1974) (wife had "ample protection of her rights in the property had she complied with the Louisiana laws relating to registry." Id. at 215.); Speights v. Nance, 142 So.2d 418 (La.App. 2d Cir.1962); Shapiro v. Bryan, 132 So.2d 97 (La. App.1961) (wife under duty to record notice of her suit for separation to prevent husband's sale of community property).

¶39 The results in these cases indicate that the law in this area is by no means settled. Furthermore, a recent statutory change in the law may affect the outcome of future similar cases.4 La.R.S. 35:11. We need not consider in this case whether the 1987 amendments to La.R.S. 35:11 are to be afforded retroactive application because plaintiff brought her action well before the six month grace period following the effective date of the statute, in fact, some several years before its enactment.

¶40 We perceive Humphreys and the case at bar to be distinguishable from Succession of James, but for reasons different from those stated by the majority in Humphreys. Furthermore, in the context here involved (prior to the 1980 Revision of Civil Code provisions on matrimonial regimes, and unaffected by 1987 statutory amendments to La.R.S. 35:11 (See footnote 4 supra)), we apply the public records doctrine here favorably to the third party purchaser and contrary to the plaintiff, former wife in community.

¶41 While the purchaser may not rely on the misstated marital status in Patrick Camel's acquisition (that he was judicially separated and thus acquiring for his separate estate), none-theless, a third party purchaser we hold, can rely upon the absence from the public record of the instrument which would have signaled that Patrick Camel was no longer in singular control of property which he might have acquired. That instrument was the judgment which terminated the community. Until such instrument was recorded the purchaser could have assumed that Mr. Camel was judicially separated, as he had declared upon acquisition, or single, in which event he could later sell the property without the participation of a wife or ex-wife, or that he was not judicially separated or single but rather married and living in community, and thus had not lost his right as head and master of the community to dispose of community property alone.

¶42 Unlike Isiah Payne, the husband in Humphreys, Mary James, the acquiring and later mortgaging "femme sole " in Succession of James, had no power to encumber or alienate community property as wife, for under the prevailing law the wife was not head and master of the community.

> "This case (Humphreys v. Royal) is not contrary to the Succession of James. Whereas the wife in the James case had no power to defeat her spouse's vested interest in the community property, the husband in the Humphreys case did have such power, and as far as third parties were concerned recordation of the judgment of divorce, like recordation of a prior sale, was necessary to destroy that power. Article 2266 of the Louisiana Civil Code requires recordation for final judgments as it does for contracts affecting immovable property."

12 La.L.Rev. at 513.

¶43 In the case under consideration, Elizabeth Camel acquired an undivided interest, albeit unrecorded, in the two properties. Yet so long as the marriage existed, her interest was subject to being defeated simply by her husband's act of conveying the community interest. Elizabeth Camel could have alerted third party purchasers to the newly acquired right of joint control attending her undivided co-ownership interest by recording her judgment of separation, if not her injunctions, in the parish "where the land or immovable is situated" (in this case the parish of matrimonial domicile-East Baton Rouge Parish). She did not do so. Consequently, "the judgment affecting immovables", that is, a judgment changing the husband's right to convey alone, to a right of joint control, is not "binding on" and does not "affect third persons". La.Rev.Stat. Ann. § 9:2721 (West 1965). In this context Elizabeth Camel's "claim", the right to enjoy joint control of property owned in indivision, which is "outside the public records" "shall [not] be binding on or affect third persons", La.R.S. 9:2721, and indeed, it is "utterly null and void, except between the parties...." La.Rev.Stat.Ann. § 9:2756 (West Supp.1988).

¶44 Consequently, the absence of the judgment terminating the community, a judgment which created in plaintiff the right to exercise control over formerly community property, permitted third party purchasers to acquire free and clear of her claims the property which her husband as head and master of the community was at liberty to convey alone, absent recorded notice to the contrary.

¶45 We hold, in this context, that plaintiff's interest, which could have been cemented by recordation, is defeated because the public records doctrine prevails.

¶46 The law is well settled that a third person can acquire a good title to immovable property from the owner of record, even though he has been appraised of the equities or rights of others in the property that did not appear of record, in accordance with the law of registry. Bell v. Canal Bank & Trust Co., 193 La. 142, 190 So. 359 (1939) (citing, inter alia, McDuffie v. Walker, 125 La. 152, 51 So. 100 (1909) (other citations omitted)).

¶47 One more noteworthy comment in this case is that recordation of the judgment of divorce after transfer of Unit # 1 (Camel and Waller to Squyres) but before the transfer from Squyres to the Barbers does not require a different result regarding plaintiff's claim against the Barbers. Since Squyres was free to rely on the absence of any recorded instrument evidencing Elizabeth Camel's right of control in the property, he acquired the property in preference to plaintiff's interest and was thereafter at liberty to transfer to the Barbers all the rights in the property which he had acquired.

DECREE

For the foregoing reasons, the judgment of the courts below is affirmed.
AFFIRMED.
LEMMON, J., concurs.
DENNIS, J., concurs with reasons.
DIXON, C.J., respectfully dissents with reasons.

DENNIS, Justice, concurring.
I respectfully concur.

It should be noted that although the recordation of the divorce judgment did not affect the transfer from Squyres to the Barbers, if Patrick Camel were to reacquire the property, then the plaintiff could claim her part.

DIXON, Chief Justice (dissenting in part).
I subscribe to this opinion in principle but dissent from that part which ignores the effect of the recordation of the divorce in the Squyres-to-Barber sale. The unrecorded judgment did not deprive Elizabeth Langley Camel of the ownership of the property; it was void "except between the parties thereto" (R.S. 9:2756) and if Patrick Camel should reacquire the property Elizabeth

could claim her part, because "[t]he recording may be made at any time ..." At the time the Barbers acquired Unit # 1, the Camel divorce was recorded. Unlike Squyres, the Barbers were not entitled to ignore it. R.S. 9:2756 gave the Camels the right to record the judgment "at any time, after which it shall ... affect third persons from the time of recording."

By such an interpretation we would give full effect to R.S. 9:2756.

LOUISIANA REVISED STATUTE 35:11

§ 11. Marital status of parties to be given

A. Whenever notaries pass any acts they shall give the marital status of all parties to the act, viz: If either or any party or parties are men, they shall be described as single, married, or widower. If married or widower the christian and family name of wife shall be given. If either or any party or parties are women, they shall be described as single, married or widow. If married or widow, their christian and family name shall be given, adding that she is the wife of or widow of . . . the husband's name.

B. A declaration as to one's marital status in an acquisition of immovable property by the person acquiring the property creates a presumption that the marital status as declared in the act of acquisition is correct and, except as provided in Subsection C of this Section, any subsequent alienation, encumbrance, or lease of the immovable by onerous title shall not be attacked on the ground that the marital status was not as stated in the declaration.

C. Any person may file an action to attack the subsequent alienation, encumbrance, or lease on the ground that the marital status of the party as stated in the initial act of acquisition is false and incorrect; however, such action to attack the alienation, encumbrance, or lease shall not affect any right or rights acquired by a third person acting in good faith.

D. The presumption provided in Subsection B of this Section is hereby declared to be remedial and made retroactive to any alienation, encumbrance, or lease made prior to September 1, 1987. Any person who has a right as provided in Subsection C of this Section, which right has not prescribed or otherwise been extinguished or barred upon September 1, 1987 and who is adversely affected by the provisions of Subsection C of this Section shall have six months from September 1, 1987 to initiate an action to attack the transaction or otherwise be forever barred from exercising his right or cause of action.

Review Civil Code Articles 2347, 2369.1, and 2369.4. In reading the following case, consider whether Louisiana Revised Statute 35:11 and the revision to the PRD have precluded findings in favor of spouses in community where the registry does not indicate that a spouse retains an interest in the immovable.

IN THE MATTER OF ROBERTSON 2000
203 F. 3D 855 (5TH CIR.)

DENNIS, Circuit Judge:

¶1   This is an appeal by the non-debtor former spouse of the debtor from the judgment by the United States District Court for the Western District of Louisiana affirming a partial summary judgment by the Bankruptcy Court. In its partial summary judgment the bankruptcy court held that the Trustee in bankruptcy could treat the former marital home as property of the bankruptcy estate, rather than as the separate property of the former spouse. The appeal by the non-debtor former spouse raises these issues: (1) whether real property received by the debtor's former spouse in a partition of former community property before the commencement of the bankruptcy case is property of the bankruptcy estate under § 541(a)(2) of the Bankruptcy Code, or, alternatively, (2) whether the Trustee may avoid the partition under section 544(a)(3) as a transfer which would be voidable by a hypothetical purchaser of real property from the debtor at the time of the commencement of the case. Upon the facts established for purposes of the partial summary judgment, we decide both questions in favor of the non-debtor former spouse, reverse the judgments of the district and bankruptcy courts, and remand the case to the district court for further proceedings.

I.

¶2   Gerald Robertson ("Debtor") and Polly Anderson ("Anderson") were married in February 1985. They acquired a family residence in Ouachita Parish, Louisiana, as their community property in 1989. Fleet Mortgage Company ("Fleet") held a mortgage on the community property home. The couple were divorced in January 1994 and the divorce judgment was filed in the Ouachita Parish, Louisiana conveyance records. They entered into a voluntary partition, with court approval, in the form of a consent judgment by the Louisiana Fourth Judicial District Court in Ouachita Parish, Louisiana in February of 1994. In the partition, Anderson acquired the former family residence as her separate property and assumed all liabilities with respect to the home, including the Fleet mortgage debt and tax liens in favor of the United States Internal Revenue Service and the State of Louisiana Department of Revenue and Taxation. The consent judgment evidencing their voluntary partition was rendered and recorded in the state district court. The partition judgment was not filed for registry in the conveyance records of Ouachita Parish.

¶3 In June 1996 Debtor filed a voluntary petition for bankruptcy under Chapter 7 of the Bankruptcy Code. John Clifton Conine ("Trustee") was named trustee of the Debtor's bankruptcy estate. In August 1997 Trustee filed a complaint to sell the former family residence as property of the estate pursuant to 11 U.S.C. § 363. In October 1997 Fleet filed a motion for relief from automatic stay under its rights as the holder of the mortgage on the home. Anderson opposed the Trustee's complaint and subsequent motion for partial summary judgment. In February 1998, the bankruptcy court for Western District of Louisiana entered a partial summary judgment for Trustee, holding that the home was properly included in the bankruptcy estate of Debtor and that Trustee would be permitted to sell the property and distribute the net proceeds according to the interest of the Debtor and Anderson. Anderson timely filed an appeal in the District Court for the Western District of Louisiana, which affirmed the decision of the Bankruptcy Court in July 1998. Anderson timely appealed to this court.

II.

¶4 We review summary judgments de novo, applying the same standards applied by the district court. See Conkling v. Turner, 18 F.3d 1285, 1295 (5th Cir.1994).

A.

¶5 Section 541 of the Bankruptcy Code defines the property of the estate, in pertinent part, as follows:

> (a) The commencement of a case under section 301, 302 or 303 of this title creates an estate. Such estate is comprised of all the following property, wherever located and by whomever held:
>
> (2) All interests of the debtor and the debtor's spouse in community property as of the commencement of the case that is-

***

(B) liable for an allowable claim against the debtor, or for both an allowable claim against the debtor and an allowable claim against the debtor's spouse, to the extent that such interest is so liable.

11 U.S.C. § 541(a)(2)(B).

¶6   Although section 541(a)(2)(B) states that the property of the bankruptcy estate includes all interests of the debtor and the debtor's spouse in community property as of the commencement of the bankruptcy case, neither that section nor any other Bankruptcy Code provision sets forth the criteria for determining whether a particular asset is community property, or, if so, whether the debtor and the debtor's spouse have interests in such property. "The term 'community property' is not defined in the Code, but clearly is used as a term of art referring to that certain means of holding marital property in those states which have adopted a community property system." (citations omitted) Generally, Congress has left the creation and definition of property interests of a debtor's bankruptcy estate to state law. See Butner v. United States, 440 U.S. 48, 54, 99 S.Ct. 914, 59 L.Ed.2d 136 (1979). The Court in Butner stated:

> Property interests are created and defined by state law. Unless some federal interest requires a different result, there is no reason why such interests should be analyzed differently simply because an interested party is involved in a bankruptcy proceeding. Uniform treatment of property interests by both state and federal courts within a State serves to reduce uncertainty, to discourage forum shopping, and to prevent a party from receiving "a windfall merely by reason of the happenstance of bankruptcy".

440 U.S. at 55, 99 S.Ct. 914 (quoting Lewis v. Manufacturers National Bank, 364 U.S. 603, 609, 81 S.Ct. 347, 5 L.Ed.2d 323 (1961)).

* * *

¶7   This Circuit has interpreted Butner to extend deference to state law whenever Congress has the authority to regulate an area under its bankruptcy powers but has chosen not to do so.

* * *

¶8   Under Louisiana law, unless spouses provide otherwise by matrimonial agreement, the legal regime of community of acquets and gains applies to them. LA. CIV.CODE ANN. arts. 2327-2329 (West 1985). Principally, the community property comprises any property acquired during the existence of the legal regime through the effort, skill, or industry of either spouse.

LA. CIV.CODE ANN. art. 2338 (West 1985). During the existence of the community property regime, the spouses may, without court approval, voluntarily partition the community property in whole or in part. In such a case, the things that each spouse acquires are separate property. LA. CIV.CODE ANN. art. 2336 (West 1985).

¶9 The legal regime of community property is terminated by the death or judgment or declaration of death of a spouse, declaration of nullity of the marriage, judgment of divorce or separation of property, or matrimonial agreement that terminates the community. LA. CIV. CODE ANN. art. 2365 (West 1985). After the termination of the community property regime by a cause other than death or judicial declaration of death of a spouse, articles 2369.2-2369.8 apply to former community property until a partition of the former community property or the death or judgment of declaration of death of a spouse. LA. CIV.CODE ANN. art. 2369.1 (West 1999); see also Katherine S. Spaht, Co-Ownership of Former Community Property: A Primer on the New Law, 56 LA.L.REV. 677 (1996).

***

¶10 The partition of the former community property between the former spouses has these effects: (1) the spouses cease to be co-owners of the former community property; (2) the former community assets are divided into separate portions or lots; (3) each former spouse becomes the exclusive owner of a separate portion or lot of the divided assets; and (4) the assets of which each former spouse acquires sole ownership is (sic) reclassified by law as the separate, exclusive property of that former spouse. See LA. CIV.CODE ANN. arts. 1382, 2335, 2336, 2341, 2369.1 (West 1999); LA.R.S. § 9:2801; MARCEL PLANIOL, 1 TRAITE ELEMENTAIRE DE DROIT CIVIL § 2498 (La. State Law Institute trans., 12th Ed.1939); MARCEL PLANIOL, 3 TRAITE ELEMENTAIRE DE DROIT CIVIL §§ 1332-1336, 2367-2410 (La. State Law Institute trans., 11th Ed.1938); AUBRY AND RAU, 4 DROIT CIVIL FRANCAIS § 625 (Carlos E. Lazarus trans., 6th Ed.1953); see generally KATHERINE S. SPAHT & W. LEE HARGRAVE, 16 LOUISIANA CIVIL LAW TREATISE: MATRIMONIAL REGIMES §§ 7.1-7.31 (2nd Ed.1997)(hereinafter SPAHT AND HARGRAVE).

¶11 Prior to the commencement of the present bankruptcy case, the community property regime was terminated, the former community property was partitioned, Anderson received the former family home from the partition as her separate property, and that asset ceased to be either community or former community property. A final judgment of divorce was entered in January 1994, dissolving the community but not partitioning the former community property. The judgment of divorce was recorded in the Ouachita Parish, Louisiana conveyance records in January 1994. In February 1994, a consent judgment was recited into the record of the court partitioning the former community property between Debtor and Anderson. Under Louisiana law, a consent judgment agreed upon by the mutual consent of the parties and approved by the court is a valid and enforceable judgment. La. Civ.Code Ann. art. 3071, 3078; see Adams v. Adams, 529 So.2d 877 (La.App. 4th Cir.1988) (citing Felder v. Georgia Pacific Corp., 405 So.2d 521 (La.1981)); In re Stouder, 164 B.R. 59, 63 (E.D.La.1994) ("[t]he consent judgment partitioned the proceeds of the sale of the former community residence ... [i]t is binding between the parties and enforceable as a partition of ... the community property."). The consent judgment recited into the record of the court therefore acted to partition the former community property between Anderson and Debtor, thus ending the former spouses co-ownership of the former community property, removing it from the former community property regime and causing the partitioned property to become the separate property of the spouses. See Crais v. Crais, 737 So.2d 785 (La.App. 4th Cir.1999); see generally 59A Am.Jur.2d Partition § 143 (1987). Thus, under the plain meaning of section 541(a)(2), Anderson's partitioned, separate property could not be included in Debtor's bankrupt estate as it was not community property at the commencement of the case.

¶12 The Trustee does not seriously dispute the conclusion that the partition vested the Debtor's former spouse with total separate ownership of her home prior to the petition date. He argues, however, that under Civil Code article 2357 Anderson's separate property home remains subject to debts which she incurred jointly with her former spouse during the community property regime, and that section 541(a)(2)(B) has the effect of making all property liable for such debts part of the bankruptcy estate. Article 2357, in pertinent part, provides that "[a]n obligation incurred by a spouse before or during the community property regime may be satisfied after termination of the regime from the property of the former community and from the separate property of the spouse who incurred the obligation." Thus, a creditor's right under state law to have such an obligation satisfied from her separate property under Article 2357 is not affected by the partition. See also La.R.S. § 9:2801(c). It does not follow, however, that separate property of the non-debtor spouse passes to the bankruptcy estate under section 541(a)(2) simply because it is subject to a pre-termination community creditor's claim under state law.

* * *

¶13 We agree with the prevailing view that former community property which has been partitioned and classified as separate property of the debtor's former spouse under state law prior to the commencement of the case does not pass into the bankruptcy estate.

* * *

B.

¶14   Alternatively, the Trustee argues that, as trustee of the Debtor's bankruptcy estate, he has, under the "strong-arm" provisions of section 544 of the Bankruptcy Code, the rights and powers of a bona fide purchaser of real property from the debtor to avoid any transfer of the property of the Debtor, including the transfer by partition to Anderson of the family homestead as her separate property. Section 544, in pertinent part, provides:

> (a) The trustee shall have, as of the commencement of the case, and without regard to any knowledge of the trustee or of any creditor, the rights and powers of, or may avoid any transfer of property of the debtor or any obligation incurred by the debtor that is voidable by-
>
> ***
>
> (3) a bona fide purchaser of real property, other than fixtures, from the debtor, against whom applicable law permits such transfer to be perfected, that obtains the status of a bona fide purchaser and has perfected such transfer at the time of the commencement of the case, whether or not such purchaser exists.

11 U.S.C. § 544(a)(3).

¶15   Under section 544(a)(3) the trustee has the right and power, as of the date of the commencement of the case, to avoid any lien or transfer avoidable by a hypothetical bona fide purchaser of real property of the debtor as of the date of the commencement of the case. These rights and powers are conferred on the trustee by federal law. See COLLIER ¶ 544.02 at 544-5 (citing Commercial Credit Co. v. Davidson, 112 F.2d 54 (5th Cir.1940)). The extent of the trustee's rights as a bona fide purchaser of real property, however, is measured by the substantive law of the state governing the property in question. See Gaudet v. Babin (In the Matter of Zedda), 103 F.3d 1195 (5th Cir.1997); COLLIER ¶ 544.02 at 544-5; 3 NORTON ON BANKRUPTCY ¶ 54.3 at 54-9, n. 22 (citing In re Clifford, 566 F.2d 1023, 1025 (5th Cir.1978); McKay v. Trusco Finance Co., 198 F.2d 431 (5th Cir.1952)) (hereinafter NORTON).

* * *

¶16   Civil Code article 2347 (1980) provides that "[t]he concurrence of both spouses is required for the alienation, encumbrance, or lease of community immovables...." The purpose of Article 2347 is to "protect one spouse against solo transactions that have the potential of depleting the community-normally transfer or encumbrance of immovables." SPAHT AND HARGRAVE

§ 5.10 at 253. Consequently, because of Article 2347, a third person who attempts to buy real property, that the conveyance records indicate is community immovable property, from one of the spouses without the concurrence of the other cannot by the solo transfer obtain bona fide purchaser status or good title to that property. See SPAHT AND HARGRAVE § 5.10 at 253-257 (citing Louisiana court decisions).

* * *

¶17   On the facts of the present case, a hypothetical buyer of the real property in question from the Debtor as of the commencement of this bankruptcy case could not have achieved bona fide purchaser status. . . .

¶18   The community regime of the Debtor and Anderson was terminated by their judgment of divorce as of the date of filing of the petition in that action on May 21, 1993. LA. CIV.CODE ANN. arts. 102, 103, 159 (effective Jan. 1, 1991). The divorce judgment was recorded in the conveyance records of Ouachita Parish on January 27, 1994 and thus became effective against third persons with respect to former community immovables in that parish from the date and time of its registry. LA. CIV.CODE ANN. art. 1839 (effective Jan. 1, 1984); LA.R.S. § 9:2721.5 Consequently, a solo transfer by the debtor to a hypothetical buyer, of the real property in question, on the June 17, 1996 bankruptcy petition date, would be a relative nullity, would not transfer valid title to such a buyer, and would not enable that buyer to obtain bona fide purchaser status. Thus, the Trustee is not authorized by section 544(a)(3) to exercise the rights and powers of a bona fide purchaser with respect to the real property in question.

* * *

¶19   For the reasons assigned, we conclude that (1) the real property in question became Anderson's separate property home through the partition of the former community property home before the commencement of the bankruptcy case and therefore is not property of the Debtor's bankruptcy estate defined by section 541(a)(2); and (2) the trustee is not entitled to obtain the status of a bona fide purchaser with respect to the real property in question under section 544(a)(3). Accordingly, the judgment of the district court is REVERSED, and the case is REMANDED to the district court, which is instructed to REVERSE the bankruptcy court's judgment and REMAND the case to the bankruptcy court for further proceedings consistent with this opinion.

2. PRD and Rights of Forced Heirs

Study Questions:

The Civil Code treats forced heirs as a protected class, much as it does spouses in community. What does the following case indicate about what may happen in a conflict between the PRD and forced heirs who have been defrauded out of their property? Might they be able to defeat the PRD just as a spouse can, if the third party is not in good faith?

LONG V. CHAILAN 1937

187 LA. 507, 175 SO. 42

O'NIELL, Chief Justice.

¶1   The plaintiffs claim an interest in a tract of land, having an area of 1,070 acres, in the parish of Rapides. They are not in possession of the land, and aver that none of the defendants-and no one else-has possession of any part of it. Hence the suit is said to be of the character which Act No. 38 of 1908 declares 'shall be known as the action to establish title to real estate.'

¶2   The defendants, Thomas O. Wells, Homer V. Smith, Woodward Wight & Co., the Union Central Life Insurance Company, and the Texas Company, filed pleas of (1) nonjoinder, or want of indispensable parties, (2) no cause or right of action; and (3) estoppel. The pleas were argued and submitted on the allegations of the petition, without the offering of evidence. The judge sustained the pleas, and dismissed the suit. The plaintiffs have appealed from the decision. There were other pleas filed, but they are not before the court on this appeal.

***

¶3   In stating the facts of the case we merely repeat, substantially, the allegations of the plaintiffs' petition, assuming, as we must assume, for the purpose of deciding whether the defendants' pleas are well founded, that the facts alleged by the plaintiffs are the true facts. The plaintiffs claim title by inheritance from Mrs. Lou Toler Cole Long, who married Henry F. Long, Sr., on June 24, 1869, and died, intestate, on December 27, 1886, leaving six children-two sons and four daughters-issue of her marriage with Henry F. Long, Sr. . . .

¶4   The plaintiffs aver that the land which they are claiming was bought by Henry F. Long, Sr., from L. P. Noland, on November 23, 1878, by virtue of a deed which was duly recorded and in which the land was described by it boundaries and by reference to the title of the seller, but was said to contain 200 acres, more or less. The plaintiffs aver that the title to the land, which, notwithstanding the area was said to be 200 acres, more or less, is the tract containing 1,070 acres, became the property of the matrimonial community then existing between Henry F. Long, Sr., and Mrs. Lou Toler Cole Long; and that at her death her six children inherited her half interest in the land.

¶5   The plaintiffs aver that, on March 2, 1901 — more than fourteen years after the death of their mother - the sheriff of Rapides parish, acting by virtue of a writ of fieri facias, under a judgment rendered against their father, in a suit entitled Stewart & Haas v. H. F. Long, seized the community property, which their father had bought on November 23, 1878, and sold it to George W. Signor, under the correct description of the 1,070 acres of land. They aver that, on May 5, 1903, George W. Signor made a sale of the 1,070 acres of land, under the correct description, to Mrs. Alice C. Love, who was the daughter of Henry F. Long, Sr., by a previous marriage, and who first married Bert Love and afterwards married Henry Chailan. The plaintiffs aver that Mrs. Alice C. Love knew of their interest in the land and 'connived' to defraud them; and that the claims of all of the defendants in this suit are derived, either directly or by mesne conveyance, from Mrs. Alice C. Love, afterwards Mrs. Chailan. They aver that the sheriff's sale to George W. Signor, and the sale by him to Mrs. Alice C. Love, were null, as far as the plaintiffs' interest in the land was concerned, because the judgment held by Stewart & Haas, to satisfy which the land was seized and sold, was a personal judgment against Henry F. Long, Sr., rendered long after the community was dissolved by the death of Mrs. Lou Toler Cole Long, for a debt which arose after the dissolution of the community, and for which neither she nor her estate was in any way liable. . . .

¶6   . . . The plaintiffs pray that, as far as they are concerned, the sale made by the sheriff to George W. Signor, and the sale by him to Mrs. Alice C. Love, and the sales made by her and by her transferees, and by virtue of which the defendants claim title-and the mortgage held by the Union Central Insurance Company, and the oil and gas lease held by the Texas Company-shall be annulled and set aside, and be cancelled from the records.

¶7   The plea of nonjoinder of the necessary parties as defendants is founded upon the theory that this is an action to annul the sheriff's sale to George W. Signor, and the subsequent sales by which the defendants claim title from Signor. Hence it is contended by the defendants that the sheriff, or his successor in office, and George W. Signor, and all who were parties to any of the subsequent sales, by which the defendants claim title from Signor, ought to be made parties, as defendants, in this suit,-even though such parties have no interest in this controversy.

¶8 It is true that all of the parties to a sale or other transaction are indispensable parties in a suit to annul the transaction. But, strictly speaking, this is not a suit to annul the sheriff's sale to George W. Signor, or the subsequent sales by which the defendants claim title from Signor. The only reason why the sheriff's sale to Signor and the titles emanating therefrom are said to be null, as far as the plaintiffs in this suit are concerned, is that the sheriff sold their property as the property of their father, and for the debt of their father. The suit is based upon article 2452 of the Civil Code, which declares that a sale of property belonging to another person-meaning a person other than the one who sells-is null. That fundamental doctrine is as appropriate to a forced sale, made by virtue of a writ of fieri facias directed against one who is not the owner of the property seized and sold, as it is to a conventional sale made by one who is not the owner of the property. In either case, the true owner of the property, in order to maintain his title, is not obliged to bring an action of nullity against the seller and the buyer, to annul the sale. If the property is real estate, and the party who bought it from one who was not the owner is in possession of it, the owner may bring a petitory action, and let the defendant set up his deed from the one who was not the owner of the property. Of course, if the defendant in a petitory action, or one who is to be made defendant in such an action, holds a deed from one who could have conveyed a valid title-and if the nullity or invalidity in the defendant's title is only a defect in the making of the sale or other transaction by which the defendant claims title-the plaintiff cannot successfully attack the transaction collaterally, but must bring a direct action to annul it, and in such a suit they who were parties to the transaction must be made parties to the suit. Graham v. Hester, 15 La.Ann. 148; Bankston v. Owl Bayou Cypress Co., 117 La. 1053, 42 So. 500; Vinton Oil & Sulphur Co. v. Gray, 135 La. 1049, 66 So. 357; St. John Lumber Co. v. Federal National Bank, 143 La. 693, 79 So. 223; Succession of Todd, 165 La. 453, 115 So. 653. But, if a person who intends to bring a petitory action knows or anticipates that the defendant will depend upon a sale from one who was not the owner of the property, the plaintiff is not obliged to set up the sale and sue to annul it.

***

¶9 We have said that the owner may ignore a sale of his property by one who had no authority to sell it, and may bring a petitory action against the party in possession. By the same token, if the party claiming the property under such a sale is not in possession of it, the owner may bring the action provided for by Act No. 38 of 1908.

***

¶10 Another argument of the defendants in support of their exception of no cause or right of action is that they acquired their titles on their faith in the public records, and that the title which the plaintiffs are asserting was not a matter of record when the defendants acquired their title. The defendants cite the leading case on the subject, McDuffie v. Walker, 125 La. 152, 51 So. 110, maintaining, according to article 2266 of the Civil Code, that a sale or other contract or a judgment affecting immovable property does not affect third persons until it is recorded. So far as that argument has reference to the imperfect description in the deed by which Henry F. Long, Sr., is said to have acquired the property in dispute from L. P. Noland, on November 23, 1878, the argument has reference to the merits of the case. So far as the argument has reference to the fact that the plaintiffs' inheriting a title from their mother was not a matter of record, the argument cannot prevail, because, according to the decisions which we shall refer to hereafter, it is well settled that article 2266 of the Civil Code, or the doctrine of McDuffie v. Walker, is not to be construed so as to defeat the rights of heirs who inherit from their mother her half interest in the community property, bought in the name of her husband.

***

¶11   The Union Central Life Insurance Company makes the further contention that the plaintiffs have no right of action without first tendering to the company the amount of its mortgage. The attorneys for the insurance company cite Denis v. Clague's Syndics, 7 Mart. (N.S.) 93, 96; Stockton v. Downey, 6 La.Ann. 581; McEnery v. Pargoud, 10 La.Ann. 497; and Farquhar v. Iles, 39 La.Ann. 874, 2 So. 791. Denis v. Clague's Syndice maintains merely that a buyer who discovers a defect in his title has not the right to rescind the sale but has the right merely to withhold payment until security is given by the seller. In Stockton v. Downey, and in Farquhar v. Iles, the defendant held title under a sale made in foreclosure of a valid mortgage granted by the owner of the property. McEnery v. Pargoud is not in point, and seems to be not the case intended to be cited. Our opinion is that a tender of reimbursement is not a prerequisite to the bringing of a suit to recover property alleged to have been illegally sold or mortgaged. Reimbursement in such a case is a matter for the defendant to set up as an alternative demand, in compensation. It was so decided in Germaine v. Mallerich, 31 La. Ann. 371; and in Heirs of Burney v. Ludeling, 41 La.Ann. 627, 632, 6 So. 248; and in Nicol v. Jacoby, 157 La. 757, 767, 103 So. 33.

¶12   Our conclusion is that the defendants' exceptions of no cause or right of action are not well founded.

***

¶13   The judgment appealed from is set aside, the exceptions of nonjoinder and of no cause or right of action are overruled, and the case is ordered remanded to the district court for further proceedings consistent with the opinion which we have expressed.

3. PRD and Simulated Sales

Review Articles 2021, 2025 through 2028, and 2035. Article 2028 provides that "Any simulation, either absolute or relative, may have effects as to third persons. Counterletters can have no effects against third persons in good faith." Comments (b) and (c) and (d) are helpful in interpreting how a simulation is treated under the PRD. Comment (b) says that "Under this Article, creditors and bona fide purchasers are among the third persons who may avail themselves of a simulation, but other third persons are not excluded provided they are in good faith." Comment (c) adds that "an act may not be attacked as a simulation against the interest of a third person who have relied on the public records." Finally, Comment (d) stipulates that

> a third person in good faith against whom a counterletter can have no effect . . . is one who does
> not know of the existence of the counterletter. Nevertheless, if the counterletter is not recorded,
> a third person's actual knowledge of it may not deprive him of protection under the principles of
> the Louisiana public records doctrine.

Study Question:

The following case is cited in the comments to Article 2028. With regard to movables, 'good faith' is a prerequisite for protection as a third party purchaser.

Consider, in reading the following two cases, whether Article 2028 provides protection for 'bad faith' purchasers, those who deliberately take advantage of the fact that a counterletter was not recorded – as opposed to those who merely are aware of the existence of a counterletter. Put another way, why specifically did Judge McClendon state that the result was 'harsh' in Tate v. Tate?

CHACHERE V. SUPERIOR OIL CO. 1939
192 LA. 193, 187 SO. 321

FOURNET, Justice.

¶1 This is a petitory action to recover a certain tract of land situated in the Parish of Acadia, State of Louisiana, and for an accounting of all of the oil or other minerals extracted therefrom.

¶2 Plaintiffs claim title as the descendants and heirs of Theodore C. Chachere, Sr., and of Perena Young, his wife, both deceased. For cause of action they allege that Theodore C. Chachere, Sr., on April 5, 1881, after the death of his wife, Perena Young, in March of the same year, acquired

300 arpents of land with funds belonging to the community formerly existing between them, which was never legally alienated by him during his life time, nor by any of his legal heirs since his demise, but that their said ancestor did execute three pretended sales without consideration which were, in fact, donations in disguise-two on January 18, 1897, one to Jackson Chachere for 80 arpents and the other to Aaron Chachere for 120 arpents, the third being executed on November 1, 1901 to Annie Chachere, for the remainder of the said property.

¶3   The defendant George Bradley deraigned his title from Aaron Chachere who acquired the same by the deed from Theodore C. Chachere, Sr., dated January 18, 1897, and the defendant Superior Oil Company is in possession of the property as his lessee. They filed a joint answer admitting the acquisition of the property by plaintiff's ancestor on April 5, 1881, after the dissolution of the community by the death of his wife during the month previous, and denying all other material allegations set out in plaintiff's petition. In the alternative they pleaded prescription acquirendi cause of ten and thirty years.

¶4   There was judgment in the lower court recognizing the title of George Bradley and dismissing plaintiffs' suit at their cost, and they have appealed.

¶5   'This being a petitory action, the plaintiffs must rely on the strength of their own title and not on the weakness of the defendants' title, which is not at issue until the plaintiffs have proved an apparent valid title in themselves.' Cook v. Martin, 188 La. 1063, 178 So. 881, 882, and the authorities therein cited. See, also, Capra v. Viola, 172 La. 731, 135 So. 41, and Doiron v. Lock, Moore & Co., 165 La. 57, 115 So. 366.

¶6   It is the well settled jurisprudence of this state that third persons dealing with immovable property have a right to depend upon the faith of the recorded title thereof and are not bound by any secret equities that may exist between their own vendor and prior owners of the land. Broussard v. Broussard, 45 La.Ann. 1085, 13 So. 699; Adams v. Drews, 110 La. 456, 34 So. 602; Adams v. Brownell-Drews Lumber Co., 115 La. 179, 38 So. 957; Vital v. Andrus, 121 La. 221, 46 So. 217; McDuffic v. Walker, 125 La. 152, 51 So. 100; Sorrel v. Hardy, 127 La. 843, 54 So. 122; Breaux v. Royer, 129 La. 894, 57 So. 164, 38 L.R.A.,N.S., 982; Schneidau v. New Orleans Land Co., 132 La. 264, 61 So. 225; Dalbey v. Continental Supply Co., 165 La. 636, 115 So. 807; Coyle v. Allen, 168 La. 504, 122 So. 596; Stamm Scheele Manufacturing Co., Ltd., v. Fontenot, 171 La. 614, 131 So. 728; Beard v. Nunn, 172 La. 155, 133 So. 429; Caskey v. Standard Oil Company of Louisiana, 181 La. 479, 159 So. 722; Hunter v. Forrest, 183 La. 434, 164 So. 163; Goldsmith v. McCoy, 190 La. 320, 182 So. 519.

***

¶7 For the reasons assigned, the judgment of the lower court is affirmed; appellants to pay all costs.

O'NIELL, C. J., concurs in the result on the ground that the prescription of 10 years is a sufficient defense.

O'NIELL, Chief Justice (concurring in the decree).

¶1 The doctrine of McDuffie v. Walker, 125 La. 152, 51 So. 100, which is founded upon article 2266 of the Civil Code, has no reference to an unrecorded title acquired by inheritance. It has reference only to contracts and judgments affecting immovable property. It was so decided in Long v. Chailan, 187 La. 507, 175 So. 42. There is nothing contrary to that decision in the prevailing opinion in this case.

¶2 I concede, of course, that one who makes a simulated sale of his property will lose it if the person in whose name he has placed the title transfers it to a third party. But I am not so sure that that rule is applicable unqualifiedly to a case where a forced heir is suing to annul a simulated sale made by his ancestor from whom he inherits. In such cases the right of action of the forced heir is founded upon Article 2239 of the Civil Code, which, as amended by Act No. 5 of 1884, reads as follows:

> 'Counter letters can have no effect against creditors or bona fide purchasers; they are valid as to all others; but forced heirs shall have the same right to annul absolutely and by parol evidence the simulated contracts of those from whom they inherit, and shall not be restricted to the legitimate.'

¶3 I have italicized that part of the article which was added by the Act of 1884. This addition is the only amendment that was made by the Act of 1884. Before the article was amended it merely provided that counter letters could have no effect against creditors or bona fide purchasers but were valid as to all others.

¶4 Inasmuch as the prescription of ten years is a sufficient defense to this suit, I consider it unnecessary to decide whether the doctrine of McDuffie v. Walker, which is merely a restatement of Article 2266 of the Civil Code, is applicable to the case.

¶5 I concur, of course, in the opinion that the plaintiffs, by alleging in their petition that their ancestor, Theodore C. Chachere, Sr., bought the land after the death of his wife, have disclosed that they have no right of action as far as their claim by inheritance from Mrs. Chachere is concerned.

TATE V. TATE 2001
42 SO.3D 439 (LA.APP. 1 CIR.)

GAIDRY, J.

¶1 In this case, the plaintiff appeals a trial court judgment dismissing her petition to rescind the sale of immovable property to defendant for failure to pay. We affirm.

FACTS AND PROCEDURAL HISTORY

¶2 On February 15, 2001, Iris Hopkins Tate executed an act of cash sale whereby she sold a tract of land containing her house and an apartment to her daughter, Pauline Tate, for $70,000.00. On the same date and before the same notary and witnesses, Iris and Pauline executed a counterletter declaring that although the parties had executed an act of cash sale, "in fact no sum was paid to [Iris] and further it was and is agreed between [Pauline] and [Iris] that [Iris] may reside on the subject property as long as she so desires...." Although the act of sale was recorded in the conveyance records, the counterletter was not.

¶3 On June 24, 2004, Pauline FN1 donated the property to her daughters, Lisa Juban Duvall and Susan Michelle J. Lozier. This donation was recorded in the conveyance records on July 2, 2004 and makes no mention of Iris's right of habitation.

¶4 On July 6, 2004, Iris filed a petition to rescind the February 15, 2001 sale to Pauline, alleging that Pauline never paid anything for the land. The petition also alleged that Lisa had threatened to use her mandate to act for Pauline to transfer the property to "other unnamed individuals." Consequently, Iris sought a restraining order to prevent the sale or transfer of the property or her removal from the property. Finally, Iris sought lost rental income from Pauline for the time period that Pauline lived in the apartment on the property rent-free. The trial court issued a temporary restraining order on July 28, 2004, prohibiting Pauline, her heirs, assigns or attorneys or anyone acting on their behalf from removing Iris from the property or from selling, transferring, or otherwise alienating the property.

¶5   On August 5, 2004, Susan donated all of her interest in the property to Lisa, and on August 6, 2004, Lisa transferred her ownership interest in the property into a limited liability company called Justification, L.L.C. Lisa was the sole member of Justification, L.L.C.

¶6   Justification, L.L.C. subsequently intervened in the suit filed by Iris. The intervention alleged that the act of cash sale executed by Iris and Pauline was actually a disguised dona- tion, as evidenced by the counterletter, and no money was owed. Justification, L.L.C. sought a declaratory judgment recognizing it as the rightful owner of the property at issue and also filed a cross claim against Iris for damages resulting from her permitting her grandson to live in the apartment on the property.

¶7   The trial court rendered judgment on April 7, 2008 decreeing that, pending resolution of the other matters, Lisa had the discretion to use the apartment as she chose, and anyone occu- pying the apartment was ordered to vacate by April 15, 2008.

¶8   The matter proceeded to bench trial, and at the close of Iris's case, the court granted Pauline's motion for directed verdict, finding that Iris had not carried her burden of proof to rescind the sale, and dismissed Iris's claims against Pauline. This appeal followed.

DISCUSSION

***

¶9   In determining whether involuntary dismissal should be granted, the appropriate stan- dard is whether the plaintiff has presented sufficient evidence on his case-in-chief to establish his claim by a preponderance of the evidence. Robinson v. Dunn, 96-0341 p. 4 (La.App. 1 Cir. 11/8/96), 683 So.2d 894, 896, writ denied, 96-2965 (La.1/31/97), 687 So.2d 410. Proof by a prepon- derance simply means that, taking the evidence as a whole, the evidence shows the existence of the fact or cause sought to be proved is more probable than not. McCurdy v. Ault, 94-1449 pp. 5-6 (La.App. 1 Cir. 4/7/95), 654 So.2d 716, 720, writ denied, 95-1712 (La.10/13/95), 661 So.2d 498.

¶10   An involuntary dismissal should not be reversed by an appellate court in the absence of manifest error. Robinson, 96-0341 at p. 4, 683 So.2d at 896. Accordingly, in order to reverse the trial court's grant of involuntary dismissal, we must find, after reviewing the record, that there is no factual basis for its finding or that the finding is clearly wrong or manifestly erroneous. See Stobart v. State, through Dep't of Transp. and Dev., 617 So.2d 880, 882 (La.1993). The issue is not whether the trial court was right or wrong, but whether its conclusion was reasonable. Id.

¶11 A contract is a simulation when, by mutual agreement, it does not express the true intent of the parties. La. C.C. art.2025. When the parties enter into a contract, but intend for that contract to produce no effects between them, the contract is an absolute simulation and has no effects between them. La. C.C. art.2026. Where the parties intend that their contract shall produce effects, although different from those effects recited in their contract, the contract is a relative simulation. A relative simulation will produce the effects intended by the parties if all requirements for those effects have been satisfied. La. C.C. art.2027.

¶12 It is clear from the counterletter executed by the parties that they did not intend for the transaction between them to be a sale, but rather a donation. Thus, the contract was a relative simulation, and as such, will only constitute a valid donation if all the requirements for a donation have been satisfied.

¶13 At the time the act of cash sale and counterletter were executed in this matter, the Civil Code contained the following form requirements for inter vivos donations: Inter vivos donations of immovable property must be made by authentic act must contain a detailed description of the property given, and must be accepted by the donee in precise terms.

¶14 The "precise terms" requirement of article 1540 obligates a donee to use express, formal, and unconditional language in his acceptance; in other words, an explicit acceptance is required. In re Succession of Jones, 43,365 p. 2 (La.App. 2 Cir. 6/4/08); 986 So.2d 809, 810, writ denied, 08-2023 (La.12/12/08), 996 So.2d 1117. Although there are no ritual words required, there must be some explicit language to signify acceptance. A signature alone cannot be construed as an acceptance, and acceptance cannot be inferred from the circumstances. Id., 43,365 at p. 3, 986 So.2d at 811.

¶15 Neither of the two documents executed by Iris and Pauline contains language which would suffice as an acceptance of a donation, and Pauline's signature alone on the two documents is insufficient to constitute acceptance. As such, there was no valid donation of the property from Iris to Pauline.

¶16 Nevertheless, unrecorded counterletters can have no effect against third parties. La. R.S. 9:2721(A).FEven a third party with actual knowledge of a counterletter is not deprived of the protections of the public records doctrine when the counterletter is unrecorded. La. C.C. art.2028, Revision Comments-1984 (d). Accordingly, Justification, L.L.C., the record owner of the property, is protected in its ownership by the failure of the parties to record the counterletter.

***

CONCLUSION

¶17 For the reasons set forth hereinabove, we affirm the trial court judgment granting an involuntary dismissal of plaintiff's claims. Costs of this appeal are assessed to plaintiff, Iris Hopkins Tate.

AFFIRMED.

***

McCLENDON, J., concurs and assigns reasons.
While the result in this matter seems harsh, I believe that the opinion is legally correct.

4. The Scope of the Public Records Doctrine

Article 3338 stipulates that an option, right of first refusal, contract to buy, real right in, or lease of an immovable is without effect as to a third person unless the instrument is registered. However, once one of those rights is recorded, subsequent effects need not be recorded – "a matter of capacity or authority, the occurrence of a suspensive or resolutory condition, the exercise of an option or right of first refusal, a tacit acceptance . . . are effective as to a third person although not evidenced of record."

Study Question:

Is the following case consistent with Articles 3338 and 3339?

AVENUE PLAZA, L.L.C. V FALGOUST 1995
654 SO. 2D 838 (LA. APP. 4TH CIR.)

LANDRIEU, Judge.
¶1 Appellants, Sandra Falgoust and Carl Chastant, appeal the trial court decision which applied the public records doctrine in granting Appellee, Avenue Plaza, L.L.C.'s eviction suit. We affirm.

¶2 Appellants operate a beauty salon (approximately 644 square feet) in property owned by Avenue Plaza located at 2115 St. Charles Avenue. This property was originally leased to the appellants by Mora-Osborne Garden District Apartments Partnership for a ten year period to commence on September 1, 1981. This lease was properly recorded. The lease contained a provision giving the appellants an option to renew the lease for an additional ten years at the expiration of its original term.

¶3   In a certified letter addressed to "Manager" of Avenue Plaza, dated April 3, 1991, appellants attempted to exercise their option to renew the September 1, 1981 lease for an additional ten years, and they continued to operate their salon on the property. This instrument was never recorded.

¶4   Ocean Development Group, Inc., the owners following the original lessor, sold the property to Avenue Plaza on February 11, 1993 and all transfers of the property were made subject to an assignment of leases clause. Again, at the time of the transfer to Avenue Plaza and, at all times prior to that transfer, it is undisputed that no instrument evidencing appellants' attempt to exercise its option to renew was recorded in the Conveyance Records of Orleans Parish. The trial court held that Avenue Plaza was not bound by this unrecorded option and consequently granted the eviction against appellants.

¶5   The manner in which to exercise the option to renew the lease for an additional ten years was set forth in the original lease. The lease required the lessee to give the lessor written notification by certified mail at 2111 St. Charles Avenue, New Orleans Louisiana regarding its intention to exercise the option not less than 120 days prior to the expiration of the primary term. Appellants contend that they exercised this option by mailing a certified letter to the "manager" of Avenue Plaza at the appropriate time. The returned receipt was made part of the record. Avenue Plaza argues that this letter did not amount to exercising the option because it was not mailed to the then lessor as required by the terms of the original lease, but rather generally addressed to the "manager." The trial court did not pass on this issue.

¶6   While there is disagreement concerning whether the option to renew the lease was properly exercised, we find the resolution of this issue unnecessary. Even if the appellants properly exercised this option, the renewal was never recorded. Thus, the sole issue on appeal is whether the trial court erred in its determination that an unrecorded option to renew was not binding on the third party purchaser of the property.

¶7   The public records doctrine clearly provides that in order for an instrument of writing relating to immovable property to bind a third party, that writing must be filed for registry in the office of the parish recorder in the parish where the land is situated. La.Rev.Stat.Ann § 9:2721 (West 1991). Further, the Louisiana Supreme Court set forth that the public records doctrine is essentially a negative doctrine and what is not recorded is not effective except as between the parties and, the actual knowledge by third parties of unrecorded interests is immaterial. Dallas v. Farrington, 490 So.2d 265, 269 (La.1986).

¶8   Accordingly, this Court has held that the exercise of a renewal option must have been recorded to be binding on a third party. Julius Gindi and Sons v. E.J.W. Enterprises, 438 So.2d 594, 596 (La.App. 4th Cir.1983). In Julius Gindi and Sons, the lessee argued that the purchaser of the property had a duty to inquire beyond the public records as to whether the renewal option had been exercised because on the face of the lease it was evident that the extension may have been exercised. Alternatively, the purchaser argued that its duty was limited to an investigation of the public records, and that because the renewal was not recorded it is not binding on the parties. This Court held that the inquiry ended with a review of the public records, and as the exercise of the option to renew had not been recorded, it was not binding on the subsequent purchaser.

¶9   Here, much of the same arguments are being urged. Appellants rely primarily on two cases; Port Arthur Towing Co. v. Owens-Illinois, Inc., 352 F.Supp. 392 (W.D.La.1972), and Thomas v. Lewis, 475 So.2d 52 (La.App. 2nd Cir.1985). Both cases essentially held that the existence of an option to renew in a lease required the purchaser to look outside of the public record to determine the status of that option. We disagree.

¶10   As we stated in Julius Gindi and Sons, the dictates of Louisiana law limits the duty of inquiry to the public records because unrecorded instruments have no effect on third parties; such an inquiry "would be fruitless for even if something did exist it would not be binding on third parties." 438 So.2d at 596.

¶11   For the foregoing reasons, we affirm the decision of the trial court.

AFFIRMED.

C. The PRD and Public Policy

Study Question:

In the following excerpt from a student comment, the author asserts that the revision has changed the public records doctrine into a "pure race" system. Do you agree? Or do the jurisprudential exceptions refute his claim? Assuming that he is correct, compare the potential harmful effect of a pure race system as against the potential harmful effect of an ineffective, inefficient system, as described by celebrated economist Hernando de Soto in the summary that follows.

COMMENT, OF REGISTRY: LOUISIANA'S REVISED PUBLIC RECORDS DOCTRINE

BY MICHAEL PALESTINA, 53 LOY. L. REV. 989, 995-998 (2007)

B. Philosophical Foundation and Basic Rules

The purpose of any recordation system is two-fold and represents a balance between two otherwise competing objectives. First, a system of public recordation should provide both security and stability for the property rights of owners. Second, it should facilitate the transfer of property between buyers and sellers such that property remains in commerce.

In order to accomplish these objectives, the American common law of property traditionally operated by a single rule: first in time, first in right. This system was very simple: whoever first acquired their interest prevailed over any interest later acquired. Over time, however, most states recognized the injustice inherent in such a draconian, absolute system, and adopted modified systems to deliver a sense of fairness by affording protection to recording first purchasers and by creating the bona fide (subsequent) purchaser doctrine. Generally, a bona fide purchaser is a subsequent purchaser who pays value for the property and has no notice of any kind of prior unrecorded claim on said property. Louisiana, however, did not evolve like most states, and today uses a modified version of the original common law system known as the pure-race system, wherein the first person to record is considered the owner of record. The pure-race system could be described as "first in time (to record), first in right."

Pure-race systems, however, are not all the same. Under the traditional pure-race system, the first purchaser for value to record his interest prevails, and non-record notice is irrelevant. Thus, traditional pure-race systems require a subsequent transferee to be a purchaser, but not to be bona fide. However, under the post-Revision recordation provisions, Louisiana is now one of only two states-the other being Delaware-that requires neither bona fide status nor value to invoke the protection of the PRD.

One hallmark of Louisiana's pure-race system, as with all pure-race systems, is the irrelevancy of non-record notice. With the Revision, Louisiana has conclusively legislated the "bona fide" requirement out of the bona fide purchaser doctrine. A subsequent purchaser is imputed to have only record notice, and is required only to check the public records for prior interests; he can assume, for all legal purposes, that the owner of record is the owner, regardless of any non-record notice he might have to the contrary, even actual notice that another person has a prior, unrecorded interest in the property. Thus, for third parties, an unrecorded instrument, for all intents and purposes, does not exist. Rather, third parties "need look only to the public records to determine [the existence of] adverse claims." To illustrate, assume Owner (O) sells Blackacre to Purchaser 1 (P1), who does not record his interest, and O subsequently resells Blackacre to Purchaser 2 (P2), who records his interest. Because Louisiana recognizes only record notice, P2 is the owner of Blackacre, even if he had non-record notice that O had previously sold Blackacre to P1. [However, if P1 had recorded his interest, P2 would be without recourse, because he would have had record notice.

The other hallmark of Louisiana's pure-race system, shared by only one other state, is the irrelevancy of value in the face of record notice. The traditional purpose of any recordation system, pure-race or otherwise, is the protection of either the current owner who recorded or a subsequent purchaser who relied on the record, the theory being that the subsequent purchaser deserves protection because he has relied on the public records to his detriment (i.e., to his financial risk). With the Revision, Louisiana has legislated the purchaser requirement out of the bona fide purchaser doctrine. In other words, under Louisiana's revised pure-race system, O can sell Blackacre to P1; and if P1 were to fail to record his purchase, O could then give Blackacre to Anyone (A), and A would become owner of Blackacre upon recordation. Under this system, A is protected despite the fact that he has not purchased for value—i.e., despite the fact that he has not relied on the public records to his detriment.

Therefore, under post-Revision Louisiana law, a subsequent transferee need not be bona fide in status nor pay value for his interest, thereby removing the only protections afforded a Louisiana first purchaser—protections that first purchasers in notice and race-notice jurisdictions still enjoy. In these alternative jurisdictions, a subsequent purchaser would have to both pay value and have no notice of any kind (record or actual) of any prior claim to the property to receive the protection of the PRD.

Nonetheless, despite this apparent injustice, the pure-race system has its benefits. Pure-race statutes are easier to administer because they minimize the potential for confusion. The criterion for determining ownership is simple, objective, and not open to judicial determination: whoever recorded first is the owner. This system also reduces the amount of litigation involved in title disputes, and, for the most part, is the best means of ensuring clear and unencumbered title such that property can remain in commerce. Consequently, land titles are almost always straightforward and seldom subject to litigation. Because it "limits inquiry to matters of record only and does not require [a] subsequent purchaser to establish that he took title without notice," the pure-race system is, in fact, the most judicially efficient and economical system available.

C. Purpose & Scope of Revision

To create this specific brand of pure-race system, the Louisiana Legislature, in Act 169 of 2005, passed the most sweeping Revision of the PRD in recent Louisiana history. Act 169 completely reorganized and consolidated the articles relating to recordation, critically changed their substance, and significantly altered their application.

The purpose of the Revision was two-fold. Arguably, the main purpose was clerical. As a result of the fragmented development of Louisiana's PRD, its codal organization was haphazard at best, lacking any pretense of uniformity or cohesion. Prior to the Revision, Code articles addressing the recordation requirement for acts affecting immovables were found in Revised Statutes sections 9:2721 through 2759. Other errant articles dealing with specific juridical acts were scattered haphazardly throughout the Code. Finally, more articles dealing with technical requirements such as form, content, and effect of recordation could be found in sections thirty-five and forty-four of the Revised Statutes. As a result, conflicting codal provisions were common, and judicial decisions, often based on similar fact patterns, were incongruous.

This organizational problem was largely solved by a mass repealing, amending, and reenacting scheme wherein a number of the Revised Statutes and errant Code articles were either repealed or significantly amended, and a new Title of the Code was created. Now, almost all of the basic provisions are in Title XXII-A, Of Registry, located in Book III of the Code, and consisting of articles 3338-3368, supplemented slightly by a few remaining Revised Statutes.

The other major purpose of the Revision was philosophical in nature. Over years of application, judicial decisions had imbued the pure-race system with the concept of non-record notice. The legislature, through the work of the Louisiana State Law Institute, rectified the inconsistencies. The result was a wholesale rejection of non-record notice. The legislature also removed the distinction between transfer via onerous sale and gratuitous disposition, thereby eliminating the value requirement as well. In short, the legislature turned back the hands of time and imposed on the state the purest of pure-race systems. While in this regard the Law Institute should be credited for doing a thorough job at eliminating any incongruencies that might plague the pure-race system in the future, with this reality comes rigid application and often unjust results.

***

C. The Post-Revision Law

Thus, at the time of the Revision, Louisiana courts generally disregarded non-record notice, often doing so even where there was reference to an unrecorded document in a recorded instrument. The post-Revision law removes whatever confusion there was regarding the issue. In short, non-record notice is simply not relevant to determining who will be afforded the protection of the public records. The public records (record notice) represent the only source of notice for the purposes of the PRD. If an interest is recorded, a third party is considered to know of that interest and purchases at his risk; if an instrument is not recorded, it simply does not exist with regard to third parties.

Article 3338 provides that rights and obligations that must be recorded are "without effect as to a third person unless the instrument is registered." There is reference only to record notice. Article 3343 defines a third person as "a person who is not a party to or personally bound by an instrument" or "a witness to an act." This construction defines a witness to a prior unrecorded act, who must therefore possess non-record notice of the act, as a third party who can invoke the protection of the PRD, thereby impliedly rejecting non-record notice. With regard to unrecorded documents referenced in recorded instruments, article 3338 specifically states that any "instrument that modifies, terminates, or transfers the rights created or evidenced" by a recorded instrument must be recorded to have effect against third parties. Any referenced document falls within this category, and needs to be recorded.

The new state of affairs appears concrete. The legislature has codified the jurisprudential rejection of non-record notice. Thus, a Louisiana purchaser who has actual, inquiry, or imputed notice that an unsophisticated buyer has purchased property but neglected to record his interest can nonetheless take advantage of a gap in the law to the disadvantage of that unsophisticated buyer.

However, the rejection of non-record notice is anomalous, as such notice is recognized throughout much of Louisiana property law. By rejecting non-record notice, the legislature has created a false dichotomy of notice requirements: the notice applicable to all other property functions (like possession and prescription) is now completely different from the notice applicable to recordation. Therefore, one cannot help but wonder how long this fabrication will be allowed to stand. Unfortunately, for now, it appears the new law is relatively airtight, and the best recourse available to the unsophisticated buyer in Louisiana is a change in the law.

However, in the absence of such change, the injured unsophisticated first purchaser must be afforded some form of recourse. Because there is a dearth of remedies available under the PRD, a significant burden is placed on alternative solutions, and Louisiana law does provide limited remedies for the disenfranchised first purchaser. For example, article 1983 stipulates that any contract must be performed in good faith. Therefore, when O sells Blackacre to P1 and then again to P2, having full knowledge of his double sale, O is in bad faith, and contractually liable. Furthermore, in a good faith sale, the seller impliedly promises not to sell the same property again and not to empower a subsequent purchaser to defeat the first purchaser's interest; any breach of this promise would lead to liability based on fraud, misrepresentation, and unjust enrichment.

Moreover, with regard to the sale of leased premises, the lessor-seller is bound by article 2700 to warrant the lessee's peaceful possession of the leased immovable. Whenever a lessor interferes with a lessee's peaceful possession—for example, by selling the premises without protecting the lessee's rights—he is in breach of his warranty obligation. Furthermore, article 2711 states that the sale of a leased immovable does not terminate the lease as between the lessor and lessee; therefore, under article 2712, the lessee would have "an action against the lessor for any loss the lessee sustained as a result of the transfer." Finally, when the seller or lessor-seller is in bad faith, article 1997 provides for recompense for all damages, foreseeable or not, that are the direct consequence of the double seller's intentional and malicious failure to perform.

Nonetheless, regardless of damages, the unsophisticated buyer or lessor can be forcibly evicted from his property, and no amount of damages is likely to make him truly whole. Furthermore, P1 would be completely unable to recover from an original owner who has left the jurisdiction—a situation that would not be unexpected given his potential liability—or who is judgment-proof by reason of insolvency. Therefore, the PRD doctrine should itself be amended to provide direct protection for a first purchaser against subsequent purchasers with notice.

Comment on Hernando de Soto

The Peruvian economist Hernando de Soto published an empirical study of systems of property in developing nations entitled The Mystery of Capital: Why Capitalism Triumphs in the West and Fails Everywhere Else (2000). He concluded:

"Nearly every developing and former communist nation has a formal property system. The problem is that most citizens cannot gain access to it, and their only alternative, consequently, is to retreat with their assets into the extralegal sector where they can live and do business. Because ownership of assets is difficult to trace and validate and is not governed by legally recognizable rules, even though these entrepreneurs work hard, those in the extralegal sector are commercially and financially invisible. So, for example, in Haiti before the 2009 earthquake, untitled rural and urban real estate holdings were together worth some $5.2 billion, i.e. four times the total of all the assets of all the legally operating companies in Haiti, nine times the value of all governmentally owned assets, and 158 times the value of all foreign direct investment. Because these assets are not registered or legally recognized, they become 'dead capital,' meaning that the extralegal entrepreneurs cannot use them to obtain loans to grow their businesses, the property can be sold out from under them, and they have little or no recourse against those who victimize them. Because extralegal entrepreneurs cannot lure investors by selling shares, they cannot secure low-interest formal credit because they do not even have legal addresses. They cannot reduce risks by declaring limited liability or obtaining insurance coverage. The only 'insurance' available to them is that provided by their neighbors and the protection that local bullies or mafias are willing to sell them. Moreover, because they live in constant fear of government detection and extortion from corrupt officials, they split and compartmentalize their production facilities between many locations, thereby rarely achieving economy of scale, and thus such nations are trapped in a cycle of poverty."

De Soto added that a major difference between the successful developed nations in the West and unsuccessful developing nations is that formal property systems developed over time, approximately 100 years ago, and that in order to bridge this gap, developing nations need to find ways to discover and formalize the informal property systems that are already in place.

Review Notes

Occasionally security of ownership collides with security of transaction when a buyer (in good faith) purchases a thing from someone that did not have the right to sell it. In those instances, if the thing is a movable, the bona fide purchaser doctrine dictates that the buyer gets to keep it. If it is an immovable, then the public records doctrine may similarly dictate that the buyer keeps it – but for a narrow exception. In both cases, the policy decision is that the protection of commerce must take precedence.

Section 1: The Bona Fide Purchaser Doctrine

As provided in Article 522, someone who purchases a corporeal movable in good faith retains ownership of the thing, even if the seller did not have the right to sell it because he obtained it from the proper owner by means of some vice of consent. Good faith is presumed, unless the buyer knew or should have known that the seller was not the owner, under article 523. If the thing was stolen, rather than transferred due to error, fraud, or duress, then the rightful owner can acquire it from the purchaser by reimbursing what the purchaser paid for the thing, if he or she purchased it in good faith at a public auction or from a merchant who customarily deals with those things. Article 524.

Brown & Root:

Plaintiff owned a wheeled loader which was stolen from him. Defendant purchased it from a Houston dealer of used equipment at a low price. The serial numbers had been filed off. Plaintiff argues it should not have to reimburse buyer for the price it paid, claiming that due to the low price and missing serial number, the buyer knew or should have known that the loader had been stolen. The court rejected the argument, finding that good faith is presumed and Brown

& Root had not established sufficient facts to show the purchaser was put on notice that the seller's ownership was questionable because there was more low-priced equipment for sale by the same dealer.

Livestock Producers v Littleton:

Littleton purchased cattle from a seller, and after rebranding them, decided to let them stay with the seller's farm manager – who stole them by illegally reselling them through an auction house. Some of them were traced to a third party. The issue is whether the auctioneer was in good faith in purchasing them from the farm manager, and the court held that he was not, that he should have found the unknown brand suspicious, and therefore had to turn over all proceeds from the cattle he had sold.

Frantz v. Fink:

Both Frantz & Fink were jewelers. Moss, another defendant, made and repaired jewelry. Frantz had entrusted (on two separate occasions) two pairs of diamond earrings to Moss on consignment. Moss, instead, pawned both pairs at two different pawn shops. Fink entrusted 171 small diamonds to Moss to be set in a pin, which he did, but then pawned it at one of the same shops. Fink figured out where his pin was and got back both the pin and the pair of earrings —- he then queried Moss further and obtained Frantz's second pair of earrings. The issue is whether Fink was in good faith. The court held that with regard to the first pair of earrings, he was, and that therefore Frantz would have to reimburse him what he paid the pawn shop in order to get them back. However, with regard to the second pair, by that time, Fink knew that Moss had stolen them, and therefore Fink had to restore them to Franz without reimbursement.

D. Registered Movables

The Bona Fide purchaser doctrine applies to registered movables like cars as well.

Trumbull Chevrolet:

Trumbull accepted a bad check for a group of cars and was able to trace one of those cars to defendant Maxwell. They sued Maxwell, wanting to be declared owner of the car. The court held in Maxwell's favor, finding that Maxwell was in good faith: "where one of two innocent parties must suffer loss through the fraud of another, the burden of such loss is imposed upon the one who most contributes thereto."

With regard to the registered title, La. Rev. Stat 32:706 provides that no sale is final until the purchaser has a certificate of title. If the title is reconstructed, that must be disclosed to the prospective purchaser, and that if no disclosure is given, the buyer is entitled to recover the price plus any fees or taxes. Any violation of this is also sanctionable by prison of up to 6 months and/or fine between $500 and $5000.

Section 2: Immovables and the Public Records Doctrine

Where an immovable is sold, the parties are bound from the time the act is made, but that sale is not effective against third parties until it is filed for registry in the parish where the immovable is located. Article 2442. Filing puts the third person on notice that there was a sale and what the recorded instrument contains; however, the PRD is a negative doctrine: what is NOT there can have effects, but what is registered may or may not be accurate, and it applies whether or not the 3d party purchaser knows about the previous transaction. Thus, Article 3341 stipulates that the recordation of an instrument does not create a presumption that what is recorded is valid, does not create a presumption as to the parties' status or capacity, has no effect unless the law expressly provides for its recordation, and is effective only with respect to immovables located in the parish where the instrument is recorded.

A party to a recorded instrument may not contradict the terms of the instrument to thee prejudice of a third person who, after its recordation acquires an interest in the immovable subject to that instrument. Art. 3342. A this person is one who is not a party to the instrument. Art 3343.

McDuffie v. Walker

This is the most famous PRD case. Walker purchased a small tract of land from McClelland and build a home on it, but neither he nor McClelland ever registered the sale. After McClelland died, his widow sold the tract to McDuffie, who registered the sale. Consequently, the people listed in the registry as having an ownership interest in the property were first McClelland and then McDuffie. Walker did not appear in the registry. When McDuffie sued, the court held that as regarded McDuffie, the sale to Walker was absolutely null (because it was never registered) – even though McDuffie knew when he purchased the tract that Walker lived in a house on it and had lived there for a number of years.

So, under the PRD, as with the bona fide purchaser doctrine, when security of transaction collides with security of ownership, security of transaction wins.

Cimarex Energy v. Mauboules

A careful oil and gas attorney noticed that Mauboules' (his client's) mineral lease contained a clause that he did not recognize and which he thought was fraudulently added to the lease. That clause provided that after the lease ended, the three-year prescriptive period for non-use could be interrupted, and if so, the former lessee had to be paid royalties. The attorney corresponded with the lessee and asked for a recordable instrument evidencing the extinction – when the lease ran out, and discussing the interruption of prescription clause. The owner then entered into a new lease, but negotiations were difficult because of that clause. They finally agreed that the new lessee would defend the case and argue that the clause was fraudulently added, should someone seek to enforce it. Sure enough, "Orange River Group" appeared once Cimarex, the new lessee struck oil. Orange River tried to argue that it was owed royalties because the previous mineral lease, with the prescription interruption clause, was properly registered. The court disagreed: what is not in the record is null with regard to third parties like Orange River, but what is in the record may or may not be valid, and in this case, the owner had a viable argument that the clause was fraudulently introduced into the contract and therefore the issue would have to go to trial.

B. PRD and other Protected Interests

The PRD, as revised in 2005, is purportedly a 'pure race theory' – allegedly, the first purchaser to register their purchase of an immovable wins, as in McDuffie, and the good faith requirement of the 'bona fide purchaser doctrine is irrelevant. However, that is overstated. Good faith is still an issue when it comes to PRD problems involving a spouse in community's unregistered interest or the interest of a forced heir. The issue is, however, whose good faith is at issue. The cases seem to swing back and forth.

Succession of James

A merchant seaman was out at sea for several months at a time, so when his wife registered the purchase and mortgage of a boarding house, she claimed she was single – though the grantor of the mortgage must have known she was married because she had a child, there was extended family around, etc. (this was in 1920). When she died, the mortgage holder tried to seize the property, but Mr. Johnson (the husband) argued that he was a spouse in community and his ½ interest should be recognized before that of the mortgage-holder. The court agreed, saying that the mortgage holder was not in good faith, and therefore Mr. Johnson's interest should be recognized.

Camel v. Waller

Mr. & Mrs. Camel separated, but did not declare a termination of the community regime. During the separation, Mr. Camel purchased to condominiums, one with Ms. Waller, but listed himself as single. Sometime after they were judicially separated, Mr. Camel and Ms Waller sold the first unit to a third party, and Ms. Waller bought the second unit from him, and then sold it to Mr. Squyres, who sold it to Mr. & Mrs. Barber. Ms. Camel sued to have her community interest in both units (or their proceeds) recognized. The court held against her, arguing that she could have (but didn't) recorded her judgment of separation in the parish where the couple lived, and thereby put potential third parties on notice, but she did not do so.

The Supreme court notes that there is a long series of cases between this decision and James, and that one has to examine the factual differences among them to discern any pattern. In James, under the old 'head and master' rule, the wife had no power to purchase immovables, so claiming that she was single was the only way Mrs. Johnson could have purchased the boarding house. There were other cases which found for the spouse in community. To the contrary, however, in Humphreys, a husband (as here) acquired property during the marriage, declaring that he was single, and he sold following an unrecorded divorce. A land speculator purchased the divorced wife's interest and championed her cause – and was unsuccessful.

Louisiana Revised Statute 35:11

This statute states that whenever a notary passes an act, they must give the marital status of all parties, and that declaration creates a presumption that it is correct in the face of an attack by an unrepresented alleged spouse in community. That spouse may, however, overcome that presumption, but that action cannot affect any right or rights "acquired by a third person in good faith."

Consequently, good faith is still a concern when it comes to a collision between the PRD and a spouse in community. The issue, however, is whose good faith? In James, clearly, the court considered the good/bad faith of the mortgage company. In Camel, however, the onus seems to be on Mrs. Camel for not preventing the problem, in the face of the fact that Ms. Waller (the third party) seems to have been Mr. Camel's 'significant other' at the time he purchased the condominiums, and therefore might not have been in such good faith . . . .

In Re Robertson

This is a more recent case (2000) from bankruptcy court involving the clash between the PRD and the community interest. Mr. & Mrs. Robertson acquired a family residence and a mortgage. Several years later they were divorced, that judgment was filed in the correct parish records, and they entered into a voluntary partition of the property under which the former Mrs. Robertson acquired the home as well as the mortgage and tax lean. That partition was recorded in court, but not filed for registry.

Two years later, Mr. Robertson filed for bankruptcy, and the trustee tried to seize the former family residence as property of his estate. Under federal bankruptcy law, state marital property law applies in such a situation. Louisiana law provides that when a former regime is partitioned, 1. The spouses cease to be co-owners; 2. The former community assets are divided into separate portions, and 3. Each former spouse becomes the exclusive and sole owner of the property contained in one of those portions.

The Trustee does not dispute the conclusion that the partition gave the former Mrs. Robertson sole and separate ownership before the petition date, but he argues that because that home remains subject to debts incurred jointly under the community regime, that makes all property liable for such debts part of the bankruptcy estate. However, Article 2357 provides that an obligation incurred during a community regime may be satisfied after it terminates from either community property or separate property of the spouse who incurred the obligation – thus, a creditor's right to have such an obligation satisfied from her separate property is not affected by the partition, but it does not follow that separate property of the non-debtor spouse passes to the bankruptcy estate simply because it was subject to a creditor's claim under state law before the partition.

The trustee also argued that under the Bankruptcy Code, the Section 544 'strong-arm' provision allowing the trustee to seize property applies wherever an obligation incurred by the debtor could be voided by a bona fide purchaser of an immovable. So, the issue, then, is whether under Louisiana Law, would a bona fide purchaser of the family home have been protected because the partition was not filed in the parish registry?

The U.S. Fifth circuit held that it could not because the divorce judgment was properly filed and therefore third persons were put on notice that former community immovables might no longer be part of a community.

2. PRD and the Rights of Forced Heirs

The Civil Code protects both spouses in community and forced heirs. Though no similar statute is in place, there is some indication that a forced heir who has been defrauded out of his or her property might be able to defeat the PRD if the third party is not in good faith, as with spouses in community.

Long v. Chailan

The plaintiffs who are forced heirs claim that their stepfather, who owned land in indivision with them (they had inherited their mother's undivided interest) allowed the land to be seized and sold and that it was sold to stepfather's daughter by a previous marriage, thus defrauding them of their undivided, unrecorded interest. The appellate court reversed the summary judgment against the plaintiffs and remanded the case to the trial court.

3. PRD and Simulated Sales

A simulation is a contract that, by the parties' intent does not express their true intention. It is an absolute simulation when the parties intend that the contract produce no effects between them, and it is relative when the parties intend that the contract will produce effects, but not the ones recited in the contract. As such, the terms of the contract are those that the parties' intended actually intended. If they had a separate document that states their true intent, then that document is called a counter letter. Arts. 2025-2027.

Students often assume that the only reason for a simulation is an attempt to defraud another person, but that is not necessarily the case. There are occasions, certainly, when a simulation is used in an attempt to defraud a creditor or someone else, in which case it is unlawful and absolutely or relatively null. However, there are other occasions when parties to a contract find that a simulation is more convenient – for example, if Mom wants to transfer land to son George, but doesn't want her other son Max to think that she is favoring George. In that case, they may write the transfer up as a sale (in authentic act form) but may actually intend a gratuitous donation. (A relative simulation). George gets the land, but doesn't actually have to pay for it, Max is none the wiser, and peace in the family is maintained.

Any simulation, whether it is absolute or relative, may be effective as to a third person. Art. 2028. This means that, especially with regard to an immovable, any counterletter that is not recorded is absolutely null, and the third person can be guided by the simulation that is recorded.

Chachere v. Superior Oil

Plaintiffs are heirs of Mr. and Mrs. Chachere, and claim that after Mom died, Dad bought land, which he then pretended to sell to two other brothers, and their descendants then leased the mineral rights to the defendant. They want their community interest in the oil revenues recognized, as in Long v. Chailan.

Their claim relies on the sale being a donation in disguise, rather than a sale, and thus being subject to community interest. However, the defendant is a third party, and thus any such donation is absolutely null with regard to it, because it was unrecorded.

Tate v. Tate

Iris Tate "sold" a tract of land with her house and an apartment to her daughter for $70,000. The two executed a counterletter declaring that the "sale" was actually a donation, and that Iris would be allowed to reside on the property as long as she desires. The act of sale was recorded, but the counter letter was not. Two years later, Pauline donated the property to her two daughters, and that donation was recorded. There was no mention of Iris's right to inhabit the property. A month later, Iris filed a petition to rescind the donation to Pauline for ingratitude, and also sought a temporary restraining order to prevent any other transfers or prevent Iris from being removed, and seeking rent from Pauline who had been living in the apartment.

While the court granted the TRO, it did not apparently grant a preliminary injunction, so once it expired, one daughter decided she wanted out of the family daughter and donated her interest to the other. The remaining daughter transferred her ownership interest to a limited liability company entitled "Justification, L.L.C." The issue is whether Iris can rescind the donation in disguise.

The court held that she could not, because the PRD trumps the unrecorded counterletter, and both the granddaughters and "Justification" were third parties.

4. The Scope of the PRD

Article 3338 stipulates that in order to be effective against a third party, any right in an immovable must be recorded, including transfers, options, rights of first refusal, contract to buy, or lease. Once one of those rights is recorded however, subsequent effects such as the exercise of the option or a tacit acceptance need not be recorded in order to be effective against a third person.

Avenue Plaza v. Falgoust

The defendants had leased a property on St. Charles Avenue, in which they operated a beauty salon from the previous owners. The lease was recorded and contained an option to renew for an additional 10 years at the expiration of the first ten-year period. In a timely fashion, they sent a certified letter to the lessor, addressed to "manager" in an attempt to exercise the option. That letter was never recorded. Two years later, the property was sold to plaintiff Avenue Plaza. The court held that even if the option was properly exercised, that renewal was never recorded. Because it was never recorded, the court held that it was not binding on Avenue Plaza, the third party.

This case was decided prior to the revision of the Public Records Doctrine in 2006. Presumably, the result would be different were the lease to have been initiated after that date.

C. PRD & Public Policy

Comment

The comment, written by a student, asserts that the Louisiana public records system is 'pure race' – i.e. whoever registers their right first wins, and that good faith (or the lack of it) is irrelevant – as in the McDuffie case – and that this is anomalous as other states' systems are not so rigid. However, given the result in the In Re James series of cases and the applicable statute, that claim is over-stated. Good faith can figure into a PRD decision if a community regime is involved.

Hernando de Soto

Economist Hernando de Soto's classic empirical study of the deleterious effects of complicated registration systems on economic development shows the need to maintain a simple, easy-to use and transparent system to record both transfers of immovables and the registration of businesses. Without such a system, property owners and business people end up owning outside the legal system, meaning that their efforts become 'dead capital' because they can neither defend their property in court nor borrow against it, and thus cannot improve their economic status.

Hypothets

1. Anna purchased some beautiful and valuable blue suede shoes at an auction last week. Today, however, she just received an email from Maria claiming that her cousin had lied, claiming that he was just borrowing them for the day, when in fact he intended to put them up for auction. Maria is demanding that Anna return the shoes to her. Must she do so?

2. Anna leased her second store from Mark Acme, for a period of only two years, but the lease contained a clause saying that she could extend the lease for an additional 5 years, as long as she notified Mark Acme within one month of the end of the lease by mail. The lease was recorded. Anna decided that she wanted the extension and send the notification as required. Five months later she received a notice from Tad Tellmi telling her that he purchased the property and as the extension was not recorded, he was terminating the lease under Avenue Plaza v. Falgoust. Can Tad, in fact, do that?

CHAPTER 9

SELLER'S OBLIGATION OF DELIVERY AND WARRANTY AGAINST EVICTION

Flowchart

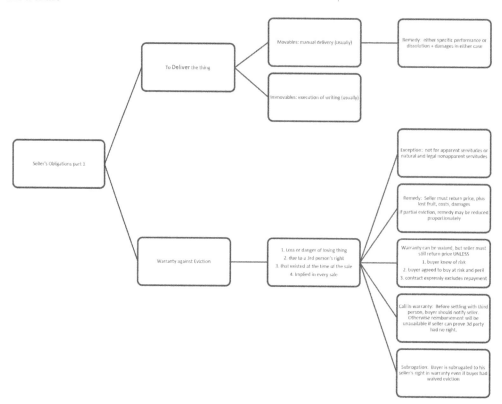

Section 1: Delivery of the Thing

A. General Concepts

Read Articles 2474-77, 2480-89, 2614 and answer the following questions:

1. If the terms of the contract of sale are vague or ambiguous, how are they to be interpreted?

2. What are the seller's four obligations?

3. When is an immovable deemed delivered?

4. How does the seller usually deliver a movable?

5. What other ways may a movable be delivered?

6. What if the thing sold remains in the seller's possession? What does the law then presume?

7. How are incorporeals delivered?

8. What if the seller is not in possession of the thing sold at the time of the sale? What obligations does he have?

9. Who pays for the costs of delivery, in the absence of a specific agreement?

10. In the case of a movable, where must the thing be delivered in the absence of an express agreement on the place of delivery?

11. If the seller fails to deliver, what is (or are) the buyer's remedies?

12. Does the seller have to deliver the thing if the buyer hasn't yet paid?

13. What condition should the thing be in at the time of delivery?

14. What can the seller do if he learns that the buyer is insolvent while the things are in transit?

B. Delivery of Movables

Study Question:

Article 2477 says that delivery of a movable takes place by manual delivery, in the absence of other arrangements. If the seller fails to deliver the thing, then the buyer has two choices under Article 2485: he can demand specific performance or seek dissolution of the sale and refund of any money paid. In either case, he can also seek incidental damages or damages for delay (i.e. moratory damages). Furthermore, the seller may refuse to deliver until the buyer pays, unless the seller granted the buyer a term for payment as per Article 2487. How do these articles operate in the following cases?

MAXWELL MOTORS V. DAVIS 1976
335 SO. 2D 74 (LA. APP. 2D CIR.)

BOLIN, Judge.

¶1 Maxwell Motors Inc., sued Fred Davis for the unpaid balance due on a chattel mortgage note. The note and mortgage were executed in connection with an alleged sale of a truck from plaintiff to defendant. Defendant answered denying liability and seeking rescission of the sale.

Defendant also reconvened for $306, the amount paid by him on the note. Following trial the lower court for brief written reasons rendered judgment for plaintiff as prayed for and defendant appeals.

¶2   The primary question on appeal is whether the transaction between Maxwell Motors and Davis constituted a valid sale of the truck, entitling the seller to enforce payment from the buyer under the note and chattel mortgage given as security for the unpaid purchase price.
      We find the facts as follows:

On February 27, 1974, plaintiff sold defendant a 1971 model truck for a price of $3,197. Defendant was credited with $650 as the trade-in value of an old truck. In payment for the 1971 truck defendant executed a promissory note and chattel mortgage in the face amount of $3,672, representing the net sale price of $2,547 plus finance and insurance charges. On the date of the sale defendant did not surrender possession of the old truck to plaintiff because he had to obtain the certificate of title to same.

Additionally, plaintiff agreed to make some repairs to the truck. Within a few days following the original agreement plaintiff made the repairs to the truck but defendant informed plaintiff he was unable to secure the title certificate to his old truck. Plaintiff and defendant agreed that plaintiff would accept $500 cash in lieu of the trade-in of defendant's old truck. Defendant being unable to secure the $500 cash payment, plaintiff offered to finance this amount if defendant would offer additional security by giving plaintiff a second mortgage on his home. The parties were unable to agree on this latter suggestion. Defendant insisted that he wanted the truck and plaintiff made several proposals to finance the down payment.

During this period of negotiation the truck remained in the possession of plaintiff and defendant made two monthly payments on the chattel mortgage note. Defendant having failed to make the down payment and having become delinquent in his installment payments under the mortgage, plaintiff filed suit by ordinary process on the note and chattel mortgage for the full amount of the note. Suit was not instituted for the alleged balance due for the down payment.

¶3   On appeal, defendant argues the sale should be rescinded and his payments on the note returned to him for plaintiff's failure to comply with its obligation to deliver the truck as required by Civil Code Article 2475: The seller is bound to two principal obligations, that of delivering and that of warranting the thing which he sells.

¶4   Defendant contends plaintiff cannot enforce the contract of sale without having complied with the seller's obligation to deliver the thing sold.

¶5 On the other hand plaintiff contends the contract of sale was complete under C.C. Art. 2456 which provides the sale is perfect 'as soon as there exists an agreement for the object and for the price thereof, although the object has not yet been delivered, nor the price paid.' Plaintiff argues C.C. Art. 2475, on which defendant relies, must be read in conjunction with C.C. Arts. 2485 and 2487:

> Art. 2485. If the seller fails to make the delivery at the time agreed on between the parties, the buyer will be at liberty to demand, either a canceling of the sale, or to be put into possession, If the delay is occasioned only by the deed of the seller. (Emphasis added)

> Art. 2487. The seller is not bound to make a delivery of the thing, if the buyer does not pay the price, and the seller has not granted him any term for the payment.

¶6 Plaintiff contends the delay in delivery was occasioned by agreement of the parties and not 'only by the deed of the seller.' Furthermore, plaintiff argues it was not required to make delivery of the truck until the price, i.e., the down payment, was paid.

¶7 From our review of the record, we find the parties agreed plaintiff would keep the truck while defendant attempted to raise enough money to make the down payment and that defendant never paid the down payment.

¶8 Accordingly, we hold plaintiff did not breach its obligation to deliver the truck, which would have entitled defendant to a rescission of the sale; there was a perfected sale of the truck by plaintiff to defendant despite the fact of non-delivery.

¶9 Although we affirm the trial court's judgment on the issue of liability, we conclude the amount of the award must be reduced because it does not reflect a refund of unearned finance and insurance charges as required by Louisiana Revised Statutes 6:958. We calculate that amount to be $575.59.

¶10 For the reasons assigned the judgment of the lower court is amended to reduce the amount from $3366.00 to $2790.41; as thus amended, it is affirmed.

¶11 Appellee is assessed with the cost of this appeal.

QUALITY PAINT, HARDWARE & MARINE SUPPLY V. CRESCENT COATING & SERVICES (2013)

123 SO. 3D 780 (LA. 3ᴿᴰ CIR.)

Opinion

SUSAN M. CHEHARDY, Chief Judge.

¶1 This is a suit on an open account, in which a paint supplier sued a paint buyer and its purported agent for the balance owed on its account. After a bench trial, the trial judge found in favor of the paint buyer and dismissed the paint supplier's action. For the following reasons, the trial court's judgment is affirmed.

Facts and Procedural History

¶2 Crescent Coatings & Services (hereinafter "Crescent Coatings") is hired by oilfield companies to apply special paints and coatings to specific pieces of machinery. If required under the contract, Crescent Coatings supplies the paint/coating for the job. [To facilitate its purchase of large quantities of paint, Crescent Coating's accountant, Billy Ray Orgeron, applied for and received a line of credit with a local paint supplier, Quality Paint, Hardware, & Marine Supply, Inc. (hereinafter "Quality Paint")].

¶3 In 2010, Crescent Coatings ordered paint from Quality Paint on February 18; March 1; March 4; and March 16, 2010. The parties agree that Quality Paint delivered thru its agent, Saia Trucking, and Crescent Coatings received and paid for each of those orders, *except* the order placed March 16, 2010. Thus, only one order is at issue.

¶4 Quality Paint sued Crescent Coatings; Billy Ray Orgeron; Max Welders, L.L.C.; and Max Welders Holding Company, L.L.C. (hereinafter collectively "Max Welders") for the balance of $11,365.40 for marine paint ordered on March 16, 2010. Crescent Coatings and its employee, Billy Ray Orgeron, answered the petition, denied responsibility for payment on the basis that Crescent Coatings did not receive, and Quality Paint failed to deliver, the paint in question.

* * *

¶5 The trial testimony further revealed that Quality Paint shipped the product from the paint manufacturer directly to Crescent Coatings' paint shed on Blackwater Court in Gibson, Louisiana. Quality Paint, as part of the delivery instructions given to the shipper, identified the sign for Max Welders, another business on Blackwater Court, as a landmark to find Crescent Coatings' location.2

¶6 John Pitre, a veteran driver for Saia Trucking, testified that, in his career, he made one delivery to Blackwater Court, which was on March 17, 2010. That day, Pitre stopped at Max Welders, where Elliott Naquin signed for the order and used a forklift to unload the order from Quality Paint. Before Pitre departed, Naquin realized his mistake, reloaded the order onto Pitre's truck, and directed Pitre toward Crescent Coatings' location at 199 Blackwater Court.

¶7 Pitre testified that he drove into the "little yard" with a warehouse next door to Max Welders, waited for a man to repair a forklift, then allowed the man to unload the order. Pitre did not obtain a signature from the man that unloaded the order because his computerized order system did not allow for a second signature.

¶8 The parties introduced the delivery ticket from Saia Trucking for the March 16, 2010 order, which was signed by Elliott Naquin, an employee of Max Welders, not Crescent Coatings. At trial, Mr. Naquin agreed that the signature was his but testified that he had no memory of this delivery and that he "never unloaded any delivery for Crescent Coatings at Max Welders." Further, it is undisputed that no employee from Crescent Coatings signed the delivery ticket for the March 16, 2010 order.

¶9 Moreover, Crescent Coatings' payroll records for its Gibson location for March 17, 2010 were introduced, which reflected that no employees were onsite at Gibson after 7:30 a.m. Finally, evidence, including photographs and satellite images, were introduced that revealed that Crescent Coatings' Gibson location was not a warehouse in a "little yard" next door to Max Welders, but a site that included a four-sided structure without a roof and several locked shipping containers about 1000 feet down a gravel road that was perpendicular to Blackwater Court.

* * *

¶10 On October 15, 2012, the trial judge issued a written judgment in favor of Crescent Coatings and Billy Ray Orgeron, dismissing Quality Paint's claims. In her Reasons for Judgment, the trial judge found credibility in Quality Paint's testimony that the paint was ordered and the order was not cancelled. The trial judge further believed Crescent Coatings' testimony that it did not receive the paint. The trial judge found the least credible testimony was presented by Saia's delivery driver, John Pitre, who contradicted testimony from several more credible witnesses, including his statement that Crescent Coatings' location was a warehouse in a "little yard," next door to Max Welders. The trial judge concluded "that the paint was more likely lost or mis-handled in transit than received and hidden by Crescent." Finally, the trial court, relying on La. C.C. arts. 2482 and 2616, found that Quality Paint failed to bear the burden of proving delivery and, thus, should bear the loss in this matter. On December 3, 2012, Quality Paint devolutively appealed the judgment rendered on October 15, 2012.

¶11   On appeal, Quality Paint argues three assignments of error: first, the trial court erred in failing to find that Max Welders was the putative agent of Crescent Coatings and delivery of the shipment of paint to Max Welders was delivery to Crescent Coatings; second, the trial court erred in failing to find that based upon equity, usage and the conduct of the parties developed in their contractual dealings that the delivery of the paint to Max Welders was delivery in accordance with the parties' contract; and third, the factual findings and conclusions of the trial court were not reasonable and clearly wrong in concluding that the delivery driver's testimony concerning the events that occurred when he delivered the paint was contradicted by the testimony of the employee of Max Welders, who signed the delivery receipt for the paint, resulting in manifest error.

* * *

Law and Argument

¶12   In its first assignment of error, Quality Paint argues that the trial judge should have applied "the doctrine of apparent authority and agency by estoppel" to find that Crescent Coatings held out Max Welders was Crescent Coatings' putative agent for receipt of goods. We have reviewed the record and find, however, that the issue of "putative mandatary" was not raised by Quality Paint in the trial court in its pleadings, in testimony, or in argument. Generally, issues not raised in the trial court will not be given consideration for the first time on appeal. *See,* U.R.C.A. Rule 1–3; *Warner v. Alex Enterprises, Inc.,* 08–0929 (La.App. 4 Cir. 1/28/09), 4 So.3d 922, 925. Therefore, we will not consider this assignment of error.

¶13   Next, Quality Paint argues that the trial court erred in failing to find that, "based upon equity, usage, and the conduct of the parties ... that the delivery of the paint to Max Welders was delivery in accordance with the party's *[sic]* contract." Quality Paint argues that *it* designated Max Welders as the destination to deliver the paint order and the shipment was delivered to Max Welders as noted on the delivery receipt; therefore, pursuant to La. C.C. 2616, the risk of loss should have transferred to Crescent Coatings when the order was delivered as instructed.

¶14   La. C.C. art. 2616 reads, in pertinent part:

"When the contract requires the seller to ship the things through a carrier, but does not require him to deliver the things at any particular destination, the risk of loss is transferred to the buyer upon delivery of the things to the carrier, regardless of the form of the bill of lading.

"When the contract of sale requires the seller to deliver the things at a particular destination, the risk of loss is transferred to the buyer when the things, while in possession of the carrier, are duly tendered to the buyer at the place of destination."

¶15 Contrary to Quality Paint's assertion, the testimony at trial reflected that Crescent Coatings required delivery of every paint order to its Gibson location at 199 Blackwater Court, not Max Welders' location at 188 Blackwater Court. Testimony revealed that, contrary to this argument, Quality Paint's President told the shipping company to look for Max Welders' sign as a landmark to help direct its drivers to Crescent Coatings but did not instruct the shipper to offload the order at Max Welders. In fact, the testimony from Max Welders' employees, Crescent Coatings' employees, and even Quality Paint's President was unequivocal that Crescent Coatings expected delivery of shipments to its isolated location at 199 Blackwater Court. The trial court did not err in finding that Quality Paint was required to deliver the goods to Crescent Coatings' Gibson location and, because the goods were not tendered at the place of destination, the risk of loss remained with Quality Paint. This assignment of error lacks merit.

¶16 In its final assignment of error, Quality Paint argues that "the factual findings ... of the trial court ... that the delivery driver's testimony concerning the events that occurred when he delivered the paint was contradicted by the testimony of the employee of Max Welders, LLC[,] who signed the delivery receipt for the paint, [were not reasonable and clearly wrong,] resulting in manifest error."

* * *

¶17 In this case, the trial judge's factual finding that Quality Paint failed to prove delivery of the order to Crescent Coatings was based on her credibility determinations. In *Rosell, supra,* the supreme court expounded on the concept of "clearly wrong" or "manifestly erroneous" with regard to credibility determinations:

When findings are based on determinations regarding the credibility of witnesses, the manifest error-clearly wrong standard demands great deference to the trier of fact's findings; for only the factfinder can be aware of the variations in demeanor and tone of voice that bear so heavily on the listener's understanding and belief in what is said. Where documents or objective evidence so contradict the witness's story, or the story itself is so internally inconsistent or implausible on its face, that a reasonable fact finder would not credit the witness's story, the court of appeal may well find manifest error or clear wrongness even in a finding purportedly based upon a credibility determination. But where such factors are not present, and a factfinder's finding is based on its decision to credit the testimony of one of two or more witnesses, that finding can virtually never be manifestly erroneous or clearly wrong.

Rosell v. ESCO, 549 So.2d at 844–45 (citations omitted).

¶18 In this case, the trial judge based her finding that the delivery was not completed on inconsistencies in the delivery driver's testimony. Upon our review of the record, and keeping in mind the correct standard of review, we find no manifest error in the trial court's factual determination. This assignment of error lacks merit.

Conclusion

¶19 Based on the foregoing, we find no error in the trial court's judgment in favor of Crescent Coatings and Billy Ray Orgeron in this case. For that reason, the judgment is affirmed. Costs of this appeal are assessed entirely to Quality Paint.

AFFIRMED

Study Question:

In both of the previous cases, the sales were perfected but the seller never delivered the object, the thing sold. In Quality Paint, the buyer was not required either to pay for the paint, while in Maxwell Motors, the buyer was still required to pay even though the truck was not yet delivered. Why did the holdings in the two cases differ?

C. Delivery of Immovables

Article 2477 states that delivery of an immovable is deemed to take place upon execution of the writing that transfers its ownership.

Study Questions:

How does Article 2477 apply in the following case? Is it true that delivery of an immovable is complete as soon as the documents evidencing ownership are transferred? What remedy did the buyer seek?

MATTHEWS V. GAUBLER 1951

49 SO. 2D 774 (LA. APP. ORL. CIR.)

McBRIDE, Judge.

¶1 By contract dated November 8, 1945, Morris Matthews, the plaintiff, agreed to purchase from Mr. and Mrs. A. J. Gaubler, and they agreed to sell to him, the property known as 2825 Arts Street, New Orleans, for the price and sum of $3000. It was stated in the contract that the property was not under lease, but was occupied by the owners, and that 'possession to be given at act of sale.' It was stipulated that the sale would be passed before the purchaser's notary public 'on or prior to Dec. 15, 1945.' By a subsequent mutual verbal understanding, the parties postponed the time for passing the act of sale to January 2, 1946.

¶2 Matthews, to finance the purchase of the property, arranged for a loan from a local homestead, and it was understood that the act of sale was to be passed before Mr. Allain C. Andry, Jr., the notary public for the homestead.

¶3 On January 2, 1946, about noon, all of the parties gathered in Mr. Andry's office. After all of the necessary documents were signed by Matthews and Mr. and Mrs. Gaubler, that is to say, the act transferring the property to the homestead, the act of resale from the homestead to the purchaser, and the purchaser's mortgage note evidencing the loan, and after Matthews had written his check for the portion of the purchase price which he would have to advance, he asked the Gaublers for the keys to the premises. They stated that they did not have the keys with them, and informed Matthews that their child was ill, and that they could not move from the premises that day. Matthews then peremptorily refused to go through with the sale. There is some testimony by the Gaublers that they told Matthews the keys could be delivered later that afternoon, but the plaintiff denies this.

¶4 Be that as it may, when Matthews insisted upon delivery of the keys and immediate possession, Mr. and Mrs. Gaubler admitted that they were not in position to turn over the keys to him at that particular moment, and after a discussion of the matter, they finally stated that they would move out of the house by eight o'clock the following morning, and would deliver the keys to Matthews then. He refused to accede to this delay.

¶5 In connection with his agreement to purchase the property, Matthews deposited with the realtors who negotiated the transaction the sum of $300, and the agreement states that: 'This deposit is to be noninterest bearing and may be placed in any bank of your selection in the City of New Orleans without responsibility on your part in case of failure or suspension of such bank pending settlement. In the event that purchaser fails to comply with this agreement within the time specified, the vendor shall have the right, either to declare the deposit, ipso facto, forfeited, without formality and without placing purchaser in default, time being the essence of this contract; or the vendor may demand specific performance. In the event that the deposit is forfeited, the commission of the agent shall be paid out of this deposit, reserving to the vendor the right to proceed against purchaser for the recovery of the amount of the commission. In the event that the vendor does not comply with this agreement to sell within the time specified, purchaser shall have the right either to demand the return of double the deposit, or specific performance.'

¶6   By this suit, Matthews, who alleges that the Gaublers are in default, seeks to recover from them double the amount of the deposit, or $600 plus $250 for his attorney's fee. After their exceptions of vagueness and no right or cause of action had been overruled, defendants answered the suit, denying that they were in default, and averring that plaintiff himself was in default, and was not entitled to the relief which he sought. The trial in the lower court resulted in a judgment in favor of plaintiff for $600, plus a $150 attorney's fee, from which the defendants have appealed.

¶7   It might be stated at this point that the stipulation 'possession to be given at act of sale' was incorporated in the agreement at the insistence of Matthews. The evidence also shows that on January 2, 1946, before proceeding to the notary's office, Matthews visited the property to examine it, and upon observing that the furniture and furnishings of the Gaublers were still in the house, he became apprehensive about getting possession at the time of the passage of the sale.

¶8   The basis of the exception of no right or cause of action, which was reurged before us, is that the plaintiff is not entitled to a return of double the deposit, as he should have accepted title, paid the purchase price, and then, in the event that the keys were not delivered to him by eight o'clock the following morning, he should have brought an action for damages against defendants. We perceive no merit whatever in the exception.

¶9   Counsel for appellants first argues that a decision of the case hinges on the meaning of the phrase, 'possession to be given at act of sale.' His contention is that the stipulation does not mean that a simultaneous delivery of the keys would be made at the signing of the formal act of sale, but that the parties, by employing such language, only intended that there would be a delivery of physical possession of the property within a reasonable time after the act was passed. Says counsel in his brief: 'Now, what are the respective rights of a vendor and a vendee? There can be no question that the vendee is entitled to obtain possession of the premises he purchases when he pays the consideration thereof, but certainly he cannot be unreasonable in his demand. What assurance does the vendor have that the vendee will have sufficient funds to complete the sale or that he will even appear at the time and place fixed for the passage of the act of sale? Must the vendor vacate his house in the absence of such assurance, or should he have a reasonable time to effect compliance with his contract when he is assured that the vendee has complied with his obligations? We submitt that when Defendants appeared in Mr. Andry's office on January 2, 1946 and agreed to deliver the keys to Plaintiff not later than either o'clock on the morning of January 3, 1946, they had effected full compliance with the contract of sale.'

¶10   Our opinion is that the words, 'possession to be given at act of sale,' which, it must be remembered, were incorporated in the agreement at the instance of Matthews, were intended to mean, and could only mean, that at the very moment of the execution of the formal act of sale, physical and corporeal possession of the property would be forthcoming to the purchaser.

¶11   Counsel states that there are no Louisiana authorities interpreting the clause, or defining the meaning of the words in question. Our research, however, discloses the case of Warfield v. Cotton, 149 La. 1004, 90 So. 374, which we think is analogous to the question posed in the instant case. The Supreme Court held that the stipulation, 'possession to be given immediately,' as used in an agreement to purchase, entitled the defendant 'by its express, explicit terms, to immediate possession,' and that when defendant took possession, he was but exercising his legal right.

¶12   It is also argued on behalf of appellants that there are extenuating circumstances in the case, which would render inhuman indeed a holding that they should have conveyed their sick child from the house before going to the notary's office, and that, because of the illness of either child, they had the natural right to retain possession of the property for the short period of time until eight o'clock of the following morning.

¶13   Again, we cannot agree with counsel. We are not at liberty to disregard the explicit terms of the agreement, which bound the vendors to deliver corporeal possession of the property to the purchaser at the very moment of the passing of the act of sale, merely because it was inconvenient for them to make delivery, or because the making of delivery would have worked a hardship upon them. Legal agreements have the effect of law upon the parties, and courts are bound to give legal effect to all such contracts according to the true intent of all the parties, and that intent is to be determined by the words of the contract, when these are clear and explicit and lead to no absurd consequences. Art. 1945, R.C.C.

¶14   Under the provisions of art. 2475, R.C.C., the seller is bound to two principal obligations, that of delivering the thing, and that of warranting the thing which he sells. In Derbonne v.

Burton, La.App., 189 So. 473, 474, it was said that 'the obligation of delivery is the primary obligation to be fulfilled.'

¶15   What is to be considered a delivery of possession is determined by the rules of law, applicable to the situation and nature of the property. Art. 1924, R.C.C. The tradition or delivery is the transferring of the thing sold into the power and possession of the buyer, and the law considers the tradition or delivery of immovables, as always accompanying the public act, which transfers the property. Arts. 2477, 2479, R.C.C.

¶16   According to art. 496, R.C.C., the ownership and the possession of a thing are entirely distinct.

¶17   Art. 3434, R.C.C. provides in part: 'Since the use of ownership is to have a thing in order to enjoy it and to dispose of it, and that it is only by possession that one can exercise this right, possession is therefore naturally linked to the ownership.'

¶18   In Ellis v. Prevost, 19 La. 251, the Supreme Court said: '* * * Possession is acquired by the actual and corporal detention of the property; this is the natural possession, or possession in fact; * * *'

¶19   The penalty for the failure of a vendor to make delivery is stipulated for in R.C.C. arts. 2485 and 2486, respectively, as follows:

> 'If the seller fails to make the delivery at the time agreed on between the parties, the buyer will be at liberty to demand, either a canceling of the sale, or to be put into possession, if the delay is occasioned only by the deed of the seller.'

> 'In all cases, the seller is liable to damages, if there result any detriment to the buyer, occasioned by the non-delivery at the time agreed on.'

***

¶20   Matthews was to have immediate physical and corporeal possession at and upon the passage of the formal act of sale, both under the express stipulations of the agreement, any by the plain import of the law. By failing to make delivery of possession at the time agreed upon between the parties, the vendors actively breached their obligation, and Matthews, the purchaser, was within his rights in receding from the agreement and refusing to pay for the property. Under the terms of the agreement, the law between the parties, which provides that in the event the vendors do not comply with their agreement the purchaser shall have the right either to demand return of double the deposit or specific performance, Matthews is entitled to maintain the present action.

¶21   On, and several times after January 5, 1946, appellants' counsel addressed letters to Matthews, offering to deliver the keys to him and demanding that he comply with his contract and purchase the property, but the plaintiff did not respond to the letters, and he denies that he received some of them. Counsel contends that when Matthews refused the Gaublers' offer to surrender the keys and pass title, he was in default, and cannot now maintain the present action, he having no further rights under the contract.

¶22   The best answer to this contention is the recent of DiCristina v. Weiser, 215 La. 1115, 42 So.2d 868, wherein the Supreme Court held that one who himself is in default on a contract for the sale and purchase of real property, cannot subsequently put the other party in default, under the provisions of art. 1913, R.C.C.

***

¶23   For the reasons assigned, it is ordered, adjudged, and decreed that the amount of the judgment appealed from be reduced from $750 to the sum of $600, and as thus amended, and in all other respects, it is affirmed. Costs of this appeal are to be borne by plaintiff-appellee.

¶24   Amended and affirmed.

D. Things Accessory to the Thing Sold

Read Articles 2461, 508, 469, 465-66. Article 2461 stipulates that "the sale of a thing includes all accessories intended for its use in accordance with the law of property." In the case of an immovable, that includes its component parts, as per Articles 465-66, 469, and 508: "in the sale of immovable property, accessories include immovables by destination and predial servitudes in favor of the property conveyed." Prados v. South Central Bell Telephone Co., 329 So. 2d 744, 750 (La. 1976).

Study Question:

What does the following case demonstrate about "accessories intended for use" and immovables by destination?

CULPEPPER, Judge.

¶1 Plaintiff purchased a dwelling owned and occupied by defendant. When defendant vacated the premises, he removed two colored glass 'doors' which were located between the den and the living room. Plaintiff filed this suit to recover the 'doors'. The city judge granted plaintiff's motion for summary judgment. Defendant appealed.

¶2 The issue is whether the alleged 'doors' were immovable within the contemplation of the relevant articles of our Civil Code If so, they were conveyed to plaintiff as part of the dwelling. Defendant contends they are not actually 'doors' but, instead, are 'schogie screens' (sic) which are movable and are the personal property of the defendant.

¶3 The affidavit attached to plaintiff's motion for summary judgment states in pertinent part: 'There were two glass doors located in the residence above described which doors were attached to and a part of the building. The said doors were located in the home between the den and the living room.'

¶4 The opposing affidavit filed by defendant states in part: 'The two colored glass fixtures located in the residence . . . were in fact not properly characterized as 'doors' but were decorative furnishings temporarily attached to the interior of the residence. The above mentioned glass furnishings are commonly referred to as 'schogie screens.' The affiant did not attach the above described schogie screens with plaster or other permanent fixings. Further, the affiant did not intend to make these decorative fixtures a permanent part of the residence and as they were not permanently attached to the residence, they remained part of affiant's personal property.'

¶5 Summary judgment may be granted only where the pleadings, affidavits, etc. 'show that there is no genuine issue as to material fact, and that mover is entitled to judgment as a matter of law.', LSA-C.C.P. Article 966. Jurisprudence holds the burden is on the mover to show clearly there is no such factual issue, and any doubt must be resolved against the granting of a summary judgment, Kay v. Carter, 243 La. 1095, 150 So.2d 27 (1963); Smith v. Preferred Risk Mutual Insurance Company, 185 So.2d 857 (La.App.3rd Cir. 1966). We ultimately reach the conclusion that there are factual issues which must be determined in a trial on the merits.

¶6 The applicable law is set forth at length in LaFleur v. Foret, 213 So.2d 141 (La.App.3rd Cir. 1968). At issue there were window air-conditioners which rested on metal racks attached to the window sills with two small screws. The first contention was that the air-conditioners were immovable by destination, under the last paragraph of LSA-C.C. Article 468 which provides: 'All such movables as the owner has attached permanently to the tenement or to the building, are likewise immovable by destination.' Article 469 explains what is meant by permanent attachment. We held that since the units could be easily removed without injury to the building, except two small screw holes, there was no permanent attachment under Articles 468 and 469.

¶7   The second contention in LaFleur v. Foret was that the air-conditioners were immovable by destination, under the first portion of LSA-C.C. Article 468 which provides: 'Things which the owner of a tract of land has placed upon it for its service and improvement are immovables by destination.' Then follows an illustrative list of unattached movables used for agricultural or industrial purposes. We held these codal provisions do not apply to residences.

¶8   The third contention in LaFleur v. Foret was that the air-conditioners became immobilized by nature, and were thus component parts of the building under LSA-C.C. Article 467. This article gives an illustrative list of articles which become immovable by nature '. . . when actually connected with or attached to the building by the owner for the use or convenience of the building . . .' We held that the air-conditioning units had not become component parts of the building under Article 467. In reaching this decision we considered (1) contemporary views as to what are component parts of a dwelling in the light of current house construction practices and (2) the degree of connection or attachment to the building. We recognized that different factual situations might warrant additional considerations. Using these tests, we found that the window air-conditioning units are portable, are often and easily moved from house to house, and are not generally considered as component parts of a dwelling. Furthermore, we found that the degree of connection or attachment to the building was minimal.

¶9   Applying these rules to the present case, it is apparent that there is a factual issue as to the degree of connection or attachment of these 'doors' or 'schogie screens' to the building. The affidavits do not show how they were attached, how easily they could be removed or the injury to the building that would result from their removal.

¶10   Furthermore, there are factual issues as to the nature of these 'schogie screens' and whether they would be considered component parts of the dwelling under contemporary views of current house construction practices.

¶11   There may be other factual issues which could develop on the trial of the merits in light of our decision in LaFleur v. Foret, supra.

¶12   We conclude there are genuine issues of material fact which preclude summary judgment.

¶13   For the reasons assigned, the judgment appealed is reversed and set aside. This case is remanded to the Lake Charles City Court for further proceedings in accordance with law and the views expressed herein. All costs of this appeal are assessed against the plaintiff appellee. Assessment of costs in the trial court must await a final decision there.

¶14   Reversed and remanded.

E. Extension of the Premises: Certain and Limited Body, Measure, and Lump Sale

Read Articles 2491 through 2499.

With regard to an immovable, the seller is obligated to deliver the full extent of the immovable sold. Article 2491. However, depending on the description of the immovable, it may be difficult to determine exactly what that means. The contract of sale may describe the immovable by name (e.g. "Blackacre," or "The Provosty Place"), or by boundaries, or by measure (e.g. 40 acres or 40 arpents), or a combination of the three. Articles 2492 through 2498 describe the legal effects when the amount of land actually delivered is either more or less than the amount described.

If the immovable is described by measure, then Article 2492 applies because the buyer's cause for the purchase was the amount of land described. Consequently, if the seller is unable to deliver the full extent, then the price must be proportionately reduced. On the other hand, if the extent delivered by the seller is greater than that specified, then the buyer must pay a proportionate supplement – though he can recede from the sale if the land actually sold is more than one twentieth larger than that specified in the contract.

If the contract for the sale of the immovable gives an indication of the extent of the premises, but gives a lump price rather than a price per measure, then t the buyer's cause for the purchase was the land being sold, but that cause was somewhat less dependent on the exact extent of the land. Consequently, under Article 2494, if the amount of land actually delivered is more or less than that described, no adjustment to the price will be made unless that discrepancy exceeds one twentieth of the extent specified in the sale. Again, if the surplus exceeds one twentieth of the specified extent, the buyer has the same choice: he can either pay a proportionate increase or recede from the sale.

Finally, if the immovable is described by name or by boundaries for a lump price, then it is presumed that the amount of land purchased was NOT important to the buyer, and under Article 2495 even if the description in the sale gives some expression of the extent of the immovable, neither party has any right to adjust the price if the actual extent of the immovable differs from that expression. The Civil Code now calls this a "sale of a certain and limited body," though it was previously termed a sale "per aversionem."

In distinguishing among the three, courts begin by determining whether the sale involves a price per measure. If the price is not expressed in terms of "so much per acre" or "so much per arpent," then Article 2492 is excluded and the price is a lump price. At this point, the court then examines the description of the property to determine whether article 2494 or 2495 applies. While the Civil Code articles are not as clear as they might be, jurisprudence is helpful. If the property is described by boundaries, or if it described by adjoining owners or a proper name, or if it is described as "as per title," or if the buyer actually saw the property and its boundaries, then it is a certain and limited body – even if it includes some indication of the amount of land.[1]

The remaining articles in the section, Articles 2497 and 2498 provide a one year prescription for actions to increase or decrease the price, and in a case where the land delivered exceeds the amount described by more than one twentieth and the buyer consequently chooses to recede from the contract rather than pay a proportionate increase, then the seller must return the price and reimburse the buyer for expenses of the sale.

In a final variation, the seller need not make any claim at all about the amount of land he is selling. Instead, the purchase agreement might state that seller will sell the Heirloom Plantation for $100 per acre. Before closing, a survey will be done, which shows, say, that the land consists of 1000 acres, from which the buyer's price is computed.

Practice Questions:

1. Suppose that the description in the act of sale is as follows: 100 Acres, for $1,000 per acre. After the purchaser has possession, he discovers that he only received 96 acres. What Civil Code article applies? May he demand a return of some of the purchase price? Why or why not?

2. Suppose instead that the act of sale read: "100 acres for $100,000," and buyer received 96 acres, can he still demand a return of some of his money?

3. What if the act of sale still read "100 acres for $100,000," and buyer received 105 acres, may the seller then demand a supplement to the purchase price for the extra five acres? If he may make that demand, and does make it, must the buyer pay the supplement?

4. What if the description stipulates: "Stravinsky Place," gives the boundaries, and says it contains 40 acres. If the property only contains 30 acres, can the buyer get a reimbursement? Why or why not?

---

1   24 La. Civil Law Treatise §9:22.

5. In once case, the Seller showed the property to the buyer, but they could not find the boundaries because it was so overgrown. The Purchase Agreement referred to it as a "beautiful 7 acres," while the Act of Sale escribed it as lying south of a named highway and as a portion of a township and range, "comprising a total of 10 acres, more or less." The Price was $80,000, and when measured, the tract was 15% short. Held: was a sale of a certain and limited body because of the reference to the adjoining highway and township and range notations. Takewell v. Masters, 117 So.3d 301 (La. Ct. App. 2d Cir. 2013).

Study Questions:

The following case seems to involve the sale of a certain and limited body; nevertheless, the court adjusts the price because the buyer found that the property as delivered contained little more than half the acreage described. What about the description indicated it was a sale of a certain and limited body? And if it was a sale per aversionem, then why did the court adjust the price? As indicated in Article 2495, in a sale of a certain and limited body, neither party has a right to adjust the price if the actual extent of the immovable differs from the description.

LASITER V. GAHARAN 1996
670 SO. 2D 395, (LA. APP. 3D CIR.)

YELVERTON, Judge.

¶1 This is an appeal by Donald Gaharan and his daughter Phyllis, defendants, from a judgment which ordered them to refund $14,750 to Charles Lasiter, the plaintiff. Lasiter had bought a piece of property from the Gaharans. The property was described as containing 80 acres, more or less. It was discovered after the sale that it actually contained only 43.20 acres. The trial court ordered a diminution of the purchase price for failure of the seller to deliver the full extent of the property. The Gaharans appealed. We affirm.

¶2 Lasiter bought the land for $50,000 cash. The Gaharans had inherited the property. What they sold to Lasiter was described in the cash sale instrument as follows:

A certain piece, parcel or tract of land, together with all buildings and improvements thereon, and all rights, ways and privileges thereto appertaining, being, lying and situated in the Parish of Catahoula, State of Louisiana, and being more particularly described as follows, to-wit:

That part of the East Half (E½) of Babin Ricquet, Section 50, Township 8 North, Range 5 East, lying North of Louisiana State Highway 8, Catahoula Parish, Louisiana, estimated to contain approximately 80 acres, being the same property acquired by Vendors by Judgment of Possession in the Succession of Philip S. Gaharan, Jr., filed October 12, 1990, under file Number 220295, and recorded in Conveyance Book 158, Page 99, of the records of Catahoula Parish, Louisiana, and by Amended Judgment of Possession, filed October 12, 1990, under File Number 220296, and recorded Under File Number 220296, and recorded in Conveyance Book 158, Page 105 of the records of Catahoula Parish, Louisiana.

¶3 Lasiter bought the land mainly for the timber. Before the sale, he hired Mike Albritton, a forestry consultant, to cruise the land for him. Albritton got a map from the tax assessor's office. He physically went to the property and estimated the timber based on the map which showed approximately 80 acres.

¶4 After the purchase, Lasiter cut what he thought was his 80 acres of timber. He learned that he had trespassed on neighboring property. Lasiter then had his purchase surveyed. The survey showed that the property he bought was actually 43.20 acres. Albritton returned and counted the stumps on the land that Lasiter had overcut. Lasiter then paid the owners who had suffered the trespass for the overcut trees.

¶5 On appeal, the Gaharans claim that this was a sale per aversionem pursuant to La. Civ. Code art. 2495, and that, accordingly, the trial court erred in ordering a diminution of the purchase price when it was discovered that the sale was short on acreage. A sale per aversionem is a sale when the object is designated by the adjoining tenements and sold from boundary to boundary. Article 2495. In such a sale, there can be neither an increase nor diminution of price on account of a disagreement in measure. Id. They claim that this was a sale per aversionem because the description of the property was from one fixed boundary to another.

¶6 The code articles dealing with the obligation of the seller to deliver the full extent of the immovable sold were amended by Acts 1993, No. 841, § 1, effective January 1, 1995. The sale in this case was in 1991. For our purposes as applied to this case, the only change in the law is that a sale hitherto referred to as a sale per aversionem is now described as a sale of a certain and limited body or a distinct object.

¶7 The Gaharans have cited the case of Cornish v. Kinder Canal Company, 267 So.2d 625 (La. App. 3 Cir.), writ denied, 263 La. 624, 268 So.2d 679 (1972), writ not considered, 263 La. 800, 269 So.2d 248 (1972), in support of their position that the above description of property is a sale per aversionem. In the cited case the property sold was described as follows:

'Also all that portion of the North East quarter of Section Twenty six in Township No. Six South Range No. Five West, that lies North of the Calcasieu River Irrigation Co.'s Canal, containing 5 acres more or less.' Id. at 628.

¶8   In that case the court found that the property conveyed was triangular shaped, with the canal crossing the northeast/northwest corner of the section, thus establishing clear boundaries. It was bounded on the north by the north line of Section 26, on the east by the east line of Section 26, and on the southwest by the canal. The court held that a section line is sufficient to constitute a "fixed boundary," and that that was a sale per aversionem.

¶9   In the present case there are only three clear boundaries. Mr. Allbritton cruised what he determined to be 80 acres, finding one good boundary, the southern boundary of La. Hwy. 8. He assumed the section lines of Section 50 on the north and east were boundaries, but there was nothing on the west side to go by except what was necessary to make up 80 acres. In fact, the property was bounded on the north and east by Section 50 and on the south by Highway 8. However, there is no clear boundary for the west. If one boundary of the four-sided tract is not identified in the deed, it is not a sale per aversionem. Deshotel v. Lachney, 465 So.2d 974 (La. App. 3 Cir.1985). This sale was not one per aversionem.

¶10   This was a sale per lump. La. Civ. Code art. 2494. In the present case the cash sale instrument showed that the sale was made in consideration of $50,000. No amount per acre was specified. Pursuant to Article 2494 the purchaser of immovable property for a lump sum can not claim a diminution of the price on a deficiency of the measure, unless the real measure comes short of that expressed in the contract by one-twentieth. In the present case, the cash sale stated that 80 acres more or less was being conveyed. One-twentieth of 80 acres is four acres. A survey of the property after it was bought revealed that 43.20 acres was actually conveyed. The property conveyed to Lasiter was short 36.8 acres. The trial court was correct in ordering that the sale price of the land be reduced.

¶11   The defendants also argue that the trial court awarded too much as a diminution in the sales price. They claim that the trial court should have considered that Lasiter made more money selling the timber than he paid for the land and therefore was not damaged. The fact that Lasiter may have profited by buying this property and selling the timber has no bearing on the agreement he reached with the sellers for the purchase of 80 acres. He bought the land for the timber. The defendants could have sold the timber but chose instead to sell the land. Lasiter simply made a good business deal. His profit would have been greater had he received the full 80 acres. We agree with the trial court that Lasiter is entitled to a diminution of the purchase price.

¶12 We also find that the trial court's determination of the amount of diminution of the purchase price was not an abuse of discretion. The trial court made a determination that the value of the land was $750 an acre. It did so based on the value of the timber that Lasiter sold off the land. In oral reasons for judgment the trial judge explained, in general although not in particular, how he arrived at the diminution figure of $14,750. He took into account what Lasiter thought he was buying, and what he actually bought; what he got for the timber; and what he recovered when he conveyed the bare land after the timber was cut. Lasiter testified that what he believed he was getting out of his $50,000 purchase of 80 acres was 80 acres at $625 an acre. Considering that his loss by this measure would have justified a diminution in price of over $20,000, we cannot say that a reduction of only $14,750 was an abuse of discretion.

¶13 For the reasons set forth in this opinion the judgment of the trial court is affirmed. All costs of this appeal are assessed against defendants-appellants.

Study Questions:

As in the previous case, the description of the immovable in the following case includes both an estimate of the acreage being delivered and a description of the property by name or boundaries. However, in this case the court does not approve a change in price when the acreage delivered is different from that described. Why? How does this case differ from the previous one, and what is it about the sales contract that makes the difference?

LONG-FORK, LL.C. V. PETITE RIVIERE, LL.C. 2008
987 SO. 2D 831, (LA. APP. 3D CIR.)

COOKS, Judge.

¶1 The Plaintiff, Long-Fork, L.L.C. (Long-Fork), brought this action seeking to compel the buyer of certain property to supplement the purchase price or to return the property. On October 31, 2003, an Agreement to Purchase and Sell Real Estate (Purchase Agreement) was executed between Long-Fork and Petite Riviere, L.L.C. involving a piece of property located in Avoyelles Parish. The property description in the Purchase Agreement provided "said tract estimated to be 2,759 acres more or less and generally described as the South Farm, less seventy-seven acres north of the center line of Little River." The Purchase Agreement set forth a price of $1,050.00 per acre and provided that the "price per acre shall control in the event of a discrepancy between the price stated below and the price as determined by the number of acres conveyed, ..." The Purchase Agreement also provided "that a survey would be performed, by a surveyor mutually agreeable to Vendor and Vendee, of the tract of land .... in order that the Vendor and Vendee may more accurately calculate the acreage of the property to be conveyed." The Purchase Agreement also provided for the consideration of the sale to be $2,896,950.00, which reflected the $1,050.00 per acre price for 2,759 acres. The Purchase Agreement further provided that the act transferring title was to be executed on or before December 31, 2003. A provision that "the Act of Transfer of the property will include the terms and provisions of this contract" was included.

¶2   When the Act of Cash Sale was executed on February 13, 2004, the property was described as "comprising approximately 2759 [acres] more or less." The Act of Cash Sale did not contain any clause with respect to the price per acre controlling as was included in the Purchase Agreement. The sales price was $2,896,950.00. Brown Realty Company of Rayville, Inc. was Long-Fork's realtor for the transaction. The property was subsequently transferred by exchange from Petite Riviere to R. Dugas Family, L.L.C. Six months after the sale it was discovered by Long-Fork that the property sold encompassed more acres (approximately 215) than originally thought.

¶3   On February 11, 2005, Long-Fork filed a petition seeking a supplemental increase in the purchase price to reflect the greater number of acres. Named as Defendants were Petite Riviere and R. Dugas Family. Brown Realty was also named as a defendant by Long-Fork. However, the allegations against Brown Realty were such that Long-Fork only sought recovery from Brown Realty if Petite Riviere and R. Dugas Family were not liable. The petition was answered by Petite Riviere and R. Dugas Family, who also filed a Motion for Summary Judgment. Long-Fork filed its own Motion for Summary Judgment, as did Brown Realty. Following several depositions and supplemental memoranda, the matter came before the trial court on the Motions for Summary Judgment filed by each party. After a hearing on the matter, the trial court took the matter under advisement.

¶4   The trial court rendered judgment, denying the Motion for Summary Judgment filed by Petite Riviere and R. Dugas Family and granting Long-Fork's Motion for Summary Judgment. Judgment was rendered in favor of Long-Fork in the amount of $226,485.00 with interest from the date of judicial demand. Long-Fork's request for attorney fees was denied. A judgment granting Brown Realty's summary judgment was also signed. Defendants filed a Motion for New Trial, contending no supplemental purchase price was due. Long-Fork also filed a Motion for New Trial seeking attorney fees. The trial court denied Defendants' motion and granted Long-Fork's motion, awarding attorney fees in the amount of $22,620.00. This appeal followed, wherein Defendants contend the trial court erred in concluding that La. Civ. Code art. 2495 was inapplicable, that La. Civ. Code art. 2498 applied, and allowing for a supplement of the purchase price and attorney fees. Long-Fork answered the appeal, and argues the trial court erred in ruling that Defendants did not violate the right of first refusal granted to Long-Fork in the Act of Cash Sale.

ANALYSIS

¶5 As noted by all the parties and the trial court, the material facts in this case have been stipulated to and, as the trial court stated, "the dispute appears to be application of applicable law."

* * *

¶6 Defendants argue, contrary to what the trial court held, that La. Civ. Code art. 2495 is applicable and controlled the Act of Cash Sale. Louisiana Civil Code Article 2495 provides as follows:

> When an immovable described as a certain and limited body or a distinct object is sold for a lump price, an expression of the extent of the immovable in the act of sale does not give the parties any right to an increase or diminution of the price in the case of surplus or shortage in the actual extension of the immovable.

¶7 Article 2495 mentions only the "act of sale" and does not reference purchase agreements. In examining the description of the property in the Act of Cash Sale, it seems clear the property was described as a "certain and limited body or a distinct object." Id. The description stated what was being sold was "[a]ll of the Seller's rights, title and interest to a certain piece, parcel, or tract of land ... SOUTH OF THE CENTER LINE OF PETITE RIVIERE ... in Sections 2, 9, 10, 11, 13, 14, & 15."3

¶8 The Louisiana Supreme Court has long held that when a sale is made pursuant to specific boundaries, it is a sale per aversionem. Johnston v. Quarles, 3 La. 90 (1831). To constitute a sale per aversionem, the buyer must acquire the land within defined boundaries. Passera v. City of New Orleans, 167 La. 199, 118 So. 887 (1928). Such a purchase "conveys all of the land within the boundaries given, whether the measure be correctly stated in the deed or not. The designation of the boundaries control the enumeration of the quantity." Id. at 202, 118 So. 887.

¶9 In Campbell v. Cook, 151 La. 267, 91 So. 731 (1922), the purchaser sought a credit on the purchase price, because the property was said to contain 177 acres more or less, but in fact only contained 123.53 acres. The act of sale described the property as being bounded by three adjoining properties and the Cane River. The court found the boundaries set forth in the legal description were accurate, even if the measurement was not. The court found "... the jurisprudence is settled that where there is error as to quantity and none as to boundary, the purchaser cannot claim a diminution of the price in the absence of concealment and fraud. [Gugliemi v. Geismar, 46 La. Ann. 280, 14 So. 501.]" Id. at 269, 91 So. 731. Citing La. Civ. Code art. 2495, the court held the sale was per aversionem and that no price adjustment was due.

¶10   Long-Fork argued below that the Purchase Agreement is the final expression of the parties' intent, and claims it evidenced a "mutual" intent that the price per acre should control. Defendants maintain that the price per acre was used to determine what the sales price would ultimately be in the Act of Cash Sale. In finding in favor of Long-Fork the trial court determined that the silence in the Act of Cash Sale of the price per acre terms did not preclude proof of the obligation that the sale was to be on a price per acre basis. The trial court found that the "obvious and apparent intent of the parties throughout this entire transaction was that the property was to be sold on a price per acre basis."

¶11   The trial court's written reasons for judgment indicate it put great import on the use of the word "approximately" in the Act of Cash Sale. Those reasons provide:

> [D]escribing a tract to be "approximately 2,759[acres] more or less" is certainly an indication that the parties to the act of sale knew that there were other terms potentially applicable concerning price, and quite naturally, those terms are the terms reflected in the purchase agreement, being a price per acre. This confirms the parties intent that the sale be on a "per acre" price.

¶12   We do not reach the same conclusion as the trial court. It was incumbent on the parties to set an acreage amount to determine a final sales price in the Act of Cash Sale. It is, at best, pure speculation for the trial court to ascribe the meaning it did to the parties' use of the word "approximately." Defendants asserted that the use of the word "approximately" was a further confirmation, along with the use of the phrase "more or less," that acreage was only incidental rather than essential to the transaction. Certainly, this is as plausible an explanation for the use of the word "approximately" as what the trial court found.

¶13   Of much greater significance to this court is the use of the phrase "more or less" when describing the property sold between the parties. A reading of the phrase "approximately 2,759 [acres] more or less" leads to a common sense conclusion that the exact acreage amount was not essential to the transaction. It would be difficult to conclude otherwise. Thus, we cannot agree with the trial court and Long-Fork that there was a mutual consent between the parties that the price per acre should control, particularly noting the Act of Cash Sale excluded the price per acre language contained in the Purchase Agreement.

¶14 Long-Fork also points to its Certificate of Authority as evidence of the parties' mutual intent that the price per acre provision survived to the Act of Cash Sale. We note that this Certificate of Authority was executed by Long-Fork alone. Further, it lists $2,896,950.00, the price listed in the Act of Cash Sale, as the "total sales price."

¶15 Defendants, in arguing the Purchase Agreement was not the final expression of the parties' intent, noted that there "were a total of thirteen (13) differences between the Purchase Agreement and the Act of Sale." They point out that such extensive differences between the two are at odds with Long-Fork's assertions that there were no changes or negotiations prior to the perfection of the Act of Cash Sale. We agree.

¶16 Long-Fork also dismisses the failure of the Act of Cash Sale to contain any clause with respect to the price per acre controlling as "unfortunate" and an "error." Although alleging "error" as the reason for the absence of any clause with respect to the price per acre controlling, Long-Fork did not sue for reformation of the Act of Cash Sale as was done in Teche Realty & Inv. Co. v. Morrow, 95-1473 (La.App. 3 Cir. 4/17/96), 673 So.2d 1145. Reformation is an equitable remedy that is available to correct mistakes when the instruments as written do not reflect the true intent of the parties. See Agurs v. Holt, 232 La. 1026, 95 So.2d 644 (1957); WMC Mortgage Corp. v. Weatherly, 07-75 (La.App. 3 Cir. 6/13/07), 963 So.2d 413. If Long-Fork believed the Act of Cash Sale did not accurately reflect the true intent of the parties, the appropriate action would have been a suit for reformation.

¶17 Furthermore, this court has held that the presence of error is irrelevant to the applicability of La. Civ. Code art. 2495. In Kile v. Louisiana Limestone Aggregates, Inc., 378 So.2d 978 (La. App. 3 Cir.1979), writ denied, 380 So.2d 71 (1980), Louisiana Limestone Aggregates (LLA) sought a piece of property of at least three acres to build a facility for storing and selling its products. Representatives of LLA examined a piece of land owned by Kile on foot and viewed it from the air. A purchase agreement describing the property by reference to boundaries was signed. This court determined the property description set forth a certain and limited body such as to fall within the scope of La. Civ. Code art. 2495. After the purchase agreement was signed, LLA discovered the tract only encompassed two acres and was insufficient to build its facility. LLA refused to purchase the property and Kile brought suit for specific performance. This court was faced with a question of what is the effect of a per aversionem sale where both parties were mistaken as to the quantity of land. We stated:

> We conclude that the description at hand is "per aversionem," as being within "fixed boundaries." LLA is obligated to purchase the property so described even though the parties to the agreement were under the impression that the area contained three acres instead of approximately two

acres as reflected by the survey. LLA's contention that the deficiency in area was an error of fact that would justify the invalidation of the agreement, must yield to the clear law of "per aversionem." Id. at 983.

¶18 Even though there was acknowledged mutual error between the parties in Kile, this court found such error was irrelevant to the applicability of La. Civ. Code art. 2495. Likewise, any error alleged by Long-Fork is equally irrelevant in this case. Long-Fork also argues the language of the Purchase Agreement should control over the language of the Act of Cash Sale. In support of this position, it cites the case of Hingle Brothers, Inc. v. Bonura, 248 So.2d 391 (La.App. 4 Cir.1971). We find Hingle distinguishable on the facts and find it inapplicable to the situation presented here. In Hingle, the issue was whether the purchaser of the land could recover from the seller the cost of certain street improvements that were made before the sale, but which were not assessed against the property until after the sale. Hingle did not deal with an action seeking a supplement to the purchase price pursuant to La. Civ. Code articles 2492 through 2495. Hingle was decided based upon the legal warranty of title as governed by the Civil Code.

¶19 Further, the court in Hingle noted the act of sale need not conform to the purchase agreement if "varied by mutual consent." The trial court in the present case concluded there was "absolutely no evidence of mutual consent to change the purchase agreement." We disagree. The description of the property in the Act of Cash Sale and the deposition testimony of Charles Mitchell indicate it was Long-Fork's intent to convey a particular piece of land for a set price. Mitchell, who was a co-managing partner of Long-Fork testified as follows:

> Q. But you came to an agreement to sell all land south of the river?
> A. Right.
> Q. And that is what you intended to convey both through the purchase agreement and the Act of Sale?
> A. Correct. ...
> Q. So correspondingly, it was your intention, Long-Fork's intention, to convey all land that Long-Fork had south of Little River?
> A. Correct.

¶20 The jurisprudence holds that the act of sale represents "the conclusion of the negotiation process and embodies the final expression of the parties' intent." Esplanade Management, Ltd. v. Sajare Interests, 498 So.2d 289, 292 (La.App. 4 Cir.1986); see also Teche Realty, 673 So.2d 1145. An authentic act constitutes full proof of the agreement it contains, as against the parties. La. Civ. Code art. 1835.

¶21 The Act of Cash Sale, unlike the Purchase Agreement, did not include any "price per acre" language. The Act of Cash Sale provides the latest and best expression of the parties' intent with respect to price. Thus, we find the presumption provided by La. Civ. Code art. 2495 serves to reinforce the "mutual intent" of the parties in this case.

¶22 Applying La. Civ. Code art. 2495 to the Act of Cash Sale confirms that the object of the sale was to include all of the property south of the centerline of Petite Riviere in specified sections. The Act of Cash Sale also states a lump price. Therefore, both requirements are met for the sale of a certain and limited body. Thus, the legal description used in the Act of Cash Sale makes the sale a transaction pursuant to La. Civ. Code art. 2495. We find, contrary to the trial court, that the language of "approximately" 2,759 acres "more or less" supports this conclusion.

¶23 Finding this was a sale pursuant to La. Civ. Code art. 2495, the one-year prescriptive period allowed for in La. Civ. Code art. 2498 is inapplicable here. Because La. Civ. Code art. 2495 is the controlling statute, the period of time to seek a supplement of the sales price ends with the act of sale. As Defendants note, since the Purchase Agreement contained the "price per acre shall control" language, Long-Fork did have the right to seek an adjustment of the purchase price prior to the closing of the sale. Had Long-Fork surveyed the property, as was its right, the total price could have been adjusted prior to closing. It is certainly reasonable to conclude that if the price per acre were the controlling factor in the setting of the sales price, Long-Fork would have conducted a survey. However, Long-Fork did not survey its property, further confirming its intent was not to sell a certain quantity of property (which would be governed by La. Civ. Code art. 2492), but to sell all of its property south of the centerline of the Little River regardless of acreage. As such, La. Civ. Code art. 2495 is controlling and Long-Fork was not entitled to "any right to an increase or diminution of the price in the case of surplus or shortage in the actual extension of the immovable the property." The trial court erred in holding otherwise, and we reverse the trial court's judgment awarding Long-Fork a supplement to the purchase price and attorney fees and render judgment granting the Motion for Summary Judgment filed by Defendants.

* * *

DECREE

¶24 For the foregoing reasons, we reverse the trial court's judgment awarding Long-Fork a supplement to the purchase price and attorney fees and render judgment granting the Motion for Summary Judgment filed by Defendants. . . .

AFFIRMED IN PART; REVERSED IN PART; AND RENDERED.

Section 2: Warranty Against Eviction

Read Articles 2500-2517, 2557, & 2560.

The seller has two principal obligations: delivering the thing and warranting the thing he sells. However, there are three kinds of warranty to which the seller is obligated under the Civil Code: the warranty against eviction (i.e. the buyer's peaceable possession of and title to the thing sold), the absence of redhibitory vices (i.e. hidden defects), and the warranty that the thing is fit for its ordinary use. This section deals with the seller's warranty against eviction.

Article 2500 defines eviction as the buyer's loss of, or danger of losing the whole or part of the thing sold because of a third person's right that existed at the time of the sale, including any undeclared encumbrances – with the exception of apparent servitudes and those natural and legal nonapparent servitudes which need not be declared.

A. General Concepts, Warranted Rights, and Loss or Danger that Constitutes Eviction

The warranty against eviction is the buyer's remedy when the seller does not own the thing he purports to sells and therefore cannot convey its ownership to the buyer. In addition, the warranty against eviction also applies when the seller's rights in the thing are somehow incomplete or are encumbered by the right of a third person. Thus, the warranty against eviction can be seen as the post-sale parallel to the warranty of merchantability discussed earlier. That warranty of merchantability means someone who has agreed to buy a thing cannot be forced to execute the purchase if he discovers that he will have to sue a third party in order to protect his right in the thing – hence the expression, "buying a lawsuit." Under the warranty against eviction, in contrast, the sale has already gone through when the buyer discovers that a third person has a right in the thing sold.

In addition, the warranty against eviction includes mortgages and other encumbrances that the seller did not previously disclose. Thus, the warranty protects the buyer even if the mortgage is recorded. It also includes non-apparent servitudes. But the warranty against eviction does not cover apparent servitudes: so the buyer cannot claim a breach of this warranty because he failed to notice the Cajun Christmas tree (i.e., oil derrick) that was in place before he bought the land.

The evicted buyer may recover from the seller the price he paid, the "value" of any fruits he had to give to the third party who evicted him, and any other damages caused by the eviction, but not any loss due to "increase in value" of the thing. Art. 2506. The buyer may also recover for products lost. Art. 2512. The seller must return the full price, even if the property's value has decreased in the interim – unless the buyer has benefited from a diminution in value caused by his own act. In that case, the amount of the benefit is subtracted. Art. 2507. Such a benefit can occur when the buyer sells off a component part of the thing, thus diminishing its value. Art. 2507, comment (b). Generally, a seller liable for eviction must reimburse the buyer for the cost of useful improvements in addition to the price, any fruits, and any other damages. However, if the seller was in bad faith (i.e. he knew of the third person's right in the thing at the time of the sale), then he must reimburse the buyer for the cost of all improvements, whether useful or not. Art. 2509.

The definition of eviction in Article 2506 includes four fundamental concepts.[2] First, the buyer's loss must result from actions of a third party whose rights were superior to and pre-existed the buyer's rights. Second, eviction refers not just to the buyer's actual loss, but also his 'danger of losing' the thing. Third, the warranty protects only against third parties with rights that pre-date the sale, not trespassers, and fourth, the warranty protects against both total and partial evictions.

The buyer who learns of a potential eviction cannot simply settle with the third party and then sue the seller, he must first give the seller timely notice of the threat or notify the seller in a timely fashion of any suit he brought against the third party. This is known as a 'call in warranty.' Art. 2517. This is so that so that the seller has a chance to defend the sale or resolve the problem. If the buyer fails to give reasonable notice to the seller, then he forfeits the warranty against eviction if the seller is able to prove that, had he been notified in time, he would have been able to prove that the third person had no right.

Study Questions:

In the case below, what is the basis of the plaintiff's claim that he was evicted?

What language in the Civil Code leads to the conclusion that he doesn't have a claim?

How is the public records doctrine involved in the court's reasoning?

RICHMOND V. ZAPATA DEVELOPMENT CORP. 1977
350 SO. 2D 875 (LA.)

DENNIS, Justice.

¶1 The question presented by this case is whether the presence of drilling structures on land, as visible evidence of a mineral lease, will prevent a buyer of the property, who made no pre-sale inspection, from recovering in warranty from his vendor, who failed to disclose the existence of the lease.

---

2   24 La. Civil Law Treatise § 10:3.

¶2   On June 9, 1972, defendant Zapata Development Corporation, conveyed to plaintiff R. Randolph Richmond, Jr., by warranty deed a parcel of immovable property located in Iberville Parish comprising some 640 acres. The act of sale declared a number of charges claimed against the property. Richmond purchased without examining the title or inspecting the premises, and later discovered that the property was being exploited for oil and gas pursuant to a mineral lease by Gay Union Corporation in favor of Gulf Refining Company of Louisiana which had been executed and properly recorded in 1930.

¶3   On October 2, 1974, Richmond filed suit against his vendor, Zapata, alleging that the extensive mineral recovery operations conducted under the 1930 Gay-Gulf lease on some 360 acres of the property rendered that portion of the property useless for any purpose other than mineral production and impaired his ability to develop and utilize the remaining 280 acres. Plaintiff alleged that the mineral lessee had placed on the property a network of pipelines, tanks, lines, canals, structures, shacks, offices, houses, drilling equipment, rigs both active and abandoned, roadways and other earthen works, ponds, pits, oil spills and pollutants. Contending that failure to declare the existence of the lease in the act of sale amounted to a breach of Zapata's warranty against eviction, Richmond originally prayed for judgment in the amount of $120,000, but subsequently amended his petition to seek an award of $2,120,000.

¶4   Defendant Zapata filed exceptions of no cause of action and prescription, and a motion for summary judgment. In support of the latter motion it attached as exhibits copies of the 1972 act of sale of the property from Zapata to Richmond, a 1971 recorded act of sale of all oil, gas and mineral interests in the property from Southdown, Inc. to Pelto Oil Company, and the 1930 mineral lease from Gay Union Corporation to Gulf Refining Company of Louisiana. [The district court granted the defendant's motion for summary judgment, and the court of appeal affirmed, holding that plaintiff had been put on notice, by inscriptions recited in the deed, of facts sufficient to provoke his examination of the title before purchasing.]

***

¶5   We granted writs to review this decision. 341 So.2d 1126 (La.1977).

¶6   In its opinion the appellate court, citing Juneau v. Laborde, 219 La. 921, 54 So.2d 325 (1951), stated our jurisprudence holds that, generally a buyer is not obliged to examine title to immovable property, but where certain facts known to him constitute a warning that further inquiry is needed, and such facts are sufficient to excite inquiry, a duty devolves upon him to investigate his vendor's title. Defendant, Zapata, has called our attention to a number of cases it says also stand for this broad proposition. We find the Juneau case and these decisions inapposite to the instant proceeding as the holding in none of them hinges on the vendor's obligation in warranty owed to the vendee.

¶7   Juneau v. Laborde, for example, involved a petitory action brought by heirs to immovable property against a possessor claiming the property on the basis of ten-year good faith acquisitive prescription. La. C.C. art. 3478. This Court found that the possessor was aware of facts which were sufficient to excite inquiry into the validity of his vendor's title, and that a duty devolved upon him to investigate the title before purchasing. However, this rule provides no defense against a vendee who seeks to enforce his vendor's obligations under a warranty deed. In fact, to allow its application in such an action would violate basic principles of warranty against eviction in the civil law and a substantial body of jurisprudence interpreting our Civil Code.

¶8   Because the registry laws are intended only as notice to third parties and have no application whatever between parties to a contract, a vendee is under no obligation to search the record in order to ascertain what his vendor has sold and what it has not, and the vendee is entitled, as between himself and his vendor, to rely upon his deed as written. Young v. Sartor, 152 La. 1064, 95 So. 223 (1923). Moreover, as a general rule, in the absence of a stipulation of non-warranty in the act of sale, knowledge of the danger of eviction does not prevent the purchaser from recovering the purchase price upon disturbance of his possession. Scott v. Featherston, 5 La.Ann. 306 (1850) citing Article 2481 of the Louisiana Civil Code of 1825 (La. C.C. art. 2505); Hall v. Nevill, 3 La.Ann. 326 (1848). See, Comment, Warranty Against Eviction in the Civil Law: Limitations on the Extent of the Vendee's Recovery, 23 Tul.L.Rev. 154, 169-70 (1948). Cf. Collins v. Slocum, 317 So.2d 672 (La.App. 3d Cir. 1975). But see, Culver v. Culver, 188 La. 716, 178 So. 252 (1938), criticized in 23 Tul.L.Rev., supra, at 170.

¶9   This accords with the view of a majority of French courts and writers that although such knowledge bars recovery of damages by an evicted buyer who purchases by a deed which does not contain a non-warranty clause, the purchaser is nevertheless entitled to a restitution of the price. 2 M. Planiol, Civil Law Treatise, pt. 1, ss 1504, 1509 (La.St.L.Inst.Transl.1959); 1 M. Troplong, Droit Civil Expliqué: De La Vente, s 482 (2d ed.1835); See, Comment, Warranty Against Eviction in the Civil Law, supra, at 160, and authorities cited therein. It is their view that this principle is not provided directly by the warranty provisions of the Code, but results from Article 1599 of the Code Napoleon (La. C.C. art. 2452) which, after declaring that the sale of the thing of another is null, adds that it can give occasion for damages "when the buyer did not know that the thing belonged to another." See, Planiol, id. at 1509.

¶10   An exception to the rule is recognized, however, regarding an alleged eviction resulting from the existence of an apparent servitude on the property. In discussing Code Napoleon

Article 1638, the French authorities have declared that the only servitudes which give rise to the warranty are those which at the same time are non-apparent and not declared. 2 M. Planiol, Civil Law Treatise, pt. 1, §§ 1493-95. The origin of the distinction drawn between visible servitudes and non-apparent charges against the property was explained by Pothier, who observed:

> "A . . . kind of real charges, of which it is the buyer's business not to be ignorant, and against which consequently he cannot claim any warranty, though they are not expressly declared by the contract, consists of visible servitudes, such as those of light and eaves-dropping; of which the buyer cannot be ignorant, since in visiting the house before purchasing it, he cannot avoid seeing the windows or the eaves.

> "Are we to include amongst the rights, which it is the buyer's duty not to be ignorant of, a right of champart not seignorial? The reason for doubting is, that the perception of the champart being public and known in the country, it is easy for the buyer to inform himself, and to ascertain before purchasing, whether the estate is subject to that charge.

> ***

> "Notwithstanding these reasons, we must decide, that the seller is bound to warrant against a champart, which is not declared by the contract. A buyer does not buy a house without visiting it in person, or sending some one on his part, nor, consequently, without perceiving the visible servitudes; but, he cannot be instructed of the charge of champart, except by being informed of it, and he may neglect to inform himself, or be deceived in the information, which he receives. . . ."

1 R. Pothier's Treatise on Contracts: Contract of Sale, §§ 200-01 at 123-24 (L. S. Cushing transl. 1839).

¶11   Louisiana courts also have adopted the view that a vendor does not warrant the property conveyed as free from apparent servitudes. Lallande v. Wentz & Pochelu, 18 La.Ann. 289 (1866); James v. Buchert, 144 So.2d 435 (La.App. 4th Cir. 1962). Cf. Collins v. Slocum, 317 So.2d 672 (La. App. 3d Cir. 1975). This conclusion may be inferred from La. C.C. art. 2515, which, as Code Napoleon art. 1638, provides that the seller is bound to warrant against undeclared, non-apparent servitudes. The rule is justified as a practical matter for the reasons stated by the French writers. Pothier, supra, and Planiol, supra, § 1494.6

¶12   In the instant case the undisputed material facts are as follows: The buyer acquired by deed containing no general stipulation of non-warranty. The existence of the Gay-Gulf lease as a charge on the property was not declared in the list of inscriptions bearing upon the property included in the act of sale. (footnote omitted) The extensive mineral development of which plaintiff complains does not flow from any of the charges enumerated in the act of sale, but rather from the 1930 Gay-Gulf lease. The alleged eviction stemmed from an undeclared mineral lease and not an undeclared apparent servitude, but there were on the property ample external signs of mineral production conducted pursuant to this lease.

¶13 Hence, if it is the vendee's duty not to be ignorant of apparent mineral leases as well as apparent servitudes, the action in warranty should be refused him, and the vendor would be entitled to judgment as a matter of law. On the other hand, if the vendee is presumed to know only of apparent servitudes, the vendor must respond in warranty because the eviction resulted from a different kind of visible charge which was not declared at the time of the sale.

¶14 The Civil Code does not expressly address the issue. It merely indicates that the buyer has a warranty against a servitude which at the same time is non-apparent and not declared. La. C.C. art. 2515. The civilian writers do not seem to have considered whether other charges equally as visible as apparent servitudes are excluded from the vendor's warranty. In discussing the special rules as to servitudes, however, the writers dwell not upon the legal classification of the charge but on the practical question of whether the premises may be examined without perceiving the visible signs of its existence. If the buyer cannot avoid seeing evidence of the charge should he visit the property before the purchase there is no need for the seller to inform him of it. In the event the purchaser is unable to learn of a charge because it is non-apparent, fairness demands that the buyer must either inform him of it before the sale or protect him against eviction.

¶15 As the treatise writers, we think paramount importance should be attached to whether the charge produces visible external effects on the property rather than upon the legal classification of the charge. In the present case, for instance, the drilling structures and other artifacts of mineral production would be equally apparent regardless of their source. A simple inspection of the premises would have apprised the buyer of the existence of a significant charge against the property whether it derived from a lease or a servitude. Furthermore, there is probably less difference between a mineral lease and a mineral servitude than between other servitudes and charges. Both are basic mineral rights, and they share many of the same attributes. See, La.R.S. 31:16, 31:21 et seq., 31:114 et seq., and comments. For all these reasons we conclude that, just as an apparent servitude, an undisclosed mineral lease which produces on the property ample signs of its existence is a real charge of which it is the buyer's business not to be ignorant and against which he cannot claim warranty.

¶16 For the foregoing reasons, we find there is no genuine issue of material fact in this case and that the defendant Zapata is entitled to judgment as a matter of law. Although we do not approve of the reasons given by the trial court and court of appeal, we conclude they reached the correct result. Accordingly, the judgment of the court of appeal is affirmed at appellant's cost.

Affirmed.

B. Disturbance: The Loss or Danger that Constitutes Eviction

Study Question:

What doe the following cases illustrate about the loss or danger that constitutes eviction? Must the buyer actually be dispossessed of the thing, or is the mere danger that he will be sufficient?

KLING V. MCLIN 1981
394 SO. 2D 1289 (LA. APP. 1ST CIR.)

EDWARDS, Judge.

¶1 On October 14, 1976, plaintiff, Leonce P. Kling, Jr., purchased a used car from defendant, Richard H. McLin. When Kling applied for a title from the Louisiana Department of Public Safety, he was informed, on December 21, 1976, that no title would issue since the vehicle was encumbered with a chattel mortgage. On October 11, 1979, plaintiff brought suit against McLin, seeking return of the purchase price, interest and costs. McLin answered, denied plaintiff's claim and named Durham Pontiac-Cadillac, Inc., a third party defendant.

¶2 McLin and Durham Pontiac-Cadillac each filed a peremptory exception of prescription, urging that plaintiff's action was in redhibition and had prescribed by the passage of one year. The trial court maintained both exceptions and dismissed both plaintiff's and third-party plaintiff's actions at their respective costs. Plaintiff appeals. We reverse.

¶3 A seller is bound to two principal obligations that of delivering and that of warranting the thing which he sells. LSA-C.C. Art. 2475. The seller's warranty has two objects the first is the buyer's peaceable possession of the thing sold and the second is the hidden defects of the thing sold or its redhibitory vices. LSA-C.C. Art. 2476.

¶4 The peaceable possession of a buyer is disturbed when he is evicted from the totality or a part of the thing purchased, due to the right or claims of a third person. LSA-C.C. Art. 2500. In the present case, the third person is Beneficial Finance Company of Hammond, the mortgage holder.

¶5 When a buyer sues his vendor for breach of the warranty of peaceable possession, the applicable period of prescription is ten years. LSA-C.C. Art. 3544. Evangeline Farmer's Co-op, Inc. v. Vidrine, 378 So.2d 604 (La.App. 3rd Cir. 1979); Hoggatt v. Halcomb, 250 So.2d 471 (La.App. 2nd Cir. 1971); Gage v. Heins, 197 So.2d 699 (La.App. 4th Cir. 1967), writ refused 250 La. 917, 199 So.2d 921 (1967); Whitten v. Monkhouse, 29 So.2d 800 (La.App. 2nd Cir. 1947), amended on other grounds 213 La. 651, 35 So.2d 418 (1948). It was, therefore, error for the trial court to apply LSA-C.C. Arts. 2498 and 2546 and to find that plaintiff's action had prescribed.

¶6 For the foregoing reasons, the judgment appealed from is annulled and reversed. The case is remanded to the trial court for proceedings not inconsistent with law and this opinion. All costs are to await a final determination on the merits.

REVERSED AND REMANDED.

Study Question

In a similar situation, Bologna Bros. v. Stephens, 206 La. 112, 18 So. 2d 914 (1944) involved the sale of three lots to a partnership, plaintiff Bologna Bros. Mr Stephens bought three lots in Baton Rouge's Bonnecaze Subdivision from Lewis Gottlieb, Lots 21, 22, and 23. Mr. Stephens later organized a realty company, Stephens Realty Company, Inc., owned in part by his wife and daughter. Stephens then sold the lots to Bologna Brothers in his own name, and they built a building on it.

Six years later, after Stephens died and his wife and daughter took over the Realty Company, they sold Cecil Bankston two parcels of ground, one of which included part of the same property that Mr. Stephens had previously sold to the Bologna Brothers.

Bankston informed the Bologna Brothers that he owned the land on which their building was built, and after some negotiations, they paid Bankston $1,000 for a deed to the property. The Bologna Brothers then sued the Stephens Realty Company for eviction and repayment of the funds expended on clearing the title.

The Louisiana Supreme Court reversed the trial court's judgment in favor of the plaintiff Bologna Brothers on the grounds that the description in the registry was unclear, and that Bankston was a necessary party to the suit. Nevertheless, assume for a moment that Bankston did not have a valid claim. **Would Stephens Realty be liable for reimbursing the money? (Hint: Read Article 2517)**

C. Apparent and Non-Apparent Servitudes

Article 2500 stipulates that the warranty against eviction "covers encumbrances on the thing that were not declared at the time of the sale, with the exception of apparent servitudes and natural and legal nonapparent servitudes, which need not be declared. An encumbrance is any real right that burdens a thing. For immovables, this includes mortgages, privileges, liens, servitudes, building restrictions, and various kinds of mineral rights.[3] It can also include rights that are not technically real rights, but which simulate them under the public records doctrine, things such as leases, options to buy, rights of first refusal, and bilateral contracts to sell. So, any such right that is not declared to the buyer would be a violation of the warranty against eviction.

If, to the contrary, the seller informs the buyer of the pre-existing right, or if the encumbrance is an apparent servitude, then there is no warranty. So, for example, an encumbrance expressly mentioned in the deed of sale is 'declared,' as are any survey maps referenced in the deed and annexed to it that indicate the existence of a servitude.[4] While the parol evidence rule precludes the admission of testimonial proof that varies or negates the contents of a written act under Article 1848, Louisiana courts have allowed oral proof to be admitted if the writing is ambiguous or leaves doubt as to the parties' intent. Apparent servitudes, such as the one at issue in *Richmond v. Zapata*, have always been excluded from the warranty against eviction. A servitude is apparent if it can be perceived by exterior signs – such as a construction, an aqueduct – or a Cajun Christmas tree. While a mineral lease is not a servitude, and the Code expressly exempts only apparent servitudes, the mineral lease was equally apparent.

The final exception in Article 2500 covers natural and legal nonapparent servitudes. For example, an estate may be bound by a servitude of passage in favor of an enclosed estate, but the owner of the estate owing passage could be completely unaware of it until the owner of the enclosed estate files suit against him. In these cases, however, it is the law and not the seller who is responsible for this type of charge, so it would be unfair to allow the seller to face an eviction suit when owner of the enclosed estate demands a roadway from the buyer.[5]

D. Sale With or Without Warranty v. Sale at the Buyer's Peril and Risk

Article 2503 provides:

The warranty against eviction is implied in every sale. Nevertheless, the parties may agree to increase or to limit the warranty. They may also agree to an exclusion of the warranty, but even in that case the seller must return the price to the buyer if eviction occurs, unless it is clear that

---

3 24 La. Civil Law Treatise § 10:8.

4 Id. § 10:9.

5 Id. at § 10:11.

the buyer was aware of the danger of eviction, or the buyer has declared that he was buying at his peril and risk, or the seller's obligation of returning the price has been expressly excluded.

In all those cases the seller is liable for an eviction that is occasioned by his own act, and any agreement to the contrary is null.

The buyer is subrogated to the rights in warranty of the seller against other persons, even when the warranty is excluded.

Thus, the Code states that the warranty against eviction is implied in every sale, though the parties may agree to increase or to limit the warranty. They may even agree to exclude it, but even in that case, the seller must still return the price to the buyer if eviction occurs, unless it was clear to the buyer that he was buying at his own risk and peril. This can happen in three ways: 1) the buyer was clearly aware of eviction, or 2) the buyer expressly declared that he was buying at his peril and risk, or 3) the seller's obligation to return the price was expressly excluded. The second paragraph of Article 2503 includes an exception to the exception, however: if the seller himself does something to evict his own buyer, then the seller is liable for that eviction, regardless of any agreement to the contrary. (The third paragraph, that referring to subrogation, will be discussed in a later section).

Study Question:

In the case below, analyze whether the sale was one with warranty, one without warranty, one at the buyer's own risk or one where (regardless of any exclusion of the warranty) the seller did something to evict his own buyer.

NEW ORLEANS & CARROLLTON RR. V. JOURDAIN'S HEIRS 1882
34 LA. ANN. 648 (LA.)

The opinion of the Court was delivered by Fenner, J.

¶1 Plaintiff sues defendants for the price of certain real estate sold to plaintiff by E. V. Jourdain, the ancestor of defendants, on May 3d, 1836, and from which plaintiff was evicted on May 27th, 1878.

¶2 The answer of defendants admits the sale but avers that the sale from Jourdain to plaintiff contained a stipulation of no warranty, and that plaintiff, at date of purchase, was aware of the danger of eviction, and purchased at its peril and risk.

¶3 The act of sale contains a warranty against all troubles, evictions, etc., "provenant de ses faits et promesses seulement."

¶4 The French authorities agree that such a clause as the above is equivalent to an express stipulation of non-warranty against troubles, evictions, etc., arising from the acts or promises of others than the vendor himself. 1 Troplong, Vente, p. 610, Nos. 478-9-80.

¶5 Warranty, as a general rule, is of the nature, and not of the essence, of the contract of sale; the only exception being that the vendor is, under all circumstances, "accountable for what results from his personal act, and any contrary agreement is void." C. C. 2504.

¶6 In all other respects, the parties may, "by particular agreement," add to, or diminish, or even abrogate, the obligation of warranty. C. C. 2503.

¶7 But with regard to the effect of such "particular agreements," the law distinguishes between the different consequences of eviction.

¶8 The mere stipulation of non-warranty frees the seller from liability for fruits or revenues, costs and damages; but with regard to the price, the case is different. Nec enim bonœ fidei contractus hanc patitur conventionem, ut emptor rem amitteret, et venditor pretium retineret, was the equitable doctrine of the Roman law. Dig. L. 11, § 18, De act. empti.

¶9 Our own Code expressly provides that "even in case of stipulation of no warranty, the seller, in case of eviction, is liable to a restitution of the price, unless the buyer was aware, at the time of the sale, of the danger of the eviction, and purchased at his peril and risk." C. C. 2505.

¶10 This Article is a literal translation of Art. 1629 of the Code Napoléon, except that the latter uses the disjunctive or, instead of the conjunctive and, in the last phrase of the Article.

¶11 Counsel for plaintiff contends that the effect of this change in our law from the French Code, is to require the concurrence of three elements in order to create an exemption from restitution of the price, viz: 1st, stipulation of no warranty; 2d, knowledge of buyer, at time of sale, of danger of eviction; 3d, express stipulation in the act that the buyer bought at his peril and risk.

¶12 We cannot adopt this interpretation. We think, with the District Judge, that our Article means the same as if it read: "Unless the buyer was aware, at the time of the sale, of the danger of the eviction, and thus or therefore purchased at his peril and risk." In other words, the law means that the buyer who acquires under a clause of non-warranty, having, at the time, knowledge of the danger of the eviction, is held, by implication from those facts to purchase at his risk and peril, and cannot, therefore, sue for restitution of the price.

¶13 When, on the other hand, the act contains an express stipulation that the buyer purchases at his peril and risk, it would seem to be of no consequence what knowledge he had of the danger of eviction, or even, perhaps, whether there was a stipulation of no warranty or not. "In that case," says Marcadé, "the object of the sale is not properly the thing itself, but merely the pretensions and claims which the vendor may have upon this thing. The seller then fulfils his promise completely by the simple fact of transferring his rights, whatever they may be, and hence the buyer can have no right to reclaim the price, on the ground of eviction from the thing itself. There is no occasion, in such case, to inquire whether the act contains the clause of non-warranty or not, because what the Article says under the assumption of the existence of this clause, would equally result, even in its absence." 6 Marcadé, p. 262; 6 Mourlon, No. 573; 1 Duvergier, 341.

¶14 Our Code expressly recognizes the sale of an uncertain hope, such as the haul of the fisher's net before he throws it, and maintains the sale, although he should catch nothing. C.C. 2151.

¶15 In this case, there is no such express stipulation, and under our construction of Art. 2505, considering the clause of non-warranty, and considering that nothing is claimed beyond the restitution of the price, we have only to inquire whether the plaintiff "was aware, at the time of the sale, of the danger of the eviction."

¶16 The record furnishes no evidence whatever that the vendor communicated to plaintiff, or that the latter otherwise had knowledge of any particular real or suspected defect of title, from which any danger of eviction might have been anticipated. The sale took place more than forty years ago, and naturally evidence outside of the act itself is wanting.

¶17 The sole ground on which defendants rely, to establish plaintiff's knowledge of the danger of eviction, is the following clause in the act: "The property presently sold belongs to the vendor, by means of the acquisition which he has made thereof from Mr. Raymond Mansana, according to an act passed before the undersigned notary, on the 24th of February last, to which the parties declare that they refer for fuller information."

¶18 Referring to the sale from Mansana, we find it to be a sale with full warranty, at the same price for which it was subsequently sold to plaintiff.

¶19 That act, however, also sets forth the origin of Mansana's title as derived by sale from syndics of the creditors of Louis Bierra, made on the 19th of August, 1823.

¶20 Bierra had acquired the property from Relf & Chew, claiming to be (but finally decided not to be) executors of Daniel Clark.

¶21 By these successive references, defendants contend that plaintiff acquired full knowledge of the authorship of Jourdain's title; that it was thus advised that the title was derived mediately from a syndic's sale, and that this was sufficient to inform it of the danger of eviction.

¶22 We cannot admit the correctness of this view. There is nothing apparent on the face of any of the acts referred to, suggesting any cause for, or danger of, eviction. Mansana, who had acquired at the syndics' sale, had held the property for thirteen years, without disturbance, and then sold to Jourdain with full warranty. The mere fact that the property was derived from a syndic's sale, does not, necessarily or naturally, import any defect of title or danger of eviction. Indeed, in many respects, titles derived from judicial sales are more secure than private titles.

¶23 A syndic's sale is analogous to the sale under execution, as to which the Code declares that "it transfers the property of the thing to the purchaser as completely as if the owner had sold it himself; but it transfers only the rights of the debtor such as they are." C. C. 2620.

¶24 The latter clause does not signify, as substantially contended by defendants, that such a sale amounts merely to a quit-claim. On the contrary, the following Article gives the purchaser, in case of eviction from the property, recourse for reimbursement against the debtor and creditor. So, in case of a syndic's sale, the evicted purchaser would have his recourse against those who had received the price.

¶25 We have carefully considered this question and can find neither reason nor authority in support of the position that mere knowledge of the sources of the vendor's title dispenses with the necessity of establishing knowledge of the danger of eviction, in order to bar the claim for restitution of the price; unless, indeed, the titles referred to have infirmities so patent on their face, that the buyer would be thereby affected with notice.

¶26 The latter feature is distinctly presented in the cases of Carrian v. Rieffel, 2 N. S. 621; Boisblanc v. Markey, 21 A. 721, and in the French case of Dulut contre Deloffre, J. P. 1846, 1, 576.

¶27 We think the knowledge of the danger of eviction, referred to in the Code, means actual knowledge, which must be brought home to him by direct proof, or by implication from references to, or proof of, collateral facts, so strong as to be equivalent thereto. See Fletcher v. Cavalier, 4 La. 274

* * *

Rehearing refused.

Study Questions:

The previous case stated that Article 2503 requires one of two things to be true for the seller's warranty against eviction to be excluded. First, the contract may declare that the buyer is buying at his own risk and peril. Or second, direct proof may show that the buyer in fact bought with the knowledge of the danger of eviction, which in turn shows that the buyer willingly accepted the risk of eviction.

But what is the effect of a waiver of the warranty against eviction? The next case involves interpretation of the language in Article 2503 stipulating that even if the warranty is waived, the seller must return the price. Though the court ultimately concludes that there was no consent and therefore no contract, which party is arguing for which language and why? What would have been the effect of the putative buyer's contractual language? The seller's?

BIELAWSKI V. LANDRY 1981
397 SO. 2D 861 (LA. APP. 4TH CIR.)

HUGHES, Judge.

¶1   This is an action for specific performance of an agreement to buy and sell immovable property. The trial court refused to grant specific performance and plaintiff appealed. We affirm. The litigation brings us into confrontation with the issue of whether a waiver of warranty of title sufficiently protects a seller from recourse, specifically the right of return of the purchase price from the purchaser where the purchaser is aware of a defective title. The purchaser was willing to take the property "as is and without legal warranty", however, the seller insisted that the act of sale proposed by the purchaser include an exculpatory clause providing that the property be sold "without legal warranties, without recourse and not even for the return of the purchase price."

¶2   On May 8, 1978, Mr. and Mrs. Zigmund Bielawski entered into a written agreement to purchase a lot from Alvin J. Landry, Jr. for a price of $15,000. The agreement indicated that the act of sale was to be passed on or before June 30, 1978. As is frequently provided in these agreements, the contract provided for a sixty-day extension for passage of the act of sale if curative title work was required. Additionally, the contract stated that:

> "The seller shall deliver to purchaser a merchantable title, and his inability to deliver such title within the time stipulated herein, *shall render this contract null and void*, reserving unto purchaser the right to demand the return of the deposit from the holder thereof and to recover actual costs incurred in processing of sale and reserving unto agent the right to recover commission. (Emphasis added [by the court])

> "In the event the seller fails to comply with this agreement for any other reason, within the time specified, the purchaser shall have the right either to demand the return of his deposit in full plus an equal amount to be paid as penalty by the seller, or the purchaser may demand specific performance, at his option."

¶3 Before the scheduled date for passing the actual sale, a title examination by the plaintiff's attorney revealed that Landry had obtained title to the property in a 1974 tax sale. After the validity of such a title was questioned, the defendant filed suit against the tax debtor, a Mrs. Estelina C. Keller, and her heirs, and obtained a judgment confirming and quieting the tax title. Subsequent investigation by the plaintiff's attorney showed however, that the judgment confirming Landry's tax title was defective because Mrs. Keller's husband was not named as a defendant, a legal description of the property was omitted from the judgment of confirmation and, the confirmation suit itself was filed before the expiration of the five year preemption period for quieting tax titles under Art. X, Section 11 of the 1921 Constitution and Art. VII, Section 25 of the 1974 Constitution of Louisiana.

¶4 Despite the fact that both parties considered Landry's tax title to be unmerchantable, arrangements were made for the passing of an act of sale on July 26, 1978. The conveyance instrument proposed by the buyers included only the waiver of warranty language suggested by them. A dispute arose when the Bielawskis refused to include the broader exculpatory recitals insisted upon by Landry. The act of sale was not passed and this suit for specific performance followed.

¶5 After trial of the matter, which largely consisted of stipulations of facts and the essentially undisputed testimony of the Bielawskis' attorney, the trial court entered judgment in favor of Landry. In written reasons, the trial judge indicated that it was his opinion that the vendor, Landry, had a valid reason for not signing the act of sale unless the Bielawski's took the property without recourse and also waived their right to ask for the return of the purchase price in the event they should at some time in the future be legally vested with such a right. The trial judge was of the view that the vendee's proposed "no warranty" clause, while offering Landry some protection, did not protect him completely in view of LSA-C.C. art. 2505, which provides that:

> Even in case of stipulation of no warranty, the seller, in case of eviction, is liable to a restitution of the price, unless the buyer was aware, at the time of the sale, of the danger of the eviction and purchased at his peril and risk.

¶6   According to the trial judge, Landry had as much justification for wanting his additional "no recourse" language included in the act of sale as the Bielawskis had for demanding that the proposed additional language be excluded. We are of the view that the trial judge was correct in dismissing the vendee's suit for specific performance.

¶7   The written agreement between these litigants specifically provides that their contract would become "null and void" if the seller was unable to deliver a merchantable title within the time stipulated. It provides further that the purchaser in such a situation has the right only to demand return of the deposit and to recover only the actual cost incurred. It also provides that specific performance may be demanded by the purchaser if the seller "fails to comply with the agreement for any other reason." (Emphasis ours.) It is our view that under this contract, inability to deliver a merchantable title within the specified period had the effect of placing the parties in the same position as if no contract to purchase had ever been entered into. We view the seller's inability to deliver a merchantable title as constituting a failure of a suspensive condition to the agreement and we believe that no rights flowed to either party upon that failure except those provided for in the contract itself.

¶8   In Lear v. Great Nat. Development Co., 215 La. 749, 41 So.2d 668 (1949), concerning a contract in which vendors were to furnish a valid record title, it was held that the vendee could not be compelled to accept a title to land upon which a claim rested and which was suggestive of future litigation. Conversely, in this case, in view of the contractual requirement that the vendor deliver a merchantable title, we hold that the vendee cannot compel the vendor to deliver a defective title, even without warranty and also without resolution of the problem presented by the provisions of LSA-C.C. art. 2505.

¶9   The Bielawskis argue that the provision in the contract that the seller is required to deliver to the purchaser a merchantable title is a provision for the exclusive benefit of the purchaser and that they were free to waive the merchantability requirement and insist on transfer of title. According to the Bielawskis, the election to consider the agreement null and void or demand specific performance rests exclusively with them. In support of this argument the Bielawskis draw an analogy to conditional financing clauses sometimes found in real estate contracts which provide that a contract to purchase realty on credit shall be null and void it the purchaser is unable to obtain financing. Citing Felder v. Terry, 351 So.2d 244 (La.App. 4th Cir. 1977) the Bielawskis point out that a provision conditioning the sale on the purchasers' ability to make a mortgage loan is a suspensive condition for the sole benefit of the purchaser who may waive it and elect to pay cash for the property.

¶10   It is our opinion that the Felder case concerning conditional financing is inapposite to this case. In conditional financing cases, the vendee may compel a cash sale of the property because the rights and obligations of the parties are clear and remain unchanged. The vendor in such a situation incurs no prejudice since he receives the full purchase price in cash and other provisions of the agreement are not affected thereby. On the other hand, in this case, the rights and obligations of the parties are not clear, even if the Bielawskis accept title "as is and without warranty." LSA-C.C. art. 2505 provides that even in a case of stipulation of no warranty, the seller in case of eviction is liable for a restitution of the purchase price, unless the buyer was aware at the time of the sale of the danger of the eviction and purchased the property at his peril and risk. Only actual, and not constructive knowledge will suffice to defeat a warranty action when a sale is made with an exception to the warranty clause. Collins v. Slocum 317 So.2d 672 (La.App. 3rd Cir. 1975). See also, "Warranty Against Eviction in the Civil Law: Limitations on the Extent of the Vendee's Recovery." 23 T.L.R. 154 (1948).

¶11   Even though it is clear in this case that the Bielawskis had actual knowledge of the unconfirmed nature of Landry's tax title and even though the signing of the proposed act of sale tendered by them would probably bar any action for a refund of the purchase price in the event of an eviction arising from the imperfect nature of the tax title, there may be other grounds for eviction apart from the tax title defects. Conceivably, other problems might surface in the future that might cause the Bielawskis or someone taking title from them to seek a refund of their purchase price from Landry. To compel Landry to convey the unmerchantable property without warranty only under these circumstances does not assure Landry that the purchaser will have no recourse at a later time. If some unanticipated problems force the Bielawskis into bankruptcy, a trustee in bankruptcy might be able to litigate the warranty issue. Unlike conditional financing cases, the rights and obligations of the parties in this case remain uncertain.

¶12   In seeking specific performance of the sale, the Bielawskis in effect are asking that we reform the contract to sell. Despite the clear wording of their agreement which provides that the agreement shall be rendered null and void upon the vendor's inability to convey merchantable title, the Bielawskis are asking the court to write out of the agreement that provision and substitute in its place a clause whereby the vendees may compel a sale without warranty. We are of the opinion that reformation of instruments is available only to correct mistakes or errors when the written contract does not express the true agreement between the parties. Fontenot v. Lewis, 215 So.2d 161 (La.App. 3rd Cir. 1968); Pipes v. Pipes, 343 So.2d 329 (La.App. 2nd Cir. 1977), writ denied, 345 So.2d 904 (1977). We are of the opinion that Landry and the Bielawskis had no meeting of the minds, other than nullity, regarding the recourse available in the event merchantable title could not be delivered within the time specified. Under the circumstances, the agreement between these parties, by its own terms, is null and void. We are of the opinion that clear and unambiguous agreement between competent majors is the law between the parties and accordingly, the judgment of the trial court is affirmed.

AFFIRMED.

GULOTTA, J., dissents and assigns reasons.
¶1   I respectfully dissent.

¶2   I interpret the contractual provision that the seller shall deliver to the purchaser a merchantable title to be for the benefit of the purchaser. As pointed out by the Bielawskis in argument, this stipulation is in the nature of a suspensive condition analogous to a conditional financing clause providing that a contract to purchase realty on credit shall be null and void if the purchaser is unable to obtain financing. See Felder v. Terry, 351 So.2d 244 (La.App. 4th Cir. 1977), which held that a purchaser may waive the financing clause for his benefit and pay cash. Likewise, in our case, the requirement that Landry warrant his title is a suspensive condition for the Bielawskis' benefit and they are entitled to waive the provision and accept title with knowledge of Landry's unconfirmed tax title.

¶3   Because I conclude the merchantability clause is for the Bielawskis' benefit and may be waived by them, I am not persuaded by Landry's argument that the contract became null and void and could not be enforced by either vendor or vendee upon discovery that his title was not merchantable. Although it is true that the contract provides that the seller's inability to deliver a merchantable title within the specified period shall render the contract null and void, there is no language in the contract limiting the purchaser to that remedy alone and the contract does not explicitly rule out an election to waive the merchantability requirement and knowingly accept a defective title.

¶4   I also reject Landry's argument that the inclusion of the broader language is necessary in view of LSA-C.C. art. 2505. Although LSA-C.C. art. 2505 provides that even in a case of stipulation of no warranty, the seller in case of eviction is liable for restitution of the purchase price, there is a proviso: "unless the buyer was aware, at the time of the sale, of the danger of the eviction, and purchased at his peril and risk." The Louisiana Supreme Court, interpreting this codal article, held in Richmond v. Zapata Development Corp., 350 So.2d 875 (La.1977) that knowledge of a danger of eviction will not prevent the purchaser from recovering the purchase price upon disturbance of his possession, in the absence of a stipulation of non-warranty in the act of sale.

¶5 In our case it is clear that the Bielawskis had actual knowledge of the uncertainty of Landry's tax title. According to the Richmond case, a stipulation of non-warranty under these circumstances would have sufficiently protected the seller from a suit by plaintiffs for return of the purchase price in the event plaintiffs' peaceful possession may have been disturbed.

¶6 As pointed out by the Bielawskis, Landry's proposed exculpatory clause confers upon a seller greater insulation against future recourse than would exist if there were no defect in the title. If we assume that no defect were discovered, title would have been warranted. With the discovery of the defect the seller is demanding greater protection than he would be entitled to if the act of sale were passed with warranty. Furthermore, purchaser could very well have not disclosed the defect and obtained title with warranty. The result of the majority's holding is that a purchaser who notifies a vendor of a title defect is in a worse position than if he remains silent and takes a defective title. Moreover, a seller by demanding the sale be without recourse or refund will be placed in a more favorable position when he transfers a deficient title than when he transfers a merchantable title. I therefore find no merit to Landry's position. A defect exists in the title. Purchasers are aware of the defect and they have waived the warranty. The seller is entitled to no further protection.

¶7 Accordingly, I would reverse the trial court's judgment and order specific performance. I therefore respectfully dissent.

Study Question

Continuing the interpretation of Article 2503, how does the second paragraph of the article apply in the following classic case?

CLARK V. O'NEAL 1858

13 LA. ANN. 381 (LA.)

Merrick, C. J.

¶1 This suit is brought upon two promissory notes given as the price of a tract of land. The defense to the action is the failure of consideration. It appears that in March, 1849, the plaintiff sold the defendant the land by an act under private signature. The act of sale not having been recorded in November, 1850, one Robert Burns instituted a suit by attachment against the plaintiff, before a Justice of the Peace in the parish of De Soto, where the land is situated. After the return of citation and attachment was made, showing that they had been served, judgment was rendered against the defendant in that suit. Execution having issued on the judgment, directed to the Sheriff, he seized the tract of land as the property of Mrs. Clark, and after advertising the sale, sold it for the sum of $75 cash.

¶2 In regard to the judgment, it does not appear that Mrs. Clark ever made any effort to have it set aside, or even took an appeal from it. It acquired the force of the thing adjudged, and must be held to have been rendered in conformity to law and for a just debt. As between herself and Burns, it was her duty to pay the debt; to acquit and discharge her obligation resulting from her debt, and the judgment of the court and the law. Instead of fulfilling her obligation in this respect, she suffered the property which she had sold, and which she had covenanted to warrant and defend, to be seized to pay her debt. The record does not show that she made any effort to relieve the property or even to substitute the promissory notes given as the price (and which she still held), in the place of the seizure of the land.

¶3 The mere fact that the vendee had neglected to record the act of sale did not release the plaintiff from her obligation to warrant the title. The unregistered act has its full force between the contracting parties, so much so. that a second sale of the same property to a third party is viewed as a fraudulent act. C. C. 2417; Rev. Stat. 453.

¶4 The sale being valid between the parties, and having force as such, the rules of law in regard to warranty, have their application.

¶5 The seller is bound to deliver and warrant the thing which he sells. C. C. 2450. The warranty respects the buyer's peaceable possession of the thing sold (C. C. 2451) and the vendor warrants the buyer against the eviction of the whole or a part of the same. C. C. 2477.

¶6 The proof shows that the defendant has violated this obligation by a neglect of her own duties, and she has suffered the property to be sold for her own debt, and thus has she been instrumental in evicting her own vendee, and thus has she bound herself to maintain the new vendee in possession. C. P. 711, 712, 713; 6 La. 737.

¶7 But it is said that Art. 2478 C. C. exempts the defendant from this sort of eviction. This Article, it is true, declares that in order that the warranty should have existence, the right of the person evicting should exist before the sale. But this evidently applies to some right acquired of persons other than the vendor himself. The last paragraph of the Article says: "If, therefore, this right before the sale was only imperfect and is afterwards perfected by the negligence of the buyer, he has no claim for warranty." Now an example or two will at once show that the Article has no application to the acts and omissions of duty of the vendor. Take this case: A sells a tract of land to B for $10,000, B, having the utmost confidence in A's integrity, omits or is prevented from recording his act of sale. Thereupon A sells the same land to C, an innocent purchaser, for $11,000, and C records his title. C sues B to recover the land. B cites A in warranty. A defends the demand of B in warranty on the ground, that C's right did not exist at the date of the sale, and cites the Article 2478 in support of his position. Will it avail him? Again, D sells E a tract of land for $10,000, but before the act is recorded, a recent judgment creditor of D seizes the land and sells the same and pays a debt of D's of $10,000. Is E to lose his money? It is apparent to every one how these questions must be answered. We think, therefore, that the obligation of warranty continued upon the plaintiff, although the act of sale was not recorded, and that the defendant has a valid defense to the notes, both under the Civil Code and the commercial law. 8 La. 547.

¶8 It is, therefore, ordered, adjudged and decreed by the court, that the judgment of the lower court be avoided and reversed, and that there be judgment in favor of the defendant, and against the demand of the plaintiff; and that the plaintiff pay the costs of both courts.

VOSS V. ROACH 1948
35 SO. 2D 142 (LA. APP. 2D CIR)

HARDY, Judge.

¶1 [This is a suit for the recovery of the sum of $350.00 paid by plaintiff to defendant as consideration for the purchase of certain timber on an eighty-acre tract of land then owned by defendant. The timber deed gave Voss 1 ½ years within which to remove the timber. It was not recorded. Six months later, Ms. Roach sold the tract to Sones, who refused to permit plaintiff to cut and remove the timber and claimed ownership of it because he had purchased the land.

Voss then paid another $350 to Sones in order to be allowed to harvest the timber, and he subsequently sued Ms. Roach for return of the $350 he had paid her, plus $100 as attorney's fees. The trial court found for plaintiff, and defendant appealed, arguing that plaintiff had failed to put her in default before filing suit, and that defendant's loss was due to his own negligence in failing to record the timber deed].

¶2 The court affirmed for plaintiff, finding that the law does not require a putting in default when such action would be a vain, futile and useless gesture; Robinson v. Clark, 20 La.Ann. 384; New Iberia Sugar Co. v. Lagarde, 130 La. 387, 58 So. 16. Under the facts in this case defendant had actively breached her contract and agreement with plaintiff, and had placed it beyond her power to carry out the said contract. It is therefore obvious that by her own action she put herself in default to such extent and degree that any demand on the part of plaintiff would have been a waste of time and effort. The facts in the case of Hart v. Adler, 19 La.Ann. 301, which case is cited in support of defendant's contention, are clearly at variance with the facts in the instant case, and the holding of the Court therefore is not applicable.

¶3 The only other issue made by defendant is that plaintiff's loss is due to his own negligence in failing to record the timber deed given by defendant. It is well established that the negligence, carelessness and laches of a party in failing to seasonably record an instrument cannot be interposed as a defense by the vendor of property who, by his own act, has been guilty of depriving such party of title. Clark v. O'Neal, 13 La.Ann. 381; Boyer v. Amet, 41 La.Ann. 721, 6 So. 734; Whitten v. Monkhouse, La.App., 29 So.2d 800.

***

¶4 For the reasons assigned the judgment appealed from is affirmed at appellant's cost.

D. The Quit-Claim deed

As just previously discussed, the warranty against eviction is implicit in every sale unless the parties limit or exclude it as set forth in Article 2503: the parties can limit the warranty; they can exclude it, which means that the evicted buyer will still get the price back from the seller, but nothing else; or they can specify that the sale is without warranty and at the buyer's "peril and risk," in which case the buyer cannot get his money back if he is evicted from the property. Article 2502 states a principle very close to a sale at 'risk and 'peril': the parties stipulate that the sale is one where the seller is transferring whatever rights he has in the thing, with the understanding that he may not in fact have any at all, whether as owner or as someone with less of an interest.

As such, this quit-claim deed, whereby the seller 'quits' any claim he might have in the property, is a kind of sale of a hope. The buyer hopes there may be some ownership interest but recognizes that might not be the case and if not that he'll have no recourse against the seller. Nevertheless, such a transfer "does not give rise to a presumption" that the seller is in bad faith, and functions as just title for the purposes of acquisitive prescription.

Study Question:

What do the following cases demonstrate about the strength of a title derived from a quit-claim deed? (Diagramming the chain of ownership and marking where the quitclaim deed came into existence will help your understanding of these cases.)

OSBORN V. JOHNSTON 1975
322 SO. 2D 112 (LA.)

DIXON, Justice.

¶1 In this petitory action, the court of appeal affirmed the judgment of the trial court in rejecting the demands of the plaintiffs, holding that the plaintiffs' ancestor had acquired no title or right of ownership by virtue of a sheriff's deed on which plaintiffs base their claim. Osborn v. Johnston, 308 So.2d 464. . . .

¶2 Plaintiffs are the heirs of Lassaline P. Briant; defendants are the assignees and mineral lessees of James and Alcide Owens. The property involved is an undivided interest in:

Lot 3, Section 1, and Lots 2 and 3, Section 2, Township 13 South, Range 11 East, Southwestern Land district, St. Martin Parish, Louisiana.

¶3 Neither plaintiffs nor defendants are in possession of the property, which apparently became swamp land shortly after the civil war. The issue, therefore, is: have the plaintiffs shown a better title to the land than the defendants?

***

The Ancient Document

¶4   Plaintiffs' claim to title is based on a sheriff's deed dated January 1, 1870 and recorded on the fourteenth day of the same month, purporting to convey the property to Lassaline P. Briant. The name of the vendee, Lassaline P. Briant, is written over another name in the instrument; the other name, almost obscured, can be determined to be 'Miss Valerie Fournet'. (The Proces verbal of the sheriff's sale recited that Miss Valerie Fournet was the vendee, and that L. P. Briant and Z. T. Fournet were her securities for the payment of the price of the 12-months credit sale.)

¶5   The deeds, of course, were written in pen and ink, and the record shows that Briant's name was superimposed over Valerie Fournet's in Briant's own hand, that the balance of the deed was not written in Briant's hand; that Briant, himself a deputy clerk, 'filed' the Proces verbal on January 10, 1870; that the sheriff's deed was 'recorded' by another deputy recorder on January 14, 1870.

[Discussion of the standard of proof governing admissibility of a copy of an ancient document is omitted].

***

¶6   The superimposition of Briant's name over that of Miss Fournet is not such an alteration that could not have an innocent explanation. It was recorded and indexed with no effort at concealment on the public records; it was assessed for tax purposes to Briant the following year and subsequently to the state for non-payment of taxes, in the name of Briant. Miss Fournet was Briant's sister-in-law. Briant is named as one of her securities for the payment of the purchase price in the Proces verbal. The deed was not recorded until four days after the recordation of the Proces verbal. It is entirely possible that Miss Fournet freely consented to the substitution of Briant's name for hers on the deed, for one of a number of valid reasons. The record contains no evidence whatsoever that the substitution of the name was not with the knowledge and consent of Miss Fournet.

***

Briant's Loss of Ownership

¶7   Nevertheless, we find that plaintiffs cannot prevail, for reasons not reached by the courts below.

¶8   In 1873, the land in dispute was adjudicated to the state for failure to pay taxes. The name of L. P. Briant appears as the owner. In 1889 the land in dispute was again adjudicated to the state for failure to pay taxes. The name of James Owens appears as the owner. In 1891 the state conveyed the land to the Atchafalaya Basin Levee District. In 1896 the Levee District conveyed the land to Pierre Angelloz. Pierre Angelloz conveyed to Arthur Angelloz in 1899, who conveyed to James and Alcide Owens in 1902. Defendants claim through the Owens.

¶9   Plaintiffs present two positions, arguing alternatively that the property either never left the patrimony of Briant or, if it did leave Briant's patrimony, that it was returned by operation of law. [the court rejects both arguments]

***

¶10   It is contended that the conveyance from the Levee Board to Pierre Angelloz was a mere quit-claim and that the Levee Board had no rights in the property. The act of transfer contains the words 'quitclaim' in the heading; the language within the act is as follows:

> "Be it Known: That for and in consideration of the sum of One Hundred & Two Dollars and Ninety Nine Cents, ($102.99/100) lawful money of the United States of America paid, and receipt of which is hereby acknowledged, the Board of Commissioners for the Atchafalaya Basin Levee District acting through its President does by these presents transfer, convey and quit claim unto

> "Pierre Angelloz all the rights, titles and privileges acquired by the said Board from the State of Louisiana . . . "

¶11   Even if this instrument is a 'quit-claim', we find that it effectively conveyed to Angelloz the ownership of the land, because the Levee Board was the owner. A quitclaim deed conveys whatever title the grantor owned. Waterman v. Tidewater Associated Oil Co., 213 La. 588, 35 So.2d 225 (1947).

¶12   Plaintiffs take the position that, for two separate reasons, the Levee Board did not own the property conveyed to Pierre Angelloz.

¶13   First, they argue that the donation from the state to the Levee Board transferred only rights obtained by the state in the 1889 tax adjudication, which plaintiffs contend is an absolute nullity, and not rights the state obtained in the 1873 tax adjudication.

¶14 We need not decide whether the 1889 tax adjudication is a nullity because we find that the state conveyed to the Levee Basin all rights in the property regardless of how or when the state acquired them.

¶15 By act 97 of 1890, the legislature provided for the donation of transfer to the Atchafalaya Basin Levee District All lands then belonging to the State within the limits of the Levee District.

¶16 The conveyance by the auditor to the Levee District reads as follows:

> I, O. B. Steele, Auditor of Public Accounts, under and by virtue of the authority in me vested by Act 97 of 189-Section 11, do hereby transfer and convey to the Board of Commission of the Atchafalaya Basin Levee District, all right, title and interest of the State of Louisiana, in and to the lands situated in the Parish of St. Martin and embraced within the limits of said Levee District which said lands have been adjudicated to the State for unpaid taxes of 1880 and subsequent years and not redeemed within the time prescribed by law. Said lands being more fully described in the list (attached hereto and made a part hereof.
>
> In evidence, whereof I have hereto set my signature and seal of office on the day and date first above written.

> Signed O. B. STEEL AUDITOR (SEAL)

¶17 This language clearly transfers 'all right, title and interest of the State of Louisiana'. The clause referring to the unpaid taxes of '1880 and subsequent years' does not limit the conveyance to those lands the titles to which were acquired for taxes subsequent to 1880. Act 97 of 1890 did not limit the conveyance. As the deed expresses, the lands conveyed were 'more fully described' in the attached list, which described the property involved here. The reference to lands described for taxes after 1880 might accurately describe some parcels, but did not limit the conveyance to certain Titles of land described particularly in attached list.

¶18 Thus the state transferred all of its rights regardless of when they were acquired; the state acquired ownership of this land in the tax adjudication of 1873.

***

¶19 Thus, plaintiffs' argument that the property returned by operation of law to Briant's patrimony is wholly without merit. Since they have no title, plaintiffs cannot prevail.

¶20 The judgments of the court of appeal and district court are affirmed at plaintiffs' cost.

What does the following case say about how the law applicable to quitclaim deeds is affected by the public records doctrine?

SIMMESPORT ST. BANK V. ROY 1993
614 SO. 2D 265 (LA. APP. 3D CIR.)

DOMENGEAUX, Chief Judge.

¶1 Simmesport State Bank filed this action to annul a quitclaim deed which was granted by Leonard R. Tanner and Lucy Tanner to Jack R. Roy and Jean Roy, all of whom were named as defendants. The quitclaim deed purportedly conveyed to the Roys an interest in a piece of land located in Avoyelles Parish. All parties filed motions for summary judgment. The trial judge granted summary judgment in favor of the Bank, declaring the quitclaim deed at issue to be null, void, and of no effect. The trial judge also granted summary judgment in favor of the Tanners, dismissing them from the litigation.

¶2 The Roys have appealed the judgment in favor of the Bank, and we affirm the trial court's decision; the judgment in favor of the Tanners has not been appealed.

¶3 The record reveals the following undisputed facts. In 1988, the Tanners went into bankruptcy. Simmesport State Bank was one of their creditors. Pursuant to a bankruptcy court order authorizing a trustee's consensual sale, the property at issue was sold to the Bank on September 14, 1988. Officials at the Bank, however, did not record the deed until August 8, 1991, probably through inadvertence.

¶4 In May of 1991, the Roys purchased the property at a tax sale. Jack Roy then checked the mortgage and conveyance records and discovered that the Tanners were the record owners of the property. While the tax assessment was still listed under the Tanners' names, the tax records did contain a reference to Simmesport State Bank. (Apparently, the tax notices for 1988, 1989, and 1990 were sent to the Tanners who forwarded them to the Bank. The Bank paid the 1988 and 1989 taxes but neglected to pay the 1990 taxes.) Jack Roy also learned from his research that a mortgage executed by the Tanners in favor of the Bank had been cancelled. When Roy talked to the Tanners, he was told they no longer owned the property because they had lost it to the Bank as a result of their bankruptcy. The Tanners showed Roy the pertinent papers evidencing the trustee's consensual sale.

¶5 Roy explained to the Tanners that he was in the process of buying the property for delinquent taxes, and he requested that they execute a quitclaim deed in his favor in exchange for $500.00. The Tanners were reluctant to execute the quitclaim deed, but after making sure they were not doing anything wrong, and were not guaranteeing title to property which they did not own, they decided to execute the deed and accept the $500.00 payment. Roy immediately filed the deed in the Avoyelles Parish conveyance records on August 5, 1991.

¶6 On August 7, 1991, Roy informed the Bank that he had purchased the property at a tax sale. Upon reviewing their records for this property, officials at the Bank discovered that the deed from the trustee's consensual sale had never been recorded. The Bank then recorded the deed on August 8, whereupon the quitclaim deed in favor of the Roys was discovered. The Bank successfully redeemed the tax sale and instituted this suit on August 20, 1991, to annul the quitclaim deed.

¶7 The Bank asserts ownership of the subject property based upon the well established principle that a quitclaim deed is one which purports to convey, and is understood to convey, nothing more than the interest in the property described of which the grantor is possessed, if any, at the time, rather than the property itself. Waterman v. Tidewater Associated Oil Co., 213 La. 588, 35 So.2d 225 (1947). The Bank contends that because the Tanners owned no interest in the property at the time they executed the quitclaim deed, the deed transferred nothing and is essentially null and void.

¶8 The Roys assert ownership based on the public records doctrine, codified at La. R.S. 9:2721 and 9:2756, which requires that all contracts affecting immovable property must be recorded in order to affect third parties. The Roys cite Dallas v. Farrington, 490 So.2d 265 (La.1986) for the long established rule that because recordation is essential for effectiveness against third parties, actual knowledge by third parties of unrecorded interests is immaterial. 490 So.2d at 269, citing McDuffie v. Walker, 125 La. 152, 51 So. 100 (1909).

¶9 The issue before us, as the trial judge pointed out in his well reasoned oral opinion, which was transcribed, is how the law applicable to quitclaim deeds is affected by the public records doctrine. In other words, in applying the law that a vendor in a quitclaim deed sells only that interest which the vendor owns at the time of the sale, a determination must be made as to what the vendor owned, but is that determination restricted to what is contained in the public records? Or can the determination be based on facts outside of the public records?

¶10 There is no question in the present case that the trustee's sale was a valid transfer of property between the Tanners and the Bank. There is also no question that the sale could have no effect on third parties until it was recorded three years after the fact in 1991. But what effect does an unrecorded sale have on a quitclaim deed which, by its very nature, transfers only an interest in property, not the property itself? The trial judge held that what is contained in the public records is not determinative of the interest held by a vendor to a quitclaim deed. He found that an unrecorded sale has the same effect as a recorded sale on the validity of a quitclaim deed. The Tanners, therefore, had no interest in the property at the time they executed the deed.

¶11 We find the trial judge's analysis to be correct. There is nothing in the jurisprudence which requires that a determination of the interest held by a vendor to a quitclaim deed must depend on what is contained in the public records. The Tanners lost their interest in the subject property when it was sold to the Bank. Therefore, they had no interest to convey when they executed the quitclaim deed. We agree with the century old case of Benton v. Sentell, 50 La.Ann. 869, 24 So. 297 (1898), which stated:

¶12 We think that a quitclaim deed reaches only to interests actually owned at that time by the party executing it; that it is of no effect whatever as to interests already gone. In the very nature of things, there is a great difference between an act of sale or donation and a quitclaim deed. It is true that through the latter interests in property may be acquired, for the party quitclaiming is ordinarily estopped from subsequently asserting rights which had been by him relinquished. A person undertaking to sell warrants the existence of and his ownership of the thing sold, and is bound to make the warranty good, but a party quitclaiming, carries out precisely what he undertook to do in simply abstaining from disturbing or questioning the rights of those in whose favor he has renounced. 24 So. at 301.

¶13 In this appeal, the Roys argue that a decision affirming the trial court's judgment would serve only to imperil or erode the public records doctrine. This argument is without merit. Our decision is based on the unique characteristics of a quitclaim deed and its inherent independence from what is contained in the public records. Indeed, more often than not, a quitclaim deed is obtained from persons who are not record owners, but who may have an ownership interest nonetheless. In order to protect himself from the uncertainty of the situation, such a vendor will transfer whatever interest he has, but only without any warranty of title. Hence, the quitclaim deed is utilized.

¶14 The Roys' reliance on the rule that unrecorded transfers of immovable property cannot affect third parties is misplaced. The focus, instead, must be on the deed which the Roys hold; it is a deed that contains no warranty of title and transfers nothing but an interest in property, the ownership of which had previously been lost. The purported interest, therefore, is nonexistent, and the deed itself is null and void and of no effect. There are many instances where a quit-claim deed does constitute a valid transfer of property because the vendor does, in fact, own an interest which can be transferred. See, Osborn v. Johnston, 322 So.2d 112 (La.1975); Clifton v. Liner, 552 So.2d 407 (La.App. 1st Cir.1989); Sabourin v. Jilek, 128 So.2d 698 (La.App. 4th Cir.1961); Armstrong v. Bates, 61 So.2d 466 (La.App. 1st Cir.1952). This, however, is not such a case, and we therefore affirm the trial court's ruling.

¶15 Finally, we note that in the instant case, both the vendor and the vendee to the quitclaim deed knew of the trustee's consensual sale to the Bank. Further, the vendee knew that sale had not been recorded. The vendee attempted to take advantage of the situation by obtaining a quitclaim deed. The questions of fraud and bad faith are relevant generally to a determination of whether a third party purchaser is entitled to the protection afforded by the public records doctrine. American Legion v. Morel, 577 So.2d 346 (La.App. 1st Cir.1991), writ denied, 580 So.2d 924 (La.1991). However, in the instant case, the question of fraud is not before us as the Bank did not allege fraud and the trial court pointed out that he was not making a finding of fraud. Our decision likewise is not based on any finding of fraud or bad faith, but rather, on the conclusion that the law governing quitclaim deeds does not support the position advocated by the Roys.

¶16 For the foregoing reasons, the judgment of the trial court is affirmed at appellants' costs.

AFFIRMED.

E. After-Acquired Title Doctrine and Partial Eviction

Article 2482 states that when, "at the time of the sale the seller is not in possession of the thing sold, he must obtain possession at his own cost and deliver the thing to the buyer." This, in the case of eviction, has led to the after-acquired title doctrine: if the seller becomes aware of a danger of eviction and corrects the title problem before it is brought to the buyer's attention, then the buyer does not have an eviction claim.

In the case of a sale by quit-claim deed, there is a somewhat odd (but logical) result: Article 2502 provides that if the transferor via quitclaim acquires ownership of the thing after having transferred his rights to it, the after-acquired title does not inure to the transferee's benefit. After all, as comment (c) indicates, "conveyance by quitclaim does not include any implication that the vendor has good title to the property, or even that he has any title at all. Thus the purchaser by quitclaim deed is put on immediate notice that he is not acquiring land but merely the interest of his vendor in the land." Thus, assuming the transferor had been in good faith in selling the property by quitclaim deed to a buyer, then the buyer was on notice, at that time, that the seller might have had no ownership in the property. If the seller subsequently acquires such ownership, then the buyer had not been deprived of anything – he did in fact acquire whatever interest the seller of the quitclaim had at the time of that sale.

Study Question:

How does the doctrine of after-acquired title apply in the following cases?

ST. LANDRY OIL & GAS CO., INC., V. NEAL 1928
166 LA. 799, 118 SO. 24

OVERTON, J.

¶1 In January, 1919, Emma Garrett and others executed a mineral lease on 5 acres of land in the parish of Claiborne to J. M. Eastham, who, on October 6, 1919, assigned the lease to T. S. Neal, one of the defendants in this case. In December of the same year, Neal assigned the lease to the St. Landry Oil & Gas Company, Inc., the plaintiff herein. The consideration for this assignment was $10,000 cash and $15,000, to be paid out of a certain part of the oil produced from the land. In November, 1920, Neal assigned to W. F. Reynolds a one-third interest in the credit portion of the consideration, stipulated in the assignment to plaintiff, and Reynolds transferred this one-third interest to the Commercial National Bank of Shreveport. In May, 1920, plaintiff assigned a one-half interest in the lease acquired by it to the Tulsa Oil & Gas Company, under a contract by which plaintiff was to pay a certain part of the cost of production. Two wells were drilled on the property under this contract, one of which produced nothing and the other $39,563.99 of oil, which was sold to the Standard Oil Company of Louisiana.

¶2 In August, 1920, Emma Garrett, the widow of William Garrett, and various others, including plaintiff, instituted a suit against the heirs of Thornton Bridgeman and his widow to have recognized as valid a correction made in a deed from the Bridgemans to Garrett, and, in the alternative, to reform two deeds to Garrett by correcting the description of the property therein conveyed. In that case judgment was rendered recognizing the Bridgemans as the owners of the land upon which Emma Garrett and others had granted the lease that was acquired by plaintiff.

¶3 Within two months after the foregoing judgment became final, the defendant Neal, who had transferred the lease to plaintiff, obtained from the Bridgemans, who had been decreed the owners of the land, a ratification and confirmation of the lease, executed by Emma Garrett and others to his assignor. Neal had the act of confirmation recorded, and notified plaintiff of its execution and recordation, but plaintiff refused to accepted the confirmation.

¶4 Some months after the foregoing act of confirmation was executed, plaintiff, urging that it had been evicted by the judgment declaring that the Bridgemans, and not Emma Garrett and others, were the owners of the land upon which the lease was granted, instituted the present suit to recover from Neal the $10,000 paid by it to Neal as the cash portion of the consideration for the assignment of the lease; to recover from him $7,500, one-half of the cost paid by it for drilling a well; also to recover from him $3,353.39, the cost of operations and production incurred by it, and also to annul and rescind the obligation, contracted by it, to pay the credit portion of the consideration for the assignment of the lease made to it by Neal. As Neal had assigned a one-third interest in that part of the consideration to Reynolds, who had assigned that third to the Commercial National Bank, that bank was made a party to the suit.

¶5 The defense is that, when Neal obtained the ratification from the Bridgemans, the ratification immediately accrued to plaintiff, and gave him a perfect title to the lease, thereby destroying any right plaintiff might have had to rescind the sale of the lease to it, and recover the purchase price with damages.

¶6 Ordinarily, where one sells the property of another-and the rule is equally applicable to the granting or sale of mineral leases-and later acquires title to the property sold by him, the title vests immediately in his vendee. Bonin v. Eyssaline, 12 Mart. (O. S.) 185, 227; McGuire v. Amelung, 12 Mart. (O. S.) 649; Woods v. Kimbal, 5 Mart. (N. S.) 246; Fenn v. Rils, 9 La. 95, 100; Stokes v. Shakleford, 12 La. 170; Lee v. Ferguson, 5 La. Ann. 532; New Orleans v. Riddell, 113 La. 1051, 37 So. 966; Wolff v. Carter, 131 La. 667, 60 So. 52; Brewer v. New Orleans Land Co., 154 La. 446, 97 So. 605.

¶7 The foregoing rule admits of exceptions. The first case, in this jurisdiction, in which it was considered when, and under what circumstances, the after-acquired title of the vendor vests in his vendee and when it does not, is the case of Bonin v. Eyssaline, supra, 12 Mart. (O. S.) 185, 227. In that case, the plaintiff, who was still in possession of the property sold him, discovered the nullity of his title, and gave public notice that he would sue his vendor for the rescission of the sale. His vendor took steps to acquire title to the property, and acquired it. Thereafter the plaintiff brought his suit to rescind the sale. The question was raised as to whether, and when, an after-acquired title vests in the vendee of the one acquiring it. The court, in passing upon the question, which was raised by defendant in order to defeat the suit for rescission, expressed the view that, while it was inclined to think that an after-acquired title vested in the vendee of the one acquiring it, if it was acquired at any time prior to final judgment rescinding the sale, yet held that it clearly did so, where the title was acquired prior to the institution of the suit to rescind, and, as the title in that case was so acquired, rejected the demand for rescission.

¶8   The same question arose in the case of Hale v. City of New Orleans, supra, 18 La. Ann. 321. In that case it appeared that the city of New Orleans sold to Thomas Hale certain real estate. In a suit instituted by A. and F. Remy, the Remys were adjudged the owners of the property. Hale then sued to rescind the sale made to him by the city of New Orleans, and to recover the purchase price. The city then acquired the title of the Remys, and urged that the new title acquired accrued to Hale, and hence that his title was perfect. But Hale resisted this contention, and it was held that, having instituted his suit to rescind before the acquisition by his vendor of the newly acquired title, and having thereby evinced his intention not to accept any such title, it could not be held in the face of these facts that the title vested in him.

¶9   A similar question arose in the case of Brewer v. New Orleans Land Co., supra, 154 La. 446, 97 So. 605, in which the facts are similar, in essential respects to those in the Hale Case. In that case, as in the Hale Case, the suit to rescind was instituted prior to the acquisition of the newly acquired title, and the same ruling was made, as was made in the Hale Case, or, in other words, it was there ruled that the new title did not accrue to the plaintiffs therein, and defeat their suit to rescind.

¶10   While there are expressions in the Hale Case and in the Brewer Case, and especially in the former, that are suggestive that it is wholly optional with one who has purchased from a person without title whether he will accept an after-acquired title, yet these expressions must be considered in connection with the particular facts of those cases. In either instance the plaintiffs therein might have accepted the after-acquired titles, but, due to their suits to rescind, they had the right to refuse those titles and continue with their suits.

¶11   In our view, at least in the absence of an actual eviction working substantial injury, where one purchases from another without title before a suit to rescind is commenced, the title thus acquired vests immediately in the vendee of the one acquiring it, and the vendee cannot sue for a rescission of the sale by which he purchased. He should not then be permitted to sue, because his vendor, under these circumstances, would have fulfilled all of his obligations to him. However, after he has instituted suit to rescined, his suit cannot be defeated by a title acquired by his vendor after the institution of the suit. the new title does not vest in him then, unless he accepts it, for he cannot be forced to retract his steps and dismiss his suit by an after occurrence.

***

¶12   For the reasons assigned, the judgment appealed from is annulled and set aside, plaintiff's demands are now rejected, ...

Study Suggestion:

It will almost certainly be helpful to sketch the movement of ownership from person to person, and through which transactions, in order to understand and follow the following case, whose holding was codified in Article 2502's exclusion of the quitclaim deed from the scope of the after-acquired title doctrine. That will also be helpful for reading the cases in the section dealing with subrogation and chain of title.

WATERMAN V. TIDEWATER ASSOC. OIL CO. 1947
213 LA. 588, 35 SO. 2D 225 (LA.)

McCALEB, Justice.

¶1 On May 13, 1942, John S. Waterman, Jr., initiated this petitory action in the Twenty-Fifth Judicial District Court, in which he claims that he is the true and lawful owner of an undivided one-fourth right, title and interest in and to the following described property in Plaquemines Parish: [description omitted].

***

¶2 Plaintiffs' main chain of title, which has been referred to as the 'Lacey' title, is as follows: Buras Levee Board to Lacey, January 4, 1896; Lacey to Buck, same date; Buck to Rectangle, October 23, 1905; Rectangle to Rose, January 11, 1923 and Rose to plaintiffs by a series of conveyances which are neither questioned nor important.

¶3 Defendants' chain, referred to as the 'Leovy' title, is as follows: State to Leovy by patents issued in 1893 and subsequent years; heirs of Leovy to Hayne, November 17, 1905; Hayne to Kranebell, November 3, 1913; Kranebell and wife to Rectangle, February 4, 1927, and Rectangle to Johnson, Pautsch and other defendants of various interests, including a mineral lease acquired by Tidewater Associated Oil Company, by a series of transactions not important to the controversy.

¶4 Since this is a petitory action, plaintiffs must recover on the strength of their own title and not on the weakness of that of their adversaries. Code of Practice, Article 43, 44; Dugas v. Powell, 197 La. 409, 1 So.2d 677; Simmons v. Carter, 186 La. 377, 172 So. 425.

***

¶5 [P]laintiffs submit (1) that the description in the Rectangle-Rose deed is sufficient and includes the land in contest; (2) that the title acquired by Rose from Rectangle is valid; (3) alternatively, that defendants are estopped to deny that Rectangle had a valid title which passed to Rose; (4) that, even if Rectangle did not have a good title, the title which it acquired from Mr. and Mrs. Kranebell in 1927 (under which all defendants claim) inured to the benefit of Rose under the doctrine of after-acquired title; (5) that, moreover, the title acquired by Kranebell from Hayne, his vendor, was nothing more than a security title since Hayne's acquisition from the Leovy heirs created an antichresis and that Rectangle was the holder of the equitable title and (6) that, at all events, Rose and his successors have a good title by the ten year acquisitive prescription.

¶6 We shall discuss the various contentions and counter-contentions in order. Preliminarily, let us consider the nature of the deed from Rectangle to Rose-that is, whether that deed conveyed any land to Rose or whether it merely quitclaimed whatever right, title and interest Rectangle may have had in and to the property described therein.

¶7 The deed recites in substance that the party of the first part has 'remised, released, sold, conveyed, and quitclaimed, and by these presents does remise, release, sell, convey and Quit Claim * * * all the right, title, interest, claim and demand which said party of the first part has in and to the following described piece of land * * *.' Obviously, the declarations do not convey the land but only the right, title and interest of the vendor. It is in the nature of an assignment of a right or an interest and as such falls squarely within the category of the common law quitclaim deed. Examination of our Civil Code discloses the absence of provisions relative to quitclaim deeds. The articles on sales of property and the obligations and rights resulting therefrom do not mention quitclaim deeds; Articles 2500 through 2504 respecting the warranty of the seller being confined to treatment of sales with warranty, express and implied, and those where warranty is specifically excluded. On the other hand, quitclaim deeds are fully recognized in the jurisprudence and have many times been considered by our courts. 26 Corpus Juris Secundum, verbo, Deeds, § 8, page 181, defines a quitclaim deed as follows:

'A quitclaim deed is one which purports to convey, and is understood to convey, nothing more than the interest or estate in the property described of which the grantor is seized or possessed, if any, at the time, rather than the property itself.'

¶8 The authorities from the Federal courts and the courts of other states are that, in determining whether a deed is a quitclaim or not, reference must be made to the language used therein for the purpose of ascertaining the intention of the parties. Williams v. Rabb, Tex.Civ.App., 161 S.W.2d 121. The fact that the deed is denominated a quitclaim is not conclusive (Wise v. Watts,

Ariz., 239 F. 207, 152 C.C.A. 195; Cook v. Smith, 107 Tex. 119, 175 S.W. 1094, 3 A.L.R. 940), nor does the fact that the words 'bargain and sell' are used necessarily imply that the grantor is absolute owner and that he is not merely quitclaiming his right, title and interest. Brown v. Harvey Coal Corporation, D.C.E.D. Ky., 49 F.2d 434; Young v. Clippinger, 14 Kan. 148. Examination must be had of all of the recitals contained therein in an effort to resolve the true intent. Here, we think, as above stated, that the recitals are clear and show merely a transfer of the interest of Rectangle in two townships and do not convey any property.

¶9 On the other hand, the title to real property may be as effectually transferred by quitclaim as by any other form of conveyance. But such a deed conveys only such title or interest that the grantor had at the time it is given 'and excludes any implication that he has any title or interest.' 26 C.J.S., Deeds, § 118, page 415. Nevertheless, it is established in Louisiana that a quitclaim deed is sufficient to support the ten year acquisitive prescription provided by Article 3478 of the Civil Code. See Smith v. Southern Kraft Corp., 202 La. 1019, 13 So.2d 335 and cases there cited.

¶10 This jurisprudence is to be regarded as an exception in favor of a good faith possessor holding under a quitclaim deed for, as a matter of fact, a conveyance of the vendor's title and interest in property does not convey the property itself. Albeit, the purchaser is put on immediate notice that he is not acquiring land but merely the interest of his vendor in the land. And, while it may be appropriate to say that the purchaser in good faith may use the conveyance to support title by prescription, he cannot otherwise acquire more than the interest conveyed. Thus, the title examiner is alerted, when confronted with such a deed, to delve further to ascertain the interest of the vendor in order to know the exact property which is embraced in the conveyance.

¶11 With these principles in mind, we approach a discussion of the title upon which the plaintiffs rely. [This discussion of the title is omitted]

¶12 Inasmuch, therefore, as the Levee Board obtained no title whatever to the lands in contest, neither Lacey, Buck nor Rectangle acquired a title to them under the subsequent conveyances and it follows that Rose did not get title by acquiring Rectangle's interest in T. 21 S., R. 30 E. in 1923.

¶13 It is therefore apparent that plaintiffs cannot succeed unless one of their alternative contentions can be maintained. The first one of these contentions is that defendants are estopped to deny that Rectangle had a valid title which passed to Rose. This point is without merit. Title to real estate cannot be acquired by estoppel (see Pan American Products Co. v. Robichaux, 200 La. 666, 8 So.2d 635), although the doctrine may be employed for the purpose of prohibiting a grantor from denying that an after-acquired title passed by the original conveyance. See 31 Corpus Juris Secundum, verbo Estoppel, § 21, page 203; Standard Oil Co. v. Allison, 196 La. 838, 200 So. 273 and Jackson v. United Gas Public Service Co., 196 La. 1, 198 So. 633.

¶14   This leads us to a discussion of plaintiffs' principal alternative contention-viz., that, even though Rectangle did not have a title to the land in controversy when it sold its interest in the two townships to Rose in 1923, its subsequent acquisition of the property from Mr. and Mrs. Kranebell in 1927 inured to the benefit of Rose under the doctrine of after-acquired title.

¶15   The doctrine of after-acquired title is recognized in the jurisprudence of this state but, heretofore, its application has been limited to cases where the vendor warranted title to the conveyed property. See Wells v. Blackman, 121 La. 394, 46 So. 437; Standard Oil Co. v. Allison, supra, and Jackson v. United Gas Public Service Co., supra. It is easy to see why one, who sells with warranty, becomes estopped from thereafter acquiring a title to the prejudice of his grantee. To hold that the title he acquires inures to his grantee is really nothing more than an enforcement of the grantor's obligation to deliver a good title. And it may even be proper to extend application of the doctrine to a sale without warranty where the land conveyed is adequately described. In such a case, it might be argued that the vendor would be precluded from subsequently acquiring an adverse title to the prejudice of the vendee under Article 2504 of the Civil Code, which declares that:

> 'Although it be agreed that the seller is not subject to warranty, he is, however, accountable for what results from his personal act; and any contrary agreement is void.'

See also Articles 2503 and 2505.

¶16   On the other hand, it is quite manifest that the doctrine of after-acquired title should not be expanded to include a quit-claim deed, primarily for the reason that a conveyance of that character transfers only the present interest of the vendor in the land and does not convey the property. It is generally accepted by the leading authorities (see 16 American Jurisprudence Verbo 'Deeds' Section 344; Chesney v. Valley Live Stock Co., 34 Wyo. 378, 244 P. 216, 44 A.L.R. 1266; 162 A.L.R. 566 and 31 Corpus Juris Secundum Verbo, Estoppel, § 22, page 205) that there is no basis for the application of the doctrine of after-acquired title where the vendee is claiming under a quitclaim deed. And this Court, in Benton v. Sentell, 50 La.Ann. 869, 24 So. 297, 301, in distinguishing the quit-claim deed from an act of sale, remarked that it 'reaches only to interests actually owned at that time by the party executing it * * *.' This being so, there is no reason why the vendor should not thereafter acquire title even though it be adverse to the vendee holding under the deed.

***

¶17 The judgments appealed from are affirmed.

F. Subrogation

The last paragraph of Article 2503 provides that "the buyer is subrogated to the rights in warranty of the seller against other persons, even when the warranty is excluded." This means that if the buyer cannot proceed against his seller because he agreed to exclude the warranty, he can step into his seller's shoes and proceed against previous sellers. In that case, however, jurisprudence provides that the extent of his remedy is limited to the price paid by that predecessor in title, as shown in the following cases. As mentioned previously, the best way to study them is to diagram the chain of transaction so that you can see the domino effect of a call in warranty.

Study Questions:

How is the buyer subrogated to the rights of the seller in the following cases?

Did the buyer waive his right to eviction in any of them?

Does the first case actually involve an eviction – where a third party has an ownership claim – or does it involve some other seller's warranty?

If it involves a different warranty, which warranty does it involve? Look at the placement of Article 2503 in the Civil Code. Does the Supreme Court's interpretation make sense in that context, or did it overreach?

AIZPURUA V. CRANE POOL CO., INC. 1984
449 SO. 2D 471 (LA.)

WATSON, Justice.

¶1 Plaintiffs, Dr. and Mrs. Aizpurua, filed this suit on May 29, 1981, to recover for defects in a swimming pool which they purchased in conjunction with a residence on December 6, 1977. Named as defendants were: Edward M. and Anna Lee Smith, the vendors of the house and pool; Crane Pool Company, Inc., and/or Cory Crane, who constructed and manufactured the pool; and Watts Brothers Buildings, Inc., which developed the lot where the residence and pool are located. The trial court sustained exceptions of no cause of action, no right of action and prescription as to the Crane defendants. The Court of Appeal affirmed. Aizpurua v. Crane Pool

Company, Inc., 439 So.2d 572 (La.App. 1 Cir.1983). A writ was granted to review the judgment. 443 So.2d 591 (La., 1983).

¶2 The trial court concluded that any claims in redhibition or tort had prescribed. Because there was no privity of contract between plaintiffs and the Crane defendants, exceptions of no cause of action and no right of action were also sustained.

¶3 At the hearing on the exceptions, photographs were introduced in evidence which showed that the pool was in very poor condition prior to its repair. Problems with the pool were first apparent in December of 1979 and became progressively worse. Crane Pool Company was contacted in February of 1980 when the liner of the pool had separated from the cement wall and started to rip. Subsequently, cracks appeared in the coping of the pool.

¶4 An employee of Soil Testing Engineers testified as an expert from his company's records that the Aizpuruas' problems with the pool resulted from a six inch differential in settlement of the soil under the pool. The compressible soil materials which caused the pool problem were below the depth of the test borings. In this expert's opinion, the condition began developing shortly after the pool was built in 1976 and continued, probably at a decreasing rate. If there had been appropriate testing prior to construction, the pool could have been placed on pilings "going down to a competent soil" or the incompetent soil could have been removed and replaced with a different material. (Tr. 70) The feasibility of both of these courses of action was open to serious question.

¶5 The trial court correctly found that any actions in tort and redhibition against Crane had prescribed. LSA-C.C. arts. 2546 and 3536. The question remaining is whether plaintiffs have a right of action against Crane for breach of any implied or express warranty in the Crane building contract with the Smiths.

¶6 Plaintiffs rely on Media Pro. Consult., Inc. v. Mercedes-Benz of N.A., Inc., 262 La. 80, 262 So.2d 377 (1972), which allowed a consumer without privity to recover against the distributor of an automobile for latent defects under the implied warranty of fitness inherent in every sale. In Media, an American automobile distributor was found to occupy the position of the foreign manufacturer.

¶7 Liability of a contractor to the owner or other contracting party is governed by a ten year prescriptive period. LSA-C.C. art. 3500. The Smiths, vendors of the house and pool, warranted to the Aizpuruas, the vendees, that the things sold were free of hidden defects. LSA-C.C. art. 2476. The Aizpuruas were subrogated to the Smiths' rights and actions in warranty against "all others". LSA-C.C. art. 2503. This article has been interpreted as including only actions against other vendors. See LeBlanc v. Ellerbee Builders, Inc., 317 So.2d 1 (La.App. 1 Cir.1975). This reading of the article erroneously qualifies its literal language. "[T]he right to sue for breach of warranty of quality is transmitted with the object of the sale." XIV Tul.L.Rev. at p. 471. The implied warranty of materials and workmanship in a building contract is one to which a subsequent purchaser is subrogated.Media, supra. Despite lack of privity, one who acquires immovable property can enforce a contract made for the improvement of the property by the person from whom he acquired it. LSA-C.C. art. 2011; Breaux v. Laird, 223 La. 446, 65 So.2d 907 (1953).

¶8   For the foregoing reasons, the judgment is affirmed insofar as it sustained the Crane defendants' exceptions of prescription. Insofar as the judgment held that plaintiffs had no cause of action and no right of action against the Crane defendants, the judgment is reversed, and the matter is remanded for further proceedings.

AFFIRMED IN PART; REVERSED IN PART; AND REMANDED.

DIXON, C.J., concurs.
LEMMON, J., concurs,
believing that the contract between defendant and Smith was a building contract, but that plaintiffs have a right of action to enforce defendant's obligation imposed by La.C.C. Art. 2762.

MARCUS, Justice (dissenting).
The majority opinion holds that La. Civ. Code art. 2503 subrogates a purchaser to his seller's rights and actions against a building contractor for breach of the implied warranty of workmanship in a building contract. Chapter 6 of Book III, Title VII of the Civil Code is divided into three sections corresponding to the three principal obligations of the seller: tradition or delivery of the thing sold, warranty against eviction and warranty against redhibitory vices. Article 2503 is located in section two, entitled "Of the Warranty in Case of Eviction From the Thing Sold," and deals exclusively with the warranty against eviction. Because plaintiff has failed to allege that either his seller or the pool contractor breached the warranty against eviction, art. 2503 is inapplicable. Accordingly, I respectfully dissent.

DENNIS, Justice, concurring.
¶1   I respectfully concur.

¶2 Since the instant case is clearly covered by the second example described by Civil Code Article 2011, I do not feel there is any necessity to construct an analogy upon the Media case.

¶3 Further, I interpret the majority opinion to hold that, although plaintiffs' causes of action in tort and redhibition have prescribed, their cause of action based on the construction contract is governed by a ten year period and therefore has not prescribed.

BLANCHE, J. (dissenting)

¶1 The majority opinion broadly interprets C.C. art. 2503 to allow a vendor of a house to subrogate to the vendee the vendor's actions in warranty against any contractor who may have worked on the home or its immediate concomitants. By so doing, any notion of privity of contract which remained after Media Production Consultants, Inc. v. Mercedes-Benz of North America, Inc., 262 La. 80, 262 So.2d 377 (1972), has been dispelled.

¶2 Regardless of the merits of disposing of the theory of privity of contract, the codal authority cited by the majority to do so is inapposite. Art. 2503 is located in the civil code under the section entitled: "Of the Warranty in Case of Eviction From the Thing Sold." Article 2500 states that eviction is the loss suffered by the buyer of the thing sold, occasioned by the right or claim of a third person. Thus, the warranty to which a vendee becomes subrogated under Article 2503 is simply the vendor' own warranty from eviction owed to him by previous vendors. LeBlanc v. Ellerbee Builders, Inc., 317 So.2d 1 (La. App. 1st Cir. 1975). Article 2503 was never intended to provide subrogation to claims of defective workmanship or implied warranties of fitness. Had it been the article would have been placed in the section of the code dealing with the vices of the thing sold, Art. 2520, et seq.

¶3 Finding no basis in the civil code for the type of subrogation created by the majority opinion, I therefore respectfully dissent.

Comments:

Aizpurua applies the subrogation provision of Article 2503 not just to eviction, but also to the construction contracts. That was (as you saw in the dissent) quite controversial at the time. Its effect has since probably been limited by the New Home Warranty Act, but the chain-of-title principle still applies in eviction cases, as you will see in the following case. As you read the following case, which incorporates a number of the eviction rules we have already considered, look for discussion of a partial eviction, as well as discussion of subrogation. Article 2511 provides that:

When the buyer is evicted from only a part of the thing sold, he may obtain rescission of the sale if he would not have bought the thing without that part. If the sale is not rescinded, the buyer is entitled to a diminution of the price in the proportion that the value of the part lost bears to the value of the whole at the time of the sale.

REVIEW NOTES

Two of the seller's obligations are to deliver the thing and to warrant the buyer's ownership against eviction. Eviction is the loss, or danger of losing the thing due to a third party's interest that existed at the time of the sale.

Section 1: Delivery of the thing

Movables

In general, the seller impliedly warrants that he will deliver the entire thing as per the contract. If the thing is a movable, then delivery generally takes place by manual delivery. Art 2477. If the seller fails to deliver it, then the buyer can demand specific performance or seek dissolution of the sale as well as incidental and delay damages. That obligation may be waived if the buyer refuses to pay, the issue then is which came first – ie. Which of the two parties defaulted?

Examples:

In Maxwell Motors, the defendant buyer was supposed to trade in his old truck as part of the agreement to buy a new one. The parties agreed on the price and had been approved for financing, and the buyer agreed to leave the new truck at the dealer's while he went to get the title to the old truck. However, defendant was unable to secure the title to the old truck and was also unable to come up with a $500 down payment as an alternative, though he did make two payments towards the mortgage. Finally, plaintiff sued on the mortgage. Defendant claimed that the plaintiff cannot enforce the contract of sale because he had never delivered the truck. The court held for the plaintiff because the one who defaulted was the defendant. The plaintiff did not deliver the truck only because the parties that he would maintain possession pending the completion of the negotiation over the down payment.

Quality Paint: Plaintiff paint supplier sued buyer for balance allegedly owed on the account. Defendant buyer, whose business it was to paint machinery, ordered large quantity of paint, which plaintiff was to deliver. The trucking company delivered the paint to Max Welders, at a 'little yard' next door, which was not defendant's property, and it was signed for by an employee of the Welding company. Crescent Coating never received the paint. The court held that it was never delivered, and therefore defendant was not required to pay for it.

Immovables

An immovable is deemed delivered when the writing that transfers its ownership is executed. Art. 2477. This does not mean, however, that the parties cannot alter this arrangement.

Example: In Matthews v. Gaubler, the parties agreed in the contract to buy that the seller would deliver possession and keys at the act of sale. At the act of sale, however, the defendant buyer refused to do so, claiming that they did not have the keys with them, that their child was ill, and that they could not move that day. The plaintiff buyer then refused to go through with that sale, and then demanded the return of his deposit. The court found that as the defendant was the one who defaulted, the plaintiff had the right to dissolve the contract.

Things Accessory to the thing sold:

The sale of a thing includes all accessories intended for its use. In the case of an immovable, that includes immovables by destination and predial servitudes in favor of the property conveyed.

Example: Vincent v. Gold – Plaintiff purchased a home from the defendant and on taking possession was upset to find that defendant had taken two colored glass doors between the den and the living room and brought suit for their return. Defendant claims that they were only "schogie screens" (sic), decorative furnishings temporarily attached to the interior of the residence. After a grant of summary judgment in plaintiff's favor, defendant appealed. The appellate court remanded for a determination of whether the screens were immovables by destination or not.

Immovables and Extension of the Premises:

Articles 2491-2499 As with all sales, a buyer deserves to receive the entirety of the thing purchased. However, when it comes to land, that may mean different things. If the buyer is purchasing farmland, it is generally important that he receive the exact acreage for which he contracted, especially when the sale indicates that the price is per measure – i.e. a price per acre or arpent. When that is the case, the price is adjusted proportionately either up or down whenever the amount of land delivered does not match the amount indicated in the contract. If, however, the amount of land delivered is a lot more than agreed-on (i.e. more than 1/20th the contractual amount), then the buyer has a choice of either paying thee proportionate increase or receding from the contract.

On the other end, if the buyer is purchasing a home, a building, or even a plantation, or by boundaries, and the price is described as a 'lump' price (e.g. $100,000), then the exact amount of acreage is not that important – even if there is some indication of the amount of land being sold. This is described as the sale of a certain and limited body (or a sale per aversionem). In this case, the law provides no adjustment of the price either up or down.

In the middle, if the buyer is buying land at a lump price, but it is not the sale of a 'certain and limited body,' – e.g. 100 acres for $100,000, then the price may be adjusted up or down if the difference between the contract and the amount of land delivered is greater than 1/20th. As with the price per measure, if the buyer receives an overage of more than 1/20th, he may choose to withdraw from the sale.

Examples:

In **Lasiter**, the property was described by boundaries, containing 80 acres more or less, for $50,000 cash. Lasiter purchased it mainly for the timber, and had gone out to physically measure the property himself. After purchasing the land and cutting the timber, he learned that the property contained only 43.20 acres, and that he had cut the neighbor's timber. He had to reimburse the neighbor for the cut timber. The reason for the mistake was that the description included only 3 boundaries of a rectangular-shaped property. He then sued the seller for a proportionate reduction in the price. Even though this looked like a sale per aversionem, the court held for the plaintiff because the incomplete boundaries meant that it was a sale per lump sum, and the shortage was much more than 1/20th.

In **Long Fork,** the purchase agreement provided that the price was per acre, and that "price per acre shall control in the even of a discrepancy between the price stated below and the price as determined by the number of acres conveyed." Otherwise, the property was described as being estimated at 2,759 acres, more or less, generally described as the South Farm. It also provided that a survey would be performed for a closer calculation, and that the price would be $2,896,950 – based on $1,050/acre and 2,759 acres.

The Act of Sale omitted any reference to price per acre and set a price of $2,896,950. Subsequent to the sale, the seller-plaintiff sued for a supplemental increase in price because it was discovered that the property had approximately 215 acres more than originally thought.

The court found for the defendant. But for the per-acre clause, the purchase agreement looked like a per aversionem sale. The court reasoned that the fact that the clause was omitted in the act of sale was because the parties had intended that any price adjustments be made before the act of sale in order to avoid exactly this situation. As the final contract, the act of sale was per aversionem, no price adjustment would be made.

Section 2: Warranty Against Eviction

The warranty against eviction is the buyer's remedy when the seller fails to deliver clear title and is the post-sale equivalent of the warranty of merchantability. It is implied in every sale. Eviction is the buyer's loss of, or danger of losing, the whole or part of the thing sold because of a third person's right that existed at the time of the sale. Art 2500. The warranty covers encumbrances on the thing that were not declared at the time of the sale (such as a mortgage). If a buyer is evicted, he may rescind the sale and recover from the seller the price paid, any fruit he had to return to the person who evicted him, and other damages and losses (except for any increase in value of the thing). Art 2506. The warranty excludes apparent servitudes and natural and legal nonapparent servitudes. Art 2500. Consequently, if the buyer would have seen an electrical tower on the land, had he inspected it before purchase, that is an apparent servitude and not covered by the warranty, as is a natural servitude such as a navigable stream or a legal nonapparent servitude such as a cable line.

Elements of an Eviction:
1. Loss of or danger of losing the thing or part of it
2. Because of a third person's right
3. The right existed at the time of the sale
4. No warranty for apparent servitudes and natural and legal nonapparent servitudes

Example: In Richmond, plaintiff purchased land from Zapata Development with the intent of building on it, but without inspecting the premises or even checking the title. When he finally looked at it, he realized that it had been largely used for mineral exploitation, as there were pipelines, tanks, canals, offices, shacks, drilling equipment, rigs, and etc. on it. He sued, claiming eviction. The court held against him because the lessee's mineral servitude was readily apparent.

B. The Loss or Danger that Constitutes Eviction

The third person's right must exist at the time of the sale. If the third person's right is only perfected because of the buyer's negligence (though the facts that gave rise to it existed before then), the buyer has no claim in warranty. Art. 2500. If the buyer is evicted from only a part of the ting, he may still obtain rescission of the sale if he would not have purchased the thing without that part. Otherwise, the buyer is entitled to a proportionate diminution of the price.

Examples:

Kling v. McLin:

Kling purchased a used car from defendant McLin, only to learn that he could not get title for it because of a pre-existing mortgage. Three years later, he sued for dissolution of the sale. Although the trial court dismissed plaintiff's claim, the appellate court reversed, finding that 1. The applicable prescriptive period is three years, and 2. Plaintiff had presented a prima facia claim that he had been evicted by a third party's pre-existing right, a violation of the warranty against eviction.

Bologna Brothers:

Plaintiff Bologna Bros. purchased a lot from Stephens Realty and built on it. When Stephens died, his wife and daughter took over the Realty Company, and because the titles were not clear, resold some of the same land to Bankston, who informed the Bologna Brothers that their building intruded on his land. The Bologna Bros. negotiated with Bankston, paying him $1,000 for a deed to their property, and then sued Stephens Realty.

Consider how the following concepts apply:

1. While the third party's right must exist before the sale, in this case the seller's own act of reselling some of the property to Bankston caused the eviction. Even if the sale had excluded the warranty against eviction, the seller would still have been liable under Art. 2503.

2 Call in warranty: A buyer threatened with eviction must notify the seller of the threat in a timely manner. If he does not, and the seller could have proven that the third party had no right, then the buyer cannot reclaim any funds buyer spent in settling the third party's claim.

C. Apparent and Non-Apparent Servitudes

Article 2500 stipulates that the warranty against eviction covers encumbrances that there not declared at the time of the sale. An encumbrance is any real right that burdens a thing such as a mortgage, a privilege, a lien, a servitude, and a mineral right. Any right not declared to the buyer and not excluded under 2500 would be a violation of the warranty.

Most of the time, however, sellers inform their buyers of any encumbrances by mentioning it in the deed of sale – though that is not necessary if, as in Richmond v. Zapata, the encumbrance is as apparent as an oil rig.

Article 2500 excludes natural and legal nonapparent servitudes as well as apparent servitudes. For example, an estate may be bound by a servitude of passage in favor of a neighboring enclosed estate – that is a legal servitude, and the seller is not responsible for it.

D. Sale with or without Warranty v. Sale at the Buyer's Risk and Peril

Article 2503 provides a two-level waiver scheme. If the agreement simply excludes the warranty, the buyer can still obtain a rescission if he is evicted but cannot get reimbursed for fruit and other damages. The only way the seller will not have to reimburse the buyer the price he paid is if he proves that 1. The buyer was aware of the danger of eviction at the time of the sale; 2. The buyer declared that he was buying at his peril and risk, or 3. The contract expressly excluded the seller's obligation to return the price. However, even if the contract excludes the warranty against eviction and even if 1, 2, or 3 is present, that waiver is null if the eviction is caused by the seller's own act.

Examples:

New Orleans & Carrollton RR v. Jourdain's Heirs:

Plaintiff Railroad purchased land from defendant's ancestor, from which plaintiff was evicted. Defendant claims that the sale expressly stipulated that it was sold without warranty, and that the buyer was aware of the danger of eviction. The court found that while the act of sale did contain an express waiver against eviction, it did not state that the buyer was buying at his risk and peril, nor was there any showing that the buyer knew of any danger of eviction. While it was aware of the sources of Jourdain's title, there was nothing in that line suggesting a danger of eviction. (Under current law, Jourdain's heirs would have to return the price paid by the Railroad).

Bielawski v. Landry:

This case is somewhat odd because the plaintiff buyer is demanding that the seller be forced to sell, knowing that he may face an eviction. The seller claims that even if the buyer waives the warranty against eviction and even if he agrees to purchase at his risk and peril, he (the seller) cannot be forced to sell. The original contract to buy provided an express warranty against eviction: if the seller was unable to deliver merchantable title within the stipulated time, that would "render this contract null and void." A title examination revealed that seller had obtained the property at a tax sale four years prior, and had filed suit and obtained a judgment confirming and quieting the tax title. Subsequent investigation by plaintiff's attorney, however, showed that that tax title was defective because it had not included the tax debtor's spouse as a defendant, the property's legal description was omitted from the judgment, and the suit itself had been filed before the expiration of the five year preemption period for quieting tax titles.

Despite the fact that Bielawski knew of the unconfirmed nature of the tax title before they signed the original contract, and they were willing to waive the warranty against eviction, Landry did not want to sell. The court found for the defendant because 1. The plaintiff is asking that the court rewrite the document – and reformation is only appropriate where the parties' original agreement differed from the document; and 2. There was apparently no meeting of the minds regarding what would happen in the event that no merchantable title could be delivered. Thus, the court finds that the contract was null and void.

The dissent argues that everything listed in the 2503 Waiver was present here, and there was no reason to nullify the contract if Bielawski is willing to assume all risks of eviction.

Clark v. O'Neal

Plaintiff sold defendant a tract of land and defendant paid with two promissory notes. The plaintiff did not record the sale, one of her creditors obtained a judgment against her, and then seized the land from the defendant and sold it. She then sued her buyer, defendant O'Neal, for payment on the notes. Clark never made any effort to have that judgment set aside. The court finds that it was her negligence that led to O'Neal's eviction, that his not recording the act of sale did not release her from her obligation to warrant his title. Thus, the sale is dissolved and he is not liable on the notes.

Voss v. Roach

Similar to Clark v. O'Neal, seller evicted her own buyer (of a right to harvest timber) by selling the tract to a third party before the plaintiff buyer had harvested the timber and failing to notify the third party that plaintiff had the right to the timber. The court reiterates that buyer cannot be accused of negligence for failing to seasonally record the timber purchase, that the seller is liable where his or her own actions or negligence after the sale lead to the buyer's eviction.

D. The Quit-Claim Deed

Article 2502 presents a different kind of contract, separate and apart from a sale with an implied warranty against eviction. A quit-claim deed is where the seller agrees to transfer whatever right he **may** have in a property, without warranting that he, in fact, has any rights. It is a variety of the sale of a hope. If the seller had ownership, then a quit-claim deed effectively transfers it. If, on the other hand, the seller had no rights, then the buyer gets none. The cases that follow contain a title battle involving a quit-claim deed.

Osborn v. Johnston

Plaintiffs and defendants both claimed the same land and thus an interest in its mineral lease – neither party has possession of the land which became swamp land shortly after the civil war. Defendants' Line of title:

Sheriff 1873

The plaintiffs claim that their ownership comes from Briant, and that the quitclaim deed between the Levee Board and Pierre Angeloz conveyed not title.

The court finds for the defendants because it determined that at the time of the quitclaim deed, in 1896, the Atchafalaya Levee Board had title to the land, and therefore effectively transferred it to Pierre Angeloz, and from there down to the derendants.

Simmesport St. Bank v. Roy

Mr. and Mrs. Tanner owned land in Avoyelles Parish. When they went into bankruptcy, the property was sold to the plaintiff Bank, but the bank failed to record the deed. It also failed to pay the taxes.

The Roys then purchased the property at a tax sale the next year. Noticing that the Tanners were still listed as the record owners, Roy approached them and purchased a quitclaim deed for the property from them for $500 – though they explained to him that the Bank now owned it. Roy immediately filed the deed in the parish conveyance records, and informed the Bank that he had purchased it at a tax sale. When they went to record the purchase, they discovered Roy's quitclaim deed. The bank redeemed the tax sale and instituted suit to annul the quitclaim deed.

The court finds for the Bank because, as the Tanners had no right in the property when they executed the quitclaim deed, they could not transfer any rights.

E. After-Acquired Title Doctrine & Quitclaim Deed

If seller who realizes that there is a title problem corrects it before his buyer realizes there is a problem, then the buyer does not have a claim for eviction Art 2482. This is the after-acquired title doctrine.

If, however, the seller sold his rights by quitclaim deed and then corrects the title problem, that after-acquired title does not inure to the quitclaim buyer's benefit: after all, he bought what the seller owned at that time – nothing. As long as the seller was in good faith, the buyer has no claim and the seller can keep the property at issue. Art. 2502.

Examples

St. Landry Oil & Gas v. Neal

Garrett 1901 mineral lease

1920 ½ interest

In 1920, Garrett sued heirs of Bridgeman because of a title problem in the land, the Bridgemans were recognized as owners of the land on which T.S. Neal had gotten the mineral lease which had been transferred to St. Landry. So, Neal went to the Bridgemans and obtained a ratification of the lease. Some months later, plaintiff St Landry claimed had been evicted by the Bridgemans and sued Neal.

Held: for Neal under the after acquired title doctrine because he had resolved the title issue before St. Landry became aware of it; consequently, St Landry was never evicted nor did he face a danger of being evicted.

Waterman V. Tidewater Assoc.

Plaintiff Waterman claims he owns a ¼ interest in land in Plaquemines Parish

Plaintiffs' chain of title: the "Lacey" title:

Buras Levee Board 1896

    Defendants' chain of title: the "Leovy" title

    State 1893

    Plaintiffs claimed first that the Rectangle-Rose quitclaim deed transferred ownership, and therefore their title is clear. Alternatively, even if Rectangle did not have any right at the time to transfer to Rose, that title was subsequently cleared when Rectangle acquired it from Kranebell in 1927.

    The court found against Waterman because the Buras Levee Board did not have title to it, neither did anyone in the Lacey chain after that, and therefore the quitclaim deed did not transfer any ownership from Rectangle to Rose. Furthermore, the after-acquired title doctrine does not apply to a quitclaim deed.

F. Subrogation

The last paragraph of Article 2503 provides that the buyer is subrogated to the seller's rights against other persons, "even where the warranty is excluded." This means that if a buyer is evicted from his purchase, he can pursue his claim against not just his seller, but also his seller's seller, and on up the line to where the fault in title occurred, even if the warranty against eviction is waived.

Examples

Aizpurua v. Crane Pool

Plaintiff Aizpurua purchased a home in 1977 from defendants Smith, who had purchased it from the contractor, Watts Brothers Buildings. Crane Pool Company had installed a swimming pool at the time the house was built that was apparently built improperly and started failing in 1979. In 1981, Aizpurua sued. The plaintiffs' claims in redhibition and tort had prescribed as against the Smiths, so the issue that remained was whether any warranties between Crane and the Smiths were breached. Relying on the common law implied warranty of fitness and Media Pro (a Louisiana Supreme court manufacturer's liability case), the Supreme court used the subrogation provision in Article 2503 to find that the claim against Crane had not prescribed rather than the more appropriate subrogation provision in Article 2548.

Justice Marcus dissented, finding that the 2503 provision should not have been applied to this, which is a defect claim. Art. 2503 it is intended to apply only to eviction claims.

Justice Dennis concurred but on different reasoning – the case was one not of sale, but of building, and as the prescriptive period for a building is 10 years, the claim had not prescribed.

Because of the odd reasoning and inconsistent interpretation of the Civil Code, the authoritative nature of this case is somewhat questionable.

HYPOTHET

This hypothet is from a final exam:

In December 2011, Audrey sold to Betsy a tract of land fronting Bayou John for $500,000 by an act of sale containing the following provision:

The property herein conveyed is sold without warranty of title but with full subrogation to all rights in warranty against all prior owners. Vendor also transfers to Vendee whatever rights and claims, if any, Vendor may have to the bed of Bayou John adjoining the property.

Betsy did not have a title examination done prior to the sale, choosing instead to rely on her knowledge that Audrey had owned the property for over thirty years. After the sale, however, Betsy learned a number of things that negatively affected her plans to develop the property as a residential subdivision. First, upon walking the entire perimeter of the property for the first time shortly after buying it, Betsy discovered that an overhead electrical line providing electrical service to a neighboring tract crossed her property. Furthermore, after her plans for the property became publicly known, Betsy received a letter from a pipeline company asserting that an underground gas pipeline crosses the property. Enclosed with the letter was a copy of a pipeline servitude agreement, which had been executed by Audrey's predecessor-in-title, establishing a pipeline servitude along a designated route and specifically providing that no improvements could be constructed over the pipeline. Betsy was surprised by this news since she had recognized no visible signs of a pipeline crossing the property. Betsy has also learned that the State of Louisiana owns the bed of Bayou John and will not grant her permission to erect a dock or several other structures that she had planned to install as amenities to her residential subdivision.

Concerned by these developments, Betsy for the first time obtained a title examination, which reflected that agreements establishing servitudes for the overhead electrical line and the underground pipeline had been properly recorded several years before Audrey had acquired the property. The title examination also revealed an agreement executed and properly recorded in 1999 by which Audrey granted Camille the right to purchase the property for $250,000 in the event that Audrey ever decided to sell it.

Determined not to abandon the plans for her residential subdivision, Betsy paid the holder of the electrical servitude $10,000 to re-route the electrical line along the perimeter of her property. She paid Camille $50,000 for a relinquishment of her claims to the property. Finally, after determining that it would be too expensive to re-route the pipeline, Betsy had her engineer re-configure her site plans so that the pipeline would run down the middle of a new boulevard rather than through any lot, thus resulting in a decrease of four in the number of lots she would be able to include in the subdivision. Unable to obtain any concession from the State concerning the dock she had planned to build over the bed of Bayou John, she abandoned those plans, though she believes that the overall value of her subdivision has decreased as a result.

Betsy has filed suit against Audrey seeking reimbursement of the amounts she paid to Camille and the holder of the electrical servitude, as well as damages from the loss of lots resulting from re-configuration of her subdivision around the underground pipeline and damages from her inability to construct the dock as she had planned. Before filing suit, Betsy did not notify Audrey of any of the title problems or the actions that Betsy had taken to address them.

A. (75 pts) Discuss whether and to what extent Betsy has rights against Audrey or others on account of the existence of the overhead electrical line and the underground pipeline.

B. (50 pts) Discuss the nature and enforceability of Camille's claim to the property, as well as whether and to what extent Betsy has rights against Audrey on account of the payment Betsy made to Camille for relinquishment of that claim.

C. (25 pts) Discuss whether and to what extent Betsy has rights against Audrey on account of the states ownership of the portion of the bed of Bayou John mentioned in the act of sale.

CHAPTER 10

REDHIBITION AND RELATED WARRANTIES

Flowchart

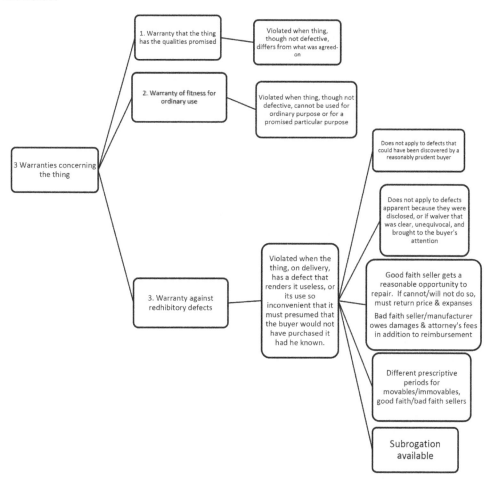

Section 1: Three Different Warranties

The previous chapter dealt with the seller's warranty that he will deliver the object of the sale and its title. This chapter deals with the sellers' obligations to warrant the fitness, quality and usefulness of the object of the sale. Read Articles 2520-2522, 2530-2548 on Redhibition, Article 2534 on Fitness for Use, and Article 2529 on Thing Not of Kind Specified in the Contract

As defined by Article 2520, the warranty against redhibitory defects applies when the thing delivered has a hidden defect that renders it useless or its use so inconvenient that it must be presumed the buyer would not have bought the thing had he known of the defect. One could compare this to a manufacturing defect as defined in a products liability action – the thing was broken when it was delivered. In fact, though they are not the same because a products liability action addresses personal injury and a redhibition action addresses monetary and consequential damages, one can bring both claims (redhibition and strict products liability) in the same action, as shown in the last section of this chapter. The warranty of fitness applies when the thing delivered, though not containing a defect, is not reasonably fit for its ordinary use or for the particular use the seller recommended it for. The warranty provided in Art. 2529 applies when the thing delivered is not the same kind or quality of thing as the thing ordered – e.g., you ordered blue suede shoes, but received red patent leather instead.

In the past, courts have consistently had difficulty distinguishing among the warranty against redhibitory defects (Art. 2520), the warranty of fitness for ordinary use or the buyer's particular purpose (Art. 2524), and the warranty that the thing sold conforms to the specifications in the contract (Art. 2529). These are three different warranties that apply in three different types of situations. It is important to be accurate in determining which warranty applies because the effects of each are different. Redhibition has its own remedies and shorter prescriptive periods. In contrast, the prescriptive period for other two warranties is ten years and the normal breach-of-contract remedies apply.

Articles 2520, 2522, and 2531 provide the basic warranty against redhibitory defects. If the thing delivered by the seller is rendered useless due to a hidden defect, or its use is so inconvenient that it must be presumed the buyer would not have bought the thing had he known of the defect, then after notice, the seller must either repair the thing or return the price to the buyer with interest. The defect must have existed before delivery. If it appears within three days of delivery, it is presumed that the defect pre-existed delivery. Art. 2530. Unless the thing sold is a commercial or residential immovable, the action prescribes four years from the day of delivery or one year from the day of discovery, whichever occurs first. Art. 2534. The prescriptive period for a residential or commercial immovable is one year from the date of delivery. As indicated in the comments, the four-year/one-year period was implemented in 1995 in order to be consistent with the Uniform Commercial Code.

Study Question:

As you read the following cases, ask yourself:

1) Does the court correctly categorize the problem with the thing delivered as a redhibitory defect, a lack of fitness, or a lack of quality? If so, why? If not, why not?

2) What prescriptive period did the court apply?

NELSON RADIOLOGY ASSOCIATES, LLC V. INTEGRITY MEDICAL SYSTEMS, INC. 2009

16 SO.3D 1197 (LA.APP. 4TH CIR.)

JAMES F. McKAY III, Judge.

¶1 Integrity Medical Systems Inc., appeals the judgment of the trial court in favor of Nelson Radiology Associates, L.L.C. and Dr. Ava Nelson, awarding the sum of Fifty-Three Thousand Eight Hundred Twenty-Eight Dollars and Twenty-Eight Cents ($53,828.28) plus court costs and attorney's fees in the sum of Twenty-Six Thousand One Hundred Twenty-Seven Dollars and Thirty-three Cents ($26,127.33).

FACTS AND PROCEDURAL HISTORY

¶2 [Dr. Ava Nelson, radiologist, after practicing in hospitals for many years, began the process of opening her own outpatient imaging center in New Orleans in 1999, where she intended to offer mammograms, x-rays, ultrasounds, and bone densitometry studies. The business would be known as Nelson Radiology Associates, L.L.C. ("Nelson Radiology"), and she needed four essential pieces of medical equipment: an x-ray machine, an ultrasound, a bone densitometer, and a mammogram unit. In November, 1999, she contacted Integrity Medical Services ("Integrity"), in order to purchase a refurbished mammography unit and a bone densitometer. with the purpose of acquiring medical equipment for Nelson Radiology. Integrity is in the business of buying and selling new and refurbished medical equipment. Though Integrity not only acquires, refurbishes, installs, and services used equipment, on November 26, 1999, Dr. Nelson agreed to purchase both pieces of equipment without installation, but with 90-day warranties. She purchased them F.O.B. Fort Meyers, Florida through a lease-purchase agreement with a financing company, HPSC, Inc. The lease-purchase agreement gave Dr. Nelson an option of purchasing the At equipment for fair market value at the end of the lease term. Based on this agreement, HPSC paid Integrity in full on January 12, 2000. The mammography unit is the issue of this lawsuit.]

* * *

¶3 [After being refurbished, it was delivered to Dr. Nelson's clinic on February 2, 2000.]

¶4 Dr. Nelson asserts that there were problems with the mammography unit which was delivered on February 2, 2000. She complains that the unit was damaged, not properly refurbished by Integrity, and improperly packaged thereby rendering the unit unusable for the purpose for which it was intended. The alleged damages were noticed only after March 9, 2000, when John Mills of Performance Medical came to the office to install the unit. Mr. Mills observed that there were parts missing and that he would be unable to install the unit until the missing parts were replaced. As noted in the trial court's reasons for judgment, Mr. Mills sent a descriptive list of damaged parts to Integrity; the unit was missing a frame nut plate, a frame spacer, a cover, a wall adapter plate, a wall bracket assembly and a broken plug. More notable, the trial court determined that Mr. Mills did not report the following damaged parts: an x-ray tube, a broken cable, cracked compression paddles, a bent column, and dust in the machine. Upon receiving Mr. Mill's list, Integrity sent an urgent request to Bennett Mammography Parts Order Department requesting the missing parts. Parts began to arrive at the clinic on March 13, 2000, with the last parts arriving on April 25, 2000. Mr. Mills did not attempt to install the missing parts and power up the unit until May 2, 2000, three months after the unit was delivered. At that time Mr. Mills informed Integrity that the unit was making noise, there was a broken cable on the unit and two compression paddles were cracked. Integrity ordered a replacement x-ray tube at its cost and shipped it to Dr. Nelson on May 30, 2000 and she received it on June 2, 2000. . . .

¶5 On June 4, 2000, Integrity requested that the unit be inspected by Mr. Louis Rodriguez of Tri-State Medical, a company that installs new and used x-ray equipment. Upon inspection, Mr. Rodriguez noticed that the equipment was damaged. He testified that the column was already bolted to the wall but it appeared that the installation was not finished. The column moved, but the compression bars did not, likely due to a broken cable. The column cover and the column itself were the only things upright. The column itself was bent. The main generator was in the room, but still sitting on the side. Some of the boxes were still sealed. Based on Mr. Rodriguez's report, Integrity suggested that Dr. Nelson return the mammography unit at her cost. Dr. Nelson rejected this offer. On August 4, 2000, Tri-State removed the unit to their warehouse for storage. It remained in their warehouse for over four years until they discarded the unit at Dr. Nelson's direction.

¶6 Allegedly, as a result of the tardiness in delivery of the missing parts, Dr. Nelson determined that it was necessary to rent a mammography unit from another company.

¶7 On December 26, 2000, Dr. Nelson filed a petition for damages against Integrity seeking to recover the return of the purchase price of the equipment, repair costs, costs incident to the sale, lost business and profits, general damages, attorney's fees, and court costs. Dr. Nelson asserts that Integrity acted in bad faith and knew that the equipment was defective.

¶8 After a two-day trial on the merits, the trial court found that Integrity had breached its warranties of sale and was a bad faith seller under Louisiana's redhibition law and awarded damages in the amount of $53,828.28, plus attorneys' fees, costs and interest. The trial court issued reasons for judgment, which included a $30,000.00 general damage award to Dr. Nelson. We agree with the trial court's application of Louisiana law and determining that the matter lies in redhibition and in assessing costs and attorney's fees to Integrity. However, we disagree with the determination that Integrity was a bad faith seller and with the trial court's award of general damages in the sum of $30,000. We further disagree with the trial court's award of incidental damages to Dr. Nelson.

***

DISCUSSION

¶9 Based on the record and more specifically the trial court's reasons for judgment, a number of issues need clarification.

***

REDHIBITORY DEFECTS

* * *

¶10 The critical issue concerning the mammography unit relevant to the claim of redhibitory defects is . . . the condition in which the unit arrived. More, importantly, is the issue of whether the condition of the unit, upon its arrival at Dr. Nelson's clinic, reached the level of a redhibitory defect.

¶11 The trial court concluded that Integrity was liable in redhibition for the plaintiffs' damages.

*　*　*

¶12   In Louisiana, "[t]he seller warrants the buyer against redhibitory defects or vices in the thing sold." La. C.C. art. 2520. A defect is redhibitory when it "renders the thing useless, or its use so inconvenient that it must be presumed that the buyer would not have bought the thing had he known of the defect." Id. The existence of this type of redhibitory defect provides the buyer with the right to obtain rescission of the sale. Id. A thing can also contain a redhibitory defect when the defect "diminishes its usefulness or its value so that it must be presumed the buyer would still have bought it, but for a lesser price." Id. This type of redhibitory defect limits the right of a buyer to seek a reduction of the price. Id. Pursuant to La. C.C. art. 2530, the warranty extends only to defects that exist at the time of delivery, and there is a presumption that the defect existed at delivery if the defect appears within three days of delivery. Proof that a redhibitory defect existed at the time of sale can be made by direct or circumstantial evidence giving rise to a reasonable inference that the defect existed at the time of sale. Boos v. Benson Jeep-Eagle Co., Inc., 98-1424, p. 3 (La.App. 4 Cir. 6/24/98), 717 So.2d 661, 663. Further, under La. C.C. art. 2521, the seller owes no warranty for defects that were known to the buyer at the time of the sale, or for defects that should have been discovered by a reasonably prudent buyer. La. C.C. art. 2522 requires that the buyer must give the seller notice of a redhibitory defect and allow time for the seller to repair the defect; however, if the seller has actual knowledge of the defect, then no notice is required.

¶13   However, not all redhibitory vices or defects justify rescission or reduction of the price. Apparent defects, which the buyer can discover through a simple inspection, are excluded from the seller's legal warranty. La. C.C. art. 2521. A defect is apparent if a reasonably prudent buyer, acting under similar circumstances, would discover it through a simple inspection of the property. David v. Thibodeaux, 04-0976, p. 3 (La.App. 1 Cir. 5/11/05), 916 So.2d 214, 217. Factors to be considered in determining whether an inspection is reasonable include knowledge and expertise of the buyer, the opportunity for inspection, and assurances made by the seller. Crow v. Laurie, 98-0648, p. 6 (La.App. 1 Cir. 2/19/99), 729 So.2d 703, 707-708.

¶14   Applicable facts to the case sub judice, are that the mammography unit arrived at Dr. Nelson's clinic on February 2, 2000, but there was no attempt to inspect the unit until March 9, 2000. This Court finds no reasonable explanation for this inaction. Dr. Nelson had hired Mr. John Mills of Performance Medical to install the mammography unit. Upon his inspection of the unit he discovered that it was missing vital parts and other vital parts of the unit were broken. John Mills made a list of parts that he said were missing and drew a sketch of a broken plug, which was faxed to Integrity. Although the defendant made numerous attempts to replace the missing and broken parts throughout the month of March, the last part did not arrive until around April 25, 2000. Mr. Mills did not reattempt to install the mammography unit until May 2, 2000, after the five missing parts had arrived. Integrity maintains that the parts were shipped timely within a reasonable time of the notification of the defects and continues to argue the failure of Dr. Nelson to inspect the unit timely.

¶15   Under the circumstances, on the date of initial delivery and even up to the time that Mr. Mills attempted to install the unit it is clear that the mammography unit was defective and could not be used for the purpose for which it was intended.

¶16   On June 4, 2000, at Integrity's request, Louis Rodriguez inspected the mammography unit. Upon inspection, Mr. Rodriguez noticed that the unit was visibly damaged. Mr. Rodriguez opined that the unit's column being bolted to the wall was indicia of partial installation, but the partial installation had not sufficiently progressed for power to be hooked up to the x-ray tube. Based upon Mr. Rodriguez's report, Integrity suggested that Dr. Nelson send the mammography unit back to them, at her cost, and that they would evaluate it to see if it had been damaged beyond repair. Dr. Nelson rejected this offer.

¶17   In July of 2000, Dr. Nelson . . . moved the clinic to a new location on Chef Menteur Hwy. She asserts that due to the condition of the mammography unit, she had no choice but to lease another mammography unit with a monthly lease of $450.00 per month, which was less than the fees on the Integrity unit. On August 4, 2000, at Dr. Nelson's request, Tri-State Medical removed the unit to their warehouse for storage. It is somewhat troubling to this Court that the unit remained in storage with Tri-State Medical for over four years until it was discarded while the current suit was pending, at the request of Dr. Nelson.

¶18   Based on the facts we find no error in the trial court's factual determination that the mammography unit had defects that reached the level of being redhibitory thereby rendering the unit unusable for its intended purpose. The buyer would not have bought the thing had she known of the defects. We further find it reasonable for the trial court to have concluded that Integrity knew of the defects prior to shipping the unit to Dr. Nelson, . . .

¶19   We find merit to appellant's argument that Dr. Nelson is not entitled to the added incidental damages outlined above for a total of $6,254.00 and amend the trial court's judgment to reflect this ruling.

***

¶20   [The Court reverses the award of general damages and attorney's fees.]

¶21 We affirm the judgment of the trial court in all aspects except for the award of incidental and general damages. Accordingly, we amend the judgment to limit monetary recovery, attributable to the cost of the mammography unit itself, $17,575. We further amend the judgment to exclude the $30,000 general damages award.

AFFIRMED IN PART; REVERSED IN PART; AMENDED IN PART AND RENDERED.

Lagniappe Questions:

1) Under general obligations rules, what damages are due for bad faith nonperformance?

2) Does this include attorney's fees? (Check Article 1997.)

3) When can one demand attorney's fees in a contract-based claim? (Check Articles 1958, 1964, & 2545.)

BO-PIC FOODS, INC. V. POLYFLEX FILM & CONVERTING, INC. 1995
665 SO. 2D 787 (LA. APP. 1ST CIR.)

KUHN, Judge.

¶1 In this appeal, buyer and seller dispute whether buyer is entitled to recover the purchase price of a metalized film paper ("film") purchased for bagging potato chips, which was found not suitable for that purpose. The trial court dismissed plaintiff's claims against defendant after determining plaintiff failed to carry its burden of proving a redhibitory defect. We reverse.

FACTS

¶2 Plaintiff-appellant, Bo-Pic Foods, Inc. ("Bo-Pic"), filed suit against defendant-appellee, Polyflex Film and Converting, Inc. ("Polyflex"), seeking to recover $7,152.45, the price paid for the film.1 The petition asserts 1) the film was sold by defendant's sales representative to meet the requirements and specifications of plaintiff for containment of plaintiff's products; 2) upon receipt of the film, Bo-Pic immediately determined the product did not meet it's requirements and specifications for the intended use of the film and was not in accordance with the representations made by Polyflex's sales representative; 3) the product was returned to Polyflex; 4) payment for the product was made in error by Bo-Pic; and 5) Polyflex has refused to refund the purchase price upon plaintiff's demand. In answer to the petition, Polyflex admitted 1) the film was sold by its sales representative to meet Bo-Pic's requirements and specifications for containment of its products and 2) the invoiced sale price of the film was paid by Bo-Pic and not refunded by Polyflex.

¶3 Representatives for both Bo-Pic and Polyflex testified during the trial of this matter. Mr. Walter Kimbrel, who was a customer sales and service representative for Polyflex, testified that Polyflex sold printed cellophane roll stock to Bo-Pic during 1987 and 1988, which was used by Bo-Pic for bagging chips and popcorn. The orders were frequently placed by Bo-Pic through Mr. Quentin Sharp, an independent broker, who sold products for Polyflex on a commission basis.

¶4 Kimbrel testified he handled "anything that required technical specifications for manufacture within the plant," while Sharp handled the "leg work" or "direct calls on the customer." Kimbrel explained technical information was required to service the Bo-Pic account with respect to the types of films used for various products, the type and size of printing cylinders used, the acquisition of printing plates and delivery schedules. Kimbrel acknowledged he had visited Bo-Pic on occasion to examine its equipment.

¶5 Kimbrel handled the order which is the subject of this dispute. He explained Polyflex had been supplying Bo-Pic with a cellophane film manufactured by another company. During the latter part of 1986 or during 1987, Kimbrel had several discussions on the telephone with Robert Bourg, Bo-Pic's president, regarding another type of film to be used for bagging the chips. Kimbrel explained Bourg was looking for a product that would be less expensive than the one he was using. The alternative product discussed was a fairly new product on the market, a light gauge metalized material, which had not been previously handled by Polyflex. This film was manufactured by Mobil Films ("Mobil"). Kimbrel testified the initial request for information regarding the film came from Bourg.

¶6 Since the new product had not been tested by Bo-Pic, Kimbrel advised Bourg to order a sample of the film. However, before the sample was received, Bourg placed an order for five hundred pounds of the film and later increased the order by an additional five hundred pounds.

* * *

¶7 Kimbrel's testimony was conflicting regarding whether he advised Bourg that the product might not be suitable for Bo-Pic's use prior to the time the order was placed. . . .

¶8 Bourg's testimony regarding the events prior to and after the order of the film was very different from Kimbrel's testimony. Bourg testified he had been doing business with Polyflex since

1981 or 1982. Sharp solicited his business and he had not had any major problems with Polyflex's products prior to ordering the new film. Bourg stated he relied on Kimbrel's advice when ordering products from Polyflex. He decided to order the new film, which was less expensive than the product he was currently using, after Kimbrel advised that another potato chip company located in the same geographical region as Bo-Pic was successfully using the product. Because he was low on film inventory, he decided to order the film immediately.

¶9 Bourg testified Kimbrel never told him he was buying the product at his own risk. He explained Kimbrel did not tell him the film would not work for bagging potato chips until after the film was ordered and en route to him. Although Bourg acknowledged receiving a letter from Kimbrel advising him that Kimbrel did not think the film was suitable for the purpose intended, Bourg indicated the letter stated the film was en route to Bo-Pic and did not advise the order could be canceled. . . .Bourg also stated he was never offered a sample of the film, never received a sample of the film and was never advised by anyone that the order could be canceled.

¶10 When Bourg received the film, he could not get it to run on his machinery. After the meeting with Kimbrel and Sharp, Polyflex agreed to put a lacquer coating on the film. After he received and used the coated product, he determined the film was not holding his product; the potato chips were going stale within a four-day period. He stated the standard shelf life for the snack food industry was six weeks. Bourg testified he attempted running a double bag with the film, but found it was not compatible with the other products he had available to him for use in double-bagging. Since Bourg had no use for the film, he returned it to Polyflex. He explained the invoice for the film was paid in error by his father, who handled some of the bookkeeping for Bo-Pic.

¶11 Stephen Schexnayder, who worked for Bo-Pic when the film in question was received, testified he was not successful in running the film on Bo-Pic's machinery. He recalled the Mobil representative, Briggs, was able to make a bag after making adjustments to the machinery. He also recalled Briggs had commented that the bag was not designed to be used on its own, but was to be combined with another film to make a bag. After Polyflex coated the film, the product was still not rigid enough to use for storing a product. He testified Bo-Pic's products required a six-to-eight-week shelf life, and the film was useless because it did not provide a six-week shelf life. In addition, he explained the end seal and the back seal on every bag were irregular. Schexnayder also testified he did not recall receiving a sample of the film and never heard Kimbrel advise Bourg that he was buying the film at his own risk.

***

PROCEEDINGS BELOW

* * *

¶12   The trial court decided the case based on redhibition law, determining the pertinent question presented was "whether or not this metalized product is absolutely useless or whether or not it might be useful for something else other than packaging potato chips." The court acknowledged some testimony showed the film could be used in a cookie box or cracker box and concluded Bo-Pic failed to carry its burden of proving the product "was absolutely useless or so inconvenient or imperfect that it must be supposed the buyer would not have purchased it."

¶13   Bo-Pic has appealed contending the trial court "committed an error of law by not properly applying Civil Code Article 2520 on redhibition to plaintiff's inability to use the product for its intended purpose."

ANALYSIS

¶14   Under the provisions of La.C.C. art. 2475,5 a seller warrants the thing which he sells, and under the provisions of La.C.C. art. 2476, the seller warrants there is no hidden defect in the thing sold. Under the provisions of La.C.C. art. 2520, a sale may be avoided where a vice or defect in the thing sold renders it absolutely useless, or so inconvenient and imperfect that it must be supposed the purchaser would not have purchased it had he known of the vice. Based on these articles, our courts have found the seller impliedly warrants the thing sold is free of hidden defects and is reasonably fit for the purpose intended. Hob's Refrigeration and Air Conditioning, Inc. v. Poche, 304 So.2d 326, 327 (La.1974), Rey v. Cuccia, 298 So.2d 840, 842 (La.1974); J.B. Beaird Co. v. Burris Bros., 216 La. 655, 44 So.2d 693, 697 (1949).6

¶15   Our courts have recognized these warranties can be limited or waived. However, they cannot be regarded as waived in the absence of a clear, unambiguous and express agreement. La.C.C. art. 2474; Hob's, 304 So.2d at 327; Rey, 298 So.2d at 840; Hendricks v. Horseless Carriage, Inc., 332 So.2d 892, 894 (La.App.2d Cir.1976). The seller bears the burden of proving the warranty has been waived. Savannah v. Anthony's Auto Sales, Inc., 618 So.2d 676, 679 (La.App.2d Cir.), writ denied, 626 So.2d 1174 (La.1993); Reilly v. Gene Ducote Volkswagen, Inc., 549 So.2d 428, 432 (La.App. 5th Cir.1989).

¶16   The trial court's reasons for judgment establish the court considered redhibition law but failed to consider the seller's implied warranty of fitness in analyzing this case. The court considered whether the product was absolutely useless but did not consider whether the film was reasonably fit for its intended purpose. Accordingly, since the trial court's judgment dismissing plaintiff's claims is based on an error of law, we are required to consider this case on a de novo basis. Lasha v. Olin Corp., 625 So.2d 1002, 1006 (La.1993).

¶17 The record establishes Bo-Pic had been a customer of Polyflex for a number of years, Kimbrel was familiar with Bo-Pic's operations, and Bourg and Sharp relied on Kimbrel's expertise in the film paper business when making decisions regarding product specifications. The record clearly demonstrates Kimbrel was fully aware Bo-Pic intended to use the metalized film for the purpose of bagging potato chips. We note Polyflex admitted in its answer that the film was sold by its sales representative to meet Bo-Pic's requirements and specifications for containment of its products. Thus, based on the circumstances presented in this case, we find Polyflex warranted the film as suitable for the purpose of bagging potato chips.

¶18 The record also clearly establishes the film was entirely unsuitable for the purpose of bagging potato chips. Bourg testified his product required a six-week shelf life, and his product became stale within four days after being bagged in the film. Accordingly, we find plaintiff established Polyflex did not satisfy the implied warranty of fitness in the sale of the film.

¶19 However, the warranty of fitness is not owed by a seller when the buyer waives that warranty. Kimbrel and Sharp testified Bourg was advised after the film was ordered it would not be suitable for the purpose intended and the order could still be canceled. However, Bourg testified he was never advised that the order could be canceled. In light of the contradictory testimony regarding whether Bourg had an opportunity to cancel the order after being advised the product might not be suitable for his use and Kimbrel's admission he never advised Bourg he was buying the product at his own risk, we find Polyflex has not carried its burden of establishing Bo-Pic clearly, unambiguously and expressly waived the warranty of fitness.

CONCLUSION

¶20 For the above reasons, we reverse the judgment of the trial court and render judgment in favor of plaintiff-appellant, Bo-Pic Foods, Inc., and against defendant-appellee, Polyflex Film and Converting, Inc., in the amount of $7,152.45, plus interest from date of judicial demand, January 19, 1989, until satisfaction of the judgment. The trial court costs and the costs of this appeal are to be paid by Polyflex Film and Converting, Inc.

REVERSED AND RENDERED.

COOK V. STOWE 2005

914 SO. 2D 1135 (LA. APP. 2D CIR.)

BROWN, C.J.

¶1 In January 2004, plaintiffs, Roger Cook and James Davis, purchased 100 cows for $625 each from defendant, Luther Stowe, Jr. The deal was made after plaintiffs viewed the cows in Stowe's Texas pasture. Stowe delivered the cows to the West Monroe Sale Barn on January 24, 2004. At that time, plaintiffs rejected two cows because of open wounds on their backs. Defendant refunded the cost of the two rejected cows. Therefore, plaintiffs took delivery of 98 cows at a cost of $61,250.

¶2 Plaintiffs contend that defendant guaranteed that all the cows were three to six years old, were five to seven months bred, meaning five to seven months into a nine-month pregnancy, and were bred by Angus or Charolais bulls. Plaintiffs also testified that defendant agreed that he would have a veterinarian check the cows before shipment.

¶3 Plaintiffs resold the cows for $60,258.40. Alleging that the cows were not the age or bred as guaranteed, plaintiffs filed this action seeking damages for loss of profit, mental anguish and the cost for feeding the cows longer than they expected.

¶4 Defendant denied that he made any guaranty. The contract was made orally, which is common in the cattle trade. The trial court awarded plaintiffs $26,821.60 representing lost profits and feeding costs. Defendant has appealed.

Facts

¶5 At delivery, plaintiffs processed the cows through a chute and recorded each cow's ear tag number, the age and month bred, which were marked on the side of the cow in blue paint, and each animal's color. Plaintiffs presumed that the blue paint markings were made by a veterinarian hired by defendant.

¶6 A "vet check" is a term pregnancy evaluation performed by a veterinarian, generally costing four dollars a cow. A cow is either "open," meaning not pregnant, or bred anywhere from one month to the end of a nine-month term. A calf born early in the year feeds on spring grass and is more valuable than one born mid to late year.

¶7 Plaintiff, Roger Cook, testified that he and Davis bought the cows cheap with the intent to quickly resell them for a profit of approximately $200 per cow. Plaintiffs resold the cows on three separate occasions. On February 16, 2004, plaintiffs took 15 of the cows to the West Monroe Sale Barn. A veterinarian checked them before the sale and concluded that 8 of the 15 were more than six years old; 4 of the cows were open; and 3 were in very early stages of pregnancy. Plaintiffs received $8,324 for the 15 cows.

¶8 On March 27, 2004, plaintiffs sold 27 cows for a total of $17,735 in Alexandria. Some of the cows were open, bred light (meaning these cows must have been bred in plaintiffs' pasture), or older than six years of age.

¶9 On May 25, 2004, plaintiffs sold 54 of the cows for $34,199.40 in West Monroe. If the cows had been five to six months bred at the time plaintiffs had purchased them, then plaintiffs contend that each one would have birthed a calf by that date; however, only 19 of the 54 had birthed calves at this time. According to the veterinarian at the sale barn, 16 cows were seven years of age or older, 21 were open, and 4 were four months bred or less, indicating that plaintiffs' own bull had impregnated them. Some of the cows were "open mouth," indicating extreme age, and some of the calves were clearly not sired by Angus or Charolais bulls.

¶10 Bob Smith owns livestock barns in Monroe and Alexandria and has worked with cattle all of his life. The court recognized him as an expert in the evaluation and sale of cows. Smith testified that he traveled with plaintiffs to Texas to view the cows. According to Smith, defendant guaranteed the cows to be six years old or younger, five and six months bred, some even seven months bred, and that defendant would have each of the cows "vet checked" before delivery. Smith told plaintiffs that the cows as presented were being sold at least $200 per cow below their worth. Smith received a commission from defendant for the sale.

¶11 The primary method of determining a cow's age is by the length of its teeth: the shorter the teeth, the older the cow. Smith testified, however, that the deterioration of the teeth depends on the type of grass the cow eats, and the subjective view of the beholder; however, this method is effective in determining if the cow is younger than five years or older than seven years.

* * *

¶12 When the deal was made in defendant's Texas pasture, Smith stated that he had not inspected any of the cows' mouths or attempted to determine their pregnancy status. He simply took defendant's word. Smith testified that he purchased some of the cows himself from plaintiffs at two of the sales and recognized them as the same cattle sold by defendant due to their 3-S or 3-5 brands (an "S" and a "5" looked the same to Smith).

* * *

Trial Court's Ruling

¶13 The district court held that there was a valid contract for $625 a cow, that the cows were to be under six years of age, five to six months bred by either Angus or Charolais bulls, and that defendant would have the cows vet checked before making delivery. The court found that there was a breach of this contract in that some of the cows were not bred, some of the cows were older than six years, and some of the cows had been bred by bulls other than Angus and Charolais.

¶14 As to evaluating the damages, the district court considered the testimony of both experts, the uncertainties of the age and gestation period of each cow, and other unforeseen events. . . .

¶15 As to the sale on February 16, 2004, the court decided that if the cows had been as guaranteed, then they would have sold for $750 per cow (for the 15 sold on that day) for a total of $11,250. Plaintiffs actually received $8,324 for the cows, for a loss of $2,926.

¶16 As to the sale on March 27, 2004, the court found that the average value for the cows should have been $850, as they should have been further into their pregnancies.

* * *

¶17 According to the trial court's calculations, the total loss for the cows was $25,241.60. The court further found that the cost of feeding the cows for longer than expected amounted to $1,580, bringing the total damages to $26,821.60.

***

Discussion

¶18 When factual findings are based on determinations regarding the credibility of witnesses, the manifest error standard demands great deference to the trier of fact's finding. Stephens v. Fuller, 39,918 (La.App.2d Cir.06/29/05), 907 So.2d 917. When there are two permissible and reasonable views of the evidence, the fact finder's choice cannot be manifestly erroneous or clearly wrong. Arceneaux v. Domingue, 365 So.2d 1330 (La.1978); Stephens, supra.

¶19   In the trial at hand, witnesses gave contradictory testimony. Most of the witnesses were either employees or family members of the parties. All of the parties agreed that there was an oral contract to sell the cows. What was in dispute was whether there was a guaranty that the cows were of a certain age and condition, and, if so, what would be the proper remedy.

***

The Award

¶20   LSA-C.C. Art. 2529 as written by the legislature in 1993 provides:

Art. 2529. Thing not of the kind specified in the contract

When the thing the seller has delivered, though in itself free from redhibitory defects, is not of the kind or quality specified in the contract or represented by the seller, the rights of the buyer are governed by other rules of sale and conventional obligations.

Acts 1993, No. 841, § 1, eff. Jan. 1, 1995.

¶21   The revision comments state:

(a) This Article is new. It does not change the law, however. It has been introduced in order to enhance the distinction between redhibition and breach of contract, and to eliminate the possibility of confusion that arose from the pertinent Articles in the Louisiana Civil Code of 1870. In addition, it gives legislative formulation to a principle implicit in the Articles of the Louisiana Civil Code of 1870 governing redhibition.

(b) The provisions of Article 2529 of the Louisiana Civil Code of 1870, to the effect that a seller's mistaken declaration as to quality gives rise to redhibition when such quality was the buyer's principal motive for entering the sale, have been eliminated. That Article was of uncertain origin. It was introduced into the Civil Code in 1825; the French Civil Code contains no corresponding provision. Revised Article 2529 provides that where a thing of a different kind or quality from that specified in the contract is delivered, but the thing is free of redhibitory defects, the rights of the buyer are governed by other rules of sales and conventional obligation but not by the Articles on redhibition.

(c) Under this Article, decisions such as the one rendered in Rey v. Cuccia, 298 So.2d 840 (La.1974), concluding that redhibition is available even though the thing sold is in itself free of defects, are legislatively overruled. In all such cases the buyer may reject the thing or may sue for damages or dissolution or both.

¶22   La. C.C. Art.1995 provides:

Damages are measured by the loss sustained by the obligee and the profit of which he has been deprived.

See Security National Bank of Shreveport v. Terrell, 482 So.2d 919 (La.App. 2d Cir.1986).

¶23   Having found a guarantee as to the age, months bred, and paternity for the cows in question, the court followed the expert testimony of Smith and Gibson in determining what the cows should have been worth. The trial court calculated the difference between what the cows should have sold for, and what they did in fact sell for, along with the cost of keeping the cows longer than expected and reached a total of award of $26,821.60 in damages. There was credible evidence at trial to support this award, thus we cannot find this ruling to be clearly wrong or manifestly erroneous.

AFFIRMED

Section 2: The Nature of the Redhibitory Defect

In order to be redhibitory, the defect must render the thing sold either useless or its use is "so inconvenient that it must be presumed that a buyer would not have bought the thing had he known of the defect." In this case, the buyer may rescind the sale. (Art 2520). If, on the other hand, the defect is such that it did not render the thing totally useless, but its usefulness or value is diminished so that "it must be presumed that a buyer would still have bought it but for a lesser price," then the buyer may not rescind the sale, but may get a reduction in price. In addition to the extent of the defect, the Civil Code also requires that the defect was not apparent and would not have been discovered by a reasonably prudent buyer. (Art 2521) And the defect must have existed at the time of delivery (it is presumed to have existed at the time of delivery if it appeared within three days). (Art 2521).

Study Questions:

Article 2521 provides that one cannot bring a cause of action for redhibition when the defect was apparent. There is no cause of action, even though the thing was defective on delivery, either the defects "were known to the buyer at the time of the sale," or "the defects . . . should have been discovered by a reasonably prudent buyer of such things."

What does the following case indicate is the standard used to determine when a "reasonably prudent buyer" should be aware of such defects? What facts are dispositive about whether or not the buyer "should" have been aware of the defect?

SPRAGGINS V. LAMBETH 2007
973 SO. 2D 165 (LA. APP. 2D CIR.)

PEATROSS, J.

* * *

FACTS

¶1 The Spraggins purchased a home located in Bossier City from Lambeth on June 30, 2005, for a purchase price of $132,000. Within a couple of months of moving into the home, the Spraggins began experiencing problems with the roof due to damage from Hurricane Rita. During the repair process, the Spraggins discovered additional damage of which they were not previously aware, including separation of the beams in the attic, inadequate bracing and unconnected rafters. The Spraggins then hired an engineer to inspect their home, who found significant foundation problems that were causing the house to sink. The Spraggins then filed this suit in redhibition seeking rescission of the sale or, alternatively, seeking a reduction in purchase price due to alleged latent defects that existed prior to the sale and which were not disclosed to them.

¶2 Lambeth answered the suit, denying all of the redhibitory allegations. He attached to the answer a copy of a "Property Condition Disclosure Form" completed by him and provided to the Spraggins prior to the closing of the sale. Lambeth subsequently filed a motion for summary judgment, arguing that the Spraggins had the benefit of the disclosure form, on which he had made full disclosure of his knowledge of the condition of the property and which had been initialed by the Spraggins. Lambeth further argued that the Spraggins had elected not to have the property inspected prior to the sale. The Spraggins opposed the motion, arguing that, although they were aware of cracks in the patio and floor of the home, they accepted the explanations of the presence of the cracks given them by their realtor and a representative of their mortgage company. In addition, the Spraggins submitted that their realtor told them that they did not need a home inspection; and, as first-time homebuyers, the Spraggins accepted the assurances. For these reasons, the Spraggins urged that this matter was better suited for a trial on the merits rather than summary judgment. The trial court disagreed, reasoning that a prudent person having seen the visible cracks in the floor and patio and armed with a disclosure form that specifically noted the cracks and indicated that the seller had no knowledge of any foundation issues would have sought out further inspection of the property prior to purchasing it. Accordingly, the trial court granted summary judgment in favor of Lambeth and this appeal ensued.

DISCUSSION

* * *

¶3 The warranty against redhibitory defects is contained in La. C.C. art. 2520:

The seller warrants the buyer against redhibitory defects, or vices, in the thing sold.

* * *

The seller owes no warranty for defects in the thing that were known to the buyer at the time of the sale or for defects that should have been discovered by a reasonably prudent buyer of such things.

La. C.C. art. 2521.

¶4 To determine whether a defect is apparent, courts consider whether a reasonably prudent buyer, acting under similar circumstances, would discover it through a simple inspection of the thing sold. A simple inspection is more than a casual observation; it is an examination of the article by the buyer with a view of ascertaining its soundness. Stuck v. Long, 40,034 (La.App.2d Cir.8/17/05), 909 So.2d 686, writ denied, 05-2367 (La.3/17/06), 925 So.2d 546, citing Amend v. McCabe, 95-0316 (La.12/1/95), 664 So.2d 1183. Whether an inspection is reasonable depends on the facts of each case and includes such factors as the knowledge and expertise of the buyer, the opportunity for inspection and the assurances made by the seller. Stuck, supra; Morrison v. Allstar Dodge Inc., 00-0398 (La.App. 1st Cir.5/11/01), 792 So.2d 9, writ denied, 01-2129 (La.11/2/01), 800 So.2d 878. If the defect is apparent and could have been discovered by simple inspection, a plaintiff has a duty to make a further investigation. A failure to do so waives the right to sue in quanti minoris. Dage v. Obed, 40,414 (La.App.2d Cir.12/14/05), 917 So.2d 713.

¶5   The material facts in the case sub judice are not in dispute. In support of his motion for summary judgment, Lambeth provided his affidavit and the disclosure form, which expressly listed in Section 3: Structure, that "defects" existed in the floor, porch and patio. Lambeth wrote "cracks in each" as a description of the "defects." Also on the disclosure form, Lambeth marked the box labeled "no knowledge" for any defects in the foundation of the home. In addition, the Spraggins acknowledge that they saw the cracks in the floor and patio. This visual inspection revealed apparent and observable defects which would have put a reasonably prudent buyer on notice that further investigation was warranted. For various reasons, the Spraggins elected not to conduct further inspection or investigation.

¶6   In some circumstances, a cracked foundation may be truly hidden, creating liability for the seller. Nesbitt v. Dunn, 28,240 (La.App.2d Cir.4/3/96), 672 So.2d 226; Collins v. Curtis, 97-2348 (La.App. 4th Cir.9/30/98), 719 So.2d 679, writ denied, 98-2755 (La.12/18/98), 734 So.2d 641. We note, however, that a crack or separation in the outer brick has been held to be readily apparent to the buyer, satisfying art. 2521. See Pickerel v. Long, 286 So.2d 430 (La.App. 2d Cir.1973). While we are sympathetic to the Spraggins as first-time home buyers, we conclude that their failure to make further inspection constitutes a waiver of any complaints of redhibitory defects in the foundation of the home. Dage, supra.

CONCLUSION

¶7   For the foregoing reasons, the summary judgment in favor of Defendant, Clyde M. Lambeth, Jr., and dismissing the claims of Plaintiffs, Arlin and Katie Spraggins, is affirmed at Plaintiffs' costs.

AFFIRMED.

Note

The Spraggins were inexperienced buyers. To see a similar treatment in the case of a more experienced buyer, see Dage v. Obed, 917 So.2d 713 (La. App. 2nd Cir. 2005).

Study Question

What does the following case tell you about the 'apparentness' of a defect and the relation-ship between the warranty against redhibitory defects and the warranty of fitness?

KITE BROS. LLC V. ALEXANDER (2019)
__SO.3D __, 2019 WL 6887259 (LA. 3D CIR)

FACTS AND PROCEDURAL POSTURE

¶1 The Alexanders previously purchased two RVs from Kite Bros. prior to October 15, 2013, when they purchased a 2014 Torque RV (the Torque) from Kite Bros. and traded in their 2006 Fleetwood Gearbox fifth wheel "toy-hauler" RV (the Gearbox). . . . Kite Bros. allowed the Alexanders $25,495.00 for the trade-in. No one at Kite Bros. inspected the interior of the Gearbox prior to perfecting the transaction, according to Mr. Kite.

¶2 Robert Kite testified that he relied upon his prior dealings with the Alexanders and, thus, did not inspect the interior of the trailer. Mrs. Alexander testified that during their October 15 meeting, Mr. Kite and his son, Jeff, left her and her husband in his office while they inspected the trailer, and Mr. Alexander confirmed this in his testimony. Mrs. Alexander denied seeing either Robert or Jeff Kite enter the trailer; however, when he returned to his office, Robert Kite complimented her on how "new" looking she kept the interior. Mr. Alexander also confirmed this.

¶3 The Gearbox was not without flaws when the Alexanders traded it in. The awning had been torn off in a storm and there was damage around the fender wells. [The parties agreed that the Alexanders would file a claim with their insurer for replacement of the awning, and the insurer subsequently paid for the replacement.]

* * *

¶4 After completing the paperwork, Kite Bros. personnel readied the Torque and the Alexanders moved their personal effects from the Gearbox into the Torque. Robert Kite entrusted the Alexanders with his credit card so they could fill the tank of the Torque's genera-tor. They then returned the credit card and drove home, the Torque in tow.

¶5   In November 2013, Kite Bros. contacted Mrs. Alexander and advised her that the roof of the Gearbox had been damaged. The Alexanders went to the dealership and were shown an area where the membrane roof material had been peeled back a corner over the garage section of the trailer, beneath which was a "hole" in the roof deck. Mrs. Alexander testified that she did not think the damage she was shown could have developed during the month Kite Bros. had owned the Gearbox.

¶6   . . . It took some months for Kite Bros. to obtain the parts needed to repair the awning. After those parts arrived in February 2014, the Gearbox was moved into a garage to be repaired, and deterioration inside the Gearbox was discovered. Robert Kite contacted the Alexanders, who agreed to file a second claim with USAA. Mr. Kite testified that the Gearbox has been stored indoors since.

¶7   USAA paid a portion of the damages but denied others as resulting from lack of maintenance or wear and tear. The Alexanders denied any responsibility for the damage.

¶8   In July 2014, Kite Bros. filed their "Petition for Breach of Contract" against the Alexanders. The petition alleged that the Alexanders traded the Gearbox and that Kite Bros. fixed the trade-in value "solely on the defendants [sic] ...description of the trade-in as having no leaks, rotten wood, water damage, and in good condition, never having a leak or being damaged in any manner." The petition further alleged that Kite Bros. inspected the Gearbox on two separate occasions and, despite that, did not discover that the Gearbox had been "leaking for a long time, had sustained water damage, and had deteriorated to the extent that is was a total loss[.]" The leaking was such, according to the petition, that it could not be detected by reasonable and simple inspection. It concluded with a prayer for adequate compensation, costs, and attorney fees.

¶9   The matter proceeded to trial in August 2018. The testimonies of the Alexanders and Robert Kite have already been discussed. The trial court also heard from Eyoul Slaydon, [a friend of the Alexanders who considered purchasing the Gearbox from Kite Bros. with full knowledge of the deterioration, which he thought he could repair. When Mr. Slaydon examined the trailer, it was sitting outside Kite Bros. Kite Bros.

¶10   Mr. Aaron Theall was offered by Kite Bros. as an expert in mobile home and recreational vehicle appraisal, damage assessment and causation, and repair. After questioning and traversal on Mr. Theall's qualification, the trial court ruled that no proper foundation had been laid to qualify him. Mr. Theall thereafter identified photographs he took of the Gearbox on June 2, 2016. These photographs show extensive deterioration of a large section of the roof, several feet in length rather than the corner of the roof shown to Mrs. Alexander. They also reflect extensive interior damage to the floor and walls in the area identified by Mr. Theall as the toy-hauler section. The exterior wall was buckled, about which no one testified.

¶11 The trial court … rendered … judgment in favor of the Alexanders. [Kite Bros. appealed.]

ANALYSIS

Redhibition

¶12 The trial court found, and the parties agree, that this matter does not sound in redhibition. We agree. Sellers—in this case the Alexanders—do not warrant against defects in a thing, such as the Gearbox, that "were known to the buyer [Kite Bros.] at the time of the sale, or for defects that should have been discovered by a reasonably prudent buyer of such things." La.Civ. Code art. 2521. The trial court concluded that Kite Bros. should have discovered all defects in the Gearbox because it has been in the RV business for many years. We could not reverse on this finding.

¶13 Findings such as the existence of a redhibitory defect and whether the same should have been detected by a reasonably prudent buyer are findings of fact and are reviewed under the manifest error standard. Under that standard, the issue is not whether the trial court was right or wrong, but whether its conclusions were reasonably supported by the whole record. *Stobart v. State, Dep't of Transp. and Dev.*, 617 So.2d 880 (La.1993). In this case, the record supports the trial court's finding. Robert Kite testified that he did not inspect the Gearbox. The Alexanders testified that he did. Either way, redhibition would be precluded as a viable cause of action.

Other remedies

¶14 In addition to an action in redhibition, a buyer enjoys remedies in contract. Louisiana Civil Code Article 2524, although it appears in Chapter 9 of Title VII, which governs redhibition, affords the buyer additional warranties (emphasis added):

> "The thing sold must be reasonably *fit for its ordinary use.*

> "When the seller has reason to know the particular use the buyer intends for the thing, or the buyer's particular purpose for buying the thing, and that the buyer is relying on the seller's skill or judgment in selecting it, the thing sold must be *fit for the buyer's intended use or for his particular purpose.*

"If the thing is not so fit, the buyer's rights are governed by the general rules of conventional obligations."

Comment (b) provides:

"Under this article when the thing sold is not fit for its ordinary use, even though it is free from redhibitory defects, the buyer may seek dissolution of the sale and damages, or just damages, under the general rules of conventional obligations. The buyer's action in such cases is one for breach of contract and not the action arising from the warranty against redhibitory defects."

"Thus, it appears that the legislature intended to separate and categorize three different types of warranties applicable to sales rather than to have all such warranties defaulted into the category of the warranty against redhibitory defects." *Cunard Line Ltd. v. Datrex, Inc.*, 05-1171, pp. 6-7 (La.App. 3 Cir. 4/5/06), 926 So.2d 109, 114.

¶15 Clearly, Kite Bros. was not relying on the Alexanders' "skill or judgment in selecting" the Gearbox. La.Civ.Code art 2524. The Alexanders did not seek out a Gearbox for Kite Bros.; they had the Gearbox and were seeking to trade that particular Gearbox for an adjustment to the amount they ultimately had to pay for the Torque. Thus, the only remaining warranty available to Kite Bros. was that the Gearbox was unfit for ordinary use. The enforcement of that remedy lay in the "general rules of conventional obligations." *Id.*

General law of sales provisions

¶16 "When the thing the seller has delivered... is not of the kind or quality specified in the contract or represented by the seller, the rights of the buyer are governed by other rules of sale and conventional obligations." La.Civ.Code art. 2529. Separate from claims in redhibition, the general law of sales gives a buyer a reasonable opportunity to inspect a thing. La.Civ.Code art. 2604. "A buyer may reject nonconforming things within a reasonable time." La.Civ.Code art. 2605. "A buyer's failure to make an effective rejection within a reasonable time shall be regarded as an acceptance of the things." *Id.* "Things do not conform to the contract when they are different from those selected by the buyer or are of a kind, quality, or quantity different from the one agreed." La.Civ.Code art. 2603.

¶17 The trial court found that Kite Bros. had a reasonable opportunity to discover the defects in the Gearbox. Kite Bros. argues that the defects were discovered within a reasonable time, that notice was properly given to the Alexanders, and that it operated in the belief that "the initially discovered nonconforming things would be fixed, or cured, since the defendants agreed to file an insurance claim, and a portion of the claim was paid." Kite Bros. also makes much of the "existence of the damages, and the extent thereof, as shown in the photographs taken by Aaron Theall." In essence, Kite Bros. is arguing that the trial court's finding that it had a reasonable opportunity to inspect and discover the defects was wrong. This finding is one of fact and subject to the manifest error standard. *See Stobart*, 617 So.2d 880.

¶18 We find that the trial court's finding is reasonably supported by the record. Kite Bros. did not contact the Alexanders about the problem for a month. We are unable to reverse the trial court's finding; if the purpose of taking the Gearbox in trade was to sell it, as evidenced by the fact that Kite Bros. offered it to Mr. Slaydon, surely Kite Bros. would have incentive to get the Gearbox turned around and ready to sell as quickly as possible.

* * *

CONCLUSION

¶19 Even a sophisticated buyer is given remedies under the law for deficiencies in its purchases. The availability of those remedies sometimes depends upon its actions. In the present case, Kite Bros. claims it performed no inspection of the Gearbox until a month after it purchased the Gearbox. The trial court determined that it did not discover the defects in a reasonable, timely fashion, and we find no error in this ruling. . . .

¶20 The judgment of the trial court is affirmed. All costs of this appeal are taxed to plaintiff/appellant, Kite Bros. LLC.

AFFIRMED.

Study Question:

The following case involves a number of redhibition concepts and is still regarded as a correct statement of the law. Consider how the court treats the defect, what the defect was and how serious it was, whether it existed at the time of delivery, and who has the burden of proving both its existence and its nature. Consider as well whether the warranty of fitness should have been applied rather than the warranty against redhibitory defects.

TATE, Justice.

¶1 The buyer ('Rey') sues to recover the purchase price paid for a camper trailer, alleging that, because of redhibitory defect, it had come apart after a short period of use. Made defendant are the seller ('Cuccia') and manufacturer ('Yellowstone') of the trailer. The court of appeal affirmed the trial court's dismissal of the action, 284 So.2d 66 (La.App.4th Cir. 1973), certiorari granted, 288 So.2d 352 (La.1974).

1.

¶2 The plaintiff Rey purchased the trailer from Cuccia on May 27, 1971, and drove it to his home, a distance of less than ten miles. It was not used again until June 4, eight days later, when Rey and his family drove to Dauphin Island, Alabama, a distance of 125 miles. On the return trip to New Orleans two days later, the trailer commenced swerving back and forth on the highway. After stopping, Rey found that the trailer body had come loose from its frame, the frame was buckled, and the right rear of the trailer body was down toward the ground.

¶3 At the time of this serious breakage, the trailer had been used in total for just slightly over 200 miles, all on major paved highways.

¶4 The previous courts held that the buyer had failed to prove that any redhibitory defect had caused the break-up of the trailer so soon after its purchase. They felt that, since the collapse occurred just four miles after the buyer's wife commenced driving the vehicle, it is likely that her inexperience may have been the cause of the mishap.

¶5 In our opinion, the previous courts held the buyer to too strict a burden in rejecting his proof of a redhibitory defect as the cause of the break-up during normal use of the recently purchased trailer. Further, as we shall note, there is absolutely no evidence that the driving of the buyer's wife contributed to the collapse.

2.

¶6 In Louisiana sales, the seller is bound by an implied warranty that the thing sold is free of hidden defects and is reasonably fit for the product's intended use. Civil Code Articles 2475, 2476, 2520; Media Production Consultants, Inc. v. Mercedes-Benz of North America, Inc., 262

La. 80, 262 So.2d 377 (1972). The seller, of course, can limit this warranty by declaring to the buyer the hidden defects at the time of the sale, Article 2522, or can otherwise limit his obligations as seller, providing he do so clearly and unambiguously, Article 2474.

¶7   A redhibitory defect entitling the buyer to annul the sale is some defect in the manufacture or design of a thing sold 'which renders it either absolutely useless, or its use so inconvenient and imperfect, that it must be supposed that the buyer would not have purchased it, had he known of the vice.' Article 2520. Upon proof of such a defect, the buyer is entitled to annul the sale and recover the purchase price, rather than being limited to recovering the cost of curing any such substantial defects. Prince v. Paretti Pontiac Company, Inc., 281 So.2d 112 (La.1973).

¶8   The buyer must prove that the defect existed before the sale was made to him. Article 2530. However, if he proves that the product purchased is not reasonably fit for its intended use, it is sufficient that he prove that the object is thus defective, without his being required to prove the exact or underlying cause for its malfunction. J. B. Beaird Co. v. Burris Bros., 216 La. 655, 44 So.2d 693 (1949); Crawford v. Abbott Automobile Co., Ltd., 157 La. 59, 101 So. 871 (1924); Stumpf v. Metairie Motor Sales, Inc., 212 So.2d 705 (La.App.4th Cir. 1968); Fisher v. City Sales and Service, 128 So.2d 790 (La.App.3d Cir. 1961).

¶9   The buyer may prove the existence of redhibitory defects at the time of the sale not only by direct evidence of eyewitnesses, but also by circumstantial evidence giving rise to the reasonable inference that the defect existed at the time of the sale. Fisher v. City Sales and Service, 128 So.2d 790 (La.App.3d Cir. 1961); Mattes v. Heintz, 69 So.2d 924 (La.App.Orl.1954); Standard Motor Car Co. v. St. Amant, 134 So. 279) La.App.1st Cir. 1931). As stated in Jordan v. Travelers Insurance Co., 257 La. 995, 245 So.2d 151, 155: '* * * proof by direct or circumstantial evidence is sufficient to constitute a preponderance when, taking the evidence as a whole, such proof shows the fact or causation sought to be proved is more probable than not.'

¶10   If the defect appears within three days following the sale, it is presumed to have existed before the sale. Article 2537. However, even where the defect appears more than three days after the sale (as here, when it appeared on the second day of use, buy ten days after the sale), if it appears soon after the thing is put into use, a reasonable inference may arise, in the absence of other explanation or intervening cause shown, that she defect existed at the time of the sale. Andries v. Nelson, 46 So.2d 333 (La.App.1st Cir. 1950); Standard Motor Car Co. v. St. Amant, 134 So. 279 (La.App.1st Cir. 1931). See, for similar principle, when a constructed thing fails shortly after being put into use. Joyner v. Aetna Casualty & Surety Co., 259 La. 660, 251 So.2d 166 (1971).

3.

¶11   Tested by these standards, the buyer Rey met his burden of proving that a redhibitory defect existed at the time of the sale. We find no difficulty in holding the seller Cuccia liable for such redhibitory defect. (The liability of the manufacturer Yellowstone presents a more difficult issue. See part 5 below of this opinion.)

¶12   Rey purchased the 18-foot 2700-pound camper trailer from Cuccia on May 27, 1961. The price of $2510.15 included the installation, at Cuccia's direction and order, of a trailer hitch on the Rey automobile which would be used to haul the trailer. Improper installation of this hitch, as will be noted, is one of the factors assigned as causing the break-up of the trailer.

¶13   As earlier stated, the trailer breakage occurred when the vehicle had been used slightly more than 200 miles, all on good paved roads. The buyer Rey had driven the vehicle to an Alabama park, a distance of some 125 miles, and for about 80 miles of the return trip, all without incident. Three-to-four miles before the accident, he and his wife changed as drivers of the automobile hauling the trailer, in order to give her some experience preparatory to a vacation trip planned for later that summer.

¶14   Mrs. Rey drove slowly, at a speed of 30-35 mph, in the right-hand lane of the Interstate highway. When another vehicle passed on her left, the trailer behind her immediately began to swing, pulling the car first to the left, then right, and then left again. The wife held the wheel straight, controlling the tandem of car and trailer, and brought it to a slow stop in the right emergency lane off the travel-lanes. At no time did the vehicles leave the highway surface. Other testimony established that neither the husband nor wife hit anything in the road while driving, nor was the trailer ever involved in any other untoward incident.

¶15   When the vihicle [sic]stopped, it was discovered that the trailer-body had pulled loose from the frame, that the frame was buckled, and that the right rear of the body dragged toward the ground. Other damage had occurred due to buckling and wrenching of the exterior and interior of the trailer. A repair estimate totalled $1,338.18, without including all the damages involved.

¶16   By a mechanic witness, the buyer Rey made some effort to prove, as cause of the incident, that the process of spot-welding the trailer body to the frame was inadequate; that the spot-welds, even if correctly done, were too far apart (18 inches) to hold the body on the frame under stress. Three to five spot-welds had, in fact, broken. The mechanic's opinion was that the frame had collapsed over the wheel, and the body had come loose from the frame, because of some structural deficiency in the rear of the trailer.

¶17   As the previous courts held, the preponderance of the evidence does not prove a structural deficiency or inadequate number of spot-welds to be the cause of the trailer break-up. (On the other hand, it does not negative the possibility that the particular three-to-five spot-welds which came loose had individually been defectively done.)

¶18   The failure to prove inadequate welding to be the cause of the trailer break-up does not defeat the buyer's cause of action. If the purchased vehicle breaks up soon after it is put into use, then this in itself (in the absence of other cause shown) may be evidence of a redhibitory defect, without the buyer being held to prove the specific cause of the vehicle's break-up.

¶19   The chief thrust of the defense against this redhibitory action is the suggestion that the vehicle-collapse occurred because Mrs. Rey, an inexperienced trailer-hauler, may have swung too sharply in an overcompensation of the sway caused when a vehicle passed her. However, the uncontradicted evidence established that no such overcompensation took place. The opinion that the incident and break-up might have been caused by such driver reaction is negated by the clear testimony that the wife did not so react and that there was no misuse of the trailer during its short period of use by either of the drivers.

¶20   Since no abnormal and unforeseeable use or other intervening cause is proved, the collapse of the trailer during normal and foreseeable use, after only 200 miles or so after the dale, raises the strong inference that the trailer would not have collapsed in the absence of a latent defect.

¶21   Additionally, the evidence of the manufacturer's expert indicates, as a possible cause of the break-up, an improper installation of the trailer hitch on the automobile by Cuccia part of the sales transaction. Installed at 24 inches above the ground, rather than at 18 inches as specified by the manufacturer's manual, such improperly installed trailer-hitch could have caused or contributed to sway and to abnormal stresses and strains during use of the trailer.

¶22   We therefore hold that the circumstantial evidence clearly proves, at least against the seller Cuccia, that a redhibitory defect existed at the time of the sale of the trailer, which included Cuccia's installation of the trailer hitch.

***

¶23 [The discussion of Rey's case against the manufacturer, Yellowstone, is omitted here, but included in the next section on Good Faith / Bad Faith sellers.]

Conclusion

¶24 The buyer is therefore entitled to recover the sum of $2510.15, the purchase price of the vehicle, plus $1,000 attorneys' fees. . . . SUMMERS, J., dissents for the reasons assigned.

SUMMERS, Justice (dissenting).

¶1 Both lower courts found, and I agree, that there is no evidence to establish any inherent defect or vice in the trailer. Each of the courts below attributed the accident to the suction effect caused by a high speed vehicle passing, which tends to result in over compensation by the driver. They found that Mrs. Rey was inexperienced and over-reacted to the swaying caused by the passing vehicle. This conclusion is corroborated by the absence of incident during the first 125 miles of the trip during which Mr. Rey, an experienced driver, was at the wheel. The laborious effort of the Court's opinion to de-emphasize these facts is unconvincing to say the least. The case presents nothing buy a factual question. This Court is not warranted in overruling both courts on this record. I agree with the opinion of the Court of Appeal. See 284 So.2d 71. I would uphold that adjudication.

Comment

Cuccia is known for establishing that the buyer need not prove the nature of the defect, only its existence and whether it is substantial enough to merit if not rescission then a reduction in price. The jurisprudence has accepted the concept that a redhibitory defect can instead consist of a number of small defects rather than one major one, each of which might be insufficient in itself. In Bruce v. Ford Motor Co., 130 So.3d 427 (La. 3d Cir. Ct. App. 2014), Mr. Bruce bought a lightly used 2007 Ford F-150, paying $30,118.63:

> "almost immediately, a litany of minor problems and others not so minor manifested themselves.
> The most significant event in the court's mind occurred when the vehicle accelerated on its own
> in traffic and once again at Mr. Bruce's residence."

The trial court expressly noted "that the throttle body and vehicle's transmission were also replaced at one point," and "a long series of complaints and attempted repairs including numerous minor repairs, or at least less serious ones, were made." Accepting Mr. Bruce's testimony that he would not have purchased this vehicle had he known it had been titled prior to his purchase, or had he known of the defects, and considering the evidence that "numerous complaints and attempts at repairs were made by both Marler and a dealership in Natchez, Mississippi," the trial court found that Mr. Bruce was entitled to a rescission of the sale.

Even though Bruce had used the truck for 3 years and 67,000 miles, the Third Circuit affirmed the trial court's finding that the sale should be rescinded. Ford was granted, however, a $15,000 credit for the use Bruce had made of the truck, resulting in an award of $20,917.72 plus reasonable attorney's fees because of the manufacturer's presumption of bad faith.

As we have seen, a sale may be rescinded not just for redhibitory defect, but also for failure of cause if the buyer wants a home that does not flood and the seller lies, claiming the house does not flood, when it in fact is prone to flooding. "Susceptibility to flooding can be a redhibitory defect."[1]

The opposite, however, is the case if the 'defect' only occurs under extraordinary circumstances. For example, in Redlauer v. Remax, No. 2019-CA-0311 (4th Cir. Ct. App. 2019), the buyer argued that the house he purchased was defective because it had admittedly sustained "a small amount of water seepage" in May 1995, four years before he purchased it, and was severely flooded in Katrina. The seller had apparently disclosed the 1995 incident, which had occurred in a separate incident of severe flooding in New Orleans. The court granted summary judgment to the seller, finding that because the two incidents related to natural disasters, and that no other flooding events were shown on the Property Loss History, the buyer could not establish that the house was susceptible to flooding.

Section 3: Good and Bad Faith Sellers, Prescription

1. The Seller in Good Faith

The seller in good faith is accorded a reasonable opportunity to repair the defect. This opportunity appears in Articles 2531, 2534, 2354, 2522, & 2545. Article 2531 states:

> If the seller is in good faith, the buyer of a defective thing must give him an opportunity to
> repair, remedy, or correct the defect. If he is unable to do so, then the seller must return the price
> to the buyer with interest, reimburse him for reasonable expenses occasioned by the sale and
> any incurred for the preservation of the thing, minus a credit for any use the buyer was able to
> make of the thing in the interim.

For example, in Arnold v. Wray Ford., Inc., 606 So. 2d 549 (La. App. 2nd Cir. 1992), plaintiff Arnold purchased a customized Ford van from defendant, including such things as a custom

---

[1] McCarthy v. E&L Dev., Inc., 54 So.3d 1143, 1148 (La. Ct. App. 2d Cir.)

stereo system, an electric sofa, a snack table, Venetian blinds and curtains, additional lighting, a large window, and a rear air-conditioning unit. There were a number of problems with the van, such that plaintiff returned the van to the dealership on at least eleven different occasions for repair between January and November 1988. She eventually sued for rescission alleging redhibitory defects. Wray Ford put forth a number of defenses, including the contention that it satisfactorily repaired the majority of the problems, the remaining problems were not sufficient to warrant rescission, and furthermore, that it did not have a reasonable opportunity to repair the van. The court posited that while Article 2531 gives a good faith seller a reasonable opportunity to repair, eleven repair orders were more than an ample opportunity.

Study Question:

How does the following case illustrate Article 2520's provision for partial redhibition, Article 2521's exclusion of apparent defects, and the provision in Article 2522 that a good faith seller must be accorded an opportunity to repair the defect?

DAVID V. THIBODEAUX 2005
916 SO. 2D 214 (LA. APP. 1ST CIR.)

GUIDRY, J.

¶1   In this redhibition action, defendant, Concepcion St. Romain Thibodeaux, appeals the trial court's judgment, ordering rescission of the April 26, 2000 Act of Sale of certain immovable property to plaintiffs, Joseph and Pamela David. For the following reasons, we reverse.

FACTS AND PROCEDURAL HISTORY

¶2   On April 26, 2000, Joseph and Pamela David purchased immovable property, including a single-family residence, in Lakeland, Louisiana from Mrs. Thibodeaux for the purchase price of $175,000.00. According to the Act of Sale, Joseph David paid $125,000.00 in cash, and executed a promissory note in favor of Mrs. Thibodeaux for the remaining $50,000.00. Prior to the sale, the Davids conducted several visual inspections of the premises. Additionally, a wood destroying insect report (WDIR) and a property condition disclosure statement were obtained. The property condition disclosure statement indicated that termite damage was discovered and repaired in 1990. Further, according to the WDIR, old termite damage and/or scars were discovered in three locations of the home. However, Mrs. Thibodeaux showed the Davids the three locations and explained that the termite problem had been taken care of and the damages had been repaired.

¶3 After moving into the home, the Davids discovered extensive active termite infestation and damage. Thereafter, the Davids filed a petition to rescind the sale and for damages, and in the alternative, for a reduction in the purchase price. Following a trial held on February 4, 5, 7, and 28, 2003, the trial court rendered judgment on May 13, 2003, ordering rescission of the Act of Sale. Mrs. Thibodeaux appeals from this judgment.

DISCUSSION

¶4 Generally, the seller of a home impliedly warrants to the buyer that it is free from redhibitory vices or defects. La. C.C. art. 2520. A defect is redhibitory, entitling the buyer to rescind the sale, when it renders the home useless, or makes its use so inconvenient that it must be presumed that the buyer would not have bought the home had he known of the defect. La. C.C. arts. 2520. A defect is also redhibitory, entitling the buyer to reduction of the price, when, without rendering the home totally useless, it diminishes its usefulness or its value so that it must be presumed that a buyer would still have bought it but for a lesser price. La. C.C. art. 2520.

¶5 However, not all redhibitory vices or defects justify rescission or reduction of the price. Apparent defects, which the buyer can discover through a simple inspection, are excluded from the seller's legal warranty. La. C.C. art. 2521. A defect is apparent if a reasonably prudent buyer, acting under similar circumstances, would discover it through a simple inspection of the property. A simple inspection is more than a casual observation; it is an examination of the article by the buyer with a view of ascertaining its soundness. Amend v. McCabe, 95-0316, p. 9 (La.12/1/95), 664 So.2d 1183, 1188. Factors considered in determining whether an inspection is reasonable include the knowledge and expertise of the buyer, the opportunity for inspection, and assurances made by the seller. Crow v. Laurie, 98-0648, p. 6 (La.App. 1st Cir.2/19/99), 729 So.2d 703, 707-708.

¶6 Whether termite damage is apparent to the buyer of a home by reasonable inspection is a question of fact. See McMorris v. Marcotte Builders, L.L.C., 98-2302, p. 6 (La.App. 1st Cir.12/28/99), 756 So.2d 424, 428, writ denied, 00-0664 (La.4/20/00), 760 So.2d 1158. Typically, when all of the termite damage is concealed within the home's structure (e.g., walls and floors) it is considered unapparent because it is not discoverable by a simple inspection. Amend, 95-0316 at p. 10, 664 So.2d at 1188. In such situations, there is no obligation on the part of the buyer to inspect further. On the other hand, when some of the termite damage detectable by a simple inspection, the buyer has a duty to investigate further. If he chooses to purchase the home without further investigation, he waives the right to sue for rescission or reduction based upon the termite damage. Amend, 95-0316 at p. 10, 664 So.2d at 1188. However, if the seller represents that suspected defects have been corrected, and simple inspection establishes these representations to be accurate, the buyer need not investigate further. Estopinal v. Bourshie, 420 So.2d 749, 751-752 (La.App. 4th Cir.1982); see also Caple v. Green, 545 So.2d 1222, 1227 (La. App. 2nd Cir.1989) and Perrin v. Kuehne, 97-196, p. 10 (La.App. 5th Cir.12/10/97), 704 So.2d 839, 844, writ denied, 98-0022 (La.2/20/98), 709 So.2d 786.

¶7   In the instant case, the Davids made at least four visual inspections of the home. According to the Davids, Mrs. Thibodeaux was present during each inspection, and controlled their access/ view of the home. Additionally, Morris Bergeron performed a professional inspection on April 14, 2000. According to the Davids, nothing from their inspection or from Mr. Bergeron's report caused any alarm, and all the notations made by Mr. Bergeron appeared to be "cosmetic."

¶8   Additionally, on April 14, 2000, Joseph David reviewed a copy of the WDIR, which noted three locations where old termite damage and/or scars were discovered. Mr. David testified that he asked Mrs. Thibodeaux for further explanation of the notations on the WDIR. Mrs. Thibodeaux brought him to all three areas listed on the WDIR and told him that the termites and damage had been taken care of and that it was not a problem any more, the spots being just old scars. Further, the property condition disclosure statement received by the Davids indicated that termite damage was discovered and repaired in 1990. Mr. David testified that based on his visual inspection, the WDIR prepared by Terminix, Mr. Bergeron's report, and the assurances made by Mrs. Thibodeaux, he felt satisfied that there was old damage that had been repaired, and that he did not see anything to suggest that there was still a problem.

¶9   According to the Davids' testimony, it was not until the outside, wooden deck collapsed in July 2000 and Mrs. David's hand went through the basement wall while moving boxes in August 2000 that they suspected something was wrong. In September 2000, the Davids hired Gary Morris to perform a structural inspection of the home, at which time some of the walls and flooring were removed, revealing hidden, active termite infestation and damage. Additionally, the Davids hired Louis Faxon, an architect, who inspected the home twice. According to Mr. Faxon, evidence of termite damage had been covered up. Both experts testified that some damage was initially observable, but that did not mean a layperson buying a home would recognize it as a problem like a home inspector or architect would. From our review of the entire record, we cannot find that the trial court manifestly erred or was clearly wrong in determining that the active termites and termite damage were a latent defect.

¶10   Mrs. Thibodeaux, however, also asserts that according to La. C.C. art. 2531, she is only bound to repair, remedy, or correct the defect; therefore, the trial court erred in ordering rescission of the sale. Louisiana Civil Code article 2522 provides that a buyer must give the seller notice of the existence of a redhibitory defect within sufficient time to allow the seller the opportunity to make the required repairs. "A buyer who fails to give that notice suffers diminution of the warranty to the extent the seller can show that the defect could have been repaired." However, this notice is not required when the seller has actual knowledge of the existence of a redhibitory defect. La. C.C. art. 2522. Additionally, La. C.C. art. 2531 provides, in part, that "[a] seller who did not know that the thing he sold had a defect is only bound to repair, remedy, or correct the defect. If he is unable or fails so to do, he is then bound to return the price to the buyer." Together, these codal provisions state that the right to an opportunity to repair is a condition precedent to rescission if the seller is in good faith. See Jordan v. LeBlanc and Broussard Ford. Inc., 332 So.2d 534, 538 (La.App. 3rd Cir.1976). The buyer has the burden of establishing that the seller was given the opportunity to repair the defect. Pratt v. Himel Marine, Inc., 01-1832 (La.App. 1st Cir.6/21/02), 823 So.2d 394, writ denied, 02-2128 (La.11/1/02), 828 So.2d 571. If the buyer fails to establish that he gave notice of the defect to the seller, he is not entitled to rescission of the sale. However, such failure to give notice does not preclude the buyer from obtaining reduction of the price. See Coleman Oldsmobile, Inc. v. Newman and Associates, Inc., 477 So.2d 1155, 1160 (La.App. 1st Cir.1985), writ denied, 481 So.2d 1334 (La.1986); see also Dunn v. Pauratore, 387 So.2d 1227 (La.App. 1st Cir.1980) and Coffin v. Laborde, 393 So.2d 915 (La.App. 4th Cir.), writ denied, 396 So.2d 915 (La.1981) (finding that notice and an opportunity to repair are not prerequisites to maintain a suit in quanti minoris).

¶11   In the instant case, the trial court specifically found that Mrs. Thibodeaux did not have actual knowledge and was not in bad faith. Therefore, in order to obtain rescission of the sale, the Davids had to show that they notified Mrs. Thibodeaux of the redhibitory defect, thereby affording her an opportunity to repair it. From our review of the record, we do not find any evidence that the Davids gave Mrs. Thibodeaux notice of the existence of the redhibitory defect. Rather, the Davids elected to file suit, seeking rescission, or alternatively, reduction of the purchase price on the basis that Mrs. Thibodeaux had actual knowledge. Therefore, because the Davids did not establish that they notified Mrs. Thibodeaux of the redhibitory defect, the trial court erred in awarding rescission of the sale.

¶12   However, as stated above, failure to give notice does not preclude the buyer from obtaining reduction of the purchase price. In an action for reduction of the purchase price, the amount to be awarded is the difference between the sale price and the price that a reasonable buyer would have paid if he had known of the defect. In the case of immovable property, the amount to be awarded is the amount necessary to convert the unsound structure into a sound one. A principle element in formulating a reduction of the purchase price is the cost of repairs. Lemonier v. Coco, 237 La. 760, 765-66, 112 So.2d 436, 438-39 (La.1959); Sanders v. Earnest, 34,656, p. 29 (La.App. 2nd Cir.7/24/01), 793 So.2d 393, 409; see also Lemoine v. Hebert, 395 So.2d 353 (La. App. 1st Cir.1980).

¶13 At trial of this matter, the testimony of three experts was introduced. The Davids introduced the testimony of Garry Morris, who performed a structural inspection of the home, and Louis Faxon. The trial court specifically found Mr. Morris's testimony not to be credible and also found that his estimated repair costs were extraordinarily high. Additionally, the trial court specifically found that the standards set by Mr. Faxon were very high, in that he thought the only way to remedy the defects was to tear the house down and start over, and that his estimate for repair costs was also high. Mrs. Thibodeaux introduced the testimony of Kenneth Jones. Mr. Jones inspected the home and testified that he prepared an estimate of repairs in the amount of $25,622.00. Mr. Jones stated that this amount estimated the cost to repair the existing damage, and included mark ups to take into account contingencies, such as undiscovered damage. The trial court considered Mr. Jones's repair estimate to be realistic and we agree. As such, we grant the Davids a reduction in the purchase price, in the amount of $25,622.00, subject to a credit of $24,000.00 in favor of Mrs. Thibodeaux for the award arising from the arbitration with Terminix.

CONCLUSION

¶14 For the foregoing reasons, the judgment of the trial court, ordering rescission of the sale, return of the purchase price, and cancellation of the promissory note is reversed. We grant the Davids a reduction in the purchase price, in the amount of $25,622.00, subject to a credit of $24,000.00 in favor of Mrs. Thibodeaux for the award arising from the arbitration with Terminix, for a net judgment of $1,622.00, together with legal interest. All costs of this appeal are to be borne equally, one-half assessed to Concepcion St. Romain Thibodeaux, and one-half assessed to Joseph and Pamela David.

REVERSED AND RENDERED.

2. The Seller in Bad Faith

In contrast with the good faith seller who must be given an opportunity to repair the defect, a bad faith seller is not owed such an opportunity and owes enhanced damages. A bad faith seller is one who knows that the thing he sells has a defect but omits declaring itm or declares that the thing has a quality that he knows it does not have. The manufacturer of a defective thing is presumed to be in bad faith. Art 2545.

In addition to reimbursing the price paid with interest from the date it was paid, and reimbursing reasonable expenses occasioned by the sale and those incurred for the preservation of the thing, a bad faith seller also owes damages and reasonable attorney's fees.

Prescription Periods Under Redhibition

Article 2534 sets out the prescriptive periods for redhibition. They are shorter than those for the warranties of kind or quality and warranty of fitness for ordinary use in order to encourage the buyer of a defective thing to act quickly.

Movables & Good Faith: The action against a good faith seller of a movable prescribes four years from delivery or one year from discovery, whichever is first.

Immovables & Good Faith: The action against a good faith seller of a residential or commercial immovable prescribes one year from delivery.

Bad Faith: The action against a bad faith seller of either a movable or an immovable prescribes one year from discovery.

Tolling of Prescription for Repairs: Prescription is interrupted when the seller accepts the thing for repairs and begins again when he tenders it back to the buyer, refuses to repair it, or is unable to repair it.

Study Question:

While the following case presents a correct statement of Article 2534's prescription of an action in redhibition, what problem might you see with the cause of action?

QUERAL V. LATTER & BLUM, INC. 2010
33 SO.3D 955 (LA.APP. 5TH CIR.)

McMANUS, Judge.

¶1 Plaintiffs, Alberto Queral and Vincente Davis, file this appeal from the trial court's grant of exceptions of prescription on behalf of the defendants, which resulted in the dismissal of all of plaintiffs' claims. For the reasons assigned below, we reverse the trial court's judgments granting the exceptions of prescription.

STATEMENT OF THE CASE

¶2 On February 12, 1998, plaintiffs, Alberto Queral and Vincente Davis, purchased a home, located at 200 Terry Parkway, from Mary and Ernest Warrendorf ("the Warrendorfs"). The property was listed and advertised for sale by Latter & Blum, Inc. realtors. A paper flyer advertising the home for sale was available and provided information about the house, including the fact that it was "custom built on pilings". Murdock Richard was the listing agent on the property for Latter & Blum. Sidney Mahoney, another agent with Latter & Blum, also worked with the plaintiffs concerning this property. According to Queral, both Mahoney and Richard assured him the house and brick fence around the yard were structurally sound and not defective.

¶3 Latter & Blum supplied plaintiffs with a property disclosure statement signed by the Warrendorfs on October 2, 1997. The statement was later signed by Queral and Davis on December 8, 1997. Amongst other things, the statement provided that no alterations had been made to the property, no building permits had been obtained for any work, and the Warrendorfs knew of no defects in the foundation of the home.

¶4 After purchasing the home, Queral noticed thin cracks in the house in approximately May or June of 1998. In November 1998, an air conditioning repairman was working in the attic of the house and noticed unusual bolts. He indicated to Queral that these bolts would only have been put there if a major repair had been done by an engineer.

¶5 In December 1998, plaintiffs hired Robert B. Anderson Consulting, Inc. to inspect the property. Anderson, a structural engineer, performed the inspection of the house on April 1, 1999. He submitted a written report to plaintiffs on April 5, 1999. The written report stated the foundation type of the house was a "[p]ost-tensioned slab on ground," meaning the house was not built on pilings. . . . With regards to the settlement of the house, Anderson found the differential movement to be average for this area and found it did not appear to be a current cause for concern. He found the slab and superstructure of the residence to be in satisfactory condition and performing adequately.

¶6 On April 4, 2000, plaintiffs filed a petition . . . [seeking] redhibition of the sale and return of the purchase price. On February 23, 2003, the plaintiffs filed a First Amended, Supplemental, and Restated Petition alleging the specific redhibitory defect was a differential settlement in the property.

¶7 On March 22, 2007, the Warrendorfs filed an exception of prescription arguing the plaintiffs' petition was prescribed on its face because it was filed over two years after the purchase of the home. Further, the Warrendorfs alleged that even if the plaintiffs proved they knew of the settlement differential at the time of the sale, the plaintiffs had constructive notice of the problem by March 1999. Therefore, the Warrendorfs argued the one year prescriptive period began to run at that time and the April 4, 2000 petition was prescribed. The Warrendorfs' exception was . . . denied by the trial court on July 9, 2007. Latter & Blum and Richard also filed an exception of prescription . . . . This exception was heard by the trial court on April 30, 2008 and granted on July 14, 2008.

¶8 On July 24, 2008, plaintiffs filed a motion for new trial on the grant of the trial court's exception of prescription in favor of Latter & Blum and Richard. The Warrendorfs then re-urged their exception of prescription on August 5, 2008. On November 13, 2008 the trial court granted the Warrendorfs' re-urged exception of prescription, dismissing all claims of plaintiffs. On December 1, 2008, the trial court denied plaintiffs' motion for new trial.

* * *

¶9 Plaintiffs now appeal the judgment granting the exception of prescription in favor of Latter & Blum and Richard, the judgment granting the exception of prescription in favor of the Warrendorfs, and the denial of the motion for new trial. On appeal, plaintiffs argue the notice of cracks is not automatic notice of a defect sufficient to start the running of prescription. They allege the defect was discovered on April 5, 1999, the date the engineers report was received. Therefore, the plaintiffs argue the April 4, 2000 petition was filed within one year of the discovery of the defect.

¶10 Plaintiffs further argue there are two different causes of action, an action for fraud and negligent misrepresentation and an action for redhibition. . . . Plaintiffs argue prescription tolls one year from the discovery of the defect for the redhibition claim and one year from the discovery of the fraudulent misrepresentation itself for the negligent misrepresentation claim. They allege the fraud and misrepresentation by defendants was not discovered until the engineers report was received on April 5, 1999.

DISCUSSION

¶11 The plaintiffs' action against Latter & Blum, its agents, and the Warrendorfs is for redhibition based on fraudulent or negligent misrepresentations made by defendants with regards to the type of foundation that existed beneath the house. La. C.C. art. 2534 governs prescription of these claims, and states, in part:

A. (1) The action for redhibition against a seller who did not know of the existence of a defect in the thing sold prescribes in four years from the day delivery of such thing was made to the buyer or one year from the day the defect was discovered by the buyer, whichever occurs first.

(2) However, when the defect is of residential or commercial immovable property, an action for redhibition against a seller who did not know of the existence of the defect prescribes in one year from the day delivery of the property was made to the buyer.

B. The action for redhibition against a seller who knew, or is presumed to have known, of the existence of a defect in the thing sold prescribes in one year from the day the defect was discovered by the buyer.

¶12   Plaintiffs allege the Warrendorfs and Latter & Blum, through its agents, knew or should have known, that the house was not built on pilings. Therefore, pursuant to La. C.C. art. 2534(B), this action prescribes one year from the day the defect was discovered by the buyer. The plaintiffs have alleged the defect is the fact that the house is not built on pilings, and their cause of action against defendants includes the fraudulent misrepresentations made prior to the purchase which led the plaintiffs to believe the house was built on pilings. Therefore, discovery of the defect would occur when the plaintiffs learned the house was not built on pilings.

¶13   Queral testified in his deposition that he began noticing cracks in the house in approximately May or June of 1998. The air conditioning repairmen was in the attic and alerted Queral to the unusual bolts, which indicated a major repair had been done, in November 1998. Queral then proceeded to investigate any possible problems by hiring Anderson to perform an inspection. The inspection was conducted on April 1, 1999. However, Anderson's written report with his findings was not presented to the plaintiffs until April 5, 1999. It was this report that actually stated the house was not built on pilings, but was instead a "[p]ost tension slab on ground."

¶14   We note that Queral had some knowledge of the cracks in the walls and possible problems before the inspection was even completed, which is what prompted him to hire Anderson. However, there is no indication the plaintiffs knew of the lack of pilings under the house prior to receiving Anderson's report. Thus, we find the plaintiffs did not discover the defect complained of, that the house was not built on pilings, until the April 5, 1999 engineer's report.

¶15   Similarly, in Gad v. Granberry, 2007-117 (La.App. 3 Cir. 5/30/07), 958 So.2d 125, the plaintiff homeowners filed a redhibition action based on fraud or negligent misrepresentation against the sellers of the home, after discovering settlement of the home and foundation problems. . . .

¶16 In this case, we find, as the Third Circuit did in Gad, that the plaintiffs did not have constructive knowledge of the defect, or the fact that the house was not built on pilings, until the engineer's report which was given to plaintiffs on April 5, 1999. As in Gad, the plaintiffs in this case noticed some problems prior to the engineer's inspection and report, but did not know the extent, or the fact that the house was not built on pilings until the report was prepared and delivered by Anderson. Thus, the claims against defendants would have prescribed one year from that date, or April 5, 2000. Plaintiffs' suit was filed April 4, 2000. Thus, it was timely filed and not prescribed.

¶17 In accordance with the above, we find the trial court erred in granting the exception of prescription in favor of the Warrendorfs, Latter & Blum and Richard. Therefore, the trial court's judgment granting these exceptions is reversed and the matter is remanded to the trial court for further proceedings.

REVERSED; MATTER REMANDED.

Study Question:

After you read and compare Articles 2531 and 2545, consider how and why Article 2545 applies in the following continuation of Rey v. Cuccia.

REY V. CUCCIA 1974 (CONT'D)

4.

¶25 The buyer's case against the manufacturer Yellowstone is not as clear. In the first place, the improper hitch-installation by the seller Cuccia may cast into doubt whether any other underlying redhibitory defect existed at the time the manufacturer delivered the trailer to Cuccia. In the second place, Yellowstone had sold the trailer to Cuccia more than a year before Cuccia sold it to Rey-although the evidence shows that, during Cuccia's possession, the trailer was not used except occasionally to move it from one part of Cuccia's lot to another, the inference is not as strong that the defect existed at the time the manufacturer Yellowstone transferred the vehicle to the seller Cuccia, as it is that the defect existed at the time of the sale, just ten days before the defect appeared after slightly over 200 miles of use.

¶26 Preliminarily, we should observe that we find no merit to the manufacturer's contention that it could not be held liable directly to the buyer for a redhibitory defect existing at the time is sold that vehicle to Cuccia. In so contending, the manufacturer relies upon the lack of privity between it and the ultimate buyer, Rey, and on the circumstance that its own sale had occurred more than a year before the re-sale by Cuccia to Rey and before the breakage.

¶27   When the sale is annulled for a redhibitory defect resulting from the original manufacture, the purchaser can recover the pecuniary loss resulting from the unusable thing sold from the manufacturer as well as the seller. Media Productions Consultant v. Mercedes-Benz of N.A., Inc., cited above. As there stated, 262 La. 80, 262 So.2d 377: 'Louisiana has aligned itself with the consumer-protection rule, by allowing a consumer without privity to recover, whether the suit be strictly in tort or upon implied warranty.' In effect, the consumer's cause of action, which is based upon the breach of the sale's implied warranty, is enforceable directly against the manufacturer, who himself is by law bound to the same implied warranty.

¶28   The consumer's action is enforceable against the manufacturer at the same time and at least within the same year following the sale to the consumer, Article 2534, as it is enforceable against the seller. The manufacturer is presumed to know of the defect in the thing made by him. Radalec, Incorporated v. Automatic Firing Corp., 228 La. 116, 81 So.2d 830 (1955); Tuminello v. Mawby, 220 La. 733, 57 So.2d 666 (1952); George v. Shreveport Cotton Oil Co., 114 La. 498, 38 So. 432 (1905). The one-year limitation on redhibitory actions does not apply where the seller (manufacturer) had knowledge of the defect bu[t] failed to declare it at the time of the sale. Article 2534. In such instance, the consumer may institute the action to recover for the redhibitory defect within the year following his discovery of it. Article 2546.

    5.

¶29   The chief witness relied upon by Yellowstone was Lawrence Drudge, Yellowstone's production manager. He was qualified as an expert in the repair and supervision of repairs for such trailers.

¶30   He testified that he found no fault in the construction or design of the camper trailer. He did testify that the trailer hitch was improperly installed on the Rey automobile at 24 inches from the ground.

¶31   The Yellowstone manual specified that it should be installed 18 inches from the ground, and Drudge testified that in no case should it be more than 19 or 19 1/2 inches from the ground. The reason is that a higher installation would cause a difference in the weight distribution between the two vehicles, tending to exaggerate any sway. This, of course, would cause more than normal stresses and strains and would tend, on the sway, to cause the body to compress the spring on one side or the other more deeply than if the hitch were installed at the proper height.

¶32 The witness opined that the damages to the Rey trailer were similar to those which resulted from severe swaying. The witness listed as principal causes of undue sway of a trailer which result in the need for repairs: (1) an improper hitch from towing vehicle to trailer (as here); (2) high winds; (3) the suction effect caused by high speed vehicles passing, which tends to result in overcompensation by the driver; and (4) 'the biggest one we have found' is inexperience of the driver of the towing vehicle.

¶33 By the last, he explained, he meant that an inexperienced driver tended to steer the opposite way the trailer was swaying, causing it to sway back. This then may result in the driver's steering the opposite way, causing an accentuated sway back again, eventually causing the trailer body to rock over hard and sometimes to 'bottom out' (the impact of the body drives the wheel through the wheel well) and, perhaps, wrench loose, similar to the damage which resulted in the present case.

¶34 The substance of Drudge's testimony is that the damage resulted when the trailer bottomed out due to severe swaying.

¶35 We may note at this point that the Yellowstone owner's guide furnished with the vehicle does not warn against such hazards, nor does the manual's suggestion as to installation of the trailer hitch ('The top of the hitch should be 18 from the ground on most models.') warn about the dire consequences resulting, according to Drudge, if the trailer is installed at higher than 18 inches. No other witness than Drudge testified as to this danger, and there is no evidence that the seller Cuccia had any reason to appreciate any undue hazard to result from installing the trailer-hitch six inches higher than recommended 'for most models'.

¶36 Under cross-examination, Drudge also admitted that the damage found could have resulted if, as the vehicle was swaying, the frame came loose and the trailer body fell on the wheel well.

¶37 Considering the evidence as a whole, we conclude that the preponderance of the evidence proves that the trailer break-up resulted from a defect in construction or design which existed at the time the manufacturer Yellowstone sold the trailer to the seller Cuccia.

¶38 The evidence indicates that, until it collapsed after 200 miles of use, it had been kept on Cuccia's lot without any use, except a move 50 or 75 feet or so to make room for another trailer. As previously noted, driver mal-use is not proven to be a cause of the collapse of the trailer.

¶39 Cuccia's improper installation of the trailer hitch may have contributed to the severe swaying and to unusual stresses and strains during the 200 miles of customer use. Nevertheless, Yellowstone should not be exonerated from liability for defective functioning of the camper-trailer because a trailer-hitch, necessarily contemplated by a sale of the camper-trailer, was installed six inches higher than weakly recommended by the manual. There is no warning that there might be such damage occasioned as was here by the failure to so install the hitch. If the trailer were so constructed that such a slight deviation from a recommended procedure of installation of the hitch would cause this type of damage, then this constitutes a defect for which the manufacturer would be responsible, absent at least some warning of the danger involved.

¶40 The evidence, in effect, negatives any other than a redhibitory defect in the manufacture or design of the trailer as the cause of the break-up of the trailer, even though Cuccia's improper installation of the trailer-hitch may have contributed to the vehicle's malfunctioning.

6.

¶41 Under the 1968 amendment to Article 2545: '*The seller, who knows the vice of the thing he sells and omits to declare it, besides the restitution of price and repayment of the expenses, including reasonable attorneys' fees, is answerable to the buyer in damages.*' (Italics ours.) A manufacturer is presumed to know of the defects of the products he sells. In this instance, the retailer Cuccia, who ordered the installation of the trailer hitch as part of his sale of the product, is presumed to know of the defect in this installation. Therefore, both Cuccia and Yellowstone are liable for such attorneys' fees.

¶42 The evidence in the record justifies an award of attorneys' fees in the amount of one thousand dollars.

Conclusion

¶43 The buyer is therefore entitled to recover the sum of $2510.15, the purchase price of the vehicle, plus $1,000 attorneys' fees. The buyer is entitled to recover this amount from the seller and the manufacturer as solidarily liable.

¶44 Accordingly, there will be judgment in favor of the plaintiff, Armand J. Rey, and against the defendants, Robert E. Cuccia and Yellowstone, Inc., holding them liable in the amount of three thousand five hundred and ten and 15/100 ($3,510.15) dollars, together with all costs and legal interest thereon from date of judicial demand, conditioned upon the return of the camper-trailer to Cuccia.

Reversed and rendered.

Section 4: Waiver of Warranty against Redhibitory Defects

Article 2548 provides:

> "The parties may agree to an exclusion or limitation of the warranty against redhibitory defects. The terms of the exclusion or limitation must be clear and unambiguous and must be brought to the attention of the buyer.

> "A buyer is not bound by an otherwise effective exclusion or limitation of the warranty when the seller has declared that the thing has a quality that he knew it did not have.

> "The buyer is subrogated to the rights in warranty of the seller against other persons, even when the warranty is excluded."

Study Question:

Is the warranty against redhibitory defects waived in the following case? If so, how? What article or articles do the courts rely upon? Did the court rely on the correct articles, in your view?

What kinds of claims can invalidate an otherwise valid waiver?

SHELTON V. STANDARD/700 ASSOC. 2005
798 SO. 2D 60 (LA. APP. 1ST CIR.)

KNOLL, Judge.

¶1 [Shelton purchased a condominium, located on the top floor of a building at 700 South Peters Street, New Orleans, from defendant Standard/700 associates. The condominium was sold "as is where is," without any warranties or right to sue in redhibition and the act of sale contained the following language:

NOTWITHSTANDING ANYTHING HEREIN TO THE CONTRARY, THE UNIT DESCRIBED HEREIN IS SOLD AND PURCHASED "AS IS WHERE IS", WITHOUT ANY WARRANTY OR REPRESENTATION WHATSOEVER WITH RESPECT TO THE CONDITION OR REMAINING USEFUL LIFE OF SUCH CONDOMINIUM UNIT OR WITH RESPECT TO ANY OF THE

COMMON ELEMENTS OF THE CONDOMINIUM, OR ANY OF THEIR COMPONENTS OR
PARTS OR CONTENTS, AND WITHOUT WARRANTY WHATSOEVER WITH RESPECT
TO THE FITNESS OF ANY CONDOMINIUM UNIT OF THE COMMON ELEMENTS FOR
ANY PARTICULAR OR GENERAL USE OR PURPOSE AND NO REPRESENTATION OR
WARRANTIES WITH RESPECT TO ANY OF THE FOREGOING ARE MADE, ALL OF THEM
BEING EXPRESSLY DISCLAIMED.

PURCHASER HEREBY WAIVES ANY RIGHT TO SUE IN REDHIBITION OR FOR RETURN OR
REDUCTION OF THE PURCHASE PRICE OR ANY PART THEREOF AS A RESULT OF THE
CONDITION OF THE UNIT OR UNITS DESCRIBED HEREIN OR THE CONDOMINIUM.

¶2   Two months after the sale, water began to leak through the ceiling of the condominium,
causing damage to the interior of the condominium and plaintiff's personal property. After
several failed attempts by defendant Standard/700 Associates to repair the roof of the building,
on April 17, 1997, plaintiff filed suit. In her petition for and redhibition and damages, plaintiff
alleged the leaks were caused by a swimming pool, a hot tub, and planters located on the roof
of the building.]

¶3   In a supplemental and amending petition, plaintiff pled fraud and inducement, alleging that
defendants had knowledge of the condition of the roof, but intentionally concealed this information from plaintiff prior to purchase. Plaintiff specifically alleged that, prior to the act of sale,
defendant Ms. Margaret Aldon Lovelace Guichard, the sales agent for defendant Standard/700
Associates, "unequivocally vouched for the soundness of the roof of the subject condominium
complex" and stated there had been no previous leaks.

¶4   After answering plaintiff's original petition and amended petition, defendants moved for
summary judgment, contending that plaintiff effectively waived the warranty against redhibitory defects when plaintiff entered the contract of sale containing the "as is where is" clause.
. . .

¶5   After a hearing, the trial court granted defendants' motion. On appeal, the Fourth Circuit
affirmed. Shelton v. Standard/700 Associates, 2000-0227 (La.App. 4th Cir.1/31/01), 778 So.2d
1265. In reaching its holding, the court of appeal relied on two findings. First, the court of appeal
found no defect existed in the condominium at the time of delivery. Consequently, the court of
appeal determined there was no redhibitory defect in the condominium. LSA-C.C. art. 2530.5
Second, the court of appeal found that plaintiff waived her right to sue for redhibitory defects.

DISCUSSION

¶6   The issue before us does not concern the "as is where is" waiver of warranties plaintiff signed. It is the allegation of fraud that prompted this court to grant this writ, as fraud in the inducement of a contract cannot be waived.

¶7   Plaintiff can only obtain relief from the harsh consequences of the waiver she signed if she can show fraud in the inducement of the contract. As such, our discussion will address the body of law pertaining to fraud in the inducement of a contract of sale.

¶8   It is clear that a seller warrants his buyer against redhibitory defects, or vices, in the thing sold. LSA-C.C. art. 2520. It is equally clear, however, that this warranty may be excluded or limited per LSA-C.C. art. 2548, which provides, in pertinent part:

> The parties may agree to an exclusion or limitation of the warranty against redhibitory defects.
> The terms of the exclusion or limitation must be clear and unambiguous and must be brought to
> the attention of the buyer.

¶9   While an exclusion or limitation of the warranty against redhibitory defects is usually effective, LSA-C.C. art. 2548 further provides that "[a] buyer is not bound by an otherwise effective exclusion or limitation of the warranty when the seller has declared that the thing has a quality that he knew it did not have." Under this article, an otherwise effective exclusion or limitation of the warranty against redhibitory defects is not effective if the seller commits fraud, as defined in the civil code, upon the buyer. Thus, although the warranty against redhibitory defects may be excluded or limited, a seller cannot contract against his own fraud and relieve himself of liability to fraudulently induced buyers. See Roby Motors Co. v. Price, 173 So. 793, 796 (La.App. 2nd Cir.1937). Indeed, such a contract would be contra bonos mores and unenforceable.

¶10   A contract is formed by the consent of the parties. LSA-C.C. art. 1927. However, consent may be vitiated by error, fraud, or duress. LSA-C.C. art. 1948. "Fraud is a misrepresentation or a suppression of the truth made with the intention either to obtain an unjust advantage for one party or to cause a loss or inconvenience to the other. Fraud may also result from silence or inaction." LSA-C.C. art. 1953. "Error induced by fraud need not concern the cause of the obligation to vitiate consent, but it must concern a circumstance that has substantially influenced that consent." LSA-C.C. art. 1955.

¶11   Nevertheless, fraud does not vitiate consent when the party against whom the fraud was directed could have ascertained the truth without difficulty, inconvenience, or special skill.

However, this exception does not apply when a relation of confidence has reasonably induced a party to rely on the other's assertions or representations. LSA-C.C. art. 1954.

¶12   In pleading fraud, the circumstances constituting fraud must be alleged with particularity. LSA-C.C.P. art. 856. However, fraud need only be proven by a preponderance of the evidence and may be established by circumstantial evidence. LSA-C.C. art. 1957.

¶13   In sum, there are three basic elements to an action for fraud against a party to a contract: (1) a misrepresentation, suppression, or omission of true information; (2) the intent to obtain an unjust advantage or to cause damage or inconvenience to another; and (3) the error induced by a fraudulent act must relate to a circumstance substantially influencing the victim's consent to (a cause of) the contract.

¶14   Appellate courts review summary judgments de novo. Doerr v. Mobil Oil Corp., 2000-0947 (La.12/19/00), 774 So.2d 119, 136. It is well established that a summary judgment shall be rendered if the pleadings, depositions, answers to interrogatories, and admissions on file, together with the affidavits, if any, show that there is no genuine issue as to material fact, and that the mover is entitled to judgment as a matter of law. LSA-C.C.P. art. 966(B). However, if the movant will not bear the burden of proof at trial on the matter that is before the court on the motion for summary judgment, the movant's burden on the motion for summary judgment does not require him to negate all essential elements of the adverse party's claim, but rather **6 to point out to the court that there is an absence of factual support for one or more elements essential to the adverse party's claim. LSA-C.C.P. art. 966(C)(2). Thereafter, if the adverse party fails to produce factual support sufficient to establish that she will be able to satisfy her evidentiary burden of proof at trial, there is no genuine issue of material fact. LSA-C.C.P. art. 966(C)(2).

¶15   In support of their motion for summary judgment, defendants submitted several documents, including a document entitled "Statements of Uncontested Material Facts," which essentially sets forth the waiver provisions in the sales documents; a copy of the Public Offering Statement for 700 South Peters Condominium; a copy of the Agreement to Purchase; a copy of the Act of Sale; and a copy of plaintiff's deposition. In opposition to summary judgment, plaintiff also submitted several documents, including a copy of her deposition; repair and maintenance records evidencing the extent and amount of repairs made on the roof before and after the date of sale; two affidavits executed by plaintiff; an affidavit executed by Ms. Carita Boutte; and the deposition of Ms. Guichard.

¶16   After carefully studying the documents plaintiff filed in opposition to summary judgment, we find that plaintiff failed to produce factual support sufficient to establish that she would be able to prove her allegation of fraud at trial. Notably, plaintiff herself conceded in deposition that defendant Ms. Guichard, the sales agent for defendant Standard/700 Associates, who represented defendants throughout the sales negotiations, and who in fact managed the condominium building, may never have known about any prior problems involving leaks in the roof of the condominium building. This admission certainly belies plaintiff's allegation of fraud because it underscores defendants' lack of intent to obtain an unjust advantage or to cause damage or inconvenience to plaintiff. In her deposition, plaintiff further stated that if Ms. Guichard was unaware of the prior leak problems, surely "somebody there knew about it." This statement is pure speculation which falls far short of plaintiff's burden on summary judgment to produce factual support sufficient to establish that she would be able to satisfy her evidentiary burden of proof at trial. Moreover, the repair and maintenance records which plaintiff relies on fail to raise a genuine issue of material fact regarding fraud. Indeed, the records evidencing the extent and amount of repairs made on the roof after the date of sale are irrelevant to plaintiff's fraud allegation. The records evidencing the extent and amount of repairs made on the roof before the date of sale are relevant, but such repairs were so infrequent and inconsequential that these records also fail to raise a genuine issue of material fact regarding plaintiff's fraud allegation.

¶17 Furthermore, the three affidavits submitted by plaintiff in opposition to summary judgment fail to raise a genuine issue of material fact regarding fraud. The first affidavit executed by plaintiff merely recounts and expounds on allegations made in plaintiff's original petition and amended petition. The second affidavit executed by plaintiff, referred to as a supplemental affidavit, contains irrelevant information regarding plaintiff's continuing problems with the leaky roof. The affidavit of Ms. Carita Boutte merely corroborates an alleged conversation between plaintiff and Ms. Guichard, wherein Ms. Guichard allegedly told plaintiff that "there had never been any reported leak in the roof of 700 S. Peters."

¶18 Finally, Ms. Guichard's deposition fails to support plaintiff's allegation of fraud. Indeed, Ms. Guichard denies having any knowledge of any roof leaks prior to September 4, 1996, the date of the act of sale.9

¶19 In conclusion, we find plaintiff's conjectural allegations of fraud are too speculative. Plaintiff has failed to produce factual support sufficient to establish that she would be able to satisfy her evidentiary burden of proof at trial. Summary judgment was properly granted in defendants' favor. Accordingly, the judgment of the court of appeal is affirmed.

AFFIRMED.

Section 5: Subrogation & Manufacturer's Strict Liability

Subrogation is the substitution of one person to the rights (not the obligations) of another. La. Civ. Code art. 1825. It can be conventional or legal. A legal subrogation is where the substitution occurs by operation of law, as compared to a conventional subrogation where the substitution occurs by agreement (as is the case generally with insurance contracts that provide that an insurance company is subrogated to its insureds rights to sue a tortfeasor for property damage). A number of instances of legal subrogation are listed in Article 1825, including (for example) an obligee who pays a creditor whose right to collect from the obligor is otherwise superior, a purchaser who uses purchase money to pay off a pre-existing secured creditor, and others. Louisiana Civil Code Article 2548 provides another instance of legal subrogation. It provides in pertinent part that despite any waiver of warranty, "[t]he buyer is subrogated to the rights in warranty of the seller against other persons, even when the warranty is excluded."

To further explain what this means, Comments (c) and (d) provide:

(c) Under this Article, the subvendee is subrogated to the rights of his vendor and his vendor's warranty against redhibitory defects from the vendor who sold the thing to him, and so on in the chain of title. DeSoto v. Ellis, 393 So.2d 847 (La.App. 2d Cir.1981).

(d) Under this Article, the buyer is subrogated to the seller's rights and actions in warranty against the manufacturer. Cotton States Chemical Co., Inc. v. Larrison Enterprises, Inc., 342 So.2d 1212 (La.App. 2d Cir.1977).

Furthermore, Comment (d) of Article 2545, which lists the damages a seller may owe the buyer on a redhibition claim, again emphasizes the buyer's right to subrogation: "[t]he buyer may bring action against all sellers in the chain of sales back to the primary manufacturer to rescind a sale for breach of implied warranty."

Study Question:

How does the buyer's right to subrogation apply in the following cases? Does a buyer's right of subrogation survive that buyer's waiver of warranty? (You will probably find it helpful to diagram the chain of title in the following cases).

MEDIA PROD'N CONSULTANTS V. MBNA 1972

262 SO. 2D 377 (LA.)

SANDERS, Justice.

¶1 We granted certiorari to review a decision of the Fourth Circuit Court of Appeal denying the purchaser of an imported Mercedes-Benz automobile warranty rights against Mercedes-Benz of North America, Inc., the American distributor that supplied the automobile to the dealer. We reverse.

¶2 [Plaintiff Media Production Consultants purchased a new 1968 Mercedes-Benz automobile from Cookie's Auto Sales, Inc., in Baton Rouge. The automobile had been manufactured in Germany by Daimler-Benze Aktiengesellschaft, a German corporation, who transferred it to importer Daimler-Benz of North America. The manufacturer included a warranty in materials and workmanship. The importer then transferred the car to distributer, Mercedes-Benz of North America (MBNA) who prepared it for sale and sold it to Cookie's. MBNA in turn included a 24,000 mile warranty that contained the following disclaimer:

> 'This warranty is expressly in lieu of all other warranties and representations, expressed or
> implied, and of all other obligations or liabilities on the part of the Seller, Mercedes-Benz of
> North America, Inc. and Daimler-Benz of North America, Inc. and Daimler-Benz A.G. Seller nei-
> ther assumes nor authorizes any other person to assume for it any other liability in connection
> with such motor vehicle. '

¶3 Cookie's sold the automobile to Media. The Mercedes-Benz Owner's Service Policy delivered with automobile contained a warranty that the vehicle was 'free from defects in material and workmanship.' In it the dealer agreed to replace or repair defective parts. The Service Policy also contains the following provision:

> 'This warranty is expressly in lieu of all other warranties and representations, expressed or
> implied, and of all other obligations or liabilities on the part of Dealer, Mercedes-Benz of North
> America, Inc., and Daimler-Benz A. G. Dealer neither assumes nor authorizes any other person
> to assume for it any other liability in connection with such motor vehicle.'

¶4 Immediately after the purchase, Media found the automobile unusable because it had the following defects: peeling off of the interior trim, interior lights that did not burn, transmission problems, stalling in traffic, a defective air conditioner, excessive brake squeal, deterioration of rear window channels, uncorrectable vibration, and paint deficiencies.

¶5   After futile efforts to obtain correction of the deficiencies, Media surrendered the car to an authorized dealer and filed this suit.]

¶6   Both lower courts found the vehicle so defective as to require an avoidance of the sale. Accordingly, the sale was set aside with judgment against Cookie's, the dealer, for the purchase price. The judgment is now final but unexecuted. It is conceded that the dealer is no longer in business.

¶7   The question before us is whether or not the automobile buyer can recover from the distributor.

¶8   The Court of Appeal held that no express or implied warranty ran from MBNA to Media, the purchaser, and denied recourse against the distributor. In our opinion, this disposition is unsound.

¶9   Two warranty obligations are inherent in every sale, the warranty of merchantable title and the warranty of reasonable fitness for the product's intended use. LSA-C.C. Arts. 2475, 2476.

¶10   The jurisprudence is well settled that warranty limitation provisions in automobile manuals and similar documents delivered with the vehicle have no effect upon the statutory warranty of fitness. Radalec, Inc. v. Automatic Firing Corp., 228 La. 116, 81 So.2d 830 (1955); Hebert v. Claude Y. Woolfolk Corporation, La.App., 176 So.2d 814 (1965); Stevens v. Daigle and Hinson Rambler, Inc., La.App., 153 So.2d 511 (1963); Harris v. Automatic Enterprises of Louisiana, Inc., La.App., 145 So.2d 335 (1962); Fisher v. City Sales and Service, La.App., 128 So.2d 790 (1961); 24 La.L.Rev. 199-200 (1964). Hence, despite the warranty limitation in the Owner's Service Policy, Media has not renounced the warranty of fitness.

¶11   More difficult is the question of whether Mercedes-Benz of North America can be held liable for a breach of the implied warranty.

¶12   MBNA asserts that it has no liability in warranty to Media, because it is neither the seller nor manufacturer of the automobile and has no contract with the purchaser.

¶13   Media asserts that MBNA occupies the position of manufacturer and, under sound legal theory, no privity of contract is required for a consumer to bring an action in warranty against a manufacturer of a defective product, relying upon Penn v. Inferno Mfg. Corp., La.App., 199 So.2d 210, cert. denied 251 La 27, 202 So.2d 649 (1967); Marine Ins. Co. v. Strecker, 234 La. 522,

100 So.2d 493 (1958); MacPherson v. Buick Motor Co., 217 N.Y. 382, 111 N.E. 1050, L.R.A.1916F, 696.

***

¶14   We see no reason why the rule should not apply to the pecuniary loss resulting from the purchase of a new automobile that proves unfit for use because of latent defects.

¶15   The Legislature has declared that the distribution and sale of motor vehicles in Louisiana vitally affect the public interest. See LSA-R.S. 32: 1251. By placing automobiles on the market, the supplier represents to the public that the vehicles are suitable for use. The intervention of a franchised dealer should not mitigate that responsibility. The dealer serves only as a conduit for marketing the automobiles.

¶16   The pecuniary loss resulting from an unusable vehicle is recoverable when there is an Express warranty without privity. Beck v. Spindler, 256 Minn. 543, 99 N.W.2d 670 (1959); Inglis v. American Motors Corp., 3 Ohio St.2d 132, 209 N.E.2d 583 (1965); Posey v. Ford Motor Co., (Fla. App.), 128 So.2d 149 (1961); Hoskins v. Jackson Garin Co., (Fla.), 63 So.2d 514 (1953). Although there is a split of authority on the question, we find no adequate reason for not applying the same rule and allowing recovery when there is an Implied warranty without privity. See Smith v. Platt Motors, Inc., (Fla.App.), 137 So.2d 239 (1962); Continental Copper & Steel Indus., Inc. v. E.C. 'Red' Cornelius, Inc., (Fla.App.), 104 So.2d 40 (1958); G.M.C. Truck Co v. Kelley, 105 Okl. 84, 231 P. 882 (1924); Santor v. A & M Karagheusian, Inc., 44 N.J. 52, 207 A.2d 305 (1965); Lang v. General Motors Corp., (N.D.), 136 N.W.2d 805 (1965); Manheim v. Ford Motor Co., (Fla.), 201 So.2d 440 (1967). See also Beck v. Spindler, supra.

¶17   *We hold, therefore, that Mercedes-Benz of North America, Inc., is solidarily liable with Cookie's Auto Sales, Inc. for the price of the automobile and other allowable expenses.*[2]

¶18   The Court of Appeal has never reviewed the amount of recovery, since it affirmed the trial court's dismissal of the suit. Hence, the case should be remanded to that court for fixing of the amount of the award. See Felt v. Price, 240 La. 966, 126 So.2d 330 (1961).

¶19   For the reasons assigned, the judgment of the Court of Appeal is reversed and judgment is rendered in favor of plaintiff, Media Production Consultanta, Inc., and against the defendant, Mercedes-Benz of North America, Inc., in such amount as may hereafter be fixed, said judgment

---

2   Since Mercedes Benz, there has been a split among circuit courts as to whether the seller and the manufacturer are solidarily liable or liable under a comparative fault scheme. [Ed.]

to be in solido with that rendered against Cookie's Auto Sales, Inc. The case is remanded to the Court of Appeal, Fourth Circuit, for the fixing of the award. All costs are taxed against the defendant.

DIXON, Justice (concurring).

¶1 I fully concur in the opinion of the majority.

¶2 An additional reason available to the plaintiff is that it was subrogated to the rights of warranty of Cookie's Auto Sales, Inc. Cookie could have waived all its rights against MBNA; the warranty of quality could have been waived but was not. The waiver must be specific. C.C. 1764; Note, 4 Tul.L.Rev. 285; see also C.C. 2503.

¶3 The limitations that MBNA attempted to place on its warranty as quoted in footnote 2 of the majority opinion did not serve as a waiver of all rights of warranty by Cookie. MBNA did not say that it sold cars to Cookie without Any warranty whatsoever, express or implied. MBNA modified the 'no warranty' clause to limit it to performance, characteristics, specifications and conditions, including merchantability and fitness for a particular purpose. The warranty of quality of C.C. 2520 (against redhibitory vices which might render a car absolutely useless or its use so imperfect and inconvenient that it would not have been knowingly purchased) was not mentioned.

¶4 This dealership contract was obviously prepared by MBNA. If any ambiguity exists as to the interpretation of limitations placed on the no warranty clause, it must be construed against MBNA. As this court said in Radalec, Incorporated v. Automatic Firing Corporation, 228 La. 116, 123, 81 So.2d 830, 833:

> 'Under Article 2476 of the Civil Code, the warranty against hidden defects and redhibitory vices is implied in every contract of sale unless expressly excluded, see Nelson v. M.C.M. Truck Lines, 209 La. 582, 25 So.2d 236, and Article 2474 declares that
>
> 'The seller is bound to explain himself clearly respecting the extent of his obligation: any obscure or ambiguous clause is construed against him'. Accordingly, even if it be liberally conceded that the defendant actually intended to restrict its entire liability to a replacement of parts, it would still be responsible, as the alleged limitation in the contract does not plainly signify such an aim.'

¶5 Under C.C. 2503, the buyer is subrogated to the seller's rights and actions in warranty. If C.C. 2503 is applicable, plaintiff Media is subrogated to Cookie's rights against MBNA. C.C.

2503 should be applicable, even though found in the section of the code dealing with warranty against eviction. This court recognized its applicability in dicta in McEachern v,. Plauche Lumber & Construction Co., Inc., 220 La. 696, 57 So.2d 405, 408. See also 14 Tul.L.Rev. 470; 23 Tul.L.Rev. 119, 140.

¶6 This principle of subrogation, long recognized as applicable to the warranty of quality, should be available to plaintiff.

AUCOIN V. SOUTHERN QUALITY HOMES LL.C. 2008
984 SO. 2D 685 (LA.)

VICTORY, J.

¶1 We granted this writ application to determine whether the manufacturer of a mobile home is liable for redhibitory defects in the mobile home. After reviewing the record and the applicable law, we find that the manufacturer is liable to the plaintiff for redhibitory defects existing at the time the mobile home was delivered to the seller and for appropriate damages thereunder.

FACTS AND PROCEDURAL HISTORY

¶2 Kelly G. Aucoin ("plaintiff") purchased a mobile home and land from Southern Quality Homes, LLC (the "seller") on July 6, 2001 for $93,980.00. The mobile home had been delivered to Southern Quality Homes' lot by Dynasty Homes (the "manufacturer") in January, 2000. A pre-occupancy inspection report listed numerous defects in regard to the mobile home; however, Southern Quality Homes assured plaintiff they were minor and would be repaired. Plaintiff alleged that after the delivery and set-up of the mobile home, he and his wife, Cindy, began to experience problems with the home. The Aucoins contacted Southern Quality Homes and Dynasty Homes numerous times regarding these defects, and several attempts at repair were made by the manufacturer.

¶3 Plaintiff ultimately filed suit against Southern Quality Homes and Dynasty Homes, alleging redhibitory defects and seeking to hold the two defendants solidarily liable for rescission of the sale, including the price of the land, damages and expenses.1 At trial, the plaintiff presented expert witness testimony that the principal defect in the home was a moisture problem that caused a proliferation of mold, and that the manufacturer was responsible for several defects that related to the infiltration of moisture, including improper installation of the vinyl vapor barrier, improper sealing of the marriage line, improper fastening and installation of the roof and roof shingles, improper installation of vinyl siding, and improper installation of drywall on the ceiling. The plaintiff also produced a document dated October 17, 2000, wherein Southern Quality Homes requested service from Dynasty Homes because the ceiling in the master bedroom had a leak and needed repair, indicating that defects relating to the moisture problem were present in the home when the home was delivered by the manufacturer to the seller.

¶4 The trial court found in favor of the plaintiff, relying heavily on the above mentioned testimony of the plaintiff's expert witnesses. Specifically the trial court gave "great weight" to Ervin Ritter's testimony that the home had a moisture problem because the roof and the top plate were not sealed properly, which was a code violation, and that the marriage line between the two sections of the mobile home had not been properly sealed. The trial court also found Alexis Mallet's3 testimony "extremely well documented, thoroughly researched and based on sound construction standards and entitled to a great deal of weight." The trial court found that "one of the main problems that Mr. Mallet noticed was that the roof and the siding had not been applied properly," and that of the 30 homes in the subdivision, this was the only one to sustain roof damage in Hurricane Rita, which the trial court found corroborated his testimony that the roof was not installed properly. In addition, when asked which party caused the air infiltration problems, Mr. Mallet testified as follows:

> Q. Okay. Air infiltration problems that you've testified to, those would not be anything the dealer did, that would be the manufacturer would it not?
> A. Yes, sir.
> Q. Okay. So you don't really see anything, anything in your finding that has any significant associations with anything the dealer did?
> A. Nothing of any significance.

¶5 The trial court also credited Mr. Mallet's opinion that repairing the home would not be an option as the cost of repairs would greatly exceed the value of the home and noted that "this is the primary reason that the Court finds that the proper remedy for this redhibition suit is refund of entire purchase price." In addition, the trial court inspected the home and noted the following:

> [t]he Court visually walked through the home at the request of all counsel and was especially troubled by the obvious condition of the siding having deflections or bowing, and the fact that the underside of the home had not been sealed properly. The Court was not able to get on the roof and look at the roof problems described by Mr. Mallet nor was the Court able to get in the attic and notice the improper sealing problems mentioned by Mr. Mallet. However, the Court finds his testimony to be credible and accepts his testimony on these issues. The 'gap' between the wall and the ceiling was obvious. You could actually see light from outside through the crack."

¶6 The trial court concluded that:

> [t]he main and principle [sic] defect in this mobile home is the moisture problem causing the
> mold and eventual deterioration of the home. The main cause of the moisture problem, the Court
> finds, is the improper sealing of the marriage lines in the roof and underside of the home and top
> plate. The construction defects in the home show poor quality workmanship throughout, and
> though some problems are minor and are easily repaired, taken as a whole, the plaintiffs have
> satisfied their burden under the redhibition articles.

¶7 Recognizing that the seller had filed for bankruptcy, the trial court held the manufacturer
and the seller solidarily liable for these redhibitory defects. Finally, the trial court held the
manufacturer liable for nonpecuniary damages under La. C.C. art. 1998, finding a "significant
nonpecuniary interest in the fact that the Aucoins decided to upgrade and buy this new mobile
home to satisfy their desire to achieve the American dream and to have a new, much finer home
so that they could live more comfortably, worry free, and entertain family and friends." The
total damages awarded were the $93,980.00 purchase price for the home and land, $4,190.33 for
closing costs, $1,000 for dirt work, $25,000 for mental pain and suffering, $25,000 in attorney
fees, $25,000 in expert fees, $288.18 for medical bills, $285.00 for prescription bills, and $6,446.13
for insurance and taxes.

¶8 The court of appeal affirmed the trial court's judgment. Aucoin v. Southern Quality Homes,
LLC, 06-979 (La.App. 3 Cir. 2/28/07), 953 So.2d 856. . . . We granted Dynasty Homes' writ application to determine whether it is liable for the redhibitory defects in this mobile home, and,
if so, the appropriate damages thereunder. Aucoin v. Southern Quality Homes, LLC, 07-1014
(La.6/29/07), 959 So.2d 516.

DISCUSSION

¶9 The statutory law relative to redhibition is contained in Title VII of the Louisiana Civil
Code governing "Sale." La. C.C. art. 2520 states the warranty against redhibitory defects as
follows:

> The seller warrants the buyer against redhibitory defects, or vices, in the thing sold.
>   A defect is redhibitory when it renders the thing useless, or its use so inconvenient that it
> must be presumed that a buyer would not have bought the thing had he known of the defect.
> The existence of such a defect gives a buyer the right to obtain rescission of the sale.
>   A defect is redhibitory also when, without rendering the thing totally useless, it diminishes
> its usefulness or its value so that it must be presumed that a buyer would still have bought it

but for a lesser price. The existence of such a defect limits the right of a buyer to a reduction of the price.

¶10 La. C.C. art. 2530 provides in pertinent part that "[t]he warranty against redhibitory defects covers only defects that exist at the time of delivery."

¶11 The extent of a seller's liability to a buyer for breaching this warranty depends on whether the seller knew, or did not know, of the defect. La. C.C. art. 2531 provides:

> A seller who did not know that the thing he sold had a defect is only bound to repair, remedy, or correct the defect. If he is unable or fails so to do, he is then bound to return the price to the buyer with interest from the time it was paid, and to reimburse him for the reasonable expenses occasioned by the sale, as well as those incurred for the preservation of the thing, less the credit to which the seller is entitled if the use made of the thing, or the fruits it has yielded, were of some value to the buyer.
>
> A seller who is held liable for a redhibitory defect has an action against the manufacturer of the defective thing, if the defect existed at the time the thing was delivered by the manufacturer to the seller, for any loss the seller sustained because of the redhibition. Any contractual provision that attempts to limit, diminish or prevent such recovery by a seller against the manufacturer shall have no effect.

¶12 On the other hand, the liability of a seller who knows of the defect is greater:

> A seller who knows that the thing he sells has a defect but omits to declare it, or a seller who declares that the thing has a quality that he knows it does not have, is liable to the buyer for the return of the price with interest from the time it was paid, for the reimbursement of the reasonable expenses occasioned by the sale and those incurred for the preservation of the thing, and also for damages and reasonable attorney fees. If the use made of the thing, or the fruits it might have yielded, were of some value to the buyer, such a seller may be allowed credit for such use or fruits.
>
> A seller is deemed to know that the thing he sells has a redhibitory defect when he is a manufacturer of that thing.

La. C.C. art. 2545.

¶13 In Young v. Ford Motor Co., Inc., 595 So.2d 1123 (La.1992), we explained the Roman origins of the redhibitory action and that its purpose was to protect buyers from latent defects undisclosed by corrupt dealers. "This important aspect of our current law on sales (i.e., this system of implied warranty against latent defects and vices) was fully incorporated into Louisiana law." Id. (See e.g., Louisiana Civil Code of 1808, Art. 669 and Art. 7110) "The purpose of the redhibition action in Louisiana, as was the case in Roman law, has been to restore the status quo." Id. (Citing Floyd W. Lewis, Comment, Warranty of Quality in Louisiana: Extent of Recovery under the Implied-In-Law Warranty, 23 Tul. L.Rev. 130, 131 (1948); Savoie v. Snell, 213 La. 823, 35 So.2d 745, 746 (1948). "The seller in good faith had only to restore the purchase price paid and any expenses incurred (Article 2509, La. Civil Code of 1825), while the seller in bad faith was also liable in damages. Article 2523, La. Civil Code of 1825)." Id. Thus, an action in redhibition entitles the buyer to annul the sale and recover the purchase price, rather than being limited to recovering the cost of curing any such substantial defects. Rey v. Cuccia, 298 So.2d 840 (La.1974); Prince v. Paretti Pontiac Co., Inc., 281 So.2d 112 (La.1973).

¶14 Although the code articles on redhibition appear to only allow a suit by a buyer against a "seller" for redhibitory defects, this Court held in Media Production Consultants, Inc. v. Mercedes-Benz of North America, Inc., 262 La. 80, 262 So.2d 377 (1972), that the buyer could recover directly from the manufacturer for breach of warranty, despite the fact that there was no privity of contract between them. In Media Production, the Court stated:

> Louisiana has aligned itself with the consumer-protection rule, by allowing a consumer without privity to recover, whether the suit be strictly in tort or upon implied warranty. Marine Ins. Co. v. Strecker, 234 La. 522, 100 So.2d 493 (1958); LeBlanc v. Louisiana Coco Cola Bottling Co., 221 La. 919, 60 So.2d 873 (1952).

¶15 We see no reason why the rule should not apply to the pecuniary loss resulting from the purchase of a new automobile that proves unfit for use because of latent defects. The pecuniary loss resulting from an unusable vehicle is recoverable when there is an Express warranty without privity. [Cites omitted.] Although there is a split of authority on the question, we find no adequate reason for not applying the same rule and allowing recovery when there is an Implied warranty without privity. [Cites omitted.], 262 So.2d at 380-81. After this analysis, the Court held "that Mercedes-Benz of North America, Inc. [the manufacturer], is solidarily liable with [the seller] for the price of the automobile and other allowable expenses." Id.

¶16 Two years later, in Rey v. Cuccia, supra, this Court relied on Media Productions to hold the manufacturer of a trailer solidarily liable with the seller for a redhibitory defect which existed at the time the manufacturer sold the trailer to the seller. See also Womack and Adcock v. 3M Business Products Sales, Inc., 316 So.2d 795 (La.App. 1 Cir.1975) (holding that "since the now famous case of Media Pro. ..., the buyer's action for breach of implied warranty has been extended to all sellers in the chain of sales back to the primary manufacturer"). The Court in

Rey held that "[t]he consumer's action is enforceable against the manufacturer at the same time and at least within the same year following the sale to the consumer, Article 2534, as it is enforceable against the seller." 298 So.2d at 845. The Court further held that because the manufacturer is presumed to know of defects, the one-year limitation of Article 2534 does not apply and the consumer may institute the action to recover for the redhibitory defect within the year following his discovery of it. Id. (Citing La. C.C. art. 2546).

¶17   Although Media Production and Rey held the manufacturer and seller were solidarily liable for the defects at issue, we need not reach the correctness of that issue, as we find that the manufacturer is independently liable under those cases for redhibitory defects that existed at the time of delivery to the seller.

¶18   Under La. C.C. art. 2520, the seller warrants the product he sells to be free of redhibitory defects, and under La. C.C. art. 2531, the seller is liable to the buyer even for redhibitory defects he was not aware of, including those that were the fault of the manufacturer. In such a case, the seller is responsible for correcting the defect, or, if he is unable to do so, he must return the purchase price with interest, plus reimburse the buyer for his reasonable expenses; however, he has an action against the manufacturer for any defects which "existed at the time the thing was delivered by the manufacturer to the seller." La. C.C. art. 2531. On the other hand, while a buyer may sue a manufacturer directly for redhibitory defects, the manufacturer is liable but only for defects "resulting from the original manufacture" of the product. Rey v. Cuccia, supra at 845.13

¶19   Thus, whether the manufacturer is solidarily liable with the seller for redhibitory defects is immaterial in this case, as the manufacturer is directly liable for redhibitory defects resulting from the original manufacture of the product. In this case, although the lower courts held that the manufacturer and seller were solidarily liable for the redhibitory defects, the trial court found, and the court of appeal affirmed, that the redhibitory defects were manufacturing defects, for which the manufacturer would be independently liable.

¶20   Dynasty Homes argues that the trial court's findings in this regard are manifestly erroneous and that other laws governing the manufacture, sale, and installation of mobile homes, namely, the "Uniform Standards Code for Manufactured Housing," La. R.S. 51:911.21, et seq., (the "USCMH"), mandate a different result.

¶21   La. R.S. 51:911.23 provides that "[a]ll new manufactured homes which are sold or offered for sale in this state must be in compliance with the Code and the requirements of this Part" and that "[i]n any redhibitory action brought against the seller of a manufactured home or mobile home, the standards set forth in the Code shall be considered in establishing and determining whether or not a defect exists." The "Code" means "the National Manufactured Home Construction and Safety Standards Act of 1974, 42 U.S.C. 5401 et seq., as amended, and federal regulations promulgated pursuant thereto, along with any construction or installation-related standards adopted by the Louisiana Manufactured Housing Commission." La. R.S. 51:911.22(1). "Seller" is not defined. The warranty required by the USCMH provides as follows:

A. Each new manufactured home, sold as such shall be covered by warranties that shall protect only the first retail purchaser of the manufactured home, for a period of one year from the date of the purchase, in accordance with the terms of the warranty:

(1) The manufacturer shall warrant, in writing, that the manufactured home was in compliance with the Code and the requirements of this Part at the time of manufacture.

Further, the manufacturer shall warrant that the manufactured home was manufactured free from any defects in materials or workmanship as outlined in the Code.

(2) The installer shall warrant that the manufactured home was installed according to the Minimum Standards for Installation of Manufactured Homes (R.S. 51:912.21 et seq.).

(3) The manufacturer, retailer, or installer shall not be liable for any defect in the manufactured home which is the result of improper setup, moving, or defects in work or materials done or furnished by persons other than the manufacturer, retailer, or installer.

B. Manufactured homes sold as used manufactured homes shall not be covered by a warranty unless provided for in writing outlining the terms and conditions of the warranty.

C. The warranty required by this Part shall be in addition to and not in derogation of any other warranties, rights, and privileges which the buyer may have under any other law or instrument. The buyer may not waive his rights under this Part and any such waiver is hereby prohibited as contrary to public policy and shall be unenforceable and void.

La. R.S. 51:911.25.

¶22 In addition, the installation may only be performed by the homeowner or a Louisiana licensed installer and must be performed in strict compliance with the Minimum Standards for Installation of Manufactured Homes. La. R.S. 51:912.27(B). To strictly comply with Louisiana's minimum standards, the licensed installer must install the home in compliance with the manufacturer's instruction and seal the marriage line on all multi-sectional homes "at the ceiling line, the floor line, and the end walls to restrict any air flow into the home." La. R.S. 51:912.22(1), (9).

¶23   Finally, La. R.S. 51:911.24.1(C) provides:

> C. Notwithstanding the terms of any franchise, sales, or other contractual agreement, each
> manufacturer shall indemnify and hold harmless its retailers against any judgment for damages,
> including but not limited to court costs and reasonable attorney fees of the retailer, arising out
> of complaints, claims, or lawsuits including but not limited to strict liability, negligence, misrep-
> resentation, express or implied warranty, or rescission of sale to the extent that the judgment
> arises out of alleged defective or negligent manufacture, assembly, or design of manufactured
> homes, parts, or accessories or other functions of the manufacturer, which are beyond the con-
> trol of the retailer.

¶24   A violation of the USCMH subjects the violator to civil penalties. La. R.S. 51:911.39.

¶25   A reading of these sections reveals that the warranty provided by the USCMH is not exclusive, but is "in addition and not in derogation of any other warranties, rights, and privileges
which the buyer may have under any other law or instrument," such as redhibition. However,
"in any redhibitory action against the seller," the standards set out by the Code must be considered in determining whether a redhibitory defect exists. Finally, the manufacturer must indemnify and hold harmless its retailers against any judgment "aris[ing] out of alleged defective
or negligent manufacture, assembly, or design of manufactured homes, parts, or accessories
or other functions of the manufacturer, which are beyond the control of the retailer." La. R.S.
51:911.24.1(C). After reviewing the USCMH, we find that it is in line with the Code articles on
redhibition, which recognize that the seller is liable for redhibitory defects even if they are, in
fact, manufacturing defects, but that the seller has an action against the manufacturer if the
defect existed at time of delivery to the seller. Since manufacturers can be sued in redhibition
in the absence of a contract, the manufacturer is liable for defects existing at time of delivery
to the seller.

¶26   Further, while the USCMH requires the installer to install the home and seal the marriage lines according to specific standards, this does not preclude a finding that the redhibitory
defects in this case were manufacturing defects. In addition to the improper sealing of the
marriage lines, the trial court found numerous other redhibitory defects based on the plaintiff's expert witnesses' testimony that were clearly attributable to the manufacturer and which
contributed to the moisture problems. As we stated in Young, supra, "[m]ultiple defects can
collectively form the basis of a redhibitory action even though many of the defects are minor
or have been repaired." 595 So.2d at 1126. Thus, we find no manifest error in the trial court's
finding that manufacturing defects were redhibitory. Because the manufacturer is presumed to
know of manufacturing defects, he is liable for "the return of the price with interest from the

time it was paid, for the reimbursement of the reasonable expenses occasioned by the sale and those incurred for the preservation of the thing, and also for damages and reasonable attorney fees." La. C.C. art. 2545.

¶27 The manufacturer next argues that the trial court erred in holding it liable for the cost of the land and closing costs. It is undisputed that the manufacturer sold only the home to the seller, while the seller sold the home and land to the buyer for $93,980.00. The Third Circuit affirmed the trial court's holding by applying La. C.C. art. 2540, which provides that "[w]hen more than one thing are sold together as a whole so that the buyer would not have bought one thing without the other or others, a redhibitory defect in one of such things gives rise to redhibition for the whole." The court of appeal's holding was in error.

¶28 As early as 1894, this Court held that the principles contained in La. C.C. art. 2540 (1870) apply "only when the things sold are dependent upon each other, so that the defect of one renders the other useless and without value." C.S. Burt Co. v. Laplace, 46 La. Ann. 722, 15 So. 293 (La.1894). In this case, there was no evidence presented that defects in plaintiff's home rendered the land useless and without value such that plaintiff will be prevented from using the land in the future. Further, the manufacturer had nothing to do with the development and sale of the land to plaintiff. There is simply no legal basis under Louisiana law for holding the manufacturer of a mobile home liable for the rescission of the sale of the land simply because it was sold jointly with the home by the seller. Further, such a holding could lead to absurd results. For example, if plaintiff had purchased 100 acres of valuable land for $1,000,000 as part of a package deal with a defective $50,000 mobile home from a seller, it would be absurd to hold the manufacturer of the mobile home liable to the plaintiff for the value of the land. Thus, we find that the lower courts erred in holding the manufacturer liable for the purchase price of the land and closing costs associated with the land.

***

[The discussion of nonpecuniary damages and expert witness fees is omitted.]

CONCLUSION

¶29 The manufacturer is directly liable to the buyer for redhibitory defects which exist at the time the manufacturer sold and delivered the product to the seller. In this case, the lower courts did not err in finding redhibitory defects existed for which the manufacturer was responsible and in holding the manufacturer liable for damages pursuant to La. C.C. art. 2545. However, in its assessment of these damages, the lower courts erred in several respects. First, the manufacturer is only liable for the return of the purchase price of the mobile home with interest from the time it was paid and for reimbursement of the reasonable expenses occasioned by the sale and those incurred for the preservation of the mobile home, plus reasonable attorney fees as were properly awarded by the lower courts. The price of the land should not be included in this amount because the evidence did not show that the requirements of La. C.C. art. 2540 were met. Accordingly, on remand, the trial court must determine what amount of the $93,980.00 was for the mobile home and what was for the land, and what amount of the closing costs and dirt work were associated with the mobile home itself. The $25,000 attorney fee award was appropriate and should not be disturbed. In addition, the lower courts erred in awarding $25,000.00 in mental pain and suffering damages because the plaintiff failed to show that the manufacturer knew or should have known that its failure to perform his obligations would result in nonpecuniary losses. Finally, the trial court did not abuse its discretion in awarding $25,000.00 in expert witness fees, but did err in awarding $20,000.00 of that amount as damages bearing interest from the date of judicial demand. On remand, the trial court must tax the entire $25,000.00 as costs bearing interest from the date of judgment.

DECREE

¶30 For the reasons expressed herein, the judgment of the court of appeal is affirmed in part and reversed in part and the case is remanded to the trial court for further proceedings.

AFFIRMED IN PART; REVERSED IN PART; REMANDED TO TRIAL COURT.

Study Question:

Read the New Home Warranty Act (NHWA), La. Rev. Stat. 9:3141 through 9:3150. It was implemented in order to provide "clear, concise, and mandatory warranties for the purchasers and occupants of new homes in Louisiana and by providing for the use of homeowners' insurance as additional protection for the public against defects in the construction of new homes." La. Rev. Stat. 9:3141.

Consider how the NHWA affects the provision made for subrogation under Civil Code articles 2545 and 2548, as demonstrated in the following case – does it help or hurt consumers?

CILIBERTI V. MISTRETTI 2004

879 SO. 2D 789 (LA. APP. 1 CIR.)

WHIPPLE, J.

¶1 This matter is before us on appeal by defendants/third-party plaintiffs, Eric and Nicole Mistretta, from a judgment of the trial court maintaining an exception of prescription filed by Bestbuilt Homes, Inc. For the following reasons, we affirm.

FACTS AND PROCEDURAL HISTORY

¶2 On January 7, 2003, plaintiffs, Louis and Patricia Ciliberti, filed a "Petition for Rescission of Sale and for Damages" seeking to rescind a cash sale entered into on July 19, 2002 with the Mistrettas, who were "sellers" of a certain lot of immovable property and residential structure thereon. In the petition, plaintiffs contended that a sewerage blockage created a situation that led to "a severe and nauseating presence of sewerage gases being present at all times within the residence and upon the immovable on which the residence sits." Plaintiffs contended that the sewerage blockage and resulting problems constituted a redhibitory defect, and that plaintiffs would never have entered into the contract of sale had they known of the defect. Plaintiffs prayed that the July 19, 2002 sale be rescinded, that the purchase price be returned to them, and that damages and attorneys fees be awarded.

¶3 On March 6, 2003, the Mistrettas filed an Answer and Third-Party Demand naming as third-party defendant Bestbuilt Homes, Inc. ("Bestbuilt"), the manufacturer/builder of the home. The Mistrettas claimed that they had purchased the home directly from Bestbuilt, and had experienced one plumbing-related incident involving the subject premises that was subsequently reported to and repaired by Bestbuilt in late September or early October of 1996. Accordingly, the Mistrettas asked that the suit be dismissed, or alternatively, that in the event they were deemed liable on the main demand, their third-party demand against Bestbuilt be granted and judgment rendered in their favor for damages, attorneys' fees, expenses and costs.

¶4 In response, Bestbuilt filed an Exception of Prescription and alternative Answer to the Third Party Demand, asserting that any claims set forth by the Mistrettas had prescribed pursuant to the provisions of LSA-R.S. 9:3144,1 the New Home Warranty Act ("NHWA"), and LSA-C.C. art. 2534. The matter was heard before the trial court on May 30, 2003, and after considering the pleadings, evidence, and argument of counsel, the trial court rendered judgment on June 4, 2003, maintaining the exception of prescription in favor of Bestbuilt, and dismissing the third party claims of the Mistrettas with prejudice.

THE APPEAL

¶5   The Mistrettas filed the instant devolutive appeal, contending that the trial court erred in dismissing their third-party claim against Bestbuilt as prescribed under the provisions of the NHWA. The Mistrettas contend that their claims for negligent misrepresentation and/or detrimental reliance and request for indemnification are independent and separate causes of action which the NWHA cannot exclude as a matter of law. The Mistrettas further contend that the trial court erred as a matter of law in applying an over-expansive interpretation of the NHWA's definition of "Owner" as neither the Cilibertis (plaintiffs) nor the Mistrettas (third-party plaintiffs) meet the definitional requirements necessary to establish either party as an "Owner" under the Act.

DISCUSSION

Assignments of Error Numbers One and Two

¶6   The standard of review controlling review of a peremptory exception of prescription requires that this court strictly construe the statutes against prescription and in favor of the claim that is said to be extinguished. Pratt v. Himel Marine, Inc., 2001-1832, p. 7 (La.App. 1st Cir.6/21/02), 823 So.2d 394, 400.

¶7   In these assignments, the Mistrettas do not challenge the trial court's finding that their third-party claims were prescribed under the NHWA. Instead, they contend that the trial court erred in failing to recognize their right to seek relief under alternative theories of recovery, i.e., negligent misrepresentation, detrimental reliance, and indemnification, which they argue are separate and independent causes of action not governed by the provisions of the NHWA. Bestbuilt counters that because the Mistrettas did not allege negligent misrepresentation or detrimental reliance in their third-party demand, or raise these arguments before the trial court, these claims are waived and the Mistrettas are prohibited from raising them on appeal for consideration by this court in the first instance.

¶8   The Mistrettas' Third Party Demand set forth the following allegations against Bestbuilt:

> In the event third-party plaintiffs are held liable to plaintiffs for any redhibitory defects in the subject premises, then Bestbuilt Homes, Inc. is concomitantly liable unto third-party plaintiffs as their predecessor in title because Bestbuilt Homes, Inc. was the manufacturer/builder of the subject property and is therefore legally presumed to know of the existence of any such "defects" therein.

Third-party plaintiffs had earlier purchased said premises directly from third-party defendant, Bestbuilt Homes, Inc., and had one plumbing-related complaint with the subject premises, which arose shortly after the premises were delivered to them for habitation and which complaint was tendered for repair to Bestbuilt Homes, Inc. and thereafter was ostensibly repaired.

¶9 The NHWA was enacted in 1986 and codified in LSA-R.S. 9:3142, et seq., for the purpose of "providing clear, concise, and mandatory warranties for the purchasers and occupants of new homes in Louisiana and by providing for the use of homeowners' insurance as additional protection for the public against defects in the construction of new homes." LSA-R.S. 9:3141. The NHWA provides a "warranty for a new home purchaser defining the responsibility of the builder to that purchaser and subsequent purchasers during the warranty provisions provided herein." LSA-R.S. 9:3141. The NHWA also provides that "all provisions of this Chapter shall apply to any defect although there is no building standard directly regulating the defective workmanship or materials." LSA-R.S. 9:3141.

¶10 Most importantly, the NHWA provides the exclusive remedies, warranties, and peremptive periods as between the builder and owner relative to home construction and statutorily sets forth that no other provisions of law relative to warranties and redhibitory vices and defects shall apply. LSA-R.S. 9:3150. Further, LSA-C.C. art. 2520, which governs claims in redhibition, specifically states in Comment (e) that, "[t]he Articles on redhibition do not apply to hidden defects discovered in a new home governed by the New Home Warranty Act, R.S. 9:3141-3150."

¶11 Nonetheless, on appeal, the Mistrettas assign as error the trial court's granting of the exception of prescription and dismissal of their third-party claim for relief under alternative theories of negligent misrepresentation and/or detrimental reliance. At the outset, as noted by counsel for Bestbuilt, we recognize that the Mistrettas' third-party demand does not assert a demand for relief on these theories.

¶12 At the hearing of this matter before the trial court on May 30, 2003, the trial court asked counsel for the Mistrettas, on at least two occasions during the hearing, what cause of action they would proceed under if the NHWA did not apply. The following colloquy occurred:

> THE COURT: Let me ask you this question: If the New Home Warranty Act does not apply, as you all claim, then what is your cause of action?
> [COUNSEL]: But do we put it in a vacuum?
> THE COURT: What is your cause of action? What are you seeking indemnity under?
> [COUNSEL]: Well, that would be just under general equitable principles.

***

THE COURT: But here's my question one more time: Let's assume the New Home Warranty Act does not apply.

[COUNSEL]: Okay.

THE COURT: What cause of action or right of action do you have to proceed six years later?

[COUNSEL]: Well -

THE COURT: Redhibition has prescribed, all right, so -

[COUNSEL]: Well, I'm not sure redhibition has prescribed because of my prescription articles, I believe it was told-First, I think it was acknowledgment by the builder when they went out to repair and then prescription–

¶13   Thereafter, the trial court dismissed the Mistrettas' claims "as prescribed according to the New Home Warranty Act." Thus, as Bestbuilt correctly notes, the Mistrettas did not allege negligent misrepresentation and/or detrimental reliance theories against Bestbuilt; instead, the Mistrettas argued they were entitled to indemnification for redhibitory defects, if proven, under "general equitable principles."

¶14   The Mistrettas argue that "indemnification" constitutes a separate and independent cause of action, which cannot be excluded by the NHWA, as a matter of law. In support of their argument, the Mistrettas cite Nassif v. Sunrise Homes, Inc., 98-3193 (La.6/29/99), 739 So.2d 183. In Nassif, the home owner brought an action in redhibition to recover damages for a defective foundation against the seller, Sunrise Homes, Inc., and the real estate developer who built the house. The builder/developer filed a third-party demand against the engineering firm that designed the foundation of the house for full indemnity for any and all sums for which the builder/developer was held liable to the home owner on the main demand.

¶15   However, the sole issue for review in Nassif was whether a defendant, whose liability to a plaintiff for the plaintiff's attorneys fees resulted from the actual fault of another, could recover, by way of indemnity, the amount of such attorneys fees from the party actually at fault, given the general rule that attorneys fees are not allowed except where authorized by statute or contract.

¶16   In Nassif, the home owner brought an action in redhibition against the builder/developer to recover for a foundation defect, and the builder/developer filed a third-party demand against the engineering firm that negligently designed the foundation of the house, for "full indemnity" for all sums for which the builder/developer was deemed "technically liable." Nassif, 98-3193 at p. 2, 739 So.2d at 185. On appeal, the Supreme Court affirmed the award of full indemnification to the home owner, but reversed the appellate court's deletion of attorneys fees that the trial court had included in the judgment in favor of the builder/developer and against the negligent engineer. In doing so, the Supreme Court reasoned as follows:

> "[W]e conclude that the equitable principle of restitution applies in an action for indemnity to allow a defendant who is only technically or constructively liable for a plaintiff's loss to recover from the party actually at fault the attorney fees it was compelled to pay the plaintiff, even in the absence of a statute or contract of indemnification. This measure of relief is in accordance with the long standing principle that "[i]ndemnity shifts the entire loss from a tortfeasor only techni-cally or constructively at fault to one primarily responsible for the act that caused the damage."

Nassif, 98-3193 at pp. 6-7, 739 So.2d at 18-188.

¶17 While the Court in Nassif stated that an action in indemnity is a "separate substantive cause of action, independent of the underlying wrong, and distinct from an action for attorneys fees," Nassif, 98-3193 at p. 5, 739 So.2d at 186-187, we do not find Nassif dispositive of the issues presented in this appeal. We find Nassif distinguishable from the instant case because in Nassif: (1) the claims arose prior to the enactment of the NHWA; and (2) the underlying suit was filed in redhibition and thus, was governed by the applicable redhibition law at the time, not the provisions of the NHWA. Moreover, we deem it significant that the contractor who sought indemnification from its engineering firm had timely filed his independent claim against the engineer for indemnity based on a breach of contract between the engineer and the builder/developer, not a homeowner and builder. Nassif, 98-3193 at p. 1, 739 So.2d at 184.

¶18 Because the NHWA provides the exclusive remedies, warranties, and peremptive periods as between the builder and owner relative to home construction and specifies that no other provisions of law relative to warranties and redhibitory vices and defects shall apply, we reject the Mistrettas' contention that their third-party claim was preserved under a theory of indemnity. See LSA-R.S. 9:3150.

¶19 These assignments lack merit.

¶20 Lastly, the Mistrettas argue that they are not subject to the exclusivity provisions of the NHWA because they are not suing the builder as an "owner" in a main demand but, rather, as non-owners asserting a claim for indemnity in the third-party demand. "Owner" is defined under the NHWA as "the initial purchaser of a home and any of his successors in title, heirs, invitees, or assigns to a home during the time the warranties provided under this Chapter are in effect." LSA-R.S. 9:3143(6). The Mistrettas claim that, in addition to not being "owners" because they no longer own the home, the peremptive warranties guaranteed by the NHWA for the plumbing system expired prior to the date of sale.3 Thus, the Mistrettas argue, since they do not meet the definitional requirements of an "owner," their claims are not within the purview of the NHWA.

¶21   Contrariwise, Bestbuilt maintains that the NHWA contemplates that the remedies against the builder are limited to the NHWA for all purchasers of a home constructed by the builder and sold to an initial purchaser. In support, Bestbuilt cites Ory v. A.V.I. Construction, Inc., 2003-72 (La.App. 5th Cir.5/28/03), 848 So.2d 115.

¶22   In Ory, the plaintiffs claimed that since A.V.I. was both the "builder" and the "seller" of the home, the NHWA did not provide their exclusive remedy and that they could proceed against A.V.I. in redhibition. Ory, 2003-72 at pp. 5-6, 848 So.2d at 118. After reviewing the record, the appellate court determined that the Orys and A.V.I. met the definitional requirements of "owner" and "builder" respectively, under the NHWA. Ory, 2003-72 at p. 6, 848 So.2d at 118. The court noted that where the cause of action had not wholly arisen from construction defects, some courts had determined that the NHWA was not the sole remedy available to home owners. Ory, 2003-72 at p. 7, 848 So.2d at 118-119. However, the court concluded that the type of damage asserted by the Orys therein, i.e., the defective installation of the corner bead, was squarely addressed by the NHWA. Ory, 2003-72 at p. 7, 848 So.2d at 119. The appellate court maintained A.V.I.'s exception of no cause of action as to any alleged claim in redhibition, concluding the suit was subject to the provisions of the NHWA, and maintained A.V.I.'s exception of prescription, as the Orys' suit was not timely filed under the provisions of the NHWA. Ory, 2003-72 at pp. 7-10, 848 So.2d at 119-121.

¶23   When a law is clear and unambiguous and its application does not lead to absurd consequences, the law shall be applied as written, and no further interpretation may be made in search of the intent of the legislature. See LSA-C.C. art. 9; Lasyone v. Phares, 2001-1785, pp. 3-4 (La.App. 1st Cir.5/22/02), 818 So.2d 1068, 1071. It is a recognized rule of statutory construction that this court must give the words of a law their generally prevailing meaning. See LSA-C.C. art. 11. When the words of a law are ambiguous, their meaning must be sought by examining the context in which they occur and the text of the law as a whole. LSA-C.C. art. 12. Furthermore, the meaning of words or phrases may be ascertained by the words and phrases with which they are associated. Words of general meaning should be applied only to such classes of things of the same general kind as those specifically mentioned. Cox Cable New Orleans, Inc. v. City of New Orleans, 624 So.2d 890, 894 (La.1993). When the language is susceptible of different meanings, it must be interpreted as having the meaning that best conforms to the purpose of the law. LSA-C.C. art. 10.

¶24 Further, it is presumed that every word, sentence, or provision in the law was intended to serve some useful purpose, that some effect is to be given each such provision, and that no unnecessary words or provisions were used. McDonald v. Louisiana State Board of Private Investigator Examiners, 2003-0773, p. 3 (La.App. 1st Cir.2/23/04), 873 So.2d 674, 675, 2004 WL 324978. The meaning of a statute is to be interpreted by looking to all sections taken together so that no section, clause, sentence or word becomes superfluous or meaningless. Barrilleaux v. NPC, Inc., 98-0728, p. 4 (La.App. 1st Cir.4/1/99), 730 So.2d 1062, 1065, writ denied, 99-1002 (La.5/28/99), 743 So.2d 672.

¶25 Finally, if a statute is not clear on its face, the meaning must be determined. Statutory interpretation is a province of the judiciary. The paramount consideration in interpreting a statute is ascertaining the legislature's intent and the reasons that prompted the legislature to enact the law. Southlake Development Company v. Secretary of the Department of Revenue and Taxation for the State of Louisiana, 98-2158, p. 4 (La.App. 1st Cir.11/5/99), 745 So.2d 203, 205, writ denied, 99-3405 (La.2/4/00), 754 So.2d 235.

¶26 Keeping in mind the rules of statutory interpretation outlined above, we recognize that the statute defines "owner" as "the initial purchaser of a home and any of his successors in title ..." (Emphasis added). See LSA-R.S. 9:3143(6). The parties do not dispute that the Mistrettas were the initial purchasers of the home or that the Cilibertis subsequently purchased the home from the Mistrettas. Applying the plain language of the statute, we conclude the Mistrettas are clearly considered the "owner" as defined by the NHWA.

¶27 Further, we conclude that the Mistrettas' third-party claim falls squarely within the purview of the NHWA. Alleged defects in the plumbing system are squarely addressed by the two-year warranty provision of the NHWA. See LSA-R.S. 9:3144(A)(2); Ory, 2003-72 at p. 7, 848 So.2d at 119. To accept the Mistrettas' strained statutory interpretation would render the NHWA and its prescriptive periods meaningless. For example, new-home purchasers who became aware of a defect after the tolling of the prescriptive period could simply sell the home to another "owner" and circumvent the statutory prescriptive periods by waiting to be sued and then claiming they were not covered by the act as they were no longer the "owner."

¶28 Such an interpretation would virtually eliminate any legal effect of the NHWA. Interpreting the sections of the statute as a whole, the NHWA contemplates that the remedies against the builder are limited to the NHWA for initial and subsequent purchasers of the home.

¶29 This assignment lacks merit.

CONCLUSION

¶30 We find no error in the judgment of the trial court maintaining Bestbuilt's Exception of Prescription, and dismissing the Mistrettas' claims with prejudice. Accordingly, for the above and foregoing reasons, the June 4, 2003 judgment of the trial court maintaining the Exception of Prescription, and dismissing Eric and Nicole Mistretta's claims against Bestbuilt Homes, Inc. is affirmed. Costs of this appeal are assessed against the appellants.

AFFIRMED.

Note

While the New Home Warranty Act is the exclusive remedy against a builder for problems with the building itself, the scope of that Act does not necessarily apply to extensions of the home, such as improvements to the lot on which the home sits. In Shepard v. Robinson Const. LL.C. , 170 So. 3d 387 (La. Ct. App. 2 Cir 2015), the Second Circuit held that the Act did not apply to an improperly graded lot's drainage problems and the normal implied warranty against redhibitory defects applied instead.

Section 6: Redhibition and Other Remedies

As was indicated in the early part of this Chapter, redhibition and other implied warranties may be used in conjunction with tort-based claims, and each cause of action leads to different kinds of remedies.

Study Question:

What do the following cases demonstrate about the relationship between redhibition and other remedies such as products liability?

DE ATLEY V. VICTORIA'S SECRET CATALOGUE 2004
876 SO. 2D 112 (LA. APP. 4TH CIR.)

MAX N. TOBIAS, JR., Judge.

¶1 Relators, Cheri Pink, Inc. ("Cheri Pink") and Victoria's Secret Catalogue, L.L.C. n/k/a Victoria's Secret Direct, LLC ("Victoria's Secret"), have filed substantially similar writ applications objecting to the denial of their peremptory exceptions of no cause of action and prescription by the trial court. For the reasons below, we grant the writ, but deny relief, and remand the matter for further proceedings.

¶2 This matter involves a suit for bodily injury arising out of a fire that occurred on 8 January 2001 at the home of the respondents Carol Chilton De Atley and Ronald R. De Atley. The fire started when Ms. De Atley's cotton flannel dress caught on fire from the nearby gas fireplace, causing severe bodily injury.

¶3 On 21 September 2001, the respondents filed suit seeking damages under the Louisiana Products Liability Act ("LPLA"), La. R.S. 9:2800.51 et seq. The respondents allege that the dress worn by Ms. De Atley, which had been purchased from a Victoria's Secret catalog in December 1999, was unreasonably dangerous in various respects pursuant to the LPLA. Cheri Pink is alleged to have sold the dress to Victoria's Secret for retail sale.

¶4 On 11 December 2003, the respondents filed a third amended and supplemental petition which added for the first time a claim in redhibition. In response to this amended and supplemental petition, the relators filed the exceptions at issue. Both were denied by the trial court.

¶5 The relators contend that the exception of no cause of action should be granted and the claim for redhibition dismissed on the basis that the LPLA provides the exclusive theories of liability against manufacturers for their allegedly defective products. Alternatively, the relators contend that the exception of prescription should be granted because the redhibition claim constitutes a completely distinct and separate cause of action from the products liability claim and, therefore, does not relate back to the filing of the original petition so as to interrupt prescription.

¶6 We first address the respondents' motion to dismiss the application of Victoria's Secret's application for writs on the basis of the failure of Victoria's Secret to attach the notice of intention of seeking a writ and an order from the trial court setting the deadline for filing the application for supervisory writs in this court, as required by Rules 4-2 and 4-3 of the Uniform Rules of the Courts of Appeal. Victoria's Secret supplemented their application with the notice and a copy of an order setting the deadline. The later demonstrates that the application is timely. Therefore, that issue is now moot.

¶7 Second, we note that Cheri Pink's application is defective for failure to conform to Rule 4-5 of the Uniform Rules of the Courts of Appeal. Our rules specifically require that a relator file a verified application for a supervisory writ. Cheri Pink's application contains no verification, which ordinarily would result in the automatic denial of the writ application on the showing made by the relator. However, only because (a) the issues in the writ applications of Cheri Pink and Victoria's Secret deal with the identical issue and (b) we have consolidated the writ applications of the relators, we find the interests of justice direct us to consider the merits of Cheri Pink's writ application.1 La. C.C.P. art. 2164.

¶8   On the merits of the applications, we first address the issue of whether the exclusivity provision of the LPLA prohibits the respondents' claim of redhibition. The LPLA, enacted in 1988 "establishes the exclusive theories of liability for manufacturers for damages caused by their products." La. R.S. 9:2800.52. The statute defines "damage" as follows:

> "Damage" means all damage caused by a product, including survival and wrongful death damages, for which Civil Code Articles 2315, 2315.1 and 2315.2 allow recovery. "Damage" includes damage to the product itself and economic loss arising from a deficiency in or loss of use of the product only to the extent that Chapter 9 of Title VII of Book III of the Civil Code, entitled "Redhibition [La. C.C. art. 2520 et seq.]," does not allow recovery for such damage or economic loss. Attorneys' fees are not recoverable under this Chapter.

La. R.S. 9:2800.53(5).

¶9   Thus, the statute defines "damage" by explicitly excluding amounts recoverable under redhibition for damage to the product and other economic loss. Courts have interpreted the LPLA as preserving redhibition as a cause of action only to the extent the claimant seeks to recover the value of the product or other economic loss. See Pipitone v. Biomatrix, Inc., 288 F.3d 239, 251 (5th Cir.2002); Thomas C. Galligan, Jr., Contortions Along the Boundary Between Contracts and Torts, 69 Tulane L.Rev. 457, 489-91 (1994). Thus, we conclude that the respondents have a cause of action for redhibition for economic loss only and not for personal injury claims.

¶10   The remedies for a claim under the LPLA and one in redhibition are different in a number of ways. The LPLA is the exclusive remedy against a manufacturer and does not allow for the recovery of attorney's fees, while attorney's fees are recoverable from the manufacturer in a redhibition claim pursuant to La. C.C. art. 2545. However, attorney's fees may be awarded only:

> [I]nsofar as those fees relate to the recovery of purely economic loss. This is because much of the proof of a "vice" for redhibition recovery overlaps with proof of a defective product for tort purposes. However, courts in such suits should be careful to realistically allocate recovery costs between the personal injury and economic loss portions of the claim.

Frank L. Maraist & Thomas C. Galligan, Jr., Louisiana Tort Law § 15-6 (1996) (citations omitted).

¶11 Thus, it will be for the trial court to determine what of the respondents' claims constitute pure economic loss and what damages for which La. C.C. arts. 2315, 2315.1, and 2315.2 allow recovery. Attorney's fees would only be recoverable for the pure economic loss and not for the damages recovered pursuant to the LPLA.

¶12 We now turn to the question of whether the amended petition setting forth the claim for redhibition relates back to the original filing. According to the original petition, the dress was purchased on 8 December 1999; the fire occurred on 8 January 2001; the original suit setting for a claim under the LPLA was filed on 21 September 2001; and the redhibition claim was added on 11 December 2003. La. C.C. art. 2534 provides in pertinent part:

> A. (1) The action for redhibition against a seller who did not know of the existence of a defect in the thing sold prescribes in four years from the day delivery of such thing was made to the buyer or one year from the day the defect was discovered by the buyer, whichever occurs first.
>
> ***
>
> B. The action for redhibition against a seller who knew, or is presumed to have known, of the existence of a defect in the thing sold prescribes in one year from the day the defect was discovered by the buyer.

¶13 Pursuant to La. C.C.P. art. 1153:

> When the action or defense asserted in the amended petition or answer arises out of the conduct, transaction, or occurrence set forth or attempted to be set forth in the original pleading, the amendment relates back to the date of filing the original pleading.

¶14 It is well established that La. C.C.P. art. 1153 permits amendment despite technical prescriptive bars where the original pleading gives fair notice of the general fact situation out of which the amended claim arises. Gunter v. Plauche, 439 So.2d 437, 440 (La.1983), citing Baker v. Payne and Keller of Louisiana, Inc., 390 So.2d 1272 (La.1980). "Where there is some factual connexity between the original and amended assertions, together with some identity of interest between the original and the supplemental party, amendment should be allowed." Baker, 390 So.2d at 1275; Gunter, 439 So.2d at 440.

¶15 We have reviewed the original and amended petitions filed by the respondents. In the original petition, it is alleged that the dress in question was purchased by Ms. De Atley and caught on fire because it is unreasonably dangerous in construction and composition, in design, and due to an inadequate warning, all claims under the LPLA. In the third amended petition, the respondents set forth the claim for redhibition. The pleading alleges that the defect in the dress rendered it so useless and/or its use so inconvenient that it must be presumed that Ms. De Atley would not have bought the dress had she known of the defect. See La. C.C. art. 2520.

¶16 We find that there is a factual connexity between the LPLA and redhibition claims in this case. In addition, we find that a products liability cause of action in which the plaintiff is a consumer of the product may sound in tort, La. C.C. art. 2315, in redhibition, La. C.C. art. 2545, or both. Firmin, Inc. v. Denham Springs Floor Covering, Inc., 595 So.2d 1164, 1170-71 (La.App. 1 Cir.1991). The primary difference between the two causes of action is the damages available under the two theories of recovery.

¶17 In the instant case, but for the sale of the dress from the relators to Ms. De Atley, the dress would not have caught on fire. Consequently, we find that the third amended petition relates back to the filing of the original pleading.

MOTION DENIED; WRIT GRANTED; RELIEF DENIED.

Study Question:

As the following case shows, the person who joins together two incompatible parts may also be viewed as a manufacturer. Examine as well the court's discussion of the interaction between redhibition and products liability..

BEARLY V. BRUNSWICK MERCURY MARINE DIV. 2004
888 SO. 2D 309 (LA. APP. 2D CIR.)

CARAWAY, J.

¶1 Plaintiff seeks return of the purchase price of a boat and motor from the wholesaler of the boat and motor. [Bearly alleges that the defendant outfitted its boat with another manufacturer's motor, knowing that the two were incompatible, and then marketed the assembled produce wholesale to plaintiff's marine dealer.] Defendant challenged plaintiff's ability to prove its advance knowledge of the defect with a motion for summary judgment which was granted by the trial court. Finding that defendant's knowledge of the defect is immaterial to plaintiff's claim under either our products liability law or in redhibition, we reverse.

Facts

¶2   Plaintiff, Floyd Bearly, purchased a Ranger boat and Mercury motor from Reeves Marine ("Reeves"), a boat retailer. Bearly . . . he immediately began experiencing problems with the motor which necessitated returning to Reeves for repair work on several occasions. He filed suit against Brunswick, Mercury Marine Division ("Brunswick"), the manufacturer of the motor, and Wood Manufacturing Company, d/b/a Ranger Boats ("Ranger"), the manufacturer of the boat. Bearly sought return of the purchase price, unspecified damages, and attorney fees.

¶3   The pertinent allegations of Bearly's petition are as follows:

> In the time spent trying to continually repair the broken and cracked reeds in the Mercury Boat, Petitioner has discovered that whenever the Mercury Motor is idling around, the reeds in the Motor get blown out or cracked. Petitioner has even spoken with representatives of Brunswick and members of its racing team, and they have indicated to him that this type of Mercury Motor on this type of Ranger Boat will not work properly.

> ***

> Petitioner was informed by representatives of Brunswick Corporation that the representatives of Wood were well aware of the fact that this particular Mercury motor was not a suitable design for this type of Ranger Boat, but that Wood decided to go ahead and market this Mercury Motor and Ranger Boat together anyway.
>
>   Petitioner alleges that Wood knew of the design problem with the Mercury Motor for this particular Ranger Boat prior to the sale of the Mercury Motor and Ranger Boat to Petitioner, but Wood failed to take any actions to solve it.

¶4   Ranger filed an answer and incidental demand, generally denying the allegations made by Bearly and countering that Brunswick indemnify Ranger for any damages arising from Bearly's suit.

* * *

¶5   The affidavit of Kevin Parker, a mechanic at Reeves, describing several telephone conversations with Brunswick's employee Randy Hankwitz was also submitted. Hankwitz informed

Parker that the motor was a performance engine, not suitable for extended idling, and thus unsuitable for the bass boat.

¶6   After the hearing, the trial court granted Ranger's motion for summary judgment and dismissed Bearly's claims against it. The trial court determined that since the affidavits of Bearly and Parker were based upon the hearsay statements of others regarding Ranger's knowledge of the alleged defect, Bearly had not shown that he could meet his burden of proof at trial. Bearly appeals the judgment on the grounds that his opposition affidavits established genuine issues of material fact based upon the personal knowledge of the affiants.

Discussion

¶7   Our review of the parties' briefs to this court and the trial court reveals the glaring omission of any discussion of the cause of action existing between Bearly and Ranger. Instead, the parties debated in a vacuum whether there was undisputed evidence that Brunswick had notified Ranger that the Mercury motor was incompatible for installation on the boat Ranger marketed wholesale to Reeves. Since we find that Ranger, as the alleged assembler of the two products, may be responsible under the Louisiana Products Liability Act (La. R.S. 9:2800.51, et seq.) (the "LPLA") or in redhibition (La. C.C. arts. 2520, et seq.) without actual knowledge of its defectively assembled product, the issue of its knowledge contested in this summary judgment proceeding is not dispositive of the case.

¶8   Initially, we will review Bearly's claim under the LPLA. The LPLA defines a manufacturer to include the following:

> (c) A manufacturer of a product who incorporates into the product a component or part manufactured by another manufacturer.

> La. R.S. 9:2800(1)(c). In stating that Ranger outfitted its boat with the Mercury motor as a component, Bearly's petition asserts that Ranger is a manufacturer under LPLA. For purposes of assessing Bearly's cause of action based on the pleadings, we accept that Ranger could be an LPLA manufacturer because of its actions in assembling the end product. See, Rey v. Cuccia, 298 So.2d 840 (La.1974); Austin's of Monroe, Inc. v. Brown, 474 So.2d 1383 (La.App. 2d Cir.1985).

¶9   Next, although Bearly is claiming no personal injury from the defective product, the LPLA provides that damage under the Act "includes damage to the product itself and economic loss arising from a deficiency in or loss of use of the product only to the extent that Chapter 9 of Title VII of Book III of the Civil Code, entitled 'Redhibition,' does not allow recovery for such damage or economic loss." La. R.S. 9:2800.53(5). Although this provision and its relation to a claim in redhibition has been questioned by commentators concerning its clarity, all seem to agree that the consumer will have a right to recover against the manufacturer for purely economic loss, whether under the LPLA or in redhibition. Thomas C. Galligan, Jr., The Louisiana Products Liability Act: Making Sense of It All, 49 La. L.Rev. 629 (1989); William Crawford, The Louisiana Products Liability Act, 36 La. B.J. 172 (1988); John Kennedy, A Primer on the Louisiana Products Liability Act, 49 La. L.Rev. 565 (1989); Revision Comments, La. C.C. art. 2545. We agree with this analysis, yet do not decide at this time whether Bearly's claim is under the LPLA, or in redhibition, or both. We will set forth the basis for the claim under both theories of recovery to show that the actual knowledge of Ranger regarding the defect is irrelevant to the viability of Bearly's claim.

¶10 In viewing the claim under the LPLA, "the manufacturer of a product shall be liable to a claimant for damage proximately caused by a characteristic of the product that renders the product unreasonably dangerous when such damage arose from a reasonably anticipated use of the product by the claimant or another person or entity." La. R.S. 9:2800.54(A). The product is unreasonably dangerous if the product is unreasonably dangerous in construction or composition. La. R.S. 9:2800.54(B)(1). This type of unreasonably dangerous condition is addressed in La. R.S. 9:2800.55, which provides:

> A product is unreasonably dangerous in construction or composition if, at the time the product left its manufacturer's control, the product deviated in a material way from the manufacturer's specifications or performance standards for the product or from otherwise identical products manufactured by the same manufacturer.

¶11 Although the use of the phrase "unreasonably dangerous" in the LPLA implies danger to the consumer or user resulting in personal injury, the Act as a whole, by its allowance for damage to the product itself and other purely economic loss, suggests that such product which does damage to itself because of its composition is "unreasonably dangerous" under the Act, subjecting the manufacturer to liability. Thus, we find that Ranger's product can be considered under the alleged facts to be in violation of La. R.S. 9:2800.55. Nevertheless, for purposes of the summary judgment ruling before us, La. R.S. 9:2800.55's definition of an unreasonably dangerous product does not require that the manufacturer have knowledge that the construction or composition of the product is defective. The liability theory underlying that section is therefore a type of strict liability, and the parties' argument over Ranger's knowledge of the defect was misplaced.

¶12 Before leaving the LPLA and considering redhibition, it must be noted that the Act provides that it "establishes the exclusive theories of liability for manufacturers for damage caused by their products." La. R.S. 9:2800.52. Ranger is a manufacturer, but it is not Bearly's seller, who under Civil Code article 2520 would warrant the buyer against redhibitory defects. Nevertheless, the Code's provisions on redhibition, which, in 1993 after the enactment of the LPLA, were revised and re-enacted, contain remedies against certain manufacturers. These redhibition remedies and their jurisprudential interpretation as to claims against manufacturers before the enactment of LPLA may be argued to conflict with the "exclusive theories of liability" provision of the LPLA. Yet, as indicated above, we need not decide that question at this stage of the proceedings. From the following review of the law of redhibition, with the assumption that the law can apply, Ranger's actual knowledge of the defect is not material to a claim in redhibition.

¶13 The two redhibition articles of the Civil Code which directly address manufacturers are Articles 2531 and 2545. Regarding the seller without knowledge of the defect, Article 2531 provides:

> A seller who is held liable for a redhibitory defect has an action against the manufacturer of the defective thing, if the defect existed at the time the thing was delivered by the manufacturer to the seller, for any loss the seller sustained because of the redhibition. Any contractual provision that attempts to limit, diminish or prevent such recovery by a seller against the manufacturer shall have no effect.

¶14 Article 2545 further provides that a seller, who is also the manufacturer of the product, is deemed to know that the thing he sells has a redhibitory defect and he is liable in redhibition.

¶15 Regardless of these limited articles, our highest court, in dealing with a clear redhibitory claim, pronounced the following in the landmark decision in Media Production Consultants, Inc. v. Mercedes-Benz of North America, Inc., 262 La. 80, 262 So.2d 377, 381 (La.1972):

> Louisiana has aligned itself with the consumer-protection rule, by allowing a consumer without privity to recover, whether the suit be strictly in tort or upon implied warranty. We see no reason why the rule should not apply to the pecuniary loss resulting from the purchase of a new automobile that proves unfit for use because of latent defects.

[Citations omitted.]

¶16   In Rey v. Cuccia, supra, the court confirmed that the Media conclusion was indeed a ruling regarding the scope of redhibition and that "the purchaser can recover the pecuniary loss resulting from the unusable thing sold from the manufacturer as well as the seller." Id. at 845.

¶17   The 1993 Revision Comments to Article 2545, again, written after the enactment of the LPLA, reflect that Media's and Rey's broad interpretation of the Code's redhibition principles still apply to a manufacturer who is not the immediate vendor of the plaintiff/vendee. Comment (i) states that "the assembler of things manufactured by another is a seller in bad faith." Comment (d) states that "the buyer may bring action against all sellers in the chain of sales back to the primary manufacturer to rescind a sale for breach of implied warranty." See also, La. C.C. art. 2548. The jurisprudence cited in support of the Revision Comments reflects that Ranger, as an alleged assembler/manufacturer without direct privity with Bearly, is nevertheless subject to claims in redhibition. Spillers v. Montgomery Ward & Co., Inc., 294 So.2d 803 (La.1974); Womack and Adcock v. 3M Business Products Sales, Inc., 316 So.2d 795 (La.App. 1st Cir.1975); see also, LeGros v. ARC Services, Inc., 03-918 (La.App. 3d Cir.2/25/04), 867 So.2d 63 and De Atley v. Victoria's Secret Catalogue, LLC, 04-0661 (La.App. 4th Cir.5/14/04), 876 So.2d 112.

¶18   From this authority, Bearly's petition reflects the allegation of a cause of action in redhibition. Accordingly, because of the manufacturer's presumed knowledge of the defect under the jurisprudential interpretation of Article 2545, Ranger's actual knowledge of the alleged defect is immaterial to Bearly's claim.

Conclusion

¶19   While we have determined that Bearly's claim states a cause of action, we leave open the question which the parties have never briefed concerning the application, vel non, of the LPLA, the law of sales and redhibition, or both bodies of law. Because of the parties' lack of articulation of the cause of action before the trial court, the court's ruling for summary judgment must be reversed. Costs of appeal are assessed to appellee.

REVERSED AND REMANDED.

In addition to delivery and warrantying against eviction, the seller has other duties, specifically three warranties dealing with the quality of the thing sold. The most widely litigated warranty is the warranty against redhibitory defects (Art. 2520), followed by the warranty that the thing delivered has the qualities and is the kind promised (Art. 2529), and the warranty of fitness (Art. 2524).

Section 1: The Differences Among the three warranties

These three implied warranties differ from each other. A redhibitory defect is one that renders the thing useless, or its use so inconvenient that it must be presumed that the buyer would not have purchased it – or if he did, it would be for a lower price. So, if the thing as delivered is defective, the warranty against redhibitory defects applies. The warranty that the thing is the kind specified in the contract is violated when the thing, as delivered, is not defective, but is not what was agreed on. So, for example, if you ordered blue suede shoes and the seller sent green suede shoes, the thing did not have the qualities agreed on. Finally, the warranty of fitness for ordinary use applies when the thing, though not defective, is not reasonably fit for its ordinary use. Art. 2524 Comment a. It is not the same as the common law concept that has the same name. In addition to the warranty of fitness for ordinary use, Article 2524 presents another implied warranty: that if a seller specifies that the thing can be used for the buyer's particular purpose which is somewhat different from the thing's ordinary use, then he is warrantying that the thing is fit for that use. To sum up: if the thing has a defect on delivery, use the warranty against redhibitory defects. If it differs from what war ordered, use the warranty of kind or quality, and if it is not defective but just not reasonably fit, then the warranty of fitness for ordinary use applies. Remedies and prescription periods differ among the three warranties – Redhibition having shorter-than-normal prescription periods.

Examples:

Nelson Radiology:

Dr. Nelson purchased a refurbished mammography unit from the defendant. When it arrived, the installer noticed that parts were bent, other parts were broken, and others simply missing. The court eventually held that the thing had at least one redhibitory defect that rendered it so unusable that the buyer would not have purchased it and the sale was dissolved. Furthermore, the remedies for redhibitory defects differ depending on whether or not the seller knew the thing had a defect. In this case, the court found that the seller knew of the defects, and therefore was bound to return the price with interest, plus reasonable expenses occasioned by the sale and needed to preserve the thing, plus damages and attorney's fees. Art. 2545.

Bo-Pic Foods v. Polyflex Film:

Plaintiff buyer was looking for a new way to wrap his potato chips, and seller indicated that though not previously used for potato chips, a new product – a light gauged metalized film would work. Plaintiff bought and paid for the film, but when it was delivered, it was found that it would not work for the purpose: it did not seal properly, and the potato chips went stale in 4 days in Louisiana's humid climate. Consequently, the buyer sued for reimbursement of the price paid. The trial court decided that the defendant was liable under redhibition law. The appellate court found instead that this was a violation of the warranty for a particular purpose: seller knew that the buyer was relying on his assurances that the film could be used for a particular purpose other than the one it was usually used for, but the film did not work. Consequently, the sale was dissolved.

Cook v. Stowe:

Plaintiffs purchased 100 cows from defendant, who warranted that they were all 3-6 years old, and 5-7 months pregnant, bred by either Angus or Charolais bulls. Unfortunately, many of the cows were not, in fact, pregnant and therefore were less valuable. Furthermore, some of them were more than 6 years old. The court found that the cows, as delivered, while not 'defective' were not of the kind or quality warranted.

Section 2: The Nature of the Redhibitory Defect

A redhibitory defect is one that 1. Exists before delivery (Art. 2530); and 2. Renders the thing sold either useless or its use "so inconvenient that it must be presumed that the buyer would not have bought the thing had he known of the defect." Art. 2520. It must not be apparent. Art. 2521.

Examples:

Apparent Defect:

Spraggins v. Lambeth:

Plaintiff first time home buyers noticed cracks in the patio and flor of the home, but were told by their realtor that they were not important and they did not need to have the home inspected. They later learned that the house had foundation problems, the roof had been damaged from Hurricane Rita, and that beams in the attic had separated and rafters were inadequately braced, and filed suit for redhibitory defects. The court held that a reasonably prudent buyer would have noticed the cracks, which were specifically noted in the disclosure form, and so as the defect was apparent, the plaintiffs had waived any claim in redhibition. The case stands for the proposition that there is no claim in redhibition where a reasonably prudent buyer would have been put on notice of a problem.

Kite Bros. v. Alexander:

The defendants, Mr. & Mrs. Alexander traded in their old Gearbox RV to plaintiff buyer Kite Brothers in October, at that time, Kite Bros. did not inspect the interior of the RV, but simply parked it in their outdoor lot pending an awning repair. One month later, Kite Brothers notified the Alexanders that the roof had been damaged, and had probably been damaged before the purchase, but they never looked in side, and they left the RV outdoors in the lot. When the awning parts arrived in February, they moved the Gearbox into the garage and finally discovered substantial deterioration inside. They then filed suit against the Alexanders for redhibitory defect. The court held that the warranty against redhibitory defects did not apply where, as here, the defects were known to the buyer or which could have been discovered by a reasonably prudent buyer – Kite Brothers had more than a reasonable opportunity to inspect the Gearbox. The court also held that neither the warranty of fitness for ordinary or particular use applied

Buyer's Burden of Proof that Defect Existed on Delivery

Rey v. Cuccia:

The plaintiff buyers purchased a camper trailer from defendant. Eight days later, they drove it to Dauphin Island, Alabama – a distance of 125 miles. On the way back to New Orleans two days later, it started swinging back and forth on the highway, and when they stopped on the shoulder of the road, the Reys found that the body had come loose from the frame, the frame had buckled, and the right rear of the trailer body was sagging to the ground, after just over 200 miles on major highways. This is one of the landmark cases in this field, and one of the first issues was whether the defect existed at the time of delivery. If the defect shows up within 3 days of delivery, the presumption is that it existed on delivery. Art 2530. The court found that as this was the first trip with the camper, it existed at the time of delivery. The case also stands for the principle that the buyer need not prove the nature of the defect, only its existence and whether or not it is so serious as to merit rescission of the contract or merely a reduction in price. The court found that the Reys had met this burden of proof.

Section 3: Good Faith and Bad Faith Sellers, Prescription

The Good Faith Seller's Reasonable Opportunity to repair: If the seller is in good faith, the buyer of a defective thing must give him an opportunity to repair, remedy, or correct the defect. If he is unable to do so, then the seller must return the price to the buyer with interest, reimburse him for reasonable expenses occasioned by the sale and any incurred for the preservation of the thing, minus a credit for any use the buyer was able to make of the thing in the interim. Art. 2531

Noted Case: Arnold v. Wray Ford:

Buyers of a customized van experienced a number of problems and returned the van to the dealer for repair on at least 11 different occasions. Court held that even assuming the seller/ manufacturer was in good faith, the buyer had given it a reasonable opportunity to repair the vehicle, repair was ineffective, and the sale should be dissolved.

Queral v. Latter & Blum

In February 1998, plaintiff Queral purchased a home. The advertisement indicated that it was custom built on pilings, and the disclosure statement indicated that no alterations had been made to the property, no building permits obtained, and the seller knew or no defects in the foundation of the home. In May or June of the same year, plaintiff noticed thin cracks in the house, and in November 1998, an A.C. repairman noticed unusual bolts in the attic that would only have been put there if a major repair had been done by an engineer. In December, plaintiffs hired a structural engineer to inspect the house, which he did on April 1, 1999, and submitted a report to them on April 5, 1999, finding that the house was not built on pilings, and though the house had settled, the slab and superstructure of the residence were in satisfactory condition.

The plaintiffs filed a petition alleging a redhibitory defect on April 4, 2000 alleging a redhibitory defect of the foundation that the disclosure statement was fraudulent.

The court held that the plaintiffs' claim was not prescribed. A good faith claim would have prescribed, as it was more than one year since delivery, but the plaintiffs were alleging bad faith, and their discovery of the alleged defect was on April 5, 1999, when they received the report from the structural engineer. Therefore, the April 4, 2000 filing was not untimely. (However, it is not clear from the opinion as to whether or not the court is likely to find a redhibitory defect)

David v. Thibodeaux – Termites & Partial Redhibition

The plaintiffs purchased a home from the defendant on April 26, 2000. Before the sale, the buyers visually inspected the premises, and they obtained a termite report and disclosure statement which showed that termite damage had been discovered and repaired in 1990, and that old termite damage were discovered in three locations. Thibodeaux showed the locations and the repairs to the buyer. After moving in, the plaintiffs discovered new termite infestation when the porch collapsed. The court found that had they known of the infestation, the plaintiffs would still have purchased the home but (they had inspected the home 4 times) and that the seller had been in good faith.

Consequently, the seller is bound to repair, remedy, or correct the defect, and the buyers had not yet given her that opportunity. Estimates indicated that repairs would cost approximately $25,622, consequently, the court reduced the purchase price in that amount, subject to the $24,000 credit Ms. Thibodeaux had received in settling her arbitration with Terminix and which was used towards the repairs.

The Bad Faith Seller:

In contrast with the good faith seller who must be given an opportunity to repair the defect, a bad faith seller is not owed such an opportunity and owes enhanced damages. A bad faith seller is one who knows that the thing he sells has a defect but omits declaring itm or declares that the thing has a quality that he knows it does not have. The manufacturer of a defective thing is presumed to be in bad faith. Art 2545.

In addition to reimbursing the price paid with interest from the date it was paid, and reimbursing reasonable expenses occasioned by the sale and those incurred for the preservation of the thing, a bad faith seller also owes damages and reasonable attorney's fees.

Prescription Periods Under Redhibition

Article 2534 sets out the prescriptive periods for redhibition. They are shorter than those for the warranties of kind or quality and warranty of fitness for ordinary use in order to encourage the buyer of a defective thing to act quickly.

Movables & Good Faith: The action against a good faith seller of a movable prescribes four years from delivery or one year from discovery, whichever is first.

Immovables & Good Faith: The action against a good faith seller of a residential or commercial immovable prescribes one year from delivery.

Bad Faith: The action against a bad faith seller of either a movable or an immovable prescribes one year from discovery.

Tolling of Prescription for Repairs: Prescription is interrupted when the seller accepts the thing for repairs and begins again when he tenders it back to the buyer, refuses to repair it, or is unable to repair it.

Rey v. Cuccia redux – manufacturer's liability

In Rey, the plaintiffs were claiming that their brand-new camper trailer had a redhibitory defect because it collapsed on the highway. This section of the opinion deals with the issue of the cause of the failure and whose fault it was. The cause of the failure seems to have been the improper installation of the hitch, but it could also be that defective welding of the frame contributed to the failure. As with eviction, the buyer is subrogated to the rights in warranty of the seller against other persons. Art 2548. In this case, Rey sued Cuccia as well as the manufacturer, Yellowstone, who had sold the trailer to Cuccia more than a year before the sale to Rey. It is not clear that the defect existed at the time the trailer was sold to Cuccia, though it is clear that it did exist when the trailer was sold to Rey, so it's not clear that Rey is subrogated to Cuccia's claim. However, Rey has his own direct claim against the manufacturer under Media Productions which held that the implied warranty against redhibitory defects is enforceable directly against the manufacturer, and the manufacturer is presumed to be in bad faith. While Yellowstone did not install the hitch (Cuccia did), and its manual specified that it should be installed 18 inches above the ground, it did not warn against installing it higher than that – which an expert witness testified would (and did) result in dire consequences.

The court held that both the retailer and Yellowstone were responsible for the defect, and thus were both in bad faith, both solidarily liable to Rey, and both owed attorney's fees as well as reimbursement of the price of the trailer, costs, & etc.

Section 4: Waiver of Warranty

The Eviction waiver is complicated (remember – two levels, even if waived, evicted buyer gets reimbursed the price unless has bought at own risk and peril, affirmatively knew of the risk, or reimbursement is explicitly excluded). In contrast, the waiver of the warranty against red-hibitory defects is straight-forward. Article 2548 stipulates that the terms of the exclusion or limitation of the warranty must be clear and unambiguous and brought to the buyer's attention. Many such clauses stipulate that the sale is "As Is Where Is." As with eviction, however, if the seller lies or is in bad faith, claiming that the thing had a quality he knew it did not have, then any such waiver is null.

Shelton v. Standard/700

Plaintiff Shelton purchased a condominium that was situated just below the building's roof-top swimming pool. The act of sale stipulated that it was "AS IS WHERE IS," in all capital letters accompanied by an explicit explanation of what that meant. When the pool started leaking into her condo, plaintiff nevertheless filed an action in redhibition, claiming that the seller had lied. No one who represented the building testified that they had any knowledge of any leaking problems, and the only evidence that the Plaintiff provided was that "someone must have known." The court found in the defendant's favor.

Section 5: Subrogation

As mentioned previously under Article 2548, the buyer is subrogated to the rights in warranty of the seller against other persons, even when the warranty is excluded. It is because of this provision that the Aizpurua decision was odd – it was a redhibition case, but was decided under the subrogation provision in the Civil Code's chapter on Eviction, instead of the appropriate provision in Article 2548.

Media Production v. Mercedes-Benz of North America

Along with Rey v. Cuccia, this is one of the most known of Louisiana cases on redhibition. Plaintiff Media Production purchased a new Mercedes-Benz from Cookies' auto sales. The car had been manufactured in Germany, and was imported into the U.S. by defendant MBNA. The car came with a 24,000 warranty and a warranty disclaimer that stipulated that it was in lieu of all other warranties and representations, expressed or implied. Cookie's included the same disclaimer in the Service Policy it delivered with the car.

The car was defective: the interior trim peeled off, interior lights did not work, transmission problems, stalling in traffic, defective air conditioning, excessive brake squeal, deterioration of rear window channels, uncorrectable vibration, pain problems. After trying to get the problems corrected unsuccessfully, Media surrendered the car to an authorized dealer (Cookies had gone out of business).

The Louisiana Supreme Court held that 1. Limitation provisions in such Service Policies have no effect on the statutory warranty of fitness; 2. Cookie's is liable to Media Production for the sale of a car with a redhibitory defect, and 3. Media Production is subrogated to Cookie's rights against MBNA, and MBNA stands in the position of the manufacturer because it was the entity that introduced the car into the U.S. stream of commerce. The court held, therefore, that MBNA was solidarily liable with Cookies for the price of the automobile and other allowable expenses.

Aucoin v. Southern Quality Homes

Aucoin purchased a mobile home and land from SQH in 2001. The mobile home had been manufactured by Dynasty homes in 2000. Although the pre-occupancy inspection report listed numerous defects, SQH assured the plaintiff that they were minor and would be repaired, however, after delivery and set-up, there were numerous defects, the primary being mold caused by moisture infiltration – the two halves of the home had not been properly sealed, nor had the roof been properly installed, the vinyl siding was improperly installed, as was the drywall on the ceiling.

The primary issue was the allocation of liability among SQH and Dynasty. Plaintiff's expert testified that the problem was caused primarily by manufacturing problems, defendant claimed that the problem was improper marriage installation by the installer hired by the seller. The trial court found both defendants at fault. The seller had filed for bankruptcy. The trial court held the manufacturer and the seller solidarily liable, and that holding was affirmed by the trial court.

The Supreme Court found that 1. Mercedes Benz held that a buyer can recover directly from the manufacturer for breach of warranty, despite the fact that there was no privity of contract between them; and 2. Rey v. Cuccia held the manufacturer solidarily liable with the seller for a redhibitory defect which existed at the time of the sale. Furthermore, 3. A manufacturer is independently liable for redhibitory defects that exist at the time of delivery to the seller. In which case, the seller has an action against the manufacturer for those defects. The Louisiana Manufactured Housing Act does not change this. The only change made was that the manufacturer was not liable for reimbursement of the money paid for the land – the plaintiff still held title to the land, it was not defective, and it was not a "matched thing" (under Art 2540, redhibition lies when more than one thing are sold together as a whole such that the buyer would not have bought one thing without the other.

A question that has arisen in some appellate courts is whether such liability is solidary or whether it should be assessed under a comparative fault scheme, but Supreme Court jurisprudence seems pretty consistently pointing towards solidary liability as this cause of action is based primarily in contract, not tort.

Ciliberti v. Mistretti

The Cilibertis purchased a home from the Mistrettis in 2003, only to find out soon thereafter that the house had a severe sewerage problem – with sewerage gasses being present at all times within the residence, caused by a blockage. The home had been built by Bestbuilt Homes in 1996, and Bestbuilt was brought in as a third party defendant. Bestbuilt claimed that the claim against it had prescribed under the New Home Warranty Act, which provides the exclusive remedy for homeowners against a home builder. That act provides a one-year prescriptive period for defects in fit and finish and building standards, two years for plumbing, electricity, and heating systems, and five years for foundational problems. The problem here falls squarely in the two year period. Consequently, the builder (who cause the problem) is excluded from liability under the New Home Warranty Act and dismissed from the case, leaving the seller, Mistretti, as the only one that Ciliberti can sue in redhibition.

Section 6: Redhibition and Other Remedies

Redhibition can be combined with other causes of action, in particular, strict liability for design, manufacturing, and warning defects. The difference is that strict liability provides remedies for personal injury, while redhibition provides a remedy against a manufacturer for the thing itself. In apportioning attorney's fees (which are awarded under both strict products liability and bad-faith redhibition claims), the court must apportion according to the amount of work done on each kind of claim.

De Atley v. Victoria's Secret

Plaintiff De Atley purchased a cotton dress from Victoria's Secret, which caught fire when she stood next to a fireplace. She was severely injured and brought suit under both strict liability for design defect and redhibition. The court held that Ms. De Atley can move forward with both claims.

Drearly v. Brunswick Mercury

Plaintiff purchased a boat and motor for bass fishing. The two components were manufactured by different companies but were assembled by the boat manufacturer and sold wholesale to the defendant Dealer. The plaintiff immediately began experiencing problems with the motor, had it repaired several times, and eventually filed suit. Apparently, defendant boat manufacturer was aware that the two (boat and motor) could not be combined together because the motor was a performance engine and not suitable for extended idling required of a bass boat. In addition to alleging redhibition, the plaintiff also alleged that the combination was unreasonably dangerous in construction or composition – though he was not injured.

At trial, the parties debated whether or not the seller had notified the boat manufacturer that the Mercury motor was an improper choice for its boat, but that is irrelevant where the manufacturer is presumed to have knowledge that his product is defective (whether under strict products liability or redhibition). The court reversed the court's summary judgment, pointing out that that the party who assembles such a defective product may be viewed as a manufacturer as discussed in comments to Articles 2545 and 2548.

COMBINATION HYPOTHETICAL

This hypothetical, drawn from a final exam, includes redhibition, eviction, and extent of the premises.

Brandi Buyer purchased a home located in Hammond along with farmland in December, 2015 from Samuel Seller: she paid $500,000 for the home, listed in the act of sale as "Samuel Place." In a separate Act of Sale, confected on the same day, she paid $100,000 for the farmland, on which she plans to raise habanero peppers. The land was described as "100 acres at $1,000 per acre." Brandi is especially pleased with Samuel Place because it had been designed by a famous California architect, who had developed a kind of roof that used extensive skylights to provide large amounts of natural light. Conny's Construction Company built it in 2009, using a roof system manufactured by Roofus Roofs.

Brandi was thrilled when she moved in – especially because she learned that the home was really worth $1,100,000! Unfortunately, her joy was short-lived. It is now November, 2017, and she has been through a lot! The eccentric next door neighbor, Martha, showed her a document signed by Sam in 2004, that granted her a right of first refusal, claiming that the land on which the house is built is actually hers because Sam never offered it to her before selling it to Brandi. Brandi paid Martha $10,000 to give up any claim she might have in the property. Furthermore, Sam is now demanding that she pay him an additional $500,000. On top of all this, Brandi had a surveyor check the farmland, and learned that she only has 90 acres, not 100.

In addition to the ownership problems, Brandi has had maintenance problems – especially with the roof. This design was not well adapted to Louisiana's wet climate, and requires frequent repairs to fix leaks, especially after exposure to high winds during tropical storms. Susan discovered this in October, 2017: she hired a roof engineering expert, who issued a report which advised that the problem could be fixed, but only with an extensive and expensive reworking of the roof that would eliminate most of the skylights, at a cost of almost $600,000. The expert believes that Sam knew about the roofing problems because he found evidence that extensive repairs had been done (and hidden) by cosmetic refinishing and painting. When she asked Sam about it, he denied any knowledge of roof problems, that he had not experienced any leaks while he owned the house, and he insisted on hiring his own expert who says that while there are some problems, but they can be fixed for a mere $60,000. Brandi even contacted Conny's Construction Company, who say they were assured by California Roofers that, though not originally designed for Louisiana weather, Roofus Roofs claimed it would work and even installed it themselves to make sure it was done right. Consequently, they deny any and all responsibility for the roof.

2.1 (50 points) Can Brandi demand that Sam repay her the $10,000 she paid to Martha on the basis that she was evicted from the property?

2.2 (20 points) Is Sam likely to win a suit based on the discrepancy between what Martha paid for the house and its value?

2.3 (30 points) Can Brandi demand that Sam pay back some of the money she paid for the farmland, and if so, how much?

2.4 (50 points) What rights does Brandi have against Sam due to the problems with the roof?

2.5 (50 points) Does Brandi have any rights against Conny's Construction or Roofus Roofs?

CHAPTER 11

THE BUYER'S OBLIGATIONS AND SELLER'S REMEDIES

Flowchart

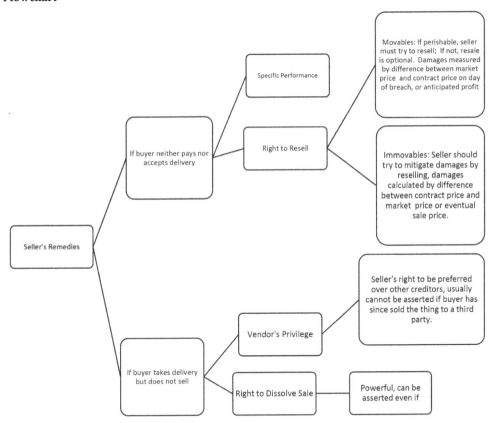

Introduction

Read Articles 2549 through 2564 and 2611 through 2615.

As Chapter 9 showed, the seller is obligated to deliver the thing sold, to warrant the buyer against eviction, to warrant that the thing is free of redhibitory defects, to warrant that it is fit for use, and to warrant that it has the qualities stipulated in the contract. The buyer's obligations are simpler: he must pay the price and take delivery of the thing sold (Art. 2549). If the buyer fails to fulfill either of these obligations, the seller may pursue either specific performance (La. Civ. Code arts. 1986-1988), or dissolution (Arts. 2561), but not both. The seller who is pursuing specific performance may also – like any obligee – seek moratory damages (Arts. 1989-1993), and the seller pursuing dissolution may seek compensatory damages. A third type of remedy the vendor may use is the vendor's privilege or other security rights he may have put in place at the time of the sale.

Section 1: The Buyer's Obligations to Take Delivery and Pay and the Seller's Right of Resale

The buyer is bound to pay the price and take delivery of the thing at the time and place stipulated in the contract. Art. 2549-2550. If the contract does not stipulate where and when payment is due, then it is due at the time and place of delivery. If he fails to pay at the time payment is due, then the buyer owes interest from that date. Furthermore, if he either fails to pay or fails to take delivery, then he is liable for expenses incurred by the seller in preserving the thing, as well as any damages incurred by the seller. Art. 2555. Damages are measured by the loss sustained by the obligee and the profit of which he has been deprived, additionally consequential damages vary in scope depending on whether the obligor's failure to perform was in good faith or bad faith. Arts. 1995-1997. A good faith obligor is liable only for damages that were foreseeable at the time of contracting, while a bad-faith obligor is liable for all damages, foreseeable or not, that are a direct consequence of his failure to perform.

Study Questions:

What remedies did the sellers choose to pursue when the buyers refused to accept delivery in the following cases?

How were damages calculated?

a. Movables

FRIEDMAN IRON & SUPPLY CO. V. J.B. BEAIRD CO. 1953
222 LA. 627, 63 SO. 2D 144

HAWTHORNE, Justice.

¶1 Plaintiff, Friedman Iron and Supply Company, instituted this suit against J. B. Beaird Company, Inc., praying that the defendant be judicially ordered and condemned to accept delivery of 500 tons of scrap steel at $41 per ton and to pay the sum of $20,500, and praying in the alternative for damages against the defendant for breach of the contract to purchase the steel.

¶2 Plaintiff's suit for specific performance was dismissed on exception of no cause of action and has now been abandoned by plaintiff. In due course, after trial on the merits, the lower court rendered judgment denying plaintiff's alternative plea for damages and dismissing its suit. Plaintiff has appealed.

¶3 The record in this case clearly establishes that during the month of February, 1949, plaintiff and defendant entered into a binding contract by which plaintiff was to sell to defendant 500 tons of scrap steel at a price of $41 per gross ton, to be delivered on various dates as specified by the defendant in its acceptance of plaintiff's offer to sell. The record also discloses that on March 7, 1949, defendant notified plaintiff not to ship any of the scrap steel until requested in writing so to do, and, according to defendant, on March 8 it cancelled in writing its order for the purchase of this scrap steel in its entirety. On March 12 plaintiff requested the defendant to accept the scrap steel which it had purchased, assembled, stockpiled, and allocated for sale to the defendant. Defendant refused to accept the steel and pay the purchase price, and plaintiff instituted this suit.

¶4 In its petition plaintiff alleged that it had retained the entire 500 tons of scrap steel on its yard, segregated, stockpiled, and allocated to fill the contract order with defendant; that this amount of steel so segregated, stockpiled, and allocated on its yard was awaiting shipment to defendant, and that delivery had been tendered and refused.

***

On Rehearing

PONDER, Justice.

¶1 The plaintiff contends that we erred in using the market value of scrap steel at the date of the trial as a criterion in determining whether it had suffered a loss or been deprived of a profit as a result of the defendant's breach of contract. The plaintiff takes the position that the true measure of damages is the difference between the contract price and the market price of the scrap steel on the date the contract was breached.

¶2 The defendant purchased 500 tons of scrap steel from the plaintiff at a price of $41 per gross ton, to be delivered in carload lots on specified dates between April 4 and June 6, 1949. On March 8, 1949, prior to the delivery of the scrap steel, the defendant notified the plaintiff, by letter, that it was cancelling the order in its entirety. On March 12th, the plaintiff requested the defendant to accept the scrap steel and the defendant thereafter refused to accept it or pay the purchase price. In this suit the plaintiff is seeking to recover damages for the breach of the contract.

¶3 Under the provisions of Article 1934, LSA-Civil Code, the damages due the plaintiff for the defendant's breach of the contract is the amount of the loss the plaintiff has sustained and the profit of which it has been deprived, except, in the absence of fraud or bad faith, the defendant is liable only for such damages as were contemplated or may have reasonably been supposed to have entered into the contemplation of the parties at the time the contract was entered into. It is presumed, in the sale of personal property, that the parties contemplated the difference between the contract price of the thing sold and the market value at the time and place at which it was to be delivered when they entered into the contract. Robinson Lumber Company v. W. O. & C. G. Burton, 128 La. 120, 54 So. 582 and the authorities cited therein. This court has on numerous occasions pointed out that the measure of damages for the breach of a contract of sale, where no fraud is shown, is the difference between the contract price and the market price of the goods on the date of the breach. See Interstate Electric Company v. Frank Adam Electric Company, 173 La. 103, 136 So. 283 and the authorities cited therein to that effect. This rule of law is based on solid grounds because neither a plaintiff nor a defendant should be permitted to select the market value of a date different from that on which the contract was breached for the purpose of determining whether any loss was suffered or profit deprived to the detriment of either party. The facts in this case amply demonstrate the reasonableness of and the necessity for this rule. The defendant breached its contract when it saw the market for scrap steel was rapidly declining. At the time the suit was tried, more than a year after the contract had been breached, the price for scrap steel had advanced in excess of the price called for in the contract. The record shows that scrap steel had continued to decline for more than two months after the contract was breached but it does not show when the prices took an upward trend. If the suit had been tried at an earlier date when the market price of steel might have been on the further decline, the defendant's liability would have been greater if the value of the steel at the date of the trial was to be used as a criterion in determining whether the plaintiff had suffered a loss or been deprived of a profit. If such were to be used as a criterion, the rights of the parties would depend on conditions arising at an uncertain future date. In fact, it would leave the rights of the parties uncertain and encourage litigants to jockey for a trial on a date when the market was favorable. The rule, that the measure of damages for the breach of the sale of personal property is the difference between the contract price and the market price at the date of the breach of the contract, is a salutary one and does not depend on uncertain events that may occur sometime in the future.

¶4 There is dispute in the evidence as to the date the contract was breached but we have arrived at the conclusion that the plaintiff received notice of the cancellation of the contract on March 9, 1949. This is borne out by the fact that the plaintiff consulted attorneys as to its rights under the contract within three or four days after that date. While there is dispute as to the market value of the scrap steel on March 9th, we have reached the conclusion that the testimony produced by the plaintiff, based on the trade journal 'The Iron Age', which is the accepted trade journal of the iron and steel industry, that the price quotations for scrap steel listed from date to date therein are accepted in the trade as being reliable and authentic and that they serve as a basis for the buying and selling of scrap steel. This publication bases its prices on the Pittsburgh market, which is the center of the buying and consuming of scrap steel, and, of course, if these prices are to be the guide it is necessary to deduct the freight charges from Shreveport to Pittsburgh in order to determine the value of this scrap steel now located in Shreveport. On March 9, 1949, No. 1 scrap steel was listed at $36.50 to $37 per ton and phosphate steel was listed at $42 to $43 per ton. The scrap steel specified in the contract involved herein is a type of scrap especially selected and prepared for small electric furnaces similar to that of defendant's which has no premium value to large mills and according to the testimony of the expert witness, who testified in behalf of the plaintiff, it is bought and sold in the market as No. 1 steel except when there exists a scarcity of scrap steel which compels the Pittsburgh buyer to pay the premium low phosphate price in order to obtain the scrap steel. At the time the contract was breached, the market was declining rapidly and a seller could only expect to receive the prevailing price of No. 1 steel. The highest price for No. 1 steel at Pittsburgh on the date of the breach was $37 per ton and the cost of freight to ship it to the Pittsburgh market on that date was $13.3248 per ton. Under the contract the defendant was to pay $41 per ton for the scrap steel. At the date of the breach of the contract, the steel was worth $37 per ton at Pittsburgh. Deducting the freight charges from Shreveport to Pittsburgh of $13.3248, the steel would have had a market value at Shreveport of $23.6752 per ton. The contract price called for $41 per ton. After deducting the present market value at Shreveport, the plaintiff suffered a loss of $17.3248 per ton on the steel. The contract calling for 500 tons, the loss suffered by the defendant would be $8,662.40. The plaintiff is entitled to recover this amount as it is the difference between the contract price and the market value of the steel at the date the contract was breached.

¶5   Under the provisions of Articles 1932 and 1933, LSA-Civil Code, damages are due from the moment that there is an active violation of the contract and the creditor is not under obligation to place the debtor in default, but when the breach is passive only it is necessary to place the debtor in default. Irrespective of whether the cancellation of the contract is considered as an active violation or a passive violation of the contract, there would be no necessity to place the defendant in default because it would have been a vain and useless thing after the defendant had notified the plaintiff that it did not intend to comply with the contract by ordering its cancellation.

¶6   For the reasons assigned, the decree heretofore handed down is reversed and set aside. The judgment of the district court is reversed and set aside. It is ordered, adjudged and decreed that there be judgment in favor of the plaintiff and against the defendant in the sum of $8,662.40 with legal interest from judicial demand. All costs to be paid by the defendant. The right to apply for a rehearing is reserved to defendant.

[The dissenting opinions are omitted, as is the opinion on second rehearing, which reduced the damages awarded.]

LEON GODCHAUX CLOTHING CO. V. DEBUYS 1929
120 SO. 539 (LA. APP. ORL. CIR.)

JONES, J.

¶1   This is an attachment suit brought on January 5, 1928, against defendant, alleged to be a resident of the city of Los Angeles, for the sum of $169.68, the unpaid purchase price of two dresses sold and delivered by plaintiff to defendant. The itemized account attached to plaintiff's petition and made a part thereof reads as follows:

May 2/27	
1 Dress	$99. 50
1 Dress	69. 50
Postage & Ins	. 68
	$169. 68

¶2 A curator ad hoc was appointed to represent the absent defendant and a writ of attachment issued and interrogatories were duly served on Stafford, Derbes & Roy, Inc., a local real estate firm. It answered that it did not know the defendant, but that it had sold on the 15th day of January, 1926, to defendant, 104 lots of ground in the parish of Jefferson, for the sum of $8,112, and had received a cash payment of $1,100, with mortgage notes for the balance. Defendant had, since that time, made an additional payment of $1,500, leaving a balance due of $5,181, with interest.

¶3 The curator ad hoc filed an answer on January 14, denying the allegations on information and belief.

¶4 On March 1, 1928, the defendant filed exceptions to the citation and to the attachment, which exceptions were overruled, and later, on April 4, 1928, defendant answered denying the allegations of plaintiff's petition specifically.

¶5 There was judgment for plaintiff as prayed, recognizing plaintiff's lien, and ordering that the property held by the garnishee be sold and petitioner's claim be paid by preference out of the proceeds.

¶6 Defendant has appealed to this court.

¶7 The evidence shows that on May 2, 1927, defendant, after trying on several dresses at plaintiff's store without satisfaction, ordered the two dresses, the price of which is herein claimed, to be sent down from New York City. Though defendant was told at the time that it would take two or three weeks to make delivery of the dresses, she insisted on ordering them. Accordingly the order was at once telegraphed by plaintiff to the manufacturing firm with which it did business in New York, and shortly thereafter the order was confirmed by letter. In about three weeks the dresses were received by plaintiff in this city, and an unsuccessful attempt was made to deliver them at the residence which defendant had given in this city. On the next day the woman who had sold the dresses telephoned defendant's alleged residence and was told that defendant had left for Los Angeles. Thereupon plaintiff secured defendant's address in Los Angeles and sent the dresses to her in that city by parcel post C. O. D. They were refused, and were returned to New Orleans. After an exchange of letters between plaintiff and defendant, plaintiff sent the dresses parcel post C. O. D. again to defendant in Los Angeles, but they were again refused. After another unsuccessful attempt had been made to deliver them in this city, this suit was filed.

¶8 Plaintiff's manager testifies that the dresses conformed in all respects to the order.

¶9 In this court defendant argues vehemently that plaintiff has not followed the right procedure. The dresses, she contends, should have been sold, and defendant should then have been sued for the loss occasioned by her breach of the contract. In support of this contention, she cites articles 1934 and 2555, R. C. C., H. T. Cottam & Co. v. Moises, 149 La. 305, 88 So. 916, and many other decisions of the appellate courts of this state.

¶10 It is thus seen that defendant contends that the sole remedy of a seller, where the buyer refuses to take delivery of movable goods, is a suit for damages after selling the goods. Such a contention is not sustained by the authorities. The case most relied on by defendant is that of H. T. Cottam & Co. v. Moises. supra, where merchandise had been sold by the grocery firm of Cottam Company to purchasers in South America, in which the Supreme Court held that the seller may sell the goods at auction or at private sale, and then sue for the balance. All the other decisions are in cases where sales had been made and damages sued for, but not one of them sustains his contention that the sole remedy is If the vendee refuses to accept delivery, the vendor becomes the "negotiorum gestor" of the vendee, and must administer the thing sold like a good administrator. If the thing sold is of a perishable nature, he must sell it within a reasonable time and credit the vendee with the proceeds of sale and sue for the balance of the price; but, if the thing sold is not perishable, he may pursue one of two courses in order to minimize the loss on both sides-either sell it, or hold it and take reasonable care of it. Gilly et al. v. Henry, 8 Mart. (O. S.) 416, 13 Am. Dec. 291; White v. Kearney, 9 Rob. 495; Id., 2 La. Ann. 639; Benton v. Bidault, 6 La. Ann. 30; Judd Oil Co. v. Kearney, 14 La. Ann. 352; Pothier's Contract of Sale, § 280. But the course above indicated fixes the amount of the vendor's claim only when he chooses to sue for damages. He may elect between one of these actions. When the vendee fails to accept delivery of the thing sold, the vendor, according to Louisiana law, may sue him for the price (R. C. C. 2549), or for the rescission of the sale (R. C. C. 2561), or for damages (R. C. C. 2555).

***

¶11 It is only where the thing sold is perishable that the law makes it the duty of the vendor to sell the thing, on the principle that the creditor must use every means to minimize his own loss and that of the debtor. In every other case, where the thing is not perishable, the right is optional with the creditor. In the present case the burden was on the defendant to prove that a sale for a reasonable price could have been effected by the plaintiff at private or at public sale, and within a reasonable time. The defense has offered no evidence on that point, and the presumption is it could not be done, since defendant's dresses had to be sent from New York.

¶12 The articles of our Code are taken almost literally from the Code Napoleon. The authors say that the duty of the vendor to sell or sue for specific performance is optional with vendor.

***

¶13   Such was the interpretation given to R. C. C. art. 2551, by this court on rehearing in the case of L'Hote Lumber Mfg. Co. v. Dugue, 2 Orl. App. 308, where the plaintiff obtained judgment against the defendant for the price of lumber, delivery of which the defendant refused to accept or to pay for.

¶14   The last expression of the Supreme Court on this point is found in the very recent case of Mutual Rice Co. of La. v. Star Bottling Works, 163 La. 159, 111 So. 661. In the last paragraph of its decision, the court uses the following words:

> "It is argued on behalf of appellant that, according to articles 2551, 2556, and 2462 of the Civil Code, when a buyer breaches the contract of sale, the seller has the option either to resell the property and bring an action in damages for the difference between the contract price and the price actually received, or to demand specific performance by tendering the property at the stipulated time and place of delivery and suing for the contract price. The right to demand specific performance in such cases is not appropriate to a sale of merchantable goods, like sugar, which is quoted every day on the commercial exchanges throughout the world, because in such case it is the duty of the seller to lighten his loss-or avoid it altogether if possible-by selling the goods on the open market as soon as practicable after the contract has been breached."

¶15   The court here distinctly recognizes that the seller has the option either to resell the property and bring an action in damages for loss, or to demand specific performance. In this case the plaintiff has exercised the option of suing for specific performance after it had taken every possible step to comply with its contract, and defendant had prevented it from doing so.

¶16   For above reasons, the judgment appealed from is affirmed.

Lagniappe Questions:

In the previous two cases, rather than dissolve the sales, the sellers chose to sue for damages or specific performance. Remember that, under Article 2022, "[e]ither party to a commutative contract may refuse to perform his obligation if the other has failed to perform or does not offer to perform his own at the same time, if the performances are due simultaneously."

Why did the sellers not simply regard the contracts as dissolved and look to sell the goods to a third party? Could they have done so?

b. Immovables

The previous cases dealt with goods that were not perishable, and which the seller kept in his possession pending the court's decision. The sellers were not obligated to do this, even though an obligee cannot sue for nonperformance unless she is ready, willing, and able to perform – Art. 1993. However, pursuant to Articles 2611, which applies specifically to sales, if the buyer fails to perform, the seller may resell the object of the sale if it's in his possession. In such a case, the seller will be entitled to recover the difference between the contract price and the resale price, in addition to consequential damages minus any costs avoided or expenses saved as a result of the buyer's failure to perform. In reselling the things, the seller must be in good faith, must resell only after a reasonable time has passed, and must have given the buyer reasonable notice of the public sale at which the things will be resold or of his intention to resell the things at a private sale. If the things are perishable, naturally, the seller's duty to wait is modified to a reasonable period under the circumstances.

Article 2612 provides the seller with yet another remedy where the buyer refuses to accept delivery of movable things: the seller may request court authority to put the things out of his possession and at the buyer's risk, after having given the buyer the appropriate notice.

Study Question:

Article 2611 provides a measure for damages when the seller resells a movable pending resolution of a claim against a buyer who refuses to accept delivery. But does the following case indicate any difference in measure of damages against the nonperforming buyer of an immovable?

DORSETT V. JOHNSON 2001
786 SO.2D 897 (LA.APP. 2D CIR.)

DREW, J.

¶1 Seller of home appeals judgment awarding seller only buyer's $500 deposit after buyer breached contract to purchase home. We amend the judgment to provide for an award of attorney fees, and as amended, the judgment is affirmed.

FACTS

¶2 Debra Dorsett and her brother Madison Formby were co-owners of a home in Bossier City. Dorsett owned a 7/8 interest in the home; Formby owned the remaining 1/8 interest. In 1996, the home was placed on the market for sale. An appraisal performed in May, 1996 showed the home had an appraised value of $94,000, subject to certain repairs. This FHA appraisal required a termite treatment certificate, replacement of rotten decking on the rear porch, a new roof over the rear porch, replacement of broken glass on the rear porch, removal of a deteriorated shed from the yard, filling of holes dug by dogs in the yard and the replacement of a broken shower door with safety glass.

¶3 On April 22, 1996, Gary and Nancy Johnson signed an agreement to purchase the home in as/is condition for $93,700. Closing was to occur before May 29, 1996, but was extended to June 7, 1996. The Johnsons performed a walk-through inspection on June 1. Five days later, the Johnsons received a letter from their insurer informing them that he would not insure the home because of a problem with the roof that he observed. The Johnson then refused to execute the closing documents. Mr. Johnson declined to use another insurer because he wanted to use his old insurer. He also never offered to allow the sellers additional time to repair the roof.

¶4 In June of 1996, Dorsett and Formby filed suit against the Johnsons, seeking damages, attorney's fees, court costs and the release of the Johnsons' $500 deposit that was being held by the Louisiana Real Estate Commission. Formby died while this suit was pending. Dorsett refinanced her mortgage on the house in November of 1996. The house was eventually sold to another party for $85,000 in May of 1998. The property had been appraised at $85,000 at that time.

¶5 Trial was held in this matter on July 16, 1999. The trial court ruled in favor of Dorsett on the issue of liability, finding that the Johnsons had breached the Buy/Sell agreement. Because Madison Formby had died prior to the time of trial, the court reduced damages by 1/8, Formby's ownership interest. The court ordered the Johnsons' $500 deposit to be released to Dorsett. The trial court found that Madison Formby had agreed to pay Dorsett a total of $8,400 as rent for living in the house after the breach.

¶6 The trial judge ruled that Dorsett was entitled to the difference between the contract price and the market value on the date of the breach. While there was no evidence of the property's market value on the exact date of the breach, the property had been appraised at $94,000 less than a month before the breach. The court concluded that Dorsett suffered no damages in this regard as the property was appraised for a value higher than the contract price. Because Dorsett refinanced her mortgage after the sale fell through, she was entitled to damages of $7,636.81 for the interest she paid on the mortgage, to be reduced by 1/8 (Formby's interest) and the number of months Formby lived in the house and it was taken off the market. The court denied Dorsett's claim for travel expenses, lost wages and long distance telephone call expenses incurred after the breach because these expenses were litigation expenses and not damages directly resulting from the breach. Dorsett was also not allowed to recover for expenses that improved or enhanced the property.

¶7   The trial court ultimately concluded that Dorsett was not entitled to any damages because the $8,400 in rent she received offset the interest she paid on the refinanced mortgage. No attorney fees were awarded as no evidence was introduced at trial to establish the amount of attorney fees. The court also denied the appraiser's $240 fee for testifying because he did not testify as an expert witness.

DISCUSSION

Measure of Damages

¶8   Appellant first argues that the trial court erred in determining that the appellants were only entitled to the difference between the market value of the house on the date of the sale and the contract price, based on this court's decision in Lockhart v. Sutton, 503 So.2d 1046 (La.App. 2d Cir.1987). Relying on Nesbitt v. Dunn, 28,240 (La.App.2d Cir.4/3/96), 672 So.2d 226, Dorsett contends that she is entitled to the difference between the contract price and the amount for which the house was eventually sold.

¶9   La. C.C. art.1995 provides that damages are measured by the loss sustained by the obligee and the profit of which he has been deprived. The measure of damages is clear when the sale involves a movable. See La. C.C. art. 2611, which provides that if the seller resells movables after the buyer fails to perform a contract of sale, then the seller is entitled to recover the difference between the contract price and the resale price.

¶10   In Lockhart, the buyer breached a contract to purchase a home for $76,000. Thirteen months later, the house was sold for $61,500. This court stated that the correct measure of damages for the breach of a contract to sell a home, in addition to the expenses incurred as a result of the breach, is the difference between the contract price and the market value of the object of the contract on the date of the breach. Id., 503 So.2d at 1049. Cited in support of this standard were Womack v. Sternberg, 247 La. 566, 172 So.2d 683 (1965) and Eanes v. McKnight, 251 So.2d 491 (La.App. 1st Cir.1971), aff'd 262 La. 915, 265 So.2d 220 (1972).

¶11   Citing Lockhart, the Third Circuit used this same test to measure damages for the breach of a contract to purchase a supermarket building in Vallot v. Champagne, 583 So.2d 549 (La.App. 3rd Cir.), writ denied, 588 So.2d 108 (La.1991). There was apparently no subsequent sale of the supermarket in Vallot. We recognize that the Third Circuit later used a different test in Natali v. Froeba, 98-1354 (La.App. 3rd Cir.3/3/99), 735 So.2d 30, writ denied, 99-1442 (La.9/17/99), 747 So.2d 1106, finding that the plaintiffs were entitled to the difference between the contract price and the later sale price of a tract of land. The Natali court cited Bordelon v. Kopicki, 524 So.2d 847 (La.App. 3rd Cir.1988) in support of this position, without distinguishing Vallot.

¶12 This court concluded in Nesbitt that the trial court did not err in awarding the difference between the contract price and the amount for which the property was subsequently sold. However, we note that no jurisprudence or law was cited in Nesbitt to support this departure from the measure of damages utilized in Lockhart. Therefore, we conclude that the trial court properly used the measure of damages set forth in Lockhart.

Damages

¶13 Dorsett next urges that the trial court erred in denying all of the allegedly consequential damages she suffered after the date of the contract breach. Specifically, Dorsett claims she is entitled to reimbursement for travel expenses, lost wages, storage costs, gas line repairs, repairs to a faucet and a fan and the cost of long-distance phone calls.

¶14 An obligor in good faith is liable only for the damages that were foreseeable at the time the contract was made. La. C.C. art.1996. An obligor in bad faith is liable for all the damages, foreseeable or not, that are a direct consequence of his failure to perform. La. C.C. art.1997. Bad faith in the context of art.1997 generally implies actual or constructive fraud or a refusal to fulfill contractual obligations, not an honest mistake as to actual rights or duties. Delaney v. Whitney Nat. Bank, 96-2144 (La.App. 4th Cir.11/12/97), 703 So.2d 709, writ denied, 98-0123 (La.3/20/98), 715 So.2d 1211. See also comment (b) to article 1997 providing that "[a]n obligor is in bad faith if he intentionally and maliciously fails to perform his obligation." The trial court never made a specific finding that the Johnsons breached the sales contract in bad faith. However, we will assume the Johnsons were in bad faith while discussing this assignment of error.

¶15 We agree with the trial court that the claimed expenses for telephone calls, travel and lost wages were litigation expenses, and therefore, were not compensable. These expenses were not directly caused by the breach. The additional repairs requested by the Johnsons enhanced the value of the house and would have been reflected in the later purchase price. Moreover, there is no evidence that these repairs were required for the subsequent sale. Compare Bond v. Broadway, 607 So.2d 865 (La.App. 2d Cir.1992), writ denied, 612 So.2d 88 (La.1993), where this court allowed the recovery of repair costs necessary to sell the house to another buyer and which would not have been incurred if there had been no breach. Finally, while Dorsett may have stored furniture in anticipation of the sale because the Johnsons required the house to be empty at the time of closing, there is no reasonable explanation as to why Dorsett did not return the furniture to the home once the sale fell through. The storage rent per month was $40, and she rented the storage unit for seven months, beginning on May 20, 1996, which was prior to the breach. The storage expenses would have been incurred even if the Johnsons had not breached the purchase agreement. The trial court was not clearly wrong in denying the claim for these damages.

Attorney's Fees

¶16 Dorsett argues in her third assignment of error that the trial court erred in denying an award of attorney fees. Dorsett seeks over $7,000 in attorney fees and expenses. She also seeks attorney fees for this appeal. The Buy/Sell agreement permitted reasonable attorney fees in the event of a breach. However, Dorsett presented no evidence at trial setting forth the amount of attorney fees. Instead, her counsel attached an invoice of attorney fees to a post-trial memorandum. After carefully reading the entire trial transcript, we do not find any indication that the trial judge held the record open to allow additional evidence to be introduced regarding attorney fees. Nevertheless, Dorsett correctly asserts that proof of the value of an attorney's services is not necessary where the services are evident from the record. See Odom v. Respiratory Care, Inc., 98-0263 (La.App. 1st Cir.2/19/99), 754 So.2d 252; Sibley v. Insured Lloyds, 442 So.2d 627 (La. App. 1st Cir.1983). Accordingly, $2,000 is a reasonable attorney fee for services rendered in this matter at the trial and appellate levels. The judgment is amended to include this award.

***

Conclusion

¶17 We amend the judgment to award attorney fees of $2,000. As amended, the judgment is affirmed.

DECREE

As amended, the judgment is AFFIRMED at appellees' cost.

Section 2: The Vendor's Privilege and Security Rights

The previous sections demonstrate what remedies the seller has if the buyer refuses both to accept delivery and to pay the price, but the more common problem is that the buyer accepts delivery but then either refuses or is unable to pay. In such an instance, the most traditional remedy for the seller is the vendor's privilege set forth in Article 3249(1) for immovables and in Article 3217(7) for movables. The privilege means that the vendor has priority over other creditors of the buyer: "a privilege is a right, which the nature of a debt gives to a creditor, and which entitles him to be preferred before other creditors, eeven those who have mortgages." Art 3186. The Vendor's Privilege dates back to the Code Napoléon and is necessitated by the concept of the perfection of a sale – that ownership is transferred on agreement. A privilege is necessary to protect the unpaid vendor, but it also enables a buyer to purchase on credit where he might otherwise not be able to do so.

The vendor's privilege secures both the price and other expenses such as interest accruing on the price and attorney's fees (if required by contract). In one case, the Louisiana Supreme Court held that the vendor's privilege even guaranteed the purchaser's obligation to pay the seller an additional amount of money if a reversionary clause in the act of sale was found to be unenforceable.

L. DAVID CROMWELL, VENDOR'S PRIVILEGE: ADHERET VISCERIBUS REI (2015)

75 LA. L. REV. 1165, 1166-68

Article 3186 of the Louisiana Civil Code, which was borrowed verbatim from the Code Napoléon, provides that "[p]rivilege is a right, which the nature of a debt gives to a creditor, and which entitles him to be preferred before other creditors, even those who have mortgages." A privilege is thus a preference established by legislation and is an exception to the general rule of the Civil Code that the proceeds of the sale of an obligor's property are distributed ratably among his creditors. A privilege is a form of real security. Privileges cannot be granted contractually; they can arise only by operation of law based upon the nature of the debt

Planiol defines a privilege as "a disposition of the law which favors a creditor." . . .

Some privileges are general and operate on all property of the debtor, such as those securing funeral charges, law charges, and expenses of the last illness. Other privileges are special; that is, they operate only on specific property. One of the most important special privileges is that in favor of the vendor as security for the unpaid purchase price. The law itself grants the unpaid vendor this privilege; it is unnecessary for the vendor to obtain a mortgage, or even to obtain written recognition of the existence of the vendor's privilege, for it to arise.

* * *

Among two or more competing privileges, the general rule is that they rank according to their nature rather than the date on which they arise [and the Civil Code includes articles that list the ranks of various privileges]. Privileges that are of the same rank are paid concurrently from the proceeds of the thing that they burden. These general rules are applied consistently only to privileges burdening movables, though there are instances under Louisiana law in which they continue to apply to immovables.

The last phrase of article 3186 is critical, for it contains the general rule of ranking of privileges upon immovables against mortgages. By their nature, privileges are preferred to mortgages, regardless of whether the mortgage may have previously arisen or become effective against third persons, unless some other provision of law provides to the contrary. It is for this reason that the general privileges that arise under the Civil Code outrank mortgages. Nevertheless, in order for most privileges upon immovables to enjoy this favored ranking, the acts that evidence them must be filed for record within the period prescribed by Civil Code article 3274. If the act evidencing a privilege is not filed within that time, it takes effect against third persons from the date of registry and affords the holder of the privilege no preference over previously recorded mortgages. . . .

It is fitting that the vendor's privilege on movables and that on immovables arise under different articles of the Louisiana Civil Code, for they are actually entirely different privileges. If these two privileges can be seen as twins that share the same family name and several common attributes, they are fraternal twins at best, for they were born at different times and of different sources. Moreover, apart from the obvious difference in the domain of things upon which they operate, they are wholly different in their status as real rights, the means by which they are made enforceable against third persons, and their ranking against competing interests.

Movables and the Vendor's Privilege

The vendor's privilege gives the seller of a movable the right to be preferred over other creditors of the buyer, art 3227: "He who has sold to another any movable property, which is not paid for, has a preference on the price of his property over the other creditors of the purchaser." This preference applies regardless of whether the sale is made on credit or without, or whether the buyer gave the vendor a note or bond or not. It applies as long as the movable remains in the purchaser's possession and is identifiable. In such an instance, the seller may demand restitution of the things themselves, and thus effective dissolution of the contract of sale or immediate payment of the price and all supplemental expenses and interest.

Things become a more complicated if the buyer has since agreed to sell the things to a third party ('the second vendee'). If the things are still identifiable (or can be returned in kind) and in the possession of the purchaser, then the vendor can prevent the second sale, provided he files his claim within eight days of delivery. Art. 3229. If the vendee sells and delivers the things to a second buyer in a cash sale, the vendor's privilege is lost (the bona fide purchaser doctrine displaces it). However, if the second sale is made on credit, the things are still identifiable, and the price for the second sale can be determined, then the vendor's privilege is still intact. Art. 3228, 3230, 3231. The vendor's privilege similarly follows the sale of the thing by a received and the proceeds of a judicial of the thing, if the court still has the proceeds. Moreover, the vendor's privilege applies to insurance proceeds paid to the vendee when the movable is destroyed by a fire or other such force majeur. (Cromwell footnote 98)

Immovables and the Vendor's Privilege

To be effective against third parties, a vendor's privilege on an immovable must be recorded in the mortgage records, not the conveyance records. Art. 3271. It must also be recorded in the parish where the property is situated, and it must be recorded within seven days from the act of sale in order to be preferred over previously recorded mortgages. Art 3274. If it is not recorded as required within that period, it does not take preference over previously filed mortgages, but it is still effective against third parties and other instruments after the date of registry. The vendor's privilege on an immovable is a real right and gives the vendor who recorded a credit sale properly the right to assert his privilege even after the immovable is transferred to a third person's possession. Timely recordation causes the vendor's privilege to outrank even the vendee's previously existing mortgages against the vendee's property.

Security Interests

In a credit sale, where the buyer is granted a term for payment of the price, a seller who extends credit to his buyer may further strengthen his position contractually by securing the sale with an accessory right. If the thing sold is movable, the permissible accessory right is a security interest created under Chapter 9 of the Louisiana UCC, which calls this particular accessory right a purchase money security interest (PMSI). If the thing sold is immovable, then the appropriate accessory right is a conventional mortgage. In such a case, the automatic imposition of the vendor's privilege and the right to dissolve the sale for nonpayment of the price are back-up positions.

Chapter 9 of the Louisiana of the Uniform Commercial Code, entitled "Secured Transactions, was enacted as part of Title 10 of the Louisiana Revised Statutes. La. Rev. Stat. 10:9-101 to 10:9-710. Civil Code articles 3287-3298 govern conventional mortgages on immovables.

Section 3: The Vendor's Right to Dissolve the Sale

The vendor's privilege is one of three rights the vendor can assert against a non-paying vendee: the vendor's privilege, specific performance, and dissolution. The vendor's privilege is something of the opposite of the right of dissolution. When the vendor dissolves the sale, he must return whatever portion of the price that has been paid. Enforcement of the vendor's privilege, instead, is an attempt to enforce the vendee's obligation to pay the price. he two are distinct remedies, and neither depends on the other's existence. Consequently, a vendor can assert them as alternatives against a non-paying vendee.

As indicated previously, unless the buyer agrees to it and it is perfected as required, the seller's interest in getting paid will not be backed up by an accessory (or security) right, whether a PMSI under Chapter 9 of the UCC or a conventional mortgage. Furthermore, the vendor's privilege can be lost if the thing is transferred to a third party. However, the Article 2561 right of the seller to dissolve a sale for nonpayment of price is a powerful remedy. Though it can only be ordered by a court and cannot be exercised by the seller on his own, it allows the seller who dissolves the sale to extinguish all encumbrances and conveyances that the buyer has entered into after the sale. It is lost only when liberative prescription has accrued or when it has been expressly waived. The vendor's right to dissolve a sale for nonpayment is separate and independent and does not depend on the availability of either the vendor's privilege or a security right. "Enforcement of the vendor's privilege is 'an affirmation of the contract,' whereas the exercise of the right of dissolution places 'matters in the same state as though the obligation had not existed.'"

Concerning movables, the right to dissolve for nonpayment under Article 2615 can be asserted against third parties, but only so long as the thing is still in the possession of the buyer – if the thing sold has since been seized from the buyer and sold in a sheriff's sale, or if it has been incorporated into a building in such a way that it belongs to a third party, then the seller's right to dissolve will be lost. Furthermore, the seller may stop delivery of movables in transit when he learns that the buyer will not perform or is insolvent.

Different rules apply if the thing sold is an immovable. Generally, under the public records doctrine, any sale of an immovable must be in writing to bind the parties to the sale and must be recorded to affect third parties. In order for the seller of an immovable to assert the right of dissolution to the prejudice of third parties who have since dealt with the buyer, the writing that evidences the sale must identify the transaction as a credit sale, but it does not have to be recorded in the mortgage records to affect third parties, while the vendor's privilege would so have to be recorded. If the instrument states that some or all of the price has not been paid, then the 'credit sale' language puts third parties who may be dealing with the buyer on notice of the seller's right to dissolve the sale for nonpayment. Consequently, even if a credit sale instrument is recorded only in the conveyance records, the seller cannot assert the vendor's privilege, but he can still dissolve the sale for nonpayment of the price – and he may even be able to dissolve the sale if the sale is not recorded at all, as in Johnson v. Bloodworth, 12 La Ann. 699 (1857).

Under articles 2652-2564, the buyer of an immovable facing action for dissolution for non-payment of price may under certain circumstances be given extra time, but not the buyer of movables. Article 2654 prohibits a court from granting an extension of time to the buyer of a movable, but Article 2562 allows a court to grant up to sixty days if there is no danger that the seller may lose the price and the thing. Even if the contract of sale provides expressly for dissolution in case of failure to pay, the buyer will still have the right to pay as long as the seller has neither notified the buyer that he's availing himself of the clause nor filed suit for dissolution.

Study Question:

Which of the Seller's rights is being exercised in the following cases, and what do the decisions add to your understanding of the underlying Civil Code articles?

PADILLA V. SCHWARTZ 2009
11 SO.3D 6 (LA APP. 4TH CIR.)

MICHAEL E. KIRBY, Judge.

¶1 Andrea Padilla appeals a Civil District Court judgment of July 17, 2006 that denied her motion for summary judgment and granted the motion for summary judgment filed by the intervenors, Ronald and Lynda Burger ("the Burgers"). The judgment dismissed Padilla's suit to quiet tax title, declared null the tax sale of the property in dispute, and cancelled Padilla's tax sale deed upon the Burgers' paying her the lawful redemption amount. In this Court, Padilla has filed peremptory exceptions of prescription, no cause of action and no right of action to the Burgers' petition of intervention.

FACTS AND PROCEDRUAL HISTORY

¶2 By Act of Credit Sale dated August 1, 1996, the Burgers sold Louis Schwartz certain property bearing the municipal address 11112 Haynes Blvd., New Orleans, LA ("the property"). The vendor-financed instrument was filed and duly registered in the conveyance records of Orleans Parish, and clearly states that the Burgers held a mortgage and vendor's privilege against the property.

¶3 On July 19, 2001, the property was declared blighted and a public nuisance by an administrative hearing officer for the City of New Orleans in a case captioned "The City of New

Orleans v. Louis Schwartz, 11112 Hayne Blvd., New Orleans, LA 70128." The notice of Judgment with respect to that adjudication reveals that a fine and costs were assessed against Schwartz. It also states that because the property was found to be blighted and a public nuisance it was eligible for expropriation by the New Orleans Redevelopment Authority; eligible for demolition; and, that failure to pay the assessed fine and costs would result in a lien being placed against the property. The notice further states that "[f]ailure to pay the lien along with your next ad valorem tax bill may result in this property being sold in accordance with laws that govern tax sales of immovable property."

¶4 Following an auction on November 14, 2001, the Collector of Ad Valorem Taxes for the city of New Orleans executed a tax deed on June 4, 2002 in favor of Padilla, transferring all of Schwartz's right, title and interest in the property for non-payment of property taxes for the years 1997, 1998, 1999 and 2000. This tax deed specifically states that the owner, Schwartz, could redeem the property at any time within three years of the filing of the deed in the conveyance records of Orleans Parish. The deed was filed on June 5, 2002.

¶5 On February 13, 2004, Padilla filed a Petition to Quiet Tax Title pursuant to La. R.S. 47:2228, which formerly provided that once three (3) years had elapsed the purchaser of property at a tax sale could file suit to quiet title. The trial court appointed a curator ad hoc to represent Schwartz based upon Padilla's allegation that Schwartz was last known to be a resident of New Orleans but his then current residence was unknown.

¶6 In May 2004, the Burgers discovered that the property had been sold at the tax sale and made a redemption request to Padilla for an accounting of the amounts owed to her. Padilla refused to provide the accounting. On July 28, 2004, the Burgers intervened in the suit to quiet tax title, naming as defendants Padilla, the City of New Orleans and Schwartz, through his curator ad hoc, to assert their claims as recorded mortgage holders on the property at issue.

¶7 On May 17, 2005, Padilla filed a motion for summary judgment, alleging that because the property had been adjudicated blighted, an eighteen month redemption period applied pursuant to La. Const. Art. VII, § 25(B)(2). Thus, Padilla contends, the Burgers had eighteen months from June 5, 2002 to timely redeem the property, but failed to so.

¶8 On November 21, 2005, the Burgers filed a motion for summary judgment based upon a violation of their due process rights as mortgage holders to receive notice of the proposed tax sale. They claimed the violation of their due process rights made the tax sale an absolute nullity. On May 25, 2006, the trial court heard the motions and determined that it first had to ascertain whether the city of New Orleans had provided notice of the pending tax sale in compliance with constitutional due process requirements. The trial court ordered the city to produce any and all information concerning notices. At a subsequent hearing, the city failed to present any evidence that the Burgers or Schwarz had received notice of the pending tax sale. The trial court then dismissed Padilla's Petition to Quiet Title, rendered the tax sale an absolute nullity, and ordered that the tax sale deed be canceled upon payment of the lawful redemption amount.

ASSIGNMENTS OF ERROR

¶9 In addition to the peremptory exceptions noted above, Padilla appeals the trial court judgment, raising four (4) assignments of error: 1) trial court erred in denying her motion for summary judgment; 2) trial court erred in hearing the Burgers' motion; 3) trial court erred in granting their motion; and, 4) trial court erred in entering a final judgment annulling the tax sale without entering a money judgment awarding her the amounts owed if the tax sale was nullified.

STANDARD OF REVIEW

¶10 Appellate courts review summary judgments de novo under the same criteria that govern the district court's consideration of whether summary judgment is appropriate. Costello v. Hardy, 2003-1146, p. 8 (La.1/21/04), 864 So.2d 129, 137; Schroeder v. Board of Supervisors of Louisiana State University, 591 So.2d 342 (La.1991). A court must grant a motion for summary judgment if the pleadings, depositions, answers to interrogatories, and admissions on file, together with the affidavits, if any, show that there is no genuine issue as to material fact, and that mover is entitled to judgment as a matter of law. La. C.C.P. art. 966(B). Summary judgment procedure is favored and is designed to secure the just, speedy and inexpensive determination of actions. La. C.C.P. art. 966(A)(2); Samaha v. Rau, 2007-1726, p. 4 (La.2/26/08), 977 So.2d 880, 883.

***

DISCUSSION

¶11 On appeal, Padilla argues the issue is not whether the Burgers' due process rights to notice were violated but whether that issue was even before the trial court. Padilla reasons that the Burgers' intervention was premised on a single issue, i.e., whether the three year redemption period of La. Const. Art. VII, § 25(B)(1) had accrued. Padilla contends that the proper redemptive period is eighteen months under Art. VII, § 25(B)(2), because the property had been declared blighted on August 3, 2001, and, therefore, the Burgers failed to timely exercise any rights they may have had to redeem the property. The Burgers, on the other hand, argue that the tax sale was absolutely null as a result of the violation of their due process right to receive notice. Since the sale was an absolute nullity, they contend the redemption periods established by La. Const. Art. VII, § 25(B) never commenced to run.

¶12   First we will address the procedural arguments, and then the substantive issues.

¶13   Louisiana Const. Art. VII, § 25(B), provides:

***

(B) Redemption.
(1) The property sold shall be redeemable for three years after the date of recordation of the tax sale, by paying the price given, including costs, five percent penalty thereon, and interest at the rate of one percent per month until redemption.
(2) In the city of New Orleans, when such property sold is residential or commercial property which is abandoned property as defined by R.S. 33:4720.12(1) or blighted property as defined by Act 155 of the 1984 Regular Session, it shall be redeemable for eighteen months after the date of recordation of the tax sale by payment in accordance with subparagraph (1) of this paragraph.

¶14   After reviewing the record, we find no merit to Padilla's argument that the Burgers had only eighteen months from the recordation of the tax sale pursuant to La. Const. Art. VII, § 25(B)(2) to exercise their right of redemption. The record contains no evidence that the property was actually sold pursuant to the city's authority to sell blighted property. The notice of judgment upon which Padilla relies uses the permissive "may" rather than the mandatory "shall" when speaking of the potential sale of the property. Further, a reading of the actual tax sale deed of June 4, 2002 reveals the sale was in fact made for non-payment of ad valorem taxes, not for failure to pay a lien associated with the blighted property declaration. There is no mention therein of the fine and costs for blighted property. Thus, we conclude the sale was for non-payment of ad valorem taxes subject to the peremptive period of three years. For the suggested eighteen month redemption period to apply, the sale would have had to occur under the statutory authority governing sales of blighted property. That did not occur in this case.

¶15   Next we address whether or not the tax sale was valid. Under the Fourteenth Amendment to the United States Constitution and La. Const. Art. I, 2, a person is protected against a deprivation of his life, liberty or property without due process of law. Hamilton v. Royal International Petroleum Corporation, 2005-846, p. 9 (La.2/22/06), 934 So.2d 25, 32 (citation omitted). The fundamental requirement of procedural due process is notice and the opportunity to be heard at a meaningful time and in a meaningful manner. Id.

¶16 In Mennonite Board of Missions v. Adams, 462 U.S. 791, 103 S.Ct. 2706, 77 L.Ed.2d 180 (1983), a case with facts similar to the present case, the U.S. Supreme Court interpreted the Due Process Clause with respect to the rights of a mortgagee and the notice requirements of an Indiana statute. In that case, the Mennonite Board of Missions ("Mennonite") was the mortgagee of record of a certain parcel of property. The property owner failed to pay her taxes and the property was sold at a tax sale. Indiana law did not require that notice be given by mail or personal service to a mortgagee and Mennonite was not given any notice of the impending tax sale. Relying on its earlier decision in Mullane v. Central Hanover Bank & Trust Co., 339 U.S. 306, 70 S.Ct. 652, 94 L.Ed. 865 (1950), the Supreme Court held that "a mortgagee possesses a substantial property interest that is significantly affected by a tax sale" and therefore "is entitled to notice reasonably calculated to apprise him of a pending tax sale." Mennonite, 462 U.S. at 798, 103 S.Ct. at 2711. Regarding the publication of notice of the impending tax sale in a newspaper and the posting of notice in the county courthouse, the Court stated:

> When the mortgagee is identified in a mortgage that is publicly recorded, constructive notice by publication must be supplemented by notice mailed to the mortgagee's last known available address, or by personal service. But unless the mortgagee is not reasonably identifiable, constructive notice alone does not satisfy the mandate of Mullane. Id.

(Footnote omitted).

¶17 The Court further held that:

> Notice by mail or other means as certain to ensure actual notice is a minimum constitutional precondition to a proceeding which will adversely affect the liberty or property interests of any party, whether unlettered or well versed in commercial practice, if its name and address are reasonably ascertainable. Furthermore, a mortgagee's knowledge of delinquency in the payment of taxes is not equivalent to notice that a tax sale is pending.

Id., 462 U.S. at 800, 103 S.Ct. at 2712.

¶18 In her Petition to Quiet Title, Padilla alleges she purchased the property at a tax sale conducted by the city. La. Const. Art. VII, 25 requires that prior to conducting a tax sale of property for nonpayment of taxes, the state and/or city must give notice to the delinquent owners in the manner provided by law. La. R.S. 47:2180 provided the manner of giving notice to delinquent owners regarding immovable property. Furthermore, pursuant to the Supreme Courts holding in Mennonite, supra, a mortgagee, who is reasonably ascertainable, is entitled to prior notice of an impending tax sale.

¶19   In support of their motion for summary judgment arguing the tax sale is absolutely null for lack of notice, the Burgers submitted a copy of the recorded mortgage instrument evidencing the credit sale of the Hayne Blvd. property to Schwartz. The document clearly identifies the Burgers as the SELLER and MORTGAGEE and lists their domicile as Orleans Parish. It identifies Schwartz as the PURCHASER and MORTGAGOR and as a domiciliary of Orleans Parish.

¶20   The Burgers also presented the affidavit of Ron Burger, who averred that on the date of the act of sale, Schwartz owed a balance of $39,000.00 with interest, and was currently in default. Burger stated that in 1998, 1999, and 2000, the Burgers never received any written notice from the city that taxes were due on the property, and they never received any prior notice, either written or by personal service, of the November 14, 2001 tax sale.

¶21   Burger averred that he made two attempts to redeem the property from Padilla, but she refused the requests. He then contacted Walter J. OBrien, Jr., Finance Operations Manager of the Bureau of the Treasury, Department of Finance for the City of New Orleans, in December 2004, to redeem the property, and presented him with a certified check in the amount of $12,783.88, the redemption price. OBrien refused the payment and declined to issue Burger a certificate of redemption. Instead he gave Burger a copy of a Notice of Judgment that evidenced the property had been adjudicated blighted.

¶22   In addition to Ron Burgers affidavit, the Burgers submitted an affidavit from Stephen C. Barnes, the abstractor retained by them to conduct an abstract of the property. Barnes averred that his search of the public records disclosed no recordation of the judgment by the Administrative Adjudication Bureau for Public Health, Housing and Environmental Violations adjudicating the property blighted. He further stated that he had requested from Mr. OBrien copies of any records that the city of New Orleans had regarding notice documents of the tax deficiency and/or the November 14, 2001 tax sale. In response, the city informed Barnes that it had no such records.

¶23   Neither Padilla nor the city submitted any evidence that disputes the evidence offered by the Burgers to prove they were never given prior notice of the November 14, 2001 tax sale. Absent any evidence that raises a genuine issue of material fact as to whether or not the city gave the Burgers prior notice of the tax sale, we conclude, as did the trial court, that, as a matter of law, the Fourteenth Amendment due process requirement was not satisfied in this case and, therefore, the tax sale is an absolute nullity.

***

¶24 This Court is cognizant of the tremendous difficulties presented to property owners and mortgage interests in the greater New Orleans area post-Hurricane Katrina. One can argue that imposing a high burden of notification on the local and state governments will greatly increase the administrative costs of establishing some degree of normalcy to the region. Nevertheless, considering the advances in information technology and other available resources, the city through reasonable diligence could have ascertained the Burgers physical and/or mailing address to give them notice of the pending tax sale. The similarity of identification between the mortgagee in Mennonite and the mortgagees in this case are such that we can conclude the city did not afford the Burgers the minimum due process protection recognized in Mennonite.

¶25 Also, we find no merit to Padillas argument that the Burgers waived their right to notice of the tax sale because they failed to request notice of the tax sale pursuant to La. R.S. 9:5201 or to comply with La. R.S. 47:2180.1 (which formerly required mortgagees to notify tax collectors if they wished to be given notice of the tax delinquency on immovable property).

* * *

¶26 Finally, we address the effect of nullifying the November 14, 2001 tax sale.

¶27 La. Civ. Code art.2033 provides, in part:

> An absolutely null contract, or a relatively null contract that has been declared null by the court, is deemed never to have existed. The parties must be restored to the situation that existed before the contract was made. If it is impossible or impracticable to make restoration in kind, it may be made through an award of damages.

(Emphasis added [by the court]).

¶28 La. Const. Art. VII, 25(C) provides that "[n]o judgment annulling a tax sale shall have effect until the price and all taxes and costs are paid, and until ten percent per annum interest on the amount of the price and taxes paid from date of respective payments are paid to the purchaser ..."

¶29 The trial court correctly found the November 14, 2001 tax sale to be absolutely null. To give the trial court judgment effect, it shall be amended to order the Burgers to pay the purchase price, and all taxes and costs, plus ten percent per annum interest on the price and taxes paid from the date of the respective payments. The amended judgment will restore all parties to the status quo ante, i.e., the State keeps its tax payment from Padilla, Padilla receives the redemption amount plus any lawful interest, and the Burgers have their mortgagee rights restored.

DECREE

¶30 Accordingly, for the aforementioned reasons, the trial court judgment is amended to order Ronald G. Burger and Lynda Ogden Burger to pay Andrea Padilla the purchase price, and all taxes and costs, plus ten percent per annum interest on the amount of the price and taxes paid from the date of the respective payments. As amended, the judgment of the trial court is affirmed.

JUDGMENT AMENDED; AND AS AMENDED, AFFIRMED

ON APPLICATION FOR REHEARING.
MICHAEL E. KIRBY, Judge.

¶1 We grant the application for rehearing of the plaintiff-appellant, Andrea Padilla, for the sole purpose of clarifying our holding that the status quo ante will be restored by payment to Padilla of the purchase price, taxes and costs, and ten percent interest from the date of each respective payment as required by La. Const. Art. VII, § 25(C). Our opinion upheld the trial court's dismissal of Padilla's suit to quiet tax title and its nullification of the tax sale of the property in dispute. As noted in the opinion, La. C.C. art.2033 requires that the parties to a contract which has been annulled be restored to the situation that existed before the contract was made. Comment (b) to La. C.C. art.2033 states, "The restoration of the parties to the situation that existed before the contract … includes restoration of fruits and revenues, as any unjust enrichment of the parties must be prevented."

¶2 In the application for rehearing, Padilla contends that since the tax sale she has spent considerable amounts of money to remediate the property to return it to commerce and to make repairs following Hurricane Katrina. Those expenses, she contends, must be considered in restoring the parties to the " status quo ante." Because the record before us contains no evidence of the amounts of money allegedly spent by Padilla in remediating the property or of the rental income generated from the property since the tax sale, we must remand the case to the trial court for the taking of additional evidence to determine the status quo of the parties prior to the tax sale as well as their current status. The record is also silent as to the amounts Padilla paid in taxes subsequent to the tax sale. Thus, remand is necessary for Padilla to offer proof of any tax payments and to allow the trial court to render a specific monetary judgment in compliance with La. Const. Art. VII, § 25(C).

¶3 Accordingly, we grant the application for rehearing and amend our decree to read as follows:

> The July 17, 2006 judgment of the trial court is affirmed insofar as it denied Andrea Padilla's motion for summary judgment; granted the Burgers' motion for summary judgment; dismissed Padilla's Petition to Quiet Tax Sale; and declared the tax sale of the property at issue an absolute nullity. The case is remanded to the trial court for further proceedings consistent with this opinion on rehearing and for entry of a judgment awarding Padilla the constitutionally mandated amount and any amount necessary to restore the parties to the situation that existed prior to the tax sale.

REHEARING APPLICATION GRANTED; DECREE AMENDED.

ROBERTSON V. BUONI 1987
504 SO. 2D 860 (LA.)

DIXON, Chief Justice.

¶1 This is a suit to dissolve a sale of immovable property. By act of sale and assumption dated April 7, 1982, Elouise N. Robertson sold Mr. and Mrs. Joseph Buoni a piece of real property identified as Lot 20, Section D, Elmwood Subdivision, now known as Northbrook Subdivision, in Jefferson Parish, Louisiana. At trial, Ms. Robertson testified that the Buonis agreed to assume the balance of the existing mortgage held by Jefferson Savings & Loan, pay an $8,000 deposit and execute a promissory note in Ms. Robertson's favor for $40,000 representing the balance of the purchase price. The note provided for the payment of $7,000 on or before July 7, 1982 and $6,000 each year thereafter payable on April 7th. Ms. Robertson did not receive any payment after the initial $8,000, and when she attempted to collect, she learned the Buonis had left the area. The property at issue was no longer in her name on the public records, and the Buonis appeared as the record owners with only plaintiff's mortgage to Jefferson Savings & Loan Association encumbering the property. In an effort to avoid foreclosure because she had no funds with which to bid on the property, Ms. Robertson continued to make the mortgage payments. At the time judgment was rendered in the trial court, Ms. Robertson had paid taxes and mortgage installments for approximately three and one-half years after the sale.

¶2 Ms. Robertson sued, and an attorney was appointed as curator ad hoc for the absentee defendants. Attempts to locate the defendants were unsuccessful, and the matter proceeded to trial with Ms. Robertson as the lone witness. The promissory note, but not the act of sale, was introduced and admitted into evidence. The trial court declined to dissolve the sale, quoting at length from Waseco Chemical & Supply Co. v. Bayou State Oil Corp., 371 So.2d 305 (La.App. 2d Cir.1979), cert. denied 374 So.2d 656 (La.1979), a case concerning dissolution of a mineral lease, and concluding that Ms. Robertson failed to meet her burden of proof in not providing the court with sufficient information to determine whether dissolution was warranted under Waseco. The court of appeal affirmed with one dissent, 494 So.2d 563 (La.App. 5th Cir.1986), citing the devastating financial effect such a dissolution could have on an innocent third party purchaser. The dissenter objected to the court's speculation about the existence of a third party purchaser. He opined that Ms. Robertson should be entitled to relief under C.C. 2561 and C.C. 2562 which read as follows:

> C.C. 2561. "If the buyer does not pay the price the seller may sue for the dissolution of the sale. This right of dissolution shall be an accessory of the credit representing the price, and if it be held by more than one person all must join in the demand for dissolution; but if any refuse, the others by paying the amount due the parties who refuse shall become subrogated to their rights."

> C.C. 2562. "The dissolution of the sale of immovables is summarily awarded, when there is danger that the seller may lose the price and the thing itself.

> "If that danger does not exist, the judge may grant to the buyer a longer or shorter time, according to circumstances, provided such term exceed not six months.

> "This term being expired, without the buyer's yet having paid, the judge shall cancel the sale."

¶3 The Louisiana Civil Code provides several remedies for a vendor who has not received payment of the purchase price. Under C.C. 3249 and C.C. 3271, the vendor has a privilege on things sold for payment:

> C.C. 3249. "Creditors who have a privilege on immovables, are:

> 1. The vendor on the estate by him sold, for the payment of the price or so much of it as is unpaid, whether it was sold on or without a credit.

2. Architects, undertakers, bricklayers, painters, master builders, contractors, subcontractors, journeymen, laborers, cartmen and other workmen employed in constructing, rebuilding or repairing houses, buildings, or making other works.

3. Those who have supplied the owner or other person employed by the owner, his agent or subcontractor, with materials of any kind for the construction or repair of an edifice or other work, when such materials have been used in the erection or repair of such houses or other works.

The above named parties shall have a lien and privilege upon the building, improvement or other work erected, and upon the lot of ground not exceeding one acre, upon which the building, improvement or other work shall be erected; provided, that such lot of ground belongs to the person having such building, improvement or other work erected; and if such building, improvement or other work is caused to be erected by a lessee of the lot of ground, in that case the privilege shall exist only against the lease and shall not affect the owner.

4. Those who have worked by the job in the manner directed by the law, or by the *862 regulations of the police, in making or repairing the levees, bridges, ditches and roads of a proprietor, on the land over which levees, bridges and roads have been made or repaired."

C.C. 3271. "The vendor of an immovable only preserves his privilege on the object, when he has caused to be duly recorded at the office for recording mortgages, his act of sale, in the manner directed hereafter, whatever may be the amount due to him on the sale."

¶4 Additionally, under C.C. 2561 and 2562, the unpaid vendor has the right to demand dissolution of sales by judicial process. This vendor's privilege and the right of dissolution are clearly distinguishable from and independent of each other. Sliman v. McBee, 311 So.2d 248 (La.1975); Stevenson v. Brown, 32 La.Ann. 461 (1880); United States v. Maniscalco, 523 F.Supp. 1338 (E.D.La.1981); Toler v. Toler, 337 So.2d 666 (La.App. 3d Cir.1976). Enforcement of the vendor's privilege is "an affirmation of the contract" whereas the exercise of the right of dissolution places "matters in the same state as though the obligation had not existed." Yiannopoulos, "Real Rights in Louisiana and Comparative Law: Part I," 23 La.L.Rev. 161, 230 quoting Heirs of Castle v. Floyd, 38 La.Ann. 583, 587 (1886) and Louis Werner Saw Mill Co. v. White, 205 La. 242, 252, 17 So.2d 264, 268 (1944). In the sale of immovables, the resolutory action of dissolution exists against the original purchaser and also third persons acquiring real rights or title to the property. 23 La.L.Rev. 161 at 232, fn. 334. See also United States v. Maniscalco, supra.

¶5 In Litvinoff, 7 Louisiana Civil Law Treatise, Book 2 at 508 (1975), the author cautions against casual dissolution of contracts, and states that the remedy of contract dissolution is not to be regarded as a convenient way for a party to unburden himself of the contract. The dissolution of the contract must be pronounced by the court, which must determine whether the rendering of only partial performance by the obligor, plus the delay attending a possible completion, or the failure to perform an accessory obligation, warrants dissolution. Litvinoff suggests several factors to be considered that were adopted by the Waseco court. These include the extent and gravity of the failure to perform alleged by the complaining party, the nature of the obligor's fault, the good or bad faith of the parties involved, and also the surrounding economic circumstances that may make the dissolution opportune or not. Litvinoff, supra at 509.

¶6   In Sliman v. McBee, supra, we addressed the issue of judicial dissolution of a contract of sale of an immovable. Among other pertinent facts and issues, in that case the agreed purchase price was $78,000, in part payment of which the purchaser paid $5,000, and executed four promissory notes for the remainder. There was no mortgage accompanying the sale. We applied C.C. 2045 which at that time read:

> "The dissolving condition is that which, when accomplished, operates the revocation of the obligation, placing matters in the same state as though the obligation had not existed.

> "It does not suspend the execution of the obligation; it only obliges the creditor to restore what he has received, in case the event provided for in the condition takes place."

(In the 1984 revisions of the articles on obligations, C.C. 2045 was incorporated into C.C. 1767). We also applied C.C. 2561 and held that the vendor was entitled to dissolution of the sale on account of the purchaser's default in full payment of the purchase price, and held the vendee to be entitled to restoration of any partial payment. See also Hollanger v. Hollanger Rice Farms, 445 So.2d 117 (La.App. 2d Cir.1984), cert. denied 449 So.2d 1028 (La.1984); Groner Apartments v. Controlled Building Systems, 432 So.2d 1142 (La.App. 3d Cir.1983), cert. denied 438 So.2d 1106 (La.1983).

¶7   Ms. Robertson had an action under C.C. 2561, C.C. 2562 and Louisiana jurisprudence to seek dissolution of the sale when full payment of the price was not made, in spite of the fact that she failed to obtain a mortgage. The remedy afforded by C.C. 2561 is in no way dependent upon the existence of a security device such as a mortgage or a privilege. Sliman v. McBee, supra; Hollanger v. Hollanger Rice Farms, supra; Stevenson v. Brown, supra and Toler v. Toler, supra. Applying the Litvinoff suggested factors to the present case, it can be determined from Ms. Robertson's unrebutted testimony that the extent and gravity of the failure to perform is quite extreme. Failure to perform has caused Ms. Robertson to lose her property and her equity in such property, and to suffer substantial financial losses as she pays off the mortgage and taxes and legal fees for this action. Second, the nature of the obligor's fault-failure to pay-goes to the very heart of the purpose of the contract. Third, the good or bad faith of the parties must be considered, and it is unrebutted that Ms. Robertson is in good faith. On the other hand, the Buonis have defaulted on their obligation and have left the area without notifying Ms. Robertson. Litvinoff states that a fraudulent intent on the part of the obligor is not necessary to produce dissolution. "Any failure to perform involving some fault on his part suffices for this purpose, ..." supra at 509-510. Leaving the area without notice or payment to Ms. Robertson constitutes more than "some fault." No economic circumstances have been shown in this case that would make dissolution inopportune. Conversely, the facts that the Buonis have not made any mortgage payments or paid any taxes on the house for the last three and one-half years when the house is in their name, and that Ms. Robertson has assumed these responsibilities, show economic circumstances that would make dissolution quite opportune. From the evidence presented, judicial dissolution of the sale is a warranted and just remedy.

¶8   The court of appeal's speculation of the presence of a third party purchaser of the property is reasonable, but is not a valid cause for denial of the remedy of dissolution of a sale of immovables. The right to dissolution of a sale of an immovable for nonpayment is not contingent on the absence of a third party purchaser. A vendor seeking dissolution of the sale may do so even after the property has left the hands of the original purchaser. Stevenson v. Brown, supra; 23 La.L.Rev., supra at 232 and cases cited therein.

¶9   C.C. 2562 provides that if there is no danger that the seller may lose the price and the thing itself, the judge may grant to the buyer up to six months to perform and make payment. Here, however, defendants' disappearance and lengthy absence would not justify further delay.

¶10   For these reasons the judgments of the courts below are reversed, and there is now judgment in favor of Elouise Neilson Robertson and against Joseph and Geraldine Buoni decreeing the sale of April 7, 1982 from Ms. Robertson to Mr. and Mrs. Buoni dissolved and of no effect, at the cost of defendants.

DENNIS and COLE, JJ., concur.
LEMMON, J., concurs and assigns reasons.

LEMMON, Justice, concurring.
¶1   I do not necessarily agree with the broad proposition that a seller's right to dissolve the sale for non-payment of the purchase price under La.C.Cr.P. art. 2561 always exists against a third person who has subsequently acquired ownership. When a sale of immovable property has been recorded, the seller's right to dissolution, as against a subsequent purchaser, may depend

on whether the recorded original sale indicates that the price has or has not been paid.1 A. Yiannopoulos, 2 Louisiana Civil Law Treatise-Property § 165 (2d ed. 1980).

¶2   Since the record in the present case does not contain the original sale, plaintiff arguably has not proved her right of dissolution as against a subsequent purchaser. However, the present litigation is solely between the original seller and the original purchasers, and plaintiff-seller is entitled to a judgment of dissolution as against these defendants.

Review Notes

The seller's obligations, as learned in Chapters 9 and 10 include delivery of the thing, warrantying the sale against eviction, and warrantying that the thing is free from redhibitory defects, is the kind and has the qualities promised, and is fit for ordinary use. The buyer's obligations are simpler. She must take delivery of the thing and pay the price. If she does not, the seller can choose among several remedies. He can sue for specific performance or dissolve the sale, and in any case demand damages. If the buyer failed to pay, he can assert his vendor's privilege to seize the thing, or if he holds a security right in the thing, he can assert the remedies under those rules, whether mortgage or Article 9 of the UCC as adopted by Louisiana. The latter two remedies are not covered in the scope of this course.

Section 1: Buyer's Obligations to Pay and Take Delivery & Seller's Right to Resell

The buyer is bound to pay the price and take delivery of the thing at the time and place stipulated in the contract. Art. 2549-2550. If the contract does not stipulate where and when payment is due, then it is due at the time and place of delivery. If buyer fails to pay when payment is due, then interest is owed from that date in addition to the price. Furthermore, whether he failed to pay or failed to take delivery, the buyer will be liable for the seller's expenses in preserving the thing as well as damages as measured (as usual) by the loss sustained and the profit deprived. Additional damages may be owed depending on whether the buyer's failure to perform was in good or bad faith, as provided by conventional obligations rules. Arts 1996-1997. One mistake students often make is to assume that every failure to perform is in bad faith. That is not at all the case. Most failures to perform are in good faith, meaning that the obligor owes only those damages that were foreseeable at the time the contract is made (which is the same as under common law). Art 1996. A bad faith breach of contract is one that involves an intentional and malicious failure to perform, or perhaps a conflict of interest. In that case, the breaching party would owe all damages, foreseeable or not, that a direct consequence of the failure to perform.

Art. 1997. So, for example, a failure to pay because one simply lacks the money to do so is not bad faith. A dressmaker's refusal to finish the bride's wedding gown because she had been the groom's former fiancée and still holds a grudge would be bad faith – and she would be liable for both bad faith damages and nonpecuniary damages (Art 1998).

Damages are measured by the loss sustained plus the profit deprived. Art. 1995. The profit deprived is generally measured in one of two ways. If the absolute potential profit was discernable at the time of the breach, then that amount is the profit deprived. For example, if Plaintiff was to buy widgits from Defendant for $2000, and then had a contract to sell them to Third Party for $6,000, then the profit of which he is deprived is $4,000 if Defendant breaches the contract and Plaintiff cannot mitigate that breach. In terms of foreseeable damages, Defendant may owe any additional amount lost because his breach forced Plaintiff to breach as well. Alternatively, if there was no second contract that set an absolute profit, then a court will use the difference between the market price of the thing at the time and place of the breach and the contract price to determine the profit lost.

Examples:

a. Movables

Friedman Iron v. Beaird:

Defendant agreed to buy 500 tons of scrap steel from plaintiff at $41/gross ton, delivery to be by carload lots on specified dates over the next few months. A few days before the delivery of the first carload, defendant notified plaintiff that it was cancelling the entire order (because the market price of scrap steel had dropped precipitously, and defendant could purchase it cheaper elsewhere). Plaintiff sued, and the court agreed that defendant had breached the contract. In determining the profit lost, the court **calculated the difference between the price as listed in the contract and the market price on the day of the breach**.

Godchaux v. DeBuys:

Defendant, a Los Angeles resident who owned immovables in Jefferson parish ordered two dresses from plaintiff's Louisiana store, The dresses were sent to her in California, where she refused to accept delivery. The trial court found that she had breached the contract and charged her for the price plus costs. On appeal, she argued that the defendant should have mitigated damages by selling the dresses. The court found against her, saying that the only time when it is the vendor's duty to sel the thing is when the thing is perishable. Otherwise, selling the thing to mitigate losses is optional on the vendor's part when the thing is not perishable.

Article 2611 stipulates that when the buyer fails to perform a contract of sale of movable things, the seller, within a reasonable time and in good faith, may resell those things that are still in his possession. In such case, the seller is entitled to recover the difference between the contract price and the resale price and other damages and expenses caused by thee breach. Unless the things are perishable or subject to a rapid decline in value, the seller must notify the buyer in reasonable time of the forthcoming sale of the things.

b. Immovables

As in Godchaux, where goods are not perishable, the seller may resell the goods and then demand the difference in value from a breaching buyer but is not required to do so. Article 2612 provides an additional remedy: after reasonable notice to the buyer, the seller may request the court's authority to deposit the things at some place out of his possession at the buyer's risk.

Dorsett v. Johnson

Dorsett and her brother Formby owned a home in Bossier city which the Johnsons agreed to buy as is for $93,700. However, when their insurer informed them that he would not insure the home due to a roof problem, the Johnsons refused to go through with the sale. Two months later, the plaintiffs filed suit seeking damages, court costs, and the buyer's deposit. Two years later, the house was sold to a third party for $85,000. The trial court held that defendant had breached the contract and awarded thee interest paid on the mortgage in the interim minus the rent received in the interim between the two sales, but refused to include travel expenses, lost wages, telephone calls as those were litigation expenses. The appellate court affirmed.

Section 2: The Vendor's Privilege, Security Rights, and the Seller's Right to Dissolve

The right to resell is appropriate where the buyer refuses to both accept delivery and pay the price, but other remedies may be more appropriate where the buyer accepts delivery but then refuses to pay. The vendor's privilege is a way for the seller to secure both the price and other expenses. Art 3186 explains that a privilege is a right given to the creditor of a debt which entitles him to be preferred before other creditors – even those who have mortgages. If there are more than one privilege that apply to the same thing, then they rank according to their nature, not the date on which they arise. With regard to immovables, any privilege must be timely recorded in order for it to preserve its favored ranking. Thus, it must be recorded in the mortgage records (not the conveyance records) Art. 3271; in the correct parish, and within 7 days of the sale to be preferred over previously recorded mortgages. Art 3274.

For movables, the vendor's privilege gives the seller the right to be preferred over other of the buyer's creditors, Art 3227. If the vendor tries to assert her privilege after the buyer has already sold the things to a third party, then things get more complicated. If the things are still in the purchaser's possession, are identifiable or can be returned in kind, then the vendor can prevent the second sale. Art 3229. If, however, they have already been sold and paid for in cash to the new buyer, then the bona fide purchaser doctrine displaces the vendor's privilege. If they were paid for by credit and the things are still identifiable, then the privilege still adheres. Arts 3228, 3230, 3231. Alternatively, a vendor could secure the sale of a movable with a chattel mortgage, as per the stipulations in La. Rev. Stat. 10:9-101-10:9710.

Section 3: The Right to Dissolve the Sale for Nonpayment

As set forth in Articles 2561 and 2615, faced with a non-paying buyer, a vendor can assert specific performance (with or without the vendor's privilege) or dissolution. The vendor's privilege is contrary to the right of dissolution because with the latter, the vendor must return whatever portion of the price that the buyer paid – so it is a mode of specific performance. Nevertheless, the right of dissolution for nonpayment is a powerful remedy. It can only be ordered by a court and cannot be exercised by self-help. It allows the seller to extinguish all encumbrances on the thing that the buyer may have entered into in the interim and is only lost due to liberative prescription or express waiver.

The right to dissolve the sale of a movable is set forth in Article 2615, and can be asserted against a third party – but only if the thing is still in the original buyer's possession or is in transit, not if it has been seized and sold in a sheriff's sale or incorporated into a building.

With an immovable, the vendor's right to dissolve in the face of a third party claim depends on whether the writing evidencing the sale shows the transaction was a credit sale, but it does not have to be recorded. Consequently, even if a credit sale instrument is recorded only in the conveyance records and not in the mortgage records (or possibly if it is not recorded at all) the seller can still dissolve the sale for nonpayment – something that cannot be done with the vendor's privilege. Articles 2652-64 provide that the buyer of an immovable facing an action for dissolution may be given more time to pay by the court, but such an extension is not available to the buyer of a movable. That extension is for a maximum of 60 days, and can only be granted if there is no danger that the seller may lose both the price and the thing if thee sale is not immediately dissolved.

Example:

Padilla v. Schwartz 2009

Mr. & Mrs. Burger sold their immovable in New Orleans to Swartz, who properly recorded both a vendor's privilege and a mortgage. Five years later, a tax lien was declared against the property. Schwartz apparently disappeared, not having finished paying the mortgage. Padilla purchased the property at a tax sale, knowing that Schwartz could redeem the property at any time within three years. Two years later, when Padilla filed a petition to quiet tax title, the Burgers discovered the tax sale and made a redemption request. Padilla tried to avoid the redemption. The court held that under the circumstances the Burgers could dissolve the sale to Schwartz (no vendor's privilege was available because they were not demanding that Swartz pay). Furthermore, given that the Burgers held a recorded mortgage on the property, the city should have notified them of the pending tax sale, that they did not waive their right to be so notified, and so the tax sale was absolutely null. On rehearing, the court provided that Padilla should be refunded the amounts spent on taxes and remediation.

Robertson v. Buoni

Ms. Robertson sold an immovable to the Buonis, who agreed to assume the existing mortgage, pay an $8,000 deposit, and execute a promissory note for $40,000. When they disappeared and could not be located, she continued paying the taxes and the mortgage for 3 ½ years. She then filed suit to dissolve the sale. The Supreme Court granted her request, noting that the unpaid vendor has the right to demand dissolution by judicial process, and is thus distinguishable from the vendor's privilege and not dependent on it. Dissolution cannot be by self-help, but must be pronounced by a court, and though there is a concern that the vendor might since have sold the property to a third party purchaser whose right would be affected is justifiable, it is not a valid cause for denial of the remedy of dissolution of a sale of immovables. Article 2562 provides a possible extension to the purchaser of an immovable, unless there is a danger that the seller may lose the price and the thing itself. The court found that the Buoni's lengthy disappearance means that there is no justification for any delay in dissolving the sale. (Notice that at the time Robertson was written, the possible extension was a maximum of 6 months, but 2562 has since reduced that to 60 days.)

Gertrude of Gertrude's Garden LLC. ("Gertrude"), cultivates and grows beautiful award-winning flowers. In fact, her flowers are so popular that she be able to obtain landscape contracts with various outlet malls. One contract in particular was with Shopper's Lane ("Lane"), a relatively new outlet mall. Gertrude contracted with Lane to plant several sets of exotic azalea bushes in various colors such as pink, purple, and blue. As for the blue azalea bushes, Gertrude must go through a special supplier obtain them. To ensure proper cultivation, Gertrude must also order special fertilizer and other gardening items.

Several weeks later when Gertrude was ready to begin the massive gardening project at Lane, the owner changed his mind as to the blue azaleas and refused to accept them. Gertrude had no other gardening projects until months later and conversely, she had no use for them herself.

Is Lane LLC entitled to reimburse Gertrude for the price of the Azaleas? What if Gertrude was able to sell a portion of the flowers to her neighbor for a much lower price than what Lane would have paid?

(Written by Ms. Brianna Golden)

CHAPTER 12

THE NATURE, FORM, AND PERFECTION OF THE CONTRACT OF LEASE

Flowchart

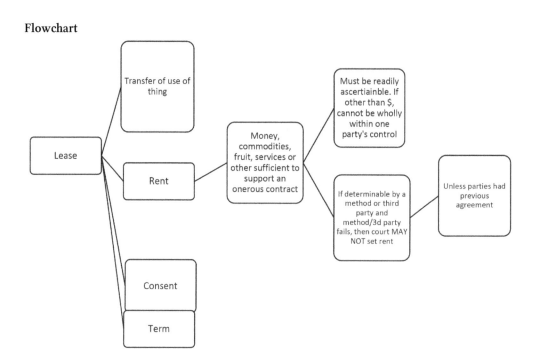

Section 1: General Concepts

Read Articles 2668-2674.
Article 2668 states:

> A lease is a synallagmatic contract by which one party, the lessor, binds himself to give to the
> other party, the lessee, the use and enjoyment of a thing for a term in exchange for a rent that
> the lessee binds himself to pay. The consent of the parties as to the thing and the rent is essential
> but not necessarily sufficient for a contract of lease.

Thus, the elements of a lease include the thing, the rent, and consent. If any of these is missing or fails, then there is no lease. As indicated in comment (a) the term rent is used, rather than price, because the rent paid need not be in money. For example, the lessee of farmland can pay rent in terms of a portion of the crop raised on the land. A lease differs from a sale in that it involves the exchange of only two components of ownership (usus and fructus), not abusus, and that the fee paid for such use need not be in money.

Title IX on Lease was revised in 2004, with the goal of modernizing and clarifying the concepts. Under the new definition, lease applies only to things, not services so articles 2645-2750 on the "Letting out of services" are unrevised and are excluded from the concept of a lease. As with the articles on sale, the lease articles are supplemented by the general obligations and conventional obligations articles. Art. 2669. Just as one can have a contract to sell, one can have a contract to lease, as provided in Art. 2670,

Article 2671 explains that there are different kinds of leases: residential, agricultural, mineral, commercial, or consumer. The first two of these involve immovables, while a consumer lease applies only to movables intended for the lessee's personal or familial use outside his trade or purposes. A commercial lease could refer to the lease either of a commercial building or commercial equipment. Note that mineral leases are governed by the mineral code, but where the Mineral Code does not expressly or impliedly provide for a particular situation, then the Civil Code provisions supplement what is not covered in the Mineral Code. Article 2672 & comments.

Just as with a sale, all things, corporeal or incorporeal, that are susceptible of ownership may be the object of a lease, unless prohibited by law. Art. 2673. However, there is a significant and logical difference: one can sell things that cannot be used without being destroyed by that very use, but one cannot lease them. For example, one can lease restaurant equipment, but not the food that will be cooked with it. One can, however, 'borrow' a cup of sugar. This is a loan for consumption, a gratuitous agreement where the borrower is bound to return to the lender an equal amount of things of the same kind and quality. Art. 2904. Thus, a loan, a gratuitous contract, is entirely different from a lease, where the lessee must pay rent, though in either case, one party gets the use of the thing and must at some point return it.

Contrary to what one might expect, the lessor need not necessarily own the thing being leased: "A lease of a thing that does not belong to the lessor may nevertheless be binding on the parties." In such case, the lessor must have the right to use the thing and the right to allow others to use it. If he does not, and his lessee is deprived of its use, then the lessee will have a claim against his lessor for breach of the warranty of peaceful possession. La. Civ. Code art. 2700. Consequently, under Louisiana lease law, a tenant may sublease residential property he has leased to a subtenant unless the original lease specifically prohibits it. As a matter of experience, most leases do prohibit subleases without the lessor's consent.

In addition to a thing, rent, and consent, a lease "shall" have a term. Article 2678. That term may be fixed or indeterminate. Id. It may be fixed, meaning that the parties set a date for its termination or agree that it will terminate when a designated event occurs. Id. In any case, a term cannot exceed ninety-nine years. Art. 2679. The term may be indeterminate, meaning that the parties did not specify a termination date. If so, then the law provides a term as per Article 2680.

A. The Rent

Read Louisiana Civil Code Articles 2464-2466 (including the revision comments) and compare them to Civil Code Articles 2675-2676. Read as well Sale Exposé des Motifs 1.6-1.8; Précis pp. 29-30, 135-36.

The payment of rent is as necessary to a lease as the payment of a price is necessary to a sale, but there are some differences. As you know, for a sale a price must be in money (or else the transaction is called an exchange). In contrast, rent can be in "money, commodities, fruits, services, or other performances sufficient to support an onerous contract." Art. 2675. The Civil Code articles on Sale provide for an open price term, and they also provide that the parties may make provision for the price to be determined by a third party. Similarly, the Article 2675 on lease similarly provides:

> The rent shall be fixed by the parties in a sum either certain or determinable through a method agreed by them. It may also be fixed by a third person designated by them.
>
> If the agreed method proves unworkable or the designated third person is unwilling or unable to fix the rent, then there is no lease.
>
> If the rent has been established and thereafter is subject to redetermination either by a designated third person or through a method agreed to by the parties, but the third person is unwilling or unable to fix the rent or the agreed method proves unworkable, the court may either fix the rent or provide a similar method in accordance with the intent of the parties.

Review Benglis Sash & Door Co. v. Leonards 387 So.2d 1171 (La. 1980) from the chapter on price, as well the Civil Code's rules on that topic. Are agreements on rent handled the same way?

Study question:

If the price is out of all proportion to the thing, then we presume that the sale is a simulation, is the same true of a lease? Consider the following hypothets and cases.

1. Seller owns a house on Audubon Boulevard. A recent appraisal was $750,000. Seller and Buyer agree that Buyer may acquire ownership of this house for payment of $1. Is it a sale? What if the payment is $10,000?

Would the rules on lesion apply to the $1 sale or the $10,000 sale (if it is a sale)?

2. Lois and Bob are fifty-fifty partners, and their partnership owns an office building. Their partnership agreement provides a buyout mechanism. "One partner may offer to buy the other partner's interest in the Partnership in writing. Within seventy-two hours of receipt of the offer, the other partner may either agree to sell at the offered price or to buy the offeror's partnership interest at that same price." Is the price certain?

3. Frank François has a 1000 Euro note. Van Vespucci has a 1000 United States dollar note. Frank promises to give Van the Euro note if Van gives Frank the dollar note. Do they have an agreement, and therefore a contract? Is the contract a sale? If so, which one of them can invoke Louisiana Civil Code art. 2487? That is, which one of them does that article empower to hold onto the note that has now become the other's property until the other delivers the note he promised to deliver?

WILLIS V VENTRELLA 1996
674 SO. 2D 991 (LA. 1ST. CIR CT. APP.)

SHORTESS, Judge.

¶1 Daniel Konrad Willis (plaintiff) owned 835 acres upon which his neighbors, G. Gary Ventrella and Dione M. Ventrella (defendants), wished to hunt. Plaintiff and defendants executed a document entitled "Hunting Lease" which was drafted by plaintiff and contained strikeouts and interlineations made by G. Gary Ventrella (Ventrella). The document is undated, but according to the parties, it was intended to be effective with the 1991 hunting season.

¶2 The draft of the document provided that each year defendants were to pay $2,000.00 plus the property taxes and were to provide 120 hours of work with a bulldozer. Defendants were also obligated to maintain all roads and creek crossings in a condition suitable for passage by two-wheel-drive vehicles and log trucks. At the time the document was executed, Ventrella struck out certain portions of the paragraph regarding bulldozer work in the "Consideration" section so that it ultimately read as follows:

> LESSEE further agrees to provide dozer work with a bull dozer of the equivalent of a John
> DEER[E] 450, provided that lessee shall have the right to select the type of dozer provided that
> it have the capacity of a John DEER[E] 450 OR EQUAL, or that lessee shall have the right to
> provide a smaller dozer, but, in the exercise of which option, the smaller dozer shall perform the

equivalent amount of work as a John DEER[E] 450 would do, for general purposes of capital improvement to the leasehold, at direction of lessor, such as building ponds, lakes, clearing rights of way, clearing land, removing stumps, or any other work that lessor shall direct.

¶3   By 1992 problems developed between plaintiff and defendants. From September 1992 throughout 1993, plaintiff complained to Ventrella that he had failed to provide dozer work, had failed to maintain the roads properly, and was hunting at close range to plaintiff's home. On December 7, 1993, plaintiff's counsel sent a letter to defendants notifying them eviction proceedings would be filed against them if they were not off the property by December 31.

¶4   When defendants refused to comply, plaintiff filed a "Petition for Damages and Injunctive Relief" seeking a declaration the "lease" had been breached, compensation for damage to the property, and an injunction preventing defendants or their invitees from using firearms within 800 meters of his home or from using "high power rifles" anywhere on the property. After a hearing, the trial court granted the injunctive relief.

¶5   Plaintiff then filed a rule for eviction in the same suit record. The trial court denied the rule in part because the rent which plaintiff claimed was unpaid was not yet due. When plaintiff filed a second rule for eviction, defendants filed an exception of improper cumulation (sic) of actions. After a hearing, the trial court granted the eviction because defendants had failed to pay the cash consideration for 1994 and had avoided or performed in a substandard manner, bulldozer work contemplated by the lease. The court also denied the exception.

¶6   Finally, the trial court tried the merits of plaintiff's claim for damages. After hearing all new testimony for this portion of the case, the court found the document was not a valid lease because the price was not certain and determinate as required by Louisiana Civil Code article 2671. The court awarded compensation to plaintiff, however, under the theory of unjust enrichment. The court also awarded plaintiff the cost of repairing road work improperly performed by Ventrella but denied plaintiff's demand for attorney fees.

¶7   From this judgment defendants have appealed. Plaintiff has answered the appeal seeking attorney fees.

I. WAS THERE AN ENFORCEABLE LEASE?

A. Law

¶8   The Civil Code defines "lease" as a "synallagmatic contract, to which consent alone is sufficient, and by which one party gives to the other the enjoyment of a thing, or his labor, at a fixed price." La. C.C. art. 2669 (emphasis added). Three elements are essential: the thing, the price, and the consent. La. C.C. art. 2670. The requisites of "price" are set forth in article 2671: "The price should be certain and determinate, and should consist of money. However, it may consist in a certain quantity of commodities, or even in a portion of the fruits yielded by the thing leased." While the price need not be in money but may consist of other considerations, Louisiana Ass'n for Mental Health v. Edwards, 322 So.2d 761, 767 (La.1975), it must be readily ascertainable and determinable from facts or circumstances not within the control of the parties. Mouton v. P.A.B., Inc., 450 So.2d 410, 413 (La.App. 3d Cir.), writ denied, 458 So.2d 118 (La.1984).

B. Analysis

¶9   A portion of the consideration section of the "lease" provides the dozer work is to be done "at direction of lessor." The amount of dozer work to be done is not readily ascertainable. Furthermore, it is determinable solely from circumstances within the control of the parties. The trial court was legally correct in finding the essential element of a certain and determinate price was absent in this case, and thus the lease was unenforceable.

* * *

III. DID THE TRIAL COURT ERR IN APPLYING THE DOCTRINE OF UNJUST ENRICHMENT?

A. Law

¶13   There is a general concept of quasi contractual obligations based upon the principle that where there is an unjust enrichment of one at the expense or impoverishment of another, the value or the enrichment must be restituted. Minyard v. Curtis Products, 251 La. 624, 205 So.2d 422, 432 (1967). Thus, when a plaintiff confers a benefit on a defendant in pursuance of a contract supposedly valid but in truth void, the plaintiff is entitled to restitution of the benefit conferred.

¶14   At common law, damages in this quasi contractual situation would be based on quantum meruit. Barry Nicholas, Unjustified Enrichment in Civil Law and Louisiana Law, 37 Tul.L.Rev.

49, 56-57 (1963). Quantum meruit is not recognized in our Civil Code, although it has been applied by our courts. A similar equitable remedy, the actio de in rem verso or unjust enrichment, is firmly rooted in our Civil Code. Gray v. McCormick, 94-1282, p. 6 (La.App. 3d Cir. 10/18/95), 663 So.2d 480, 486.

¶15   Civil Code article 2055, in pertinent part, contains this moral maxim: "Equity ... is based on the principles that no one is allowed to take unfair advantage of another and that no one is allowed to enrich himself unjustly at the expense of another." The supreme court has enumerated five distinct prerequisites for the application of the doctrine of unjust enrichment: (1) an enrichment; (2) an impoverishment; (3) a causal relationship between the enrichment and the impoverishment; (4) an absence of justification or cause for the enrichment or impoverishment; and (5) the absence of any other remedy at law. Kirkpatrick v. Young, 456 So.2d 622, 624 (La.1984); Minyard, 205 So.2d at 432.

¶16   Civil Code article 2298 refers to these principles as "enrichment without cause." Although this article was effective January 1, 1996, and thus was not in effect when the benefit was conferred or the subject judgment was rendered, it expresses principles based on existing civilian doctrine and jurisprudence. This article provides:

> A person who has been enriched without cause at the expense of another person is bound to compensate that person. The term "without cause" is used in this context to exclude cases in which the enrichment results from a valid juridical act or the law. The remedy declared here is subsidiary and shall not be available if the law provides another remedy for the impoverishment or declares a contrary rule.

¶17   The amount of compensation due is measured by the extent to which one has been enriched or the other has been impoverished, whichever is less.

¶18   The extent of the enrichment or impoverishment is measured as of the time the suit is brought or, according to the circumstances, as of the time the judgment is rendered.

B. Analysis

¶19   The trial court found the principle of unjust enrichment required plaintiff be compensated for the fair lease value of the 835-acre tract. Although the court did not specifically discuss the five prerequisites, we find they were met. Defendants were enriched by enjoying the benefit of hunting rights on plaintiff's property for three years. Plaintiff was impoverished by the loss of revenue from leasing the property at fair market value. Plaintiff's loss was directly related to defendants' gain; he could not lease the property to another when he believed he had validly leased it to defendants.

¶20   The late Justice Tate explained the fourth prerequisite, the absence of legal cause, as existing when no lawful contract or provision of law permits the enrichment or prevents the impoverishment. Albert Tate, Jr., The Louisiana Action for Unjustified Enrichment, 50 Tul.L.Rev. 883, 887 (1976). In this case, as there was no lawful lease, there was no legal cause for the enrichment and resulting impoverishment. Finally, there was no other remedy at law as plaintiff could not enforce an invalid lease.

¶21   Thus, the trial court correctly applied the principles of unjust enrichment or enrichment without cause to the facts of this case. Defendants' contentions that these principles should not have been utilized are without merit.

IV. ARE THE DAMAGES AWARDED SUPPORTED BY THE RECORD?

A. Law

¶22   In the assessment of damages in cases of quasi contracts, much discretion must be left to the trier of fact. La. C.C. art. 2324.1. The trial court's award of damages is supported by thorough written reasons. His finding of a fair lease price of $12.00 per acre is supported by testimony that the "going rate" in the area is $10.00 to $12.00 per acre, that plaintiff's sister leases adjoining property for $15.00 per acre, and that plaintiff now leases his property for $15.00 per acre.

¶23   Regarding damages for road repairs necessitated by Ventrella's improper road maintenance, defendants contend in their brief that the trial court "placed too great a weight on the evidence adduced by the [plaintiff] with respect to damage to the roads." The weight accorded plaintiff's evidence was a credibility decision which will not be disturbed by this court in the absence of manifest error. Rosell v. ESCO, 549 So.2d 840, 844 (La.1989).

¶24   Plaintiff's claim of damage to the roads was supported by his testimony and photographs of the roads, and the cost to repair them was supported by the testimony of plaintiff and a heavy equipment operator, William Buckley. We find no manifest error in the factual findings, and no abuse of discretion in the amount of damages awarded.

V. SHOULD PLAINTIFF HAVE BEEN AWARDED ATTORNEY FEES?

¶25 The trial court denied plaintiff's claim for attorney fees because the claim was based on a provision in the invalid lease. Plaintiff has answered the appeal seeking a reversal of that portion of the trial court's decision.

¶26 Attorney fees may not be awarded except where authorized by statute or contract. Maloney v. Oak Builders, 256 La. 85, 235 So.2d 386, 390 (1970); Burns v. McDermott, Inc., 95-0195 p. 5 (La.App. 1st Cir. 11/9/95), 665 So.2d 76, 79. Plaintiff cites no statutory provision allowing attorney fees in a quasi contractual situation, and the trial court correctly held the attorney fees provision in the invalid lease was unenforceable. Plaintiff's answer to the appeal has no merit.

VI. CONCLUSION

¶27 For these reasons, the judgment of the trial court is affirmed. Defendants are cast with all costs of this appeal.

AFFIRMED.

Study Questions:

Does Article 1816 of the Civil Code of 1870 ("OA 1816") decide the Benglis facts or does it address a slightly different situation? If you'd written (or dissented from) the Benglis opinion, would you have cited it?

OA 1811.

The proposition as well as the assent to a contract may be express or implied:

Express when evinced by words, either written or spoken;

Implied, when it is manifested by actions, even by silence or by inaction, in cases in which they can from circumstances be supposed to mean, or by legal presumption are directed to be considered as evidence of an assent.

OA 1812.

Express consent must be given in a language understood by the party who accepts, and the words by which it is conveyed must be in themselves unequivocal; if they may mean different things, they give rise to error, which, as is hereinafter provided, destroys the effect of a contract.

OA 1813.

Even when words are unequivocal and expressive of assent, they are not always obligatory, when from the context, if in writing, or from what in speech is equivalent to it, the words which immediately precede, or follow, it appears that the party did not intend to obligate himself.

OA 1814.

Unequivocal words, expressive of mere intent, do not make an obligation.

OA 1815.

A positive promise, that, from the manner in which it is made, shows that there was no serious intent to contract, creates no obligation.

OA 1816.

Actions without words, either written or spoken, are presumptive evidence of a contract, when they are done under circumstances that naturally imply a consent to such contract. To receive goods from a merchant without any express promise, and to use them, implies a contract to pay the value. If an offer is made of an article in deposit, and the article is received, the contract of deposit is complete. If a mandate is acted on, the mandatary is bound in the same manner as if he had accepted in writing. In all those cases and others of the like nature, all the conditions, which he, who gives or proposes, annexed to the delivery or the acceptance of the proposition, are also presumed to have been accepted by the act of receiving. If the merchant, in delivering the goods, declare that they must be paid for by a certain time; if the depositor designate how the deposit is to be kept, or the mandator in what manner his commission is to be executed, he who receives and acts is obligated to the performance of all these conditions.

OA 1817.

Silence and inaction are also, under some circumstances the means of showing an assent that creates an obligation; if, after the termination of a lease, the lessee continue in possession, and the lessor be inactive and silent, a complete mutual obligation for continuing the lease, is created by the act of occupancy of the tenant on the one side, and the inaction and silence of the lessor on the other.

OA 1818.

Where the law does not create a legal presumption of consent from certain facts, then, as in the case of other simple presumptions, it must be left to the discretion of the judge, whether assent is to be implied from them or not.

Study Questions:

What articles apply in the following cases? Consider Articles OA 1812-1818 as they might have applied to the following cases involving lease. Would their application result in a different decision?

MYERS V. BURKE 1939

189 SO. 482 (LA. APP. 1ST CIR.)

[Defendant Burke gave plaintiff Myers permission to occupy defendant's land on the Calcasieu River and build a dwelling on it for payment of $1/year. Defendant subsequently sold the land and the purchaser evicted the plaintiff upon his refusal to pay $1/week rent. Plaintiff is now suing for the $500 value of the improvements. The defendant's position is that the improvements (i.e. the dwelling) were to become his property. Plaintiff claimed that was not true, that he was to be allowed to remove them. Only the portion of the opinion dealing with the issue of whether the agreement constituted a lease is included.]

OTT, Judge.

* * *

¶1 It is obvious that these plaintiffs were not occupying this property as lessees under a lease. The essentials of a lease are the thing, the price and the consent. Civil Code, Article 2670. The price should be certain and determinate, and unless there is a price fixed in money, or some commodity or fruits of the land, so that the price can be determined, there is no lease. Civil Code, Article 2671; University Pub. Co. v. Piffet, et al., 34 La.Ann. 602. The consideration of one dollar per year that is mentioned was not a serious consideration as rent. If defendant had so considered it, he would have been bound for one year on the payment of the one dollar by plaintiffs, and they could not have been evicted by defendant before the end of year. The whole tenor of defendant's answer and his testimony goes to show that he considered the plaintiffs nothing more than licensees occupying the land at his will.

* * *

¶2 As the relations of the parties are not to be considered from the standpoint of lessor and lessee, the articles of the Code relating to lease have no application to the case. The right of the plaintiffs to recover the value of their houses arises under Article 508 of the Civil Code which gives a third person who places improvements on the land of another the right to recover for the value of the material and workmanship when these improvements are kept by the owner of the land. Kibbe v. Campbell, 34 La.Ann. 1163; Womack v. Womack et al., 2 La.Ann. 339.

* * *

T. B. GUILLORY INC. V. NORTH AMERICAN GAMING ENTERTAINMENT CORP. 1999

741 SO.2D 44 (LA.APP. 3D CIR.)

SULLIVAN, Judge.

¶1   This suit is based upon a written lease of immovable property for use as a truck stop, restaurant, and video gaming parlor. The lessee appeals a judgment declaring that an option to renew the lease is unenforceable because it lacks a determinate price. The lessor has also appealed, objecting to the trial court's finding that the lessee was not in default when it attempted to exercise the option to renew. For the following reasons, we affirm the judgment of the trial court in all respects.

Facts and Procedural History

¶2   On April 28, 1992, Tonas B. "Bill" Guillory and T.B. Guillory, Inc., leased King's Truck Stop and Lucky Lady Casino (King's) in St. Landry Parish to O.M. Investors, Inc. for the operation of a truck stop, restaurant, and video gaming parlor. T.B. Guillory, Inc. is a closely-held corporation owned by Mr. Guillory and his son, Blane Guillory. The principal shareholders in O.M. Investors, Inc. were Lamar Ozley and Don Williams. Subsequently, O.M. Investors, Inc. merged with North American Gaming Entertainment Corporation (North American), a publicly-traded company in which Mr. Ozley and Mr. Williams also have a significant ownership interest. (Mr. Ozley is North American's acting chief executive officer.) North American then transferred its interest in the lease to O.M. Operating, L.L.C. (O.M. Operating).

¶3   The lease provided for a primary term of five years, from May 1, 1992 through April 30, 1997, with rent equal to "20% of the net revenue from the Video Poker Machines on the premises." "Net Revenue" was defined as the "total money played in all machines, less all payout on winnings to players and less the fee paid the State of Louisiana as provided by Law." The lessee assumed the obligations of renovating and operating the premises as a "first class twenty-four (24) hour restaurant and truck stop" and of purchasing between twenty and fifty video poker machines.

¶4   The lease also contained the following option that forms the basis of this dispute:

14. OPTION TO RENEW: Provided that Lessee is not in default in the performance of this lease, Lessee shall have the option to renew the Lease for three (3) additional five (5) year terms commencing at the expiration of the initial lease term or any renewal term. All terms and conditions

of the lease shall apply during any renewal term except that the monthly percentage due Lessor shall be negotiable. The option shall be exercised by written notice given to Lessor not less than ninety (90) days prior to the expiration of the initial lease term or any renewal term. If notice is not given in the manner provided herein within the time specified, this option shall expire. (Emphasis added.)

¶5   On January 16, 1997, O.M. Operating timely notified Mr. Guillory of its intention to exercise this option. Between January and July of 1997, the parties exchanged several written proposals concerning the rent during the renewal term, but they failed to reach an agreement. On April 10, 1997, Mr. Guillory and T.B. Guillory, Inc. filed a petition to evict North American and O.M. Operating from the premises. In their answer, Defendants alleged that Plaintiffs refused to negotiate the price of the option in good faith. Defendants also filed a reconventional demand seeking specific performance of the option at a price set by the court or through negotiations by the parties or, alternatively, damages under unjust enrichment and attorney fees as provided in the lease. Plaintiffs later amended their petition to allege that Defendants breached their obligation to perform in good faith by opening another truck stop and video casino that directly competed with King's.

¶6   Pat Willis, Jr., an attorney from Opelousas, Louisiana, negotiated the King's lease on behalf of Mr. Guillory and T.B. Guillory, Inc. Mr. Willis also drafted the final document. He testified that Mr. Ozley and Mr. Williams initially proposed a ten-year primary term with rent at ten percent of net gaming revenue and a ten-year option at the same rental rate. The parties eventually negotiated a five-year primary term at twenty percent of net gaming revenue and three five-year options, but at the time the lease was executed they were still unable to agree on the rent during the option periods.

¶7   Mr. Willis drafted the option to reflect the failure to agree on the price, believing that the parties would negotiate in good faith at the time of renewal because they had done so initially. When Mr. Willis drafted the lease, he believed that the option was enforceable, although he admitted that if the parties did not reach an agreement there would be no option. Mr. Willis later drafted similar contracts concerning the right to place video poker machines at other truck stops. In those documents or in his notes concerning those transactions, he used the terms "industry standards" or increases in "small increments" when referring to rent during renewal periods. However, Mr. Willis did not recall these terms in any discussions about the King's lease.

¶8   Mr. Guillory testified that Mr. Ozley and Mr. Williams approached him about leasing King's after the truck stop had been closed for six to eight months. (Mr. Guillory had decided to close

King's when Blane Guillory, its manager, returned to college.) Mr. Guillory believed that the lessee did not fulfill its obligation of operating a "first class" truck stop during the primary term of the lease. He often complained about the condition of the building's appearance, the bathrooms, and the parking lot, eventually resurfacing the parking lot at his own expense. He also believed that Mr. Ozley and Mr. Williams breached their duty to perform in good faith when a corporation that they owned, Ozdon, Inc., opened the I-49 Truck Stop and Gold Rush Casino (Gold Rush) within eight miles of King's and which competed for King's customers. (Ozdon, Inc. later sold full ownership of the Gold Rush to North American.) Although Mr. Guillory believed that the option required him to negotiate in good faith, he did not believe he would be forced to agree to terms that he found unacceptable.

¶9 Mr. Ozley testified that he initially proposed a ten-year lease with a ten-year option. Although he did not succeed in securing this commitment, he testified that he was happy with the lease that was negotiated. During the primary term, his corporation invested approximately $300,000 to improve the existing premises and another $300,000 to purchase the video poker machines. He stated that he would not have invested that amount of money for only a five-year commitment. He believed that the option would be negotiated at a "reasonable" price or at one that was not "artificially high." However, he admitted that the parties had never discussed what would happen if they could not agree on a price at the time of renewal.

¶10 To address Mr. Guillory's concern about competition from the Gold Rush and Mr. Ozley's concern about continuing the business beyond the five-year primary term, the parties attempted to amend the lease in 1993. They drafted an agreement in which Mr. Guillory would receive forty percent of King's net gaming revenue for twenty years, but he would then return the additional twenty percent to Mr. Ozley and Mr. Williams in exchange for twenty percent of the profits at the Gold Rush. They never implemented this arrangement, however, because of a misunderstanding about whether Mr. Guillory's interest in the Gold Rush would be based on gaming revenue only or on profits from all concerns on the premises.

¶11 In a bench trial, the trial court limited the issues to whether the option was valid and whether the lessee was in default, leaving the questions of good faith, damages, and unjust enrichment to be determined at a later date. In written reasons, the trial court found that the option was unenforceable because it lacked a determinate price. Although not necessary to its holding, the trial court also determined that the lessee was not in default. From this ruling, both sides have appealed.

Opinion

¶12   La. Civ. Code art. 2670 provides that three things are "absolutely necessary" to the contract of lease: thing, price, and consent. "The price should be certain and determinate, and should consist of money. However, it may consist in a certain quantity of commodities, or even in a portion of the fruits yielded by the thing leased." La. Civ. Code art. 2671. La. Civ. Code art. 2672 provides that the price may be left to a "third person named and determined," but if this third person cannot or will not fix the price, there is no lease. Further, the contract is null "if the price were left to be fixed by a person not designated." Id.

¶13   Defendants argue that this case is governed by Benglis Sash & Door Co. v. Leonards, 387 So.2d 1171 (La.1980), in which the supreme court upheld a contract of sale, notwithstanding the parties' failure to set a price at the time of the sale. In Benglis, the defendant's agent placed a special order for windows with a vendor that he frequently patronized. The vendor sued when the defendant refused to accept delivery of the windows. In finding that the parties consented to buy and sell the windows at a reasonable price, the supreme court relied on the history of prior dealings between the parties and the fact that the defendant did not object to the price that was charged.

¶14   Although Benglis involved the contract of sale, its rationale has been applied to the contract of lease. See Carmichael v. Gene Allen Air Service, Inc., 532 So.2d 407 (La.App. 3 Cir.), writ denied, 534 So.2d 447 (La.1988) (where circumstances, including the parties' prior dealings, supported the finding of a lease of an airplane, even though no price was discussed at time of rental). However, we find both Benglis and Carmichael readily distinguishable from the present case. First, we note that the parties to the King's lease had no prior business dealings. Second, and more important, the amount of the price in the Benglis and Carmichael cases was never at issue, whereas here it forms the basis of the dispute. Indeed, the present parties' inability to agree on the price of the option has persisted throughout their business relationship. They could not agree in 1992 when they executed the lease, in 1993 when they attempted to amend it, and in 1997 at the conclusion of the primary term. In Benglis, the supreme court specifically distinguished those cases "in which the parties negotiated price but failed to agree, thereby creating circumstances under which one could not reasonably infer the parties implied consent to a reasonable price." Id. at 1173 (emphasis added).

¶15   Defendants next argue that the option is enforceable because it provides a method of reaching a "certain and determinate" price, i.e., through negotiation. We disagree. In Louis Werner Sawmill Co. v. O'Shee, 111 La. 817, 821, 35 So. 919, 921 (1904) (emphasis added), the supreme court offered the following guidance in determining whether a price has been set:

"What is essential," says Marcadé, Comm. on art. 1592, C. N., "is that the parties should have bound themselves in such way that the price may be thereafter determined as a mere consequence of the consent given by them, without any new act of volition on their part. If, for example, after the parties had said that the sale was made for a price as to which they would agree thereafter, they added, or which, in case of disagreement, should be fixed by an expert to be appointed by the parties themselves or by the judge of the district, it is clear that there would be a sale, since it would no longer be within the power of the parties to prevent the fixing of the price.. ."

¶16   In Mouton v. P.A. B., Inc., 450 So.2d 410, 413 (La.App. 3 Cir.), writ denied, 458 So.2d 118 (La.1984) (emphasis added), we stated that "[a]s long as the rent can be determined from factors or circumstances not within the control of the parties, the rent is certain." Thus, in Mouton, we held that, where the rent was fixed at a percentage of net profits, one party could not unilaterally change the method of determining profits that had previously been used. In Bonfanti v. Davis, 487 So.2d 165 (La.App. 3 Cir.1986), we found that excess rent tied to a cost of living index was determinable, even though two such indexes resulted in slightly different figures. See also Sealy v. Physicians & Surgeons Hosp., Inc., 480 So.2d 832 (La.App. 2 Cir.1985), writ denied, 483 So.2d 1024 (La.1986) (where an option reserving the landlord's right to recalculate rent based upon the Department of Labor Consumer Price Index was held enforceable). In the instant case, similar provisions removing the determination of rent from the parties' control are simply not present. Additionally, even if we agreed that such terms as "industry standards," "going rate," and increases in "small increments" could have produced a certain price, these words do not appear in the lease and were not discussed in the initial negotiations.

¶17   We also reject Defendants' argument that setting a price by negotiation is tantamount to establishing a price by arbitration or through experts. Relying on experts or arbiters "provide[s] a method by which a price could be determined by third parties in future negotiations, one that could not be frustrated by any act of commission or omission of buyer or seller." I.P. Timberlands Operating Co., Ltd. v. Denmiss Corp., 93-1637, p. 52 (La.App. 1 Cir. 5/23/95); 657 So.2d 282, 313, writ denied, 95-1958 (La.10/27/95); 661 So.2d 1348 (emphasis added) (quoting Shell Oil Co. v. Texas Gas Transmission Corp., 210 So.2d 554, 560 (La.App. 4 Cir.), writ denied, 252 La. 847, 214 So.2d 165, 166 (1968)). Negotiation by the parties does not place the final determination into the hands of a third party, and the courts cannot assume that role. See La. Civ. Code art. 2762.

¶18   In their final argument, Defendants request that we remand the case for a determination of whether the Guillorys negotiated the price of the option in good faith. We find that such a remand would be futile. Mr. Willis, Mr. Ozley, and **9 Mr. Guillory all stated that in 1992 everyone negotiated the lease in good faith, yet even then they could not agree on a price for the option. Good faith negotiations in 1997 would not necessarily have resulted in a later agreement, and bad faith negotiations would not have changed the fact that the option, as written, was never enforceable. For these same reasons, we also find that we need not address Plaintiffs' appeal on the issue of default.

Decree

¶19   For the above reasons, the judgment of the trial court is affirmed. Costs of this appeal are assessed to North American Gaming Entertainment Corporation and O.M. Operating, L.L.C.

AFFIRMED.

HUNT V. GULFTRUST FUND NO. FIFTEEN, INC. 1992
606 SO.2D 25. (LA. APP. 5TH CIR.)

BURNS, Judge Pro Tem.

¶1   Gulftrust Fund No. Fifteen, Inc. (Gulftrust) appeals a judgment declaring the purported sale of immovable property situated in Kenner, Louisiana to be null and void. We affirm.

¶2   On September 1, 1989, Gulftrust and Ernest E. Hunt executed in authentic form an agreement entitled a "Sale Subject to Mortgage." Under that agreement, Gulftrust supposedly acquired title to immovable property owned by Mr. Hunt but encumbered with first and second mortgages. The agreement provided that, while ownership of the property passed to Gulftrust, Mr. Hunt remained personally liable for payment of the mortgages on the property. The sales price was recited to be $33,068.77, of which Mr. Hunt was to receive $1,000.00. The remaining portion of the sales price represented the balance due on the two mortgages.

¶3   Mr. Hunt filed suit against Gulftrust in district court, seeking to have the property sale declared a nullity. The parties concurred at the trial that Mr. Hunt only received $400.00 of the $1,000.00 cash payment specified by the agreement. However, the testimony of the parties conflicted regarding any further understandings as to the sales price or its payment. At the trial's conclusion, the judge ruled in favor of Mr. Hunt and declared the sale null. He also ordered the return of the $400.00 paid by Gulftrust to Mr. Hunt.

¶4   Gulftrust first contends that the trial judge erroneously concluded the transaction between the parties to be a sale with assumption of mortgage, as opposed to a sale subject to mortgage.

In its appellate brief, Gulftrust correctly notes the legal distinction between these two types of sales. See Leisure Villa Investors v. Life & Cas. Ins., 527 So.2d 520, 523 (La.App. 3rd Cir.1988), writ denied, 532 So.2d 157 (La.1988). The trial judge did not conclude, however, that the transaction at issue constituted a sale with assumption of mortgage. Rather, he commented on the convoluted nature of this purported sale [FN1] and referred to the parties' apparent disagreement over assumption of the mortgages as illustrative of that comment. This specification of error therefore lacks merit.

¶5   The remaining error assignments challenge the district court judgment declaring this sale null for lack of consideration. Gulftrust argues that the parties to this case entered into an enforceable sale supported by adequate consideration.

¶6   A valid sale in Louisiana requires concurrence on three elements: the thing sold, the price, and the consent of the parties. La. Civ. Code art. 2439. The specific amount of the sales price need not be stated at the time of contracting. The parties are free to agree upon a price to be fixed by computation, arbitration or any other method of calculation. The essential factor is that the parties reach a meeting of the minds as to price. Benglis Sash & Door Co. v. Leonards, 387 So.2d 1171, 1172 1173 (La.1980).

¶7   The sale of immovable property must be made by authentic act or under private signature. La. Civ. Code art. 2440. An authentic act constitutes full proof of the agreement contained in it as against the contracting parties. La. Civ. Code art. 1835. Under the parol evidence rule, embodied in Article 1848 of the Louisiana Civil Code, testimonial or other evidence may not be admitted to negate or vary the contents of an authentic act or an act under private signature. However, Article 1848 recognizes an exception to that rule: parol evidence may be admitted, in the interest of justice, to prove such circumstances as a vice of consent, or a simulation, or to prove that the written act was modified by a subsequent and valid oral agreement. A party to an authentic act who alleges that the act was executed through fraud, error or mistake may be permitted to introduce parol evidence to support such allegations. Mitchell v. Clark, 448 So.2d 681 (La.1984); Billingsley v. Bach Energy Corp., 588 So.2d 786 (La.App. 2nd Cir.1991).

¶8   Although the property sale at issue was executed in authentic form, neither party invoked the parole evidence rule in this case. During trial parol testimony was admitted, without objection, to explain the dealings and intentions of the parties. Mr. Hunt testified that the agent of Gulftrust with whom he negotiated the sale advised that the company would make the mortgage payments after acquiring the property. The Gulftrust representative who appeared at trial unequivocally denied any such understanding with Mr. Hunt. The sale agreement executed by Gulftrust and Mr. Hunt specified $33,068.77 as the price to be paid by Gulftrust for the property.

However, $32,068.77 of that sales price represented the balance due on the two mortgages for which the sale agreement obligated Mr. Hunt to remain personally liable. The agreement itself thus refutes the validity of its own price provision.

¶9 The conflicting testimony of the parties and the invalid price provision contained in the sale agreement establish that Gulftrust and Mr. Hunt failed to reach a meeting of the minds as to price. Benglis Sash & Door Co. v. Leonards, supra. As a result, there was no contract of sale between these parties which can be given legal effect. First National Bank of Ruston v. Mercer, 448 So.2d 1369, 1375 (La.App. 2d Cir.1984). The trial judge correctly declared the purported sale between Gulftrust and Mr. Hunt to be a nullity, and he properly returned the parties to their original positions by ordering repayment of the $400.00 Mr. Hunt received from Gulftrust.

¶10 Accordingly, the district court judgment is affirmed with Gulftrust to bear costs of this appeal.

AFFIRMED.

B. Consent

Study Questions:

Read Article 2669. Review the conventional obligations articles on consent, Articles 1927-1947, especially Article 1942, Acceptance by Silence, which states:

> When, because of special circumstances, the offeree's silence leads the offeror reasonably to believe that a contract has been formed, the offer is deemed accepted.

> Were there special circumstances in the following cases such that the court should have found acceptance by silence?

> Why does one case hold that there was consent and the other find that there was none?

H. W. AYRES, Judge.

¶1 By this action, plaintiffs seek to recover of the defendant the sum of $276 allegedly due as rent on certain of plaintiffs' property occupied by the defendant. The defense is there was no contract of lease upon which a claim for rent may be predicated. From a judgment in favor of plaintiffs, as prayed for, defendant appealed.

¶2 The factual situation upon which plaintiffs' claim for rent is predicated may be briefly stated. Plaintiffs, as the owners of Lots 48 and 49, Square 428, 2d District, of the City of New Orleans, on August 18, 1959, sold a portion thereof to the State of Louisiana for right-of-way purposes in connection with the construction of an interstate highway. Plaintiffs retained that portion of the lots fronting 50.04 feet on Catina Street, 62.95 feet in width in the rear, by a depth of 58.04 feet on Homedale Avenue, and 20.20 feet on Florida Avenue. The State, however, acquired, by the sale, the improvements located partially on the property acquired by it and partially on the portion retained by plaintiffs.

¶3 The improvements as purchased by the State were sold by it to the defendant in December, 1959, without a specified time for removal. Defendant, at the time of his purchase, was unaware that plaintiffs had retained a portion of the realty and, consequently, was unaware of the fact that the improvements were located partially on plaintiffs' property. Through subsequent correspondence, defendant's counsel advised plaintiffs' counsel the improvements would be removed by April 30, 1960. Notwithstanding the fact that the defendant had promptly, on making his purchase of the improvements, instructed a house-moving concern to move them, delays were encountered due to the number of houses to be moved and, in this particular case, to the presence of trees for which permission to cut had to be obtained. The removal, however, was carried out on June 9, 1960.

¶4 In the meantime, plaintiffs had requested of defendant, by letter, that the improvements be removed from their property on or prior to April 1, 1960, or, in the event said improvements had not been removed by that date, that the defendant pay rental at the rate of $120 per month. The record does not establish that defendant in any wise or manner assented to plaintiffs' proposition or agreed to pay rent in any amount. For the period from April 1 to June 9, 1960, plaintiffs charged defendant rent in the sum of $276.

¶5 No claim, alternately or otherwise, predicated on a basis of a quantum meruit is made.

¶6 The legal proposition advanced in brief by plaintiffs, in justification of their claim, is that the use of their land by the defendant permits the recovery of rent under the relationship of lessor and lessee (or in quasi contract). This proposition, for the reasons hereinafter assigned, is, in our opinion, untenable.

¶7 A lease in a contract imposing reciprocal obligations on the parties by which one party gives to the other the enjoyment of a thing at a fixed price. LSA-C.C. Art. 2669. To a contract of lease, there are three absolute essentials; namely, the thing forming the subject matter of the contract, the price for its enjoyment, and the consent or agreement of the parties. LSA-C.C. Art. 2670; Caldwell v. Turner, 129 La. 19, 55 So. 695; Myers v. Burke, La.App.1st Cir., 1939, 189 So. 482. Thus, there can be no contract of lease in the absence of a stipulation or agreement between the parties as to the amount of rent to be paid. LSA-C.C. Art. 2671; McCain v. McCain Bros., 165 La. 884, 116 So. 221; Weaks Supply Co. v. Werdin, La.App.2d Cir., 1933, 147 So. 838. Two parties are necessary in order to form a contract, one proposing something and the other accepting and agreement to it; and the will of both parties must unite on the same. LSA-C.C. Art. 1798; Succession of Aurianne, 219 La. 701, 53 So.2d 901; Superior Merchandise Corporation v. Oser, La.App.Orleans, 1942, 8 So.2d 770.

¶8 The terms of plaintiffs' letter to the defendant, upon which they rely as fixing the amount of rent allegedly due them, were, as heretofore pointed out, neither accepted nor agreed to by the defendant. Consequently, there clearly was no meeting of the minds of the parties, and, hence, no contract. LSA-C.C. Art. 1798; Collins v. Louisiana State Lottery Co., 43 La.Ann. 9, 9 So. 27. Plaintiffs' letter to defendant, without an acceptance of the proposal made, is insufficient to constitute a contract between the parties. Hearne v. De Generes, La.App.2d Cir., 1932, 144 So. 194.

¶9 Thus, the unity of will necessary for the formation of a contract is not present here.

¶10 Nor will occupancy alone imply a relationship of lessor and lessee. Terzia v. The Grand Leader, 176 La. 151, 145 So. 363; Weaks Supply Co. v. Werdin, supra; Jordan v. Mead, 19 La.Ann. 101; Blanchard v. Davidson,7 La.Ann. 654.

¶11 At most, all that can be inferred from the record is that defendant was the mere occupant of plaintiffs' property, and, as we have pointed out, it has been repeatedly held that the proof of mere occupancy alone is insufficient to establish the relationship of lessor and lessee.

¶12 As heretofore observed, no basis of recovery under a quasi contract or on a quantum meruit has been alleged or established. Particularly noted is the fact that plaintiffs' petition fails to allege and the record is devoid of any proof as to the rental value of plaintiffs' property which was occupied by the defendant. One cannot, under such circumstances, where there is no lease, sue for an arbitrary amount. The value of the use or occupancy of the property must be established by the evidence.

¶13   The conclusion is therefore inescapable that plaintiffs have failed to establish their claim to that degree of legal certainty and by a preponderance of the evidence which would entitle them to judgment. . . .

Reversed.

Section 2: The Nature of a Lease

Read Article 2671, and Article 2713.

Article 2671 lists several kinds of leases: a residential lease, and agricultural lease, a mineral lease, and a consumer lease, and it specifies that the list is not exclusive, meaning that there may be other kinds of leases. Article 2713 stipulates that a lessee has a right to sublease the thing, unless the contract prohibits it.

MEANS V. COMCAST, INC. 2009
17 SO.3D 1012 (LA. APP. 2D CIR.)

MOORE, J.

¶1   Jesse Means appeals a judgment rejecting his suit to evict his lessee, Comcast, Inc. Comcast answers the appeal, seeking contractual attorney fees. We affirm on the principal demand and amend the judgment to award reasonable attorney fees.

Factual and Procedural Background

¶2   The property involved is a 3,000-sq. ft. tract on Main Street in Gilliam in north Caddo Parish. Means's sister, Mrs. Lay, previously owned the property. In August 1990, Mrs. Lay leased it to Cablevision of Shreveport for the installation of a satellite dish and other transmission and reception facilities. The term of the lease was 15 years, with an option (¶ VII) for the lessee to renew for one additional 15-year term by giving written notice any time prior to the end of the initial term. Rental was set at $1,000 per year, with the lessee to pay all property taxes. The lease also provided for reasonable attorney fees (¶ XII) in the event of legal proceedings. Mrs. Lay did not record the lease.

¶3 In 1992, Time Warner acquired the cable franchise from Cablevision and continued making lease payments to Ms. Lay.

¶4 In May 1998, Means and his wife bought the property from Mrs. Lay's trust. On December 30, 1998, Means sent a letter to Cablevision's manager, advising him of this. The letter concluded: "We are the legal owners of the ground where your cable television facility is located; therefore, please make your lease payment to Jesse L. and Marie S. Means." Time Warner made seven annual lease payments to Means and his wife.

¶5 On March 23, 2005, Time Warner advised Means by letter that it would exercise its option to renew the lease for another 15 years, tendering a check for the first five months' rent. Means refused the check, telling Time Warner that he was not bound by the lease because it was never recorded. In November 2005, Means sent Time Warner a notice to vacate.

¶6 In early 2006, Comcast acquired the cable franchise from Time Warner. Comcast sent Means rent checks for the years 2006, 2007 and 2008, but he refused them.

¶7 Means filed the instant suit to evict Comcast in October 2006. Comcast reconvened, seeking attorney fees under ¶ XII of the lease.

¶8 At trial in October 2008, the parties stipulated to most of the facts outlined above, and Comcast filed exhibits including the unrecorded lease. The elderly Means testified, but he did not remember much. He did not recall ever reading the lease, but admitted he probably knew about it when he bought the property. He admitted that Time Warner sent him a copy of the lease, and that Mrs. Lay's lawyer, the late Sid Galloway, probably told him about it when he bought the property, but he was not certain of this. He admitted writing Time Warner in 1998 and directing them to send all future rent to him, but he could not recall the duration of the lease.

¶9 The district court commended Means's candor but found that by knowingly accepting seven years' rent, he tacitly ratified Mrs. Lay's lease and thus was bound by its renewal provision. The court therefore rejected the claim for eviction. The judgment was silent as to Comcast's prayer for attorney fees.

¶10 Means appealed. His appellate brief was untimely, but this court denied Comcast's motion to dismiss the appeal while Means obtained new counsel. Comcast answered the appeal, seeking contractual attorney fees.

Discussion: Lease and Ratification

¶11   By three assignments of error, Means contends that he was not bound by the terms of an unrecorded lease. First, he asserts that only a recorded lease binds subsequent owners of the property, citing former La. C.C. art. 2733 (now art. 2712), former C.C. arts. 2265 and 2266 (now art. 1839), R.S. 9:2721, and McDuffie v. Walker, 125 La. 152, 51 So. 100 (1909). He shows that Mrs. Lay's lease was not recorded, and contends that because he lacked either actual or constructive notice of its terms, he is not bound by it. Second, he argues the court erred in finding him bound to the renewal option in the unrecorded lease. He cites Julius Gindi & Sons Inc. v. E.J.W. Enterprises Inc., 438 So.2d 594 (La.App. 4 Cir.1983), and Judice-Henry-May Agency Inc. v. Franklin, 376 So.2d 991 (La.App. 1 Cir.), writ denied, 381 So.2d 508 (1980), which restate the basic rule of McDuffie v. Walker but add that even if a recorded instrument refers to an unrecorded lease, the third party is not bound. Third, he contends the court erred in finding a tacit ratification. In support he cites La. C.C. art. 1843 but urges that ratification is essentially an agency relationship in which the burden is on the party asserting the ratification. Fleet Finance Inc. v. Loan Arranger Inc., 604 So.2d 656 (La.App. 1 Cir.1992). He submits there was insufficient proof of agency in that Mrs. Lay made no manifestation of authority to Means and Means relied on none. Broadway v. All-Star Ins. Corp., 285 So.2d 536 (La.1973). He concludes that his 1998 letter to Comcast, requesting payment of all future rent, was insufficient to prove ratification.

¶12   Comcast concedes that under art. 2712, Means would not have been bound by the unrecorded lease, but urges that under art. 1843, he ratified it by accepting the benefits thereof. Comcast cites Pirkle & Williams v. Shreveport Jitney Jungle Inc., 19 La.App. 729, 140 So. 837 (La.App. 2 Cir.1932), and P.J.'s Army Surplus & Co. v. G.D. & G., 93-609 (La.App. 5 Cir. 3/16/94), 635 So.2d 1217, to show that ratification of an unrecorded lease occurs when the new owner allows the lessee to remain on the premises and accepts the rents for a time. Comcast contends that proof of ratification was strong in that Means asserted ownership in 1998, accepted rent payments for seven years, and benefitted from Comcast's tax payments on the tract. Comcast also shows that Means's testimony was equivocal, never excluding the fact that he was indeed aware of the renewal clause when he bought the property from his sister. Finally, Comcast disputes the theory that ratification applies only to agency, as art. 1843 appears in Title III, Chapter 5, "Proof of Obligations," and plainly applies to all obligations.

¶13   Both parties are correct as to the general effect of an unrecorded lease. "An instrument involving immovable property shall have effect against third persons only from the time it is filed for registry in the parish where the property is located." La. C.C. art. 1839. "A third person who acquires an immovable that is subject to an unrecorded lease is not bound by the lease." La. C.C. art. 2712.

¶14 Nevertheless, the law provides for the ratification of obligations, as stated in La. C.C. art. 1843:

> Ratification is a declaration whereby a person gives his consent to an obligation incurred on his behalf without authority.
>
> An express act of ratification must evidence the intention to be bound by the ratified obligation.
>
> Tacit ratification results when a person, with knowledge of an obligation incurred on his behalf by another, accepts the benefits of that obligation.

See also Frazier v. Harper, 600 So.2d 59 (La.1992).

¶15 Although art. 1843's mention of "without authority" suggests an application to agency questions, courts have long applied it to sales and leases. Landry v. Connely, 4 Rob. 127 (1843); Pirkle & Williams Inc. v. Shreveport Jitney Jungle Inc., supra; P.J.'s Army Surplus & Co. v. G.D. & G., supra. In Pirkle & Williams, supra, this court stated:

> Although we should hold that the lease in question was not assumed in the deed of purchase by plaintiff, the record clearly shows that plaintiff and defendant affirmed the lease by their actions, defendant, in occupying the building and paying rent in accordance with the terms of the lease, and plaintiff, in accepting the payment of rent. There was no other lease contract between plaintiff and defendant, and by their acts they both ratified the written lease, and it was binding on them both.

¶16 More recently, this court held that in order for a lease agreement to be binding on third parties, it must be recorded or the purchaser must intend to purchase the property subject to the unrecorded lease. Hill v. Doctors Park of Minden, 501 So.2d 987 (La.App. 2 Cir.1987). In Hill, we found that the purchaser's "simple knowledge" of the existence of the lease would not suffice to show an intent to assume the lease.

¶17 In the instant case, the record shows much more than simple knowledge on Means's part. As in Pirkle & Williams, supra, Means allowed Comcast to keep its equipment on the property, advised Comcast to pay him all future rent, and accepted several years' rent; he also received the benefit of another lease provision whereby Comcast paid annual property taxes. Moreover, Means candidly admitted that he received a copy of the lease at some unspecified time, and he "probably" knew about its provisions when he bought the property from his sister's trust, as his sister's lawyer "probably" told him. On these facts, the district court was not plainly wrong to find that Means ratified and adopted Mrs. Lay's unrecorded lease, including the renewal option. With the finding of ratification, we need not consider the issue of indirect reference to an unrecorded instrument, as discussed in Julius Gindi & Sons, supra, and Judice-Henry-May Agency v. Franklin, supra.

¶18   The judgment rejecting Means's claim to evict Comcast is affirmed.

Study Question:

While the previous cases had to decide whether all three elements of a lease (thing, rent, and consent) were present, consider what the following case shows, not just about mineral leases, but also about the nature of a lease and a sublease, and the requirement that a lease have a term.

PHOENIX ASSOC. LAND SYN., INC. V. E.H. MITCHELL & CO., L.L.C. 2007
970 SO.2D 605 (LA. APP. 1ST CIR.)

PETTIGREW, J.

¶1   This appeal challenges a partial summary judgment rendered by the trial court on September 15, 2006. In granting partial summary judgment, the trial court ruled in favor of defendant, E.H. Mitchell & Co., L.L.C., and against plaintiff, Phoenix Associates Land Syndicate, Inc. ("Phoenix"), declaring that the operating agreements between Phoenix and Pontchartrain Materials Corp., L.L.C. ("Pontchartrain") and Michael Ellinger ("Ellinger") were subleases. The trial court further declared that in executing these subleases, Phoenix had breached the provisions of a sand and gravel lease that had been assigned to it by L. Murphy's Trucking Service, Inc. ("Murphy's Trucking") as well as the Addendum to an Extension of Lease that Phoenix had entered into with E.H. Mitchell & Co., L.L.C. Accordingly, the trial court ruled that E.H. Mitchell & Co., L.L.C. was entitled to dissolution of the subject leases. From the judgment, Phoenix has appealed, and for the reasons that follow, we affirm the trial court's judgment of September 15, 2006.

FACTS AND PROCEDURAL HISTORY

¶2   The record reveals that Elbert H. Mitchell, the grandfather of defendants, Steven M. Furr, Brian Furr, and Michael Furr, owned approximately 820 acres of land with sand and gravel deposits situated along the Pearl River in St. Tammany Parish. Upon Elbert Mitchell's death, his grandsons became the owners of the land in question. The Furr brothers formed E.H. Mitchell & Co., L.L.C. ("Mitchell"), and Steven Furr ("Furr") became its president. Mitchell thereafter entered into a lease with Murphy's Trucking on August 8, 1996, regarding the mining of the sand and gravel on a portion of the property. Said lease contained, in pertinent part, the following paragraphs:

> 6. It is agreed that during the term of this lease there will be no mining, excavation, and removal of sand and gravel from the hereinbefore-described property other than those permitted under the terms and provisions of this lease.
>
> ....
>
> 10. This lease may not be sub-let, in whole or in part, without the written permission of Lessor.

¶3 On May 14, 1997 and August 28, 1997, Mitchell and Furr gave written consent to Murphy's Trucking and Murphy Construction Company, Inc. ("Murphy Construction") to assign or sub-lease to Phoenix upon such terms and conditions as Murphy's Trucking and Murphy Construction shall deem fit and proper. Said authority was "granted with the full understanding that the terms of the original lease shall not be changed and shall remain intact and that any sub-lease or assignment of this said lease shall be made subject to all the terms and conditions of the original lease dated August 8, 1996." Phoenix purchased Murphy Construction's entire sand and gravel operation through an act of assignment dated August 29, 1997.

¶4 On June 23, 1998, Mitchell and Phoenix entered into an addendum to and extension of the original sand and gravel lease between Mitchell and Murphy's Trucking dated August 8, 1996. This lease was subsequently assigned to Murphy Construction, which in turn assigned the lease to Phoenix on August 29, 1997. The June 23, 1998 addendum and extension of lease, contained several key provisions. First, paragraph one, provided:

> 1. All the provisions of the original sand and gravel lease between E.H. MITCHELL & COMPANY, L.L.C. and L. MURPHY'S TRUCKING SERVICE, INC., and assigned to PHOENIX ASSOCIATES LAND SYNDICATE, shall remain in full force and effect except as modified herein.

¶5 The addendum and extension of lease also provided for a change of the beginning of the primary term and extensions thereof and other conditions, to read as follows:

> 4. Lessor grants unto Lessee, from the date of execution hereof and in lieu and substitution of the chronological terms contained in the original lease a renewal of the sand and gravel lease beginning as of this date an initial term of five (5) years. Lessee shall have the option to renew the sand and gravel lease after said initial five (5) years period for additional five (5) year terms, but

in no event shall the Sand and Gravel Lease be extended in excess of twenty-five (25) years from this date; i.e., there shall be no more than four (4) extensions of the initial five (5) year term.

¶6   The addendum and extension of lease also dealt with potential changes of royalties to be paid as follows:

> 5. The provisions concerning royalties in the sand and gravel lease are hereby modified as fol-
> lows: The royalties paid for waste concrete sand, concrete sand, mason sand, washed gravel,
> road gravel, pea gravel and waste pea gravel shall remain the same. The issue of royalties shall
> be addressed every five (5) years and shall be increased in proportion to the market price of the
> materials, should the price thereof increase. It is the intent of the parties that E.H. MITCHELL &
> COMPANY, L.L.C., shall receive the same percentage in royalties for the aforementioned materi-
> als should the market price increase.

[Emphasis supplied]

¶7   Phoenix later ran into financial difficulties and filed for bankruptcy reorganization on November 18, 1999. The bankruptcy court rejected Phoenix's plan of organization and dismissed the bankruptcy on January 22, 2001. Problems developed between Phoenix and Mitchell regarding Phoenix's operations, including, but not limited to, the alleged lack of payment of royalties, underpayment of royalties, the alleged taking of overburdened soil without remuneration to Mitchell, and the allowance of third parties on the premises to mine same without Mitchell's written permission.

¶8   Prior to the expiration of the primary term on June 23, 2003, Phoenix sent a letter to Mitchell, notifying Mitchell of Phoenix's desire to exercise its option to renew the lease on the property for another five years. The parties however could not come to an agreement as to the royalties owed pursuant to paragraph five (5) of the Addendum to and Extension of Lease executed on June 23, 1998. Phoenix nevertheless continued its operations on the leased premises without a written extension of said lease or an agreement with Mitchell as to the amount of royalties owed. Due to its inability to negotiate the price to be paid for a renewal lease, Phoenix sued Mitchell on June 17, 2003.

¶9   Subsequent to this, Phoenix entered into certain "Operating Agreements" with two other companies to mine part of Mitchell's property. The first of these "Operating Agreements" was dated August 15, 2004, and involved Phoenix and Pontchartrain, while the second agreement dated June 15, 2005 was entered into between Phoenix and Ellinger. Mitchell never consented to these "Operating Agreements" either orally or in writing.

¶10 Phoenix filed the instant suit on June 17, 2003, naming Mitchell and Furr as defendants therein. Phoenix sought to recover damages for Mitchell and Furr's alleged breach of their obligations pursuant to the lease, as well their alleged tortious interference with Phoenix's operations on the property owned by Mitchell. On July 3, 2003, Mitchell filed an answer setting forth affirmative defenses together with a reconventional demand against Phoenix. Mitchell sought a cancellation of its lease with Phoenix, an accounting of materials removed by Phoenix from the premises, and damages for Mitchell's lost opportunities to lease the property to other prudent operators. On June 25, 2003, Furr responded by filing peremptory exceptions that raised objections of no cause of action and prescription with respect to Phoenix's claims against him.

* * *

¶11 The trial court rendered judgment on September 15, 2006, declaring that Phoenix's operating agreements with Pontchartrain and Ellinger constituted subleases, which amounted to a material breach by Phoenix of its lease with Mitchell. The trial court further dissolved and cancelled the sand and gravel lease between Mitchell and Phoenix. Thereafter, on October 10, 2006, Phoenix filed for a suspensive appeal from the trial court's judgment of September 15, 2006, and it is that judgment that forms the basis of the instant appeal.

* * *

ISSUES PRESENTED FOR REVIEW

¶12 In connection with its appeal in this matter, Phoenix has presented the following issues for review and consideration by this court:

1. Whether the district court erred in concluding that the Operating Agreements were prohibited subleases, where the Operating Agreements were "internally inconsistent" in material respects by Mitchell's own admission, and therefore ambiguous, and where the evidence before the court was highly disputed.

2. Whether the district court improperly resolved material factual issues in dispute on summary judgment in terminating a sand and gravel lease where the lease did not provide for automatic termination in the event of a breach, Louisiana law requires consideration of numerous fact-intensive factors before a lease can be cancelled, and the proper resolution of those fact issues was hotly contested.

* * *

[The standard for appealability of judgments and sections of the standard for summary judgment are omitted.]

DISCUSSION

¶13 In support of its motion for partial summary declaratory judgment, Mitchell introduced its memorandum together with the affidavit of its president, Furr, that referred to, and which by reference included, the following exhibits:

* * *

[The court lists Mitchell's original Sand and Gravel Lease, the 1997 consent to the sublease granting permission to Murphy to assign the lease to Phoenix, and the Operating Agreements between Phoenix and Ellinger and Phoenix and Poncharttrain].

¶14 It is an undisputed fact in this litigation that Mitchell did not orally or in writing consent to the various "Operating Agreements" dated August 16, 2004, between Phoenix and Pontchartrain; dated June 15, 2005, between Phoenix and Ellinger; dated December 22, 2005, between Ellinger and The Dirt Connection; and dated February 10, 2006, between Ellinger, Ron Omelian, and Lakeshore Materials. Therefore, there is no material issue of fact in dispute concerning same.

¶15 There is no material issue of fact in dispute in that Phoenix is prohibited from subletting the property without the written permission of Mitchell, pursuant to paragraphs 6 and 10 of the Act of Sand and Gravel Lease, dated August 8, 1996, between Mitchell and Murphy; the Consent to Sublease or Assign Lease, by Mitchell to Murphy, by acts dated May 14, 1997, August 28, 1997; the Assignment of Lease, dated August 29, 1997, by Murphy to Phoenix; and the Addendum to and Extension of Lease, dated June 23, 1998, between Mitchell and Phoenix.

* * *

¶16 As between Mitchell and Phoenix, the prohibition against Phoenix subleasing the premises set forth in paragraphs 6 and 10 of the August 8, 1997 lease between Mitchell and Murphy; the assignment of that lease, dated August 29, 1997, by Murphy's Trucking to Phoenix; and the addendum to and extension of lease, dated June 23, 1998, between Mitchell and Phoenix, makes paragraphs 6 and 10 the law between Mitchell and Phoenix. The obligation imposed upon Phoenix by paragraphs 6 and 10 of the Mitchell mineral lease is unequivocal and express. "[T]he mineral lease constitutes the law between the parties and regulates their respective obligations." Terrebonne Parish School Board v. Castex Energy, Inc., 2004-0968 (La.1/19/05), 893 So.2d 789, (quoting Caskey v. Kelly Oil Company, 98-1193 p. 8 (La.6/29/99) 737 So.2d 1257, 1262); see Frey v. Amoco Production Co., 603 So.2d 166, 171 (La.1992).

¶17   The key issue in this appeal turns on whether the "Operating Agreements," executed by Phoenix with Ellinger, on June 15, 2005, and Pontchartrain, on August 15, 2004, are in fact subleases and a direct breach by Phoenix of its Mitchell lease and the addendum to and extension of said lease, dated June 23, 1998.

¶18   The covenant in the lease against subletting is for the benefit of the landlord, because it is regarded as for his interest to determine who shall be a tenant of his property. See Montecon v. Faures, 3 La. Ann. 43 (1848). If the operating agreements are truly subleases, then Phoenix, by executing these agreements with Pontchartrain and Ellinger without Mitchell's consent, has caused a "subletting-without-consent" breach of the Mitchell to Murphy lease, assignment of said lease by Murphy to Phoenix, and the addendum to and extension of the lease between Mitchell and Phoenix. See Major v. Hall, 251 So.2d 444, 449 (La.App. 1 Cir.1971), partially reversed on other grounds, 262 La. 243, 263 So.2d 22 (1972). This would cause Phoenix to be in active breach of paragraph 10 of the Mitchell to Murphy lease. The division of breaches into active and passive violations is preserved under La. R.S. 31:135 of the Louisiana Mineral Code. Violations of mineral leases may be either passive or active is established. Hunt v. Stacy, 25,578, p. 5 (La.App. 2 Cir. 2/23/94), 632 So.2d 872, 875, (citing comments to La. R.S. 31:135 of the Louisiana Mineral Code).

¶19   Phoenix takes the position that it was never its intention to enter into a sublease or to transfer any of its rights on the lease to Pontchartrain and Ellinger. Pontchartrain and Ellinger, according to Phoenix, were independent contractors engaged to perform certain specified services in the same way Phoenix contracted out other services, such as, trucking services. In support of this position, Phoenix referred to a particular paragraph in the recital portions of the "Operating Agreements" with both Pontchartrain and Ellinger that provide:

> Whereas, Phoenix and Pontchartrain agree that this Operating Agreement is not and shall not be constructed as a lease or a sublease and that Phoenix does not surrender, transfer, or in any other matter assign to Pontchartrain its rights or obligations as Lessee under the aforesaid Sand and Gravel Lease, Consent to Sub-Lease or Assignment of Lease, and/or Addendum to and Extension of Lease.

¶20   Phoenix argues that the expression of intent by Pontchartrain and Ellinger not to consider their agreements as assignments or subleases legally binds the court and Mitchell in characterizing these contracts or at the minimum creates a material issue of fact to prevent summary judgment.

¶21 Whether the "Operating Agreements" between Phoenix, Pontchartrain, and Ellinger are really subleases is a question of law. Louisiana Supreme Court has repudiated Phoenix's argument. "Questions of law cannot be confessed or admitted; the characterization of the contracts in issue is preeminently of that nature." Howard Trucking Co., Inc. v. Stassi, 485 So.2d 915, 918 (La.1986), cert. denied, 479 U.S. 948, 107 S.Ct. 432, 93 L.Ed.2d 382 (1986). The intent of Phoenix, Ellinger, and Pontchartrain cannot determine the character of the operating agreements because "the legal character of a contract must be determined by its substance, by its effect on the parties, what the law-not the parties-says it is; so the parties' intent is not conclusive." Major, 251 So.2d at 448. "The intent of the parties to a contract should govern its interpretation ..., the best evidence of the parties' intent is what the parties agreed to do." La. Civ. Code art.2045. (Citations omitted.) Howard Trucking Co., 485 So.2d at 918. The trial court is entitled to apply the law to the legal documents before it without being hindered by erroneous assumptions of law by the parties. Cities Service Oil & Gas Corp. v. State, 574 So.2d 455, 461 (La.App. 2 Cir.), writs denied, 578 So.2d 132, 133 (La.1991). The effects on Mitchell's rights control the character of the operating agreements. Although the parties entered into a written contract in which they were identified as independent contractors, and this designation may have some validity between the parties, it is not binding or controlling on the rights of third persons. The rights of third persons are controlled by the substance, rather than the title, of the contractual relationship between the parties. Hughes v. Goodreau, 2001-2107, pp. 11-12 (La.App. 1 Cir. 12/31/02), 836 So.2d 649, 659, writ denied, 2003-0232 (La.4/21/03), 841 So.2d 793.

¶22 Under La. R.S. 31:4, the provisions of the Louisiana Mineral Code are applicable to all forms of minerals, including oil and gas. Said provisions also apply to rights to explore for, or mine, or remove from land the soil itself, gravel, shells, subterranean water and other substances. Provisions of the Mineral Code are supplementary to those of the Louisiana Civil Code and are applicable specifically to the subject matter of mineral law. La. R.S. 31:2. Individuals may renounce or modify what is established in their favor by the provisions of the Mineral Code unless they are expressly or impliedly prohibited, and the renunciation or modification does not affect the rights of others and is not contrary to the public good. La. R.S. 31:3.

¶23 Ownership of land includes all minerals occurring naturally in a solid state. Solid minerals are insusceptible of ownership apart from the land until reduced to possession. La. R.S. 31:5. Pursuant to La. R.S. 31:114, a mineral lease is a contract by which the lessee is granted the right to explore for and produce minerals, and in accordance with La. R.S. 31:2, mineral leases are construed as leases generally, and whenever pertinent codal provisions applicable to ordinary leases are applied to mineral leases. See Frey, 603 So.2d at 171.

¶24 The codal requirements for a sublease are the same as for the lease, since a sublease is a lease between the original lessee and a third party. A lease is a contract by which one party gives to another the enjoyment of the thing for a fixed price. La. Civ. Code arts. 2669, 2674 [now 2668]. A lease, which may be oral (La. Civil Code art. 2683 [now 2681]), requires an object, a certain and determinate price, and consent. La. Civ. Code arts. 2670, 2671 [now 2668 and 2678, respectively]. Major, 251 So.2d at 447. The "Operating Agreements" between Phoenix, Pontchartrain, and Ellinger contain all three of these elements.

¶25 Phoenix contends the agreements with Pontchartrain and Ellinger were operating agreements. An "operating agreement" implies Pontchartain and Ellinger were operating the mine for Phoenix, and Phoenix was still the owner of the minerals produced. That is contrary to the very agreements between Phoenix, Pontchartrain, and Ellinger. Under both agreements, Pontchartrain and Ellinger became owners of the gravel, soil, and minerals produced. This fact is made clear in paragraph 16 of both the Pontchartrain and Ellinger agreements with Phoenix, which obligates Pontchartrain and Ellinger to sell their mined minerals, if any available, when Phoenix requests.

¶26 In paragraph 15 of the Mitchell lease to Phoenix, Mitchell granted Phoenix a singular right-of-way to reach the leased premises insofar as such right-of-way may be required. In paragraph 2 of the agreements between Phoenix, Pontchartrain, and Ellinger, Phoenix granted to Pontchartrain and Ellinger the right to use all existing roads on the subject property including the right to build additional roads.

¶27 In the original lease by Mitchell to Phoenix, Phoenix did not acquire the right to bring outside materials onto Mitchell's property for reprocessing. In paragraphs 1, 8, 16, and 23 of Pontchartrain's agreement, and paragraphs 8, 16, and 23 of Ellinger's agreement, Pontchartrain and Ellinger were given the right to bring outside materials onto the Mitchell's property for reprocessing. Further, Phoenix, in its agreements with Pontchartrain and Ellinger, granted to Pontchartrain and Ellinger the use of all existing electrical utilities on the subject property-a grant of authority that Phoenix did not possess.

¶28 Phoenix dismembered Mitchell's ownership by conferring upon Pontchartrain and Ellinger specified rights of use on the property. The operating agreements between Phoenix, Pontchartrain, and Ellinger provide that Pontchartrain and Ellinger shall have the sole and exclusive use of the area designated as Pontchartrain's and Ellinger's mining and dredging plan. These rights to sole and exclusive use of Mitchell's property were for the purpose of allowing Pontchartrain and Ellinger to dredge and/or mine various materials on and from the property, including access to the soils and minerals. They further gained the right to bring other scales and equipment on Mitchell's property.

¶29 A "personal servitude" is a charge on a thing for the benefit of a person. La. Civ. Code art. 534. Right of use is one of three types of personal servitudes recognized by the Civil Code. A right of use servitude confers on a favorable person a specified use of an estate less than full enjoyment. La. Civil Code art. 639. A "mineral lease" on the other hand, is a contract by which the lessee is granted the right to explore for mine, or remove minerals from the land; it is a real right with some characteristics in the nature of a limited personal servitude or right of use. La. R.S. 31:4. La. R.S. 31:16. The operating agreements imposed charges on Mitchell's land for the benefit of Pontchartrain and Ellinger. By executing the "Operating Agreements," Phoenix conferred to Pontchartrain and Ellinger the right to specified uses of Mitchell's land less than full enjoyment. This created a dismemberment of the ownership of Mitchell's land, whether by lease or personal servitudes. Phoenix, pursuant to its mineral lease with Mitchell, possessed no authority to create real rights or personal servitudes on Mitchell's property in favor of third persons. A land owner may convey, reserve or lease his right to explore and develop his land for production of minerals and to reduce them to possession. La. R.S. 31:15. Basic mineral rights that may be created by a landowner are the mineral servitude, the mineral royalty, and the mineral lease. La. R.S. 31:16. The executive right is the exclusive right to grant mineral leases of specified land or mineral rights. La. R.S. 31:105. Phoenix is neither the landowner nor owner of the executive right to create mineral leases or servitudes. The effects of dismemberment support the trial court's finding of a material breach. See Quinn Properties, Inc. v. Sabine River Realty, Inc., 95-1714 (La.App. 3 Cir. 5/29/96), 676 So.2d 639.

¶30 After a thorough de novo review of the record and all exhibits included herewith, we conclude that the assignment of error of appellant is without merit, and the trial court did not commit error in declaring that the operating agreements between Phoenix, Pontchartrain, and Ellinger to be in truth and in fact subleases. We further find the trial court did not commit error in declaring that the execution by Phoenix of these subleases with Pontchartrain and Ellinger constituted a breach of the Act of Sand and Gravel Lease assigned from Murphy to Phoenix and the Addendum and Extension of Lease between Mitchell and Phoenix, and further granting a dissolution of that Act of Sand and Gravel Lease assigned from Murphy to Phoenix and the Addendum to and Extension of Lease between Mitchell and Phoenix.

¶31 For the foregoing reasons, we do hereby affirm the judgment of the trial court rendered September 15, 2006. All court costs of this appeal shall be assessed against Phoenix.

AFFIRMED.

The following case is still good law, judging by the fact that it was cited in an appellate brief as recently as 2006 for setting forth a principle of Louisiana 'hornbook law.'

What does that principle state about a lessee's claim that he is, in fact, the owner of the leased premises?

GRAVE V. SCOTT 1959
107 SO.2D 808 (LA. APP. ORL. CIR.)

YARRUT, Judge ad hoc.

¶1 This is an ordinary suit for the eviction of a tenant, for cancellation of the lease, and for past due rent. Plaintiffs are residents of New York and defendants are residents of Jefferson Parish. Only defendant Dave Scott has taken an appeal. Defendant Leon Dukes was never cited, nor did he appear.

¶2 Defendant resists all demands on the ground that he, and not plaintiffs, is the owner of the property. On the trial of the case the District Court refused to permit defendant to prove his ownership of the property and rendered judgment for plaintiffs as prayed.

¶3 Defendant only challenges the ruling of the court in prohibiting him to prove his ownership of the property.

¶4 The ruling of the trial judge was entirely correct. It is an established doctrine in Louisiana that a person may lease property of which he is not the owner. Stinson v. Marston, 185 La. 365, 169 So. 436; Spence v. Lucas, 138 La. 763, 70 So. 796; Town of Morgan City of Dalton, 112 La. 9, 36 So. 208; Tippet v. Jett, 10 La. 359.

¶5 It is likewise well established that a lessee, in undisturbed possession of leased premises, cannot contest lessor's title as long as he remains in possession. Weil v. Segura, 178 La. 421, 151 So. 639; Lacaze v. Beeman, La.App., 178 So. 660; Federal Land Bank of New Orleans v. Spencer, La.App., 160 So. 175; Defelice v. Autin, La.App., 159 So. 648.

¶6 Defendant, however, urges that, as plaintiffs are nonresidents, he has the right to reconvene for any cause of action.

¶7   Pleading and procedure is not an issue here. Defendant may have a cause of action in a proper proceeding, but he has no right of action to assert that cause of action so long as he remains in possession of the premises under lease from his plaintiff-lessor.

¶8   Accordingly, the judgment of the District Court is correct and is affirmed.

Section 3: Form

Reread Article 2681.

While Article 2681 provides that a lease may be made orally or in writing; nevertheless, an unrecorded lease of an immovable is not effective against third persons. Consequently, a lessee, in order to protect his possession of the premises, may want to record a lease to prevent a third-party purchaser of the property from evicting him.

Study Question:

What do the following cases show about the requisite form for a contract of lease? The term?

MCWILLIAMS V. COURTNEY 2006
945 SO.2D 242 (LA. APP. 2D CIR.)

DREW, J.

¶1   Troy Courtney seeks reversal of the trial court's judgment awarding $1,270.00 in general damages and $500.00 in attorney fees and costs to Ronnie McWilliams. For the following reasons, the judgment of the trial court is affirmed.

FACTS

¶2   In November 2001, Ronnie McWilliams and Troy Courtney entered into an oral agreement under which McWilliams leased a wood splitter and trailer to Courtney so that Courtney could cut, haul, and sell firewood. The splitter and trailer remained in Courtney's possession for four to five months. In June 2003, McWilliams, through his attorney, presented Courtney with a demand letter for $1,500.00. Courtney refused to pay the bill.

¶3   On June 22, 2004, after making amicable demand, McWilliams filed a suit on open account for $1,500.00 plus attorney fees and costs against Courtney. In his answer to the petition,

Courtney denied that he owed the debt on the basis that the parties' agreement only called upon Courtney to cut firewood for McWilliams, which Courtney alleged that he had done. His answer further claimed that he had four witnesses to the agreement.

¶4 The matter came for trial on March 23, 2006. McWilliams testified that he and Courtney had entered into the rental agreement at McWilliams' place of business, the Porterville Country Store. According to McWilliams, Courtney agreed to pay $40.00 per day for use of the wood splitter and $30.00 per day for use of the trailer. He testified that over the next several months he kept track of the days on which his equipment was being used by driving past Courtney's house. If the equipment was in use, he would charge Courtney for it, but if it was sitting idle, he would not charge Courtney for it. As to Courtney's claim that McWilliams had been provided four cords of firewood in return for the use of the equipment, McWilliams testified that Courtney had only delivered a load of unmarketable limbs to his house.

¶5 Without any objection from Courtney, who was not represented by counsel at the time, McWilliams introduced a copy of the ledger notes where he kept track of the use of his equipment. The notes reflect a total amount due and owing of $1,470.00. However, in his testimony, McWilliams admitted that the starting balance of $200.00 did not reflect accurate record keeping but merely an estimate of what he "figured" Courtney owed when he began to keep track of his equipment's use. Also offered and admitted into evidence without objection was a copy of the demand letter sent to Courtney by McWilliams' attorney.

¶6 The court then heard testimony from Kenneth Coleman, who was with Courtney on the day the arrangement between the parties was made. Coleman indicated that he only heard McWilliams offer to make Courtney a "deal," but he did not hear anything regarding the terms of that deal. He confirmed that he had been with Courtney when he made deliveries of two cords of firewood to both McWilliams' home and the home of McWilliams' son. There was no testimony as to when these deliveries took place.

¶7 Courtney testified that the original agreement was proposed by McWilliams and that the only request McWilliams had made in return for Courtney's use of the equipment was that he provide McWilliams and McWilliams' son each with two cords of firewood. Courtney testified that he cut and delivered the wood as agreed and that there was never any discussion regarding the payment of money for the rental of the equipment. On cross-examination, he asserted the sales price for a cord of firewood was $225.00. When asked the whereabouts of the four witnesses to the agreement identified in his answer, he indicated that Coleman was one of them, two others were in prison, and the fourth was in Houston.

¶8 After hearing the testimony, the trial court rendered judgment awarding McWilliams $1,270.00 on the open account, and $500.00 in attorney fees and court costs. The court stated that it did not believe Courtney's testimony as to the nature of the agreement and therefore awarded McWilliams the amount reflected on the invoice minus the $200.00 estimated balance. A judgment to that effect was signed on June 30, 2006. The instant appeal followed.

DISCUSSION

¶9 On appeal, Courtney makes two assignments of error. First, he contends that the trial court erred in allowing hearsay into evidence in the form of McWilliams' ledger notes regarding the dates that his equipment was in use by Courtney. Second, Courtney argues that the trial court was manifestly erroneous in concluding that the terms of the agreement between the parties were those testified to by McWilliams.

Evidentiary Issue Regarding McWilliams' Ledger Notes

[discussion of this issue is omitted.]

Erroneous Finding of Fact

¶10 Courtney argues that the factual inconsistencies in the evidence support a finding that the trial court manifestly erred in rendering judgment in favor of McWilliams. Specifically, Courtney cites the discrepancy in the amount claimed by McWilliams and the amount ulti-mately awarded, the lack of an explanation as to why McWilliams and his son were provided firewood, and the lack of specificity as to the terms of the contract.

¶11 Whether or not an oral contract has been confected between the parties is a finding of fact and, as such, is subject to the manifest error standard of review. An appellate court may not set aside a trial court's finding of fact in the absence of manifest error or unless it is clearly wrong, and where two permissible views of the evidence exist, the fact finder's choice between them cannot be manifestly erroneous or clearly wrong. Cole v. Department of Public Safety & Corrections, 2001-2123 (La.9/4/02), 825 So.2d 1134; Stobart v. State through Dept. of Transp. and Development., 617 So.2d 880 (La.1993). Even though an appellate court may feel its own evaluations and inferences are more reasonable than the fact finder's, reasonable evaluations of credibility and reasonable inferences of fact should not be disturbed upon review where conflict exists in the testimony. Cole, supra; Rosell v. ESCO, 549 So.2d 840 (La.1989). To reverse a fact finder's determination, the appellate court must find from the record that a reasonable factual basis does not exist for the finding of the trial court and that the record establishes that the finding is clearly wrong. Stobart, supra.

¶12 McWilliams testified that the parties had agreed to the rental of his wood splitter and trailer for $40.00 per day and $30.00 per day, respectively. He further testified as to how he tracked the use of his equipment by noting the days it was not sitting idle at Courtney's property. McWilliams explained that the reason he did not charge for the rental on those days was because if he had wanted to use the equipment, it was available to him. He also testified that the beginning balance of $200.00 on his ledger was strictly an estimate and not a reflection of actual knowledge as to Courtney's use of the equipment. This evidence not only explains the alleged discrepancy between the amount awarded and the amount originally claimed, but supports the trial court's finding that McWilliams was owed $1,270.00 for the rental of his equipment.

¶13 Courtney's argument that the agreement testified to by McWilliams fails to explain why Courtney delivered four cords of firewood to McWilliams and his son is also without merit. Courtney's argument assumes that the trial court believed that such deliveries had been made. We see no indication of such a finding in the record. McWilliams admitted to receiving only one pickup truckload of what he considered to be unmarketable wood. Furthermore, even if such a finding had been made, Courtney's suggestion that it constitutes irrebuttable evidence of the nature of the agreement is unconvincing. Courtney's actions in this regard could have been motivated by gratuity or conscience since he was in possession of McWilliams' wood splitter during the winter months. That the record does not evidence what other motive there might have been is of no moment. McWilliams did not acknowledge that the delivery of four cords of firewood was made. Accordingly, he was not likely to offer an explanation for an event he did not acknowledge ever occurred in the first place.

¶14 Lastly, Courtney's complaint as to the lack of specificity in the contract also fails. A lease is a synallagmatic contract by which one party, the lessor, binds himself to give the other party, the lessee, the use and enjoyment of a thing for a term in exchange for a rent that the lessee binds himself to pay. La. C.C. art. 2668. The essential elements of a lease are the thing, the price (rent), and consent of the parties. Southern Treats, Inc. v. Titan Properties, L.L.C., 40,873 (La. App.2d Cir.4/19/06), 927 So.2d 677, writ denied, 2006-1170 (La.9/15/06), 936 So.2d 1271. The form of a lease may be written or verbal. La. C.C. art. 2681; Southern Treats, supra.

¶15 Courtney's complaints as to the absence of a term, payment arrangements, and a proper method of accounting for his use are inapposite. Courtney has not cited and we are not aware of any authority supporting the proposition that a lease agreement must contain specifics as to the accounting method to be used or as to the manner in which payment will be made. Courtney offered no evidence to contradict the assertion that he was using McWilliams' equipment on the days alleged. Accordingly, he will not now be heard on appeal to complain that McWilliams' method for determining it was unreliable.

¶16   As to the absence of a lease term, the law clearly provides that for a lease agreement wherein the parties have failed to agree as to the duration of the term, the duration is supplied by law. See La. C.C. art. 2678. In the case of the lease of movables, the term is day to day, unless the rent is fixed by longer or shorter periods. La. C.C. art. 2680. Accordingly, we find no manifest error in the trial court's findings.

CONCLUSION

¶17   For the foregoing reasons, the judgment of the trial court is hereby AFFIRMED. The costs of this appeal are to be borne by appellant.

Section 4: Perfection of the Contract of Lease

Read Articles 1947 and 2670

Study Question:

In Chapter 6 we discussed contracts to sell and suspensive conditions. We concluded that a contract to sell is not the same as a contract of sale, and if they intended not to be bound until a written contract is perfected, then parties are not bound until the contract is formalized. Consider the following case – do the same principles apply to a contract to lease?

LAROUSSINI V. WERLEIN 1899

52 LA. ANN. 424, 27 SO. 89

BLANCHARD, J.

1   Plaintiff sues to enforce a verbal contract of lease on valuable real property in New Orleans, for the term of five years, at $750 per month, or $9,000 per annum. His contention is that there was entered into between himself and defendant a complete and final verbal contract of lease, for the more secure proof of which an act in writing was to have been executed, but that the binding obligation of the agreement was in no manner to depend upon the said writing, or to be

suspended or revocable in the meantime. The contention of the defendant is that, while the lease of the property was negotiated at personal interviews between himself and plaintiff, the verbal agreement was only preliminary to a written contract intended to be passed, and, until the latter was consummated, neither party was bound by the verbal agreement. The parties sustained at the time the relation of lessor and lessee towards each other. The defendant was occupying the identical premises under a previous five-year lease, which was drawing towards its close; and the contract now declared on was in renewal of the lease for another five years, at a rate of rental $50 per month greater than the then existing lease called for. The latter was in writing,-an authentic act,-and rent notes for the monthly payments of $700 had been given. It was in contemplation that rent notes for the renewed lease were to be given. About a week after the verbal agreement of renewal had taken place, the plaintiff called at the office of a notary public, and, informing the latter that he had leased his store to the defendant,-mentioning the terms of the new lease and the monthly rental,-requested him to draw up an act of lease substantially similar to the one then existing between the parties, for the same premises. The notary did so, and also prepared 60 rent notes, at $750 each to cover the five-year lease. He then notified defendant that the lease and notes were ready for signature. Some delay ensued, but in the course of a week or ten days later the plaintiff, with the notary, repaired to the office of the defendant. The lease, as prepared by the notary, had been handed to the defendant, at his request, for his inspection, some days before, and he had it in his possession when the notary and the plaintiff called. The notary informed him that the object of the call was to formally execute the lease, and obtain his signature to the rent notes, whereupon defendant replied that he had changed his mind, and would not execute the lease, and handed the written instrument and the unsigned notes back to the notary. Following this, the plaintiff brought an action to enforce the specific performance of defendant's promise to sign the act of lease, in execution of the verbal agreement. That suit was dismissed on exception, and the judgment of dismissal, on the ground of no cause of action, was affirmed here. See Laroussini v. Werlein, 48 La. Ann. 13, 18 South. 704. The present suit was then instituted, basing recovery on the verbal lease. It was met by the plea of res judicata, filed by way of exception, predicated upon the judgment in the first case. The plea was sustained by the trial court, and the suit dismissed; but on appeal here that judgment was reversed, the case ordered reinstated on the docket, and a trial upon its merits directed to be proceeded with. See Laroussini v. Werlein, 50 La. Ann. 637, 23 South. 467. Trial followed, with the result that plaintiff's demand was rejected. He appealed, and this appeal is now before us.

2 The question presented is whether there was a valid, binding agreement, amounting to a completed contract, verbally made between the parties, which is enforceable, irrespective of the fact that the same was not followed by the execution of a written contract of lease, or whether there was only a bargain between the parties to lease, or a completed negotiation to that end, or an understanding and agreement as to terms, conditions, duration, etc., which was to attain

to the dignity and importance of a contract of lease, and obligatory, only after the same had been reduced to writing, and signed by the parties. If the first, the case is with the plaintiff; if the latter, with the defendant.

3 A verbal contract of lease, complete in itself, independent of any writing, and unaccompanied by an intention to have the same reduced to writing, as perfecting it, is an enforceable contract. And if such a verbal contract be made, and subsequently the parties agree that the same shall be reduced to writing and be signed, and afterwards there is a failure to so reduce it to writing and to signature,-one of the parties refusing,-it is still enforceable as a binding contract. Carlin v. Harding, 10 La. 225; Avendano v. Arthur, 30 La. Ann. 321. But if, when a verbal contract of lease is agreed on, it is understood, contemplated, and intended that it should be reduced to writing, that there should be a written lease, and that the written lease should take the place of, and stand for, what has been agreed on verbally in respect to the leasing of the property, then until the writing is drawn up and signed the contract is inchoate, incomplete, and either party, before signing, may recant, retract, recede, withdraw, decline to go further, refuse to consummate. Fredericks v. Fasnacht, 30 La. Ann. 117; Villeré v. Brognier, 3 Mart. 349, 527; Bloeker v. Tillman, 4 La. 80; Wolf v. Mitchell, 24 La. Ann. 434; Fernandez v. Soulie, 28 La. Ann. 31; Des Boulets v. Gravier, 1 Mart. (N. S.) 421, 422; Meyer v. Labau, 51 La. Ann. 1729, 26 South. 463. Judged by the rule thus laid down, the case at bar is with the defendant. Undoubtedly these parties litigant did agree verbally upon a contract of lease in renewal of the then existing lease; but that this was to be followed by a writing setting forth the same, and to be signed by the contracting parties, which writing should take the place of, and stand for, what had been agreed on verbally, is established beyond peradventure. This was, we think, the understanding and intention of the parties, and this understanding and intention was contemporaneous with the verbal agreement made. After agreeing verbally with the defendant about the lease, plaintiff left the store, where the interview had been held, to have, later, the contract drawn by his notary. Defendant had suggested that it be merely indorsed upon the then existing written contract of lease, but plaintiff had not consented to this. He desired a formal contract drawn in renewal of the lease, with accompanying notes; and such contract was drawn, and the notes prepared. Whether the renewal contract was to be indorsed upon the old contract of lease, and signed by the parties, or whether a fresh contract was to be drawn and signed, equally evidences the intention that a written contract was to be made. The agreement reached as to the renewal of the lease was to be reduced to writing, in some form or another. The law is not particular as to this form, nor as to the verbiage used, nor as to the length of the contract; and, however brief the writing, if it were part of the understanding that there should be a writing, as we hold was the case, such writing suffices, provided it sets forth the intention of the parties, and until it is drawn up and signed no contract of lease was perfected. Plaintiff does not deny that a writing setting forth the lease was contemplated and intended at the time the verbal agreement was made, but contends that

this was to serve only as proof of the agreement, and that, the contract being complete without it, the parties remained bound, even though the written act was not executed. Considering the many circumstances disclosed by the record militating against it, we cannot accept this view of the case. Nor do we think it can be pressed with consistency, in face of the fact that, having failed to obtain the signature of defendant to the new contract and notes, plaintiff first brought suit to compel the signing of the same. The contract was to be reduced to writing. The lease had yet to be executed. There is no contradiction as to that. This understanding, contemplation, and intention as to the writing-as to the execution of a written lease-was part of the transaction that went to make up the verbal agreement, and the same cannot be held to have been completed until the written lease was prepared and signed. The plaintiff had had a long experience in leasing real estate, and is a conservative business man. A five-year verbal lease of high-priced property was not a reasonable business transaction. He had never finally closed a contract of lease, except in writing, and had never put a tenant in possession of premises, except under a written contract of lease. These are strong circumstances militating against the probability of a completed verbal contract having been made. In Wolf v. Mitchell, 24 La. Ann. 434, where a verbal lease of property for five years at the price of $9,000 for the first year, $10,000 for the second year, and $12,000 for the three following years was sought to be enforced, it was held, 'It being shown that it was the obvious intention of the parties to reduce the terms of the lease to writing before it was considered as complete, the defendants, as lessees, could not be held on the plaintiff's showing a verbal lease merely.' And in this connection it was said: 'In making a contract to the extent, amount, and importance of the one under consideration, it is reasonable that the parties should have reduced it to writing, so as to make it binding, in all its stipulations, before considering it fully closed.

4 In the lease under consideration, as shown by the copy plaintiff had drawn up by the notary, there were many and drastic stipulations, such as that the nonpayment of any one of the rent notes at maturity should cause all the remaining notes to become due and demandable, payment of attorney's fees (5 per cent.) in case of suit to collect the rent, keeping of the premises in good order at the expense of the lessee during the lease, the nondissolution of the lease in the event the building should be destroyed by fire, and the reservation of the right by the lessor to cancel the lease in the event of the violation of any of its conditions by the lessee, etc. It surely was not intended that a contract of lease embracing concessions, rights, and obligations of this character was to be left to the doubts and uncertainties of a mere verbal agreement. And that the written instrument which was to follow was only to furnish proof of a completed, anterior, verbal contract of lease, is not, we think, sustained by the evidence. Nor does it comport with what is usual among business men in transactions of that character. We incline to the conviction that the written act which the parties intended to execute between themselves was to be the contract itself. This being so, the law fixed their rights and responsibilities; and neither

party was bound until the written instrument was passed, and either had the right, before consummation, of receding. Judgment affirmed.

Study Questions:

If the parties to a sale fail to set a price, or if the method for setting a price fails, then a court may impose a reasonable price if it determines that the parties intended to be bound.

What insight does Article 2676 on the method of determining rent provide into the following hypothet?

Assume the following facts:

Scott Ferris and his sister and brother-in-law Cindy and Stan Rogers formed a business, Southern Treats, with the aim of opening and operating a combination TCBY/Mrs. Fields franchise in Shreveport.

The parties negotiated with Mark Porter who owns property in a good location at the intersection of Youree Drive and East Bert Kouns Industrial Loop. Porter did not want to sell his location, but was interested in building it to suit Southern Treats and leasing it to them.

Ferris first met with Mark Porter in April 2002. They discussed the square footage needed for the business and agreed that Porter would own the structure and lease it for twelve percent of the cost of building.

Relying on that agreement, Ferris prepared a business plan to obtain financing to open the business. The plan, which was admitted into evidence, included a projected monthly rent of $2,000 based on the agreed upon rate of twelve percent of the estimated building cost of $200,000. After getting loan approval, the parties, including Porter, met with a TCBY representative to get approval for the building site. Porter suggested an architect for the project, and Southern Treats paid $10,000 for the architect to design the building to suit the needs of the business. In October 2002, Ferris received franchise papers to sign. He needed to obtain a lease for 15 years. He drafted an agreement in the form of a letter to be sent to Jerry Nisbet, the vice-president of leasing with Mrs. Fields Famous Brands, and made an appointment to meet with Porter on October 28, 2002. At the meeting, Porter and Ferris signed the agreement which states:

"An agreement is made between Mark Porter, LESSOR and Scott Ferris, LESSEE, dated this 28th day of October, 2002."

The agreement provided a lease term of five years with two options of five years each. Both parties signed the agreement, but did not specifically include a statement of rent. Ferris stated that he made a mistake in neglecting to specify the rent agreed to in the letter. He testified that he took Porter at his word regarding their agreement as to rent and explained that their lease agreement consisted of the verbal agreement as to rent and the written agreement of October 28, 2002.

The building was built and TCBY moved in, but then problems arose. Southern Treats alleges that it had a lease for an initial term of 5 years with two options to renew for 5 years each. Rent was $2,250 per month in accordance with the parties' agreement that rent would be calculated at twelve percent of the cost of the building up to $225,000. It claims that at the opening of the business, Porter presented it with a second lease with an increased monthly rent of $3,600, which Southern Treats refused to sign, so Porter then presented yet a third lease with a monthly rent of $2,250 and a five year term, but with an option to renegotiate as opposed to the two options to renew. After paying the agreed-upon rent of $2,250 for twenty months, Porter then sent Southern Treats a letter notifying it that it was a month-to-month tenant and must vacate by April 1, 2005 unless it was willing to sign a written lease with monthly rent set at $4000.

Porter counters that the parties never executed a written lease and claimed there had been no meeting of the minds as to lease terms, particularly rent. He alleged that the parties entered a verbal month-to-month lease in July 2003 that he now wished to terminate. Furthermore, Porter claimed that the October 28, 2002, agreement signed by him was meaningless. He described it as a letter of intention which he signed to help Ferris speed up the franchise process. He asserted that Ferris drafted the letter from an example sent in a packet by TCBY stating it was not intended to be a lease. However, he admitted that the document he signed did not include that language. He stated that he looked at the letter and realized it was wrong, but he considered it to be insignificant and signed.

For which party would you decide? Why?

Would your answer change if you were given the following additional facts?

After securing the fifteen year agreement with Porter, Ferris paid a franchise fee of $35,000. Southern Treats and Porter worked together to obtain construction bids from contractors recommended by Porter. He testified that the first bid offered was for $321,000. Because the rent was to be based on the cost of construction, Ferris told Porter the bid was too high. At a meeting, Porter told the same thing to the bidder, indicating that rent would be based on the building cost. The parties obtained two other bids and accepted a bid of $215,000 by Brian Builders submitted on March 1, 2003. At a meeting with Porter to discuss accepting the bid, the parties again discussed rent being twelve percent of the building cost. Cindy Rogers suggested setting the cost at $225,000 to take overages into account. Thus, rent would be $2,250 per month. Porter did not object to the amount of rent or mention any increases. Construction began on March 10, 2003. Southern Treats put $7,000 into the construction of the building to keep the cost basis of their rent at $225,000, the amount paid by Porter for construction.

Ferris's testimony was corroborated by that of Stan and Cindy Rogers. Stan recalled that when they met with Porter to discuss the construction bids, they also discussed rent being twelve percent of the building cost. He specifically recalled using his cell phone's calculator to determine the amount of rent after Cindy mentioned setting the cost at $225,000 to take overages into account. Porter said nothing at the meeting about increasing the rent to reflect land value. Stan also recalled the subsequent meetings with Porter after the opening at which he tried to get Southern Treats to enter a new lease for more rent.

Cindy Rogers likewise recalled meeting with Porter to discuss the bids and agreeing to set rent at twelve percent of the building cost. She suggested adding $10,000 for overages to the bid by Brian Builders. They agreed that Southern Treats would pay costs over $225,000 so that their rent would not go up. She testified that Porter did not mention anything about increasing the rent to reflect land value. She also recalled meeting with Porter after the grand opening when he tried to increase the rent to $3,600 on account of the land value. When they disagreed, he said that he would honor his word regarding their agreement. She testified that he never mentioned anything about entering a two year lease, and the first she heard of such a lease was at trial. She stated that their agreement had always been a five year term with two options. Cindy also testified that she had worked for TCBY for over 14 years. She recalled rent for two different shops being $1,800 a month for about 1800 square feet of space and $2,600 a month for about 3,000 square feet.

The Second Circuit's opinion is excerpted below. Is it consistent with yours?

SOUTHERN TREATS, INC. V. TITAN PROPERTIES, L.L.C. 2006
927 SO.2D 677 (LA. APP. 2D CIR.)

¶1 Having thoroughly reviewed the record, including the trial court's ruling at the close of the hearing, we find legal error in its application of the law in determining whether there was a lease between the parties. The trial court found "no written evidence" of an agreement on the amount of rent. The court also determined that the written agreement of October 28, 2002, was not a lease, because it did not have the "necessary parts that one would expect in a lease" and the parties had not "put the finishing touches on their agreement." The law provides that the form of a lease may be oral or written. La. C.C. art. 2681. The trial court restricted its analysis to whether there was written evidence of the lease agreement between the parties and failed to address whether there was an oral agreement as to any of the lease terms. It also appears that the trial court was looking for something other than agreement as to the essential elements required to confect a lease. The trial court's finding of a two-year lease "by Mr. Porter's agreement" is also contrary to the very definition of a lease which is contract between two parties requiring the consent of both as to the essential elements. See La. C.C. art. 2668; La. C.C. art.

1906. These legal errors were clearly prejudicial as they materially affected the outcome of the litigation and deprived Southern Treats of substantial rights. In light of the legal errors apparent from the trial court's ruling, a de novo review of the record is warranted.

¶2 Even in the absence of legal error, we also find manifest error in the trial court's ruling. The trial court's finding of a two-year lease was based on a credibility determination in favor of Porter. However, this credibility determination was clearly inconsistent with the documentary evidence, particularly the October 28, 2002 agreement and the two leases prepared by Porter, all of which had an initial term of five years. The credibility determination was also inconsistent with the testimony of every other witness, including Porter's former assistant who contradicted his claim that he asked her to change the term from five to two years. Finally, the credibility determination was inconsistent with the trial court's own conclusion that all the witnesses testified credibly as to how they viewed the facts. If all the witnesses were found credible, it is bewildering that the trial court would accept the testimony of the sole witness whose testimony was contrary to the others on the alleged existence of a two-year lease. We also find manifest error in the trial court's finding of no lease agreement for the reasons explained in our de novo review.

¶3 Our law requires courts to give legal effect to all written contracts according to the parties' intent as determined by the words of the contract when they are clear, explicit, and lead to no absurd consequences. First South Farm Credit, ACA v. Gailliard Farms, Inc., 38,731 (La.App.2d Cir.8/18/04), 880 So.2d 223. Signatures on an agreement are not mere ornaments. A person who signs a written agreement is presumed to know its contents and cannot avoid its obligations by claiming that he did not read it, that he did not understand it, or that it was not explained. Id. See also St. Andrews Place, Inc. v. City of Shreveport, supra.

¶4 Porter and Ferris signed a written agreement on October 28, 2002. Although in the form of a letter to the franchisor's vice-president of leasing, it is still an agreement as indicated by the unambiguous phrase "[a]n agreement is made." The written agreement sets forth the thing to be rented and the term. The term agreed upon is five years with two five year options. The agreement is signed by Mark Porter and Scott Ferris. Porter even testified that he signed it as a letter of intention. As will be addressed, the parties had already agreed on a formula for calculating rent. Thus, with the oral rent agreement and the written agreement, they confected a valid lease and / or a binding and enforceable contract to lease at a future time.

CONCLUSION

¶5   For the reasons stated in this opinion, the trial court's judgment is reversed, judgment is rendered as stated above, and costs are assessed to appellee, Titan Properties / Mark Porter.

REVERSED.

REVIEW NOTES

The Nature, Form, and Perfection of the Contract of Lease

A lease is a

> 'synallagmatic contract by which one party, the lessor, binds himself to give to the other party, the lessee, the use and enjoyment of a thing for a term in exchange for a rent that the lessee binds himself to pay. The consent of the parties as to the thing and the rent is essential but not necessarily sufficient for a contract of lease. Art. 2668

The elements of a lease include the thing, the rent, and consent. A lease must also have a term, but that can be supplied by either the parties or the law. The articles covered include Articles 2668-2729. (The lease of labor, articles 2746-2777, are not covered by this chapter, some articles have been discussed under the concept of distinguishing between a sale and a contract to build).

The lease articles are short, consisting of only 4 chapters: General Provisions, Essential Elements (the thing, the rent, the term), The Lessor's and Lessee's Obligations, and Termination and Dissolution. A number of the concepts should seem familiar because they parallel similar concepts in sale. For example, the articles pertaining to rent are quite similar to those pertaining to price (be sure to note the differences)! This Chapter will cover the first two chapters.

General Provisions

In addition to defining a lease in Article 2668, this chapter explains that the provisions of conventional obligations and obligations in general apply where not displaced by specific lease provisions. One can have a contract to sell followed by a sale. Similarly, you can have a contract to lease followed by the actual lease itself. (In both cases, the first contract is a precursor of the second and can be enforced by specific performance.) Art 2669. There are different kinds of leases: residential, agricultural, mineral, commercial, consumer (the list is non-exclusive). Art. 2671. Mineral leases are covered as well by the Mineral Code. Art. 2672.

A lessor need not necessarily own the thing being leased, Art 2700. However, he must have the right to use the thing and the right to allow others to use it. In other words, a lessee can sub-lease the thing – unless the lease prohibits it. (Most leases prohibit subleasing as a matter of habit).

Essential Elements

The essential elements of a lease are the thing and the rent (as peer Article 2668) AND the term. Article 2678 stipulates that "A lease shall be for a term. Its duration may be agreed to by the parties or supplied by law."

A. The Rent

Rent may consist of money, commodities, fruits, services, or other performances sufficient to support an onerous contract. Art. 2675. So, for example, if the lease at issue is an agricultural lease, then the parties can agree that the rent will consist of a portion of the crops (i.e. a share-crop, no longer a 'bad word,' as commonly used, modern farmers generally keep up to 98% of their crop, paying only 2% to the landowner.)

Rent must be fixed by the parties in a sum certain or determinable through a method agreed by them or set by a third party designated by them. If the method proves unworkable or the third party unavailable or unwilling, then there is no lease. Art 2676. (Notice that this differs from Sale, wherein the court MAY set a reasonable price. Art. 2465). However, there is an exception with regard to lease: if the rent was previously established and only needs to be redetermined by the method or the third party, and neither is available, then the court MAY fix the rent or provide a similar method. This last provision changed the law in 2004 by allowing the court to intervene in limited circumstances.

Short Review:

Consider the following Hypothets. Identify the kind of contract at issue and what rule applies

1. Seller owns a house on Audubon Boulevard. A recent appraisal was $750,000. Seller and Buyer agree that Buyer may acquire ownership of this house for payment of $1. Is it a sale? What if the payment is $10,000?

Would the rules on lesion apply to the $1 sale or the $10,000 sale (if it is a sale)?

2. Lois and Bob are fifty-fifty partners, and their partnership owns an office building. Their partnership agreement provides a buyout mechanism. "One partner may offer to buy the other partner's interest in the Partnership in writing. Within seventy-two hours of receipt of the offer,

the other partner may either agree to sell at the offered price or to buy the offeror's partnership interest at that same price." Is the price certain?

3. Frank François has a 1000 Euro note. Van Vespucci has a 1000 United States dollar note. Frank promises to give Van the Euro note if Van gives Frank the dollar note. Do they have an agreement, and therefore a contract? Is the contract a sale? If so, which one of them can invoke Louisiana Civil Code art. 2487? That is, which one of them does that article empower to hold onto the note that has now become the other's property until the other delivers the note he promised to deliver?

Rent v. Price
Benglis Sash

You should remember this case from the Price chapter. Mrs. Leonards ordered custom-made windows from plaintiff Benglis Sash for an apartment building she and Mr. Leonards were renovating, no price was mentioned. They had ordered from them before. Mr. Leonards got back in town, was displeased with the amount of progress that had been made, and allegedly cancelled the windows order claiming that they had not been delivered within the allotted time. Plaintiff denied ever receiving the letter and manufactured the windows. Then he contacted Leonards for delivery, Leonards refused to accept them, claiming they were not delivered within the agreed-upon time.

The court found that no specific time for delivery was indicated in the contract, that they had been delivered within a reasonable time, and that by refusing to accept delivery, Leonards had breached the contract. In determining the price, the court adopted an open price term – as with UCC Article 2, if the seller is a merchant and the parties fail to agree on a price or say nothing about a price, then the price is a reasonable price for that time and place. This case led to the coordinating Civil Code Article.

So, is there an equivalent for lease?

Willis v. Ventrella p 5

Facts: Willis owned 835 acres, which the defendants Ventrella wanted to use for hunting. So the parties agreed on a lease. In payment for the use of the land, each year the defendants were to pay $2,000 plus property taxes and provide 120 hours of bulldozer work at the plaintiff's direction for doing things like digging lakes, clearing rights of way, removing stumps, etc. . The parties even agreed on the size of the bulldozer to be used.

Problems began in the second and third years of the lease. Willis complained that Ventrella had failed to provide the dozer work, had failed to properly maintain the roads, and (worst of all) were hunting at close range to plaintiff's home. Consequently, in December, 1993, plaintiff began eviction proceedings.

The issue was whether this was an enforceable lease. If it was not, then defendants could be ordered to leave as trespassers, but either evicted or ordered to perform under the lease. The court held that the lease was invalid because it failed to set a proper rent.

The problem: The rent was neither fixed nor determinable by some OBJECTIVE method or a third party: Rent must be readily ascertainable and determinable from facts or circumstances not within the parties' control." Consequently, as the parties did not have a contract in place, plaintiff could be compensated only under unjust enrichment: the unfair loss sustained by one party or the unjust enrichment of the other, whichever is less. Notice the factors on of Unjust enrichment:

1. An enrichment

2. An impoverishment

3. A causal relationship between the two

4. An absence of justification for either the enrichment or the impoverishment, and

5. The absence of any other remedy.

Under this theory, the plaintiff was compensated for the fair lease value. No attorney's fees were awarded because no statute or contract stipulated that they be paid. (and even had there been bad faith involved, no attorney's fees or punitive damages are provided under the general damages provisions of Obligations).

So, how are the two cases similar? How are they different?

Myers v. Burke p9

Defendant Burke gave plaintiff Myers permission to occupy defendant's land and build a dwelling on it for $1/year. Defendant subsequently sold the land, and the purchaser evicted the plaintiff. Plaintiff is suing his former 'landlord' for $500 – the value of his dwelling, [implicitly arguing that as it was a lease, the defendant owed him a warranty of peaceful possession, which he violated by selling the land].

Held: This was not a lease because the 'rent' was 'not sufficient to support an onerous contract.' As a licensee, the plaintiff can recover the value of the material and workmanship of his dwelling from the owner of the land under Article 508.

Guillory v. North American Gaming

Guillory leased King's Truck Stop and Casino to O.M. Investors, who subsequently merged to become defendant NAG. The lease gave a primary term of 5 years, rent was 20% of the proceeds from the Video Poker Machines. Lessee was tto renovate and operate the premises as a "First Class 24-hour restaurant and truck stop" and purchase between 20-50 video poker machines, AND it contained an option to renew:

> If no default, then at the expiration of the initial lease term or any renewal, the lessee has the
> option to renew for 3 additional 5-year terms. All terms apply, except that the monthly percent-
> age due Lessor is negotiable. To exercise the option, lessor must receive written notice no less
> than 90 days before expiration . . .

NAG notified Guillary as required of its intention to exercise the option, but the parties got stuck on the renewal rent amount. Defendant alleged that plaintiffs refused to negotiate the price of the option in good faith. Plaintiffs claim thee opposite, and that defendants breached good faith by opening a competing truck stop.

Issue: was the lease valid?

Held: no, affirmed that the option was invalid because it lacked a price term

Rationale:

> 1. This is not Benglis – in that case, the parties failed to even mention price. Here, the parties
> negotiated, but failed to agree, so one cannot reasonably infer implied consent to a reasonable
> price.

> 2. No reason to litigate good faith negotiation – even had the parties negotiated before the first
> term, there is no reason to conclude that they would have reached an agreement.

Question: 1. Why isn't the option valid? 2. Would the result be the same under the current articles? (See Art. 2676, esp comment e)

Hunt v. Gulftrust

Defendant Gulf Trust 'bought' an immovable from plaintiff Hunt encumbered by 2 mortgages. The agreement was that he would remain personally liable for the mortgages. The sale price was $33K, and Hunt was to receive $1K – reflecting the difference between the price and the outstanding mortgages.

Hunt sued to have the sale declared null, TCT found in Hunt's favor, and Gulftrust appeals.

Issue: was the sale valid?

Held: Affirmed, no.

Rationale:

> A valid sale must have thing, price, consent. The specific price need not be stated, but there must be a meeting of the minds. Sale of an immovable must be inwriting, and generally testimonial or other evidence may not negate or vary the terms of the contract. UNLESS to prove a vice of consent, a simulation, or a subsequent modification.
>
> Neither party raised the issue of parol testimony, the parties used it to explain the parties' intentions. Hunt testified that Gulf Trust promised to make the mortgage payments after acquiring the property, but defendant Gulf Trust denied that. The price specified in the agreement was $33K, of which $32 was the balance due on the two mortgages, for which Hunt was to remain personally liable --- [so in essence, Gulf Trust was paying $1,000 for the property, not $33K).
>
> This shows that they failed to reach a meeting of the minds as to price . . .
> So, is this like the previous Gaming case or not??? If so, why?

B. Consent

Article 2669 says one should fill in with Obligations in General and Conventional Obligations rules. Art 1942 stipulates that "when, because of special circumstances, the offeree's silence leads the offeror reasonably to believe that a contract has been formed, the offer is deemed accepted"

How does this article play into the following case?

Faroldi v. Nungesser

Plaintiffs owned an immovable in New Orleans on two lots, of which a portion was sold to the state for the building of the I-10 (1950's and Eisenhower). The state acquired the buildings that were located partially on their part of the lots and partially on the plaintiffs.

The state then sold the buildings to the defendant, but without stating when defendant had to remove them. Defendant did not know that the buildings were partially on plaintiff's property, until plaintiffs informed him that he needed to remove them before April 1, 1960, or they would charge him rent of $120/month (defendant had made arrangements to move them, but had been confronting delays)

Issue: Was there a lease?

Held: NO, there was no consent to a lease – defendant never accepted or agreed to the rent nor was there any meeting of the minds.

Hence, no contract, no quasi contract nor quantum meruit – the presence of the buildings remaining on plaintiff's lot did not cost plaintiff anything . . .

Section 2: The Nature of a lease

Article 2671 lists several kinds of leases: residential, commercial, agricultural, consumer, mineral . . not exclusive. Article 2713 stipulates that a lessee has a right to sublease the thing.

Means v. Comcast

Means wants to evict lessee Comcast. Means sister previously owned the property and leased it to Cablevision to use as a satellite dish and reception facilities for a term of 15 years with an option to renew for another 15 years by giving written notice any time prior to the end of the initial term, rent at $1,000/year + property taxes + reasonable attorney fees. Time Warner acquired Cablevision & continued to pay Ms. Lay. Then Means bought the property from Ms. Lay's estate, sending a letter to Cablevision's manager saying "we are the legal owners, therefore please make your payment [to us]. Time Warner made 7 annual lease payments to Means.

7 years later, Time Warner sent written notice exercising the option to renew, and tendering a check for the first five months' rent. Means refused the check, claiming that he was not bound by the lease because it was never recorded.

TCT: Tacit ratification, therefore plaintiff bound by the lease.

Issue: Is he bound?

Held: Yes, affirmed.

Rationale: Means claims that only a recorded lease binds subsequent owners (citing McDuffie v. Walker) As the lease was not recorded, he is not bound by it.

HOWEVER, Ratification (1843) occurs when a person declares that he gives his consent to an obligation incurred on his behalf without authority. It must evidence his intent to be bound. Tacit ratification results when a person, with knowledge of an obligation incurred on his behalf by another, accepts the benefits of that obligation."

Means letter to Comcast & acceptance of 7 years of rent = tacit ratification.

(Compare Art 1843 on ratification to confirmation, art. 1842)

Phoenix Land v. Mitchell (sublease)

Mitchell (defendant's grandfather) owned land with sand and gravel deposits in St. Tammany. When the grandfather died, the defendant for Mitchell & Co. and leased out the land to Murphy's Trucking in 1996. The lease said that during its term there will be NOT mining, excavation, or removal of sand and gravel OTHER than as per the terms of this lease AND **the lease may not be sublet without written permission of Lessor**

In 1997, Mitchell gave such permission to sublease to Phoenix on the same terms and conditions. Phoenix purchased All of Murphy's Sand and Gravel operation. In 1998, Mitchell and Phoenix added an addendum, adding an option to renew after the initial 5 year period, for 5 additional 5-year terms, but no more than a total of 25 years. It also provided that royalties paid on sand and gravel be paid.

Phoenix ran into financial difficulties and filed for bankruptcy reorganization, the bankruptcy court rejected its plan, and then Mitchell and Phoenix started having disputes about how Phoenix was conducting business, underpayment of royalties, improper mining, allowing 3d parties to mine on Mitchell's land without Mitchell's permission.

Prior to the expiration of the first term, Phoenix sent a letter indicating a desire to exercise the option to renew, but the parties could not agree on the amount of royalties. Nevertheless, Phoenix continued its operations without a written extension. Phoenix sued Mitchell to get a price set re the royalties, and then entered into "operating Agreements" with two other companies to mine part of Mitchell's property. When Mitchell objected, Phoenix added to the original suit over royalties a claim that Mitchell was interfering with its contracts with other parties.

Issue: Were the 'operating agreements' subleases in violation of the original agreement?

Held: Yes., affirmed.

Phoenix's argument (p24): "this Operating Agreement is not and shall not be constructed as a lease or sublease . . . ."

BUT "whether the operating agreements are really suleases is a question of law. Questions of law cannot be confessed or admitted. The characterization of the contracdts . . is preeminently of that nature. The legal character of a contract must be determined by its substance, by its effect on the parties, what the law (not the parties) says it is . . .

Here, the provisions of the Mineral Code apply, and supplement the provisions of the Civil Code. Ownership of land includes all minerals, including solid minerals. "A mineral lease is a contract by which the lessee is granted the right to explore for and produce minerals . . ." A sublease has the same elements as a lease: an object, a determinate price, and consent. Under both agreements, Ponchartrain and Ellinger became owners of the gravel, soil, and minerals produced. Mitchell granted Phoenix a singular right of way to reach the premises. Thus, Phoenix did sublease to Ponchartrain and Ellinger.

The original lease did not give Phoenix the right to bring outside materials onto Mitchell's property for reprocessing, but thee Pontchartrain and Ellinger Operating Agreements allowed them.

Phoenix dismembered Mitchell's ownership by giving Pontchartrain and Ellinger rights of use on the property that Phoenix itself did not have.

Grave v. Scott

Facts: Plaintiffs are residents of New York, and defendants are residents of Jefferson Parish. Defendant is resisting plaintiff's efforts to evict him as tenant, claiming that he, not the plaintiffs, is the owner of the property.

Held: for Plaintiff

Rationale: 1. One can lease a property even though one does not own it; and 2. If one is a lessee in undisturbed possession of the leased premises, one cannot contest lessor's title.

Section 3: Form

A lease may be made orally or in writing, but an unrecorded lease of an immovable is not effective against a third party. Art 2681.

McWilliams v. Courtney

Facts: McWilliams leased a wood splitter and trailer to Courtney so that Courtney could cut, haul, and sell firewood. Courtney had possession of both items for 4-5 months, and McWilliams sent him a demand letter for $1,500.

Courtney denies he owes the debt, claims that all he was required to do under their agreement was supply McWilliams with firewood. McWilliams testified that the parties entered into an oral agreement at McWilliams shop, a Country Store, and Courtney agreed to pay $40/say for the splitter, and $30/day for the trailer. Over the next several months, McWilliams kept track of the days Courtney was using the equipment by driving past Courtney's house, marking down in a ledger when he saw it being used, reflecting a total amount due of $1,470. Another party, Coleman, said he only heard McWilliams offer to make Courtney a 'deal,' but did not hear the details, though he saw Courney deliver two cords of firewood to McWilliams and his son. Courtney could not produce any witness other than Coleman (2 were in prison, one was in Houston).

Issue: Was the rent agreed-on? And if so, what was it?

Courtney's argument depends on the trial court believing that he had actually delivered wood to McWilliams, but there is no indication of that in the record, McWilliams did not acknowledge any delivery of wood. Courtney complains that there was no term, no payment arrangements, and no proper method of accounting, so this should not have been regarded as a lease – however, there is nothing requiring that the lease must contain specifics as to the accounting method used. Furthermore, where the parties don't supply a term, the Civil Code will do so – Art 2680 specifies that the lease of a movable shall be from day to day. The fact is, the Trial Court found Mr. McWilliams' arguments, as supported by his ledger, credible and did not find Courtney's defense credible.

Section 4: Perfection of the Contract of Lease

Laroussini v. Werlein (1899)

Facts: Plaintiff wants to enforce an oral lease of an immovable for the term of 5 years at $750/month. Apparently, the parties had a pre-existing 5-year lease which was drawing towards a close. The contract at issue was allegedly a renewal for another 5 years at a rent $50 higher per month. About a week after the parties reached an oral agreement, plaintiff asked a notary to draw up a written lease reciting those terms. The written lease was handed to the defendant, but he refused to execute it, and plaintiff brought an action for specific performance.

Issue: was there a valid agreement?

Held: No

Rationale: A lease can certainly be verbal, regardless of whether it was followed or not by the execution of a written lease – if there is no intention to follow it with a written lease. If, on the other hand, the parties do not intend to be bound until the lease is reduced to writing, then they are not bound.

That was apparently the case here. Defendant was willing to re-endorse the original lease, but plaintiff insisted on a formal contract to be drawn up (p 31) – that being the case, as per the parties' own intention, the contract was not valid until written. (furthermore, the written lease contained a number of draconian measures, which probably put the defendant off, in part because it was not in accord with what he had previously agreed-to.

Study Question

Southern Treats

1. (partially integrated lease, rent was agreed-to orally)

Southern Treats wanted to open a TCBY/Mrs. Fields franchise in Shreveport, and negotiated with Mr. Porter who owned a suitable property. They discussed the size, that Porter would own the building and lease it for 12% of the cost of the building, and Southern Treats, on that basis, prepared a business plan, which included an estimated monthly rent of $2000 based on the agreed-upon rate of 12% of the estimated building cost ($200K). They met with TCBY to get approval for the building site, agreed on an architect, and then Southern Treats received the franchise papers.

The franchise papers required a 15-year lease, which Porter agreed to in the form of 5 years and 2 5-year options. The parties signed an agreement stating: "An agreement is made between Porter, Lessor & [ST]Lessee, dated 28 Oct. 2002" and it provided a 5-year lease with 2 5-year options. ST noted that the lease didn't specify rent, but Porter admitted that the parties had discussed 12% of building costs. Porter started paying $2,250 in rent (increased cost of the building). At the grand opening, Porter came by with a written lease stipulating $3,600/month. ST refused to sign. He then came by with a $2,250 for 5 years, rent to be renegotiated after that, no 2 5-year options. ST. refused to sign. Then Porter sent a letter stating that was a month-month lease, and he wished to terminate, that the Oct 28 writing was a mere letter of intent for purposes of obtaining a franchise. (Though admitting it did not contain any such language.

For which party would you decide? Why?

The parties considered a number of bids before settling on a $225,000 cost of construction & 12% rent, ST's testimony was corroborated by other witnesses who remembered his, using a cell phone calculator to determine rent after suggestion of $225K to cover potential overages.

Trial court held for Porter, because the writing did not include an essential term (rent), and was therefore only month-to-month.

Appellate court overturned, finding that writing was supplemented by oral agreement as to the rent of 12% of $225,000/month.

(Parol evidence rule provides an exception when a written contract is 'not fully integrated' – in other words, the writing on its face is incomplete – as it was here.)

Hypothet (Written by Brianna Golden)

Mary and Susan have been best friends since middle school and even planned on starting law school together. Mary knew Susan was having some difficulties living at home with her parents so Mary offered to let Susan stay in her spare bedroom in a condominium owned by her parents subject to Susan paying Mary $400.00 for rent on a monthly basis for the entire time they would be in law school and spending 2 hours/week cleaning the condo from top to bottom. Their agreement was never written down, but Susan continued to pay Mary $400.00. Susan paid Mary in cash but kept the receipts from all her withdrawals. Susan moved in July 2016 and both women started law school the following month.

1. Is this a valid lease agreement? Why or why not?

2. What happens if Mary's parents subsequently sell the condo to a third party before Susan graduates from law school and the new owner subsequently kicks Susan out?

CHAPTER 13

THE TERM OF A LEASE

Flowchart

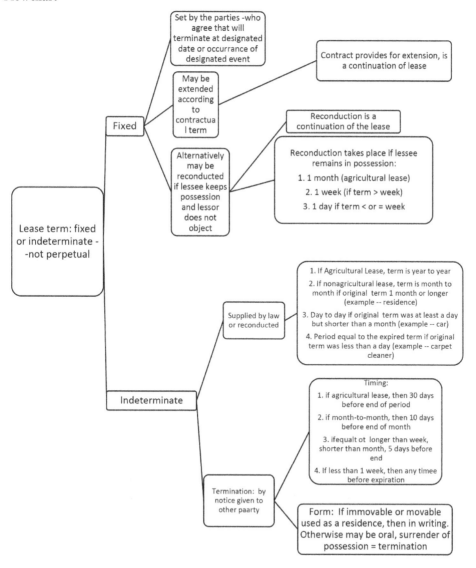

Section 1: Duration

Read Articles 2678-2680, 2720-2726, and 2727-2729

As mentioned in Chapter 11, in addition to consent, a thing, and rent, a lease must have a term, which means that it may not be perpetual. Art. 2678 cmt. (c). Nevertheless, the parties have a choice of either setting a term themselves or allowing the law to set a term. Art. 2678. If the parties set a term, then it is 'fixed,' which means that it terminates at a designated date or upon the occurrence of a designated event. A fixed term may not exceed ninety-nine years, and if a longer term is provided or the lease contains an option to extend the term to more than ninety-nine years, then the term must be reduced to ninety-nine years. Art. 2679.

Alternatively, if the parties do not set a term, then the term is 'indeterminate,' which means that Article 2680 supplies a legal term. Thus, in the absence of a fixed term, the term of an agricultural lease is from year to year, the lease of any other immovable or a movable used as a residence is from month to month, and a lease of other movables is generally from day to day. If the rent for a movable is fixed for a period other than from day to day, then the term, unless otherwise agreed, is one such period not to exceed one month.

Articles 2720 through 2726 explain how to terminate fixed-term leases, while articles 2727 through 2729 explain how to terminate indeterminate-term leases.

Study Question:

In the following case, is the term of the lease fixed or indeterminate? If it is indeterminate, then what would the term be under current Article 2680, and why? The current Lease articles were revised in 2004 (effective Jan. 1, 2005). Would the result in the next case be any different if it were decided today?

HERRING V. BREEDLOVE 1953
222 LA. 1088, 64 SO. 2D 441

HAWTHORNE, Justice.

¶1 Plaintiff Jolly F. Herring instituted this suit seeking to recover damages in the sum of $10,576.07 from Edward C. Breedlove. The lower court dismissed his suit on an exception of no cause or right of action, and he appealed to the Court of Appeal, Second Circuit, which transferred the case to this court because it lacked appellate jurisdiction.

¶2   In considering the exception which was sustained by the lower court, all well pleaded allegations of plaintiff's petition must be accepted as true. The material allegations are as follows:

> In December of 1945 plaintiff discussed with defendant the possibility of obtaining a lease on a filling station owned by the defendant in Natchitoches, Louisiana. In January of 1946 Breedlove, the defendant, advised plaintiff that, if he wanted to take over the filling station, he could do so as of February 1, 1946. Plaintiff requested a written lease, but was informed by the defendant that one was not necessary, and that he, plaintiff, could have a lease on the filling station as long as he wanted it provided he 'ran it right'. Thereafter, relying on the representations of Breedlove, the plaintiff and his wife gave up their employment in Houston, Texas, where he was earning approximately $4,000 per annum and his wife $1,000, and moved to Natchitoches in order to run the filling station. He operated the filling station during the months of February and March, 1946, and during March made a net profit of $489.13. On April 5 he received a written notice from the defendant to vacate the premises and deliver possession at the end of the month. On the same day defendant executed a written contract of lease of the filling station to the Billups Petroleum Company, effective May 1, 1946. In view of the fact that plaintiff had no written contract from Breedlove but only a verbal lease, he was forced to vacate the premises and on April 30, 1946, turned them over to Billups Petroleum Company.

¶3   Plaintiff itemized his damages as follows:

> For loss of his job in Texas and loss of his wife's employment in Texas and loss of anticipated profit of this filling station during the next two years had he been permitted to operate it for this period of time, $10,000;
>   for expenses in moving to Louisiana, $125;
>   for loss in the value of the filling station equipment purchased by him which he would be forced to sell at 50 per cent of its cost, $451.07 --
>   or a total of $10,576.07.

¶4   Under the allegations of plaintiff's petition he had a verbal lease of the filling station, but he does not allege that the lease had a fixed duration. On the contrary, his allegations show that its duration was not fixed, for he alleged that defendant had told him he 'could have a lease on the filling station as long as he wanted, provided that he 'ran it right". Since the verbal contract between the plaintiff and the defendant for the renting of the filling station did not fix the duration of the lease, the law provides that it shall be considered as having been made by the month, under Article 2685 of the LSA-Civil Code: 'If the renting of a house or other edifice, or of an apartment, has been made without fixing its duration, the lease shall be considered to have been made by the month.'

¶5   According to plaintiff's allegations he was damaged because, after occupying the leased premises for only two months under the verbal lease, defendant gave him notice to vacate and deliver possession, but defendant had a right to do this under Article 2686 of the Code, which provides: " . . .If no time for its [the lease's] duration has been agreed on, the party desiring to put an end to it must give notice in writing to the other, at least ten days before the expiration of the month, which has begun to run.' Since no time for the lease's duration had been agreed upon by these parties, either had the legal right to terminate the lease at the expiration of any month by complying with the provisions of the above quoted article.

¶6   Plaintiff in brief states that the whole theory of his case is that the defendant made representations to him upon which he relied, and caused him to suffer the damages claimed, citing in support thereof Article 2315 of the LSA-Civil Code. The damages to plaintiff were caused by termination of the lease contract by the defendant, but the defendant under the allegations of the petition has a legal right to end the lease, and consequently is not responsible in damages.

¶7   For the reasons assigned, the judgment appealed from is affirmed at appellant's costs.

Section 2: Reconduction

Read Louisiana Civil Code articles 2720-2726.

The lease involved in the Herring case had an 'indeterminate' term, not a fixed one Consequently, the law supplied a term of one month under Article 2680, and Article 2728 supplied the notice of termination requirement. The results are similar where a lease with a fixed term ends but the lessee stays in place with the lessor's agreement. Generally, a lease with a fixed term ends upon the expiration of that term, without need of notice. Art. 2720. The parties are free, however, to continue the lease either explicitly or implicitly. So, if the lease contract contains an option to extend the term and the option is exercised, then the lease continues for the term and under any other provisions stipulated in the option. Art. 2723.

Alternatively, if the lessee simply remains in possession after the expiration of a fixed-term lease for a certain period of time without notice to vacate or terminate or any other opposition by the lessor, then the lease is implicitly reconducted. Art 2721. This means that the lease continues, but is now for an indeterminate term: year to year for an agricultural lease (Art. 2722), month to month for a non-agricultural lease whose term was a month or longer (Art. 2723), day to day where the original term was at least a day but shorter than a month (id.). When reconduction occurs, all of the provisions of the lease continue for the length of the indeterminate term.

Be sure to distinguish among a reconducted lease, an extension that was provided-for in the original lease, and a novated lease that is substituted in place of the original lease.

Study Questions:

The Civil Code articles quoted in the following case have since changed. Would the result in the following case be the same under the new articles or not? What current Civil Code articles would apply?

COMEGYS V. SHREVEPORT KANDY KITCHEN 1926
162 LA. 103, 110 SO. 104

BRUNOT, J.

¶1   John M. Comegys leased the premises known as 719 Texas Street, in the city of Shreveport, La., to the Shreveport Kandy Kitchen, a business conducted under that name but owned and operated by G. F. Eltife. Before the expiration of the lease Eltife executed and recorded a chattel mortgage in favor of Fred Martel upon the property and fixtures he had placed in the leased premises. After the expiration of the lease Eltife continued to occupy the property at the same monthly rental. He paid the rent for the two months succeeding the expiration of the lease, but for three months thereafter he defaulted in his payments, and plaintiff sued for the sum due and provisionally seized all of the debtor's property found on the premises. Fred Martel intervened, alleged that the rent sued for accrued subsequent to the expiration of the lease and subsequent to the recordation of his chattel mortgage upon the debtor's property, and therefore his privilege, as mortgagee, upon the property seized, was superior to the privilege asserted by the plaintiff.

¶2   The learned trial judge held that when the lease expired and the lessee continued to occupy the premises at the same monthly rental, what is known as reconduction resulted, and the original lease, with the term thereof changed, by operation of law, from two years to a monthly lease, was continued for an indefinite time, terminable, at the option of the lessor, by service upon the lessee of a notice to vacate. Judgment was therefore rendered in favor of the plaintiff and intervener and against the defendant for the amounts of their respective claims, and in favor of the plaintiff and against the intervener, subordinating the lien of the intervener, as the holder of the chattel mortgage, to the plaintiff lessor's lien.

¶3   From this judgment the intervener appealed. The Court of Appeal reversed the judgment in part. It decreed that the lien of the mortgagee was superior in rank and primed the plaintiff's lien and privilege for rent accruing after the expiration of the lease. A rehearing was refused, and plaintiff thereupon applied to this court for certiorari or writ of review. The writ issued, and the record is now before us.

¶4　The sole question presented is whether or not the chattel mortgage became effective at the date the lease expired and, from that date, was superior in rank to the privilege of the landlord upon the property of the tenant for the rent thereafter accruing.

¶5　Counsel for intervener contends that this question is directly and affirmatively answered by the Court of Appeal of Orleans in the case of Remedial Loan Society v. Fredrick Solis and Robert E. Trepagnier, Patrick J. Morris, Intervener, C. of A. Repts. vol. 1, 164, in which case the court held that:

> '(1) A contract of lease which either party may terminate on giving 15 days' notice does not fix its duration, and under article C. C. 2685, is one by the month.

> '(2) Holding over after the expiration of each month creates a tacit reconduction from month to month and a new contract for each month.

> '(3) A chattel mortgage yields a preference to a contract of lease and to every tacit reconduction thereof made prior to recordation of the amount of mortgage but enjoys a priority over every lease or tacit reconduction made subsequent thereto.'

¶6　Counsel for plaintiff differentiates the cited case from the case at bar. The only difference is that in one case there was a month to month lease; in the other the original lease was for two years, but this lease had expired and thereafter the occupancy of the premises was held under a tacit reconduction from month to month. Counsel for plaintiff concedes that the principle of law involved is the same. The Orleans Court of Appeal specifically held that a tacit reconduction from month to month creates a new contract for each month, and that a chattel mortgage primes a lease or tacit reconduction thereof made subsequent to the recordation of the mortgage.

* * *

¶7　But, in the case now before us, it is contended, and the district judge held, that the old lease was continued by what is known as reconduction, or operation of law; that the lessee's retention or possession of the premises after the conventional lease expired had the effect of continuing that lease in full force and effect except as to the terms thereof. The learned district judge says:

'Under article 2689, where two parties enter into a contract of lease for a definite term, they do so with a full realization (legally speaking) that the law writes into that very lease the provision that that very lease shall continue in force and effect, after the expiration of the term agreed upon, for an indefinite time, saving to the parties the right to put an end to it on the expiration of any month. This being true, then the very moment the chattels are placed in the leased premises under the term lease, the lessor's lien attaches not only for the term specified in the lease but for an indefinite term thereafter.

'And one taking a chattel mortgage on the property in the leased premises, during the existence of the term lease, is legally bound to know that the lessor's lien rested against the same property for whatever rent might become due in the future so long as the lessee remained in the same premises without executing a new lease.

'It is true that the lessor and lessee in this case could not have entered into any conventional renewal of the old lease, or any new lease, and thereby cut off the rights of the holder of the chattel mortgage, and it might well be argued that what they could not do by agreement, they cannot do as a result of the law. This would be correct if the law wrote into their contract this provision at the expiration of the term lease, but the law does not do that, but writes it into their contract at the very beginning, and every person, dealing thereafter with the lessee must do so with this in view.

'We think a reconducted lease is not a new lease or even a renewed lease, but is a continuation of the old lease, and in this particular case when the fixtures were placed in the leased premises, the lessor's lien attached for all rent to become due in the future, and therefore primed the chattel mortgage.

'Counsel for intervener has cited article 2690 to show that the lien did not attach except for the specific term of the lease. This article provides that the security which may have been given for the payment of the rent shall not extend to the reconduction period. This plainly refers to any conventional security that may have been given and does not refer to legal security such as the lessor's lien.'

¶8   In answer to the cogent and persuasive reasoning of the district judge, the Court of Appeal says:

'The conventional lease expired at midnight on December 31, 1924, and at that moment all the right and privileges of the lessor under that lease expired also, except for the rent which became due under it. One moment after the conventional lease expired there was no lease on the property and the landlord had no privilege on the property then in the leased premises, except for the payment of rent already accrued. The lessee's occupation of the premises thereafter under reconduction constituted a new lease for each month. Whatever privilege the landlord had on the chattels in the premises for his rentals under the reconducted or new lease accrued subsequently to the expiration of the old lease.'

¶9   The court then quoted C. C. art. 2689, and in support of its conclusions it gives the following reasons:

'The law creates a presumption of a continuance of the lease only in case the landlord permits the tenant to occupy the premises for one week subsequent to the expiration of the old lease. It therefore follows that during the period of the week immediately following the expiration of the lease the landlord could have evicted the tenant without notice, for the Code provides that notice must be given only if the lease tenant remained a week, and the tenant could, during the same period of time vacate the premises without notice. There is no presumption of continuance of the lease unless the landlord permits the tenant to remain a week. During that week there is no tie, either conventional or legal, between the landlord and the tenant. In the case at bar, the conventional lease expired on December 31, 1924. For a period of one week immediately thereafter there was no lease-the old one had expired and there was no presumption of a continuance under article 2684 of the Code. There was therefore no tie, either legal or conventional, between the parties during this time.'

¶10   The fallacy of this reasoning strikes us as apparent. Article 2684 of the Code merely establishes a period of abeyance during which time either party to the contract may consider it at an end and act accordingly, but if neither so acts within that time the original contract is continued from month to month, terminable at the option of either party to it by simply giving the required notice. It is not a new contract or a renewal of the old contract; it is merely a tacit reconduction of the original contract with the term thereof changed, by operation of law, from a two-year lease to a monthly lease, and the same tacit reconduction takes place from month to month during the tenant's occupancy of the premises under those conditions. When neither party to the contract exercises his option to terminate the lease within one week after the expiration of the term stated therein, there arises a legal presumption that the lease is continued. Article 2689 of the Code is as follows:

'If the tenant either of a house or of a room should continue in possession for a week after his lease has expired, without any opposition being made thereto by the lessor, the lease shall be presumed to have been continued and he cannot be compelled to deliver up the house or room without having received the legal notice or warning directed by article 2686.'

¶11   The foregoing article has been interpreted to mean that a tacit reconduction continues the lease from month to month. Dolese v. Barberot, 9 La. Ann. 352; Geheebe v. Stanby, 1 La. Ann. 17. Murrell v. Lion, 30 La. Ann. 255.

¶12   In this case the lessee occupied the premises without objection or protest on the part of the lessor for several months after the term of the conventional lease expired. He paid the rent for two months, but thereafter defaulted in his payments, and this suit and seizure followed.

¶13   For the reasons stated, we are of the opinion that the judgment rendered in this case by the district judge is correct and that it should have been affirmed. It is therefore ordered and decreed that the judgment of the Court of Appeal, Second Circuit, which subordinates the plaintiff's lessor's privilege for rent to the lien under the chattel mortgage in favor of the intervener be avoided and set aside, and that the judgment as rendered in the district court be reinstated and made the final judgment of the court. It is further ordered and decreed that the district court costs be paid by the defendant, the Court of Appeal costs to be paid by the plaintiff, and the costs of this court be paid by the intervener.

Study Question:

What does the following case show about distinguishing between reconduction, an extension or amendment of an existing lease, and a new, renegotiated (novated) lease?

Was the case properly decided, or is the dissenting opinion more persuasive than the majority?

Consider Articles 1880, 1881, 2726, and the comments to Article 2726.

WALLER OIL CO. V. BROWN 1988
528 SO. 2D 584 (LA. APP. 2D CIR.)

NORRIS, Judge.

¶1   This is a suit for breach of a lease contract that was allegedly reconducted. The lessor, Waller Oil Co. Inc., sued the lessee, Loyd T. Brown, d/b/a The Sound Company, for damages due to a fire on the leased premises. Waller alleged that Brown failed to carry fire insurance, in violation of the lease. The case went to jury trial and yielded a verdict that Brown had breached a contractual duty and Waller had sustained damage as a result. Judgment was entered accordingly and Brown appeals, raising three issues:

(1) Whether the doctrine of reconduction applied to the case.

(2) Whether the lessor's failure to notify the lessee promptly of default in the latter's obligation to maintain fire insurance estopped the lessor from claiming damages.

(3) Assuming the lease was in effect and the insurance clause had not been waived, was the penalty for lessee's breach the cost of the insurance or the amount of the fire loss.

¶2   Finding merit in the first argument, we reverse.

FACTS

¶3   In April 1978, Waller Oil Company executed a contract of lease with Brown, covering a portion of a commercial building in Minden. The lease had a term of seven years, from July 1, 1978 to June 30, 1985, at a monthly rental of $500. The lease also contained an option to renew for an additional seven years under the same terms and conditions. The lease further imposed on Brown the duty of procuring and maintaining fire and extended coverage insurance on the premises for its full insurable value during the time of the lease. Waller was obligated to notify Brown promptly and in writing of any default except payment of rent; upon notification, Brown would have 20 days to cure the default, after which Waller was authorized to effect the cure and charge the cost to Brown as part of the rent.

¶4   Sometime in June 1985, shortly before the contract was to expire, Brown telephoned Mr. Waller, president of Waller Oil, to inform him specifically that he would not exercise the option to renew. Waller admitted this and testified that it was not in the parties' best interests for Brown to vacate immediately, as Waller planned to be out of state on business until September. After discussion, both parties agreed that Brown would continue to rent the premises for a term not exceeding three months. Brown asked if he would have to pay a higher rent; Waller said no. They therefore reached a verbal agreement whereby Brown would stay in the store at the same monthly rent he had been paying. No other provisions of the lease were discussed or settled. Three months later, in September, Brown again telephoned Waller to say he had still not found a new location. Waller had not yet found a new lessee, so they verbally agreed that Brown would stay another month, through October. Once again, nothing was discussed except the term and the rent. On October 28, a fire engulfed the building, causing substantial damage. Brown was not at fault in causing the damage..

¶5   Waller learned that Brown was not carrying fire insurance the day after the fire. An insurance agent testified he could have sold Brown fire insurance on the leased premises for the term of the lease. Waller also presented evidence concerning the cost of repairing the building and his legal expenses. At the time of trial, he had not repaired the building.

¶6　Brown testified he was not aware of the fire insurance clause in the original lease contract and that he never maintained the coverage. He also testified about his conversations with Waller in June and September 1985; his testimony was substantially the same as Waller's. Other witnesses also testified about Brown's intention not to renew the lease.

¶7　As noted, the jury found in response to special interrogatories that Brown had a duty under the lease to provide fire insurance and that Brown's failure to do so made him liable for the property damage. The court entered judgment in favor of Waller for $16,500 for the cost of repairs, $500 for lost rent and $4,000 for attorney fees. Brown has appealed.

DISCUSSION

¶8　Brown's first argument is that his lease was not reconducted at the end of June 1985. Tacit reconduction is the continuation of a lease after the expiration of its term by operation of law. LSA-C.C. arts. 2688, 2689. In Ashton Realty Co. v. Prowell, 165 La. 328, 115 So. 579 (1928), the supreme court interpreted the principle of reconduction as follows:

> If the tenant either of a house or of a room should continue in possession for a week after his lease has expired, without any opposition being made thereto by the lessor, the lease shall be presumed to have been continued, and he can not be compelled to deliver up the house or room without having received the legal notice or warning directed by article 2686.
>
> 　[I]f both parties to the lease remain silent and inactive for the space of one month [one week, under art. 2689] after the expiration of the lease, they shall be presumed to have acquiesced in, and tacitly consented to, a renewal of the lease for another year [another month, under art. 2689]. It has no application whatever when either party has clearly announced his intention not to renew the lease on the same terms or for a full year, for the purpose of the law is not to force a contract upon parties unwilling to contract, but merely to establish a rule of evidence, or presumption, as to their intention in the premises.

115 So. at 581.

¶9　We have closely examined the evidence in this case. It is abundantly clear that the parties were not "silent and inactive," such as would activate the presumption of reconduction. Rather, toward the end of the term Brown communicated to his lessor that he would not renew the existing lease. Waller never denied he understood Brown's intention to terminate the lease.

This testimony from the parties themselves shows that both agreed that the old lease would expire. Aware that the written lease would have no effect, they reached an oral agreement as to the basic elements of a new lease: the thing leased and the price. LSA-C.C. arts. 2670, 2683. Later, they reached yet another new agreement. There would be little point in striking these new agreements unless the old one was considered abandoned. Furthermore, the term of the first new agreement was different from that of the typical reconducted lease. The parties' stated intent not to be bound by the expired lease, together with their consent to the new leases, undermines the jury's implicit finding that the old lease was reconducted and that Brown was bound by it. This finding is manifestly erroneous. Arceneaux v. Domingue, 365 So.2d 1330 (La.1978).

¶10   Since Ashton Realty, supra, the courts have repeatedly held that evidence of intent not to renew the old lease circumvents the presumption of art. 2689 and renders it inapplicable. Prisock v. Boyd, 199 So.2d 373 (La.App. 2d Cir.1967); Misse v. Dronet, 493 So.2d 271 (La.App. 3d Cir.1986); Metzler v. Rising T Racing Stables, 461 So.2d 1219 (La.App. 1st Cir.1984); Rosedale Rental Inc. v. Fransen, 427 So.2d 620 (La.App. 5th Cir.1983); Eames v. Goodwin, 337 So.2d 909 (La.App. 3d Cir.1976). These cases reiterate that when one party expresses an intent not to renew, tacit reconduction does not apply.

¶11   We are aware of the facts in other cases cited in brief that might arguably distinguish them from the instant case. For instance, in Rosedale Rental Inc. v. Fransen, supra, the lessors showed their intent not to reconduct by seeking judicial termination of the lease and eviction of the lessee. Such an expression of intent is strong and persuasive. In Kogos v. Lemann, 285 So.2d 548 (La.App. 4th Cir.1973), writ denied 288 So.2d 648 (La.1974), and Jacobi v. Toomer, 164 So.2d 610 (La.App. 3d Cir.1964), the original lease agreements contained clauses stating that if the lessee retained possession of the leased premises after expiration of the term, then reconduction would not occur. The parties' stated intent was bound to be upheld. LSA-C.C. art. 1971. In the instant case, the parties' intent was also clearly stated and admitted at trial. They agreed that the written lease would end on its termination date and not be renewed. LSA-C.C. art. 1906. Their will was expressed just as well by oral agreement as by the instigation of legal process or by written contract. The parties' subsequent dealings were wholly independent of the lease agreement. The evidence in the instant case will not support the presumption of reconduction.

¶12   Because there was no reconduction, the parties are bound by the terms of their new agreement. As already noted, they had agreed on a thing and a price. LSA-C.C. art. 2670. Nothing more is necessary to the confection of a valid lease. There was no agreement as to fire insurance coverage. In the absence of such an agreement, the lessee is not liable for the loss. LSA-C.C. art. 2723; Gen'l Acc., Fire & Life Assur. v. Glenn, 261 So.2d 78 (La.App. 3d Cir.1972); Litvinoff, Smith's Materials on the Louisiana Law of Sales and Leases (1st ed., 1978), 468. Furthermore, silence as to a particular issue in the agreement must be construed against the lessor. Exxon Corp. of Robichaux, 393 So.2d 224 (La.App. 1st Cir.1980), writ denied 397 So.2d 1358 (La.1981). This rule of interpretation would require imposing on the lessor, not the lessee, the burden of carrying fire insurance. Metzler v. Rising T Racing Stables, supra. Brown was not obligated under the new agreement to carry it.

¶13 In sum, Brown was not bound by the terms of the written contract, which would have obligated him to carry fire insurance but had admittedly expired. The original contract was not reconducted and the new contract did not impose the obligation on him. For these reasons, the jury's verdict and the trial court's judgment are reversed. The plaintiff's claims are dismissed. Costs of appeal are assessed to appellee, Waller Oil Co. Inc.

REVERSED.

FRED W. JONES, Jr., Judge, dissenting:

¶1 Under the reasoning of the majority, the lessor released the lessee from all obligations under the lease (except for payment of rent) simply because the lessee did not choose to remain on the lease premises another seven years. The essence of tacit reconduction is legally presumed continuation of the old agreement under all the same conditions except for duration. The "express intent to the contrary," which is jurisprudentially required to defeat reconduction, contemplates more than mere repudiating the original term of duration, as occurred here. Thus, in the absence of any evidence in the record tending to show either party's desire to be free of any obligations under this lease except for the seven-year term, the lessee's continued occupancy tacitly reconducted the original agreement on a monthly basis.

¶2 According to Waller, prior to expiration of the written lease the lessee telephoned the witness and stated that he did not wish to exercise his option to renew the lease because he expected to sell his business in three or four months. Lessor voiced no objection to lessee remaining on the lease premises for that period of time. It was agreed that the lessee would continue occupying the building for three months, through September 1985, at the same rental. No other changes in the lease were discussed. The lessee contacted the lessor again in late September, requesting that he be allowed to remain for an additional month. The lessor agreed.

¶3 Defendant Brown testified concerning his lack of knowledge about the insurance clause in the lease and his consequent failure to procure that insurance. His testimony concerning his expressed intent not to renew the lease and remaining on the premises on a monthly basis after the expiration was substantially the same as Waller's.

¶4 After considering the evidence, the jury answered affirmatively to the following interrogatories:

1) Did defendant Loyd T. Brown have a duty under a lease agreement to provide fire insurance on the building owned by plaintiff, Waller Oil Co., Inc.?

2) If so, did the failure of the defendant to provide fire insurance cause defendant to be liable to plaintiff for the damage resulting from the fire?

¶5 Tacit reconduction of a lease is a continuation of the lease after the expiration of its term by operation of law. In Louisiana, tacit reconduction requires that the lease has expired, that the lessee remain in possession for more than one week, and that the lessor consent to the lessee remaining in possession or not have given notice to vacate. La.C.C. Art. 2689; 39 Tulane Law Review 798, 813-814; Governor Claiborne Apartments, Inc. v. Attaldo, 256 La. 218, 235 So.2d 574 (1970); Misse v. Dronet, 493 So.2d 271 (La.App. 3d Cir.1986).

¶6 The reconducted lease is a continuation of the original lease under the same terms and conditions except that the fixed term or period of duration of the old lease is voided and the reconducted lease is considered to be by the month. Comegys v. Shreveport Kandy Kitchens, 162 La. 103, 110 So. 104 (1926); Weaks Supply v. Werdin, 147 So. 838 (La.App. 2d Cir.1933).

¶7 A lease is presumed to be reconducted on a monthly basis if the lessee continues in possession for more than one week beyond the term of the lease. The purpose of this presumption is not to force a contract upon unwilling parties, but merely to establish a rule of evidence, or presumption, as to their intention when a contrary intent has not been expressed. The presumption is inapplicable, however, in the face of a clear intention of the parties to the contrary. Ashton Realty Co. v. Prowell, 165 La. 328, 115 So. 579 (1928); Prisock v. Boyd, 199 So.2d 373 (La. App. 2d Cir.1967); Talambas v. Louisiana State Board of Education, 401 So.2d 1051 (La.App. 3d Cir.1981); Eames v. Goodwin, 337 So.2d 909 (La.App. 3d Cir.1976); Jacobi v. Toomer, 164 So.2d 610 (La.App. 3d Cir.1964); Kogos v. Lemann, 285 So.2d 548 (La.App. 4th Cir.1973), writ refused 288 So.2d 648 (La.1974).

* * *

¶8 [A] finding of reconduction in the present cause does not operate to force a contract on anyone, as both parties obviously desired that the contractual relationship continue on a monthly basis after the expiration of the term. The record is devoid of any evidence supporting an intention on the part of either party to change any terms of the written lease except for the 7 year term.

¶9 Moreover, in Garner v. Perrin, 403 So.2d 814 (La.App. 2d Cir.1981), this court held that a written lease continued (was reconducted) on a month to month basis where the record did not support a conclusion that the lessor opposed possession of the leased premises by the tenant during the week after the lease expired.

¶10 In light of this jurisprudence, it appears that where a fixed-term lease expires and the lessee without opposition continues to occupy the premises for more than a week, and there is no evidence of an intent by either party to change any provision of the lease other than its duration, the lease is reconducted. Consequently, I would hold that the lease in this case was reconducted or continued with its same conditions, except for the term.

¶11 For these reasons, I respectfully dissent.

Study Questions:

The following case was decided under the revised articles. Is the decision consistent with the Waller majority or with the dissent? If it is consistent with the dissent, then has the law changed under the Civil Code as revised? Or did the Waller majority get it wrong? Why or why not?

GRANGER V. TRI-TECH, LLC 2008
981 SO.2D 88 (LA. APP. 3D CIR.)

AMY, Judge.

¶1 The plaintiff filed a Rule to Evict, asserting that the defendant's lease of commercial property had reconducted to a month-to-month basis and was, therefore, subject to termination. The defendant argued that it had exercised an option to extend the five-year term of the initial lease and that the extended term had not yet expired. The trial court found in favor of the plaintiff, citing a lack of proof that the defendant availed itself of the term extension. The defendant appeals. We affirm.

Factual and Procedural Background

¶2   Jacqueline Granger filed the present Rule to Evict as the Administratrix of the Estate of Justin Boudreaux and asserted that, by virtue of a written lease, Tri-Tech, LLC, was the tenant of property owned by the Estate. Ms. Granger alleged that, although the lease's initial five-year term ended on November 17, 2004, Tri-Tech continued to occupy the premises on a month-to-month basis. She observed that the defendant had been provided with notice to vacate due to Mr. Boudreaux's death and the need to settle the estate. Ms. Granger also argued that the lease was terminated due to a failure to make repairs and violations under the Sanitary Code.

¶3   In response, Tri-Tech argued that it had exercised its contractual option to extend the lease for an additional five-year term. It denied the failure to repair and Sanitary Code allegations.

¶4   In considering the Rule to Evict, the trial court considered the contract of lease, which provides in part:

> 2. TERM: The original term of this lease shall be from November 18, 1999, to November 17, 2004.

> 3. RENTAL: As rental for the premises, LESSEE agrees to pay a monthly rental of $4,000.00 payable by the 5th day of each month, beginning November 18, 1999 until November 17, 2001. The monthly rental will increase to $5,000.00 per month beginning November 18, 2001 until November 17, 2004. No rent payment shall be considered delinquent and subject to a late charge if it is mailed postage prepaid to the LESSOR's address given above by the 5th day of each month. If LESSEE decides not to purchase the property at the end of the five-year period, LESSEE have [sic] the option to renew the lease for a 10% increase in the rental price for another five year period.

> * * *

> 16. OPTION TO PURCHASE: LESSOR and LESSEE agree that LESSOR grants unto LESSEE, the right after the first two years from this date, and subject to the conditions hereinafter set forth, exclusive right, privilege or option to purchase for the price and sum of $1,000,000.00, the above described leased property.
>
> In the event LESSEE desires to exercise the option herein granted, he shall send a letter addressed to the LESSOR at his residence. The taxes for the year the sale is closed shall be pro-rated as of the date of the Act of Sale. All expenses incidental to the passing of the Act of Sale, are to be paid by LESSEE/Purchaser.

¶5   The trial court granted the eviction finding inadequate evidence that Tri-Tech renewed the lease. Tri-Tech appeals.

¶6   Petitioner cites to the court two articles of the Civil Code in support of his position that the lease was reconducted as one from month-to-month. Art. 2721 provides that a lease with a fixed term is reconducted if, after the expiration of the term, and without notice to vacate or terminate or other opposition by the lessor or the lessee, the lessee remains in possession. Article 2723 provides that the term for a reconducted nonagricultural lease with a fixed term of more than a month is month-to-month.

¶7   In opposition, the defendant claims that the petitioner's acceptance of rental checks, and a cryptic undated note in petitioner's decedent's hand, is evidence that the petitioner's decedent agreed and the defendant actually exercised his option to renew. The defendant asserts that the exercise of an option need not be in writing but may be evidenced by the actions of the parties. Defendant cites to the court the cases of Enterprise Property Grocery, Inc. v. Selma, 38,747 (La. App. 2 Cir. 9/22/04) and Meaghan Frances Hardcastle Trust v. F[l]eur de Paris, Ltd., 2004-1371 (La.App. 4 Cir. 6/26/2005)[917 So.2d 448.]

¶8   The cases cited by the defendant are factually distinguishable. In both, the documentation of a new agreement existed but was incomplete. In both, the facts reflect that the parties clearly intended to enter into a new lease after the terms of the original lease had expired. In the present case there is no evidence of the written notice required by the contract or evidence that the parties expressed an agreement to extend for an additional term. The payment and acceptance of monthly rent does not prove the exercise of an option but is equally consistent with reconduction on the basis of month-to-month.

¶9   It is the opinion of the court that although the lease contained an option to renew, the defendant has not carried his burden to prove the exercise of the option. The lease continued month-to-month from November 17, 2004, until notice of termination dated January 27, 2007.

¶10   Evidence of violation of the sanitation codes was not admitted into evidence at the hearing of the Rule but is not necessary for a finding in favor of the petitioner on the present claim.

Discussion

¶11   It is not disputed that Tri-Tech remained on the premises after the expiration of the initial lease period set forth in the contract of lease. Neither do the parties appear to dispute that Tri-Tech continued to pay, and the plaintiff continued to receive, rental payments. Rather, the question presented to the trial court, and the one now at issue, was whether Tri-Tech's continued presence was due to an extension of the lease, and therefore subject to a fixed term, or was on a month-to-month basis by virtue of reconduction and therefore subject to termination.

¶12 As for reconduction and/or extension of a term of lease, the Louisiana Civil Code provides:

> Art. 2720. Termination of lease with a fixed term
>   A lease with a fixed term terminates upon the expiration of that term, without need of notice, unless the term is reconducted or extended as provided in the following Articles.
>
> Art. 2721. Reconduction
>   A lease with a fixed term is reconducted if, after the expiration of the term, and without notice to vacate or terminate or other opposition by the lessor or the lessee, the lessee remains in possession:
>
> * * *
>
> (2) For one week in the case of other leases with a fixed term that is longer than a week[.]
>   Art. 2723. Term of reconducted nonagricultural lease
>   The term of a reconducted nonagricultural lease is:
>
> (1) From month to month in the case of a lease whose term is a month or longer[.]
>   Art. 2725. Extension
>   If the lease contract contains an option to extend the term and the option is exercised, the lease continues for the term and under the other provisions stipulated in the option.

¶13 The contract of lease in this case anticipates the type of extension as provided for by Article 2725 as it provided Tri-Tech with "the option to renew the lease for a 10% increase in the rental price for another five year period." However, Tri-Tech had the burden of proving that it exercised the option to extend the lease. See Governor Claiborne Apartments, Inc. v. Attaldo, 256 La. 218, 235 So.2d 574 (1970). We find no indication that the trial court was required to find that it met this burden.

¶14 Tri-Tech asserted that the lease was extended due to the plaintiff's acceptance of continued rental payments. However, it offered no evidence surrounding these payments indicating that they were made in pursuit of the option to extend the lease. Evidence as to these payments was scant at best and did not reveal that the payments included a 10% increase in the rental price as is anticipated in the contract for such an extension.

¶15 In Governor Claiborne Apartments, 235 So.2d 574, the Louisiana Supreme Court considered a case in which a lessee held a written lease for a five-year term with an option to renew for one additional five-year term. The lessee exercised the renewal option and, as the extended term was about to expire, sent a letter requesting to renew the five-year lease term. He received no response from the lessor, but continued to occupy the premises. The lessor accepted the monthly rental payments. When the lessor eventually filed a rule to evict the lessee, the lessee asserted that he held a fixed-term lease due to renewal, or extension, of the five-year fixed lease term. The supreme court rejected the argument finding that:

> While assent to a contract may be implied, that implication must be established and cannot be presumed. Defendant's burden was to establish a lease for a fixed term. He had to prove a meeting of the minds of the contracting parties that their relationship as lessor and lessee was for the alleged fixed term, by either express language or by circumstances (action or inaction) that necessarily implied the proposition. The facts and circumstances of the instant case establish only the existence of a lease by the month between the parties because of the reconduction of the written lease.

Id. at 577.

¶16 The present case is similar insofar as Tri-Tech failed to offer proof regarding the nature of its continued presence on the property. In light of its failure to establish that it availed itself of the option to renew, the trial court correctly found that the lease reconducted to a month-to-month lease pursuant to La. Civ. Code art. 2723. Accordingly, the lease was subject to termination, and the granting of the rule to evict was not in error.

¶17 We note that a portion of Tri-Tech's argument in its brief relates to the trial court's observation in its reasons for ruling that Tri-Tech did not produce a writing by which it exercised "the option to renew the lease for a 10% increase in the rental price for another five year period." However, the contract only specifically refers to a writing in the paragraph establishing the option to buy. On this point, we observe that, although reasons for judgment define and elucidate a case, they form no part of the judgment from which the appeal is taken. See Peters v. Harmsen, 03-1296 (La.App. 1 Cir. 4/2/04), 879 So.2d 157. Regardless of such findings, a correct judgment should be affirmed. Id. As noted above, we have found the trial court's judgment to be correct.

DECREE

For the foregoing reasons, the judgment of the trail court is affirmed. All costs of this appeal are assigned to the defendant, Tri-Tech, L.L.C.

Section 3: Dissolution

Read Civil Code articles 2686, 2704, 2714-2720, and 2727-2729 of the Louisiana Civil Code.

A lease may terminate or be dissolved in a number of ways. If the leased thing is lost or totally destroyed without the fault of either party, or if it is expropriated, then the lease terminates and neither party owes damages to each other. Art. 2714. If either the lessor or the lessee violates his obligations (which will be discussed in detail in Chapter 13), then the other party may dissolve the lease. So, for example, if a lessee misuses the thing (i.e. uses it for a purpose other than that for which it was leased, or in a manner that may damage it), or fails to pay rent when due, then the lessor may dissolve the lease. Arts. 2686, 2704. If the lessor fails to maintain the thing in a condition suitable for the purpose for which it was leased or fails to protect the lessee's peaceful possession, then the lessor has failed to perform and the lessee may dissolve the lease. Art. 2719. Thus, termination occurs when the lease cannot remain in effect for reasons for which neither party is responsible. One party, however, may sue to dissolve a lease because the other has violated its duties under the lease – has breached the lease. The party who obtains a dissolution of the lease, then, not only ends his own obligations under the lease but also may be able to recover damages from the party in breach.

The death of either party does not terminate the lease. Art. 2717. If a lease provides either or both parties with a right to terminate the lease before the end of the term, then the lease may be terminated by giving the notice specified in the lease contract itself, or by giving the notice provided in Articles 2727-2729, whichever period is longer and the right to receive this notice may not be renounced in advance. Art. 2718.

If a lease has a fixed term, then it terminates upon the expiration of that term, without need of notice – unless it is reconducted or extended. Art. 2720. If a lease has an indefinite term, then the party desiring to terminate the lease shall give notice of termination to the other party. Arts. 2727-2728. If the lease's term is measured by a period longer than a month, then notice must be given thirty calendar days before the end of that period (most likely, this would be an agricultural lease). In a month-to-month lease, notice must be given ten days before the end of the month; if the term is equal to or longer than a week but shorter than a month, five calendar days are needed, and if the lease term is shorter than a week, notice must be given at any time prior to the expiration of that period. If the leased thing is an immovable or a movable used as a residence, the notice of termination "shall" be in writing. Art. 2729. In any case, surrender of possession to the lessor acts as notice of termination. Art. 2729.

Study Questions:

What do the following cases teach about the termination of a lease?
What current Civil Code articles would now govern the issue?

LAFAYETTE REALTY CO. V. TRAVIA 1913
11 ORL. APP. 275

His Honor, EMILE GODCHAUX, rendered the opinion and decree of the Court, as follows:

¶1 Plaintiff sued for and recovered in the trial Court 12 months' rent, under an alleged oral lease from month to month, beginning September 18th.

¶2 On appeal defendant's first contention is that no rent at all is due because plaintiff failed to put the premises in repair as it had agreed to do as a condition precedent to the taking effect of the lease.

¶3 This defense is not sustained; for if there was any agreement at all upon the subject of repairs, the evidence shows that it was made during the term of the lease and while defendant was in the possession and enjoyment of the property. And conceding that plaintiff did, during the term of the lease, agree to repair the property, its failure to comply therewith did not terminate the lease, defendant's remedy being to notify his landlord and to make the repairs himself if the latter should fail to do so. R. C. C., 2694.

¶4 It appears however, that at the end of the first month, namely on October 18th, defendant, without having given the legal notice of his desire to terminate the lease as required by R. C. C., 2686, vacated and abandoned the property to the full knowledge of plaintiff but against the latter's protest; and upon this state of facts defendant urges that he cannot be held for more than two months' rent, that is, not beyond the month ending November 18th.

¶5 Upon the other hand plaintiff contends that as the lessee has never given notice "in writing at least 15 days before the expiration of the month," as provided by R. C. C., 2686, the lease continued in effect and the judgment for the 12 months rent is proper.

¶6 The contrary, however, has directly been held in the case of Waples vs. City of New Orleans, 28 An., 688, when the principle was laid down that the landlord's actual knowledge of the abandonment of the property by the lessee was the equivalent of the written notice required by the Code and was as effective in putting an end to a monthly lease.

¶7 The judgment will consequently require amendment so as to confine plaintiff's recovery to the rent for the two months ending November 18th.

¶8 The judgment appealed from is accordingly amended and to that end it is set aside and recast so as to read as follows, to-wit:

> It is ordered and decreed that there be judgment in favor of the Lafayette Realty Company, plaintiff, and against Thomas Travia, defendant, for one hundred and twenty ($120.00) dollars with 5% interest on $60.00 thereof from October 18th, 1912, and with 5% interest on the balance thereof from November 18th, 1912, the defendant to pay the cost of the lower Court and the plaintiff those of the appeal.

Judgment amended.

Study Note

While the following case concerns the dissolution of a lease, it also concerns the potential violation of one of the lessor of a residential property's three duties: 1. To warranty that the thing leased is suitable for the purpose and free from defects (art 2696); 2. To warranty that there are no vices or defects that seriously affect health or safety (a warranty that cannot be waived) (Art. 2699); and 3. To warranty the lessee's peaceful possession (art 2700). Which warranty is at issue in the case below? What is the effect of the breach of that warranty? Which current article would apply with regard to the termination of the lease? (Hint: See art. 2719).

PURNELL V. DUGUE 1930
129 SO. 178 (LA. APP. ORL. CIR.)

JANVIER, J.

¶1 Plaintiff, owner of an apartment which was rented to and occupied by defendant, seeks to recover on twelve rent notes, each for the sum of $70.

¶2   Defendant had occupied the apartment for two years, under a written lease for the term of three years, when, during the early days of October, shortly after the commencement of the third year, he abandoned the premises.

¶3   He admits that he signed the notes and executed the lease, but refuses to pay them, and bases his refusal on the assertion that the heating system with which the apartment was provided was inadequate and that it was impossible, during the winter months, to raise the temperature sufficiently high to make the premises habitable.

¶4   Plaintiff denies that the heating system was inadequate and also denies that she, as the owner of the apartment, was under any obligation to provide a heating apparatus of any particular size or type and contends that, as the heating system, such as it was, was in proper working order, her duty as landlord was fully complied with, and that she did not guarantee, and that, as a matter of law, an owner is not called upon to guarantee, that an apartment can be heated to any particular temperature.

¶5   It thus appears that two questions are presented:

One of fact, viz., Was the heating apparatus adequate and capable of heating the apartment to a reasonable temperature?

And the other of law, viz., Is it the duty of a landlord who rents an apartment containing a heating system to see to it that the system will maintain a reasonable temperature?

¶6   The question of fact is the more easily disposed of, so we will consider that first.

¶7   The testimony of Mrs. Dugue, defendant's wife, and of defendant himself, of their servant and of a gentleman who was a frequent visitor in the apartment and who later married defendant's niece, is to the effect that, during the two winters the apartment was occupied, they were never able to maintain on cold days a reasonable temperature. A physician who treated Mrs. Dugue states that he, on one occasion when he called upon her professionally, found the rooms very cold and that he kept his overcoat on.

¶8   Various heating experts who examined the heaters testified that they were entirely inadequate and could not furnish sufficient heat for rooms so large as those composing the apartment and the figures given by one of these experts with reference to the cubic capacity of the rooms and the heating capacity of the heaters show that in order to heat the place in accordance with what is recognized in this climate as proper practice there would have been required heaters either almost double in size, or practically double in number.

¶9 Against this evidence we find but little testimony and that of a rather negative character. Mrs. Poitevent, who occupied the premises after Mr. and Mrs. Dugue left, states that the heaters were sufficient for her needs, except that sometimes she had to employ oil heaters to supplement the regularly installed heating system. Mrs. Dugue, defendant's wife, stated that she on several occasions had tried the use of oil heaters, but that she was subject to headaches and that the effect of the oil heater increased her headaches to such an extent that she had to discontinue their use.

¶10 Other persons occupying various other apartments in the same building state that their respective heating systems are and were adequate, but the fact is that only one of the other apartments was at all similar in size and arrangement to that involved here, and the tenant of that one demanded and received at least one additional heater.

¶11 We are thoroughly convinced from the evidence that the apartment could not be even reasonably comfortably heated because of the inadequate heating system, and that the defendant and his wife were most uncomfortable during the winters they occupied the place.

¶12 We now approach the question of law to which we have referred. Plaintiff maintains that a tenant who has the opportunity of seeing and examining the type of heaters or radiators contained in an apartment cannot complain if those heaters or radiators, when working properly and to their full capacity, are not able to heat the leased premises to a comfortable temperature; in other words that a landlord does not warrant that his premises can be heated to any particular temperature, even to a reasonable temperature, but merely that such heaters as he furnished have no mechanical defects and will operate. We are told of the far-reaching effects which will attend a holding that a landlord warrants the efficiency of his heating system and that, if we so hold, all leases of houses containing only old-fashioned open grates may be immediately broken. We do not believe that any such dire result will follow a decision that a landlord, who furnishes a modern apartment without open fires, but containing what seems to be a modern heating system, warrants to his tenant that that system is of sufficient size and efficiency to maintain a reasonably comfortable temperature.

¶13 In Scudder v. Marsh, 224 Ill. App. 355 we find a case involving facts strikingly similar to those presented here. The property leased was a two-story dwelling.

¶14 A heating system was contained in the dwelling but, as the court found:

"In November, when the weather became cold, the furnace failed to heat the dwelling although it was run properly with a good fire; the average temperature in the rooms was from 48 to 56 degrees. Defendant's children became ill and a physician found the room so cold that his breath congealed in every room. He examined the furnace and describes it as in full blast; an experienced man in heating plants examined the furnace at this time and testified that it was only 60 per cent. adequate to furnish sufficient heat for the building."

¶15   The court said:

"The insufficiency of the furnace cannot be determined by merely looking at it, especially by one not expert in the matter of furnaces, and its inadequacy in heating capacity can only be determined by an investigation by an expert and by an actual experience with it in cold weather. Do such circumstances amount to a constructive eviction by the landlord justifying the removal from the premises of the tenant and his discharge from any obligation to pay rent thereafter?

"Plaintiff invokes the general rule of caveat emptor which throws upon the lessee the responsibility of examining as to the existence of defects and providing against their consequences. Experience, however, has shown that under circumstances like these under consideration, the strict application of this rule tends to work an injustice upon the tenant. From the very nature of the case, it would be almost impossible for a tenant by merely looking at a furnace in the summer time to have any informed judgment or opinion as to its heating sufficiency."

¶16   We have quoted somewhat at length from the opinion in the above case because of its remarkable similarity both of fact and in legal principle.

* * *

¶17   Here we think both the law and the facts warrant us in holding that defendant was within his rights in abandoning the premises.

¶18   Plaintiff complains that, as the written lease makes no mention of a heating system, to allow evidence to be introduced showing that the system was insufficient, is to permit the varying of a written contract by parol. We do not think so. All modern apartments contain heating systems and it is contemplated in any such lease, whether actually written into it or not, that, where an apartment contains a heating system, as a matter of fact that system is included in the lease and the reasonable adequacy of that system is warranted. That even plaintiff interpreted her lease as including a heating system is evidenced by her many promises that she would remedy the defect by the installation of additional heaters.

¶19   It was held in Bliss v. Clark, 104 Misc. Rep. 543, 172 N. Y. S. 112, that even in the absence of a covenant to furnish heat if "the means of furnishing the heat are in the control of the landlord, the lessee of a living apartment may, for failure of landlord to furnish proper heat, abandon the premises. . . ."

* * *

¶20   We think that the reasoning above set forth is sound and is applicable here and that, as we have stated, where a leased dwelling contains a supposedly modern heating system, there is implied a warranty, even if it be not expressed, that that system is reasonably adequate.

¶21   Plaintiff also contends that the installation of additional heaters would have cost only about $35 or $40 and that therefore defendant should have installed them himself and would have been entitled to deduct the cost thereof from the rent due or to become due. Civ. Code, art. 2694. We do not think that either the right or the duty of a tenant requires that he go so far as to tamper with the piping and fundamental structure of his landlord's building; his right is limited to the making of repairs and, in our judgment, does not include the right to remedy defects which were in the building when he first went into possession of it.

* * *

¶22   It is therefore ordered, adjudged, and decreed that the judgment appealed from be, and it is, annulled, avoided, and reversed, and that there now be judgment in favor of defendant and against plaintiff, dismissing this suit at her cost.

Reversed.

Study Question:

What leads to the termination of the lease in the following case and which Civil Code article applies?

LUCKY V. ENCANA OIL & GAS 2010
46 SO.3D 731 (LA. APP. 2D CIR.)

LOLLEY, J.

¶1 In this appeal, plaintiffs, Frederick Lucky and Lucky-Moore Farm Trust (collectively "Lucky"), appeal the judgment of the 26th Judicial District Court, Parish of Bossier, State of Louisiana, which sustained the dilatory exception of prematurity filed by Fite Oil & Gas, Inc. ("Fite"). Lucky's claims against Fite were dismissed without prejudice. For the following reasons, we affirm the trial court's judgment.

FACTS

¶2 Lucky owns immovable property in Bossier Parish, Louisiana. In May 2005, he entered into various oil, gas and mineral leases with Fite. The leases included various provisions, among those that the lessee must: access the lease from Mayflower Road across Red Chute Bridge; maintain adequate fencing around the wells to prevent cattle and livestock from entering the drilling area; and, maintain Red Chute Bridge in a reasonable condition. Further, paragraph 12 of the leases specifically states that:

> [I]n the event Lessor considers that operations are not being conducted in compliance with this contract, Lessee shall be notified in writing of the facts relied upon as constituting a breach and Lessee shall have sixty (60) days after receipt of such notice to comply with the obligations imposed by virtue of this instrument.

¶3 In June 2008, EnCana acquired from Fite all of its right, title and interest in and to the 2005 leases between Lucky and Fite, limited to the depths deeper than 100 feet below the Petit Formation.

¶4 On August 18, 2008, Lucky sent a letter to EnCana advising it of Fite's alleged breaches of the leases and calling for [their] termination . . . . EnCana responded to Lucky's letter on September 2, 2008, by denying liability with respect to the wells. EnCana also stated in its letter that the claims should be directed to Fite and that it had forwarded Lucky's letter to Fite.

¶5 On September 15, 2008, Lucky responded in a letter to Fite and EnCana again noting certain alleged breaches of the leases and demanding a cancellation of the leases. Lucky also requested a recordable act evidencing extinction of the leases from Fite and EnCana, which refused to provide the releases.

¶6   Subsequently, Lucky filed this petition against Fite and EnCana for the dissolution of the leases. Fite and EnCana responded with various exceptions, including these exceptions of prematurity. After a hearing on the exceptions, the trial court entered judgments sustaining the exceptions of prematurity based on the relevant lease provisions, statutory law and jurisprudence. The trial court also ordered that all of Lucky's claims be dismissed without prejudice. Following entry of the judgments in favor of Fite and EnCana, Lucky compromised and settled his claims with EnCana. This appeal by Lucky against Fite ensued; to which EnCana is not a party.

DISCUSSION

¶7   Louisiana C.C.P. art. 926 provides for the dilatory exception raising the objection of prematurity. The exception of prematurity addresses the issue of whether a judicial cause of action has yet come into existence because a prerequisite condition has not been fulfilled. White v. St. Elizabeth B.C. Bd. of Directors, 43,329 (La.App.2d Cir.06/04/08) 986 So.2d 202, writ denied, 2008-1440 (La.10/10/08), 993 So.2d 1284. An action will be deemed premature when it is brought before the right to enforce it has accrued. LaCoste v. Pendleton Methodist Hosp., L.L.C., 2007-0008 (La.09/05/07), 966 So.2d 519. Prematurity is determined by the facts existing at the time the lawsuit is filed. White, supra. The burden of proving prematurity is on the exceptor. LaCoste, supra.

Lucky was Contractually Bound to Provide Notice

¶8   In his first assignment of error, Lucky argues that the trial court erred as a matter of law in sustaining Fite's dilatory exception of prematurity. Lucky argues that its claims against Fite were related to the destruction of the property, not a breach related to the operations under the leases, which breach would require notice under the terms of the lease. Further, Lucky maintains that his claims were not those which require a "putting in default" as stated in La. R.S. 31:136.

¶9   Lucky's lawsuit against Fite was premature because Lucky was contractually bound to first notify Fite of any breach of the lease. In this case, Lucky and Fite entered into four separate mineral leases, each of which contained the following provision:

> [I]n the event Lessor considers that operations are not being conducted in compliance with this contract, Lessee shall be notified in writing of the facts relied upon as constituting a breach and Lessee shall have sixty (60) days after receipt of such notice to comply with the obligations imposed by virtue of this instrument.

(Emphasis added).

¶10 It is undisputed that Lucky informed EnCana, Fite's sublessee, by letter on August 15, 2008, of Fite's alleged breaches under the leases. However, this August 15th letter to EnCana was not sufficient notice . . , even if EnCana subsequently forwarded the letter to Fite, because the lease provision clearly envisions notice provided by the "Lessor" (i.e., Lucky) to the "Lessee" (i.e., Fite). Fite remained the lessee under the mineral leases, despite the assignment of certain, limited rights to EnCana -- the assignment did not change the terms of the lease as between Lucky and Fite. Thus, Lucky and Fite continued to be bound by the terms of the leases, including the Paragraph 12 obligation to notify Fite, the lessee, of any breach under the leases.

¶11 The trial court characterized the application of the provision as a "technicality," given the fact that EnCana subsequently forwarded the letter to Fite. However, contracts have the effect of law for the parties, even if the contractual terms are "technicalities." La. C.C. art.1983. The leases between Fite and Lucky created a legal relationship with contractual duties between the parties, and as stated, Lucky was legally bound to provide written notice to Fite of any alleged breach. The August 15th letter was not sent by Lucky to Fite; in fact, the only written notice sent by Lucky to Fite was inside the sixty day window created by the leases. Therefore, Lucky did not properly notify Fite of its alleged breaches pursuant to the terms of the leases.

* * *

Dismissal of Lucky's Claims

¶12 Lucky also argues that the trial court erred in dismissing all of the claims, because he presented claims separate and apart from and outside of the leases. Again, we disagree.

¶13 Our examination of Lucky's petition and amended petition indicate that all of his claims are related to Fite's alleged breach of the lease terms. As alleged by Lucky in Paragraph 5 of the petition, "Fite's operations have been conducted in direct contradiction of the specific terms and conditions of the Leases." The petition then proceeds to enumerate some of the conduct by Fite that Lucky alleges served to breach the contract. In fact, Fite describes the conduct in subsequent paragraphs as "breaches" of the lease agreements. Even if Fite's conduct in allegedly breaching the leases resulted in claims outside of the lease, those claims were not so alleged, and the trial court properly dismissed without prejudice all of Lucky's claims against Fite. This assignment of error is without merit.

CONCLUSION

¶14 Considering the foregoing, we affirm the trial court's judgment sustaining the exception of prematurity filed by Fite Oil & Gas, Inc. and dismissing without prejudice the claims of appellants, Frederick M. Lucky and Lucky-Moore Farm Trust. All costs of this appeal are assessed to the appellants.

AFFIRMED.

Study Questions:

As has been seen, a lease may be terminated by the expiration of its term, the failure of one of the parties to fulfill his obligations, or a provision in the contract itself.

Although the termination of the lease in the following case, like the previous one, depended on a provision of the lease itself, if the contract had not contained that provision, could the result have been the same under the Civil Code? (Hint: reread Article 2714).

Why do you think the lessors were arguing that the lessees had violated the contract by allowing the building to go to ruin, instead of merely acknowledging that it had been destroyed by Hurricane Katrina?

KUEBEL V. CHARVET'S GARDEN CENTER, INC. 2009
30 SO.3D 885 (LA.APP. 5 CIR.)

JUDE G. GRAVOIS, Judge.

¶1 The plaintiffs have appealed the trial court judgment in favor of the defendants involving the termination of a lease. For the reasons that follow, we affirm.

FACTS AND PROCEDURAL BACKGROUND

¶2 Plaintiffs, Robert and Kenneth Kuebel ("the Kuebels"), leased property located at 123 Metairie Road to Charvet's Garden Center, Inc. ("Charvet's"), one of the defendants, for operation of a retail nursery. The initial lease, which commenced on March 1, 1996, was for a term of sixty months with monthly rental payments of $4,200 per month. Pursuant to an option contained in the lease, on March 1, 2001, the lease was renewed by Charvet's for another sixty months with monthly rental payments of $5,200 per month. The lease, as renewed, called for an expiration date of February 28, 2006. The leased property contained two buildings, a large building which housed Charvet's retail business, and a smaller building used for storage.

¶3 According to testimony elicited at trial, Charvet's was owned by Marilyn Charvet ("Marilyn") and her husband, Carol Charvet ("Carol"), with their children, Winston Charvet ("Winston") and Michele Charvet ("Michele"), being minor stockholders in the corporation. Charvet's also owned and operated a garden center located on Clearview Parkway in Metairie, which was run by Michele. The second garden center located on Metairie Road in Metairie, referred to as "Charvet's Garden Center number 2," which is the subject of this suit, was run by Winston. Although each location maintained separate bank accounts, Marilyn did the book-keeping, payroll and accounting for both locations.

¶4 Charvet's Garden Center number 2 located at 123 Metairie Road operated continuously under the lease, originally and as renewed, until it closed on August 28, 2005 prior to the arrival of Hurricane Katrina ("Katrina"). On October 15, 2005, Winston gave notice to the Kuebels that he was canceling the lease due to damages resulting from Katrina.

¶5 On November 3, 2005, the Kuebels filed a petition naming Charvet's, Winston and Carol as defendants, alleging that the premises were not unfit for occupancy and operation of Charvet's business. The Kuebels sought to recover the remaining payments under the lease as well as insurance payments made for damages to the property resulting from Katrina. In their petition, the Kuebels also sought a writ of sequestration on Charvet's movables to enforce their lessor's lien. In their pretrial order, the Kuebels alleged that damages to the property caused by Katrina was negligible in contrast to the damages that cumulated during Charvet's occupancy of the property. Specifically, the Kuebels alleged that Charvet's failed to maintain the roof, allowing water to leak into the structure, failed to treat termites, and abandoned the building in a condition that left it exposed and subject to rapid decay. The Kuebels sought recovery of the damages to the property due to Charvet's neglect, lost rental revenue from the lost opportunity to obtain rental income, as well as attorney's fees and interest.

¶6 Prior to trial, the defendants moved for summary judgment arguing that there were no genuine issues of material fact because its termination of the lease was proper under paragraph 23 of the lease. The defendants also requested that Winston and Carol be dismissed personally from this action because they did not execute or guarantee the lease personally. The trial court denied summary judgment on the issue of whether the lease was properly terminated and granted summary judgment dismissing Winston and Carol individually from the suit.

* * *

ASSIGNMENT OF ERROR NUMBER THREE -- RIGHT TO TERMINATE THE LEASE

¶7   In this assignment of error, the Kuebels argue that Charvet's used Katrina as a ploy to terminate the lease and hide years of damage from neglect to the leased premises. The Kuebels contend it was the damage caused by Charvet's' neglect that rendered the premises unfit for occupancy rather than Katrina. They contend that paragraph 23 of the lease absolving the lessee from repairing damages caused by a casualty during the last 12 months of the lease must be read together with paragraph 19 of the lease that provides the damage must not be caused by the fault or neglect of the lessee. The Kuebels reason that taking these two paragraphs together results in a two-part test to cancel the lease-there must be damages caused through no fault of the lessee and the property must be damaged to such an extent as to render it unfit for occupancy.

¶8   Charvet's responds that the language in paragraph 23 stating "with regard to Paragraph 19 of this Lease and notwithstanding anything contained therein" means that paragraph 19 is not applicable to paragraph 23. Charvet's contends that under paragraph 23 since there was damage to the property from a casualty that occurred within the last 12 months of the lease, Charvet's had a right to terminate the lease. Charvet's contends that proper notification of termination was given pursuant to paragraph 23.

¶9   Paragraph 19 of the lease states:

> If through no fault, neglect, or design of Lessee, the premises are destroyed by fire or other
> casualty or damages to such an extent as to render them wholly unfit for occupancy, then
> this lease shall be canceled. The premises shall be deemed "wholly unfit for occupancy" if the
> premises cannot be repaired within 120 days from the date of casualty or fire. If the premises can
> be repaired within 120 days from the date of fire or casualty and such fire or casualty is covered
> by Lessee's insurance, then this lease shall not be canceled and Lessee shall notify Lessor, or its
> agent within 30 days from date of fire or casualty that Lessee will repair the damage and Lessee
> shall not be entitled to a reduction or remission of rent during the period of reconstruction.

¶10   Paragraph 23 of the lease states:

> With regard to Paragraph 19 of this lease, and notwithstanding anything contained therein,
> Lessee shall not be responsible to so repair, and either part[y] may cancel and terminate this
> lease upon giving the other party 30 days prior written notice of its desire to so cancel and ter-
> minate, if such fire or other casualty occurs during the last 12 months of the terms of this lease.

¶11 The trial court found:

> The destruction caused by Hurricane Katrina was the reason for Charvet's desire to cancel the lease. The Court finds that the defendant fully complied with the terms and conditions of the lease and that under Paragraph 23 of the lease the defendant had a right to terminate said lease. Hurricane Katrina is considered a casualty, it occurred during the last 12 months of the lease term, and it rendered the lease property "wholly unfit of occupancy" (sic).

¶12 Having previously determined that the condition of the premises following Katrina was not due to the fault or neglect of the defendants, we must determine whether the evidence supports the trial court's finding that Katrina rendered the property "wholly unfit for occupancy." Winston and Avery testified as to the condition of the premises when they returned to the business after Katrina. Avery described the premises as a "disaster" with sheetrock falling down and water entering the building. Winston testified that there were branches on the roof, broken pipes, broken doors, and debris everywhere. Robert testified that he went to the premises and "saw the disaster." Robert also testified that two rental houses that were located on the property were destroyed by Katrina. Thus, we find no error in the trial court's finding that the damage caused by Katrina rendered the premises wholly unfit for occupancy.

¶13 Under Paragraph 23 of the lease, if a casualty occurs during the last 12 months of the lease that renders the property wholly unfit for occupancy, either party can terminate the lease by giving the other party 30 days notice. There is no dispute that Charvet's gave the Kuebels proper notice of their intent to terminate the lease and vacated the premises. Accordingly, we find that Charvet's properly exercised its right to terminate the lease by giving 30 days notice to the Kuebels pursuant to the terms of paragraph 23 of the lease.

ASSIGNMENT OF ERROR NUMBER FOUR -- PERSONAL LIABILITY

¶14 Having found no error in the trial court's determination that damage to the leased premises was due to Katrina rather than the neglect of defendants, the plaintiffs' assignment of error claiming the trial court erred in holding Winston and Carol were not personally liable for the condition of the premises is moot.

CONCLUSION

¶15 For the foregoing reasons, the judgment of the trial court is affirmed. All costs of this appeal are assessed to appellants.

AFFIRMED.

Section 1: Duration

As mentioned in Chapter 11, in addition to consent, a thing, and rent, a lease must have a term, either fixed or indeterminate (art 2678), but not perpetual. Art. 2678 cmt. (c). The parties have a choice of either setting a term themselves or allowing the law to set a term. Art. 2678. If the parties set a term, then it is 'fixed,' which means that it terminates at a designated date or upon the occurrence of a designated event. A fixed term may not exceed ninety-nine years, and if a longer term is provided or the lease contains an option to extend the term to more than ninety-nine years, then the term must be reduced to ninety-nine years. Art. 2679.

Alternatively, if the parties do not set a term, then the term is 'indeterminate,' which means that Article 2680 supplies a legal term. Thus, in the absence of a fixed term, the term of an agricultural lease is from year to year, the lease of any other immovable or a movable used as a residence is from month to month, and a lease of other movables is generally from day to day. If the rent for a movable is fixed for a period other than from day to day, then the term, unless otherwise agreed, is one such period not to exceed one month.

Fixed term leases and Reconduction: Articles 2720-2726

As one would expect, a lease with a fixed term terminates upon the expiration of that term, without need of notice. Art. 2720. If, however, the lessee keeps possession of the thing and the lessor does not object, then the lease may be reconducted, as per art. 2721. If no notice to vacate or opposition is given by either party, and the lessee remains in possession for 1) 30 days if the lease is agricultural, 2) 1 week if the lease had a fixed term > a week, or 3) one day if the lease had a fixed term ≤ 1 week. Once reconducted, the term of an agricultural lease is one year (art. 2722), the term of a reconducted nonagricultural lease is month to month, if the lease's fixed term was a month or longer, day to day if the lease's fixed term was at least a day but shorter than a month, and if the fixed term was less than a day, then the reconduction is for an equal term. Art. 2723. So, if a farmer rented a farm for one year, and then overstayed the lease by 30 days, he now has the farm for an additional year. If you rented an apartment for six months and overstayed one week, then you get an additional month (well, 3 weeks from the end of that week). If you rented a car for a week and kept it for one day beyond that week, then the reconducted period is one day, and if you rented a carpet cleaner from Winn Dixie for 4 hours and kept it over that time, then you are likely to be charged for another 4 hours.

When a fixed term lease is reconducted, all provisions of the lease continue, until the lease is terminated. Art. 2724. If, on the other hand, the lease contains an option to extend the term, and the option is exercised, then the lease continues for the term stipulated in the option. Art. 2725. An amendment to a provision of a lease contract made without any intent to effect a novation does not create a new lease. Art. 2726.

In order to terminate a reconducted lease, or to terminate any lease with an indeterminate lease, notice must be given to the other party, as per articles 2727-2729. If the lease is for a period longer than a month (or an agricultural lease), notice must be given 30 calendar days before the end of that period. If the lease is month-to-month, notice must be given 10 calendar days before the end of that month. In a lease with a term equal to or longer than a week, but shorter than a month, 5 days before the end of the term, and if the term is shorter than a week, notice must be given any time before the expiration of that period. The notice given terminates the lease at the end of the period specified in the notice, or if no term specified, then at the end of the first period for which the notice is timely. Art. 2728. So, for example, if notice is sent less than 10 calendar days before the end of the month in a month-to-month lease, then it would be effective for the following month. If the lease thing is an immovable or a movable used as a residence, the notice must be in writing, but otherwise, it may be oral. In all cases, the lessee can surrender the thing at the same time as he gives notice of termination as per Article 2728, and that will constitute notice of termination. Art 2729.

Herring v. Breedlove

Plaintiff Herring wanted to lease a gas station from defendant Breedlove in Natchitoches. In January, 1946, Breedlove told Herring that he could take it over as of February, 1946. Herring wanted a written lease, but defendant said that wasn't necessary, and plaintiff could lease it as long as he wanted, 'as long as he ran it right.' So, plaintiff and his wife gave up their jobs in Houston, moved to Louisiana, and took over the filling station in February. On April 5 (two months later), Breedlove sent him a notice to vacate by the end of the month. That same day, Breedlove signed a written lease with Billups Petroleum. Plaintiff is suing for breach of contract. He claims he lost a total of $10,000 in profits for the two years he anticipated leasing the station, moving expenses of $125, loss in value of the filling station equipment he purchased of $451.07, for a total of $10,576.07.

Is he likely to collect those damages or was Breedlove entitled to terminate the lease?

Did Breedlove terminate the lease properly as per the current Civil Code?

Section 2: Reconduction

To fully understand the following case, you need to be aware that there is a Lessor's privilege that, like a vendor's privilege, attaches on agreement. It provides that if the lessee is in default, the lessor can seize movables that are on the premises. Art. 2707.

Comegys v. Shreveport Kandy Kitchen

Defendant Eltife of SKK leased a storefront from Plaintiff Comegys for his candy store. Sometime after he moved in, he recorded a chattel mortgage for store fixtures in favor of Martel. After the initial term of the lease expired, Eltife continued to occupy the property, paying rent for two months. However, apparently the candy business was no longer successful because he then failed to pay rent for three months (and failed to make payments on the chattel mortgage as well), so Comegys seized the fixtures, using his lessor's privilege. Martel then intervened.

The issue is whether the chattel mortgage outranks the vendor's privilege or whether the vendor's privilege outranks the chattel mortgage. Once the property is sold, the highest ranking secured creditor gets to take whatever is necessary out of the funds to fulfill the debt. Then the second ranking secured creditor, and on down the line. Normally, the secured right that is first filed wins, which would mean the lessor's privilege comes first. However, here Martel argues that once the lease expired, the original lessor's privileged did as well, which means that his chattel mortgage now moves to the top.

The trial court found that while Eltife owed both Comegys and Martel, Comegys ranked first because a reconduction is merely a continuation of the same lease. The appellate court reversed, finding that a tacit reconduction from month to month creates a new contract each month. The Louisiana Supreme Court agreed with the district court – and so does the current civil code (art. 2724, which cites Comegys in the comments).

Waller Oil v. Brown

While it is pretty clear in Comegys that all terms of the lease are continued due to a reconduction, the facts in this case are not as clear. Begin by rereading Articles 2725 and 2726:

If a lease is extended and the option is exercised, the lease continues for the term and under the provisions provided in the option. An amendment to a provision in a lease without an intent to novate does NOT create a new lease.

Plaintiff Waller Oil leased a commercial building to Brown. The written lease contained a clause requiring that Brown carry fire insurance. It also contained an option to renew for an additional seven years under the same terms and conditions. Sometime before the first term was to expire, Brown telephoned Waller and informed him specifically that he would not exercise the option to renew, but it was not in Brown's or Waller's interest that Brown vacate immediately. Consequently, the parties agreed that Brown would continue to rent the premises for another three months at the same rent. Nothing else was discussed. Three months later, Brown again telephoned, and asked for another three months, and the parties again agreed. One month or so after this second oral extension, a fire caused substantial damage. The fire was not Brown's fault, but he was not carrying fire insurance – and in fact, was not aware that the original lease mandated that he do so.

The issue: Was Brown in breach of the lease by not carrying fire insurance at the time of the fire? Or was this a new lease that did not require him to do so?

The court held that there was no extension of the original lease, nor was there no reconduction because the parties were not 'silent and inactive' as would activate the presumption of reconduction. Instead, they negotiated two entirely new oral leases, settling the term and the rent. As no one mentioned any other terms of the old lease, they were not in effect at the time of the fire. So, there was no agreement as to fire insurance coverage, and in the absence of either fault or such an agreement, the lessee is not liable for the loss.

Dissent: In the absence of any evidence showing that either party wanted to be free of any obligations under the lease except for the seven-year term, the majority should have found that this was a reconduction.

Granger v. Tri-Tech

Tri-Tech leased a commercial building from Boudreaux. The lease provided a five-year term, and had an option to buy the property or to extend the lease for an additional five-year term at a 10% increase in rent. If the lessee wanted to exercise the option, he was to send written notice to lessor at his residence.

The original term of the lease ended on November 17, 2004. Sometime after that date, Boudreaux's successor, Granger, filed suit to evict, claiming that Tri-Tech was on a month-to-month lease and she wanted to terminate it in order to settle the estate, and also that Tri-Tech had failed to make required repairs.

Tri-Tech claimed that it had renewed the lease as per the provision. While he did not present as evidence, he did present cancelled rental checks and a "cryptic undated note" in Boudreaux's handwriting.

The court, however, found for Granger because there was no evidence of the written notice required by the contract, (no evidence that Tri-Tech paid the additional 10%), and no evidence that the parties had agreed to the extension. Mere payment and acceptance of the rent did not prove the exercise of the option, but only a reconduction. Consequently, Granger can evict Tri-Tech.

Section 3: Dissolution

Article 2686, 2704, 2714-2720, and 2727-2729

A lease may terminate or be dissolved in a number of ways. If the leased thing is lost or totally destroyed without the fault of either party, or if it is expropriated, then the lease terminates and neither party owes damages to each other. Art. 2714. If either the lessor or the lessee violates his obligations (which will be discussed in detail in Chapter 14), then the other party may dissolve the lease. So, for example, if a lessee misuses the thing (i.e. uses it for a purpose other than that for which it was leased, or in a manner that may damage it), or fails to pay rent when due, then the lessor may dissolve the lease. Arts. 2686, 2704. If the lessor fails to maintain the thing in a condition suitable for the purpose for which it was leased or fails to protect the lessee's peaceful possession, then the lessor has failed to perform and the lessee may dissolve the lease. Art. 2719. Termination occurs when the lease cannot remain in effect for reasons for which neither party is responsible. It can also be terminated by one of the parties who may sue to dissolve a lease because the other has violated its duties under the lease – has breached the lease. The party who obtains a dissolution of the lease, then, not only ends his own obligations under the lease but also may be able to recover damages from the party in breach.

The death of either party does not terminate the lease. Art. 2717. If a lease provides either or both parties with a right to terminate the lease before the end of the term, then the lease may be terminated by giving the notice specified in the lease contract itself, or by giving the notice provided in Articles 2727-2729, whichever period is longer and the right to receive this notice may not be renounced in advance. Art. 2718.

If a lease has a fixed term, then it terminates upon the expiration of that term, without need of notice – unless it is reconducted or extended. Art. 2720. If a lease has an indefinite term, then the party desiring to terminate the lease shall give notice of termination to the other party. Arts. 2727-2728. If the lease's term is measured by a period longer than a month, then notice must be given thirty calendar days before the end of that period (most likely, this would be an agricultural lease). In a month-to-month lease, notice must be given ten days before the end of the month; if the term is equal to or longer than a week but shorter than a month, five calendar days are needed, and if the lease term is shorter than a week, notice must be given at any time prior to the expiration of that period. If the leased thing is an immovable or a movable used as a residence, the notice of termination "shall" be in writing. Art. 2729. In any case, surrender of possession to the lessor acts as notice of termination. Art. 2729.

Lafayette Realty v. Travia

Plaintiff Lafayette Realty sued the defendant Travia for 12 months rent under an alleged oral lease. The defendant claimed initially that he does not owe rent because the plaintiff did not repair the property as promised, but in reality, defendant vacated and abandoned the property one month after he rented it (on October 18th). As there was no term, defendant claims that he cannot be liable for more than two month's rent.

Plaintiff contends that while it was initially a month-to-month lease, as he was never given notice in writing at least 15 days before the end of the month, so the lease continued in effect for an entire year.

The court agrees with defendant, that he owes rent only for the two full months: October and November.

Purnell v. Dugue

Note: the lessor has three duties towards the lessee:

1. To warrant that the thing leased is suitable for the purpose and free from defects (art 2696);

2. To warrant that there are no vices or defects that seriously affect health or safety (in a residential lease) – a warranty that cannot be waived (Art 2699)

3. To warrant the lessee's peaceful possession against disturbances created by one with lessor's permission to be on the premises (Art 2700).

Dugue had rented Purnell's apartment for two years under a three-year lease when he abandoned it early in October. He claims that the heating system was inadequate and it was impossible to keep warm in the winter, it was so cold that the apartment was uninhabitable.

Purnell denies that the heating was inadequate, and she also denies that she has any obligation to provide any particular kind of heating system. The heating system that was in the apartment was in working order.

Defendant's wife, their servant, and their friend all testified to the effect that in the two winters they lived there, they were never able to maintain a reasonable temperature. A doctor who treated Mrs. Dugue testified that he had to keep his overcoat on in the apartment, it was so cold.

Various heating experts found the heaters inadequate.

On the opposing side, the tenant that took that took the apartment after the Dugues left said that sometimes she had to supplement the heating system with oil heaters, but usually it was fine (Mrs. Dugue said the oil heaters gave her headaches). Other tenants claimed that their systems were adequate, . . . though one demanded and received from the landlord an additional heater. Furthermore, plaintiff claims that the lease does not mention a heating system, or that Dugue could have installed more heaters himself at a low price and subtracted the cost from the rent.

Held: for defendant, who had a right to abandon the premises as uninhabitable.
Question: What current civil code article would apply?

Lucky v. Encana Oil & Gas

Lucky owns land in Bossier Parish and entered into various mineral leases with Fite. Those leases required Fite to access from a specific road and bridge, maintain cattle-proof fencing, and maintain the bridge. Furthermore, if there are problems, Lucky agreed to give Fite 60 days notice to comply. Fite was acquired by Encana, which took over the lease.

On August 18, 2008, Lucky sent a letter to EnCana advising that they (and/or Fite) had breached the lease and demanding termination. EnCana responded on September2, denying liability and stating that claims should be directed to Fite. On September 15, 2008, Lucky sent a letter to both parties, again noting alleged breaches and demanding cancellation. When Fite and EnCana refused to release the mineral leases, Lucky filed suit. The defendants claim that dissolution cannot be granted because they were not given the requisite 60 days to remedy any problems.

Lucky argues that its claims against Fite were related to the destruction of property, not a breach related to operation of the leases, and that his claims are not such that require a 'putting in default.'

The court finds that the lease provision requires 60 days' notice to comply. The August 15 letter was not sufficient because it was addressed to EnCana, not Fite, who remained the lessee. Lucky also argued that the trial court should not have dismissed all of its claims – however, reading the petition shows that all of the claims are related to Fite's alleged breach of the lease "Fites operations have been conducted in direct contradiction of the specific terms" – however, the dismissal was without prejudice.

Affirmed.

Question: What Civil Code article is at issue here? Or was the dismissal related to something else?

Kuebel v. Charvet's Garden Center

(No-fault dissolution due to force majeur, under Art. 2714)

The Kuebels leased a commercial property in Metairie to the Charvets to house their gardening store, Charvet's Garden Center, The initial lease was for a term of five years with rent of $4,200/month. The lease was renewed in March 1, 2001 for another five years at an increased rent and was to expire on February 28, 2006.

The Charvets operated their gardening store continuously, until August 28, 2005 (when Katrina hit). On October 15, 2005, Charvet notified the Kuebels that he was canceling the lease due to hurricane damage.

The Kuebels filed suit, claiming that the damage to the property was caused by the Charvet's failure to maintain the roof, failure to treat termites, and that they abandoned the building in an exposed condition subject to rapid decay, and that the Charvets used Katrina as a ploy to hide years of damage from neglect to the leased premises.

Two paragraphs of the contract are at issue. Paragraph 19 states that if the premises are destroyed by some fire or other casualty without the lessee's fault or neglect, and are rendered wholly unfit for occupancy, then the lease shall be cancelled. Paragraph 23 states that, with regard to paragraph 19, the lessee shall not be responsible for repair and can cancel the lease on 30 days prior written notice as long as the event occurred within the previous 12 months.

The trial court found that the condition of the premises after Katrina was not due to the defendants neglect, so the next issue was whether it was 'wholly unfit for occupancy.' The Charvets testified that when they returned, there were branches on the roof, broken pipes, broken doors, and debris everywhere. Two rental houses located on the property were also destroyed. So, the trial court found that Katrina rendered the premises wholly unfit for occupancy. Consequently, the Charvets properly exercised its right to terminate the lease by giving 30-days notice.

HYPOTHETICALS

1. Anna's cousin Walter raises Scotch bonnet peppers in Mamou. Recently, there has been such a high demand for them that he leased a second field for a year, beginning January 1, 2019. The rent was 2% of his net crop proceeds, which he paid. He was so busy, he did not realize how time had flown, and the next thing he realized, it was already February 15, 2020. He has had no contact with the lessor since he paid the rent back in December, and his equipment is still out in a shed on the property. He'd just as soon plant another crop, as he did so well last year. How

can he renew his lease? If he decides at the end of the year to end the lease, is there anything special he should do?

2. Anna leased a storefront in Lafayette in order to open yet a third Blue Suede Shoestore. The lease was for a five-year term, which ran out yesterday. What should she do if she would like to continue the lease for another five years?

3. The store in Metairie is not doing well, and as it is on a month-to-month lease, Anna has decided to close it down. What does she need to do in order to terminate it?

4. Anna received a huge order of shoes from "Don't Mess with Mamou" at her New Orleans store, but she decided that the Lafayette store could use them, so she rented a truck from You-Haul for one week but is going to need it for longer. Assuming that there is nothing in the lease papers from You-Haul about extending the lease, and they had said something about 'keep it for as long as you need it,' how will the reconducted period be if she keeps it for an extra day or two?

5. In order to do a deep cleaning in her New Orleans store before opening up after COVID-19, Anna leased a carpet cleaner from Winn Dixie for five hours, but her worker did not finish using it. How long is the reconducted term?

CHAPTER 14

THE LESSOR'S RIGHTS AND OBLIGATIONS

Flowchart

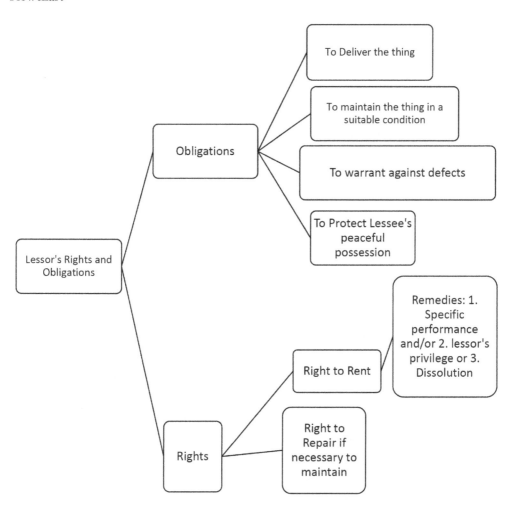

Introduction

Read Articles 2682-2685, 2690-2691, 2693, 2696-2699, 2703-2702, 2707-2709

The lessor has four obligations under a lease:

1. To deliver the thing to the lessee;
2. To maintain the thing in a condition suitable for the purpose of which it was leased;
3. To warrant the thing against vices and defects, and
4. To protect the lessee's peaceful possession for the duration of the lease.

With these obligations, the lessor has certain rights: he has a right to the rent, and a privilege to seize the lessee's property if rent is not paid or alternatively to evict the lessee, and he has a right to repair the thing if necessary to maintain it.

Section 1: The Obligation to Deliver

Just as a seller is bound to deliver the thing sold to the buyer, the lessor is bound to deliver the premises leased to the lessee. If the premises as delivered differ in extent from what was promised, then Articles 2492-2495 (sale of immovables per aversionem, per measure, and by lump sum) apply. See for example McVea v. Vance & Logan, 110 La. 998, 35 So 262 (1903). For an annual rent of $5,500, McVea leased to defendant a plantation "containing about 1, 100 or 1,200 acres in cultivation." However, because the plantation only contained 823.54 acres, a shortage in excess of 5%, the court held that the defendant lessees were entitled to a proportionate abatement of rent.

Section 2: Lessor's Obligations to Maintain and Repair

Prior to 2005, there was a somewhat elaborate (and counterintuitive) scheme allocating repairs between lessor and lessee. Since the revision became effective in January 2005, however, the allocation of repairs is quite easy to understand. The lessor's duty to maintain the premises is described in several articles that must be interpreted together. Article 2691 provides that "During the lease, the lessor is bound to make all repairs that become necessary to maintain the thing in a condition suitable for the purpose for which it was leased, except those for which the lessee is responsible." The lessee is responsible for repairing damage caused by his fault, or by persons who are on the premises with his consent, and he's obligated to pay for repairs beyond normal wear and tear. (Art. 2692). Thus, your landlord is obligated to fix the broken toilet in your apartment – unless, of course, the reason it's broken is that your inebriated guest tripped over your blue suede shoes in the bathroom doorway and broke the toilet when he fell.

Assuming this did not happen and the landlord is obligated to fix the toilet, Article 2690 shows that the landlord cannot add a new bathroom during your lease or make other unnecessary repairs or alterations (without your consent): "During the lease, the lessor may not make any alterations in the thing." If something breaks, and it's not your fault, then you must notify the lessor so that he can effectuate the repairs.

If the lessor fails to make the necessary repairs within a reasonable time after the lessee's demand, then Article 2694 provides that the lessee may cause them to be made and may then demand immediate reimbursement of the amount extended for the repair, or she may deduct that amount from the rent – but only to the extent that the repair was necessary and the expended amount reasonable.

If the repairs are intrusive, that disturbs the peaceful possession of the lessee.

If substantial repairs are needed because, for instance, a hurricane damaged the leased premises, then Article 2693 provides that

If during the lease the thing requires a repair that cannot be postponed until the end of the lease, the lessor has the right to make that repair even if this causes the lessee to suffer inconvenience or loss of use of the thing.

In such a case, the lessee may obtain a reduction or abatement of the rent, or a dissolution of the lease, depending on all of the circumstances, including each party's fault or responsibility for the repair, the length of the repair period, and the extent of the loss of use.

On occasion, a lessee makes improvements to a leased property, and the issue then becomes what happens to those improvements once the lease ends. Article 2695 provides that (unless the parties agreed otherwise) the lessee may remove all improvements to the leased thing, as long as he restores it to its former condition. If the lessee does not remove the improvements, then the lessor may appropriate them by either reimbursing the lessee for their costs or paying her the enhanced value, whichever is less. Alternatively, the lessor may demand that the lessee remove the improvements and restore the thing to its original condition within a reasonable time. If the lessee then fails to remove the improvements, the lessor can either remove them himself, charging the lessee for the cost of doing so, or appropriate ownership of the improvements – after notifying the lessee by certified mail that he is doing so.

Study Questions:

Refer back to article 2693, what if your apartment was so badly damaged by a hurricane that you had to move out during the repairs, can the landlord force you to move back in once the repairs were made? Would you have to pay rent in the interim? Reread Articles 2693 and 2715 – would the following case still be good law under the current Civil Code?

PONTALBA V. DOMINGON 1837
11 LA. 192

MARTIN, J., delivered the opinion of the court.

¶1 The plaintiff leased a house to the defendants for ten years. Considerable repairs being wanted, he employed workmen to effect them. The defendants, finding their stay in the house inconvenient while the repairs were going on, left it, and handed the key to the workmen. The repairs being completed, and the key being offered to them, they declined to receive it and return to the house.

¶2 The present action was brought for rent. The defendants, by a plea in reconvention, prayed for a dissolution of the lease and for damages, and there was verdict for the defendants, and the plaintiff appealed . . . .

¶3 It appears to us that the judgment ought to be reversed. The repairs were necessary, and the lessee was bound to suffer them to be made, and was entitled to no allowance therefor, except a suspension of the rent during the time he was obliged to quit the house. Louisiana Code, 2670.

¶4 The record shows that he was obliged to leave the house, but it does not appear at what period the repairs were completed, so as to allow him to return. As he had the verdict of the jury in his favor, and it does not appear to what diminution of the rent he is entitled, the case must be remanded.

¶5 It is, therefore, ordered, adjudged and decreed, that the judgment be annulled, avoided and reversed, the verdict set aside, and the case remanded for a new trial; the defendant paying the costs in this case.

Study Question:

The next case deals with repair issues as well, but is it lessor or lessee, in this case, who has the obligation to complete the repairs? Notice that although this is a mineral law case, the law at issue is that of lease within the Civil Code.

MARIN V. EXXON MOBIL CORP 2010

48 SO.3D 234 (LA.)

VICTORY, J.

¶1 We granted writ applications in this oilfield contamination "legacy litigation" primarily to consider complicated issues of prescription, subsequent purchaser rights, restoration obligations, punitive damages, and ground water remediation obligations. After considering the record and the applicable law, we find the lower courts erred in applying the doctrine of contra non valentem to suspend prescription on plaintiffs' tort claims. Further, the oilfield contamination at issue does not constitute a continuing tort. Accordingly, plaintiffs' tort claims have prescribed. However, as mineral and surface leases are still in effect as to the "Marin plaintiffs," Exxon Mobil Corporation ("Exxon") owes a duty to remediate the contaminated property which they have failed to do; therefore, the Marin plaintiffs have a valid contract claim against Exxon. However, because there is no lease in effect on the land now owned by the "Breaux plaintiffs" and any tort claims they may have had have prescribed, we need not analyze their rights as subsequent purchasers. Further, as the Marin plaintiffs' tort claims have prescribed, they are not entitled to punitive damages. The Marin plaintiffs are entitled to compensatory damages as awarded by the trial court. ...

FACTS AND PROCEDURAL HISTORY

¶2 This suit involves two pieces of property in St. Mary Parish upon which Exxon, or its predecessors, conducted oil and gas exploration, production and transportation activities. [One piece, the "Marin Property" consisted of 204 acres of marsh and fields owned by the Marin siblings who had inherited it from their father, E.F. Marin, Sr., In 1936, E.F. Marin, Sr., granted a mineral lease to W.S. Mackey in exchange for payment of 1/8 of all oil and gas production (the "Marin Lease"), which was later acquired by Humble. In 1941, E.F. Marin, Sr. granted a surface lease to Humble on approximately twenty acres of the Marin Property, where it built a canal and a landing/terminal for coastal operations. This lease, as amended and novated in 1994, 1997 and 2001, is referred to as the "Surface Lease." The second piece of property, owned by one of the Marin heirs and her husband, the "Breaux Property" consisted of approximately 70 acres very near the Marin Property. This property was also subject to a mineral lease granted by Canal Bank and Trust Company ("CBT") to Humble (the "CBT Lease") in 1937. E.F. Marin, Sr., lived on the Marin Property until his death in 1987, and one of his sons has lived there all his life. The Breauxs have lived on their property ever since they built their home there in 1986. When Humble Oil was absorbed into Exxon, so were the Marin and Breaux mineral leases. In addition to the oil and gas activity conducted by Exxon, these properties have been used for sugarcane cultivation.

¶3 Pursuant to the Marin, CBT, and Surface Leases, Exxon installed and operated oil and gas facilities and a landing/dock terminal on plaintiffs' properties. In conjunction with the various production facilities, Exxon built separators, oil gathering systems, and pits used for skimming oil from saltwater and other fluids routinely produced with oil and gas. As oil was skimmed from saltwater in the pits, byproducts of oil and gas operations, including oil, sludge, barium, chlorides, and other contaminants, were accumulated inside the pits in varying amounts. These pits were open and unlined, as was the industry practice and custom at that time. The produced water in these pits was discharged into a nearby waterway.

¶4 By 1958, sugarcane farmers on the Marin Property were aware that sugarcane growth was affected on and near former unused pit sites. In the 1980s, plaintiffs were concerned that sugarcane would not grow properly in the pit areas. E.F. Marin, Sr.'s son-in-law, Clyde Breaux, acted as the "family representative" on matters involving Exxon and demanded that Exxon clean the fields and make them usable for cane farming. Breaux characterized the problems they saw as follows:

> We had pipe in the field. We had cement in the field. We had something in the field that wouldn't allow us to grow cane in spots. We didn't know what it was, though. We just knew we had bare spots in the field.

¶5 Between 1988-1990, Breaux made numerous demands upon Exxon to clean up the property so that they could continue to grow sugarcane, including that "every bit of contamination [be] removed from the site and new dirt hauled in."

¶6 At about the same time, in 1986, the Louisiana Department of Natural Resources ("DNR") amended Statewide Order 29-B to require the registration and closure of existing unlined oilfield pits. The amended regulations also required that various enumerated contaminants in the soil be remediated to certain standards. Between 1987 and 1991, Exxon closed all of the remaining pits on the Breaux and Marin properties and represented that it was remediating the pit areas to Statewide Order 29-B standards. During the pit closure process, Breaux routinely communicated with Exxon employees regarding the remediation work. The last efforts to remediate the pits occurred in 1991. On September 4, 1991, Exxon instructed Breaux that in order to have his land returned to him for farming, he would have to sign a release, which he did. Thereafter, on May 18, 1994, the Marin plaintiffs and Exxon entered into a Lease and Novation Agreement that superseded the 1941 Surface Lease. This agreement was amended in December, 1997 and April, 2001. In conjunction with these amendments and leases, Exxon compensated the plaintiffs for sugarcane loss. Although production on the properties began to dwindle in the 1980s, the Marin Lease and the Surface Lease as amended and novated remained in effect at the time suit was filed.

¶7   On February 23, 2003, this Court issued its decision in Corbello v. Iowa Production, 02-0826 (La.2/25/03), 850 So.2d 686. Evidently prompted by that decision, plaintiffs hired an environmental expert, Gregory Miller, who began an assessment of the property in July of 2003. Miller reported that there was significant contamination at both the Breaux and Marin properties.

¶8   On November 26, 2003, the plaintiffs filed suit against Exxon asserting claims for remediation of the soil and groundwater and other damages arising out of Exxon's oil and gas activities. Plaintiffs alleged that Exxon knowingly disposed of oilfield wastes in unlined earthen pits and/or released the waste directly into waterways, resulting in contamination to their property. Plaintiffs alleged that the oilfield wastes deposited into these pits and water bodies contained naturally occurring radioactive material ("NORM"), produced water, drilling fluids, chlorides, hydrocarbons, heavy metals and other toxic substances. Plaintiffs claims were in tort and breach of contract including: negligence under La. C.C. art. 2315; strict liability under La. C.C. arts. 667, 2317 and 2322; continuing nuisance and trespass; breach of oil, gas and mineral leases, breach of the Mineral Code; breach of the obligation to restore the property to its original condition under La. C.C. arts. 2719 and 2720; punitive damages under La. C.C. art. 2315.3; injunctive relief; and liability under La. C.C. art. 486 for fruits of continuing trespass and unjust enrichment.

¶9   At trial, plaintiffs produced evidence of extensive contamination of soil and groundwater arising out of Exxon's operations on the plaintiffs' property, primarily caused by Exxon's use of unlined earthen pits to store and dispose of produced water and other oilfield wastes. The evidence showed that although it was the common industry practice, Exxon knew as early as the 1930s that environmental damage, particularly saltwater seepage, resulted from the use of unlined earthen pits. By 1970, Exxon knew of "chronic pit pollution problems" on plaintiffs' property but continued to use the unlined pits to handle produced water and drilling water for decades and ignored best industry practices for handling this waste.

* * *

¶10   In addition, by 1986, Exxon knew that produced water contained NORM radiation and by at least 1993, learned that NORM radiation existed in the area of its pipe cleaning facility on the Marin property.

* * *

¶11 Further, after the government ordered the pits closed by 29B, Exxon's remediation and closure did not meet 29B requirements and the property remains contaminated today.

* * *

¶12 After a five-day bench trial, the trial court found that continuous contamination of various chemicals deposited by Exxon on the Breaux and Marin Properties was unreasonable and constituted negligent operations by Exxon, resulting in breach of contract and negligence. ... The trial court rejected Exxon's claims that the plaintiffs' action had prescribed, finding that the doctrine of contra non valentem applied such that prescription did not begin to run until 2003, when plaintiffs received an expert report delineating the scope and magnitude of the damage. The trial court reasoned that even though plaintiffs knew there were some problems associated with the pits and that cane would not grow in pit areas, the average person would have no knowledge of whether a pit was properly cleaned or the extent of any damage, and further, that plaintiffs relied on Exxon's assertions in 1991 that it had remediated the pits in compliance with state regulations. The court found the release signed by the Breauxs in 1991 was obtained by Exxon by fraud and misrepresentation, because Exxon deceived Breaux with misleading lab results. The trial court terminated the Surface Lease, finding that the Surface Lease provided the lessors had the right to immediately terminate the lease upon any violation of any applicable environmental standards. The Marins were awarded compensatory damages in the amount the court found it would take to remediate the soil to state regulatory standards, $15,115,390.65. In addition, the Marins were awarded $3,481,317.62 to remediate groundwater that would accumulate in the excavated soil during soil removal and $2,408,868 for canal contamination. The court awarded the Marins punitive damages under La. C.C. art. 2315.3 for activities occurring during the time period that statute was in effect, 1984-1991, in an amount equal to the amount of compensatory damages, $21,005,576.27. Punitive damages were awarded because the trial court found the chemicals left on the property were hazardous and toxic and that Exxon's conduct constituted a wanton and reckless disregard for the environment. ...

¶13 The judgment was affirmed on appeal.

* * *

¶14 We granted Exxon's writ application, which assigned as error that the lower courts (1) committed legal error in holding that plaintiffs' claims survived prescription under contra non valentem; (2) erred in awarding punitive damages under repealed Civil Code article 2315.3, and (3) erred in allowing the Breauxs to sue for property damage that occurred before they bought the land. Marin v. Exxon Mobil Corp., 09-2368 (La.2/26/10), 28 So.3d 262. We granted plaintiffs' writ application to consider whether Exxon has an obligation to restore the soil to its original condition as existed at the time the leases were executed and whether Exxon is liable for damages for remediation of the groundwater. Marin v. Exxon Mobil Corp., 09-2371 (La.2/26/10), 28 So.3d 262. The writs were consolidated.

DISCUSSION

Prescription
Contra non valentem

¶15 Exxon urges that plaintiffs' tort claims have prescribed because plaintiffs were aware that the pits were contaminated and sugarcane would not grow on the area around the pits sites by at least 1991, yet they did not file suit until 2003.

¶16 [The liberative prescription period for a tort is one year, but that can, in exceptional circumstances, be extended under the doctrine of contra non valentem. The Court concludes that the contra non valentem exception does not apply here because in 1991 the plaintiffs were well aware of the continuing pollution problems and that Exxon's attempts to remediate had been unsuccessful but did not file suit until 2003. Nor was the prescriptive period tolled by a continuing tort because Exxon discontinued the actions that caused the damage a number of years ago: "the operating cause of the injury sued upon was the deposit and storage of oilfield wastes into unlined pits which conduct terminated when the pits were closed. Any dissolution of this contamination unto and into plaintiffs' property is the resulting damage of the damage-causing conduct, and does not give rise to a continuing tort pursuant to our previous holdings." Consequently, the Court holds that plaintiffs' tort claims have prescribed.]

Leases in effect

¶17 Regarding the contract claims, the Marin Lease and the Surface Lease, as novated, were still in effect at the time of trial. The CBT Lease, under which the Breaux's purport to sue, was not in effect at the time of trial. Plaintiffs argue that as a lessee, Exxon has continuing obligations under both the mineral and surface lease that cannot prescribe as a matter of law. Exxon argues that any restoration obligations it may have under these leases do not go into effect until the lease is terminated, making any such claims premature. The plaintiffs' position is correct.

¶18 A lessee's obligations under a mineral lease are governed by the Mineral Code and the Louisiana Civil Code. La. R.S. 31:2 (providing that the provisions of the Mineral Code are supplementary to the Civil Code and when the Mineral Code does not expressly or impliedly provide for a particular situation, the Civil Code or other laws are applicable).

¶19 La. R.S. 31:122 provides:

> A mineral lessee is not under a fiduciary obligation to his lessor, but he is bound to perform the contract in good faith and to develop and operate the property leases as a reasonably prudent operator for the mutual benefit of himself and his lessor. Parties may stipulate what shall constitute reasonably prudent conduct on the part of the lessee.

¶20 The Civil Code lease provisions require the mineral lessee to perform certain restoration obligations during the lease term, and these obligations are governed by Civil Code articles 2683, 2686, 2687, and 2692. La. C.C. art. 2683 defines the lessee's principal obligations as follows:

¶21 The lessee is bound:

> (1) To pay the rent in accordance with the agreed terms;
> (2) To use the thing as a prudent administrator and in accordance with the purpose for which it was leased; and
> (3) To return the thing at the end of the lease in a condition that is the same as it was when the thing was delivered to him, except for normal wear and tear or as otherwise provided hereafter.

¶22 La. C.C. art. 2686 provides "[i]f the lessee uses the thing for a purpose other than that for which it was leases or in a manner that may cause damage to the thing, the lessor may obtain injunctive relief, dissolution of the lease, and any damages he may have sustained." La. C.C. art. 2687 directs that "[t]he lessee is liable for damage to the thing caused by his fault or that of a person who, with his consent, is on the premises or uses the thing." Finally, La. C.C. art. 2692 provides "[t]he lessee is bound to repair damage to the thing caused by his fault ... and to repair any deterioration resulting from his ... use to the extent it exceeds the normal or agreed use of the thing."

¶23 While La. C.C. art. 2683 contains obligations that only arise at the end of the lease, i.e., "to return the thing at the end of the lease in a condition ...," there is absolutely no language to suggest that the other obligations imposed by these codal provisions are not operational until termination of the lease. These provisions continue throughout the term of the lease and a lessor need not wait until the end of the lease to sue a lessee for damage to his property. The damage in this case is the contamination of the soil and groundwater caused by Exxon's oil and gas operations on the leased property. Because the Marin Lease and the Surface Lease as novated were still in effect at the time of trial, the Marin plaintiffs' claims for damage to their property have not prescribed.

¶24 The situation with the Breaux plaintiffs is different. Although it is unclear when the CBT Lease expired, the parties in brief indicate that this lease is no longer in effect and was not in effect at the time the suit was filed. It evidently was in effect at the time the Breauxs purchased their property, but there has been no evidence presented that the Breauxs were third party beneficiaries of the CBT Lease. Further, even assuming the Breauxs had a right to sue Exxon under the lease, this contractual action has prescribed. The prescriptive period on a personal action, such as an action for breach of a lease contract, is 10 years. La. C.C. art. 3499. As this contract claim has prescribed on its face, plaintiffs had the burden of proving it had not prescribed, and they failed to do so.

Section 3: Lessor's Implied Warranty Against Vices and Defects and the Waiver thereof

Under Louisiana Civil Code art. 2696, the lessor warrants the lessee that the thing is suitable for the purpose for which it was leased and that it is free of vices or defects that prevent its use for that purpose. This warranty also extends to vices or defects that arise after the delivery of the thing and are not attributable to the fault of the lessee. In such cases, as we saw in Pontalba, the landlord has a right to repair the thing even though it may inconvenience the lessee, though the lessee may have a reciprocal right to abatement of the rent during that period. As with price and rent, the lessor's implied warranty against vices and defects parallel's some of the seller's warranties, such as the warranty against redhibitory defects and the warranty of usefulness for the purpose.

Study Questions:

What does the following case show about what the lessee must prove in order to establish that the lessor violated the Warranty against Vices and Defects, and is the lessor then liable only for defects he knew about, or only for defects caused by his negligence, or is he strictly liable for all defects? Once the lessee establishes the presence of a defect and causation, what must the lessor prove in order to avoid liability?

GREAT AMERICAN SURPLUS LINES INS. CO., V. BASS 1986

486 SO. 2D 789 (LA. APP. 1ST CIR.)

ALFORD, Judge.

¶1 This is an appeal from a judgment dismissing both the principal and incidental demands for damages sustained in a fire which occurred on July 23, 1980, in a building owned by George Bass and occupied by Bass Tire Service and Caribbean Pools, Inc.

¶2 In the original action, the plaintiffs, Caribbean Pools, the lessee of the damaged building and their property insurer, Great American Surplus Lines Co., sought recovery from the defendants, George Bass and his corporations, Bass Industries, Inc. and Bass Refrigeration and Marine Supply, Inc., under the theory of lessor-owner strict liability. In the reconventional demand, Home Insurance Company, the principal defendants' insurer, sought recovery from Caribbean and its liability insurer, Great Southwest Fire Insurance Company, alleging that the lessee's negligence caused the fire and that lessee had contractually assumed responsibility for its portion of the building's electrical system. After hearing testimony and reviewing the evidence, the trial judge determined that neither the original plaintiffs nor the plaintiffs in reconvention proved their cases by a preponderance of the evidence. Therefore, the court dismissed all demands. We disagree in part and reverse as to the principal demand.

FACTS

¶3 On February 18, 1980, George Bass leased a portion of a building owned by him individually to Caribbean Pools, Inc., a company that was wholly owned by William Lerwick. Caribbean was to use the leased portion of the building for the manufacture and sale of above ground swimming pools.

¶4 The area leased to Caribbean was an empty shell. Mr. Bass agreed to have employees of one of his corporations, Bass Refrigeration and Marine Supply, Inc., renovate the premises to meet the physical layout, electrical and plumbing requirements of Caribbean. The written lease executed by both parties contained the following provisions in regard to the premises, once the renovation was completed.

¶5 Lessor agrees to maintain the structural soundness of the building, including the roof, exterior walls, and the slab, except for conditions or damage caused by the negligence or acts of lessee, their agents or persons acting pursuant to their direction and control. Lessee agrees to maintain the interior of the building, in good repair, including the walls, floors, plumbing, electrical wiring, fixtures, heating and air-conditioning units, and plate glass.

¶6   Lessee may install or cause to be installed such equipment and trade and other fixtures as are reasonably necessary for the operation of his business.

¶7   Shortly after occupying the premises in February, Caribbean experienced trouble with the air conditioning system tripping the circuit breakers. Employees from Bass Refrigeration repaired the system, a process which took more than a month. Caribbean also started experiencing trouble with circuit breakers tripping while its employees were using electric power tools such as saws and drills. Testimony showed that whenever the blade of a saw would bind, it would trip the corresponding circuit breaker.

¶8   Caribbean started business with two employees in addition to Mr. Lerwick. As summer approached, business increased and Caribbean hired additional personnel, up to a total of 14. In June of 1980, Caribbean rented additional space in the same building in an effort to expand its production facilities. In order to reach the additional space, employees of Caribbean tore down part of a partition to which electrical receptacles were attached. The operation required Caribbean personnel, including Mr. Lerwick, to relocate the receptacles to a position on a post near a workbench.

¶9   Because of the increase in Caribbean's business, the electric power tools and several extension cords were in continual use during working hours. The constant use of this equipment caused the circuit breakers to trip more often, to the point of seven to eight times during a work day. Mr. Lerwick complained to Mr. Bass several times about Caribbean's electrical problems. As a result of these complaints, one of Bass Refrigeration's non-licensed electricians, Kim Burton, inspected Caribbean's facility several times and determined that the existing circuits were overloaded due to the machinery in use. Two days before the fire, Mr. Burton installed two additional 110 volt circuits and two 20-amp circuit breakers in Caribbean's work area. Mr. Burton placed the receptacles for the two additional circuits on the same post as the relocated receptacles. Mr. Burton's supervisor at Bass Refrigeration, Lee Bergeron, testified that he inspected Mr. Burton's work and that it was done properly.

¶10   After working hours on July 23, 1980, a fire caused extensive damage to the building. Approximately one month after the fire, Mr. Lerwick left the state and moved to New York where he had previously resided. . . . Mr. Lerwick has never attempted to reestablish his business in Louisiana.

¶11 As a result of the fire, Great American, as Caribbean's property insurer under a contents policy, determined that Caribbean had suffered a contents loss of $80,674.18. They paid Caribbean their policy limits of $70,000 and secured the salvage and subrogation rights. Home Insurance Company, as the building and contents insurer of Mr. Bass's corporations, determined that the property had suffered a loss in the amount of $87,889.15. They paid $72,768.75 to Mr. Bass after applying their co-insurance penalty and the $100 deductible, and secured subrogation rights. The suit before us now is an attempt by both insurance companies to recover under their subrogation agreements and by Caribbean and Mr. Bass to recover for their uncompensated damages.

ORIGIN OF FIRE

¶12 In his reasons for judgment, the trial judge made the following determination:

> The totality of the evidence indicates that the fire was caused by improper matching of breakers and wiring. Amperage ratings in the breakers exceeded what it should have been, given the gauge of the wire. This proximately caused the fire and resulting damage.

¶13 The trial court's findings of fact should not be disturbed on appeal, absent a finding of manifest error. Arceneaux v. Domingue, 365 So.2d 1330 (La.1978).

* * *

¶14 Thus from the evidence in the record, we cannot say that the trial court's finding as to the cause of the fire is clearly wrong.

LIABILITY

¶15 Having determined the cause of the fire, the trial judge made the following findings:

> It is the finding of the Court that the Plaintiffs, Great American Surplus Lines Insurance Company and Caribbean Pools, Inc. have failed to bear the burden of proof that the Defendants, or any of them, installed the breaker switches that were found after the fire to be improperly matched to the wiring.
> The Court, therefore, dismisses the principal demand.

¶16 In the reconventional demand filed by Bass Refrigeration and Marine Supply and the Home Insurance Company against Caribbean Pools, Inc., the Court finds that the Plaintiffs in reconvention have likewise failed to bear the burden of proving that the fire was caused by the negligence of Defendants in Reconvention therefore, the Court also dismisses the Reconventional demand.

¶17 Plaintiffs on the principal demand contend the trial court erred in finding that plaintiff must show negligence on the part of the owner-lessor in order to recover. We agree.

¶18 An owner-lessor is held to "strict liability" for injuries sustained by a tenant through a defective condition of the premises. This liability attaches whether or not specific knowledge on the owner-lessor's part can be shown so that neither his ignorance of the defect nor its latency will defeat the injured person's recovery. La. Civ. Code arts. 2322, 2695. Smith v. Hartford Accident and Indemnity Co., 399 So.2d 1193 (La.App. 3d Cir.1981), writ denied, 406 So.2d 604 (La.1981). Thus the burden of proof which the plaintiffs must meet in an action arising under either Civ.Code art. 2322 or 2695 is to show by a preponderance of the evidence that a defect in the building caused the injury complained of. Freeman v. Thomas, 472 So.2d 326 (La. App. 3d Cir.1985). No showing of negligence is required. Barnes v. Housing Authority of New Orleans, 423 So.2d 750 (La.App. 4th Cir.1982).

¶19 In the instant case, we noted previously that the court found that a defect in the premises caused the fire. Therefore, for the defendants to escape liability in this case under either of the cited codal articles, they must prove that the fire was caused by the fault of the lessee1, or that the lessee had assumed responsibility for the condition of the premises under LSA-R.S. 9:3221 with the lessor having no knowledge of the defect.

¶20 The trial court specifically noted that the original defendants had not proved negligence on the part of Caribbean. The record shows that all the involved parties deny placing the oversized breakers in the circuit breaker box. Mr. Bass admits that his employees did the initial wiring of the facilities for Caribbean. Caribbean admits moving some of the wires and receptacles near where the fire originated. Both parties admit knowledge that the circuits were overloaded, and that the overload was causing the breakers to trip. Caribbean employees reset the breakers whenever they tripped. However, as noted earlier, there was expert testimony that overloads which cause repeated tripping of breakers do not create hazardous situations in regard to fires. There was no testimony adduced to show that Caribbean's employees had performed any electrical work in or near the circuit breaker panel box. Thus, we are unable to say that the trial court's finding of no proof of negligence on the part of Caribbean is manifestly wrong.

¶21 Defendants also allege that the lessee had assumed all responsibility for the electrical wiring as part of the written contract of lease, and that the electrical system was in the lessee's care and custody. The pertinent statute provides that the lessee who assumes responsibility for the premises can not recover from the owner for any injury caused by defects therein, "unless the owner knew or should have known of the defect or had received notice thereof and failed to remedy it within a reasonable time." LSA-R.S. 9:3221 (emphasis ours). Even if Caribbean had assumed responsibility for the electricity, the record is replete with evidence that the lessor continued to be involved with the electrical problems encountered by Caribbean. Mr. Burton, the lessor's employee, made several trips to the leased premises because of complaints about the circuit breakers tripping. He determined that the circuits were overloaded and reported this to his supervisor. Two days before the fire, Mr. Burton installed additional circuits and wiring in the area where the fire started as well as adding two circuit breakers to the panel box which housed the mismatched breakers. He testified that he did not notice anything out of the ordinary in the circuit breaker panel box, but that he did not inspect the other breakers at that time. Nevertheless, Mr. Burton was actively involved with working on the electrical system on the lessee's premises. Thus the lessor-owner knew or should have known of the defect, and is liable for the damages suffered by Caribbean.

* * *

CARTER and LANIER, Judges, dissenting.

CARTER, Judge.

¶1 We cannot join in the opinion of our learned brothers of the majority because of what we perceive to be factual and legal error therein.

LEGAL ERROR

¶2 The majority has erroneously interpreted and applied La.R.S. 9:3221 to the facts of the instant case. Specifically, the majority fell into legal error by holding that, although Caribbean as lessee contractually assumed responsibility for the wiring on its leased premises, nevertheless, Bass as lessor was still liable to Caribbean for the mismatched circuit breakers and wires if he knew or should have known of these defects. The history of La.R.S. 9:3221 shows that the notice provisions contained therein are only applicable in cases between the owner-lessor and third persons; the notice provisions of the statute are not applicable to change the contractual relations between the owner-lessor and the lessee.

Study Questions:

The seller's warranty against redhibitory defects can be waived. Is the same true of the land-lord's warranty against vices and defects? Which Civil Code article provides for such a waiver? Are there any exceptions that would make such a waiver null? What are they? Must the waiver of warranty in a lease be as explicit as the waiver of warranty against redhibitory defects? Must it, too, be brought to the other party's attention?

Great American Surplus Lines Ins. v. Bass introduced you to Revised Statute 9:3221.

The dissent in that case argued that it was inapplicable to a lawsuit between tenant and lessor where the tenant is the injured party because it was intended to apply only where a third party is the one who was injured.

For example, in Terranova v. Feldner, 28 So. 2d 287 (La. App. Orl. Cir. 1946), the plaintiff, a cashier at a drug store, was injured when she fell down the drug store's broken back stairway. She sued her employer (who had leased the premises), and also the landlord. Because the lease contained an indemnity clause consistent with Rev. St. 9:3221, the landlord was dismissed from the lawsuit. Rev. St. 9:3221 was most recently revised in 2005. What do the following cases indicate about the meaning of the phrases "Notwithstanding the provisions of Louisiana Civil Code Art. 2699" (which was added in 2005), and ""unless the owner knew or should have known of the defect or had received notice thereof and failed to remedy it"?

TASSIN V. SLIDELL MINI-STORAGE 1981
396 SO.2D 1261, 1264 (LA.)

MARCUS, Justice.

1 Mr. and Mrs. Byron Tassin and Jacqueline Carr instituted this action for damages sustained to furniture and related items stored in units leased by them in a storage facility known as Slidell Mini-Storage, Inc. Made defendants were Slidell Mini-Storage, Inc., Sidney Tiblier III and Rodney Zeringue, owners of the storage facility, and their insurer, Aetna Insurance Company. . . .

2 Defendants (owners/lessors) and their insurer answered generally denying the allegations of the petition and further answered by affirmatively asserting no liability on their part on the ground that the contracts entered into between plaintiffs and Slidell Mini-Storage explicitly provided that Slidell Mini-Storage would not be responsible for any loss caused by water.

3 The trial judge found that the damage to the goods was caused by water that found its way into the leased units. He further held that despite the clause in each agreement exculpating

the lessor for the loss of property stored on the premises caused by "water," the owners of the storage facility were nevertheless liable to plaintiffs under La.R.S. 9:3221 since they knew or should have known that the doors on the units were defective inasmuch as they would not withstand the heavy rains and thunderstorms that are common, natural phenomena in southeast Louisiana. Further finding that plaintiffs clearly proved the amount of damages to their property, he rendered judgment in favor of Mr. and Mrs. Tassin for $4,802 and in favor of Jacqueline Carr for $3,140 and against Slidell Mini-Storage. . . .

4 The court of appeal reversed, finding that the clause in each lease exculpating the lessor for loss of property by water controlled and precluded the imposition of liability on Slidell Mini-Storage. The court further held that, even assuming that La.R.S. 9:3221 was applicable, there was no evidence in the record supportive of a finding that Slidell Mini-Storage knew or should have known of the alleged defect. Upon plaintiffs' application, we granted certiorari to review the correctness of this decision

5 The record reflects that plaintiffs entered into identical warehouse lease agreements with Slidell Mini-Storage. The Tassin lease, executed by Byron Tassin, was for unit 16 and was dated April 29, 1976. The Carr lease, executed by Alfred E. Carr, Jr. as agent for his daughter, Jacqueline Carr, was for unit 15 and was dated February 16, 1977. Each agreement contained the following provision under "2. Insurance":

> Insurance on property stored on said premises for loss caused by fire, water, theft, Acts of God, or otherwise, shall be obtained at Depositor's option and expense and Warehouseman shall not be responsible for any such losses, whatsoever.

6 Both Mr. Tassin and Mr. Carr testified that they read the contracts in their entirety including the clause regarding insurance; however, no insurance was obtained on the goods stored in the warehouse.

7 Subsequent to the execution of the agreements, plaintiffs moved furniture and related items into the units for storage. Upon opening their respective units on or about March 11, 1977, plaintiffs found them to be very damp and most of the items were mildewed and discolored. Ms. Carr and her father testified that items in the back of the unit were sitting in approximately two to three inches of water. Mr. Carr noted that there was no water in the front by the door.

8 Mr. Carr, qualified as an expert in the building industry, testified that the overhead doors on storage units 15 and 16 did not close flush with the concrete slab flooring despite the rubber stripping on the bottom of the doors, thereby leaving a gap between the door and concrete of

about one-fourth inch when the doors were fully closed and locked. Photographs received in evidence revealed that a person could reach a hand and part of an arm under the door and into the unit even when the door was fully closed and locked. Further testimony by Mr. Carr and other witnesses as well as photographs taken of the area showed the concrete slabs of these particular units sloped toward the back of the units. Mr. Carr opined that the cause of the water getting into the unit was the fact that the "door did not seal properly" and that water that entered by rain or otherwise would remain on the floor because the "slab was not level, or sloping toward the front." Testimony by several witnesses as well as certified National Weather Service records indicated that while there was considerable rainfall and thunderstorms during the three weeks prior to March 11, 1977, the weather conditions were not unusual for that time of the year in southeast Louisiana.

* * *

9 It is clear that the relationship existing between plaintiffs and Slidell Mini-Storage pursuant to the warehouse agreements was one of lease and is therefore governed by the rights and obligations under Louisiana law pertaining to lease agreements. La. Civ. Code art. 2695 provides:

> The lessor guarantees the lessee against all the vices and defects of the thing, which may prevent its being used even in case it should appear he knew nothing of the existence of such vices and defects, at the time the lease was made, and even if they have arisen since, provided they do not arise from the fault of the lessee; and if any loss should result to the lessee from the vices and defects the lessor shall be bound to indemnify him for the same.

10 Nevertheless, the owner can shift responsibility for condition of the premises including liability for injury caused by any defect therein to the lessee pursuant to La.R.S. 9:3221.

11 However, the codal articles and statutes defining the rights and obligations of lessors and lessees are not prohibitory laws which are unalterable by contractual agreement, but are simply intended to regulate the relationship between lessor and lessee when there is no contractual stipulation imposed in the lease. General Leasing Co. v. Leda Towing Co., Inc., 286 So.2d 802 (La.App. 4th Cir. 1973), cert. denied, 290 So.2d 334 (La.1974). All things that are not forbidden by law may become the subject of or the motive for contracts and, when legally entered into, the contracts have the effect of law between the parties who have made them. La. Civ. Code arts. 1764, 1901. Our jurisprudence is that the usual warranties and obligations imposed under the codal articles and statutes dealing with lease may be waived or otherwise provided for by contractual agreement of the parties as long as such waiver or renunciation does not affect the rights of others and is not contrary to the public good.

* * *

12 Plaintiffs proved by a preponderance of the evidence that the doors and concrete flooring of storage units 15 and 16 were such as to allow water to blow or seep into the units. The doors did not close properly and the concrete sloped to the rear rather than to the front. Moreover, we consider that the clause in each lease agreement clearly and unambiguously transferred liability of the owners/lessors for loss caused by water to property stored on the premises to the lessees including water loss caused by a vice or defect in the premises. The lessees assumed this responsibility by freely entering into the warehouse agreements, thereby dispensing with the implied warranty in their favor established by La. Civ. Code art. 2695.

13 Although plaintiffs assumed responsibility for water damage caused by a vice or defect in the premises, we are convinced that the owners/lessors knew or should have known that the storage units were defective in that they did not secure against the entering of water into the units resulting from rain normally occurring in southeast Louisiana. It should have been obvious to them that, since the doors did not close flush with the concrete flooring which sloped to the rear, water would enter the units and cause damage to property located therein. Moreover, since the units did not contain shelving, they should have been aware that property would be placed on the flooring and would be affected by any water that might enter and accumulate in the units.

14 Under the circumstances, even though the lessees assumed responsibility for water damage caused by a vice or defect in the premises, La.R.S. 9:3221 did not relieve the owners/lessors of the responsibility imposed on them by La. Civ. Code art. 2695 because they should have known of the defects in the premises. This is the conclusion reached by the trial judge. We are unable to say that it is clearly wrong. Arceneaux v. Domingue, 365 So.2d 1330 (La.1980). To the contrary, we consider that the record fully supports this conclusion. Accordingly, we must reverse the judgment of the court of appeal and reinstate that of the trial judge.

DECREE

For the reasons assigned, the judgment of the court of appeal is reversed and the judgment of the district court is reinstated and made the judgment of this court. All costs of this appeal are assessed against Slidell Mini-Storage, Inc.

DIXON, C. J., and CALOGERO, DENNIS, WATSON, LEMMON and BLANCHE, JJ., concur.

Comment:

The previous case concerned the application of a R.S. 9:3221 waiver in a commercial lease. Consider the following with regard to a residential lease.

STUCKEY V. RIVERSTONE RESIDENTIAL 2009
21 SO.3D 970, (LA. 1ST CIR. CT. APP. 2009)

[An apartment lease provided as follows:

> 11. Insurance. Owner recommends that Resident secure Renter's insurance to help protect Resident and Resident's property. Owner is not responsible for, and will not provide fire or casualty insurance for, the personal property of Resident or occupants of the Unit.... Neither Owner nor Owner's managing agent shall be liable to Resident, other occupants of the Unit or their respective guests for any damage, injury or loss to person or property (furniture, jewelry, clothing, etc.) from ... flood, water leaks, rain, ... or other occurrences unless such damage, injury, or loss is caused exclusively by the negligence of Owner .... (Emphasis added.)

[Paragraph 17 of the lease agreement is captioned "Delivery of Unit," and concludes with the following provision:

> TO THE FULLEST EXTENT ALLOWED BY APPLICABLE LAW, OWNER EXPRESSLY DISCLAIMS ANY AND ALL WARRANTIES, WHETHER EXPRESS OR IMPLIED RELATING TO THE UNIT OR ANY FURNITURE, FURNISHINGS, EQUIPMENT OR APPLIANCES, IF ANY, IN THE UNIT INCLUDING, BUT NOT LIMITED TO, WARRANTIES OF FITNESS FOR A PARTICULAR PURPOSE, MERCHANTABILITY, HABITABILITY OR SUITABILITY.

[Furthermore, Paragraph 26(a) specifically provides the following:

> Mold & Mildew Resident(s) acknowledges that the apartment is located in a State which has a climate conducive to the growth of mold and mildew. It is, therefore, necessary to provide proper ventilation and dehumidification to the apartment to minimize the growth of mold and mildew. The only effective method to properly condition the air is to operate the heating and/or air conditioning ventilation system at all times throughout the year, even during those times when outside temperatures are moderate. Please understand that Management is not responsible for any injury, illness, harm or damage to the apartment or any person or property caused by or arising from, in whole or in part, mold or mildew. (Emphasis added)

[The plaintiff-tenants, Crystal, Ashley, and Austin Stuckey, a grandmother, her daughter, and minor grandson, claim that they complained to the apartments' property manager on two occasions of a leak in one of the upstairs bathrooms. After repairs were attempted, Ms. Stuckey delivered a handwritten letter to the property manager, in which she complained about the continuing leak and the accumulation of a "black substance" on the air conditioning vents. She expressed her concern that there might be "a possible mold problem," and claimed that "we have all been sick with symptoms that are associated with mold exposure." The property manager promptly contacted Ashley Stuckey upon receiving the letter to discuss the situation.

[On May 9, 2005, Riverstone arranged to have its professional cleaning contractor inspect the apartment for mold. None was reported. The following day, an industrial hygiene technician employed by Air Environmental Services tested the apartment, and found no toxic levels of mold.

[On June 14, 2005, the plaintiffs arranged for their own testing of the apartment. On June 27, 2005, the plaintiffs vacated the apartment, apparently after receiving notice of institution of eviction proceedings for nonpayment of rent. Plaintiffs then instituted suit, claiming that while residing in the apartment from February 12 through June 24, 2005, they and Austin were exposed to toxigenic molds due to the defendants' negligence and fault, and that the water leaks resulted in the growth of the toxigenic molds, which caused them and Austin to suffer various health problems due to that exposure, including bronchial infections, persistent nose bleeds, headaches, nausea, and other conditions.]

GAIDRY, J.

DISCUSSION

Legal Principles

¶1 Louisiana Civil Code article 2696 establishes the lessor's warranty against vices or defects in the leased thing:

> The lessor warrants the lessee that the thing is suitable for the purpose for which it was leased and that it is free from vices or defects that prevent its use for that purpose.
>
> This warranty also extends to vices or defects that arise after the delivery of the thing and are not attributable to the fault of the lessee.

¶2 Louisiana Civil Code article 2697 further provides that:

The warranty provided in the preceding Article also encompasses vices or defects that are not known to the lessor.

However, if the lessee knows of such vices or defects and fails to notify the lessor, the lessee's recovery for breach of warranty may be reduced accordingly.

¶3   Louisiana Civil Code article 2699 provides for the lessee's waiver of the warranty against vices or defects in certain circumstances:

The warranty provided in the preceding Articles may be waived, but only by clear and unambiguous language that is brought to the attention of the lessee.

Nevertheless, a waiver of warranty is ineffective:

(1) To the extent it pertains to vices or defects of which the lessee did not know and the lessor knew or should have known;

(2) To the extent it is contrary to the provisions of Article 2004;

(3) In a residential or consumer lease, to the extent it purports to waive the warranty for vices or defects that seriously affect health or safety.

(Emphasis added)

¶4   Louisiana Revised Statutes 9:3221 provides:

Notwithstanding the provisions of Louisiana Civil Code Article 2699, the owner of premises leased under a contract whereby the lessee assumes responsibility for their condition is not liable for injury caused by any defect therein to the lessee or anyone on the premises who derives his right to be thereon from the lessee, unless the owner knew or should have known of the defect or had received notice thereof and failed to remedy it within a reasonable time. (Emphasis added.)

¶5   The emphasized introductory phrase of the last-cited statute was added effective January 1, 2005, as part of the same act that amended and reenacted La. C.C. art. 2699. Although La. C.C. art. 2699 and La. R.S. 9:3221 are in pari materia, article 2699 deals with the contractual obligations between the parties to the lease, rather than with delictual obligations that may arise related to the leased property. See La. C.C. art. 2699, Revision Comments—2004, (h). Thus, La. C.C. art. 2699 does not supersede the provisions of La. R.S. 9:3221 that govern and allocate such delictual obligations between the parties. Id. Louisiana Revised Statutes 9:3221 is a statutory exception to the strict liability of La. C.C. art. 2696, and is expressly recognized as not subject to the provisions of La. C.C. art. 2699.

¶6 Louisiana Civil Code article 2004 provides that "[a]ny clause [in a contract] is null that, in advance, excludes or limits the liability of one party for causing physical injury to the other party." However, its provisions do not supersede La. R.S. 9:3221. La. C.C. art.2004, Revision Comments—1984, (f).

¶7 We therefore conclude that the trial court did not commit legal error in finding La. R.S. 9:3221 legally applicable to the facts of this case.

The Terms of the Lease Agreement

¶8 The initial term of the lease agreement was for a period of slightly over six months, ending August 30, 2005, with monthly rent of $685.00. Paragraph 11 [reproduced above], although primarily directed to the subject of insurance, also contains language relevant to the issues presented.

¶9 It is certainly open to question whether the first and second paragraphs quoted above sufficiently express the intent that Ashley Stuckey assumed general responsibility for the condition of the apartment for purposes of La. R.S. 9:3221. We note that the first paragraph's stated title, "Insurance," and its context might suggest that it relates only to responsibility for securing insurance. At any rate, we conclude that Paragraph 26(a) clearly and adequately expresses the parties' intent that, as between them, the responsibility for any condition or defect involving mold or mildew in the apartment would rest upon Ashley Stuckey, for purposes of application of La. R.S. 9:3221. The paragraph describes necessary preventative measures, the operation of the apartment's individual heating and air conditioning system, obviously within the primary control and responsibility of the resident tenant, and specifically and unambiguously provides that the lessor will have no responsibility for mold or mildew in the apartment.

¶10 As previously noted, La. R.S. 9:3221 operates as an express statutory exception to La. C.C. art. 2699 where the lessee assumes responsibility for the condition of leased premises. Where the language of a provision transferring delictual liability under La. R.S. 9:3221 is clear and unambiguous, the law does not require that the provision be brought to the lessee's attention or explained to him. Greely v. OAG Properties, LLC, 44,240, p. 4 (La.App. 2nd Cir.5/13/09), 12 So.3d 490, 494. See also Ford v. Bienvenu, 00–2376, pp. 6–9 (La.App. 4th Cir.8/29/01), 804 So.2d 64, 68–70, writ denied, 01–2688 (La.12/14/01), 804 So.2d 639. Thus, La. C.C. art. 2699's requirement that a waiver of the lessor's warranty against vices or defects be brought to the attention of the lessee does not apply to a provision transferring responsibility for purposes of La. R.S. 9:3221.

* * *

¶11 Whether the defendants had the obligation to maintain the apartment and to repair reported problems is not determinative of their duties for purposes of tort liability under the standards imposed by La. R.S. 9:3221. There is a distinction between liability for damages occasioned by defects in leased premises and who has the obligation to repair such defects. Hebert v. Neyrey, 445 So.2d 1165, 1168 n. 3 (La.1984).

¶12 The plaintiffs contend on appeal that Ms. Campbell, as property manager of the complex, should have performed a "reasonable inspection" of Apartment No. 2907 prior to leasing it to Ashley Stuckey. In the first place, the record does not affirmatively show that the defendants failed to inspect the apartment prior to the plaintiffs' occupancy. As the parties alleging that circumstance as a basis for the defendants' negligence, the plaintiffs would bear that burden at trial. Secondly, the record confirms that Ashley Stuckey herself inspected the apartment, signed the required apartment move-in inspection form acknowledging that all items were in good condition, and reported no problems with it prior to occupancy. Most importantly, however, the jurisprudence interpreting La. R.S. 9:3221 does not support the imposition of a duty on the part of a lessor to inspect conditions over which a lessee has assumed responsibility.

* * *

¶13 The plaintiffs' opposition affidavits do not show that the defendants knew or should have known of any unusual "humidity problem" with Apartment No. 2907, nor any unusual potential for mold or mildew beyond that typical to Louisiana's climate. At best, the plaintiffs put forth evidence suggestive of the possibility that the defendants should have known of the potential for the development of mold or mildew. But such evidence simply does not rise to evidence creating a genuine issue of material fact on the issue of whether the defendants should have known or received adequate notice of the presence or even probability of development of mold or mildew, the defect of which the plaintiffs complain.

¶14 We agree with the trial court's conclusions that the defendants did not know and did not have reason to know of the alleged mold until their receipt of Ashley Stuckey's letter of May 6, 2005, and that upon receiving such notice, the defendants sought to investigate and remedy the claimed condition within a reasonable time. See, e.g., Meyers v. Drewes, 196 So.2d 607, 611 (La. App. 4th Cir.1967). The plaintiffs do not dispute that the defendants even offered them the use of another apartment while the report of suspected mold was being investigated. The failure of the plaintiffs to meet their burden of proof on this element is fatal to their opposition to summary judgment.

DECREE

The judgment of the trial court is affirmed. All costs of this appeal are assessed to the plaintiffs-appellants, Ashley Stuckey and Crystal Stuckey.

AFFIRMED.

Section 4: Peaceful Possession and Vices and Defects

The previous sections discussed the lessor's warranty that the thing leased is not defective, set forth in articles 2696 and 2697, as well as the waiver of that warranty and the indemnification provision set forth in the Revised Statutes. The cases used to illustrate these articles concerned physical vices and defects such as walls that fall down, leaky doors, and allegedly moldy apartments, but vices and defects also include anything that might interfere with the lessee's enjoyment of the premises, including actions of the lessor himself.

Article 2700 similarly provides protection against actions that disturb the lessee's enjoyment of the premises, but in this case, the actions are by a third party. Specifically, Article 2700 provides that the lessor warrant's the lessee's peaceful possession of the leased thing against any disturbance caused by a person who asserts ownership, or right to possession of, or an other right in the thing. In a residential lease, this includes any disturbance caused by someone who has been given access to the premises with the lessor's consent. Thus, the landlord of your apartment building warrants that the kid upstairs will not disturb you by playing his electric guitar at all times of the day and night. If there is such a disturbance, then under Article 2701, you should inform your landlord of the problem. If he fails to take action, then you, as lessee, may file any appropriate action against your upstairs neighbor with the guitar as well as the landlord, if the disturbance is egregious, and the landlord failed to take steps to remedy the situation after you notified him, then you have three potential remedies: damages, injunctive relief, or dissolution of the remedy. La. Civ. Code art. 2700 comment (b). Logically, the landlord does not have an obligation to protect his lessees from disturbance by persons who do not have any right to be on the premises. La. Civ. Code art. 2702.

Study Questions:

In the following case, who is disturbing the lessee's possession of the premises? Is the lessee's cause of action therefore based on Articles 2696 or 2700?

KEENAN V. FLANNIGAN 1925

157 LA. 749, 103 SO. 30

O'NIELL, C. J.

¶1   This is a suit by a landlord against his tenant for a balance claimed for rent. There is no dispute about the facts. The defendant leased, for a residence, for the term of two years, the upper floor of a two-story or duplex dwelling. The lower apartment was then vacant, but was afterwards leased, also for a residence, to another tenant, who moved in soon after the defendant had moved into the upper apartment. The tenant in the lower apartment conducted such a noisy and disorderly house that the occupants of the upper apartment could not sleep. A victrola played music from 8 o'clock every night until 2 or 3 o'clock in the morning, while a party of drunken merrymakers indulged in loud and obscene language. The defendant complained to his landlord, but the latter said that it was not his duty to interfere, and suggested that the defendant complain to the police. He did complain to the chief of police, but got no relief. After spending nearly four months of sleepless nights in the house, he and the other members of his household, his wife and her mother, moved out. He paid promptly for the 4 months' rent. This suit is for the remaining 20 months, less the rent which the landlord afterwards collected from other tenants, to whom he rented the lower apartment during a part of the unexpired term of defendant's lease.

¶2   It is not denied that the continuing nuisance in the lower apartment made it unbearable for the defendant or his family to continue living in the upper apartment. The only question is whether it was the duty of the landlord, or of the tenant in the upper apartment, to take action to suppress the nuisance in the lower apartment. The district court held that it was the landlord's duty, and rejected his demand for the unearned rent. The court of appeal affirmed the judgment.

¶3   The case depends upon an interpretation of two articles of the Civil Code. The defendant relies upon article 2692, and the plaintiff relies upon article 2703. Article 2692 declares that, in a contract of lease, 'the lessor is bound from the very nature of the contract, and without any clause to that effect,' to maintain the property in such condition as to serve the purpose or use for which it is rented, and to maintain the lessee in the peaceable possession of the premises during the term of the lease. But article 2703 declares:

> 'The lessor is not bound to guarantee the lessee against disturbances caused by persons not claiming any right to the premises; but in that case the lessee has a right of action for damages sustained against the person occasioning such disturbance.'

¶4 The argument of the landlord in this case is that, inasmuch as the tenant in the lower apartment, who caused the disturbance, was not claiming any right to the upper apartment, he, the lessor, was not bound to protect the lessee of the upper apartment against the disturbance. The argument resolves itself into this: That the word 'premises' in the expression 'disturbances caused by persons not claiming any right to the premises' means only the premises leased to the person disturbed-the upper apartment in this case. We agree with the Court of Appeal that article 2703 should not be given such a restricted meaning. What it means is that a lessor is not bound to warrant his lessee against a disturbance caused by a person who does not claim, under covenant with the lessor, a right to be in a position to carry on the disturbance; e. g., a lesson is not responsible for a disturbance inflicted upon his lessee by a trespasser. In our interpretation of articles 2692 and 2703 of the Code it would perhaps make no difference if the two apartments were adjacent residences belonging to the same landlord, instead of being under the same roof.

¶5 It is conceded by the learned counsel for plaintiff that it would have been a violation of the landlord's implied guaranty to the lessee of the upper apartment if the landlord, after leasing the upper apartment to him for a residence, had leased the lower apartment to the other tenant for a purpose that would necessarily disturb the tenant in the upper apartment. The argument of the learned counsel is that the landlord was not obliged to suppress the nuisance in the lower apartment because it was committed in violation of the contract of lease of the lower apart-ment. Our answer is that the violation of the contract of lease of the lower apartment was a matter which concerned the landlord, not the tenant in the upper apartment; but the nuisance in the lower apartment, so far as it disturbed the peaceable possession of the tenant in the upper apartment, was a matter which concerned him, and against which the landlord had guaranteed him. When the landlord was notified that the manner in which the tenant in the lower apart-ment was using the premises was a continuing disturbance of the peaceable possession of the tenant in the upper apartment, the landlord had no more right to sanction or tolerate such violation of his contract with the tenant in the lower apartment than he had to authorize the disturbance.

* * *

The judgment is affirmed.
AFFIRMED.

Section 5: Lessor's Remedies

The lessor's rights or remedies include the lessor's privilege, the right to recover the rent due, the right to evict the lessee who is in breach, and the right to dissolve the lease.

Article 2704 stipulates:

> If the lessee fails to pay the rent when due, the lessor may, in accordance with the provisions of
> the Title "Conventional Obligations or Contracts" dissolve the lease and may regain possession
> in the manner provided by law.

Faced with a lessee who is delinquent in paying the rent, the lessor can demand that the rent
be paid, or (after proper notice) he can dissolve the lease and evict the nonpaying tenant. Once
the tenant is evicted, however, the lease is dissolved and he cannot continue to demand rent
when the lessee no longer has possession of the property. Additionally, a lessor can exercise
his privilege to seize any of the non-paying lessee's movables found on the premises and either
release them on payment of rent or have them sold, Civil Code articles 2707-2710. The Lessor's
Privilege will be discussed in the following section.

Study Question:

What does the following case indicate about whether a lessor can demand both payment of
the rent and dissolution of the lease when a lessee fails to pay?

HENRY ROSE MERCANTILE & MFG. CO. V. STEARNS 1923
154 LA. 946, 98 SO. 429

OVERTON, J.

¶1 Plaintiff leased to defendant two warehouses for the period of three years, beginning
September 1, 1920, for a monthly rental of $275, payable in advance. Defendant failed to pay all
of the installments that fell due, and as a consequence plaintiff, in February, 1921, sued him for
the installments that had fallen due, subject to credits for payments made, and for those that
had not matured, and, in addition thereto, sued for the recognition of its privilege as lessor on
the movable property found on the leased premises, and also prayed for the issuance of a writ
of provisional seizure.

¶2 The writ issued as prayed for, and under it the sheriff provisionally seized all of the personal property found on the premises, as well as some that had been removed therefrom, and
used the warehouses for the purpose of storing the property found in them, closed their doors,
and thereby dispossessed defendant. The latter, representing that he had made arrangements
to sublease a part of the premises, requested plaintiff to have the sheriff remove the property

seized, and to restore to him the possession of the warehouses, pending the seizure, but plaintiff refused to comply with defendant's request. As a result of the action of the sheriff, and of the refusal of plaintiff to restore him to possession, defendant contends that he has been evicted from the premises, and therefore that he is not liable for rent from February 13, 1921, the date of the eviction, and demands, in reconvention, that the lease be dissolved as of that date.

¶3   By the terms of article 2692 of the Civil Code it is the duty of the lessor to maintain the lessee in the peaceable possession of the property let, during the continuance of the lease. If the lessor, instead of complying with this obligation, evicts the lessee, it seems clear that by doing so he gives to the latter good cause to dissolve the contract, and thereby to defeat any demand for rent made for the period following the eviction. If the lessee fails to pay his rent as it matures, the lessor may hold him liable for the rent due for the expired term of the lease, and may sue to dissolve the contract and evict the lessee, or, if he should so elect, he may hold the lessee for the rent, both for the expired and the unexpired terms of the lease, and may sue accordingly. If, however, he elects to avail himself of the latter right, he elects to continue the contract in force, notwithstanding the default of the lessee in his payments, and thereby accords to the latter the right to remain on the premises and to use them in accordance with the terms of the lease, and continues in force the obligation imposed by law upon him to maintain the lessee in the peaceable possession of the property. Therefore a lessor, in causing the personal property on the premisses to be seized, under a writ of provisional seizure, for installments of rent due and for those that have not yet matured, should exercise care to see that the lessee is not unnecessarily disturbed in the possession of the premises, and that he is not evicted, by permitting the premises to be taken away from him to be used as a place to store the property seized. In the case at bar, as we have observed, the plaintiff gave its sanction to the sheriff's executing the writ in the manner in which he did, by refusing to direct that official to remove the property seized, when it was in plaintiff's power to have thus directed she sheriff, and by refusing to restore defendant to the possession of the premises, pending the seizure.

¶4   The action of plaintiff and of the sheriff amounted to, and in fact resulted in, the eviction of defendant, and, since plaintiff is responsible therefor, defendant is entitled to have the lease dissolved, and to the rejection of plaintiff's demand for the rent accruing after the eviction. If plaintiff had waited until the recovery of judgment before evicting defendant, and under a writ of fieri facias had seized the lease for the installments due, a different case might have been presented, but plaintiff did not so wait; nor did it seize the lease, under the writ of provisional seizure; nor could the lease have been legally so seized, for the lessor's privilege, the existence of which is the only ground alleged for the issuance of the writ of provisional seizure, does not attach to the lease. See Brunner Mercantile Co. v. Rodgin, 130 La. 358, 57 South. 1004.

¶5 The rejection of the demand for the rent claimed, for the period following the eviction, will leave, as due, $1,356.04, subject to said credit of $375.

¶6 For the reasons assigned, it is ordered, adjudged, and decreed that the judgment appealed from be amended, by reducing the amount allowed plaintiff to $1,356.04, subject to said credit of $375, with legal interest on the balance from judicial demand until paid, and by dissolving said lease, and, as thus amended, that said judgment be affirmed, plaintiff to pay the costs of this appeal. It is further ordered and decreed that this judgment shall not be construed as affecting the right of interveners with respect to their separate appeals.

Comment and Study Questions:

Some leases provide an acceleration clause should the lessee fail to pay rent on time, an example of which follows:

> 'Should lessee at any time violate any of the conditions of this lease, or fail to comply with any
> of lessee's obligations hereunder, or fail to pay the rent or water bill or similar charges, punctu-
> ally at maturity, as stipulated, and remain in default after 10 days written notice thereof, . . . the
> rent for the whole unexpired term of this lease shall, without putting lessee in default, at once
> become due and exigible, and in any such event, lessor shall have the option either at once to
> demand the entire rent for the whole term or to immediately cancel this lease without putting
> the lessee in default. . . .'

How should such a clause be read?

Does the lessor have the option of suing the lessee for back rent if she misses a payment?

Villere & Co. v. Latter, 171 So. 705 (La. 1936) said no, the plain language of the contract left the lessor with only two options, and when he instead sued for the missed payment, he waived the acceleration / immediate cancellation clause.

Comment:

The previous cases discuss what the lessor can do when the lessee fails to pay rent, giving him a choice of either recovering the rent or eviction. But suppose the nonpaying lessee simply abandons the premises, what remedy can the lessor pursue at that point?

WEIL V. SEGURA 1933

178 LA. 421, 151 SO. 639

ROGERS, Justice.

¶1 Under a written contract dated April 20, 1932, plaintiff leased to defendant the premises described as 'gasoline service station with three rooms and paint shop, all known as 3901 and 3911 Banks Street,' New Orleans. The lease was for a term of two years beginning on the 1st day of May, 1932, and ending on the last day of April, 1934, at a monthly rental of $120, payable in advance.

¶2 Defendant paid the rent due on May 1, 1932, and went into possession of the gasoline station on May 2, 1932. Defendant removed from the leased premises on May 27, 1932, and refused to pay the rent due June 1, 1932. Plaintiff, alleging defendant's refusal to pay, brought this suit for the recovery of the rent for the unexpired term of the lease. Defendant admitted the execution of the lease, but denied any indebtedness for rent, and averred that he vacated plaintiff's premises, because plaintiff failed to deliver to him the entire premises covered by the lease.

¶3 After defendant vacated the premises, plaintiff leased them to another tenant, from whom he received $225 in rents. The court below held the defendant was entitled to credit for these rents, and gave plaintiff judgment for the amount sued for, less the $225 collected by plaintiff from the new tenant. From this judgment, defendant has appealed.

¶4 The record satisfies us that defendant examined the premises before he signed the lease and knew they were occupied by tenants. The gasoline station was occupied by one Palmisano and the paint shop by one Knauss.

¶5 The contract of lease contains a stipulation that, in the event possession of the leased premises cannot be given owing to delays in obtaining possession from the tenants, the lease shall not be affected thereby, but the lessee shall be entitled to the remission of the rent for the term during which he is deprived of possession.

¶6 The filling station was delivered to defendant on April 30, 1932, and on May 2, 1932, defendant began business, the intervening day falling on Sunday. Knauss had agreed with plaintiff to remove from the paint shop on May 7, 1932. When that day arrived, Knauss refused to move, and tendered plaintiff the rent for another month. Plaintiff declined to accept the rent until he had obtained defendant's permission for Knauss to remain until June 7, 1932. Defendant was called to the telephone and agreed to this, provided plaintiff would credit defendant with the rent he was to receive from Knauss. Plaintiff received $50 from Knauss, and on May 23, 1932, he sent defendant a check for the amount. Defendant vacated the premises on May 27, 1932, and only a few days thereafter, namely, on June 7, 1932, Knauss vacated the paint shop, and the whole of the leased premises was at defendant's disposal.

¶7   The judge of the district court reached the conclusion, we think correctly, that defendant became dissatisfied with his contract, and thought he could abrogate it by abandoning the premises and setting up the claim that defendant had neglected to fulfill his obligation by failing to deliver plaintiff possession of the paint shop. But the lease itself expressly provided for such a contingency by stipulating that delays resulting from the failure to obtain possession from former tenants should not affect the lease and by providing for a rebate of rent in accordance with such delays. As parties choose to bind themselves in their business agreements, so must they be held bound.

¶8   The abandonment by the lessee of the leased premises matures the whole amount of rent under the lease. Sliman v. Fish, 177 La. 38, 147 So. 493.

¶9   Where the lessee abandons the leased premises, the lessor may rent the property to other tenants without impairing his recourse against the lessee, though lessee is entitled to credit for the rent received. Bernstein v. Bauman, 170 La. 378, 127 So. 874; Sliman v. Fish, supra.

¶10   Therefore plaintiff is entitled to judgment for the rent for the unexpired term of the lease, subject to a credit to the lessee of the rent received from the new tenant, unless plaintiff by his own act has forfeited his right of recovery, either in whole or in part.

¶11   On the trial of the case, it developed that plaintiff by formal notarial act executed on November 14, 1933, had sold the leased premises to one Mrs. Theresa Guelp. And defendant contends that, in any event, plaintiff is not entitled to recover any rent after the date he sold the property. We think the contention is sound.

¶12   It is true, as argued by plaintiff, that ownership is not essential to make a lease valid.

¶13   He who possesses a thing belonging to another may let it out to a third person. Civ. Code, art. 2681. In such a case, the lessor warrants the enjoyment of the thing leased against the claim of the owner. Civ. Code, art. 2682. And a lessee sued for rent, and in undisturbed possession of the leased premises, cannot contest the lessor's title. Sientes v. Odier & Co., 17 La. Ann. 153.

¶14   While the lessor is not required to own the thing which he leases, he is required to possess it. And, although the lessee in undisturbed possession cannot contest the title of his lessor, he is entitled to claim the remission or reduction of the rent if he is wholly or partially evicted from the leased premises. Wood v. Sala y Fabrigas, 105 La. 1, 29 So. 367.

¶15 When plaintiff resumed possession of the leased premises after they had been abandoned by defendant, he was acting for his tenant, and his possession was that of his tenant, and he was required to account to his tenant for any rent he received from the property. But, when plaintiff sold the property to Mrs. Theresa Guelp free of incumbrances, he conveyed to the vendee full dominion, including the exclusive right of possession, of the property which he owned. Plaintiff's possession for account of his tenant was converted necessarily into possession for his own account for the purpose of making the sale. Thereafter it is clear that defendant could not reoccupy the premises, nor could defendant, nor plaintiff for defendant's account, sublease to another or sell the right of occupancy from the proceeds of which defendant might extinguish or diminish his obligation to plaintiff.

¶16 In the case of Roumage v. Blatrier, 11 Rob. 101, where, pending an action to enjoin the execution issued upon a judgment obtained by a lessor against the surety of his lessee for the amount of the lease for years, to be paid from time to time as the rent may become due under the lease, the lessor sold the property without any stipulation that the sale was made subject to the lease, the court apparently thought the lease should be dissolved from the date of the sale; and the court remanded the case for the purpose of inquiring into the fact of the sale and to liquidate the balance due the lessor for rent up to the time of the sale, after deducting the rent collected by the lessor's agent from various tenants during the period the lease was abandoned by the lessee; and to make the purchaser a party to the proceeding.

¶17 A similar principle is involved in this case, but we see no necessity for remanding the case, as the sale of the property free from all obligations of the lease is admitted, and no good reason is suggested for making the purchaser of the property a party to this suit.

¶18 Our conclusion is that the sale of the leased premises terminated the lessor's rights, and precludes him from recovering from the lessee any rent beyond the date of the sale.

¶19 Defendant defaulted on the rent due for the month of June, 1932. The property was sold by plaintiff on November 14, 1932. Therefore defendant is indebted to plaintiff for rent for the months of June, July, August, September, October, and one-half of the month of November, 1932-say, for five and one-half months-at $120 per month, or a total of $660, subject to a credit of $225 for the rent collected by plaintiff for defendant's account, making the net amount due plaintiff $435, together with the interest thereon.

¶20   For the reasons assigned, the judgment herein appealed from is amended by reducing its principal sum from $2,711, to $435, and, as thus amended, it is affirmed; costs of appeal to be paid by plaintiff.

Lagniappe Question:

The principle that if the lessee abandons the premises, then the lessor can demand the rent for the entire term (minus any rent received from a subsequent lessee) is still good law. Consequently, if a lessee realizes that he will be unable to pay the rent, is he better off abandoning the premises or waiting until the lessor evicts him?

Section 6: Lessor's Privilege

Read Civil Code articles 2707-2710 which provide another remedy for a lessor.

To secure payment of rent, the lessor has a privilege over the lessee's movables that are found on the leased property. In an agricultural lease where rent is based on a share of the crop, this privilege would include a security interest in the crop itself.

Unless something else is provided in the contract of lease, or the debtor voluntarily surrender's his property, enforcement of the privilege requires a judicial seizure and sale of property, see Article 2707 comment (d). If there is a sublessee, the lessor's privilege extends to sublessee's movables, but only to the extent that the sublessee is indebted to his sublessor at the time. Art. 2708. The lessor may even seize movables that belong to a third person if they are present upon the leased property, unless he knows that they do not belong to the lessee. If a third party's property is seized, then that person may recover it before judicial sale as provided in Article 2709.

A lessor may seize those movables over which he has a privilege while they are in or on the leased property, and for fifteen days after they have been removed, if they remain the property of the lessee and can be identified. Furthermore, he may enforce his privilege against such movables even when they have previously been seized by the sheriff without the necessity of a further seizure, as long as the movables or their proceeds remain in the custody of the officer.

Study Questions:

A vendor's privilege means that the vendor's right to seize the object of the sale for non-payment ranks above other creditor's rights. In reading this case, consider whether a lessor's privilege gives the same power. What kinds of events will interrupt a lessor's privilege? Read the current articles on renewal of a lease and reconduction carefully. Would the decision below be the same today?

ACADIANA BANK V. FOREMAN 1977

352 SO. 2D 674 (LA.)

DIXON, Justice.

¶1 This case involves the ranking of privileges on movables in a drive-in restaurant. The contest is between Acadiana Bank, which holds a chattel mortgage on the furniture and fixtures, and intervenor, Wilson J. Moosa, owner and lessor of the building. The trial court rejected the demands of the intervenor-lessor, holding that the bank's lien under the chattel mortgage was superior in rank. The Court of Appeal, with one judge dissenting, affirmed (343 So.2d 1138 (La. App.3d Cir. 1977)), and we granted writs to review that ruling.

¶2 Helen Doty operated a "Frostop" restaurant in Eunice in a building owned by Wilson J. Moosa. Kimball Aubrey Foreman and his wife arranged with Mrs. Doty and Moosa to take over the business. Mrs. Doty sold the movables to Foreman and his wife, who agreed with Moosa to rent the building for $160.00 a month through December 31, 1974. These agreements were completed on September 18, 1974, at which time a written lease was executed between the Foremans and Moosa for a period of five years at a rent of $400.00 a month, to begin on January 1, 1975. On the same day, September 18, 1974, the Foremans borrowed $12,000 from Acadiana Bank, evidenced by a hand note. The Foremans also executed a collateral mortgage on the equipment Mrs. Doty sold them, and pledged a collateral mortgage note in the amount of $17,000, to secure the hand note.

¶3 The officers of the Acadiana Bank participated in the arrangements, and were aware that the mortgaged property was in the building owned by Moosa and leased to the Foremans. The lease, which was to have commenced on January 1, 1975, was recorded on September 20, 1974. The collateral chattel mortgage was not recorded until October 3, 1974.

¶4 The indebtedness to the bank was reduced from $12,000 to $5000 by August 14, 1975. On that date Mrs. Foreman executed a $5000 hand note and delivered it to the bank; the September 18, 1974 note for $12,000 was apparently marked paid and returned to the Foremans.

¶5 Matrimonial difficulties between the Foremans resulted in a dissolution of their marriage later in 1975. Apparently, as a part of the settlement of the community property, arrangements were made, and the bank returned Mrs. Foreman's $5000 note to her on October 6, 1975, and took a note from Mr. Foreman on October 7, 1975 in the amount of $6234.24. Each note was secured by a continuing pledge of the collateral mortgage note, which never left the hands of the bank.

¶6   Foreman did not make the payments on the $6234.24 note dated October 7, 1975, and the bank proceeded to foreclose by executory process. Moosa intervened, contending that his lessor's lien and privilege for unpaid rent primed the bank's chattel mortgage.

¶7   The privilege of the chattel mortgage is effective as to third persons from the date of its recordation. R.S. 9:5354.

¶8   Since it was recorded on October 3, 1974, the chattel mortgage primes only those liens arising thereafter. The oral lease between Moosa and Foreman, commencing on September 18, 1974 and ending December 31, 1974, gave the lessor a lien superior to that of the bank's chattel mortgage.

¶9   The questions, then, are

(1) did Moosa's lien continue without interruption, even though the written lease superseded the oral lease on January 1, 1975?

(2) did the bank's privilege arising from the chattel mortgage continue without interruption in spite of renegotiation of Foreman's indebtedness during the term of the written lease?

¶10   The affirmative answer to the second question is supplied by (former) C.C. 3158. When a collateral chattel mortgage note is pledged to a creditor, and when the note remains in the hands of the creditor, to secure a particular loan or any other obligation, existing or thereafter arising (as provided in the chattel mortgage note in the instant case), the pledge continues against third persons, and the new liabilities or loans are "secured by the collateral to the same extent as if they came into existence when the instrument or item was originally pledged and the pledge was made to secure them . . ." C.C. 3158. New Orleans Silversmiths, Inc. v. Toups, 261 So.2d 252 (La.App. 4th Cir. 1972), cert. den. 262 La. 309, 263 So.2d 47 (La.1972), noted in 47 Tul.L.Rev. 211). Nathan and Marshall, "The Collateral Mortgage," 33 La.L.Rev. 497, 510; LeVan, "Security Devices," 33 La.L.Rev. 228.

¶11   The answer to the first question, however, is negative. Except in cases of tacit reconduction, the life of the lessor's privilege, in effect, spans only the duration of the lease in existence when the privilege first attached, to secure only the rent arising under the lease. If one lease is superseded by another lease, the effectiveness of the old lessor's privilege ends and a new lessor's privilege arises.

¶12   (Tacit reconduction (C.C. 2688, 2689) is said to result in a continuation of the old lease and the security of the privilege. Comegys v. Shreveport Kandy Kitchen, 162 La. 103, 110 So. 104

(1926); McKesson Parker Blake Corp. v. Eaves & Reddit, Inc., 149 So. 294 (La.App. 1st Cir. 1933). This interpretation of the civil code provisions was criticized in "Tacit Reconduction A New Lease," Lapeyre, 1 La.L.Rev. 439).

¶13   In the absence of reconduction, however, the lessor's privilege is dependent upon a particular lease. The conflict between the privilege of the chattel mortgage and the lessor's privilege is discussed in "Problems of Chattel Mortgages," Dainow, 13 La.L.Rev. 537, 543:

> "Lessor. The existence of the lessor's privilege is dependent upon two elements: (1) a lease
> between the parties, (Fisk v. Moores, 11 Rob. 279 (La.1845)) and (2) the presence of the effects
> in the premises. (Arts. 2705-2709, 3217(3), 3218, La.Civil Code of 1870). Accordingly, the earliest
> point of time when these two elements concur is the date on which the lessor's privilege arises.
> (Youree v. Limerick, 157 La. 39, 101 So. 864 (1924)). This is not dependent upon any rent being due,
> (Ibid.) the privilege is protection for a continuing relationship.

¶14   The lessor's privilege is predicated upon a lease; therefore, it must be a particular lease. Consequently, if either by agreement or operation of law there comes into existence a new lease, that also means a new privilege with a new date of creation. Thus, if the lessor and lessee (under a monthly lease for an indefinite term) agree upon a change in the rent, they are deemed to have made a new lease, (McGuffin v. Barkett, 44 So.2d 195 (La.App.1950); Weaks Supply Co. v. Werdin, 147 So. 838, and 154 So. 378 (La.App.1933, 1934), criticized in Note, 9 Tulane Law Review 124 (1934)) and the privilege deriving from the new lease cannot have a date of creation any earlier than the concurrence of the new lease and the presence of the effects on the premises. This means that a chattel mortgage which came into existence after the first lease but before the new lease thereby moves into first rank ahead of the lessor's privilege. (Cf. Easterling v. Brooks, 213 La. 519, 35 So.2d 132 (1948)).

¶15   In Youree v. Limerick, 157 La. 39, 101 So. 864 (1924), the operator of a restaurant borrowed money from Papas and gave his note, secured by a chattel mortgage on the furniture and fixtures. Limerick subsequently bought the business and assumed the obligations under the chattel mortgage, but arranged for the cancellation of the prior lease, and the execution of a new lease, apparently on the same terms. Since these facts resulted in the superior rank of Papas' chattel mortgage, the court found it necessary to pass on the landlord's "plea of estoppel" (which was decided in favor of the landlord).

¶16   The three requisite elements to a contract of lease are the thing, the price, and the consent. C.C. 2670. It has been held that when by agreement the price is changed, there is a new price and a new consent, and therefore a new lease. Weaks Supply Co. v. Werdin, 147 So. 838 (La.

App.2d Cir. 1933), affirmed, 154 So. 378 (La.App.2d Cir. 1934), criticized, 9 Tul.L.Rev. 124; Thigpen v. Wall Printing Corp., 145 So. 714 (La.App.2d Cir. 1933).

¶17 In Weaks, supra, a written lease was entered into at a monthly rate of $100 without a definite duration having been agreed upon. Some time later the monthly rental was reduced to $80 by verbal agreement. Before the rent was reduced the lessee executed a chattel mortgage. The court held that a new lease was created by the rent reduction even though no new written agreement was executed. The original lease would have primed the chattel mortgage, but the continuity of the lessor's privilege was broken when the new lease became effective; therefore, the chattel mortgage prevailed. In Thigpen, supra, after the lessee had stayed on the premises on a month-to-month basis after expiration of the lease's three year term, a new lease was executed for the same rental and same duration. A chattel mortgage recorded during the period the first lease was in operation was held to prime the lessor's lien acquired under the new lease.

¶18 In Easterling v. Brooks, 28 So.2d 523 (La.App.2d Cir. 1946), plaintiff, on December 1, 1943, leased to defendant twenty acres for two years. Brooks used a truck in the farming operation, and mortgaged it to Walling on March 3, 1944, during the first term of the lease. Although part of the rent under the first lease was not paid, a new (oral) lease was agreed on by plaintiff and defendant. Another lease was made for the main dwelling, which had been excepted from the original lease. The court held that the landlord's privilege arising from the original lease primed the chattel mortgage, but that the privilege of the mortgage primed the landlord's lien arising under the leases made after the recordation of the chattel mortgage.

¶19 In McGuffin v. Barkett, 44 So.2d 195 (La.App.2d Cir. 1950), the tenant mortgaged movables during a month-to-month lease. Later the rent was raised, and then reduced. The court held that the continuity of the lease ceased when the rent was changed, and the chattel mortgage primed the subsequently arising lessor's lien.

¶20 The jurisprudence is uniform that the lessor's privilege depends on the existence of the lease. There is no landlord-tenant relationship without the lease. As observed by Dr. Dainow above, the earliest time that the lessor's privilege can effect movables is that time when the lease is in effect and the movables are on the premises. The lease in effect when Foreman defaulted was for a term beginning January 1, 1975. The bank's chattel mortgage was recorded October 3, 1974, and therefore primed the lessor's privilege.

For these reasons, the judgment of the Court of Appeal is affirmed, at relator's cost.

CALOGERO, J., dissents for the reasons assigned by the dissenting judge in the Court of Appeal.

Would the following case be decided the same way under the current Civil Code? What article or articles would apply? Why?

WILLIAMS V. HILL, HARRIS & CO. 1939
190 SO. 157 (LA. APP. 2D CIR.)

DREW, Judge.

¶1 The lower court in a well written opinion has correctly set forth the issues of this case and found the facts and arrived at the proper legal conclusion. The opinion is as follows:

"This is a suit for damages arising out of an alleged illegal provisional seizure. The aggregate amount sued for is $1652.50, itemized as follows:

1. For embarrassment, humiliation and mental pain and suffering	$ 500.00
2. For inconvenience and physical discomfort sustained by plaintiff and his family	500.00
3. For injuries and damage to petitioner's credit	500.00
4. Storage and drayage	2.50
5. Attorney's fees	150.00
Total	$1652.50

The defendant had leased one of its dwelling houses in the City of Alexandria to a Mrs. G. O. Lowell, said dwelling consisting of some five bedrooms and located at Texas Avenue and Harris Street, said City. Plaintiff alleges that he had subleased from Mrs. Lowell one of the rooms in said dwelling at a monthly rental of $8.00, payable in semi-monthly sums of $4.00 each in advance, and that he owed no rent at the time. Hill, Harris & Company, Inc., provisionally seized plaintiff's property along with the property of Mrs. Lowell in satisfaction for rent due by Mrs. Lowell.

Mrs. Lowell having become delinquent in her rent payments, defendant Company, on May 19, 1938, seized the following property belonging to plaintiff and located within the room occupied by him and his family under said sub-lease from Mrs. Lowell, to-wit: 1 vanity dresser; 1 Philco radio; 1 2-piece living room suite, composed of couch and chair; 1 large congoleum rug, and 1 ice box. It is alleged that the couch seized was being used by him and his family as their bed on which they slept. It is alleged that plaintiff's rent being paid in advance on May 6, 1938, up to May 21, 1938, the defendant company had no right to seize his said property in payment of a rent claim against Mrs. Lowell.

Said seizure was made in plaintiff's absence at work, and that his wife was present and vehemently protested against the seizure, but without avail; that his said property was removed from the premises on the same day it was seized, and when plaintiff arrived from his work he found his wife out on the street completely distraught and in a state of hysteria.

Plaintiff alleges that it was late in the day, and it was with great difficulty that he finally arranged for another house near by which he and his wife and child had to occupy by sleeping on the floor which was quite filthy and badly infested with mosquitoes; that it was not until late next day that he was able to secure another house to move to and it was not until the 25th of the month (May) that he was able to secure the release of his said seized furniture from defendant and moved to the house he had secured from another party, and then had to pay $2.50 drayage charges to have it moved from the storage where defendant had had it moved to, to be kept in custody, or rather that said furniture had been so moved and stored by Mr. Blalock, the City Marshal, in the execution of the writ of provisional seizure. Plaintiff also alleges that he was compelled to secure the service of an attorney in order to get his furniture released. He also alleges that as a result of the seizure of his furniture, his credit was greatly impaired.

Defendant filed exceptions of no cause or right of action along with its answer of general denial, and at the suggestion of its counsel, the exceptions were referred to the merits.

Trial of the case was proceeded with to the point where it developed that plaintiff had secured from Mrs. Lowell one of the rooms in the dwelling house which the latter had under lease from defendant company, said one single room not constituting an apartment, nor was the dwelling as a whole an apartment house. All of the rooms appeared to have a common entrance from the outside and the same used by all the occupants in common. At this point the defendant urged its exceptions on the ground that since the building did not appear to be an apartment house there could be no relationship of lessee and sublessee between the plaintiff and Mrs. Lowell, but that plaintiff should be deemed as merely a roomer in the building, and that under the law the property of a roomer in a leased dwelling is subject to the rent of the lessee of such building. After considering the law as applied to the circumstances in this case, the court overruled the exceptions for the reason that it appeared from the evidence that plaintiff and his family had full control over the particular room occupied by them, to the exclusion of any supervision or control thereof by Mrs. Lowell, and in such cases it appears to be the law that the relation of lessee and sublessee exists. See Pembrook v. Goldman, La.App., 176 So. 888; and Revised Civil Code, art. 2692.

While there is some dispute as to whether plaintiff had in fact paid his rent in advance to Mrs. Lowell for the room in question, taking the testimony as a whole on that point, the court thinks that it fairly preponderates in favor of plaintiff. The court will, therefore, conclude that plaintiff had, in fact, paid on May 6, 1938, the sum of $4.00 to Mrs. Lowell as rent to cover the period of two weeks in advance, which would extend to the 21st of the month.

Under the provisions of article 2706 of the Civil Code, the lessor's right of pledge extends to the property of the under-tenant only when the latter is indebted unto the tenant for rent at the time when the lessor chooses to exercise his right. Under the evidence, therefore, Hill, Harris & Co., Inc., had no such right of pledge on the 19th day of May upon plaintiff's property on the leased premises, and the seizure was, in the opinion of the court, illegal.

Article 295 of the Code of Practice plainly states that a privilege holder shall be personally responsible for all damages suffered by the defendant in provisional seizure, should the seizure have been wrongfully obtained. The defendant in the present case makes some contention that plaintiff did not notify defendant, nor the Marshal making the seizure, that his rent was paid up in advance. Mr. Harris, President of the defendant company, testified that he came to the premises late the afternoon of the day the seizure was made and was present when the Marshal made the seizure; that, while he did not go into the house, Mrs. Williams, plaintiff's wife, came to the front and talked with him, and that she did not say anything about the rent having been paid. Mr. Blalock, the Marshal, testified that while he was back in the room he heard a conversation between Mrs. Williams and Mrs. Lowell who was present, concerning rent and heard Mrs. Lowell state that she could furnish a receipt, but that he did not understand from the conversation that any rent had been paid, or else he would not have seized the plaintiff's property. Mrs. Williams and Mrs. Lowell both testified that Mrs. Williams did tell Mr. Blalock that the rent had been paid; that a semimonthly rent of $4.00 was paid on May 6th to cover rental from that date until May 21st. Mrs. Lowell testified that she wrote out a receipt for the $4.00 on the 6th and gave it to Mrs. Williams. Mrs. Williams testified that her husband gave her the $4.00 to pay the rent in advance, and that she gave Mrs. Lowell the money, and received the receipt and that she gave the receipt to her husband, who had it in his pocket where he was at work at the Arkansas Oak Flooring Company on the day of the seizure.

Mr. Williams testified to the same thing regarding his giving the money to his wife with which to pay the rent, about her paying it and giving him the receipt and his having it in his pocket while absent from home at work on that day. The receipt was produced in court, identified by Mrs. Lowell and by Mr. and Mrs. Williams, and filed in evidence.

Mr. J. A. Ingstrum, apparently a disinterested witness testified that he was present when Dr. Blalock was making the seizure, and that he heard Mrs. Williams tell Mr. Blalock that she had paid the rent but that she did not have a receipt. This witness also testified that he heard Mrs. Williams tell Mr. Blalock that the furniture in that particular room belonged to her and her husband.

Taking the testimony as a whole on this point, it appears to the court that it fairly preponderates in favor of the plaintiff on the question of notice to the Marshal of payment of rent in advance and ownership of the property. Besides, in Macias v. Lorio, Sheriff, 41 La.Ann. 300, 6 So. 538, the court held that the sheriff in making a seizure of the property, must know that the property belongs to the defendant in execution, and the defendant is not bound, on being notified thereof, to give any notice to the Sheriff,--citing a number of authorities for so holding.

In suits for damages for illegal seizure, the amount that is recoverable under the law is actual pecuniary loss sustained, plus expenses incurred. Burglass v. Sheperd, La.App., 144 So. 67.

* * *

For the reasons assigned, there will be judgment in favor of plaintiff in the sum of $302.50, with legal interest from judicial demand and all costs; and the demands in other respects will be denied.

REVIEW NOTES

Lessor's Rights and Obligations

The lessor has four obligations under a lease:

1. To deliver the thing to the lessee;
2. To maintain the thing in a condition suitable for the purpose of which it was leased;
3. To warrant the thing against vices and defects, and
4. To protect the lessee's peaceful possession for the duration of the lease.

With these obligations, the lessor has certain rights: he has a right to the rent, and a privilege to seize the lessee's property if rent is not paid or alternatively to evict the lessee, and he has a right to repair the thing if necessary to maintain it.

Section 1: The Lessor's Obligation to Deliver – the extent of the premises rules apply, just as they do in sales

Section 2: Lessor's Obligation to maintain and repair

The lessor is obligated to maintain the thing in a condition suitable for the purpose for which it is leased. If the thing needs to be repaired, the lessee must let the lessor repair it, even if it inconveniences the lessee for a period of time. This does not include modifying the thing, nor does it include repairs necessitated by the lessee's fault (the lessee is responsible for those). If the lessor fails to make necessary repairs within a reasonable time after notice, the lessee has a right to have those repairs made at a reasonable price and then either demand immediate reimbursement or deduct that amount from the rent. (Articles 2691-2694).

If the repairs necessitate that the lessee not have use of the thing for a period of time, either rent may be abated, or depending on the length of time, the lease may be dissolved.

Example: Pontalba v. Domingon

Plaintiff leased a house to the defendants for ten years. Repairs being necessary, defendants decided to give the key to the workmen and leave the house pending their completion, rent was suspended during that time.. Once they were completed, plaintiff demanded that defendant return to the house, defendant refused. The court essentially finds that the lease was not dissolved, but returns the case to the trial court to determine the length of time rent should have been abated.

Marin v. Exxon

Complicated oil and gas lease over the course of some 30 years, lessees severely damaged the land with various pollutants. Lessors, who were sugarcane farmers, noticed that growth was affected near former pit sites. Louisiana Department of Natural Resources ordered abatement in 1986, Exxon did some remdiation to standards, and the plaintiffs entered into a new lease agreement, Exxon compensated the plaintiffs for the loss of sugarcane..

Then in 2003, Lessors filed a new suit asserting more claims for remediation, producing evidence of extensive contamination of soil and groundwater – Exxon knew as early as the 1930s that it was damaging the land, but continued the same practices of using unlined earthen pits. The trial court found that Exxon had continuously and unreasonably contaminated the plaintiffs land, that contra non valentem tolled prescription until 2003, when plaintiffs received an expert report delineating the scope and magnitude of the damage and awarding the plaintiffs $15 million in compensatory damages. The Supreme Court granted Cert. (Contra non valentem tolls prescription where there are exceptional circumstances preventing the plaintiffs from filing suit)

The Supreme Court held that contra non valentem does not apply because the plaintiffs were well aware of the continuing pollution in 1991, and aware that Exxon's attempts to remediate had been unsuccessful, but still did not file suit until 2003.

A mineral lessee is bound to perform the contract in good faith and develop and operate the property as a reasonably prudent operator for both parties' mutual benefit. The Civil Code lease provisions require the lessee to perform restoration obligations during the lease term, and Art 2683 also requires the lessee to pay rent, use the thing as a prudent administrator in accord with the purpose for which it was leased, and return it in the same condition but for normal wear and tear. Lessor need not wait until the end of the lease if the lessee is damaging his property. So, because one lease as novate was still in effect at the time of trial, one plaintiff's claim is still live, but the Breaux' claim is not because the lease was no longer in effect and was not in effect when the suit was filed.

Section 3: Lessor's Implied Warranty against Vices and Defects

Article 2696 provides that the lessor warrants that the thing is suitable for the purpose and free of vices or defects that prevent its use for the purpose.

Great American Surplus Lines v. Bass

Plaintiffs Caribbean Pools (and their insurer, GAS) are suing their lessor for damage to their business from a fire. They leased the building from defendants to use in building swimming pools, and shortly thereafter had problems with the electrical system. The lease provided that the lessor would maintain the structural soundness of the building, but the less would maintain the interior – including electrical wiring. However, Caribbean Pools was successful, and kept drawing more electricity, and it kept shorting out. So, they contacted the lessee, who sent an (unlicensed) electrician who installed a new line. Shortly thereafter, the building burned down due to an electrical short. Caribbean Pools' business was destroyed, and they claim it was due to defendant's negligent repair.

Question: Why, if lessee had assumed responsibility for the electricity, did the court hold lessor liable?

The decision was in 1986, would the result be the same – is the owner-lessor still 'strictly liable' for injuries sustained by a tenant through defective condition of the premises? (See art. 2004, limitations on liability, 2322, ruin of a building, La. Rev. Stat 9:3221).

9:3221: Notwithstanding the provisions of Civil Code art 2699, the owner of premises leased under a contract whereby the lessee assumes responsibility for their condition is not liable for injury caused by any defect therein to the lessee or anyone on the premises who derives his right to be thereon from the lessee, unless the owner knew or should have known of the defect, or had received notice thereof and failed to remedy it within a reasonable time.

Civil Code art 2322: The owner of a building is answerable for the damage occasioned by its ruin, when this is caused by neglect to repair it, or when it is the result of a vice or defect in its original construction. However, he is answerable for damages only upon a showing that he knew or, in the exercise of reasonable care, should have known of the vice of defect which caused the damage, that the damage could have been prevented by the exercise of reasonable car, and that he failed to exercise such reasonable care.

Tassin v. Slidell Mini-Storage:

Ministorage leaked, damaging Lessee's property. The contract between the parties explicitly provided that the Mini-Storage would not be responsible for any loss caused by water.

Is it? Why or why not?

Stuckey v. Riverstone Residential

Again, the lease explicitly recommended that Resident secure renters' insurance, and that lessor would not be liable for loss unless it was 'caused exclusively by owner's negligence." It also warned that mold is a part of Louisiana, that the lessor does the best it can to ventilate and dehumidify, and that the lessee should do so – management is not responsible for any injury, illness, harm of damage to any person or property caused by, or arising from mold.

A mother and daughter claimed that there was a leak in an upstairs bathroom and that black stuff was accumulating on the AC vents. She eventually brought suit.

Did she win? Why or why not? Does special law apply?

Section 4: The lessor's warranty of Peaceful Possession

The lessee warrants that the thing is not defective, art 2696, 2697. Art 2700 provides protection against disturbance by a third party – but not all third parties. Which?

Keenan v. Flannigan

Lessee wants to dissolve the lease because the tenant in another apartment plays the Victrola and has loud parties often in the middle of the night.

Can he do so?

Section 5: Lessor's Remedies

Art 2704: The lessor can dissolve the lease if the lessee fails to pay rent and may then regain possession of the premises.

He can seize the lessee's movables under his lessor's privilege

Or he can demand that the lessee pay rent

However, there is one thing he cannot do, as exemplified in the following case:

Henry Rose Mercantile v. Stearns

Lessee failed to pay rent on two warehouses, and lessor sued him for rent past due, for accelerated rent, and for recognition of its lessor's privilege on the lessee's movable property. It also, to prevent lessee from taking those movables, padlocked the warehouses against him.

What problem does lessor have now, according to the court? (Rent or eviction, not both)

Comment – an example of an acceleration clause

Weil v. Segura

Lessee leased a gas station with three rooms and a paint shop in New Orleans. He went into possession, but within one month refused to pay the next months rent. Lessor filed suit, asking for recovery of the rent for the unexpired term of the lease. Lessee admitted the lease, but claims he dissolved the lease because he had not received the full extent of what he had been promised – that the paint shop was occupied by another tenant.

So, why is the lessee held liable for abandoning the premises?

How much rent must he pay? Why is the amount reduced from the rest of the length of the lease?

Is it important that the lessor does not own the premises?

Acadiana Bank v. Foreman

The Formans leased a building toperate as a Frostop in Eunice from Moosa. After signing a lease, they executed a chattel mortgage for the restaurant equipment with Acadiana Bank. Thee lease was recorded on September 20, 1974, the chattel mortgage on October 3, 1974.

Apparently, they had both financial and marital difficulties. They divorced in 1975, and Mr. Foreman took over the restaurant and its debts. When he did not pay on the chattel mortgage, the bank proceeded to foreclose, and Moosa intervened, exerting his lessor's privilege.

Who wins? And why? (Novation of the lease)

Williams v. Hill, Harris & Co.

Defendant leased a home to Lowell in Alexandria. Plaintiff subleased one of the rooms in the 5-bedroom home for himself and his wife, and paid his rent to the lessee promptly. Unfortunately, lessee was behind in her rent, and the landlord had plaintiff's movables seized – leaving wife "completely distraught and in a state of hysteria."

Was the lessor's privilege properly executed against sublessee's property? Which Civil Code Article applies? (See Articles 2708-2709)

Hypothetical (written by Brianna Golden)

Bobby Boudreau of Boudreau Bayou Tours is running the risk of closing its doors because people aren't that interested in Bayou tours anymore. Since he is losing money, he decided to lease part of the bayou that he owns to a crawfish farmer. Chris Crawdaddy, a career crawfisher, hears about Boudreau's offer and contacts him. Both parties signed and executed a 3-year lease agreement which enables Chris to farm on the northern portion of the bayou. In return, Chris must pay Bobby $1,000.00 monthly rent or 1% of his gross, whichever is more. For Chris's convenience, Bobby marked off the northern portion with bright yellow stakes. The lease agreement made no mention of the possibility of alligators inhabiting the area. One alligator, "Carl Mauldin" (named after an actor with a big bump on his nose) in Boudreau's Bayou is considered a family pet, and Bobby regularly feeds him marshmallows, so he's not afraid of humans. Bobby orally told Chris he shouldn't run into any problems out there, but if he did to "holler at him." For the first few months everything was peaceful and Chris both enjoyed the beautiful bayou and caught plenty of crawfish.

Eighteen months into the lease, Chris was trying to empty one of his crawfish traps when Carl Mauldin came from out of nowhere and bit two of Chris's fingers off. After leaving the emergency room, he was livid and decided to confront Bobby about his pet alligator. Bobby refused to chain up his Carl because the Bayou is his home and he needs to be able to hunt and feed himself. Visibly upset, Chris storms out and leaves. He does not remove his traps which have already accumulated a lot of crawfish. Chris refuses to pay Bobby any more rent and was in fact two months behind when he left. In return, Bobby fenced off the access road so Chris could not return, refused to return Chris' traps and in fact ate the crawfish that were in the traps, and demanded that Bobby pay the rent for the entire 18 months left on the lease because, although he tried to find another lessee, he was unable to do so. Bobby also sold Chris's pirogue and kept the proceeds.

Does Chris have a cause of action? Is he required to pay Bobby both past and future?

Under what rights, if any, did Bobby have to sell Chris's belongings?

CHAPTER 15

THE LESSEE'S RIGHTS AND OBLIGATIONS

Flowcharts

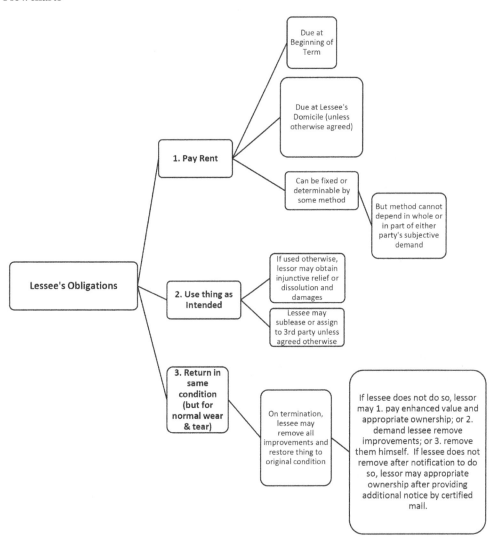

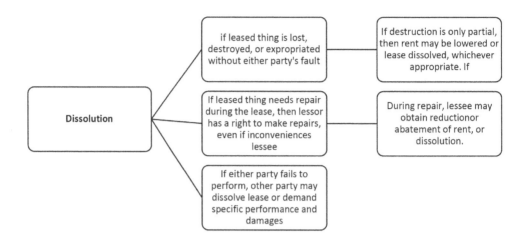

	if leased thing is lost, destroyed, or expropriated without either party's fault	—	If destruction is only partial, then rent may be lowered or lease dissolved, whichever appropriate. If
Dissolution	If leased thing needs repair during the lease, then lessor has a right to make repairs, even if inconveniences lessee	—	During repair, lessee may obtain reductionor abatement of rent, or dissolution.
	If either party fails to perform, other party may dissolve lease or demand specific performance and damages		

Introduction

Read Articles 2686-2689, 2692, 2694, 2703-2706

The lessee has only three obligations: to pay the rent, to use the thing as intended or contemplated in the lease, and to return it in the same condition at the end of the lease (but for normal wear and tear), as delineated in Article 2683. We have previously seen instances demonstrating the lessee's liability for damages caused by his fault (Maron v. Exxon), and need not discuss it further. We have also discussed the lessor's remedies when the lessee fails to pay the rent, though not when rent is due. In addition to discussing when rent is due, this Chapter will also discuss the lessee's obligation to use the leased thing as intended, how he can sublease the property, his right to dissolve the lease when the lessor cannot or will not fulfill his obligations, and what happens to the lessee's improvements and additions upon termination of the lease.

Section 1: Obligation to Pay Rent

Unless the parties agree otherwise, under Civil Code article 2703, rent is due at the beginning of the term. If rent is payable in intervals shorter than the term of the lease, then rent is due at the beginning of each interval. Thus, if your lease does not indicate when your monthly rent is due, it's still due at the beginning of each rental period. Furthermore, rent is payable (normally) at the address provided by the lessor. If none is provided, then it is payable at the lessee's address. As discussed in Chapter 13, if the lessee fails to pay the rent, then under Civil Code Article 2704, the lessor may dissolve the lease and regain possession. Rent is not always a fixed amount of money, nor is it always money. For example, in some commercial leases, rent includes a percentage of gross sales as well as a stipulated minimum monthly rent. With an agricultural lease, often rent is calculated as a certain percentage of the crop – this is called "sharecropping," and despite what you may have read in novels, is not a derogatory term. As we saw in Losecco, crops can fail. If the crop is lost and that loss is not caused by the fault of either party, then under Article 2706, the loss is borne by both parties in accordance with their respective shares. In the absence of a contrary agreement, an agricultural lessee may not claim an abatement of the rent for the loss of his unharvested crops unless the loss was due to an unforeseeable and extraordinary event that destroyed at lease one-half of the value of his crops. Any compensation he receives in connection with the loss such as insurance proceeds or government subsidies is taken into account in determining the amount of abatement.

Study Questions:

If the following case were decided today, how would Article 2703 apply? Would the result be any different?

EDWARDS V. STANDARD OIL CO. 1932
175 LA 720, 144 SO. 430

ST. PAUL, J.

¶1   [Plaintiff lessor claims that he leased a filling station in Ponchatoula to defendant lessee for two years. The monthly rent was one cent per gallon of gasoline or oil sold and was payable on the 15th day of the next month following the sale. He claims that the rent due January 15, 1931 rent was not paid until the 21st of the month and that for that reason he asks the court to order that the defendant be evicted.]

¶2   The lease does not set forth where the rent is to be paid; and the petition does not allege, but on the contrary inferentially negatives that any demand for payment was ever made on defendant. And the fact is that a check for the amount of the rent was mailed by defendant to its agent at Ponchatoula on July 10th; but, owing to some oversight, or perhaps some fault in mail deliveries, it did not reach plaintiff until July 21st, as aforesaid.

¶3   The district court gave judgment for plaintiff as prayed for; and the Court of Appeal affirmed the judgment. 141 So. 513.

¶4   Article 2712, Rev. Civ. Code, declares that 'The lessee may be expelled from the property if he fails to pay the rent when it becomes due.'

* * *

¶5 And article 2157, Rev. Civ. Code, provides, that 'The payment must be made in the place specified in the agreement. If the place be not thus specified, the payment, in case of a certain and determinate substance, must be made in the place where was, at the time of the agreement, the thing which is the object of it. These two cases excepted, the payment must be made at the dwelling of the debtor.'

¶6 Hence, it is a rule that, 'where the lease is silent as to where the rent shall be paid, the payment is to be made either at the leased premises or at the domicile of the debtor, and this presupposes, of course, that the lessor is to call for his rent.' Saxton v. Para Rubber Co., 166 La. 308, 117 So. 235, 237. So that, 'where . . . there is no specification in the lease as to the place where the rent should be paid, the law prescribes that 'payment must be made at the dwelling of the debtor.' . . . R. C. C., 2157 [hence]. By formally tendering the rent after maturity, but prior to default and to the filing of this action, the defendant effectively stripped the landlord of his right to cancel the lease on the ground alleged.' Lafayette Realty Co. v. Joseph Puglia, 10 Orleans App. 105.

¶7 Moreover, where 'defendant was offered its money, and could have had it before it even brought suit to annul the contract [lease],' he cannot annul the lease for alleged nonpayment of the rent. 'Our law does not contemplate that contracts shall be annulled by one party, where the other is able and willing to perform his own part of it as soon as demanded of him.' Hemsing v. Wiener-Loeb Grocery Co., 157 La. 189, 102 So. 303, 304.

¶8 Hence, although 'it is true that ordinarily a lessor may dissolve a lease for failure on the part of the lessee to pay the rent promptly when due, [nevertheless] the right to dissolve a lease is subject to judicial control according to circumstances." Brewer v. Forest Gravel Co., 172 La. 828, 135 So. 372, 373, citing, Sieward v. Dencechaud, 120 La. 720, 45 So. 561; Prude v. Morris, 38 La. Ann. 767, 769. See, also, Saxton v. Para Rubber Co., 166 La. 866, 118 So. 64; Schnaider v. Graffagnini, 154 La. 363, 97 So. 491; Bonnabel v. Metairie Cypress Co., 129 La. 928, 57 So. 271; Standard Brewing Co. v. Anderson, 121 La. 935, 46 So. 926, 15 Ann. Cas. 251.

Decree.

¶9 For the reasons assigned, the judgment of the district court, and that of the Court of Appeal affirming the same, are reversed and set aside, and it is now ordered that the demand of the plaintiff be rejected at his cost in all courts.

Study Questions:

What kind of rent is at issue in the following case? What standard is used to determine whether the lessee breached a percentage lease? What duty of the lessee is at issue here and what current Civil Code article sets forth that duty (Hint: read Article 2686).

QUALITY MFG. CO., INC. V. DIRECT FACTORY STORES, INC. 1989
540 SO.2D 419 (LA. APP. 1ST CIR.)

CRAIN, Judge.

¶1   This is an appeal of a judgment granting rent payments between lessee-lessor in accordance with the lease agreement.

FACTS

¶2   In February, 1981, Quality Manufacturing Company (Quality) leased space in its clothing factory by oral agreement to Direct Factory Stores (Direct) to operate a clothing outlet. The agreement provided for ten percent of the net sales as rent. This agreement was later reduced to writing and supplemented by a guarantee by Direct that net sales would exceed $20,000 per month or, in effect, that rent would be a guaranteed minimum of $2,000 per month. Direct sold various brands of clothing but the mainstay of its business was "Sans Souci", manufactured on site by Quality. In the spring of 1982 the on site manufacturing of the Sans Souci line was shut down by Quality. In August of 1982, Direct opened a new retail outlet near the present one. Direct shifted all of its first-run business to the new store and sold second-quality goods at the original store. After opening the new store, sales at the old store decreased and rental payments were substantially less than those of the prior year. Direct tendered payments of 10% of the net sales for those months exceeding $20,000 and the minimum rental payment of $2,000 for those months that did not. Quality refused to accept the tendered payments. Quality filed a suit for the month of August, 1982, and supplemental amendments and suits for rental through August 1983. These suits were consolidated.

¶3   The trial court held that Quality was only entitled to receive either the base rental of $2,000 per month or ten percent of net sales of the defendant in excess of $20,000. The court further awarded no interest on these rental payments if a replacement check was tendered by Direct within ten days of the judgment.

¶4   Quality appeals the decision of the trial court. The issues for review are whether Direct breached its implied obligation of good faith performance to conduct its operations for the mutual benefit of the parties by transferring the first quality business to another location; whether the provision in the lease agreement providing for a minimum base rental in a percentage rental lease abrogates a lessee's implied obligation to conduct its operations for the mutual benefit of the parties; whether the trial court erred in failing to award interest on the tendered payments.

BREACH OF THE LEASE

¶5   The trial court found that there was no written obligation in the lease agreement that would restrict the defendants operation or change of operations. The court did not find a breach of the implied obligation of good faith performance.

¶6   La.C.C. art. 2710 states: "The lessee is bound: 1) To enjoy the thing leased as a good administrator, according to the use for which it was intended by the lease. 2) To pay the rent at the terms agreed on."

¶7   "In his occupancy of the property the tenant is obligated not to use the premises for a purpose inconsistent with that contemplated by the parties at the time they confected the lease." Tullier v. Tanson Enterprises, Inc., 367 So.2d 773, 776 (La.1979).

¶8   The lease agreement provides that the lessee is to use the leased premises "for the purpose of operating a retail business". There was no evidence of any other agreement or requirements as to use or the anticipated use of the premises. The trial court refused to admit parol evidence regarding the purpose of the lease. This ruling was not objected to or assigned as error and is not before us.

¶9   The crux of the appellant's argument is that the implied obligation of good faith performance imposed on all contracts by La.C.C. art. 2710 created a duty on the part of Direct to maintain a first quality clothing outlet at the leased premises. The trial court found an absence of evidence to prove this allegation. The only evidence of the parties intentions regarding the leased premises in the record is the lease agreement.

¶10   As stated by the Louisiana Supreme Court in Tullier:

> Accordingly, where the lease is silent as to the intended use of the premises, we hold that the
> circumstances must clearly show that the parties intended only a certain use of the property in

order for such use to be deemed the exclusively 'intended' use within the meaning of Articles 2710 and 2711. Evidence of the contemplated initial use is relevant in this regard, but it is not decisive. Where the silent lease and the surrounding circumstances are ambiguous concerning intended use, this ambiguity must be resolved in favor of the lessee. 367 So.2d at 779.

¶11   The lease agreement is silent as to the intended use of the leased premises other than "operating a retail business". There is no evidence that the parties agreed otherwise. These parties were sophisticated businessmen. Had they intended to restrict the use of the leased premises it would have been an easy matter to incorporate a provision to this effect in the lease agreement. The lack of evidence showing otherwise requires that we resolve this matter in favor of the lessee. In addition, Direct was injured when the San Souci line of clothing was no longer manufactured at the premises. Direct had insisted that a window be installed between the outlet and the work area so that customers could see the production process. It would be inequitable to allow recovery by the lessor in these circumstances. This assignment lacks merit.

¶12   Having found that the lessee in this case did not have an implied obligation to maintain a first-quality clothing outlet we need not consider the effect of the base rental provision on the implied obligation of good faith performance imposed by La.C.C. art. 2710.

INTEREST

¶13   The appellant next argues that it was error for the trial court to fail to award interest on the award of the tendered rent payments.

¶14   Direct tendered payment, in the form of a check, for the minimum rentals for those months in which net sales were less than $20,000 and checks for 10% of the net sales for those months in which net sales exceeded $20,000. Quality refused to accept these payments.

¶15   The trial court's judgment awarded interest if the award was not paid within ten days from date of judgment. Quality alleges that interest should have been awarded from the date the monthly payments were due or, at the least, the date of judicial demand.

¶16   La.C.C. art. 2000 states in part:

> When the object of the performance is a sum of money, damages for delay in performance are measured by the interest on that sum from the time it is due, at the rate agreed by the parties or, in the absence of agreement, at the rate of legal interest as fixed by article 2924.

(Emphasis supplied)

¶17   The parties agreed that rent was due on the tenth day of each month.

¶18   However, La.C.C. art. 1869 states:

> When the object of the performance is the delivery of a thing or a sum of money and the obligee, without justification, fails to accept the performance tendered by the obligor, the tender, followed by deposit to the order of the court, produces all the effects of a performance from the time the tender was made if declared valid by the court.
>
> A valid tender is an offer to perform according to the nature of the obligation.

(Emphasis supplied).

¶19   A formal tender is not required where it would be of no avail. Louisiana Highway Commission v. Bullis, 197 La. 14, 200 So. 805 (1941).

¶20   Quality refused to accept the rental payments because of a dispute in the amount tendered. It would have been useless for Direct to tender the same payment in cash. Consequently, we find that formal tender was not required. This produced the liberative effect of relieving Direct of the obligation of paying interest from the due date of the rental payments. However, Direct did not follow La.C.C. art. 1869 and deposit the tendered payments in the registry of the court. A tender must be followed by deposit in order to produce total liberative effects. Pichauffe v. Naquin, 241 So.2d 574 (La.App. 1st Cir.1970). Therefore, it was error on the part of the trial court to fail to grant interest on the amount awarded from judicial demand.

¶21   We reverse the judgment of the trial court insofar as it grants interest from the date of judgment and grant interest on the amount awarded from the date of judicial demand.

¶22   All costs of this appeal are assessed against the appellant.

AFFIRMED IN PART, REVERSED IN PART AND RENDERED.

Lagniappe Question:

What general obligations principles are at issue in this case, in addition to the lease-specific issues? (Hint: Review Civil Code Articles 1759 and 1869-1872.)

Section 2: Obligation to Use as Intended or Contemplated

Article 2686 states that "[i]f the lessee uses the thing for a purpose other than that for which it was leased or in a manner that may cause damage to the thing, the lessor may obtain injunctive relief, dissolution of the lease, and any damages he may have sustained. While the Quality Manufacturing opinion discussed misuse, the court found that there was no misuse under the facts of the case. However, the following cases demonstrate instances when a lessee misuses the thing lease.

Study Questions:

What misuse of the property is at issue in the following case?

Would it be decided the same way under current Article 2686?

What conundrum faces both the plaintiff and the defendant in the following case because of the court's decision to enforce the permanent injunction but not to dissolve the lease?

NEW ORLEANS & CARROLLTON RY. V. DARMS 1887
39 LA. ANN. 766, 2 SO. 230

FENNER, J.

¶1 This action invokes the remedy of injunction to prevent the improper use of property leased by plaintiff to defendant, and seeks to annul the lease on the ground of such improper use. The use complained of is the establishment of a bar-room or coffee-house and a gaming-house. The evidence clearly establishes that, some months after taking possession of the leased premises, the defendant did fit up and open a public bar-room for the sale of spirituous drinks, with a room attached, provided with card-tables, where visitors played cards for drinks.

¶2 Article 2710 Civil Code provides: 'The lessee is bound- First, to enjoy the thing leased, as a good administrator, according to the use for which it was intended by the lease; second, to pay the rents at the terms agreed on.' It is not necessary that the use according to which the thing is to be enjoyed should be expressed in the lease; nor does it follow, if the lease is silent as to the use, that the lessee may make of the thing leased any use which he pleases. On the contrary, this court used the following language in a case of this sort: 'The lease is silent as to the destination or object to which the building was to be affected. The inference is that the parties intended that it should be used for one of the purposes to which it had previously been put, etc.; the question of determination to be determined according to surrounding circumstances.'

Murrell v. Jackson, 33 La. Ann. 1342. In an earlier case the court said: 'The evidence establishes that the plaintiff's right of action was well founded; that the store rented to defendant was never intended by plaintiff to be used as a kitchen; that no such use was in contemplation at the time the lease was contracted,' etc. Caffin v. Scott, 7 Rob. (La.) 205.

¶3 We quote these decisions to show that, notwithstanding some difference between the language of our article and that of the corresponding article of the French Code, 1729, they have been construed as substantially identical in meaning, and hence that the French authorities are fully applicable. Those authorities are quite unanimous in support of the doctrine announced by Marcade in the following language: 'The destination of the thing will be sometimes fixed by the agreement; but often the contract will be silent in this respect; and it is then by the situation of the place, by the use to which the thing had been previously put, and by the character under which the lessee presents himself, that the destination shall be gathered. That destination, in whatever manner it shall appear, the lessee is bound to respect. Thus, not only shall the lessee, in default of an express stipulation, not be permitted to establish in a private dwelling a house of prostitution or gambling house, but he cannot transform a private apartment into a restaurant or coffee-house, a club, nor a private house into an inn or hotel.' 6 Marcade, 459; 3 Delvincourt, 192; 17 Duranton, No. 98; Duvergier Louage, No. 308; 25 Laurent, No. 257.

¶4 It is held that the establishment of a house of prostitution or of a gaminghouse would in no case be sustained, unless the lessor has positive knowledge that such was the use for which the lessee rented the premises. Duvergier, No. 402; Troplong, No. 302.

¶5 In a lease which authorized the lessee to sublease, 'a qui bon lui semblera ou lui plaira,' it was still held that he could not sublease to one who would use the thing in a manner contrary to its destination. Poth. Louage, No. 281; Troplong, Louage, No. 1276; Duvergier, Louage, No. 391.

¶6 Now, in the instant case, the evidence shows that the building leased was contiguous to the depot and stables of plaintiff, at the corner of Napoleon and St. Charles avenues, and was built to serve as a boarding-house and lodginghouse for drivers and other employees; that it had been used to some extent for that purpose, and had never been otherwise used, except, partially, as business offices; that plaintiff had received numerous offers to rent it as a bar-room and coffee-house, at much higher rent than was paid by defendant, but had always refused; that no bar-room or other place for sale of spirituous liquors had ever been permitted; that defendant, prior to the lease, had kept a private market not far from this place, in which business he had been engaged for many years, and that he had never kept a bar-room or coffee-house; that, when he applied to rent the place, he asked permission to open a private market there, which was at first refused, and only granted after discussion and intervention of friends; that for the first three months of the lease he used the house simply for the purpose of a private market, and for offices and lodgings, and that it was only after that time that he indicated his purpose of opening the bar-room; and finally that, as soon as plaintiff heard of such purpose, it promptly protested against and prohibited it.

¶7   The foregoing surrounding circumstances would be amply sufficient to establish that the opening of a bar-room in the house was contrary to 'the use for which it was intended by the lease.' But, in addition thereto, the plaintiff offers evidence to prove that, during the negotiations for the lease, defendant was expressly notified that under no circumstances would the selling of spirituous liquors be permitted on the premises. This evidence was rejected on the ground that parol evidence was inadmissible to contradict or vary a written contract.

¶8   We think the ruling was error, and that the evidence fell within the familiar exception to the general rule which admits parol, in order to ascertain the nature and qualities of the subject-matter of the contract, e. g., to identify or define the extent of the premises leased or sold, when not sufficiently described in the written contract, and the like. 1 Greenl. Ev. §§ 286, 298a; Sargent v. Adams, 3 Gray, 72; Falcon v. Boucherville, 1 Rob. (La.) 337; Moore v. Hampton, 3 La. Ann. 193; D'Aquin v. Barbour, 4 La. Ann. 411; Corbett v. Costello, 8 La. Ann. 427; McLeroy v. Duckworth, 13 La. Ann. 410.

¶9   In this case the use of the premises is the cause or consideration of the conduct; and we have shown that, in the silence of the contract as to the nature and kind of use contemplated between the parties, resort must be had to parol evidence of the surrounding circumstances to ascertain the intentions and define the rights of the parties. No circumstance could be of so much significance as the express notice given to the lessee that a certain use, foreign to the destination of the premises, would not be allowed. The evidence is found in the record, and although, perhaps, unnecessary to our decision, we may give it effect, and it confirms the conclusions arrived at.

¶10   2. Plaintiff claims a dissolution of the lease under article 2711 of the Code, which provides: 'If the lessee makes another use of the thing than that for which it was intended, and if any loss is thereby sustained by the lessor, the latter may obtain the dissolution of the lease.' In this case, the improper use was stopped by the injunction almost as soon as it had begun, and the lessor has suffered no loss. Under the similar article 1729 of the French Code it is held that the right to dissolution for this cause is not absolute, but is left to the discretion of the court according to the circumstances. Troplong, Louage, No. 316; Duvergier, Louage, No. 107.

¶11 We think in this case the right of plaintiff will be sufficiently vindicated by perpetuating the injunction, without dissolving the lease, which runs for five years. It is therefore ordered, adjudged, and decreed that the verdict and judgment appealed from be annulled and set aside; and that there be judgment in favor of plaintiff, and against defendant, perpetuating the injunction granted therein, and rejecting the reconventional demand of defendant; defendant to pay all costs in the lower court and of this appeal.

Hypothet and Discussion Questions:

Mr. Tolar granted a hunting and fishing lease to the Spillers family on rural property adjacent to the Ouachita River. The tract traverses Lapine Bayou at its intersection with the Ouachita River. Lapine Bayou is a large waterway as it feeds as a tributary into the river at the site.
The lease provided that:

> The parties further agree that in the event Lessee constructs any buildings and/or other improvements he, or his heirs, shall have the right to remove such buildings and/or improvements.
> Further that in the event this lease is terminated for any reason, then Lessee shall have 6 months from the date of written demand to remove such buildings and/or improvements, in default of which, such buildings and/or improvements shall become the property of the land owner.

Over several years, the Spillers did the following: used the property as a campground, moved two camping trailers onto the property (attaching one permanently), constructed a sewage treatment plant to handle the sewage from the trailers, piled trash around the encampment, placed a gate on the property, nailed "Posted" signs into numerous trees, placed water lines and light poles on the property, built a concrete boat ramp, pier, floating dock and a and burned trash.

Does Mr. Tolar have grounds for arguing that the lease should be terminated for misuse? If so, on what basis?

Consider the contractual interpretation principles set forth in Louisiana Civil Code art. 2045-2057 in reaching your answer.

(Hypothet based on Tolar v. Spillers,2 So.3d 560 (La. App. 2nd Cir 2009.)

Section 3: Subleases, Assignments, and Transfers by Lessor or Lessee

Read Articles 2642 and 2713.

Article 2642, which is a sale article, states that all rights may be assigned, unless they are strictly personal, and the assignee is thereby subrogated to the rights of the assignor against the debtor. Thus, it stipulates that any right can be sold, exchanged, or otherwise transferred to someone else. If it is transferred, then the transferee gets the same rights that the transferor had. Article 2713, like article 2642, addresses freedom of contract, but applies specifically in the context of a lease. It stipulates that the lessee has the right to sublease the leased thing or to assign or encumber his rights in the lease, unless expressly prohibited by the contract of lease. Moreover, any such prohibition will be strictly construed against the lessor.

CAPLAN V. LATTER & BLUM, INC. 1985
468 SO.2D 1188 (LA.)

WATSON, Justice.

¶1   In this dispute over commercial real estate, the issue is whether the plaintiff-lessor, Dr. Harry B. Caplan, unreasonably withheld his consent to a sublease by his lessee, Latter & Blum, Inc.

FACTS

¶2   The primary lease between Caplan and Latter was for a term of five years commencing January 15, 1981, and ending January 14, 1986, for a monthly rental of $1,973.48. The printed lease form states:

> "Lessee is not permitted to rent or sub-let or grant use or possession of the premises to any other party without the written consent of the Lessor, and then only in accordance with the terms of this lease. Should Lessee desire to sub-let, permission must be obtained in writing through Lessor or Agent and such sub-lease shall be handled by Lessor's agent at expense of the herein Lessee." (Tr. 4)

¶3   A typed insert in the printed form provides: "said consent shall not be unreasonably withheld." From the inception of the lease, the parties had understood that Latter would have about 500 square feet of extra space which it intended to sublease.

¶4   Latter subleased approximately 538 square feet to Health Care Associates, Inc., for a period of twelve months at a cost of $494 a month. Dr. Caplan signed a consent to the sublease on May 19, 1981. The printed form provided that: "the lessee under said primary lease shall not be released of the obligation to pay the rent due thereunder or any renewal or extension thereof or any other obligations of said lessee thereunder."

¶5   A letter to Dr. Caplan dated May 13, 1981, from the president of Latter confirmed a prior verbal agreement under which, if Latter entered into a sublease, one-half of the profits above the basic rent, plus utility charges, renovation costs, and a six percent real estate commission would be split with Dr. Caplan. The amount was calculated at $11.17 per square foot. The letter was termed a notification of Latter's intent to live-up to the " 'gentleman's agreement' or verbal agreement" made by Latter's agents.

¶6 Dr. Caplan did not require any financial information on Health Care Associates, Inc., but testified that he knew them by reputation. The differential between the Latter lease and the Health Care sublease was an insignificant amount.

¶7 In April of 1982, Latter attempted to sublease the remainder of the property leased from Caplan. An associate realtor with Latter, John E. Ellis, obtained a sublease agreement from Duke Advertising Agency, Inc., on April 13, 1982, using the standard Latter form signed by Health Care. It provided for a term of forty-three and a half months and rental of $1,873.33 per month. Duke gave a security deposit and a check for the first month's rent. Latter sent Dr. Caplan a letter with a copy of the sublease requesting Caplan's approval. In response, Dr. Caplan's attorney sent Latter a letter in which he declined to consent to the proposed sublease because: (1) Duke did not meet the financial criteria required for his tenants; (2) the improvements proposed by the sublessee, which included a sink, would increase water usage and expense; and (3) the lease was not in strict accordance with the terms of the primary lease because it called for a higher rental to be paid by the sublessee.

¶8 The parties engaged in further correspondence. Evidence of Duke's financial responsibility was provided and Latter was threatened with a damage suit by Duke if the sublease was not approved. Reimbursement was offered as to any increased water expense. Mrs. Duke testified that she then agreed to forget about the sink. It was stipulated that there was nothing in the sublease concerning a sink. Regarding Dr. Caplan's refusal to approve the sublease as arbitrary and unreasonable, Latter abandoned the leased premises and refused to pay further rent. Dr. Caplan filed suit for the accelerated balance due on the lease plus fifteen percent as liquidated damages under the contract.

¶9 The trial court decided that Latter was unjustified in abandoning the leased premises and gave Dr. Caplan judgment for the full amount of the lease plus fifteen percent as attorney's fees.

¶10 The court of appeal affirmed, concluding that the trial court was not clearly wrong in finding that Dr. Caplan was reasonable and prudent in refusing to consent to the sublease. 462 So.2d 229 (La.App. 5 Cir., 1984). A writ was granted to consider the matter. 462 So.2d 1255 (La., 1985).

LAW

¶11 LSA-C.C. art. 2725 provides:

> "The lessee has a right to underlease, or even to cede his lease to another person, unless this power has been expressly interdicted.
>
> "The interdiction may be for the whole, or for a part; and this clause is always construed strictly."

¶12 Illinois Cent. R. Co. v. International Harvester, 368 So.2d 1009 (La., 1979) held that the lessor did not impliedly consent to a sublease and ordered dissolution of the lease. However, there was good faith bargaining and no abuse of the lessor's right to withhold permission for the sublease. A lessor cannot unreasonably, arbitrarily, or capriciously withhold his consent to a sublease when subleasing is not prohibited or interdicted. Gamble v. New Orleans Housing Mart, Inc., 154 So.2d 625 (La.App. 4 Cir.1963), writ denied 244 La. 1027, 156 So.2d 229 (1963). Here, it was expressly stipulated that the lessor's consent could not be unreasonably withheld.

CONCLUSION

¶13 Dr. Caplan's excuses for declining to consent to the proposed sublease with Duke were not valid. First, Duke's financial status was immaterial because Latter would have remained bound for the rental. Next, the sink issue was not critical to the transaction, Mrs. Duke having agreed to forget about the sink. Finally, Dr. Caplan had already prepared for the possibility of a sublessee paying a higher rental in his negotiations with Latter. It is clear that Dr. Caplan unreasonably withheld his consent to the lease. Since none of the pretexts he advanced were sufficient grounds for a reasonably prudent business person to deny consent, the conclusion is that he "unreasonably withheld" consent and violated the terms of the lease.

¶14 LSA-C.C. art. 2725 provides that interdictions on the power to underlease are strictly construed. It does not follow that the right to underlease, as opposed to an interdiction, is also strictly construed. Gamble, supra. Like the lessor in the Illinois Central case, Dr. Caplan refused to consent to the sublease in order to negotiate a new lease with Latter on more favorable terms. However, Latter had guarded against that contingency by the insert in the printed lease form which prohibited Dr. Caplan from unreasonably withholding his consent to an underlease.

¶15 The trial court and the court of appeal were clearly wrong in finding that Dr. Caplan was justified in refusing to consent to the sublease.

DECREE

¶16 For the foregoing reasons, the judgment of the court of appeal is reversed; the judgment of the trial court is vacated and Dr. Caplan's suit is dismissed at his cost.

REVERSED; SUIT DISMISSED.

Comment:

As we have seen, the lessee has a right to transfer the lease (unless expressly prohibited). The lessor has a similar right: he can transfer the leased thing. However, the transfer of the leased thing does not terminate the lease, unless lease provides otherwise. Louisiana Civil Code art. 2711. Article 2674 provides that the lease of a thing that does not belong to the lessor may nevertheless be binding on the parties. Consequently, if the lessor sells the leased thing to a third party, the lease is still in effect, but that does not mean that the buyer is bound by the lease: the two parties to the lease would remain the seller/lessor and the lessee. Under Article 2712, a third person who acquires an immovable subject to an unrecorded lease is not bound by the lease. So, that third person can evict the lessee. But since the lease is still in effect, the evicted lessee has a cause of action against his lessor because of the violation of the warranty of peaceful possession. Article 2701 provides that when a lessor fails to protect his lessee's possession, the lessee may file any appropriate action against the person who caused the disturbance.

Question:

If a lessor is free to sell the leased property and the buyer of the property can evict the lessee, the 2701 remedy may be too little, too late. What can a lessee do to protect himself from this?

Section 4: Lessee's Right to Dissolve Lease

Read Civil Code articles 2693, 2714, and 2715.

In Edwards v. Standard Oil, you learned that when a lessor claims that a lessee has breached the lease and demands dissolution, a court will consider all the facts and circumstances before granting the eviction. Is the same true when a lessee wants a lease dissolved because the leased thing has been damaged? Reread Article 2693: if repairs cannot be postponed until the end of the lease, the lessor has the right to make the repair even if it inconveniences the lessee. In turn, however, the lessee "may obtain a reduction or abatement of the rent, or a dissolution of the lease, depending on all the circumstances, including each party's fault or responsibility for the repair, the length of the repair period, and the extent of the loss of use."

Article 2714 provides "If the leased thing is lost or totally destroyed, without the fault of either party, or if it is expropriated, the lease terminates and neither party owes damages to the other." If the thing is only partially destroyed, however, or its use is otherwise substantially impaired, Article 2715 provides that the parties may obtain a diminution of the rent or a dissolution of the lease, "whichever is more appropriate under the circumstances. If the lessor was at fault, then the lessee may also demand damages."

But if the problem was caused by "circumstances external to the leased thing," the lessee may dissolve the lease, but may not obtain a reduction of the rent.

Study Question:

How do Articles 2714 and 2715 apply in the following case?

BOSSIER CENTER, INC. V. PALAIS ROYAL, INC. 1980
385 SO. 2D 886 (LA. APP. 2D CIR.)

JASPER E. JONES, Judge.

¶1   A violent tornado which struck Bossier City on December 3, 1978, is the underlying cause of these consolidated cases. The Bossier Center, Inc. (Center) leased premises in its shopping center to Palais Royal (Palais) whose clothing store was heavily damaged by the tornadic forces. Shortly after the tornado, Jay Kline, President of Palais Royal, informed the Center that Palais Royal would be vacating the premises because it elected to declare the lease to be null due to the extensive damage sustained by the leased premises in the tornado. Palais filed a declaratory judgment action seeking a determination that the lease was ended because of the damages done to the leased premises by the tornado. The Center filed a separate suit against Palais to accelerate the rental payments for the remaining years of the lease and for loss of revenue, future loss of revenue, merchants' dues, and damages to the leased premises caused by Palais while moving from the building. The cases were consolidated for trial.

¶2   The trial court held Palais did not have the right to cancel the lease because although the premises were seriously damaged, they were not partially destroyed. The trial court found Center was not entitled to accelerate the rent installments because of its failure to repair the leased premises. It also held Center did not prove it was entitled to damages, either in the form of lost income or reimbursement for any alleged damage done to the premises. Both parties appeal.

¶3   On December 19, 1974 the Center leased 20,500 sq. ft. to Palais within its shopping center to be used as a men's, ladies', and children's ready-to-wear clothing store. The lease period was ten years. The Palais area was remodeled by the Center in preparation for occupancy by Palais at a cost of approximately $275,000. Palais then spent about $150,000 on decorative and merchandising fixtures.

¶4   Palais was severely damaged by the tornado. Part of the roof was blown off and other portions were so severely damaged that over 1/3 of the roof had to be replaced at a cost of almost $50,000. The wind and rain destroyed substantially all Palais' merchandise and stock. The floor was inundated and there was substantial evidence that all parquet wood flooring and carpeting would have to be replaced. The electrical system was heavily damaged and one electrical contractor would not guarantee the system unless he replaced all wiring and fixtures. The air conditioning units located on top of the building were heavily damaged. The ceiling tile and insulation were blown out or exposed to rain, humidity, and moisture. One witness testified that much of the interior sheet rock walls would have to be totally replaced because of water damage. The large sign in front of the store was razed by the tornadic gusts.

¶5   The issues on appeal are (1) did Palais establish the leased premises were partially destroyed and for that reason it was entitled to cancel the lease? (2) if the lease is not subject to cancellation is the Center required to repair the premises as a condition precedent to accelerating all unpaid rent? and (3) did Center prove it was entitled to recover damages from Palais?

¶6   LSA-C.C. art. 2697 provides:

> "If, during the lease, the thing be totally destroyed by an unforseen (unforeseen) event, or it be taken for a purpose of public utility, the lease is at an end. If it be only destroyed in part, the lessee may either demand a diminution of the price, or a revocation of the lease. In neither case has he any claim of damages."

¶7   LSA-C.C. art. 2700 states:

> "If, during the continuance of the lease, the thing leased should be in want of repairs, and if those repairs can not be postponed until the expiration of the lease, the tenant must suffer such repairs to be made, whatever be the inconvenience he undergoes thereby, and though he be deprived either totally or in part of the use of the thing leased to him during the making of the repairs. But in case such repairs should continue for a longer time than one month, the price of the rent shall be lessened in proportion to the time during which the repairs have continued, and to the parts of the tenement for the use of which the lessee has thereby been deprived.

"And the whole of the rent shall be remitted, if the repairs have been of such nature as to oblige the tenant to leave the house or the room and to take another house, while that which he had leased was repairing."

¶8   A review of these two Articles establishes that where partial reconstruction is required to the leased premises, the lease may be cancelled but if only repairs are necessary the lease may not be subject to cancellation. The lessee is given the exclusive right to cancel the lease if the premises are partially destroyed. See Chivleatto v. Family Furniture & Appliance Center, 196 So.2d 298 (La.App. 4th Cir. 1967).

¶9   The distinction to be drawn between a partial destruction requiring reconstruction and a mere damage requiring only repair has been considered many times in our jurisprudence in cases involving deterioration, fire, floods, and other cas fortuit. The jurisprudence allows expert testimony as to the extent of restoration (whether repairs or reconstruction is required) to help distinguish between injury and partial destruction. See XXX Tulane Law Review 474. The case law sets out other criteria to be used to determine whether a partial destruction or a mere injury has occurred, such as (1) length of time the repairs would take, (2) the partial or absolute deprivation of lessee's use of the premises, (3) the length of time lessee would be displaced, (4) damage done to the lessee's stock, goods and merchandise, (5) the amount paid by the insurer of the building to the insured (as compared with the value of the building prior to damage), (6) the cost of repairs to the premises (as compared with the total value of the pre-damaged premises), and (7) to what degree and which parts of the building are damaged. See Chivleatto, supra; Treigle Sash Factory v. Saladino, 211 La. 945, 31 So.2d 172 (1947); Meyer v. Henderson, 49 La.Ann. 1547, 16 So. 729 (1894); Bernstein v. Bauman, 170 La. 378, 127 So. 874 (1930); Caffin v. Redon, 6 La.Ann. 487 (1851); Brunies v. Police Jury of Parish of Jefferson, 237 La. 227, 110 So.2d 732 (1959); Vincent v. Frelich, 50 La.Ann. 378, 23 So. 373 (1898); Viterbo v. Friedlander, 120 U.S. 707, 30 L.Ed. 776, 7 S.Ct. 962 (1887); Jackson v. Doll, 109 La. 230, 33 So. 207 (1902); Goldberg v. Porterie, 2 La.App. 645 (2d Cir. 1925); Thomas v. Soodhalter, 19 So.2d 885 (La.App. 2d Cir. 1944).

¶10   All the cases cited turn on the individual facts and circumstances. They variously found partial destruction and terminated the lease or concluded only damage not amounting to a destruction had occurred and refused to end the lease, but all used one or more of the above criteria in making this determination.

¶11   In Meyer v. Henderson, supra, damage that was construed as partial destruction entitling a lessee to demand cancellation was described as follows:

"But when the partial destruction has been of such a nature as to menace discomfort to the tenant during the entire term; to cause the tenant to abandon the premises, in order that repairs may be made; when the premises are no longer suitable for the purposes for which they were leased, in such cases it is clear that the lease should be annulled. The partial destruction of the building leased by plaintiffs from defendants made it entirely unfit for the purposes for which it was leased. It was a wreck. It was not habitable. It was unfit for the storage of goods and merchandise. The necessary repairs to it required some months for their completion."

Meyer, supra, 16 So. at 729-730. The court here annulled the lease which had two years remaining of its term.

¶12   The Center offered testimony of numerous witnesses who qualified as experts in construction, all of whom minimized the effect of the tornado upon the leased premises. The purpose of this testimony was to establish there had been no partial destruction of the leased premises. This evidence was offered to establish only repairs were necessary for the restoration of the premises which Palais was required to endure under the provisions of LSA-C.C. art. 2700.

¶13   The testimony of the two architects offered by Palais and Center was inconclusive on the issue of repair versus reconstruction.

¶14   Pictures in evidence revealed a large hole in the roof (testified by one of Center's experts to be 750 sq. ft.) where the entire roof structure was blown away. Other pictures show large holes in the roof and extensive areas where only a few pieces of sheet iron across steel beams remain, the wind having removed the zonite and other material used in the construction of the roof. Pictures also establish extensive electrical conduit and light fixture damage. These photographs also reveal extensive air condition conduit damage and substantial destruction to interior ceilings. The testimony of Palais' witnesses, who included electrical, air conditioning, and acoustical tile contractors, further established the scope and extent of the damage. The preponderance of the evidence established almost total destruction to 1/3 of the roof, substantial damage to the floor, interior ceiling, walls, electrical and air conditioning system.

¶15   The totality of the damage ($200,000 plus) in relation to the value of the building ($1,000,000 plus) shows 20% or more of this modern retail store was destroyed, exclusive of $150,000 interior decorating costs incorporated into the leased premises by Palais, all of which were destroyed. The leased structure and component parts of it essential to the operation of a modern clothing store were so extensively damaged that Palais would have been totally evicted from the premises for four to seven months while the necessary rebuilding of its store was being accomplished.

¶16 We conclude that because of the severity and nature of the damages, with the resulting total eviction of the premises for some months (because of the time required for restoration), a partial destruction of the leased premises has occurred. Partial reconstruction will be necessary within the contemplation of LSA-C.C. art. 2697 rather than only repairs which are referred to in LSA-C.C. art. 2700. This conclusion is not incompatible with the factual findings of the trial judge as reflected by the following quote from his reasons for judgment:

> "There is no question but that the leased premise were severely damaged. Part of the roof was blown off and the wind and rain substantially ruined all the merchandise belonging to Palais Royal. Much of the floor was completely under water. Much of the ceiling tile was either blown out, displaced, or exposed to moisture. There was damage to the electrical system and the air conditioning units which were located on top of the building, a large display sign in front of the building was blown away. Substantial damage was done to the interior and cost of repair 'approximately $150,000 to $250,000' and that the total value of the leased premises is approximately $1,125,000 . . .
>
>   "The evidence also shows that it will take approximately two to four months for the necessary repairs to be made to the lease premises and that another two to three months would be required by Palais Royal for repairs by its design specialist. Thus the premises would not be ready to use for several months."

¶17 The only error made by the trial judge was he concluded the building was structurally sound and he characterized the havoc wrought by the tornado as severe damage when he should have found it was partial destruction.

¶18 In the case of Caffin v. Redon and Brunies v. Police Jury of Parish of Jefferson, supra, substantial replacement of weight-bearing walls was construed to be reconstruction of "partially destroyed" leased premises within the contemplation of LSA-C.C. art. 2697. We find the roof of Palais analogous to the walls in those cases. It is the top of the four sides of a building and its function is no less important than is the purpose served by the walls. The roof is essential to the protection of all the interior of the building and no doubt the partial destruction of the roof of Palais subjected the interior of the building to the winds and rain of the tornado resulting in a substantial portion of the other damage described.

¶19 Palais is entitled to have the lease cancelled under the provisions of LSA-C.C. art. 2697 and therefore we find no need to decide its contention that it is entitled to have the lease cancelled under the provisions of LSA-C.C. art. 2699.

¶20 Because the lease is a nullity due to Palais' election to terminate, the Center is not entitled to the acceleration of the unpaid rent installments.

¶21 The trial judge found that the Center failed to establish any of the damages sought by it and the evidence fully supports this factual determination.

¶22 The judgment appealed in Palais Royal, Inc. v. Bossier Center, Inc., No. 14,167, is REVERSED and we render judgment therein cancelling the lease.

¶23 The judgment appealed in Bossier Center, Inc. v. Palais Royal, Inc., No. 14,166, rejecting plaintiff's demands for rent and damages is AFFIRMED.

¶24 All costs in these consolidated cases in the trial court and on appeal are assessed against Bossier Center, Inc.

Hypothet and Discussion Questions:

Kelly and Kevin Huff wanted to open a coffee house on a busy highway and signed a five-year lease with M1E, Inc. for space in a new shopping center. They opened their coffee house, but approximately two months later, road construction began on the highway adjacent to the shopping center, requiring the closure of portions of the roadway and a nearby bridge. The bridge closure and other roadwork greatly reduced the number of customers frequenting the coffee shop, allegedly to the extent that revenue was insufficient to pay the rent.

M1E agreed to a rent abatement for the Huffs and several other businesses that were similarly affected. The parties agreed that when the bridge reopened, payment of rent would resume. Despite the reopening of the bridge, the Huffs were unable to meet their rent obligations, declined to enter into a new lease, and closed the coffee shop. M1E filed suit seeking to recover rent, penalties, and attorney fees it claimed were due under the lease. The defendants argued that M1E was aware of the upcoming road construction at the time the lease was signed, but failed to disclose that fact to them.

On what basis can the Huffs argue that the lease was terminated? Are they likely to succeed? (Based on M1E Properties-La, L.L.C. v. Huff, No. 2011 CA 0258 (La. App. 1st Cir., April 9, 2012) (unpublished opinion).

Section 5: Removal of Improvements and Additions

Read Article 2695, as well as Articles 493, 493.1, 493.2, and 495.

Article 2695 provides for the disposition after the lease ends of additions, attachments, or other improvements made by the lessee, unless the parties agree on the destiny of such things. It states:

In the absence of contrary agreement, upon termination of the lease, the rights and obligations of the parties with regard to attachments, additions, or other improvements made to the leased thing by the lessee are as follows:

(1) The lessee may remove all improvements that he made to the leased thing, provided that he restore the thing to its former condition.

(2) If the lessee does not remove the improvements, the lessor may:

(a) Appropriate ownership of the improvements by reimbursing the lessee for their costs or for the enhanced value of the leased thing whichever is less; or

(b) Demand that the lessee remove the improvements within a reasonable time and restore the leased thing to its former condition. If the lessee fails to do so, the lessor may remove the improvements and restore the leased thing to its former condition at the expense of the lessee or appropriate ownership of the improvements without any obligation of reimbursement to the lessee. Appropriation of the improvement by the lessor may only be accomplished by providing additional notice by certified mail to the lessee after expiration of the time given the lessee to remove the improvements.

(c) Until such time as the lessor appropriates the improvement, the improvements shall remain the property of the lessee and the lessee shall be solely responsible for any harm caused by the improvements.

Study Questions:

What effect do Civil Code Articles 493, 493.1, 493.2, and 495, have on Article 2695?

Would the following case be decided the same way under current Article 2695? Why or why not?

RIGGS V. LAWTON 1957

231 LA. 1019, 93 SO. 2D 543

HAWTHORNE, Justice.

¶1   This is a suit by a lessee to recover from his lessor the $3,145.47 spent by the lessee to improve the lessor's property; or in the alternative $4,000, which represents the amount the lessor's property has increased in value because of these improvements.

¶2   During the winter of 1953-54, J. H. Riggs rented a room with board from Mrs. Ida C. Lawton of Shreveport, Louisiana, at a monthly rental of $90, and with her consent built an additional room and bath out of brick veneer onto Mrs. Lawton's house to use as his office. During 1954 Riggs became dissatisfied with the arrangement and moved out, and in May of 1955 he brought this suit to recover the amount spent by him on the room and bath or the increased value of Mrs. Lawton's property due to this addition. Mrs. Lawton answered Riggs' petition by alleging, among other things, that she had no need for the office which he had built on her property while he was her lessee, that he had the right to remove the improvements provided he left her house in its original state, and she concluded by praying that his demands be rejected and that he be ordered to remove the improvements which he had constructed on her property.

¶3   After trial on the merits there was judgment for Riggs in the amount of $1,500 with interests and costs, upon payment of which Mrs. Lawton was to be decreed owner of the improvements. Riggs appealed to this court praying that his award be increased to the amount sought in his main demand. Mrs. Lawton answered the appeal asking that the lower court judgment be reversed, and that Riggs be ordered to remove the improvements which he had made to her property. Pending appeal Riggs died, and the executory of his will, Ralph H. Riggs, was substituted as plaintiff-appellant in the case.

¶4   Mrs. Lawton has filed in this court a plea of estoppel, alleging that the legal representative of J. H. Riggs is now estopped to claim the cost or value of the improvements or their ownership. The principal basis of this plea is that J. H. Riggs testified at the trial of the case on its merits in the court below that at his death the Lawtons 'would inherit the house (improvements)'. We find no merit in this plea, nor does counsel for Mrs. Lawton cite any law applicable in support of it, and we know of none.

¶5   In the lower court and in brief filed in this court counsel for appellant seems to rely on the fourth paragraph of Article 508 of the Civil Code. Under the provisions of this paragraph the owner of the soil does not have a right to demand demolition of the works made by a possessor in good faith, but only has the choice either to reimburse the value of materials and the price of workmanship or to reimburse a sum equal to the enhanced value of the soil.

¶6 However, this article has no application here. As said in Hammonds v. Buzbee, 170 La. 573, 128 So. 520, 521, quoting from Alexius v. Oertling, 13 Orleans App. 216,

> "Defendant is not entitled to the value of his improvements. He is not a 'possessor in good faith,' for the sole reason that he is not a possessor at all. For those only are possessors who hold for themselves believing themselves owners. C.C., 3441. The term 'possessor in good faith' is purely technical, and has no application to one who acknowledges another owner than himself. (C.C. 3441). And none but possessors in good faith, in this technical sense, can compel the owner to reimburse the value of improvements placed upon the land. C.C., 508."

(Italics ours.)

¶7 The articles which we think are applicable to this case are Articles 2719, 2720, and 2726. Under Articles 2719 and 2720 the lessee must return the thing leased in the same state in which it was when taken possession of by him, except, of course, for ordinary wear and tear and unavoidable accidents. Under Article 2726 the lessee has the right to remove the improvements that he has made to the thing let provided he leaves it in the state in which he received it, but if these additions be made with lime and cement, the lessor may retain them upon paying a fair price. However, the lessee cannot force the lessor to compensate him for the improvements which he leaves on the property. Pecoul v. Auge, 18 La.Ann. 614; Dreyfuss v. Process Oil & Fuel Co., 142 La. 564, 77 So. 283, 285; see Note, 23 Tul.L.Rev. 177 (1948).

¶8 In the Dreyfuss case, supra, this court said:

> ' . . . A lessee knows when he makes improvements that his right at the termination of the lease will not be to claim compensation for them, but only to remove them, in case it can be done, and yet the premises be left in the condition in which they were when leased, and if they have been made with lime and cement, in the event the lessor does (not) elect to retain them. C.C. 2726.'

(Italics ours.)

¶9 In Superior Syndicate v. Willis, 155 La. 444, 99 So. 397, 398, it was said:

> 'As to R.C.C. art. 2726, it means no more than this: That the tenant has the right at the expiration of the lease, to remove all his improvements and additions, unless the lessor chooses to retain

such as may be made 'with lime and cement,' and pay the tenant the value thereof.' See Talley v. Alexander, 10 La.Ann. 627.

¶10   In the instant case the lessor shows and avers that she has no need for the office built by the lessee in connection with her home and that the improvements were made solely for his convenience. There is no evidence that the lessor has made any use of the additions, and she seeks to have the lessee ordered to remove them and asks that the house be left in the same state in which he received it. Since the lessor has thus elected not to retain the improvements and additions to her home, the lessee cannot recover their fair value.

¶11   The additions and improvements were made with Mrs. Lawton's full consent and approval although for Mr. Riggs' convenience. In fact, she even helped select the materials, was present during the work, approved the general plan of construction, and even paid invoices for some of the materials from funds furnished by Mr. Riggs. In other words, she approved a change, to the extent of these improvements, in the state of the thing leased, and by doing so released her lessee of the obligation imposed by law of returning the premises in the same state in which he received them insofar as these improvements were concerned. Under these facts and circumstances the lessor is not entitled to an order for the removal of these additions and improvements at the lessee's expense.

¶12   For the reasons assigned the judgment appealed from is reversed and set aside, and plaintiff's demands are rejected at his costs.

Section 6: Return of Deposit

Read Revised Statutes 9:3251-9:3254.
   Revised Statute 9:3151 provides in part that:

> Any advance or deposit of money furnished by a tenant or lessee to a landlord or lessor to secure the performance of any part of a written or oral lease or rental agreement shall be returned to the tenant or lessee of residential or dwelling premises within one month after the lease shall terminate, except that the landlord or lessor may retain all or any portion of the advance or deposit which is reasonably necessary to remedy a default of the tenant or to remedy unreasonable wear to the premises. If any portion of an advance or deposit is retained by a landlord or lessor, he shall forward to the tenant or lessee, within one month after the date the tenancy terminates, an itemized statement accounting for the proceeds which are retained and giving the reasons therefor. The tenant shall furnish the lessor a forwarding address at the termination of the lease, to which such statements may be sent.

If the landlord fails to return the deposit or account for the withholding within thirty days, then the lessee has the right to recover actual damages or two hundred dollars, whichever is greater, from the lessor. La. Rev. St. 9:3252. Failure to remit within thirty days after written demand constitutes a willful failure, the court may grant costs and attorney's fees to the lessee as well as the damages, any waiver of this right is null and void. La. Rev. St. 9:3253-9:3254.

Study Question:

How do Revised Statutes 9:3251-9:3254 apply in the following case?

GOLDEN V. RIVERSIDE APARTMENTS, INC. 1986
488 SO.2D 478 (LA. APP. 3D CIR.)

RONALD D. COX, Judge Pro Tem.

1 Riverside Apartments, Inc. has appealed a judgment from Pineville City Court requiring a return of a $125 security deposit and a $150 pet fee posted by their tenants, Mr. and Mrs. Alan Golden. The judgment also ordered defendant to pay $200 in damages and $500 in attorney's fees for willfully withholding the deposits without justification. We affirm as amended.

2 Appellant urges five grounds upon which the trial court erred:

1.) Awarding the return of a nonrefundable pet fee when not an issue before the Court;

2.) Finding the retention of part of the security deposit unjustified;

3.) Applying the punitive provisions of LSA-R.S. 9:3252 and 9:3253;

4.) Awarding both actual and punitive damages; and

5.) Awarding attorney's fees to an attorney appearing in proper person.

3 Plaintiffs leased a one bedroom apartment from defendant at 328 Main Street, Apartment Number 112 in the City of Pineville from May 4, 1984 through October 31, 1984. They posted a $125 security deposit, refundable at termination of the lease if the apartment was in the same condition as when they first moved in, aside from normal wear and tear. The lease also specifically provided, "Lessor agrees to deliver the premises broom clean and free of trash at the beginning of this lease and Lessee agrees to return same in like condition at the termination of the lease." In addition to the security deposit plaintiffs also paid a $150 pet "fee" or "deposit", to be forfeited upon vacating the apartment if a pet was allowed.

4 At the end of the lease term the plaintiffs gave notice of their intent to vacate. Mrs. Golden cleaned the apartment thoroughly. Before returning the key she contacted Lois Williams, the apartment manager, for an apartment inspection. Mrs. Williams did not inspect the apartment before the plaintiffs moved out.

5 By check dated November 6, 1984 defendant returned $67 of the $125 security deposit. Mr. Golden made written demand on November 9, 1984 for the remaining $58. By letter dated November 15, 1984 defendant refused to return the remaining deposit.

RETURN OF PET FEE WHEN NOT AT ISSUE

6 We first consider whether the return of a nonrefundable pet fee was proper when not made an issue before the trial court. In written reasons the trial judge stated: "No demand is made for the return of the $150 pet fee though it seems to the Court that this was clearly a deposit ... The lessee (sic) calls the $150 a 'pet fee,' the addendum calls it a 'deposit,' this conflict is to be resolved in lessee's favor since lessor obviously prepared and furnished the ambiguous documents."

7 Plaintiffs never alleged ambiguity in the lease language, nor raised the question of refundability of the pet fee at trial, nor made demand for return of the pet fee. Because the pet fee was never at issue, we feel the trial court erred in ordering its return. Accordingly, we reverse the trial court's judgment which ordered the defendant to return the $150 nonrefundable pet fee to plaintiffs.

RETAINING SECURITY DEPOSIT

8 We next consider whether the trial court erred in finding defendant unjustifiably retained $58 of the security deposit. Lessor must on demand either return the damage deposit, or if used to offset lessee's damage, provide lessee with an itemized statement accounting for the proceeds. LSA-R.S. 9:3251 et. seq.

9 Defendant withheld $5 from the security deposit to "clean stove hood." Cleaning the stove hood exceeded the normal cleaning necessary to restore the premises to the same condition as when first moved in, aside from normal wear and tear. The trial judge did not specifically address this $5 charge; however, he seems to give great weight to Mrs. Golden's testimony. In written reasons for judgment the trial court noted "... the apartment was in better condition at the time that it was vacated than it was when they received the apartment for occupancy, and she described her cleaning of the apartment including washing down the mildewed walls of the

closets, cleaning bugs from the cabinets and cobwebs from the corners of the rooms and installation of new shelf paper on the shelves in the apartment."

10   Mrs. Williams testified that because of the plaintiffs' kittens it was necessary to deflea the apartment, wash and wax the tile floor, and shampoo the carpets. Defendant withheld $53 from the security deposit for these pet related items. Defendant had $150 available in the nonrefundable pet fee from which to deduct the total pet charges.

11   Under these circumstances we do not find the trial court manifestly erred in finding the defendant unjustifiably retained part of the security deposit.

PENALTIES FOR FAILURE TO REFUND DEPOSIT

12   We now consider whether the trial court erred in applying the penalty provisions of 9:3252 for willful failure to refund a deposit. The purpose of this statute is to provide tenants with a mechanism to recover rent deposits and to prevent arbitrary withholding of deposits. Calix v. Whitson, 306 So.2d 62 (La.App. 4th Cir.1974); Cantelli v. Tonti, 297 So.2d 766 (La.App. 4th Cir.1974). When a landlord cites any specious, arbitrary and capricious, unjustifiable or clearly wrong reasons for withholding a deposit, the statute provides relief. Even if there is a valid dispute over a lease, the lessor must comply with the statutes or suffer the penalties provided. Bradwell v. Carter, 299 So.2d 853 (La.App. 1st Cir.1974); Moore v. Drexel Homes, Inc., 293 So.2d 500 (La.App. 4th Cir.1974), writ denied, 295 So.2d 812 (La.1974).

13   We do not find the trial court erred in imposing the statutory penalty.

DAMAGES

14   The next issue is whether the trial court properly ordered the return of the security deposit in addition to awarding statutory penalties. The defendant owed plaintiff the full security deposit of $125 and unjustifiably refused to return it. Because plaintiffs had no proof of actual damage caused by the defendant's willful noncompliance, the trial court imposed the statutory amount of $200. The statute provides for an award of actual damages or $200, whichever is greater, in addition to the return of the security deposit. Cantelli v. Tonti, supra. We find no error in the trial court awarding both the return of the security deposit and damages for willful noncompliance with the statute. Lugo v. Vest, 336 So.2d 972 (La.App. 4th Cir.1976).

15 The final issue is whether the trial judge erred in awarding attorney's fees to an attorney appearing in proper person. We are of the opinion that the attorney's fees of $500 should not have been awarded since plaintiffs have not incurred the out-of-pocket expenses of retaining an attorney as contemplated by LSA-R.S. 9:3253. In fact, we note that the plaintiff, Alan J. Golden, has represented himself and his wife, in proper person, during these proceedings and has, therefore, incurred no attorney's fees. Makar v. Stewart, 486 So.2d 166 (La.App. 3rd Cir.1986). For this reason we find the trial court erred in allowing attorney's fees in this case, and we reverse this award.

16 For the foregoing reasons, the judgment of the trial court is reversed to deny recovery to the plaintiffs of the $150 nonrefundable pet fee and $500 in attorney's fees. In all other respects the judgment is affirmed. All costs of the proceeding are taxed to the defendant-appellant.

AFFIRMED IN PART, REVERSED IN PART AND RENDERED.

REVIEW NOTES

The lessee's obligations (art 2683):
1. Pay rent
2. Use the thing as intended
3. Return in same condition but 4 normal wear & tear

Section 1: Obligation to pay rent

1. Due at the beginning of the term, unless otherwise agreed Art 2703
2. At lessee's domicile, unless otherwise agreed Art 2704

Rent can be a fixed amount of money but can be a percentage of gross sales or a percentage of a crop. If the latter, then if a crop is damaged (without fault), then loss borne by both proportionately. Art 2706. Adjustment includes government insurance proceeds or subsidies, if any. If a method is agreed-on to set the rent, that is fine, but if that method fails, a court may not set the rent (unless parties had previous existing lease). Method must not depend in whole or in part of a party's subjective demand (e.g. bull-dozing hunting lease). If the lessee fails to pay the

rent when due, the lessor may dissolve the lease and regain possession or sue for specific performance (perhaps demanding accelerated rent, if the lease provides), or use lessor's privilege
to seize lessee's movables.

Edwards v. Standard Oil

Lessor leased filling station to lessee for 2 year term. Lease does not set forth where rent is
due, but stipulates that it is due on the 15th of the month. Defendant mailed rent on the 10th, but
it did not arrive until the 21st. Plaintiff now wants to dissolve the lease.

Held: As the lease does not stipulate where rent is to be paid, it is at defendant's domicile, and
was fulfilled when defendant put the money irretrievably away from himself by mailing it.

Quality Manufacturing

Percentage lease issue: plaintiff lessor leased store-front to defendant lessee for $2,000/
month base rent plus a percentage of net sales when they exceeded $20,000/month. Original
concept was for defendant to sell plaintiff's clothing in the front of the building, while plaintiff
manufactured it in the back, and customers at this outlet store could see the clothes being manufactured. At some point, plaintiff moved the factory elsewhere, and defendant decided to move
its first-run lines to a different, lest costly location and sell only lower-priced clothes at the property in question. Plaintiff sued, claiming breach of the duty of good faith and fair dealing. Court
held for plaintiff, there was no implied obligation to maintain a first-quality clothing outlet.

Secondary issue: tender and deposit: defendant tendered base rent, but plaintiff refused to
accept. However, defendant did not deposit the tendered payments in the court's registry, and
therefore owes rent from the date of judicial demand. Had it deposited the funds, it would have
owed interest only from the date of judgment.

Section 2: Obligation to Use as Intended

Art 2685: "If the lessee uses that thing for a purpose other than that for which it was leased or
in a manner that may cause damage to the thing, the lessor may obtain injunctive relieve, dissolution of the lease, and any damages sustained."

N.O. & Carrollton RR v. Darms

Plaintiff wants an injunction to stop defendant from using its property as a bar and gambling
establishment. The building is next to plaintiff's depot and stables at the corner of Napoleon and

St Charles and was originally built as a boarding-house for plaintiff's drivers and other employees. Plaintiff had received man offers to lease it as a bar and coffee house, at much higher rent than defendant was paying, but had always turned them down. Defendant was told at the time they were negotiating that under no circumstances should he open a bar there, and in fact had rented it to use as a private market, which was the business he had previously ran at another location, but sometime after renting it, he said he wanted to open a bar – and plaintiff immediately protested it.

Parol evidence concerning whether the defendant had been told that the use as a bar was prohibited had been excluded by the trial court, and the appellate court reversed that (p 7). Defendant claimed that parol was inadmissible to contradict or vary a written contract, appellate court holds that an exception applies: to identify or define the extent of the premises, when not sufficiently described in the written contract. (weak – but could be admitted under another exception, 1. That K was not fully integrated; or 2. To explain parties' intent.)

Held: Reversed – permanent injunction granted.

Discussion Question

Hunting and fishing lease provided that defendants could construct buildings on the site, provided they removed them within 6 months of termination or otherwise the buildings would become plaintiff's property.

Defendants used the property as a campground initially, then moved 2 camping trailers onto it, one permanently, constructed a sewage treatment plant, piled trash around, put a gate on the property, nailed "posted" signs on numerous trees, placed water lines and light poles on the property, built a concrete boat ramp, pier, floating dock, and burned trash.

Did they misuse the property? (I.e. not use as intended?)

Section 3: Subleases, Assignments, and Transfers

Art 2642: all rights may be assigned, unless strictly personal. Similarly, 2713 says that all leases may be transferred – i.e. subleased unless expressly prohibited, and such prohibition will be **strictly construed against the lessor.**

We saw one such case – where a lessee was strictly prohibited from subleasing a sand-and-gravel lease by the terms of the contract, and had subleased to 2 other companies, calling them 'operating agreements' – court held for lessor.

Caplan v. Latter & Blum

Issue: Did lessor unreasonably withhold consent to a sublease?

Lessor Caplan agreed to lease a building in New Orleans to defendant. Contract stipulated that lessee could not sublet to anyone else without lessor's written permission, that such consent shall not be unreasonably withheld, that lessee would split the rent from the sublease with plaintiff.

Property is quite large, and defendant intended to sublease out 500 square feet. Plaintiff consented to the first sublease to Health Care Associates for 12 months, $494/month.

Then defendant wanted to sublease more of the property to Duke Advertising Agency, 43 months, $1873/month. Caplan refused, claiming 1. Sublessee did not meet the financial criteria; 2. Improvements proposed by sublessee (additional sink) would increase water usage and expense, and 3. Sublessee was not in strict accord with the primary lease because it called for a higher rental. When Caplan refused, defendant abandoned the premises and refused to pay further rent, Caplan filed suit for accelerated balance due plus contractual 15% liquidated damages.

Held: for defendant, plaintiff's refusal was unreasonable (and clauses prohibiting subleases are to be strictly construed against the lessor)

Rationale:

1 Duke's financial status immaterial – Latter & Blum would still remain bound

2 Sink – not critical to transaction, sublessee had agreed to forego

3 Caplan had already prepared for the possibility of sublessee paying HIGHER rent by term mandating that Latter & Blum would split the rent.

Lessor's Right to Dissolve the Lease

Arts 2693, 2714, and 2715

Art 2693: Lessor has a right to make repairs if necessary during the lease, even if it inconveniences the lessee. During that period, the lessee may obtain a reduction or abatement of the rent, or a dissolution – depending on all the facts and circumstances (Remember Pontalba)

Art 2714: If the leased thing is lost or destroyed without either party's fault, or if it is expropriated, the lease terminates.

Art 2715: If the leased thing is only partially destroyed, parties may lower the rent or dissolve the lease, whichever is more appropriate under the circumstances. If the lessor is at fault, then the lessee may demand damages.

Bossier Center v. Palais Royal

Tornado struck Plaintiff's mall in Bossier City. Defendant lessee had a clothing store in it which was heavily damaged: part of the roof was blown off, most of defendant's merchandise was destroyed, the floor was inundated, all parquet flooring and carpeting had to be replaced, electrical system heavily damaged, AC units heavily damaged, ceiling tile and insulation blown out or exposed to rain, interior sheet rock walls had to be replaced, store fixtures as well. Defendant had spent $150K on fixtures before the tornado struck, and Center had remodeled it for them at a cost of $275K. 20% or more of the store was destroyed, not counting the interior décor.

Issue: Was the damage so severe that the lease should be cancelled, or was it only partially destroyed?

PH: trial court concluded mere damage, that building was structurally sound – abatement of rent, tenant appealed.

Held: Reversed. Lease should be cancelled.

Rationale: The difference between partial and mere damage requiring repair has been considered many times. One considers the length of time repairs would take, partial or absolute deprivation of lessee's use, length of time lessee would be displaced, damage done to lessee's goods, amount paid by insurer of the building to insured, cost of repais to the premises, and the degree to which parts of the building are damaged.

Here there was partial destruction because of the damage to the roof:

When partial destruction is of such a nature as to menace discomfort to tenant during entire term, to cause tenant to abandon the premises in order for repairs to be made, when premises are no longer suitable for purposes for which they were leased . . .

Here, large hole in the roof, sheet iron gone, extensive damage to AC, interior ceilings, electrical, $200K+ damage to the store, in a $1Million+ building, not counting the $150K Defendant had spent on interiors.

Discussion Question

Defendant huff wants to cancel lease of coffee house – signed a 5-year lease in a new shopping center, but 2 months later, highway construction blocked entrance to coffee shop, defendants could not make rent, declined to adjust lease, and closed the shop. Landlord sued, defendants claims that landlord knew about upcoming road construction but did not disclose that to them, that (despite a preclusion of unwritten modifications), the parties had agreed to reduce the rent because of the construction.

In the instant case, the trial court ruled that the lease agreement between the parties was terminated in 2007, when MIE ceased charging Ms. Huff rent (at the time of the road closure near the MIE shopping center), by mutual agreement of the parties. In support of the trial court decision, Ms. Huff asserts that the road closure was a fortuitous event that prevented her performance under the lease contract, . . .

On appeal, MIE argues, in essence, that any verbal agreement to terminate the written contract of lease was insufficient to accomplish such a result, as the contract expressly required that any modification to the agreement be done in writing. Specifically, Section 26 of the contract provides: "This lease contains the final and entire agreement between the parties hereto, and neither they nor their agents shall be bound by any terms, conditions or representations not herein written." MIE further contends that its prior failure to enforce the lease requirement as to payment of rent did not constitute a waiver of their right to future enforcement of the lease or evidence an intent on their part to terminate the lease. On this point, Section 24 of the lease provides: "It is agreed that the failure of [MIE] to insist in any one or more instances upon a strict performance of any covenant of this Lease or to exercise any right herein contained shall not be construed as a waiver or relinquishment for the future of such covenant or right, but the same shall remain in full force and effect, unless the contrary is expressed in writing by [MIE]."

While this appellate court is not convinced that the parties *mutually agreed* to a dissolution of the April 2006 lease, we are unable to say the trial court manifestly erred in its finding. We conclude the trial court reached the correct result in this case, particularly in light of Art. 2715 which provides:

> If, without the fault of the lessee, the thing is partially destroyed, lost, or expropriated, or its use is otherwise substantially impaired, the lessee may, according to the circumstances of both parties, obtain a diminution of the rent or dissolution of the lease, whichever is more appropriate under the circumstances. If the lessor was at fault, the lessee may also demand damages.

> *If the impairment of the use of the leased thins was caused by circumstances external to the leased thing, the lessee is entitled to a dissolution of the lease but is not entitled to diminution of the rent.* [Emphasis added.]

It was established at the trial of this matter that an important cause, which had motivated Ms. Huff to lease space in MIE's shopping center for her coffee shop, was its location on a well-traveled highway. Ms. Huff anticipated that the busy highway would provide accessibility to and visibility for the coffee shop by potential customers. With the closure of the roadway for some six months, traffic decreased significantly and the coffee shop was deprived of the accessibility and visibility it needed to attract customers, thereby resulting in the impairment of the use of the leased premises caused by circumstances external to the leased premises. We conclude that the curtailment of the traffic flow amounted to the elimination of a cause for Ms. Huff's agreement to contract and resulted in the dissolution of the lease contract.

* * *

After a thorough review of the record presented in the instant appeal and applicable law, we conclude that the impediment to Ms. Huff's customers accessing her new coffee shop premises, because of the extended period of time the road construction affected same, was a fortuitous event caused by factors external to the leased premises, which rendered Ms. Huff's performance impossible and resulted in the dissolution of the contract of lease due to the partial failure of cause. Therefore, we find no error in the result reached by the trial court; i.e., in ruling that the April 2006 lease agreement was terminated, along with the accompanying personal guaranty, and in awarding rent to MIE against Ms. Huff, after the rent abatement period ended, in accordance with the Louisiana Civil Code's general lease provisions for the months of January, February, and March 2008.

Section 5: Removal of Improvements and Additions

Art 2695, 493, 493.1, 493.2, 495

2695: Unless the parties otherwise agree, on termination of the lease,

1 The lessee may remove all improvements he made to the lease thing and restore it to its former condition.

2 If he does not do so, the lessor may

a. Appropriate ownership by paying the enhanced value or cost of improvement, whichever is less;

b. Demand that lessee remove improvements within a reasonable time and restore the lease thing to its former condition OR remove them himself at lessee's expense, or

c. Appropriate improvement by providing additional notice by certified mail – until the lessor appropriates improvement, improvements remain the lessee's property, and he is solely responsible for any harm they cause.

493 & etc.: 493 is consistent; 493.1 provides that things incorporated into an immovable become component parts and belong to the owner, but that the one who loses ownership of a thing in that way may have a claim against the owner. 495: One who incorporates things to an immovable with the owner's consent may remove them as long as he restores the property to its former condition. If he does not remove them after demand, the owner may have them removed at his expense OR elect to keep them and pay either current value of materials or enhanced value of the immovable (at his choice).

Riggs v. Lawton

Plaintiff Lessee spent $3,145 to improve the lessor's property ($4K increase in value) – he rented a room from defendant Lawton, and with her consent added an additional room and bath to use as his office. He became dissatisfied and moved out, and then sued to recover the money he spnt. She answer that she had not need for the office, that he had a right to remove and restore – wants him ordered to do just that.

PH: TCT for plaintiff for $1500, landlord to be declared owner. Plaintiff appealed asking for additur. Defendant appealed asking for removal –Plaintiff Riggs has since died, and his executor is pursuing.

Lower court seems to rely on Art. 508 – possessor in good faith. That does not apply, must go to lease articles. Lessee cannot force lessor to compensate him for improvements which he leaves. She says she doesn't need them, and is no contrary evidence. However, they were made with her full consent an approval, and she even helped select the materials, was present during the work, approved of it, and paid invoices. Therefore, she is NOT entitled to an order for removal.

Practical point: Don't build onto someone else's building and expect to get reimbursed for it.

Section 6: Return of Deposit

Revised Statute 9:3151: Lessor MUST return deposit within one month of termination (minus reasonably necessary to remedy default or remedy unreasonable wear and tear). If retains any portion, must within one month send an itemized statement accounting for retained goods.

3252: if landlord does not comply – Punitive damages!

$200 or actual damages if fails to remit within 30 days of written demand for refund, file recovery of such damages in parish of lessor's domicile or parish where property situated

Court MAY add costs and attorney's fees

Lessee cannot waive this right.

3259 landlord of an apartment building or hotel can demand attorneys fees when lessee does not pay delinquent rent within 20 days of delivery of written demand – sent to last known address via certified mail, personal delivery, or tacking demand on door.

3260 If immovable, and lessee constructively evicted or uninhabitable through no fault of lessee, lessor must mitigate damages.

3260.1: Lessor must disclose to lessee any pending foreclosure action to which residential dwelling is subject

3261.1: Special provisions for domestic abuse victims

Golden v. Riverside Apartments

Lessee posted a $125 security deposit on renting the apartment, promised to leave it broom clean, free of trash, and return in same condition but for normal wear and tear. At end of lease, gave notice of intent to vacate, cleaned the apartment thoroughly, invited manager to inspect

– manager refused. Defendant returned only $67 of the $125, and plaintiff made written demand for the remainder, defendant refused.

Pet fee: sometimes called pet fee, sometimes called deposit in the contract, but as plaintiff did not appeal holding, defendant should not have been ordered to return it.

Security deposit: Defendant: $5 to clean stove hood – exceeded normal wear and tear; – $53 to clean up after pets

Plaintiff: vs apartment was in better condition when I left than when I received; pet clean-up should have been deducted from Pet fee

TCT found defendant unjustifiably retained part of the security deposit, App. Ct affirmed:

No proof that plaintiffs were actually damaged by defendant's willful noncompliance, trial court awarded the $200 (which was greater than the amount deducted from the security deposit) AND the trial court also awarded the security deposit. Attorneys fees --.plaintiff had appeared on her own, but trial court awarded $500 attorney's fees anyway – reversed.

HYPOTHETICAL (ADAPTED FROM A FINAL EXAM)

150 points/ 1 1/2 hour (300 words/3/4 page per subpart)

Mario just purchased a small trailer park with two trailers from Harold, which were already rented out: John lives in one trailer, while Timothy lives in the other. Each lessee pays $500 per month in rent.

A. (30 points) Mario would like to evict both John and Timothy so that he can lease the trailers to his relatives. John's lease was recorded in the parish registry, but Tim's was neither written nor recorded. Can he give either tenant proper notice of termination? Will Mario be liable for anything if he follows through? Will Harold? Explain.

B. (30 points) John's lease provided that it ended on October 31, 2019, but he was still there when Mario purchased the property on November 7, 2019. What does this mean, and does it change (in part) your answer to question A? Explain.

C. (30 points) Assume that Mario changes his mind and decides that he wants Tim to stay, so he and Tim sign a new, written lease stating that Tim can lease the trailer for another year in exchange for $500/month plus 100 hours of help harvesting his sugar crop. Is there any problem with this?

D. (30 points) Assume that both John and Tim are leasing their trailers from Mario, but then Tim complains that John formed a new heavy metal band with his friends and they are practicing until 3 am. This is a problem because the trailers are only 20 feet apart from each other, anchored permanently to cement pads. Tim doesn't like the 'music' but John contends that he has a right to do anything he wants in his trailer, whenever he wants, as long as it's not criminal. Is there anything that Mario can or should do to solve the dispute between his two tenants?

E. (30 points) Mario resolved the music issue, and the 2 tenants are now getting along so well that Tim invited John over for a jam session (Tim plays the bagpipes . . .). In the midst of their jam session, John (who weighed 300+ pounds) tripped over Tim's St. Bernard and smashed into his sink, toilet, and shower, breaking everything. Now Tim wants Mario to repair everything. In order for Mario to do so, Tim will have to vacate the premises for 1 month. Who has to pay for all this under lease rules– Mario, Tim, or John?

CPSIA information can be obtained
at www.ICGtesting.com
Printed in the USA
BVHW052325060222
628059BV00005B/42